LEO BAECK INSTITUTE
YEAR BOOK
1969

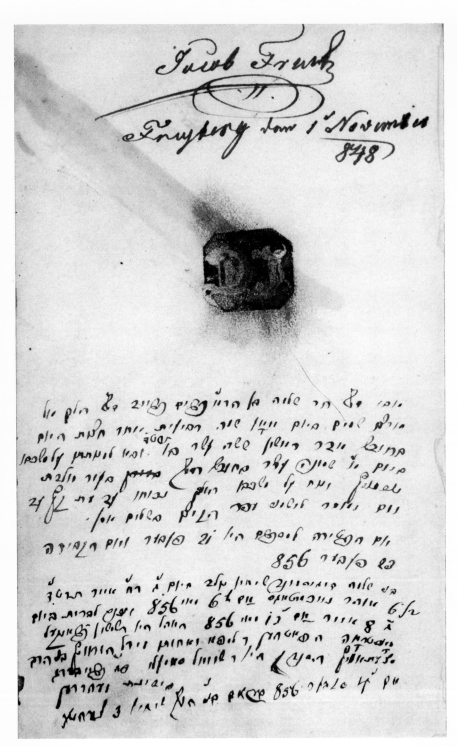

A RECORD OF SIGMUND FREUD'S BIRTH

A page from his father's Prayer Book. See page XIV

By courtesy of Mr. Ernst Freud, London

PUBLICATIONS OF THE
LEO BAECK INSTITUTE

YEAR BOOK XIV

1969

EAST AND WEST LIBRARY
PUBLISHED FOR THE INSTITUTE
LONDON · JERUSALEM · NEW YORK

EDITOR: ROBERT WELTSCH

OFFICES OF THE
LEO BAECK INSTITUTE

JERUSALEM (ISRAEL): 33, Bustanai Street
LONDON: 4, Devonshire Street, W. 1
NEW YORK: 129 East 73rd Street

THE LEO BAECK INSTITUTE
was founded in 1955 by the
COUNCIL OF JEWS FROM GERMANY

for the purpose of collecting material on and
sponsoring research into the history of the
Jewish community in Germany and in other
German-speaking countries from the Emanci-
pation to its decline and new dispersion. The
Institute is named in honour of the man who
was the last representative figure of German
Jewry in Germany during the Nazi period.

The Council of Jews from Germany was established
after the war by the principal organisations of Jews
from Germany in Israel, U.S.A. and U.K. for the
protection of their rights and interests.

THIS PUBLICATION WAS SUPPORTED
BY A GRANT FROM THE
MEMORIAL FOUNDATION FOR JEWISH CULTURE

Contents

Two Promoters of our Cause VII

Introduction by ROBERT WELTSCH IX

I. EMANCIPATION

ERNEST HAMBURGER: One Hundred Years of Emancipation 3

REINHARD RÜRUP: Jewish Emancipation and Bourgeois Society 67

ROBERT A. KANN: Assimilation and Antisemitism in the German-
French Orbit 92

II. A FINANCIAL TYCOON

KURT GRUNWALD: "Windsor-Cassel" — The Last Court Jew 119

III. VOCATIONAL TRAINING

E. G. LOWENTHAL: The Ahlem Experiment 165

GERTRUDE VAN TIJN: Werkdorp Nieuwesluis 182

IV. MEMOIRS AND DOCUMENTS

H. G. REISSNER: Daniel Lessmann in Vienna and Verona 203

A. W. BINDER: Isaac Offenbach 215

RAHEL LIEBESCHÜTZ: August Belmont and the House of Rothschild . . 224

PEREZ LESHEM: Rescue Efforts in the Iberian Peninsula 231

V. CORRESPONDENCE

WALTER BRESLAUER: Notes on Organizational Problems of German
Jewry 259

Letters to the Editor 266

VI. BIBLIOGRAPHY 269

VII. LIST OF CONTRIBUTORS 327

VIII. INDEX 331

Illustrations

Record of Sigmund Freud's birth	Frontispiece	
Max Gruenewald and Max Kreutzberger . .	opp. p.	VIII
Eduard Lasker, Eduard von Simson . . . . Leopold Sonnemann, Hugo Preuss	between pp.	24—25
Conference of Workers' and Soldiers' Councils	opp. p.	40
Ludwig Frank, Hugo Haase, Rosa Luxemburg, Kurt Eisner . . . . Paul Levi, Ernst Heilmann, Paul Hirsch, Hans Schäffer	between pp.	56—57
Ernest Cassel, Cassel's daughter, Cassel and grand-daughter . . . . Jacob H. Schiff, Henry Louis Bischoffsheim	between pp.	136—137
Ernest Cassel, Albert Ballin, Felix Cassel and Max M. Warburg . . . . . . Beerbohm Cartoon	between pp.	152—153
Moritz Simon . . . . Facsimile of Ahlem report . . . . . . Ahlem prospectus . . . . Ahlem school garden, Ahlem orchard . .	between pp.	168—169
View of Werkdorp, Jewish youth at work Opening of Community Centre	between pp.	184—185
Daniel Lessmann . . . . Facsimile of Lessmann letter	between pp.	208—209
Isaac Judah Offenbach . . . . . . Facsimile of Offenbach Composition	between pp.	216—217
Card of acknowledgment signed by Leo Baeck . . . . Embarkation, SS "NYASSA", David Blickenstaff, Farewell celebration . . .	between pp.	232—233
Facsimile of German Embassy dispatch . .	between pp.	248—249

Two Promoters of our Cause

It is not the general custom to take notice in these pages of purely personal events in the life of active members of our Institute. If we make an exception in a particular case we are doing this for convincing reasons. We are choosing the seventieth birthday of both Rabbi Max Gruenewald (4.12.1969) and Dr. Max Kreutzberger (31.1.1970) as an occasion to express to these two men the gratitude of the members of the Board of the Leo Baeck Institute for the decisive part they played in building up the Institute, especially in the United States.

Dr. Gruenewald, who has been President of the New York branch of the Leo Baeck Institute from its very beginning, is well-known to the readers of this Year Book from his contributions which were devoted to the establishment of the *Reichsvertretung* in Germany in 1933 and its activities, and also to the place of a rabbi in modern society. In both these fields he had personal experience. A graduate of the Breslau Seminary, Dr. Gruenewald never ceased in his pursuit of Jewish learning. He is a theologian of high standing and author of several important Judaistic works. In Germany he was the spiritual leader of the Mannheim Jewish community. But to a wider public he became better known during the dark days of the Nazi regime when he was not only a pillar of strength to his community in Mannheim and active in all kinds of rescue work but also, by joining the *Reichsvertretung,* he had a larger scope of activity in the whole of Germany. Some of his reminiscences of those days were published in the memorial volume dedicated to Hugo Hahn, New York 1963, in an essay 'The First Days, the First Years'. After his emigration to the United States Gruenewald, having become rabbi of an American congregation, kept in close contact with those refugees from Nazi Europe who were in need of help and advice. But more than anything else he was interested in keeping up the great traditions of German Jewry in the spiritual and intellectual field. So it was only natural that, apart from being President of the American Federation of Jews from Germany, he became a Vice-President of the Council of Jews from Germany, and, above all, President of the Leo Baeck Institute in New York. This is not the place to enumerate in detail the achievements of Dr. Gruenewald in this office but it is no secret that to him we owe the implementation of the plan of endowing the Institute with its own beautiful building in New York to serve as a centre of Jewish learning and to house its great collection of books and manuscripts.

This plan was the brain-child of Max Kreutzberger who conducted the affairs of the Leo Baeck Institute in New York from its inception up to 1967. He is now General Consultant to the Institute. Always full of ideas and initiative, not sparing any effort, Kreutzberger created this Institute and from nothing developed it to its present splendid status, with its unique library containing old and new books on German Judaism and German Jews, their history, their creative contribution to Jewish and general culture, their battles against hostility and their final catastrophe. It is very doubtful whether such a collection of books and documents on this subject as Kreutzberger has brought together in a comparatively short time can be found today anywhere else in the world. At the same time Kreutzberger was the initiator of a whole series of scholarly works which were carried out under his guidance and with his unstinting help. We cannot attempt here a full biography of Dr. Kreutzberger, but this appreciation would be incomplete if we were not to mention, at least in a few words, Kreutzberger's former role as one of the leading social workers in pre-Hitler Germany and during the first years of Nazi rule and later in Palestine (now Israel). As Director of the *Zentral-wohlfahrtsstelle* and editor of its periodical he must be regarded as one of the pioneers of modern social work in the Jewish orbit. It was only logical that he subsequently administered the relevant department during the first years of the *Reichsvertretung* prior to his emigration to Palestine. In Palestine under the British Mandate he was the director of the organization of German immigrants *(Hitachduth Olej Germania)* which, thanks to his energy and humanity, helped innumerable people to find their place in the new homeland. Immediately after the war Kreutzberger, as delegate of the Jewish Agency in Munich, was engaged in the crucial work of reclaiming Jewish property in Germany.

The story of the merits of these two men could, of course, easily be prolonged but these few lines may suffice to indicate the measure of gratitude German Jewry and especially the Leo Baeck Institute owe to Max Gruenewald and Max Kreutzberger.

TWO SEPTUAGENARIANS

Max Gruenewald (right) and Max Kreutzberger at a function
of the New York Leo Baeck Institute

Introduction

BY ROBERT WELTSCH

When just a hundred years ago, in 1869, the Law of Emancipation was passed, this was regarded as the final codification of equal rights for the Jews in Germany. Looking back today, it seems amazing how quickly the new legal situation was taken for granted and accepted as the normal status in which Jews could feel secure, notwithstanding the antisemitic undertone always present in the public atmosphere. To a large degree the Law was only the confirmation of a state of affairs which already existed. Nevertheless, the legal act was of enormous importance. German Jews had no longer to fight for their own recognition; they were now in a position to claim a similar status for Jews in other countries where equality and full citizenship were denied to them. At the Berlin Congress of European Powers in 1878, which had to deal with the so-called Oriental Question (the term "Orient" or "Near East" including also the Balkans as former Turkish territory), German Jews, hardly a decade after their own emancipation, were able, together with their correligionists from Western democracies, to help to persuade the leading statesmen of the day, above all Prince Bismarck as President of that Congress, into insisting upon citizens' status and equal rights for the Jews in the newly established Balkan states.[1] True, emancipation had been decreed in Prussia already by Hardenberg's Edict of 1812, but, as we know, this law did not remain valid for very long. The process of full emancipation, to which a large part of the present Year Book is devoted, took longer in Prussia and in the other German states than elsewhere in the West. In the words of Eugen Täubler it "was of universal significance and unique character, persisting longer in Prussia than in any other country, extending over a wider territory, displaying a greater variety, and embracing all walks of life, because the history of the Jews in Germany represents the classic example of Jewish emancipation in Western Europe".[2]

Thus, although the centenary is an obvious occasion for surveying and evaluating the developments of this period, we do not overlook the fact that the Law of 1869 had a long drawn-out prelude; this was concerned with what Dr. Selma Stern-Täubler called the "complicated problem" of "the spiritual and mental transfiguration of the Ghetto Jew into the European Jew".[3] It began in the eighteenth century, and it must not be seen solely in terms predominant during the second half of the nineteenth century, i.e. as the demand for civil equality and political rights as they are understood in a modern democracy or would-be democracy. Such rights were in any case not attainable in an era of

[1]See N. M. Gelber, 'The Intervention of German Jews at the Berlin Congress 1878', in *LBI Year Book V* (1960), pp. 221 ff.
[2]Selma Stern-Täubler, 'The German Jew in a Changing World', in *LBI Year Book VII* (1962), p. 4.
[3]*Ibid.*, pp. 3-4.

absolutism. The first aim of the Jews at that time was the abolition of disabilities, of restrictive regulations regarding movement, entering various trades and professions, special Jewish taxes, and other humiliations. This was achieved gradually, though general equality was not yet in sight. At the same time the actual life of the Jews underwent a fundamental transformation, not only because they could fulfil certain functions in the rapidly changing industrial society, but also because, in the wave of enlightenment, the Jews themselves, in increasing numbers, turned to secular education, a course abhorred by their fathers or grandfathers. They soon acquired the qualifications to take part in various economic and intellectual activities and became de facto members, albeit without legal status, of the non-Jewish society. Gradually they adjusted themselves to the general life beyond the confines of their community. Their progress in this respect, as far as the upper strata were concerned, was startling. Individual Jews were not only accepted by the elite of the German intelligentsia, but at the same time also tried to pave the way for the advancement of the younger generation, primarily by establishing suitable schools and institutions, intended to supplement the purely Jewish learning of the past.

In the popular view this whole revolution is closely linked with the name of Moses Mendelssohn, often described as the first modern German Jew. The emancipated generations after him looked on him with gratitude, and his role in Jewish history was extolled, sometimes perhaps in an exaggerated manner, when he, as a sort of redeemer, was compared with the other Moses of Biblical time. Mendelssohn was highly esteemed and reputed in his lifetime, famous also for his defence of Judaism in discussions such as that with Lavater. But as far as the encouragement of secular education was concerned he was not as solitary a figure as is sometimes assumed. The urge for that was a trend of the time. Mendelssohn as a thinker is a combination of general philosopher and pioneer of modern Jewish thought; to say that he represents a landmark in Jewish history is almost a platitude. Forty years ago, the *Akademie für die Wissenschaft des Judentums* in Berlin[4] decided on a new complete scholarly edition of his works to celebrate the 200th anniversary of his birth; this vast enterprise, in which the most competent scholars took part, could not be completed before the advent of the Nazi regime in 1933 put an end to such plans. Anyhow, seven volumes appeared before the war; they are exceedingly difficult to obtain today. It is therefore of great interest that a German publishing house has announced that not only the previously published volumes of this Berlin edition would be re-issued in a photostatic print, but also that a continuation of the original project is now under way.[5] Perhaps this can be taken as a sign of revival of interest in Mendelssohn

---

[4]The *Akademie für die Wissenschaft des Judentums* had been founded in Berlin in 1920, following the initiative of Franz Rosenzweig and its support by Hermann Cohen shortly before his death in April 1918. The first director of the *Akademie* was Eugen Täubler, who also drafted the first programme of research. See Selma Stern-Täubler, 'Eugen Täubler and the *Wissenschaft des Judentums*', in *LBI Year Book III* (1958), pp. 49-53.

[5]The publisher Friedrich Fromann, Stuttgart, says in his announcement that in addition to these seven volumes nine new ones are to be published, edited by Professor Alexander

and his time. In this respect the Leo Baeck Institute New York, which is also entrusted with a large part of the archives of the Mendelssohn family and has among its Board-members and Fellows some outstanding Mendelssohn scholars, must be given due credit. A central part in this endeavour is taken by Professor Alexander Altmann; under his editorship a new collection of Mendelssohn's early writings is being published this year.[6] Professor Altmann has devoted several years to intensive Mendelssohn studies in European libraries and archives, which have resulted in the unearthing of new material, and two essays which can be described as fruits of this occupation have been published in the Leo Baeck Institute's German-language periodical.[7]

In the process of "Europeanization" in Mendelssohn's time, and later on, a fierce debate about the position of Judaism went on not only in Jewish circles but also between Jews and Christians, especially when Christian theologians or philosophers wanted to persuade enlightened Jews to convert to Christianity and in this way facilitate their full integration into the Christian German state. To a certain extent they were successful, especially among the upper strata of Jewish society, the families of the so-called Court Jews, where conversion occurred more often for social than for religious reasons. This was helped by the rapidly increasing ignorance in Jewish matters. Many prominent Jews of that age, themselves still firmly rooted in Jewish tradition, showed lassitude in the Jewish education of their children, perhaps because instinctively they felt the paramount importance of secular learning.[8] Certainly towards the end of the eighteenth century there already existed a considerable section of well-educated Jews passionately interested in the intellectual life of the day and alienated from Judaism. With them Jewish knowledge had practically disappeared. While the traditional Jewish way of life was regarded as an inferior remnant of the Middle

---

Altmann in co-operation with other scholars such as Dr. Chaim Bar-Dayan (Jerusalem) and Professor Leo Strauss (Chicago), who were both among the original group of editors in 1929. - Professor Altmann, formerly Communal Rabbi of Manchester, England, where he also founded the Institute of Jewish Studies (now in London), is Professor of Jewish Philosophy at Brandeis University in U.S.A. He is also a contributor to this Year Book, vols. I and VI.

[6]Moses Mendelssohn's *Frühschriften zur Metaphysik*. Untersucht und erläutert von Alexander Altmann, J. C. B. Mohr, Tübingen 1969.

[7]*Bulletin des Leo Baeck Instituts*, Tel-Aviv, Editor Hans Tramer, No. 40 (1967), 'Moses Mendelssohns Kindheit in Dessau'; No. 42 (1968), 'Moses Mendelssohns Gesammelte Schriften', Neuerschlossene Briefe. Zur Geschichte ihrer Herausgabe. Both essays are by Alexander Altmann.

[8]Mendelssohn's own attitude towards the Jewish education of his children "was more indulgent than energetic". About his son Joseph (who at that time must have been very young as he was fifteen when his father died) M.M. wrote to Homberg: "He . . . has forgotten nearly all of the Hebrew you taught him. I let him go his own way; as you know, I am no friend of coercion." Quoted from Michael A. Meyer, *The Origins of the Modern Jew. Jewish Identity and European Culture in Germany 1749-1824*, Wayne State University, Detroit 1967, p. 51, - an outstanding book which is most relevant to the subject briefly discussed here. Joseph was the only one of M.M.'s children who remained a Jew. About his concern for the edition of his father's works cf. Alexander Altmann's above-mentioned essay in *Bulletin des Leo Baeck Instituts*, No. 42 (1968).

Ages incompatible with modern needs, the fact of Jewish origin, though rarely overlooked by the outside world, seemed to many individuals of this group to be a deplorable mishap or even a curse.

One of the most impressive testimonies revealing the close ties between this kind of Jew and the aristocratic and intellectual elite of society — and their limits — and also of the tribulations emerging therefrom is, of course, the legacy of Rahel Levin Varnhagen. Of this we are reminded by the great new edition of her correspondence and diaries published recently in four big volumes by the *Kösel-Verlag*.[9]

Rahel is a phenomenon *sui generis;* she reacts spontaneously and exuberantly to experiences and encounters. She lives in a permanent state of tension in her relations with other people, and all her utterances are a sort of dialogue. Her ardent interest in matters of intellect and art, and her devotion to the genius of Goethe, set her apart from the environment from which she sprang, not to speak of the lower strata of the Jewish community with which she apparently had no connection at all. This is not the place to evaluate Rahel ("the Ralle" as her Christian friends called her) as a personality and as a woman — certainly a subject of great relevance when approached with the devices of modern psycho‧logy. Many regarded her as muddle-headed in her emotional exaggerations, others saw in her a genius. Alexander von der Marwitz, in a letter to a friend written in August 1809, called her "the greatest woman living at present on this earth".[10] Her literary output consists exclusively of letters and diaries, in an epoch when letter-writing was developed as an art, hardly matched by anything in our time. In her outbursts one can find signs of exaggerated sentimentalism and sensitivity; there are, however, also many hints of despair and frustration, which some com‧mentators link, at least partly, with her Jewishness. This sometimes created an invisible distance even within the most exalted friendship.

What concerns us here is the fact that she and most others of her circle were completely detached from Judaism. There are hardly any references of significance to anything Jewish in her letters except occasional lamentations about the mis-

---

[9]Rahel Varnhagen, *Briefe in vier Bänden.* Herausgegeben von Friedhelm Kemp, Kösel-Verlag, Munich 1967/68. The first volume contains correspondence with men to whom she had been engaged, like Karl Alexander von der Marwitz, Karl von Finkelstein, Raphael d'Urquijo; the second volume, correspondence with her husband August Varnhagen von Ense; the third volume, 'Rahel Varnhagen im Umgang mit ihren Freunden, (1793-1843)' and the fourth volume, 'Rahel Varnhagen und ihre Zeit (1800-1833)' present not only a fascinating selection of letters to and from prominent contemporaries but also many excerpts from her diaries. The fact that not only Rahel's own letters have been printed but also those of her contemporaries, adds considerably to the value of the books. All persons involved are described in short biographies and a chronological record of Rahel's life and family with many biographical details of interest is included. However one may judge Rahel's colourful personality, this work appears to be an indispensible guide to the understanding of an epoch when a particular section of Jews believed themselves to have been - in spite of some difficulties - finally accepted by the elite of Germany, whose intellectual interests they shared in so passionate a manner.
[10]*Briefwechsel mit Alexander von der Marwitz*, p. 248.

fortune of being born a Jewess.[11] Nevertheless, no-one would mention her even now, almost two hundred years after her birth (1771), without referring to her Jewishness. She remained the Jewess in spite of the conversion of herself and of all her family, descendants of the orthodox Jew Levin Marcus of Berlin. An instructive pamphlet of the *Kösel-Verlag*[12] calls her "the first Jewess of German literature". When this admirable new edition of her Letters and Diaries appeared, German reviewers were fascinated by Rahel's versatility and exuberance, her powerful style and her universal intellectual interests to which she so ably gave expression. But, as one commentator remarked, "she did not realize that it was just as a Jewess that she was interesting". Did she or did she not? Her life and the rich — though not always wholly reliable — material that we possess about her whole circle of friends offer an opportunity of analysing the position of a Jewess (or Jew) within that kind of society to which she was attracted. One critic describes it as remaining "beside" society, not being absorbed by it, and that makes the whole position somewhat doubtful.[13] What she wanted to achieve was status. The first step towards this was the severance of all bonds with the Jewish people, and this she carried out without hesitation. She believed — or pretended to believe — that she had liberated herself from this burden. It did not work out that way, as she seems to have realized at the end of her life. Anyhow, to posterity she has always been a Jewish phenomenon.

For the Jewish historian Rahel's correspondence remains a mirror of the sort of integration with society which a small group of German-educated Jews had achieved at that pre-emancipation time. We also know, however, that this almost inevitably led to a break-away from the Jewish community, thus confirming the warnings of orthodox Jewish leaders, who always suspected that modern education and acculturisation would lead to apostasy. Even most of the descendants of Mendelssohn himself, and many others of similar social background, cut their ties with Judaism.

It was to a large extent in order to prevent this flight from Judaism that the drive for emancipation assumed such an urgency. As long as only baptism could provide the "entrance ticket" to full participation in European culture, the temptation would be paramount, especially at the beginning of the nineteenth century when so many intelligent young Jews acquired *Bildung* and could find no outlet for their literary ambitions. This section of the Jewish population was in

---

[11]On Rahel's attitude to her Jewish origin, to Judaism and to religion in general cf. also Meyer, *op. cit.*, pp. 108-114. - Hannah Arendt, in her portrait of Rahel, lays particular stress on her Jewishness to which Rahel is said to have returned on her death-bed when she described herself as a "fugitive from Egypt and Palestine". See Hannah Arendt, *Rahel Varnhagen. The Life of a Jewess*. Publication of the Leo Baeck Institute, London 1957.

[12]*Auf frischen kleinen abstrakten Wegen. Unbekanntes und Unveröffentlichtes aus Rahels Freundeskreis*, Dezember 1967.

[13]Hermann Meier-Cronemeyer in a remarkable review in *Germania Judaica*, Köln, VII/4 (1968), which is largely devoted to Rahel's relation to her own Jewishness. This critical essay - as well as many of the admirable explanatory notes of the editor himself - throws additional light on the problematic character of this significant chapter in the history of Jewish-German relations.

some respects breaking new ground. A few decades later people from this group were not only integrated with the life in Germany but were also critical of the political climate; they became fighters for political and human emancipation, not only of Jews, but in that wider sense indicated in Dr. Rürup's article in this volume, and referred to below. Men like Heine and Börne, both baptized, are obvious cases in point. A lesser known member of this group is Daniel Lessmann, originally of the *Culturverein* circle,[14] some of whose letters are reproduced in this volume. They are in the possession of the Archives of the Leo Baeck Institute which preserves in New York many precious documents illustrative of all stages of Jewish historical development in Germany.

In the middle of the nineteenth century Hebrew was still employed for recording solemn occasions by people who were otherwise already completely accustomed to the use of pure German in their daily life. Also, German was often written in Hebrew characters. Hannah Arendt mentions that Rahel used Hebrew script in her letters to her brother long after they had both left the Jewish community. Twenty-three years after Rahel's death, when assimilation had advanced much further, Jacob Freud of Fryberg (Freiberg, Czech name Příbor) in Moravia (then Austria) made a note in Hebrew in his prayer book, recording the death of his father and the birth and circumcision of his son, Sigmund Freud, later to become one of the most famous Jews of the century. The Editor expresses his gratitude to Mr. Ernst Freud, London, for the permission to reproduce this interesting page.*

It is generally assumed that the initiative for emancipation came from France. But while it is true that the first legal proclamation in this direction was made by the French National Assembly in 1791, there was in this field a close inter-dependence of France and Germany, especially in the ideological field. This may have to do with the fact that an important part of French Jewry, the Alsace community, was German-speaking. France had to deal with two rather different kinds of Jews, one being the Sephardic community of Western France (Bordeaux) and Avignon, the other the Ashkenasi Jews of Alsace. These two groups had a different past and had lived for centuries in different environments. It is only

---

[14]See H. G. Reissner, 'Rebellious Dilemma: The Case Histories of Eduard Gans and some of his Partisans', in *LBI Year Book II* (1957), p. 189.

*See Frontispiece. The text of the Hebrew inscription reads in (slightly shortened) English translation as follows: "My father, of blessed memory, Rabbi Shlomo, son of R. Ephraim Freud, went to the Kingdom of Heaven at 4 p.m. on Friday, 16th Adar Rischon 616 [5616]. He was buried at Tismenitz, his birthplace, on the 18th day of the same month. The date of my father's death according to the usual calendar is the 21st of February; the funeral took place on 23rd February 856 [1856].

My son Shlomo Sigismund was born on the first day of the month Iyyar 616 [5616], at 6.30 p.m., 6th May 856 [1856]. He entered the Covenant on Tuesday, 8th of Iyyar, 13th May 856. The Mohel [Circumciser] was Rabbi Shimshon Frankel of Mährisch Ostrau. The godparents were R. Lippa Horovitz and his sister Mirl, children of the Czernovitz rabbi. Sandek [who holds the child during the operation] was R. Shmuel Samueli of Freiberg in Moravia."

There is another Hebrew entry in a Bible dedicated to his son Sigmund on the occasion of his 35th birthday in 1891.

one example confirming the thesis, recently again stressed by Professor Ferdynand Zweig,[15] that Jews cannot *a priori* be regarded as a uniform entity; culturally each group is a product of the historic encounter with that part of the Gentile world which exerts its formative influence on the Jews living within its boundaries. While in the eighteenth century the Sephardim of Western France were already culturally and linguistically almost fully assimilated, the Jews of Eastern France (Alsace) preserved their traditional community life and religious orthodoxy and were socially and demographically separated from French society. Dr. Rürup draws our attention to the *enquête* arranged in 1782 by the Academy of Metz on the question: "Are there means to make the Jews in France happier and more useful?" It was influenced by the discussion aroused in Germany by Christian Wilhelm Dohm's epoch-making book *Über die bürgerliche Verbesserung der Juden* (1781). That the developments in France and in Germany at the time of enlightenment were mutually complementary, is also lucidly shown in Professor Arthur Hertzberg's recent brilliant study on *The French Enlightenment and the Jews*.[16] He presents a comprehensive analysis of the ideological background, the evolution of philosophical and social ideas in the agitated pre-revolutionary age with its abundance of searching minds. These ideas influenced, directly or indirectly, also the attitude to the Jews. Dohm, he says, "was a mercantilist and a free trader, and he imagined the Jews as a useful economic element in the light of the kind of principles that had appealed to enlightened French royal administrators in the middle of the century ... He envisaged an economic policy by the state that would shift the Jews away from trade and towards the crafts and agriculture."[17] An adequate vocational distribution was one of the principal changes to be desired. In France this argument was even extended to the discussion of the position of the Jews of Poland. The stress laid on vocational distribution and its impact on social standing emerges also from Professor Kann's comments on the subject in this volume. They are based mainly on statistics from the Alsatian territory, but — as far as statistics go — are characteristic also for other regions.

Culturally, what Professor Hertzberg calls "the older way of life" made a more persistent stand against assimilation in Eastern France than in the region of Bordeaux where westernization proceeded without much resistance. While in the first part of the eighteenth century the Sephardi intellectuals were leading in the fight for full legal emancipation, the Jews who appeared on the scene after 1776 to argue the case for their rights were all "German" Jews from Eastern France. There the enlightened intelligentsia relied on Moses Mendelssohn. The Ashkenasi leader in France, Cerf Berr, turned to Mendelssohn for literary help. He asked him to compose a memorandum on behalf of the Alsatian Jews as an answer to the local antisemites, to be submitted to the French authorities. Mendelssohn was

---

[15]Ferdynand Zweig, *Israel - The Sword and the Harp*, Heinemann, London 1969, p. 36 ff.
[16]Columbia University Press, New York 1968.
[17]*Op. cit.*, p. 75.

too ill to comply and asked Dohm to draft this petition, but instead of dealing with the particular local issue Dohm preferred to discuss the whole complex in the book mentioned above.[18]

We cannot pursue here in detail the steps taken by Alsatian Jews even before the Revolution. In France the whole problem was primarily regarded as a legal one; emancipation had to be achieved once and for all by law, giving the Jews as individuals equal rights and status, while the further development was left to the practice of integration into society. In Germany, on the other hand, more stress was laid on the "educational" process. The object, as stated in the government papers of Bavaria quoted by Rürup, was conceived as "recasting of a whole nation", a metaphor reminding us of the button-moulder in Peer Gynt. But if Professor Kann says that emancipation in France was the victory of a principle, not the result of a prolonged Jewish struggle, we have to bear in mind as well that prior to the National Assembly's Resolution Jews in France fought for emancipation in petitions, memoranda and literary pamphlets in a way very similar to that in Germany. Nevertheless Professor Täubler was right in stating that the protracted struggle on the political and intellectual level in Germany was unique; it extended to the year 1869, or, if we prefer, we may say until 1919, with many vicissitudes and ups and downs. It produced the pattern of discussion of the modern Jewish question generally, as we know it up to this day.

Nowhere else were all the aspects of the question, religious and social, political and cultural, universalist and nationalist, treated with such thoroughness on both sides as in Germany. This is the reason why modern German-Jewish history is of outstanding importance in a world-wide Jewish context, beyond national frontiers. It must be added, alas, that the ultimate disaster to which this attempt at full integration led, is also part of the general picture. In the view of many commentators in the vast ensuing literature, this tragic end has something to do with the character of German nationalism, not only because of its innate romantic trend but also because of the political complexities of German history. Dr. Hamburger points out that it is very questionable whether what actually happened in the middle of the twentieth century was an inevitable outcome of historical necessity. It is better to heed Sir Isaiah Berlin's repeated warning and keep aloof of historical determinism.[19]

But even if we are aware of the contingency of history and if we do take into account the accumulation of unfortunate circumstances and personal errors which finally brought about the ascent to power of the Nazi party, there still remains enough which points in the other direction.

What, then, was the actual motive power of emancipation? One point made by

---

[18]Oddly, the shipping of the French translation of the book to France was delayed because no permit had been obtained. Cf. Dohm's letter to Mendelssohn of 28th December 1784, published by Fritz Bamberger in 'Four Unpublished Letters to Moses Mendelssohn', in *Living Legacy. Essays in honor of Hugo Hahn*, New York 1964, p. 94.

[19]Isaiah Berlin, *Four Essays on Liberty*, Oxford University Press 1969, especially the essay 'Historical Inevitability', of 1953.

Dr. Hertzberg, which conflicts with popular views, is particularly significant. Stressing the fact that many of the most prominent pioneers of enlightenment were also undisguised Jew-haters, he goes so far as to venture the thesis that Voltaire is the actual inventor and patron of modern — racist — antisemitism. Voltaire himself did not conceal his dislike of Jews. As an unbeliever he could not base his anti-Jewish feelings on the traditional Christian motives, so he returned to the pagan attitude. Nor could he be expected to show more indulgence to the Jewish than to the Christian religion. His secularised antisemitism, which also inspired the attitude of Alsatian antisemites like Hell and Foissac,[20] was to become the legacy for future generations and to bear fruit in the twentieth century.

This accusation, which has aroused a stimulating controversy among Hertzberg's critics, helps to elucidate the ideological background of emancipation. Emancipation undoubtedly owes its practicability to the victory, or semi-victory, of enlightenment at the time of the Revolution and at later intermittent stages, but it was not a result of so-called pro-semitism, or of a pro-Jewish attitude. It was the incidental outcome of the political philosophy of the day. In the assessment of the character of Jews there were prominent thinkers in the eighteenth century who differed from Voltaire's, Diderot's and Holbach's adverse views; men like Montesquieu and Mirabeau took the opposite stand. On the other hand, many advocates of emancipation in France were inspired by the hope that the emancipated Jew might ultimately embrace Christianity.

Why the Jews were emancipated by the French Revolution is summarized by Hertzberg as follows: "The majority of *les philosophes* sincerely believed that it was their moral duty to extend equality to all men and that even the Jews would be regenerated by the new order... The economic thrust of the Revolution was towards the creation of a modern economy, and it was impossible to maintain regulations and exclusions from an earlier time and apply them only to Jews..."[21] The same motives are evident in Germany at a later stage. One example is the most influential philosopher of the time, Georg Wilhelm Friedrich Hegel, who established a school of thought, or rather two schools of thought, which were of decisive impact for philosophy and politics in the nineteenth century and beyond. Hegel's attitude towards Jews and Judaism was analysed by Professor Hans Liebeschütz in a special chapter of his book on the image of Judaism in the work of German historians.[22] At the World Congress of Jewish Studies, an international gathering concerned with all aspects of Judaism and Jewish history, last summer in Jerusalem, this writer heard a Hebrew lecture by Dr. Shlomo Avineri in which

---

[20]Hertzberg, *op. cit.*, p. 307.
[21]*Ibid.*, p. 338.
[22]*Das Judentum im deutschen Geschichtsbild von Hegel bis Max Weber*, Schriftenreihe wissenschaftlicher Abhandlungen des Leo Baeck Instituts 17, Tübingen 1967. Professor Liebeschütz also contributed a paper on 'The position of Judaism in Hegel's early philosophy of History' to the Hegel Congress in Paris in spring 1969.

the speaker clearly elaborated the dualism of Hegel's attitude.[23] Hegel despised Judaism for theological reasons, in accordance with his interpretation of Christianity. He did not regard the Jews as a desirable element of Christian society. At the same time, Hegel was a definite partisan of the idea of the state as a universal structure that has to include all its inhabitants as citizens with equal formal rights. Hegel's footnote to Par. 270 of his Philosophy of Law, quoted by Avineri, states that "the fierce outcry against the Jews ignores the fact that they are, above all, men" and therefore entitled to the possession of civil rights. In this respect he echoes Dohm's time-honoured argument that a Jew is still more a man than a Jew. So it happened that Hegel, in spite of his hostility towards the Jews, was an advocate of emancipation on the strictly formalistic grounds of his political philosophy. The dualism of Hegel in this matter was reflected in a famous controversy between two of his disciples, representing the two opposing factions of his school. Bruno Bauer in his pamphlet *Die Judenfrage* of 1843 relies on Hegel's theological thinking and rejection of Judaism when he passionately argues against emancipation. On the other hand, Karl Marx, in his polemics against Bruno Bauer, although he himself has many unsavoury things to say about Jews, joins Hegel in his positive attitude to emancipation, as a logical conclusion to be drawn from the master's political interpretation of the nature of the state.[24] This vacillation of motives in the Great Debate makes the evolution of emancipation such a fascinating story also from a general point of view. It also explains perhaps why antisemitism did not disappear with the granting of emancipation, and why the full utilization by the Jews of the new possibilities offered by citizenship resulted in resentment and later in open hostility against them. The fully integrated Jews had not really been absorbed into the larger society, even when they had given up the Jewish way of life and their religious separatism altogether. When the Jew-hatred became an emotional force of unprecedented strength, and its fanning became a profitable political weapon, Hegel's aversion to the Jews proved a stronger element in the national consciousness of the Germans than his idea of the *Rechtsstaat* (State based on the Rule of Law).[25]

---

[23]An English version of Dr. Avineri's analysis of Hegel's position with regard to the Jewish question, 'A Note on Hegel's views on Jewish Emancipation', was published in *Jewish Social Studies*, New York, April 1963. Doctor Avineri is Senior Lecturer in Political Theory at the Hebrew University and author, among others, of *The Social and Political Thought of Karl Marx*, Cambridge University Press 1969. His illuminating essay on 'Marx and Jewish Emancipation' appeared in *Journal of the History of Ideas*, vol. XXV, No. 3 (1964); it is very relevant to the subject discussed here.

[24]On this controversy cf. Nathan Rotenstreich, 'For and against Emancipation. The Bruno Bauer Controversy', in *LBI Year Book IV* (1959).

[25]It is also a wrong but widespread assumption that revolutionary movements directed against reactionary regimes are by implication friendly to the Jews because these are one of the underprivileged classes of society. That the revolution of 1848 was accompanied by considerable anti-Jewish riots is shown by Jacob Toury in his (Hebrew) book *Turmoil and Confusion in the Revolution of 1848. The anti-Jewish riots in the 'Year of Freedom' and their Influence on Modern Antisemitism*, Moreshet, Tel-Aviv 1968. Toury himself seems baffled by these anti-Jewish manifestations of revolutionary forces, which are difficult to reconcile with their slogans of freedom and equality; *ibid.*, p. 15.

An interesting example of a Hegelian supporter of full emancipation, quoted by Avineri, is to be found in the pamphlets of F. W. Carové of Heidelberg. In 1837 Carové wrote that "the emancipation of the Jews is the universal problem of the emancipation of humanity itself"; and in 1844 he advocated Jewish emancipation not only as a means of making the Jews full members of society, but also as a way of enabling them to continue and to develop their own life as Jews.[26]

These are only some incidental details. But the centenary of the Emancipation Law of 1869, which stipulated full civic equality for Jews in Germany just on the eve of the unification of the German Empire, is an opportunity to see unrolled before us, in the mind's eye, the diversified history of the post-emancipation century. For several decades German Jews were able to enjoy the fruits of their age-long endeavours. The abrogation of the principles of humanity in 1933 was the more stunning as fifty years after the Law of 1869 — i.e. in 1919 — the rights which emancipation had produced had been confirmed in the Constitution of the Weimar Republic. This climax and anticlimax constitute a drama of momentous dimensions. The Weimar Republic was — or seemed to be — the peak of democratic achievement, the opening of a new era; it occurred to no-one at that time that the new framework would prove so fragile. An annulment of emancipation seemed unthinkable. Yet only fourteen years later the whole structure collapsed, under circumstances which only an apocalyptic visionary could have foreseen.

It is unavoidable that this outcome is in our mind when we devote this Year Book to the double event of the two anniversaries; but in historical research we have to look at events as they were when they happened, without imposing standards gained from later experience. The Editor is fortunate in having found an author of great distinction for this survey. Professor Ernest Hamburger is not only a man of scholarly ability and scrupulous accuracy, but one of the few among our contemporaries who during a considerable part of this period was in a position to observe the legislative machinery and the workings of party strife at close quarters. It is sensible that he does not confine himself to the bare facts of legislation and public discussion but familiarizes the reader with the whole political, social and cultural background of the battle for emancipation and for its implementation.

Hamburger is, of course, the author of the standard work on Jewish officials and politicians in Imperial Germany.[27] Now in his eightieth year, he is a man of unique practical experience in political life, both as longstanding member of the Social Democratic Party and as a parliamentarian. He is bound to view the events with an eye different from that of younger students who can rely only on

[26]Avineri, 'Hegel's views . . .', pp. 150-151.
[27]Ernest Hamburger, *Juden im öffentlichen Leben Deutschlands - Regierungsmitglieder, Beamte und Parlamentarier in der monarchischen Zeit 1848-1918*, Schriftenreihe wissenschaftlicher Abhandlungen des Leo Baeck Instituts 19, Tübingen 1968.

documents. This makes his comprehensive evaluation of the period the more remarkable.

There is, perhaps, an element of literary piquancy in having this work supplemented by the essay of a much younger German scholar who has devoted extensive studies to the problem of Jewish emancipation in the various German states, assiduously digging for pertinent documents in German archives. Dr. Reinhard Rürup already published, some time ago, a treatise on the approach to the Jewish question in Baden,[28] with ample reference to the contradictory opinions on the subject expressed in the Diet, in writings and in speeches, over half a century, until the final legal settlement. It may be of special interest to our readers to observe how such a liberal-minded German historian sees the subject in the context of multi-faceted German history in the nineteenth century.

Perhaps it has not always been duly appreciated that the emancipation actually set a complicated problem for the Germans, which cannot be simplified as a conflict between good and evil, or between pro-Jewish and anti-Jewish, but had a bearing on all the intricacies of an unsettled national consciousness. For a progressive German it was one of the many issues waiting for solution, or at least for reform, at a time when in many parts of Germany the police state was still prevalent. The average enlightened citizen, and especially the intellectual, felt himself politically outlawed, deprived of true citizen's rights, frustrated in an authoritarian country which knew nothing of democratic institutions. No wonder that he considered himself in need of "emancipation". In the discussions of that time the word "emancipation" has been used in this comprehensive sense, indicating the struggle for participation of the people in political decisions and for abolishing anachronistic institutions. Semantically, this may be surprising to a Jewish public which has tended to monopolize the word "emancipation" as a term for the liberation of Jews from the status of second class citizens. In fact, many other restrictions were still valid in various areas, remnants of the Middle Ages, of a corporate organization, and of such bodies as guilds which restricted freedom of occupation and trade not only for Jews.

Dr. Rürup's above-mentioned essay on the prolonged debate in Baden gives also a whole range of antisemitic arguments used by the opponents of emancipation. Some regarded the Jews as foreigners intending to establish a separate nation within the nation,[29] for some they were a kind of "bacillus", a term reminding us of the language to be used a hundred years later by the executors of the Nazi extermination policy; in the view of a priest cholera was preferable to emancipation.[30] More moderate opponents, on the authority of the Heidelberg theologian H. E. G. Paulus, demanded that emancipation be made conditional on a radical religious reform. These demands included abolition of the Sabbath, of

[28]Reinhard Rürup, 'Die Judenemanzipation in Baden', in *Zeitschrift für die Geschichte des Oberrheins*, Band 114, 1966, pp. 241-300.
[29]*Ibid.*, p. 272.
[30]*Ibid.*, p. 273.

the dietary laws and of circumcision, renunciation of Hebrew as the language of prayer, and condemnation of the Talmud.[31] At a later stage, the liberal leader in the Badensian Diet, the historian Ludwig Häusser, voiced doubts as to Dohm's version that the (repellent) character of the Jews had been moulded exclusively by the treatment they had suffered. It would have to be examined, he said, to what extent their character was the effect of their natural disposition and how far it was the result of oppression. In this context he introduced the new concept of *Race*[32] which proved of wide consequence for the future.

The two articles published in this volume, and in addition Dr. Rürup's essay on Baden, give an idea of the complexities of the obstacles which had to be overcome. To a large extent they derived from prejudices or attitudes partly to be explained by social developments from the Middle Ages onwards. The objections and doubts were not extinguished by the legal act of granting civil equality to the Jews, when this was finally decreed. This antinomy between law and reality — in Hamburger's words between the *pays légal* and the *pays réel* — may explain the later events when ruthless propaganda unlocked the floodgates through which these inveterate inclinations of the people could pour forth again without inhibition. Yet in the heyday of the liberal bourgeois civilization at the end of the nineteenth century most people, and especially the Jews, had forgotten that equal rights had been granted so reluctantly, and nobody considered it feasible that in an enlightened world they could be abolished again.

But, as Rürup says, it could be assumed "that a more thorough inquiry into the connection between emancipation and antisemitism would produce new points of view for the history of modern antisemitism. One would have to study the question whether the nature and development of the emancipatory process in Germany has not contributed considerably to the fact that Germany became the country of origin of modern antisemitism."[33]

Some of the views expressed in this century-long Great Debate and some of the facts and circumstances mentioned in the three articles printed here seem to confirm this view. Perhaps this could be a starting point for a new methodological approach. Beyond its scholarly value, such an objective study of all relevant factors may even produce results of some practical impact for the understanding of the ever-present issue of co-existence between Jews and Gentiles in many countries.

Among the other contributions to this volume are records of some of the enterprises concerned with one practical problem which, as mentioned above, occupied the minds of most fighters for emancipation on both sides: the aim of achieving a more "normal" vocational distribution.

At the turn of the century, Ahlem was perhaps the most important institution

---

[31]*Ibid.*, p. 273.
[32]In the German Text the word is spelled *Race* (French) and not *Rasse*.
[33]*Loc. cit.*, p. 297.

in Germany for the training of Jews in horticulture. We are very much indebted to Mr. S. Adler-Rudel for placing at our disposal his collection of material relating to this institute, which was enriched by the archives entrusted to him by the late Dr. Ernst Tuch, the son of one of the founders of the *Bodenkulturverein*.[34] In historical perspective it is clear that men like Baron Hirsch and *Konsul* Alexander Moritz Simon were pioneers in an effort which became of fundamental importance for German Jewry in the hour of disaster, if only because many countries of refuge were not willing to accept immigrants other than those qualified for agricultural work. The Nazi authorities initially viewed such Jewish efforts with a kind of benevolence. A circular of the school management of Ahlem, outlining the details of the subjects taught, bears the remark *Gemäss Genehmigung des Reichsbauernführers II E 2/6712/35 vom 13. 12. 1935*.[35] Another circular of 1936, in the possession of the Wiener Library in London, hints at grave difficulties which had arisen with regard to the conducting of the school. They had, however, been settled by negotiations with the *Reichsnährstand* and the *Reichsbauernführer*. The circular gives a verbatim extract of the letter of the *Reichsbauernführer* in which he approves of the school programme but says that he will not himself preside over the examinations; from time to time he will send a representative who will not take part in the examinations but will observe their character.

When the *Chalutz* movement with its idea of preparing young Jews for immigration to Palestine and settlement on the land spread to Central Europe after the First World War, Ahlem became one of the centres where such plans could be pursued. That such ideologies fell on fertile soil is illustrated by a passage in the printed letters of Franz Kafka. In February 1920 Kafka started a correspondence with a girl called Minze,[36] who was one of several girls desiring to be admitted to a school of this kind. He recommended to her the *Ahlemer Gartenbauschule* of which he had just obtained an illustrated report. "It is wonderful there", he wrote, "and for my next birthday I would wish nothing better than to be nineteen and to enter Ahlem." (He was thirty-six at the time.) For Minze, however, it was difficult because Ahlem was full, and she was admitted only after some time. She had to leave after a short while because of illness. But Kafka, in these letters, showed great enthusiasm for the idea of agricultural training for young Jews. He mentioned also a similar school for girls at Opladen near Cologne, but there, too, there were no vacancies. In 1920 Kafka's

---

[34]An article, 'A. M. Simon', by S. Adler-Rudel, in *Jüdische Rundschau*, 29.1.1936, written in Germany under Nazi rule, gives full credit to the foresight of men like Baron Maurice Hirsch and Alexander Moritz Simon, who almost unwittingly created instruments which were bitterly needed forty years later.

[35]Among the subjects, in addition to the agricultural training, there are mentioned, inter alia, languages (German, English, Hebrew), Bible study, Jewish history, information on Palestine.

[36]See Franz Kafka, *Briefe 1902-1924*, Schocken Books, New York 1958, p. 263 and passim.

own sister Ottla had unsuccessfully tried to be admitted to Opladen (she later went to work at a farm in the village of Zürau).

During the first years of the Nazi regime, before the Nazis were committed to wholesale extermination of the Jews, farms for what was then generally called *Hachsharah* (training) were established on a much wider scale not only in Germany but also in other countries where Jewish youth from Germany had been admitted for this purpose. One case in point was the Werkdorp Nieuwesluis in Holland, described in this volume by one of its veteran promoters. Like other experiments of the same sort, which were depicted or referred to in earlier contributions in the Year Book,[37] this farm, too, served a useful purpose until the moment when political events caused its closure.

Some of the refugees stranded on the Iberian Peninsula during the war were inclined towards pioneering agricultural work. Although their lives were no longer in danger, these young people — more purposeful than others — were imbued with what was called *Chalutzic* spirit. To encourage them in this aim, without deceiving them with false expectations, was one of the tasks which Mr. Perez Leshem, the author of the report in this book, had to fulfil.

German-Jewish historiography suffered a grave loss when one of the lecturers and writers in this field, Dr. Eleonore Sterling, died on the 27th December 1968. Born Elli Oppenheimer in Heidelberg in 1925, she had emigrated alone to America at the age of thirteen; her parents perished later in a concentration camp. After some difficult years she managed to study political science and wrote, in America, a thesis on 'Anti-Jewish excesses in Germany in 1819'. This later served as the basis for her doctoral dissertation in Frankfurt after she had returned there in 1953. It appeared as a book, *Er ist wie Du. Aus der Frühgeschichte des Antisemitismus in Deutschland (1815-1850)*. To our Year Book III (1958) Dr. Sterling contributed an essay 'Jewish Reaction to Jew-Hatred in the First Half of the 19th Century'. She also undertook to revise and supplement Ismar Elbogen's *History of the Jews in Germany* which had originally been published in English in the USA. Eleonore Sterling brought this work up to date in a German version.[38] A small textbook she had prepared, outlining Jewish history from the Enlightenment to the State of Israel, was published posthumously in 1969.[39]

---

[37]Werner T. Angress, 'Auswandererlehrgut Gross-Breesen', in *LBI Year Book X* (1965), pp. 168-187; Joseph Walk, 'The Torah va'Avodah Movement in Germany', in *LBI Year Book VI* (1961), pp. 236-256; Eliyahu Maoz, 'The Werkleute', in *LBI Year Book IV* (1959), pp. 165-182.

[38]Ismar Elbogen, Eleonore Sterling, *Die Geschichte der Juden in Deutschland. Eine Einführung*, Frankfurt a. M. 1966.

[39]Eleonore Sterling, *Kulturelle Entwicklung im Judentum von der Aufklärung bis zur Gegenwart*, with a preface, 'In Memoriam Eleonore Sterling', by Professor Dietrich Goldschmidt, Berlin, Wuppertal 1969.

Emancipation

One Hundred Years of Emancipation

BY ERNEST HAMBURGER

FOUR LEGAL TEXTS

The year 1969 marks the anniversaries of two decisive events in German-Jewish history, both of them sadly memorable in view of what was to follow later. A hundred years ago, on July 3, 1869, the emancipation law of the *Reichstag* of the North German Federation was promulgated. It repealed all remaining restrictions on civil and political rights due to differences in religious creed. During or immediately after the Franco-German war of 1870/71, through various legal enactments, the law became applicable to the states of Southern Germany which had not been part of the Federation, i.e. Bavaria, Wurttemberg, Baden and the southern part of Hesse. Fifty years after that noteworthy enactment and thus, half a century ago, after the military defeat of Germany in World War I and the emergence of the first German Republic, the principle of equality of rights regardless of religious affiliation was restated in the Weimar Constitution of August 11, 1919.

Such a coincidence of dates may serve as an occasion for examining again the texts which were significant for the emancipation of the Jews in Germany, as well as the actualities which arose from, but were often also in contradiction to these texts.

The above-mentioned enactments were not the first measures intended to bring the status of the Jews under a unified German jurisdiction instead of leaving it entirely to the several German states. They were preceded by the often remembered Article 16 of the German Federal Act of 1815 which dealt with the rights of the religious denominations. This Act was incorporated into the General Act of the Congress of Vienna and thereby made part of a new European order established on the ruins of the Napoleonic Empire. The German problem and, with it, the question of the rights of the Christian denominations and of the Jews in the German Confederation, were thus made a concern of Europe. The principle of a European involvement in the protection of freedom of religion and equal rights regardless of faith was repeatedly revived until promotion of human rights and fundamental freedoms found world-wide recognition by its embodiment in the Charter of the United Nations.

When the German nation attempted, in 1848, to assert itself and to shake off the existing regimes, the Jewish problem came again to the surface. The first written German constitution, adopted by the National Assembly in Frankfurt in March 1849, contained a comprehensive section on the rights and the duties of the citizens among which the right to religious liberty and to the enjoyment of all civil and political rights regardless of religious belief was included. Although the

3

Constitution became obsolete a few months after its adoption, the text and, more particularly, its chapter on the rights of the citizens were often remembered and referred to.

There were thus in recent German history four legal enactments relating explicitly or by implication to the emancipation of the Jews in Germany. They were drafted in four different places — in Vienna in 1815, in Frankfurt in 1848/49, in Berlin in 1869, and in Weimar in 1919. Each place denotes a distinct reorientation of German history and each attempt influenced the fate of Germany for a longer or shorter period. None took the problem completely out of the jurisdiction of the individual states with which it rested until 1869 and even, to a considerable extent, thereafter. All four documents, however, were intended to bring about certain conditions common to the whole of Germany, which had been absent before 1815 and which lasted until, after the advent of the Nazi regime, the history of German Jewry was brought to a terrible end.

EARLY STAGES AND LIMITATIONS OF EMANCIPATION

When in 1815 the princes and statesmen convened in Vienna, the status of the Jews in the several German states had undergone far-reaching transformations. The French Declaration on the Rights of Man and of the Citizen of 1789, its incorporation into the Constitution of 1791 and its application to the status of the Jews, ascertained by a resolution of the French Constituant Assembly, had an important effect. The problem of Jewish emancipation, to be sure, had arisen in the territories of Northern and Southern Germany as a result of international humanitarian thought before the French Revolution. More than forty years earlier Gotthold Ephraim Lessing had raised his voice on behalf of the Jews for the first time, portraying them in his plays in sympathetic terms. The Prussian Councillor Christian Wilhelm Dohm supplied juridico-philosophical arguments for their emancipation. Prussian officers and administrators mingled freely with Jewish businessmen and intellectuals in the *salons* of educated Jewesses. Moses Mendelssohn, Lessing's friend, opened the way to the use and mastery of the German language by the Jews and so to a life beyond the ghetto, by his translation of the Pentateuch.

However, all this became politically relevant only in the wake of French military expansion. When Napoleon asserted his power in Central Europe and redrew the map of Germany, all states felt compelled to re-examine their legislation in the light of French political and constitutional thought. Different trends evolved, as usual in similar cases in world history: how far did a powerful state go in imposing ideological and political features of its regime on other states in its orbit of influence; how far did defeated nations go or have to go in adapting their legislation to that of the victor; how far did they strive to preserve their traditional governmental concepts in the hour of turmoil?

For the Jews — and of course not for them alone — a confusing variety of solutions ensued. Full equality was bestowed on them in those territories which were made part of the French Empire, especially on the left bank of the Rhine, except for certain economic restrictions which, in 1808, were imposed for a period of ten years. The Jews were also granted full equality in the Hanseatic cities when they were incorporated into France, and in the satellite states of Western Germany, first of all in the kingdom of Westphalia which extended far beyond the boundaries of the later Prussian province of that name. A special case was the newly established Grand Duchy of Frankfurt where the Jews were granted equality after the redemption of their annual dues for the right to governmental protection, by the payment of a lump sum and annuities.

While in these territories the impact of French power led to the imposition or complete emulation of the French example, new ground was broken in Prussia when Baron Karl vom Stein, in his law on the reform of city government, granted the right to vote and to stand for election to municipal bodies to all citizens regardless of religious affiliation. Stein considered the participation of the Jews, a rising element of the urban population, as indispensable for a healthy development of industry and trade, but did not venture into a full-scale reform of the status of the Jews, whom he personally disliked and distrusted.

Here, after the unproductive interlude of the Dohna-Altenstein ministry, Stein's successor Karl August von Hardenberg, more impressed than his predecessor with modern French legislative trends, took the decisive step. By the law of 1812, which he wrested from the reluctant King, he granted the Jews citizenship and full civil rights. He thereby enabled them to benefit from the recently secured freedom of trade and commerce, and by the Prussian Customs Union, achieved in 1818, six years after the law of emancipation. Thus the Jews were granted full equality with the exception of access to the officer corps, to public administrative offices and to the judiciary which the king, against Hardenberg's advice, left to future legislation. At that time Prussia was a country of not more than five million inhabitants. The number of Jews hardly exceeded 40,000, one third of the number to which they amounted after the reintegration of the Grand Duchy of Posen into the kingdom and the incorporation of the provinces of Rhineland and Westphalia. They lived mostly in small towns. In Berlin where a century later about 30 per cent of the German Jews resided, their percentage only slightly exceeded their share in the total population of Prussia.

The states of Southern Germany did not grant their Jews all the civil rights enjoyed by their correligionists in Prussia, especially the right to full freedom of trade and to free movement and residence. In Wurttemberg and Baden they were admitted to a limited number of localities only. The same holds true for Bavaria. One of the purposes of the Bavarian law of emancipation of 1813 was to prevent the increase of the Jewish population and, should it appear too large, to enforce its decrease. This is the reason why, leaving aside the Jewry of Posen where special rules applied, the emigration of German Jews was for fifty years overwhelmingly from the states of Southern Germany.

In the Kingdom of Saxony, finally, which before 1815 included the later Prussian province of the same name, the Jews did not enjoy equality of rights in trade and industry and were not allowed worship in public. Only a tiny number of Jews were admitted to residence in the country and they were restricted to Dresden, later to Dresden and Leipzig. Only more than twenty years after the Congress of Vienna was some progress made toward greater equality.

After the fall of the Napoleonic Empire, the Prussian law of 1812 was the most progressive instrument of Jewish emancipation in a German state. For about half a century, on the basis of this law and as a result of Prussia's liberal economic policy, the Prussian Jews advanced in the socio-economic field more than in any other German state. This was all the more important since, in 1816, 50% of all German Jews lived in Prussia and this percentage rose to about 70% in 1866 and remained so as a result of the proportional decline of the Jewish population in Southern Germany and of the integration into Prussia of formerly non-Prussian territories.

REVERSAL IN VIENNA

German Federal Act of June 8, 1815

"Article 16. The belonging to differing parties of the Christian religion shall not cause any difference in the enjoyment of civil and political rights in the states and regions of the German Confederation.
The Federal Assembly will deliberate on a procedure as uniform as possible by which a civil betterment of those who profess the Jewish faith can be brought about in Germany and how especially the enjoyment of civil rights can be secured to them, they assuming correspondingly all civil duties, in the confederate states. Until then, however, those who profess the Jewish faith shall retain those rights which they have already been granted by the several confederate states."[1]

Currents and cross-currents determined the political climate of the Congress of Vienna. Liberal ideas and the longing for German unification pervaded important sections of the population. Though they were not disregarded, they were not shared by the representatives of the German states in Vienna. Old Germany, consisting as it did of several hundred principalities, was dead, but the governments of the thirty-six new units were interested in their sovereignty rather than in the establishment of powerful central authorities and liberal institutions.

The Jewish problem did not escape the effects of this situation. Austria, Prussia and Hanover joined in working out drafts the adoption of which would have significantly advanced the Jewish cause. These drafts of the future Article 16 of the Federal Act were intended to ensure civil rights regardless of religious affiliation not only to the adherents of the Christian denominations, but also to the members of the Jewish faith. Their approval would have made the Prussian law of 1812 the basis of policy towards the Jews and would have ensured a more enlightened reform legislation in the states of Southern and South Western Germany and in the Hanseatic cities.

---

[1]Author's translation.

That Prussia favoured a solution founded on its legislation is not astonishing. In proposing supra-state and international law, every state usually sets out by suggesting the adoption of its own rules, as far as applicable to the international community. Austria had had a liberal tradition since the Josephian Edict of Toleration of 1782. In Hanover, as a part of Jerome's Kingdom of Westphalia, the Jews had enjoyed full equality of rights and had gained some influence. This carried weight at least at the beginning of the negotiations. Prussia also looked forward to the creation of a free trade area in Northern Germany. Prussian economic legislation was, therefore, to be shaped so as to be applicable also beyond the boundaries of Prussia; and the regime relating to the Jews had strong economic implications. Jews married, migrated and traded beyond the state boundaries. Frictions were bound to ensue from contradictory laws, a point brought home by Hardenberg to the Free Cities. The Prussian State Chancellor, however, encountered a strong resistance from these and other governments. The medium-sized and small states were not primarily interested in free trade, but in the protection of the Christian artisans, craftsmen and tradesmen who brought pressure to bear on their governments to help them against their Jewish competitors.

This decided the issue. As long as Prussia and Austria had to take into account liberal public opinion, neither wanted to go against popular currents. The body of liberal public opinion, however, was not yet sufficiently organized; nor was there a real consensus on which a constitution could be created.[2] As soon as liberal attitudes waned and the period of reaction was foreshadowed, each of the contenders for leadership in Germany qualified its stand. They now courted the favour of the delegates of the other states. Hanover added an escape clause to its draft referring to hindrances which might arise from the constitutions of the contracting states and which should be removed "as far as possible". As a result, the draft presented by the "Big Three" was weaker than the preceding Prussian and Austrian proposals.

The other states, however, were not prepared to accept even a text so cautiously worded. Under these conditions a time-honoured solution was found. Nothing was resolved by the Congress, everything was left to the Federal Assembly envisaged by the Federal Act. For the Christian denominations equality was declared; for the Jews it was postponed. The Assembly was to decide how the lot of the Jews could be "improved" and how, in a way on which the state members could agree "as far as possible", the Jews could be accorded and assured the enjoyment of civil rights. Austria and Prussia succeeded in writing their objective, civil rights for the Jews, into the article. The other states succeeded in putting off the decision. No time limit was set for its implementation. The wording of the article was weakened and made almost meaningless by the approval of an amendment

---

[2]*December 1918. The Congress of Vienna.* Handbook prepared under the direction of the Historical Section of the Foreign Service (1814-1815), pp. 128 ff. Salo Baron's book *Die Judenfrage auf dem Wiener Kongress* Berlin/Wien 1920, is the classic guide for the treatment of this subject.

proposed by Saxony, the hardest foe of Jewish emancipation, which stipulated that by unanimous vote only was the Federal Assembly empowered to take decisions relating to religion. As the only immediately effective measure the Jews were guaranteed the rights accorded to them previously by the individual states. The last words were substituted for the words "in the individual states", hastily and without discussion, as all were pressed for time. This amendment was considered by some as a change of substance, excluding from the guarantee the rights granted under French law or under the law in French-dominated and now dissolved territories, by others as a modification of mere drafting. Vagueness, uncertainty and confusion were further heightened.

As finally adopted, the text constituted a serious retreat from the position gained by the Jews as a result of the French Revolution. For about twenty years the tendency had been towards equality of rights. Now the trend had been reversed. The article did not preclude further advancement but was hardly conducive to it. The two leading states of the German Confederation favourable to Jewish emancipation had yielded to the pressure exercised by most other states and could not be expected to act in the future without great circumspection. A common progressive solution was, if not openly disavowed, at least abandoned in fact. The German states remained far apart in their approach to the Jewish status. As the trend towards greater German unity and the establishment of liberal institutions slackened, the possibility of any strong action intended to further Jewish emancipation became remote.

THIRTY YEARS OF POLITICAL REGRESSION

What the Congress of Vienna could not accomplish, the *Bundestag* did not achieve either, between 1815 and 1848. It did not harmonize the legislation on civil rights or even discuss the means to come closer to this objective. What was worse, the *Bundestag* did not intervene when the minimum guarantee was violated. Prussia, reversing her former attitude, became the worst offender, but other states also disregarded the provision ensuring the Jews those rights which they had been accorded previously.

In one case only the *Bundestag* took action. In 1816, the Free City of Frankfurt deprived the Jews of their citizenship. This led to a protracted struggle between the Senate and the Jewish Community of the Free City in the course of which the *Bundestag* appointed a commission which was to reconcile the opposing points of view. Since strong pressure was exercised simultaneously by four great European powers, the Senate, anxious to avoid a decision of the *Bundestag,* proclaimed in 1824 a new law restoring citizenship to the Jews and according them civil rights subject, however, to certain, in part severe, restrictions. Despite its restraint the action of the *Bundestag* appeared serious enough to the anti-Jewish states of Saxony and Wurttemberg for them to register a protest and to condemn any intervention in the domestic affairs of a German state. Their worries were unfounded, however. Frankfurt's case remained an exception; there the success was due mainly to the able diplomacy of the Jewry of the Free City and the rising influence of the House of Rothschild.[3]

Within the German states some progress was upheld or made. On the left bank of the Rhine, in the territories incorporated into Prussia, Bavaria and Hesse-Darmstadt, the Jews retained not only their civil but also their political rights; administrative measures, however, curtailed their exercise. When the effects of the French Revolution of 1830 made themselves felt and the people of Electoral Hesse and Brunswick obtained a written constitution, the Jews achieved equal rights with the other citizens. In many other states, however, advancement was arrested by the resistance of the Christian lower middle class. Anti-Jewish riots in Bavaria prevented the government from revising the backward law of 1813. Such riots were frequent also in other, mainly South German states. In Wurttemberg, the law of 1828 granting the Jews citizenship and civil rights subject to restrictions, was adopted only after the King had let it be known that he would not promulgate the version of the Legal Committee of the *Landstände* which had modified the text to the disadvantage of the Jews. In Baden the attempt to improve their status was defeated by the *Landstände* under the leadership of Karl von Rotteck, a liberal who had won fame. The government had difficulty even in upholding the existing situation. At that time the governments, feeling that the political and economic interests of their country were best served by the unfettered participation of the Jews in the national economy, were broader-minded than the people and the parliaments.

Prussia's conduct was ambivalent. On the one hand, she stuck to her previous policies, supported the cause of the Jews of Frankfurt and continued to recommend the law of 1812 for adoption by other states. On the other hand, within her own frontiers, she was swamped by the wave of reaction. As early as 1816, several of Hardenberg's ministers claimed that the law of 1812 had gone too far and should be revised. Hardenberg resisted, but could not avert the erosion of the law. In 1822, some months before his death, he yielded to the pressure of his ministers and acceded to the deletion of the article which opened academic teaching positions to the Jews. Likewise, contrary to Article 16 of the Federal Act, access to many other posts, state as well as municipal offices, was denied to Jews. The plan, pressed in 1814 and 1815, to extend the application of the law to the newly-acquired Prussian territories was abandoned. Instead of a German-wide agreement the status of the Jews differed from region to region and from city to city often in the same state.

THE SOCIAL AND ECONOMIC RISE OF THE JEWISH POPULATION

To resume, in the thirty-odd years between the Congress of Vienna and the Revolution of 1848 the promise of Article 16 of the Federal Act was not fulfilled.

---

[3]Lübeck is a case in point. The Jews of Lübeck were deprived of the right of residence and the intervention of the great European powers on their behalf was disregarded (Baron, *op. cit.*, pp. 197 ff.).

Subject to minor exceptions, the legal and administrative status of the Jewish population did not improve or even took a change for the worse. This statement, true as far as it goes, does not, however, tell the whole story. During the same period the Jews made remarkable social and economic progress. Germany remained an overwhelmingly agrarian country and the stagnant society reflected this immobility which was in strange contradiction to the flourishing intellectual life. The Jews, in contrast, improved their social and occupational stratification. They benefited by compulsory education, since 1833 compulsory also in the province of Posen. Instead of a small elite of court bankers and businessmen and a few physicians at the top and the great mass of pedlars at the bottom, they entered trade and crafts in growing numbers wherever this course was open to them, or earned their living as shopkeepers. Some acquired wealth and became big landowners, others developed industries for the domestic and foreign markets. The Jewish private banker emerged, banking firms sprang up in Frankfurt, Karlsruhe, Mainz and elsewhere. In many states they placed most of the state loans and financed the building of the railroads, indispensable instruments and themselves products of the burgeoning industrial revolution.[4] The number of Jewish physicians increased; Jews also pursued studies of law and philosophy long before they had a chance of being admitted to the bar or to teaching positions. Jewish writers and journalists made their first appearance.

This development was more significant than the restrictions to which the Jews were still subjected. Their image changed in the eyes of German society. Even men of the right like the future Chancellor Otto von Bismarck recognized that they were almost exclusively "honourable" people in the cities and that respectable Jews did not constitute "exceptions" in the countryside. The betterment of the climate was brought into the open when, less than a year before the Revolution of 1848, the Prussian government submitted a draft law relating to the status of the Jews to the first Prussian United Diet, a consultative body of noblemen, sitting in the First Chamber, and of the representatives of the Estates (the landed gentry, the towns and the rural communities) in the Second Chamber. A large part, in many cases a majority of the members of the Chamber of the Estates were favourable to the Jewish cause and voted for equality of rights. However, the Diet expressed itself against the admission of Jews to teaching posts in elementary and secondary schools and to positions as judges.

The government, which was not bound by the advice of the Diet, made the new law applicable to the entire kingdom except for Posen. Otherwise the progress was held in narrower confines than the Second Chamber of the Diet had suggested. It also lagged behind Hardenberg's intentions and even behind the law of 1812. Thus, access to academic positions at universities was restricted to the

---

[4]See Kurt Grunwald, 'Europe's Railways and Jewish Enterprise', in *LBI Year Book XII* (1967), pp. 163-209.

faculties of medicine and to some departments of the faculties of philosophy.[5] With the approach of the Revolution of 1848, there was, therefore, a definite contradiction between the social and economic status of a growing number of Jews and their legal situation.

THE CONSTITUTIONAL LAWS OF 1848/49 AND THE FACTS OF LIFE

Constitution of March 28, 1849.

"Part VI. The Fundamental Rights of the German People.

Art. V.

144. Every German has full freedom of faith and conscience. No one is bound to disclose his religious conviction.
145. Every German is unrestricted in the common private and public practice of his religion...
146. The enjoyment of civil and political rights is neither dependent upon, nor restricted by religious creed. Civic duties may not be impaired thereby.
147. Every religious body regulates and administers its affairs independently, but remains subject to the general laws of the state.
No religious body shall be granted privileges over others by the state; moreover, there is no State Church...
148. No one shall be compelled to take part in a religious act or ceremony."

Art. XIII.

188. Sections of the population of Germany not speaking the German language shall be guaranteed their popular development, in particular equal rights with regard to their languages, as far as the domains of these languages extend, to ecclesiastical matters, education, internal administration and courts of law.[6]

The Revolution of 1848 marked a new departure. The Federal Act of Vienna was produced by chiefs of government and their aides. The Constitution of 1849 emanated from an Assembly whose members were elected by the German people. In Vienna the problem of religion was singled out and articles relating to other rights were omitted with the exception of noncommittal references to freedom of movement and of the press and to copyright. The Parliament of the *Paulskirche* devoted a comprehensive chapter to the Fundamental Rights of the German people. In Vienna the emphasis was on civil rights for the Jews, with which the Federal Assembly was invited to deal. In Frankfurt political rights were added and granted, together with civil rights, by the National Assembly itself and unconditionally. Article 16 of the Federal Act treated the question of the members of the Jewish faith separately from those of the Christian denomination. The Assembly of Frankfurt enunciated principles common to all: every German shall enjoy full freedom of faith and conscience. No German shall be subjected to limitations with regard to the practice of his religion in private or in public. The enjoyment

---

[5]For the text of the law of July 23, 1847 see Ismar Freund, *Die Emanzipation der Juden in Preussen,* Berlin 1912, vol. II, pp. 501 ff. Bismarck's speech in *Vollständige Verhandlungen des Ersten Vereinigten Preussischen Landtags über die Emanzipationsfrage der Juden,* Berlin 1847, pp. 224 ff.
[6]Author's translation.

of civil and political rights shall be neither dependent upon nor restricted by religious faith. No religious body shall be privileged by the state; there shall be no established church.

When, after protracted discussions, the Fundamental Rights were proclaimed on December 26, 1848, the revolution had passed its climax and the governments of the states were again or soon were to become masters of the situation. The large states, Austria, Prussia and Bavaria did not incorporate the Fundamental Rights into their statute books. The other states made them the law of the land. Now they were either compelled to purge their legal systems of all vestiges of the revolution or did so voluntarily after the revolutionary movement had run its course.

This did not signify, however, a return to the pre-revolutionary status. Many articles relating to fundamental freedoms did not innovate; they rather consolidated laws of the several states as they had been shaped at the beginning of the revolution. As to the political rights, the composition of the Assembly of the *Paulskirche* itself was determined by the decision of the so-called Preliminary Parliament *(Vorparlament)* of March 30, 1848 which granted the right to vote to all Germans irrespective of birth, property and religion. The formula, due to Gabriel Riesser who presented it in a widely noted speech, clearly influenced the Prussian ordinance issued a week later which declared the exercise of political rights independent of religious affiliation. The Prussian National Assembly and the constituent assemblies of the other states were elected in accordance with these rules. Equality before the law, freedom of religious belief and of the practice of religion and the enjoyment of all civil and political rights regardless of creed were guaranteed in Articles 4 and 12 of the Prussian Constitution of 1848 and the guarantee was upheld in the revised Constitution of January 1850. The other states followed suit. Though the Frankfurt Constitution lapsed, these laws lasted.

Even the Constitution of Frankfurt, however, short-lived as it was, had at least some moral results. For the first time an elected body speaking for the whole of Germany had alerted the German people to the justified claim of the Jews to civil and political equality. Riesser's intervention in favour of political rights regardless of religion and his emotion-laden speech against a special status for the "Jewish tribe", as recommended by deputy Moritz Mohl, were well received and successful; and even Mohl had been careful to state that the Jews should not be denied the right to vote and to be elected.[7] The Parliament, consisting mostly of professors, lawyers and civil servants, declared equality of rights irrespective of religious belief, meeting hardly any resistance in its midst. This set a powerful precedent.

Other happenings of the year of the revolution, however, were less propitious and distinct precursors of the reaction to come. The governments acted reluctantly and under revolutionary pressure only. This was not everywhere as clear as in the Free City of Frankfurt and in Hesse-Darmstadt where formidable obstacles had

---

[7]Ernest Hamburger, *Juden im öffentlichen Leben Deutschlands - Regierungsmitglieder, Beamte und Parlamentarier in der monarchischen Zeit 1848-1918*, Tübingen 1968 (Schriftenreihe wissenschaftlicher Abhandlungen des Leo Baeck Instituts 19), pp. 21, 120 f.

to be overcome to secure equal rights for the Jews, but it was apparent also in other states. Thus, the promise of complete emancipation, given by the King of Bavaria, was not fulfilled; access to public office was not among the rights granted to the Jews. Their disabilities in the exercise of certain civil rights in the states of Southern Germany were not, or not fully, removed. Restrictions on freedom of residence and movement in Southern Germany, among which, for instance, the degrading *Matrikelzwang* in Bavaria, survived.

These governmental obstructions were accompanied by ominous signs of popular resistance to Jewish emancipation. In the very year of the revolution, Jewish newspapers had to report not only petitions, speeches and resolutions favourable to full equality, but also riots directed against the Jews. They were lumped together with princes, high officials and priests as enemies and exploiters of the people. Bavaria, Baden and Hamburg were the main centres of anti-Jewish riots in the course of which Jewish shops were plundered, workshops stormed, letters of credit burned. The movement also extended to Wurttemberg and the Prussian district of Upper Silesia, although it was less widespread there.

To conclude, then, signs of hostility towards the Jews were not missing in the year of the revolution. It did not engulf the National Assembly, but it permeated the governments and the people of the lower middle class, of which the Parliament of Frankfurt was not representative, and it prepared the ground for the period of a second reaction.

BETWEEN 1849 AND 1869: REACTION AND LIBERALISM

The period between 1849 and 1869, the year in which the law of the North German *Reichstag* was promulgated, was marked by two partly contradictory trends.

Economically and socially the status of the Jews improved steadily. This was the time in which Germany began transforming herself from a prevailingly agrarian to an overwhelmingly industrialized country. This process was accompanied by migration from the countryside to the cities, from Eastern Germany (parts of which remained largely agrarian) to Central and Western Germany, by urbanization, by the origin and increase of an urban proletariat and new political trends arising out of changed working and living conditions.

The opportunities of the Jews grew markedly as a result of this transformation. As soon as they had gained freedom of movement, Jews left the small towns, especially in the province of Posen in which they had been crowded, and integrated themselves in the urban societies of Berlin, Breslau and Königsberg in the East and the Hessian and Rhenish-Westphalian centres in the West. Jewish bankers financed the newly-developing industries. Jews ventured into industrial pursuits. The brothers Reichenheim purchased the largest textile works in Middle Silesia, the Grünfelds introduced the linen industry in Lower Silesia. Upper Silesia's coal and steel industry was developed by Jews. The Ludwig Löwe Company in Berlin became a leading weapon manufacturing firm; Emil Rathenau started the business from which the German General Electric Company sprang up.[8] The "Jew at the market place" of the small and medium-sized towns, fore-shadowed the role of the Jews as founders of large department stores in the big cities. The Jewish occupational distribution came closer to that of the German urban society while retaining important special features. The Jews were less represented in industry and far above average in banking and commerce, especially in the trading of metals, grains and textiles. Their numbers were small among the manual workers and large among the independent businessmen and the white-collar workers. They had no foothold in agriculture.

Complementary to and helped by this social stratification, and corresponding to the traditional esteem of the Jews for learning and knowledge, the percentage of Jewish high school and university students increased to remarkable proportions. By 1860, the number of Jewish students in secondary schools had grown to almost six per cent of the total, to increase still more in the later decades of the century. The trend was similar in the institutions of higher learning. There was an abundant supply of Jews qualified to fill posts for which academic training was required. Jewish participation in economic and cultural life, as it was known in Germany before 1933, took shape during that period.

Politically, however, the development was more complicated. From 1849 to 1858 political reaction, as is usual after an abortive revolution, was indicative of the spirit of the times. The disabilities of the Jews in the realm of civil rights in Southern Germany persisted or were only partly removed. As far as the exercise of political rights was concerned, the status gained by the Jews in 1848 was repeatedly put to the question, but in most states they succeeded in preserving the right to vote and to be elected. With the emergence of parliaments in the North and the transformation of *ständische* (corporative) representations into truly parliamentary bodies in the South, they won support among the Liberals who, after 1848, systematically espoused the cause of Jewish emancipation. But even in parliaments in which conservative forces were strong, attempts to deprive the Jews of their political rights were beaten back. The stubborn resistance of the German middle class to the emancipation of the Jews again became apparent, however. In the Prussian Parliament, dominated by the nobility and members of the aristocratic civil service, plans to withdraw political rights from the Jews were supported by a small minority only and failed twice. In Bavaria, in contrast, a draft law which would have made Christian faith one of the foundations of a new electoral law was approved by a majority of the Second Chamber. It was not passed only because it did not reach the constitutionally prescribed two-thirds majority. In other parts of Southern and South Western Germany, in Wurttemberg, Electoral Hesse and Frankfurt the Jews temporarily even lost their political rights.

All these restrictions were lifted when liberalism regained stature, for which the pace was set by the movement for Italian unification. In the early sixties, full

---

[8]Kurt Zielenziger, *Juden in der deutschen Wirtschaft*, Berlin 1930, pp. 103 ff., 125 ff., 155 ff.; see also *Das Leinenhaus Grünfeld. Erinnerungen und Dokumente von Fritz V. Grünfeld*, eingeleitet und herausgegeben von Stefi Jersch-Wenzel, Berlin 1967.

political rights were restored to the Jews in those states in which they had been deprived of them and their disabilities in the field of civil rights were abolished wherever they still existed. Except for some vestiges of earlier discrimination full equality was bestowed on them in law and, as far as civil and electoral rights were concerned, also in fact.

In contrast, the right of access to public office remained on paper. Appointments of Jews made here and there were distinctly exceptional. Jews continued to be excluded from administrative positions and judgeships. They were not admitted to teaching posts in primary and secondary schools and exceptionally only to professorships in the universities. Gabriel Riesser's appointment as a judge in Hamburg, the promotion of Moritz Ellstätter to Minister of Finance in Baden — the only Jewish minister in a German state until 1918 — and Levin Goldschmidt's admission as a full professor to the Faculty of Law in the University of Heidelberg show Baden and Hamburg ahead of the other states.[9] The Prussian government, disregarding petitions and resolutions of the Diet, remained adamant in refusing Jews access to positions of authority and hopes for a change were shattered when Bismarck was called by the King, in 1862, to preside over the Ministry and took up his four-year-long fight against the liberal majority of the Prussian House of Deputies.

Thus, the prestige gained by the Jews in the social and economic sphere did not cause the governments to accept them as bearers of authority in the Executive, the administration and the judiciary. The road leading thereto was thrown open to them legally in 1848 but, notwithstanding some exceptions, it remained barred to them in fact.

A HUNDRED YEARS AGO: THE ACT OF 1869

"All remaining restrictions of civil and political rights derived from the difference in religious creed are hereby abolished. In particular, eligibility for participation in municipal and state representation and for the holding of public office shall be independent of religious creed."[10]

Act of the *Reichstag* of the North German Federation of July 3, 1869.

When the North German *Reichstag* convened in 1867 after the defeat of Austria in the Austro-Prussian war, a new era began for German unification. It was marked by the emergence of the National Liberals as the strongest political party in the *Reichstag* and in the Prussian Chamber of Deputies. They supported Bismarck's foreign policy while striving to pursue a moderately liberal domestic policy. It was the period of co-operation between Bismarck and the Liberals who, after having tried in vain to bring about German unification, acknowledged Bismarck's leadership. He, in turn, conceded to them that measure of liberal reform which he deemed compatible with his foreign policy and acceptable and

[9]In the departments of mathematics and natural science a few Jews were appointed full professors before Goldschmidt. Moritz Abraham Stern, f.i. warmly supported by Karl Friedrich Gauss, became a full professor in Göttingen in 1859.
[10]Author's translation.

even unavoidable for the shaping of the institutions of the coming *Reich*. The penal code, the codes of civil and criminal procedure, the law on the constitution of the courts of law, the industrial code and the monetary reform in the *Reich* as well as the administrative reform in the Eastern provinces of Prussia and many other laws of a similar kind which Bismarck either approved without taking much interest in most of them or which he accepted grudgingly, were due to the work of the North German and the German *Reichstag* between 1867 and 1877. In the preparation, discussion and adoption of these laws Eduard Lasker, Ludwig Bamberger and Levin Goldschmidt played a leading part in the *Reichstag,* Lasker and the baptized Jew Rudolf Friedenthal, a Free Conservative who later became Prussian Minister of Agriculture under Bismarck, also in the Prussian Diet.

The Act of 1869 on the removal of all remaining civil and political disabilities based on religious belief was a fruit of the alliance between Bismarck's power politics and the representatives of the liberally-minded majority of the voters. It was initiated by the Parliament, sanctioned by the Federal Council, the representatives of the state governments whose approval was required to bring it into force, and signed by the King over Bismarck's countersignature. The law was thereby different from Article 16 of the Viennese Federal Act which was a product of governmental action only, and from its Frankfurt precedent which was based on the will of the National Assembly alone.

The four Jews among the 295 members of the North German *Reichstag* — not counting the three baptized Jews, one of whom was Eduard Simson, its president and the former president of the Frankfurt Assembly — did not play a prominent part in the adoption of the Act of 1869. Eduard Lasker was the only Jew who briefly addressed the *Reichstag* in order to reject the suggestion of a Conservative deputy that the Jews themselves were not in favour of this draft. Nevertheless, the parliamentary action was due to the petitions of hundreds of Jewish communities demanding an enactment of this kind. Although there was no mention of the Jews in the text, these initiatives and the debate between Lasker and the Conservative opponent of the law prove that the Jewish problem was uppermost in the minds of the members of the Parliament of the North German Federation during the discussion.

Although in establishing equality of civil and political rights regardless of faith, the law was not an innovation but rather put the seal on matters and rights as they had evolved during the last sixty years, it was of primary importance. It was the definitive legal text on the emancipation of the German Jews. It applied expressly also to elected bodies and to the holding of office on the state and municipal level. It was a basis of action and a barrier against discriminatory legislation. The governmental approval was expressed in the strongest possible terms in the speech of the King of Prussia on the closing of the *Reichstag:* "The bill... first prepared in your House, anticipated the unanimous intention of the Federal Council, and has received its assent".[11] The law was a unique concession

[11]English translation in *British and Foreign State Papers* LX (1869-1870), London 1876, p. 394.

by Bismarck in a matter in which he was otherwise intransigent: it introduced into the legislation of the North German Federation and, thereafter, of the German *Reich,* an article relating to human rights and affected the jurisdiction of the individual states in which the Chancellor, as a matter of principle, otherwise carefully avoided intervening.

Bismarck, for whom the Jewish question was of secondary importance and for whom antisemitism, though he was affected by it, was mainly a tactical weapon, emphasized later that he had contributed to the enactment of the law "at least by my signature". This was an understatement, as is proven by the strong terms of the above-quoted speech of the King of Prussia. Bismarck wished to accommodate the Liberals who, during these years, took a determined stand in favour of the equality of rights for the Jewish population. The law was part and parcel of the measures taken by the Liberals to do away with the still considerable feudal remnants in the legislative texts of the German states. Bismarck's assent, however, was mainly rooted in his own Prussian thought of *suum cuique* rather than in modern national and liberal ideas. As the army officers and the civil servants had to be recruited from the ranks of the nobility, the big landowners and the sons of the high officials, the problems which arose in connection with banking and international finance, and which were to become more complex in the new *Reich* in a period of economic change, were to be solved with the assistance of financially influential and knowledgeable Jews with useful international connections. The Chancellor did not want to antagonize a community able to contribute to the success of his policy and to assist him in the solution of economic and financial matters.

AFTER 1869: THE EXECUTIVE AND THE DENIAL OF POSITIONS OF PUBLIC AUTHORITY TO THE JEWS

During the sixties of the nineteenth century the emancipation was legally completed. The Act of 1869 of the North German Federation and, subsequently, of the German *Reich* was also designed to give an impulse to the implementation of the right of access to public office which, as we have seen, had remained barred to Jews, with only rare exceptions. In 1869, the already mentioned outstanding scholar and specialist of commercial law, Levin Goldschmidt, was appointed judge at the Supreme Commercial Court of the North German Federation, later included in the Supreme Court of the *Reich.* In 1870, for the first time in Prussian history, three Jews became judges at local courts, while the Bavarian government appointed the first Jewish *Amtsrichter* in 1879. Some Jewish teachers were included in the staff of secondary schools in the Prussian province of Posen. This was a special case since the Jews appeared as useful allies to the German authorities in their fight against Polish nationalism; nonetheless it was a breakthrough and a forerunner of some similar appointments in other provinces.[12]

[12]A more detailed survey on Jews in the general administration, the administration of justice, public education and in technical services may be found in Hamburger, *op. cit.,* pp. 32-66.

However, access to, not to speak of promotion in public office was far from satisfactory. As set forth above, Hardenberg's law of 1812 had ruled out admission of Jews to the officer corps, administrative positions and judgeships and left the matter to future legislation. The article of the law allowing access to academic teaching posts was repealed by the amendment of 1822. An observer of the scene between 1869 and the end of the monarchy notes an astonishing consistency. In spite of the legislation of 1848 and of the sixties the situation did not change with regard to the officer corps and those administrative agencies with which the wielding of authority was connected. Moreover, little progress was made in access to teaching positions below university level. On the whole, the attitude of the Executive toward the admission of Jews to public office was only slightly affected by the political swings of these fifty years. During the period of co-operation between Bismarck and the Liberals appointments of Jews had just cautiously begun and the personnel of the higher echelons of the administration continued to be drawn from the nobility and the conservative-minded members of the upper class to which the Jews did not belong.

In the ministries of the *Reich* and the several states Jews were not to be found. Two exceptions aside, they were not admitted to the foreign service. The general state administrations, i.e. the chiefs and their staffs administering, on a larger or smaller district level, multiple tasks — political, police and municipal affairs, educational matters etc. — did not include Jewish officials. No Jewish public prosecutor ever served in Prussia, Wurttemberg, Hesse, Saxony and smaller states of Northern Germany. Jews were promoted to the ranks of officers in the three wars waged by Bismarck, as they had been in the war of 1813 against Napoleon I. Thereafter, with the exception of Bavaria, they were not admitted to the officer corps and, after 1885 not even to the reserve officer corps. The presence of Jewish teachers in primary schools was no more than symbolic, in secondary schools infrequent, while they were better represented in institutions of higher education. The number of Jewish full professors, however, who alone were faculty members and, as such, in control of educational matters and in charge of making proposals for the filling of academic posts, was small and even decreased in the course of time; there were many universities without a Jewish full professor. For some categories, such as public prosecutors and high school teachers Bavaria, and still more Baden, showed some liberal tendencies. The overall picture, however, was not affected thereby.

Access was easier to *Reich* and state technical services, such as postal and railroad as well as medical and construction offices and in libraries in which specialized knowledge was paramount rather than the wielding of public authority. The Jews were also granted judgeships without great difficulty. This is explained by the fact that the social standing of a judge was inferior to that of a civil servant and of a public prosecutor in the German *Obrigkeitsstaat*. Jews were not promoted in the judiciary, however, before the turn of the century and attained positions of a presiding judge in exceptional cases only and not earlier than shortly before the outbreak of the war, these in Bavaria and Baden. It is significant that the most anti-Jewish governments, those of Saxony, Brunswick, Wutrtemberg and Hesse did not appoint a single Jewish official and that the two former never, the two latter hardly ever admitted a Jewish judge. Baptized Jews obtained access to administrative positions more easily, were granted full professorships and more frequently promoted in the judiciary. The small number of baptized Jews in the officer and reserve officer corps, however, proves the impact of the racial point of view on the military establishment.

JEWS IN LEGISLATIVE BODIES

After 1869 the right to stand for election was never legally contested. Its implementation fell to the organs of the political parties and, therefore, mirrored public opinion. While, as we have seen, the attitude of the Executive, determined by the measure and kind of antisemitism among the ruling circles, remained relatively stable, the willingness to nominate Jewish candidates depended upon the general political tendencies and the force and trends of popular antisemitism. As a consequence, nominations of Jews as candidates, and their elections to parliaments, had fluctuated widely already before 1869. In the constituent assemblies of the years 1848/49, in Frankfurt and Berlin, as well as in some of the smaller states Jews had their place: Riesser and Moritz Veit, among others, in Frankfurt, Johann Jacoby and Raphael Kosch in Berlin, Fischel Arnheim and David Morgenstern in Munich. Eduard Simson, a baptized Jew, won fame as president of the National Assembly in Frankfurt. In the decade of reaction they disappeared almost totally from the parliamentary scene with the decline of the Liberals to whom they mostly belonged. In the sixties and seventies, when newly-emerging parties, the Progressives and the National Liberals, pursued the aim of German unification and the liberalization of the laws and institutions, Jews were nominated as candidates by both parties and entered the *Reichstag* and the *Landtage*. Eduard Lasker, already mentioned, a member of the National Liberal group of the *Reichstag* and of the Prussian Diet, began a spectacular political career and became a leading figure and the most popular parliamentarian for a decade. Ludwig Bamberger, a member of the same party in the *Reichstag,* was nationally and internationally renowned as an outstanding expert in financial, banking and monetary matters and widely admired as a speaker and writer. The stature of Leopold Sonnemann, a lone Democrat of distinction who represented Frankfurt for thirteen years in the *Reichstag,* was enhanced by the fame of the *Frankfurter Zeitung,* the outstanding newspaper of the left of which he was the owner, publisher and chief editor. The period of the co-operation between Bismarck and the Liberals, from 1866 to 1878, was the high mark of the participation of Jews in the liberal groups of the *Reichstag,* the Prussian Diet and the *Landtage* of other states.[13]

This period was brought to an end, when, in the late seventies, Bismarck parted

---

[13]*Ibid.*, pp. 178-209 (for 1848); pp. 251-337 (with tables II and III, pp. 252 ff.) for the time since the foundation of the *Reich.*

ways with the Liberals, divided and crushed them. Political antisemitism emerged as a demagogic companion of his new policy and was cautiously encouraged by the Chancellor. It was first reflected by the movement of Court Chaplain Adolf Stoecker who temporarily enjoyed the Chancellor's support. In the nineties the racial features of antisemitism which the Christian Chaplain had been hesitant to emphasise were supplied by Hermann Ahlwardt and other protagonists of the revival of the fight against Jews, priests and high officials. It was a resumption of the antisemitic propaganda peculiar to the year 1848. This movement benefited by the agrarian crisis of these years and by the discontent of the small farmers and artisans. Pursuant to the imperialist policy of William II, several years after he had dismissed Bismarck and established his *persönliches Regiment* (his own style of rule), political associations which were either antisemitic from the outset or became so in the course of their existence were founded and gained influence: the pan-German League whose leader, Heinrich Class, conceived and published in the pre-war years the first systematic programme for the ousting of the Jews and of people of Jewish descent from citizenship; the Association for the Marches of the East *(Ostmarkenverein),* supported by the political right and the National Liberals and directed against the Poles, and the Navy League *(Flottenverein),* set up for the promotion of German sea and world power through naval armament.

As an autonomous party movement, antisemitism had no large-scale following. The outspokenly antisemitic parties remained splinter groups. In Berlin, which became the centre of an ever-increasing Jewish affluence and where the Jewish population rose to over 100,000, neither the antisemites nor the Conservatives succeeded in winning a seat in the *Reichstag.* In 1912, about 509,000 ballots were cast in the six electoral districts of Berlin; not more than 30,000 could possibly have come from Jewish voters. A negligible figure, less than one per cent, went to the antisemites and less than three per cent to the Conservatives allied with them.

However, if antisemitism was not the first consideration of the German citizens of that period at the polls, it penetrated and poisoned minds and had therefore a wide impact on the Conservatives as well as the Liberals when they chose their candidates. In 1892, the powerful Conservative Party supplemented its programme by an article condemning "the destructive and forward-pushing influence of the Jews on the life of our people" and urging "Christian authorities and Christian teachers for our Christian people". No less noteworthy was the conduct of the liberal parties which had been the political home for most Jewish voters. Nominations of Jews by these parties ceased, or were restricted to electoral districts which Liberals had anyway no chance of winning. Since 1881 there had not been a single Jew among the National Liberals and between 1893 and 1912 no Jewish member of the Progressive Party in the *Reichstag.* Even nominations of baptized Jews were exceptions. Likewise, for thirty years no Jew was among the National Liberals and for twelve years, from 1886 to 1898, among the Progressives in the Prussian Diet. Only around the turn of the century, when the long economic depression yielded to years of prosperity and political antisemitism lost somewhat in attraction, were the nominations of Jewish candidates cautiously resumed; in 1912 two Jewish members of the Progressive Party were elected to the *Reichstag*. In Prussia and some other states in which plutocratic electoral laws favoured the less narrow-minded wealthy urban bourgeoisie against the lower middle class, they were more easily nominated and elected after a temporary decline of antisemitism set in. Two prominent leaders of the National Liberal Party in the Prussian Diet, Robert Friedberg and Eugen Schiffer, were baptized Jews. On the other hand, in the states of Southern Germany in which electoral reforms were carried through, the chances of nomination decreased for Jews for the same reason for which they increased in Prussia.

Only the Socialists remained unaffected by the ups and downs of the antisemitic movement. Steadfast opponents of the regime and of all other political parties, they interpreted antisemitism as an abhorrent by-product of the capitalist order and bound to disappear with it. Consequently they did not shun the nomination of Jews. In the *Reichstag*, Jews amounted on average to about ten per cent of the Socialist group and constituted a remarkably high proportion, sometimes even a majority among its academically trained members.[14]

The change, therefore, could not have been greater. In the decade of the foundation of the *Reich* most Jewish members of the *Reichstag,* some of them outstanding party leaders, belonged to the National Liberals, then the largest governmental party. Thirty years later, in the last two decades of the existence of the same *Reich,* most Jewish members of the *Reichstag* belonged to the Social Democrats, the largest opposition party. The Jews Paul Singer and, after him, Hugo Haase served as party leaders together with August Bebel. Two other Jews, the prominent reformist Ludwig Frank and the champion of the revisionist movement, Eduard Bernstein, were nationally and internationally known. This change in the allegiance of Jews in Parliament did not, however, modify the attitude of the Jewish voters. Most of them maintained their preferences and continued to support one of the liberal parties. The contrast is due to the fact that within the Socialist camp politically able Jews were not discriminated against when seeking a nomination; they were sometimes entrusted with it without any special effort on their own part. The liberal parties, however, made the candidacy of a Jew after 1881 extremely difficult and most of the time even impossible.

A THOUGHT-PROVOKING BALANCE SHEET

The preceding surveys show that the German governments, and the governments of most German states, remained opposed to the exercise of public authority by Jews and to their admission to positions in the Executive, to the officer corps and to those administrations which carried a special prestige. They prove furthermore that during at least part of the time most people had misgivings as to the exercise

[14]*Ibid.*, pp. 404-522, with table on p. 406.

of public authority by Jews in legislative bodies. With the exception of the Socialists, all political parties took this attitude of the voters into consideration.

Beyond these two sectors of the life of the nation, however, Jews were not prevented from acceding to important positions. The industrialization which had spread rapidly during the fifty years of the Empire enabled Jews to rise to prominence in certain industrial branches and in the tremendously expanding domestic and foreign trade. Their traditional leadership and experience as bankers were propelling them to major posts in other branches of the national economy. Jews actively participated in the development of Germany's industrial society as successful and respected businessmen. The well-known publication *Juden im deutschen Kulturbereich* devotes almost eighty pages to the enumeration and brief characterisations of Jews in banking and in finance, industry and trade.[15]

Likewise, as a result of the increase of the Jews among the high school and university student population, Jewish participation in the professions and the cultural life of the German nation rose steadily. By 1890, a Prussian Minister of Education was troubled by the fact that the Jews amounted to ten per cent of the educated classes. Statistical surveys prove indeed that, in 1907, about fourteen per cent of the German attorneys-at-law, six per cent of the physicians and eight per cent of the writers and journalists were Jewish. These percentages, while lower in small and medium-sized towns, were still higher in the big cities, especially in Berlin, and aroused all the more attention.[16] The professional success of the Jews points to the fact that their advice and assistance were eagerly sought by large sections of the population and that their writings and journalistic activities were widely appreciated. It was well known that even hardened antisemites consulted Jewish physicians and lawyers to serve their personal and business interests.

To define correctly the situation of the Jews in the Wilhelminian period, however, it is not sufficient to consider the "ten per cent" and the proportionately great number of those who succeeded remarkably well in the national economy. Two developments were of primary importance as precursors or beginnings of a shift in the status of the Jews: the decline of economic opportunities for the Jewish middle class, more particularly for the small tradesmen and the salaried employees, and the anti-Jewish trend of the German students' movement.

When Germany made the transition from an agrarian to an industrial society at an extremely rapid pace, the Jews, not entrenched in agriculture, and excluded from officialdom and the academic world, were, as we have seen, in the lead. Helped by their social and intellectual mobility, they were pioneers in the development of the techniques of banking, property and stock market business; they also were prepared to take risks in trade and industrial pursuits. The ensuing concentration process in the national economy, the depersonalization of the enterprises and the establishment of purchase- sales- and consumer co-operatives,

---

[15]Siegmund Kaznelson (ed.), *Juden im deutschen Kulturbereich*, Geleitwort von Richard Willstätter, 3rd ed., Berlin 1962, pp. 720-797.
[16]Jakob Segall, *Die beruflichen und sozialen Verhältnisse der Juden in Deutschland*, Berlin 1912, pp. 47 f.

however, was not equally suited to the application of their basically individualistic business abilities. This led to a decline of their importance in the national economy. The emergence of big joint stock companies in the field of banking deprived the private Jewish bankers of their quasi-monopolistic positions. The co-operatives threatened the existence of small merchants, middlemen, commissioners, cattle dealers etc. in the small towns and in the countryside. In the province of Posen, in part also in West Prussia, Germans as well as Poles boycotted the Jews and contributed thereby to their mass exodus to the big urban centres outside these provinces. The Jews were mostly able to grow roots again, but dangers were inherent in the ensuing crowding of the Jewish population and in their occupational distribution in Berlin and some provincial capitals. Since the turn of the century, Jewish organizations had tried, without much success, to devise means for stabilizing the life of, and providing work for members of the Jewish middle class in the provinces.[17]

As the demand for white-collar workers increased in the expanding industrial economy non-Jewish manpower became readily available in branches in which it was not abundant and partly lacking before. These workers, desirous of drawing a sharp line, politically and socially, between themselves and the manual workers founded, in 1893, the German National Association of Salaried Employees *(Deutschnationaler Handlungsgehilfenverband)* which did not admit Jews as members.[18] Its antisemitic inclinations were shared by a widening sector of big business. A Jew won easier access to the board of directors of a joint stock banking corporation than to clerical work in the same firm. Jewish white-collar workers found it increasingly difficult to obtain jobs in the heavy and chemical industries and in engineering. Since Jewish and a certain number of non-Jewish firms absorbed most of them, their situation was far from critical. The Jewish organizations, however, surveying the field of business and employment, were rightly shocked by the discovery of the three newly emerging factors: the uprooting of the Jewish small businessmen, traders and craftsmen; the intensification of competititon of non-Jewish manpower in clerical jobs; and the increasing penetration of antisemitism into German big business and the most important union of salaried employees.

Outside the world of business and employment the rapid expansion of antisemitism among the German student body was noteworthy. Many, if not most students, whose attitudes so often herald changes in political and social life, were

---

[17]Hermann Becker in *Im Deutschen Reich, 1913,* pp. 433 ff.; Hans Goslar in *Jüdisches Gemeinde-Jahrbuch 1913/14-5674,* Berlin 1913, pp. 70 ff. and in *Im Deutschen Reich, 1913,* pp. 516 ff.

[18]See Hans Irwahn, *Bilder aus der Urgeschichte des Deutschnationalen Handlungsgehilfen-Verbands,* Hamburg 1920; Albert Zimmermann, *Der Deutschnationale Handlungsgehilfen-Verband,* Hamburg 1921; Iris Hamel, *Völkischer Verband und nationale Gewerkschaft. Der Deutschnationale Handlungsgehilfenverband 1893-1933,* Veröffentlichungen der Forschungsstelle für die Geschichte des Nationalsozialismus in Hamburg, Band VI, Frankfurt a. M. 1967.

impressed by Stoecker's Christian Social movement and by the teachings of the historian Heinrich von Treitschke, his academic companion. Both Paul de Lagarde, the scholar and moralist, and later Julius Langbehn, author of *Rembrandt als Erzieher,* the most popular best-seller of the Wilhelminian period, were ardent antisemites. They prophesied impending doom as a result of the alleged activity of destructive forces of modernity, championed by the Jews.[19] The anti-Jewish petition submitted to the government in 1881 was signed by 4,000 students, proportionately ten times as many as came from other sections of the population. The Association of German Students *(Verein deutscher Studenten),* formed in the same year, excluded persons of Jewish ancestry from membership. For a long time the colour-wearing feudal *Corps* had not admitted Jews; the *Burschenschaften,* after liberal beginnings early in the century severely scrutinized Jews requesting admission until, in 1896, they declared that *Reich* subjects of Jewish descent were not to be considered Germans. The German students travelled the road leading to the Third *Reich*[20] more than fifty years before Hitler was to assume power.

Rejected everywhere, Jewish students established from 1886 onwards their own colour-wearing fraternities, forming the *Kartell-Convent der Verbindungen deutscher Studenten jüdischen Glaubens* (K.C.). As from 1895 also Zionist students' organizations sprang up. Segregation in out-of-class student life became almost complete. The administrators, judges, university professors and secondary school teachers of the Weimar Republic were reared in this atmosphere of virulent antisemitism. It should also be mentioned that antisemitic currents in the best-known and most renowned youth organisation *Wandervogel* were growing steadily well before the First World War.[21]

The antisemitic mood of the students was stronger in degree, but not different in kind from the antisemitism of the middle class in general. In 1893, Ludwig Bamberger, after twenty-five years of service in parliament, decided not to stand again. He pointed to antisemitism as the main reason and spoke with disgust and horror, not so much of the violent language and poisonous attacks of the members of the antisemitic parties, but of the "three-fourths of my colleagues who are not at all disturbed thereby." When eight years later the *Reichstag* discussed the murder of a high school student, alleged by the antisemites to be a ritual murder perpetrated by Jews, only members of the left rejected the scandalous accusation; again three-fourths of the parliament remained ominously silent. The indignant reaction of the Jews to the trial of Menahem Mendel Beilis for alleged ritual murder in Russia caused even a leading National Liberal newspaper to declare that it could

---

[19]Fritz Stern, *The Politics of Cultural Despair,* University of California Press, Berkeley and Los Angeles 1961. Stern analyzes the ideas of Lagarde, Langbehn and Moeller van den Bruck in his remarkable book.

[20]Hans Peter Bleuel, Ernst Klinnert, *Deutsche Studenten auf dem Wege ins Dritte Reich,* Gütersloh 1967.

[21]See Walter Laqueur, 'The German Youth Movement and the "Jewish Question" ', in *LBI Year Book VI* (1961), pp. 193-205.

EDUARD von SIMSON

President of the Frankfurt Assembly of 1848

EDUARD LASKER

Spokesman of the National Liberal Party

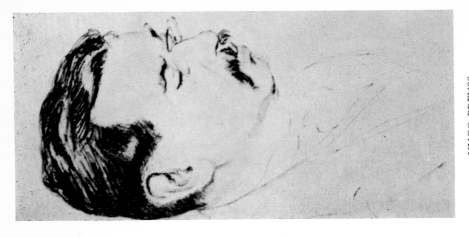

HUGO PREUSS

"Father" of the Weimar Constitution

LEOPOLD SONNEMANN

Editor-in-Chief of the *Frankfurter Zeitung*

well be ritual murder and that it was "a serious mistake of the Hebrews of all Europe to adopt innumerable resolutions in favour of Beilis."[22]

The balance sheet of the period of the Empire is, therefore, less propitious than it is generally represented. The majority of the population did not wish to see Jews as their representatives in the legislative bodies and in the administration. The Executive did not admit Jews to certain branches of the administration and in others not to leading or otherwise important positions. Comparing the situation in Prussia and Bavaria, it must be stated that the governments of Prussia carried antisemitic attitudes farther than those of Bavaria, but that the people of Bavaria were more hostile to the appearance of Jews in official positions than those of Prussia. Popular antisemitism penetrated deeply those strata of society in which Jews had gained important footholds: the professions and salaried employees as well as some of the people in big concerns who were responsible for the hiring of employees. It also appeared among high school students and members of the youth organizations. Antisemitism was essentially absent from the labour movement. It was the only stratum which nominated Jewish candidates for parliaments; the Social Democrats and the Progressive Party fought for the admission of Jews to the administration and to the judiciary on equal terms with non-Jewish candidates, but the credibility of the Progressives was impaired by their refusal, throughout decades, to consider Jewish candidacies to the *Reichstag* and to the *Landtage*.

As the academic youth was vehemently antisemitic and the majority of the population at best coldly indifferent to the Jews, any basic change in the political situation of Germany could cause antisemitism to break out of the intellectual and political confines in which it moved into the German *Obrigkeitsstaat*. If this change came about, the huge antisemitic potential could easily be stirred to activity.

THE BASIC CHANGE IN THE FIRST WORLD WAR

During the First World War the basic change of the situation occurred. It brought about a significant activation of the antisemitic potential.

At first, patriotic enthusiasm animated the population. The authorities proclaimed domestic peace *(Burgfrieden)*. The government softened its antisemitic practice and intervened whenever harmony among the citizens seemed threatened by sporadic polemical utterances. The antisemitic newspaper of Berlin, *Staatsbürger-Zeitung,* declared that it had abandoned antisemitism for good because of the patriotism of the entire population. Jews were again elevated to officer rank. William II consented to the promotion of Jewish judges to leading positions. In 1918, a Jew was called to serve in the Prussian Ministry of the Interior, a reversal of a century-old policy. In Bavaria Jewish teachers were given auxiliary posts in primary schools. Although warnings were not lacking that these were exceptions

---

[22]*Schwäbischer Merkur*, Stuttgart, October 20, 1913. See also Robert Weltsch in his Introduction to *LBI Year Book XIII* (1968), p. XI.

for the duration only, willingness to come closer to the implementation of the Act of 1869 was on the whole apparent.

However, only for a short period of time was the conduct of the government matched by a corresponding attitude of the population. As the hopes for a speedy victory faded, the war dragged on, sacrifices in human life increased and shortage of food became critical, antisemitic tendencies came to the fore again. The Jews were accused of shunning service at the front, profiteering and abusing their positions in business for acquiring special privileges. The number of Jews working in commercial war corporations was considered too high and a consequence of corrupt practices. As far as these reproaches were true, the Jews did not behave any more or less immorally than the landowners and the non-Jewish businessmen, who claimed relatives and friends for work at the homefront, and the workers who made all possible efforts to be recalled to their plants for skilled work. Wild accusations were directed against Walther Rathenau who, at the outbreak of the war, had convinced the government of the necessity of organizing the national economy in accordance with war needs and who, from August 1914 to April 1915, had headed the department established in the War Ministry to this effect. Although the highest German officials, beginning with *Reich* Chancellor Theobald von Bethmann-Hollweg and the Prussian Minister of War, Adolf Wild von Ho-henborn, heaped lavish praise on Rathenau and pointed to his extraordinary merits,[23] the attacks continued against the convenient Jewish scapegoat for all the sufferings of the population.

A scapegoat was badly needed, indeed, in the late spring and in the summer of 1916. The German armies, massed for the conquest of the fortress of Verdun, did not attain their objective. The British and Russian armies started successful offensives. Rumania entered the war. As the situation of the Germans was for the first time almost desperate and they fared badly internationally, the Jews fared equally badly on the market of national evaluation, as Felix Waldstein, a Jewish member of the Progressive Party in the *Reichstag,* illustrated the case.

Thus in the course of the first two years of the war two different trends were clearly discernible. Governmental antisemitism was restrained and demands for equal rights, submitted for decades by the Jewish middle and upper middle class, were at least partly met. In contrast, popular antisemitism was again on the rise and reached proportions such as had not been seen since Ahlwardt's days.

August 29, 1916 was a fateful day for German politics, in general, and for the good name of the Jews, in particular. General Erich von Falkenhayn, Chief of the General Staff, accused of weakness and indecision and held responsible for the military failures of spring and summer 1916, was dismissed and replaced by Field Marshal Paul von Hindenburg, with Erich Ludendorff as his principal aide and in reality, the leading figure. The appointment was made under popular pressure and on the demand of the officer corps whose confidence in the two heroes of the battle of Tannenberg was unlimited. A kind of military dictatorship ensued,

[23]Walther Rathenau, *Deutschlands Rohstoffversorgung*, Berlin 1917. The letters commending Rathenau, after p. 52.

exercised by Ludendorff, covered by Hindenburg's authority and based on a quasi-plebiscitarian consent. It was hidden behind the continued but less and less meaningful functioning of the traditional authorities. In essential matters Ludendorff became the true policy maker. When his picture appeared on the screen in films shown behind the front, he was acclaimed. The quasi-dictatorship of the Supreme Command was supported by the political parties of the right, by the Catholic Centre and the National Liberals.

The official attacks on the Jews started in September 1916, promptly following the appointment of Ludendorff, an ardent antisemite who was to become a follower of Hitler already in the early days of the Weimar Republic. The War Ministry ordered a statistical inquiry into the religious affiliations of the employees of the war corporations as well as of the members of the armed forces, separately for front- office- and garrison service. Colonel Ernst von Wrisberg, who was instrumental in promoting and carrying out the investigation, was imbued with the same antisemitic feelings as Ludendorff and worked as his right-hand man, starting the inquiry and causing the political parties to join in the witch-hunt. In October 1916 an antisemitic member of the *Reichstag,* feigning unawareness of the administrative measures already taken, requested a statistical survey for the armed forces, based on religious affiliation, and a member of the Catholic Centre Party moved the same investigation for the war corporations, thereby providing parliamentary support for the action of the ministry. All parties which ranged behind Ludendorff's policy supported the inquiry. It was an initiative of the parliament unheard of since the foundation of the *Reich.* The Centre Party representing, as it did, a religious minority which had suffered in the *Kulturkampf* and was disadvantaged in Prussia and some other states had for quite some time shed its antisemitic beginnings and showed circumspection in dealing with the Jewish question. The National Liberals who forty years before had been marked out as protectors of the Jews by the antisemites and among whose leaders Jews had been conspicuous, had later repeatedly exploited the antisemitic prejudices of the voters whenever it had suited their electoral purposes. However, like their antagonists, the Catholic Centre, they had never before sustained an openly antisemitic motion. They hid behind Wrisberg's pious assertion that the ministry was not inspired by antisemitism but aimed at rejecting unfounded accusations against the Jews by statistical evidence.

Supporting the ministry, the National Liberals acted under the leadership of Gustav Stresemann, later Foreign Minister of the Weimar Republic. Stresemann was no antisemite. His campaign speeches and his addresses in the *Reichstag* were devoid of antisemitic slogans and allusions. He had a Jewish wife. His political aims, however, nationalistic, imperialist and annexionist, his admiration for Ludendorff and his close co-operation with the War Ministry caused him to disregard any harm which was to result necessarily from the action of the *Reichstag,* not only for the Jews but also for the Rule of Law *(Rechtsstaat)* which Eduard Lasker, once a leader of the party which was now misguided by Stresemann, had been anxious to promote. Stresemann's conduct once more confirmed Hugo

Preuss' ironical statement that it was "the vocation, perhaps very honourable but by no means pleasant, of the Jews to serve as an advanced and perhaps lost outpost of liberalism".[24]

Although the statistical survey was not published during the war, the common military, governmental and parliamentary action brought antisemitic feelings to an unprecedented climax. The complaints about the behaviour of the Jews appeared officially confirmed. An antisemitic measure had been approved by a majority of a Committee of the *Reichstag*. For the first time since the short interlude of co-operation between Bismarck and Stoecker in 1881, the authoritarian and popular representatives of antisemitism joined hands. Ludendorff, wielding semi-dictatorial powers, the military establishment, dominated by the Prussian aristo-cracy, and a comfortable majority of the Parliament, elected on the basis of common suffrage, co-operated in administering a fatal blow to the idea which was at the basis of the Act of 1869. The forces which brought about this new constellation founded less than a year thereafter, the Party of the Fatherland *(Vaterlandspartei)* in which the imperialist, nationalistic and antisemitic elements of the population united and which was later qualified by the historian Friedrich Meinecke as the exact prelude to Hitler's ascendancy. "There is an atmosphere of pogrom also in Germany", complained the periodical of the *Centralverein deut-scher Staatsbürger jüdischen Glaubens* shortly before the revolution. "During the last two years almost every issue of this periodical had to deal with antisemitism getting ever wilder in speech and in the press".[25]

As the Bismarckian structure of the *Reich* was shaken to its foundations by the abdication of the political authorities to Ludendorff's quasi-dictatorship, the forces which had sustained an antisemitism suited to their interests and peculiar to monarchical Germany weakened and lost in influence. The majority of the *Reichstag*, resisted by the Socialists and Progressives only, surrendered abjectly to the ruthless antisemitic tendencies of the military, on the one hand, and those rife amongst the populace, on the other. When the defeat approached, the barriers against antisemitic extremism with mob appeal broke down. While Hitler was still the "unknown corporal" of the World War, the aristocratic and popular forces which were to carry him to power found for the first time common ground by exploiting the propagandistic potential of the Jewish question.[26]

ACCESS TO POSTS OF AUTHORITY IN THE REVOLUTIONARY PERIOD

The total military defeat arrested and reversed the political trends of the last two war years. Ludendorff resigned shortly before the end of October 1918. Imperial

[24]Hugo Preuss, 'Das Bekenntnis des Kultusministers und die Konfessionalität der Berliner Schulen', *Die Nation*, 1899, p. 390. About the statistical survey, the antisemitic motives and objectives and the distortions of the results by antisemites see Jakob Segall, *Die deut-schen Juden als Soldaten im Kriege 1914/1918. Eine statistische Studie*, Berlin 1922; Franz Oppenheimer, 'Die Judenstatistik des preussischen Kriegsministeriums', in *Gesammelte Reden und Aufsätze II, Soziologische Streifzüge*, Munich 1927; Franz Oppenheimer, *Erlebtes, Erstrebtes, Erreichtes. Lebenserinnerungen*, Düsseldorf 1964, p. 224.

Germany collapsed, the *Kaiser* fled and the kings, dukes and princes of the German states and their governments disappeared overnight. The *ancien régime* as well as Ludendorff's warlordship were thoroughly discredited. The *Obrigkeitsstaat* of the old order was dead; and the Conservatives compromised. The Social Democrats assumed the leadership of the revolution which they had tried hard to avoid. They were joined by the Independent Social Democrats who had voted against the war credits and considered the revolution inevitable and desirable, but had been cautious in promoting it. The Spartacists were the only true revolutionaries, who formed the left wing of the Independents until they established the Communist Party on December 30, 1918; they stood ready to transform the war between nations into an international civil war, but had no notable following. The Communist leaders, Karl Liebknecht and Rosa Luxemburg, lacked authority over the members of the new Party. When they urged participation in the election to the National Assembly and when in particular Rosa Luxemburg opposed the uprising of early January against the provisional government of the moderate Socialists as a hopeless adventure, they were defeated by the rank and file. The Communists were unable to give direction to the historical events of these months if only because their policy hinged on the hope of a rapid expansion of revolutionary movement to the victorious countries. This proved a delusion — as every reasonable person could foresee — and the Allied Powers could never permit a defeated and powerless Germany to become Communist and thereby an outpost of Soviet Russia.

When the revolution swept the Socialists to power, Jews were among those who acceded to important positions. The policy which had withheld governmental and administrative posts from Jewish citizens broke down with the Imperial Germany which had practised it, and was reversed by the left which had condemned it. For reasons explained above, leading Jews in political life were to be found mainly in the Socialist camp. They contributed talent and ability not easily found in the Social Democratic ranks. Moreover, the hundreds of Jews who had not been promoted to officer rank in the army because of their religious affiliation were the natural choice for election to the soldiers' councils. They were more articulate than most of their comrades in arms. No wonder, then, that Jews appeared conspicuously among the leading governing and representative figures of the revolutionary period.

Jews who emerged as political leaders during the revolution, often for a short period only, held widely differing views; among them were radicals, moderates and conservatives. Their access to leading positions was frequently caused by the

---

[25]*Im Deutschen Reich*, 1918, p. 454. About the *Vaterlandspartei* see Friedrich Meinecke, *Die deutsche Katastrophe*, Zürich and Wiesbaden 1946, p. 50. - The words *"also in Germany"* are to be explained by the pogroms in the Ukraine in 1918.

[26]Cf. Martin Broszat's remarks on antisemitism, used by Hitler as one of the most effective vehicles of ideological equalization *(Gleichschaltung)* in Hungary and Rumania during the Second World War ('Deutschland - Ungarn - Rumänien', in *Historische Zeitschrift*, vol. 206, 1968, p. 93).

pleas of, or their appointment by the men who, suddenly placed in power, badly needed their experience and knowledge. Others, however, owed their prominent position to their own revolutionary initiative.

Some examples may illustrate these often strange careers. Friedrich Ebert chose two highly-gifted Jewish aides, Otto Landsberg and Hugo Preuss. Landsberg, a right-wing Socialist member of the *Reichstag,* trained in law and a man of independent judgment, was selected for one of the three seats which fell to the Social Democrats in the Council of People's Delegates, the revolutionary Executive. Preuss, a sincere Democrat and an acknowledged authority on constitutional law, was made head of the Department of the Interior and instructed to prepare the draft of a democratic constitution; the Socialists had no competent person for this task and most of the non-Socialist experts were compromised by their political conduct during the war. The leader of the Independent Socialists, Hugo Haase, was the automatic choice for one of their seats on the Council of People's Delegates, while Emanuel Wurm was selected to become chief of the *Reich* Food Ministry which he headed with distinction.[27] At the other end of the political spectrum Eugen Schiffer, who had risen to the rank of undersecretary of the Treasury in Imperial Germany, was appointed Secretary of the same Department by Ebert. He became the centre of resistance to all attempts to change Germany's socio-economic structure. Within the soldiers' councils Max Cohen-Reuss, a right-wing Social Democrat, rose to prominence. In the *Reich* Conference of Workers' and Soldiers' Councils of December 1918 he gave an excellent performance in a speech which was decisive for an overwhelming vote in favour of electing and convening a National Assembly and for the rejection of a councils system for Germany.

On the state level, Paul Hirsch, chairman of the Social Democratic group in the Prussian Diet, was the self-evident choice as head of the Prussian government while Kurt Eisner, an Independent Socialist of moderate socialist and radical pacifist views, assumed the leadership in Bavaria after having led the revolutionary forces of Munich to victory. In Saxony, Georg Gradnauer was the leading figure; in Wurttemberg Berthold Heymann, a follower of Eduard Bernstein, and August Thalheimer, a radical, were members of the provisional government. In Mecklenburg the Socialists, unable to find a more mature candidate, turned over the Ministry of Justice to Ludwig Barbasch, who had not yet completed his legal training.[28] It was not surprising that the officials of the ministry and the lawyers of Mecklenburg frowned on the appointment of the young Jew who, incidentally, proved later to be an excellent and selfless attorney-at-law. In other states Jews as members of the Progressive (later Democratic) Party, such as Ludwig Haas in

[27]Walter Gross, 'Das politische Schicksal der deutschen Juden in der Weimarer Republik', in *In Zwei Welten. Siegfried Moses zum 75. Geburtstag,* Tel-Aviv 1962, p. 546, believes that Landsberg, Haase and other academically-trained people were selected for their positions in order to assure the bourgeoisie that the new state would be governed by knowledgeable men. However, this consideration did not play any part in the choice of the above-mentioned political leaders.

[28]I am indebted to Dr. E. G. Lowenthal, Berlin, for information about Barbasch.

Baden and Hermann Cohn in Anhalt, were associated with provisional councils in which they strove to ensure the rapid and smooth transition to a democratic regime.

Those Germans who had supported the nefarious policy of Imperial Germany sat passively by, when the rulers responsible for the lost war were ousted, but they disliked the revolutionaries who did the job. Still more than the new leaders who rose to high positions from the ranks of labour, the Jews appeared as an extraneous and unwelcome element within the traditional ruling class. The fact that Jews now held positions of public authority in which they had not been noticeable before, did not create but certainly added a new dimension to antisemitism. General Wilhelm Groener, the successor of Ludendorff, wrote to his wife six days after the revolution that Jews in Germany as well as in Russia held the reins, a remark which, as the editor of his memoirs explained, showed the temper which had seized him as well as large circles in the months of the revolution.[29] Theodor Heuss sadly recalled the deep resentment felt by many Germans because a Jewish fellow-democrat was entrusted with the drafting of the constitution; doubtless the expression *Judenrepublik,* which quickly gained acceptance, aimed not least at Preuss and his work. The leading Bavarian Federalist Georg Heim, ranking member of the Centre Party in the Reichstag, referred to Landsberg and Preuss who strove for the dissolution of the states and a unified Germany with self-administering provincial units as "die Zentraljuden von Berlin". In a crowded meeting of the Federation of Jewish Youth Associations in December 1918 the chairman indignantly condemned the wave of shameful antisemitism and was shocked by the fact that the government had even had to warn against pogroms. A non-Jewish democratic speaker joined him and there was little consolation in the assurance of Rudolf Breitscheid, then Prussian Minister of the Interior for a few weeks, that the antisemitic attacks against Landsberg, Haase and other Jews were directed in reality against the Socialists and their newly-won power.[30]

Strong as the tide ran and rampant as antisemitism was, it did not break out of the area of emotional feeling. As a political movement antisemitism was disorganized and compromised for the time being. The disastrous end of the war and the inglorious exit of the monarchs and their governments were uppermost in the minds of the voters who set the pace for the election to the National Assembly, and of the members of the Assembly themselves.

[29]Wilhelm Groener, *Lebenserinnerungen,* ed. Friedrich Freiherr Hiller von Gärtringen, preface by Peter Rassow, Göttingen 1957, p. 471 f. About Groener's attitude in the later years of the Weimar Republic and under Hitler see footnote 6a to p. 472; the significant information contained in this footnote was supplied by Dr. Liselotte Reinken, a young historian who assisted Groener in writing his memoirs. See also below p. 43.

[30]Hugo Preuss, *Staat, Recht und Freiheit,* Geleitwort von Theodor Heuss, Tübingen 1926, p. 15; Otto Landsberg, 'Der Rat der Volksbeauftragen', in *Friedrich Ebert und seine Zeit. Ein Gedenkbuch über den ersten Präsidenten der deutschen Republik,* Charlottenburg, n.d., p. 201 ("Zentraljuden"); *Die parteipolitischen Neubildungen in Deutschland und die Juden. Stenographischer Bericht über einen Erörterungsabend des Verbandes der Jüdischen Jugendvereine Deutschlands und seiner Berliner Ortsgruppe, des Jüdischen Jugendbundes Berlin e.V. am 18. Dezember 1918,* Berlin 1919, pp. 3, 27, 37.

FIFTY YEARS AGO: THE WEIMAR CONSTITUTION

Constitution of the German *Reich* of August 11, 1919.[31]

"Second Principal Part
Fundamental Rights and Duties of the Germans
First Section: The Individual.

Art. 113. Sections of the population of the *Reich* speaking a foreign language may not be restricted, by means of legislation and administration, in their free, popular development; this applies especially to the use of their mother-tongue in education as well as in questions of internal administration and courts of law.

Third section: Religion and religious bodies.

Art. 135. All inhabitants of the *Reich* enjoy full freedom of faith and conscience. The undisturbed practice of religion is guaranteed by the Constitution and is under State protection. The general laws of the State remain unaffected hereby.

Art. 136. Civil and political rights and duties are neither dependent upon nor restricted by the practice of religious freedom.
The enjoyment of civil and political rights, as well as admission to official posts are independent of religious creed.
No one is bound to disclose his religious convictions. The authorities have the right to make enquiries as to membership of a religious body only when rights and duties depend upon it, or when the collection of statistics ordered by law requires it.
No one may be compelled to take part in any ecclesiastical act or ceremony, or to participate in religious practices, or to make use of a religious form of oath.

Art. 137. There is no State Church.
Freedom of association is guaranteed to religious bodies . . .
Each religious body regulates and administers its affairs independently within the limits of the general laws. It appoints its officials without the co-operation of the state or of the civil community."

In the elections of January and February 1919 the German voters rejected extremism of any kind and expressed their preference for a coalition of moderates of the left and the centre. Accordingly, Social Democrats, Democrats and the Catholic Centre Party *(Zentrum)* of the National Assembly constituted a government of a political colouring which, from then onwards, was called the Weimar Coalition. The same coalition was formed in Prussia. No antisemitic party competed for seats in the National Assembly. Had the Communists taken part in the elections, they would hardly have won a single seat. The Independent Socialists, who were to become the opposition of the left, were torn by internal strife; they had to be content with a membership of 22 out of a total of 423. Still more shattering was their defeat in Bavaria — three seats out of 180; Eisner's authority was badly shaken by the verdict of the voters. The opposition of the right, consisting of the *Deutschnationale Volkspartei* (DNVP) in which many Conservative leaders reappeared, and the *Deutsche Volkspartei* (DVP) under Stresemann's guidance held 42 and 22 seats respectively. The DNVP was led by moderates. Klemens von Delbrück, *Staatssekretär* of the *Reichsamt* of the Interior under

---

[31]Translation based on the text in *British and Foreign State Papers,* vol. CXII (1919), London 1922, p. 1063 ff.

Bethmann-Hollweg's chancellorship, and Adelbert Düringer, last archducal minister of Justice in Baden, set the tone, not racialist fanatics like Albrecht von Gräfe who later complained bitterly about the soft policy of the leaders of his party in Weimar.[32] The provisional party platform of November 22, 1918, the proclamation of November 24 and the directives for the election, issued on December 27, were devoid of antisemitism.[33] The living forces of Christendom and a strong German *Volkstum,* independent of alien influences, were invoked. This allusion was a far cry from the antisemitic paragraph of the Conservative Party programme of 1892 and from the party programme and the proclamations of 1920 and of subsequent years.

When the draft constitution was discussed in Weimar, no-one was opposed to the two fundamental concepts which had evolved in the nineteenth century: freedom of religion and its practice were to be guaranteed and protected. The enjoyment of political and civil rights in general, and access to public office in particular, were to be independent of religious creed. Civil and political rights and duties should be neither dependent upon nor restricted by the practice of religion. This was the law as it had been shaped between 1848 and 1869. No one wanted to go back on the wording which had been initiated by the *Reichstag* fifty years before and had received Bismarck's assent.

Differences of opinion between Preuss and the law-makers about the incorporation and formulation of fundamental rights did not touch upon the substance of the law. Preuss, recalling the long-drawn-out exchanges of views on this score in 1848, was averse to a comprehensive chapter on the rights of the citizens. Yet, his own first draft, which did not spell out more than three rights and alluded to three others, included the principle of freedom of religion and equality of the citizens regardless of faith. These rights were re-incorporated in the draft submitted to the Assembly and in which the provisions on the rights and duties of the citizens were enlarged in accordance with requests made by the Social Democrats and members of Preuss' own party. In his introductory speech Preuss stressed the constitutional guarantee inherent in these articles on fundamental rights and the guidance offered by them for the further development and the legislation of the member states. There was, therefore, consensus between the author of the draft and the constituents on this score.Every one also recognized that the proclamation of rights in the Constitution of 1848 was intended to inaugurate an era of freedom, whereas the corresponding principles which reappeared in the Constitution of 1919 had already been enshrined in legal texts.[34]

[32]Albrecht von Gräfe-Goldebee, *Damals in Weimar*, Berlin 1929.

[33]Werner Liebe, *Die Deutschnationale Volkspartei 1918-1924.* Düsseldorf 1956, pp. 8, 107 ff.

[34]Hugo Preuss, 'Begründung des Entwurfs einer Verfassung für das Deutsche Volk' (speech of February 24, 1919 in the National Assembly), in Preuss, *Staat, Recht und Freiheit,* pp. 394 ff.; about fundamental rights p. 419; Eberhard Kuntze, *Die Nachwirkungen der Pauls-kirche und ihrer Verfassung in den Beratungen der Weimarer Nationalversammlung und in der Verfassung von 1919,* Historische Studien, Heft 203, Berlin 1931, pp. 23, 69 ff., 102 ff.

As promulgated on August 11, 1919, the Constitution enunciated the principles relating to religion and religious bodies in the third section of its second part. Wilhelm Kahl, a distinguished Professor of Law in the University of Berlin and a venerable figure in the National Assembly, drew attention to the interdependence of the two main provisions: if the equality of rights regardless of faith was not ensured, freedom of conscience was not secure; it would be impaired by the temptation to enjoy privileges of a favoured creed. Freedom of religion and conscience and the undisturbed practice of religion were guaranteed to all inhabitants of the *Reich* while the Constitution of 1848 extended this guarantee to Germans only. Otherwise the two sets of provisions — religious freedom and non-discrimination — were almost literally copied from the Constitution of the *Paulskirche*. So were most of the other principles: There was no State Church. Religious bodies could be freely established and regulate and administer their affairs independently within the limits of the law applicable to all. This provision excluded any law favouring or detrimental to certain denominations only, but other articles guaranteed the continuation of the state subsidies for the payment of the clergy and other purposes of the Christian churches. These privileges, which the Socialists tried in vain to abolish, did not interfere, however, with freedom of religion and equality of rights regardless of creed.

Contrary to the three precedents of 1815, 1848 and 1869, the Jewish question was not brought up during the discussion on freedom of religion. Equality of rights for the Jews was taken for granted. Attention was drawn to their situation, however, on another occasion. The section on individual rights included an article which prohibited legislation and administrative measures restricting the free, popular *(volkstümlich)* development of those parts of the population which spoke a foreign language *(fremdsprachige Volksteile)*. Use of the mother tongue should be allowed especially in education, in internal administration and in courts of law. This article, too, was essentially copied from the Constitution of Frankfurt.

When these provisions were discussed, Oscar Cohn, the representative of the Independent Social Democrats on the Constitutional Committee, took the floor at the first and second reading as well as in the Committee itself. He found the language of the article unduly restrictive. Language, he held, was not the only criterion of a nationality. All national minorities should enjoy this protection even when their mother-tongue was German. Cohn referred to the Sorbs in Lusatia and some other splinter groups and dwelt at length on the Jews. He claimed that there existed a national Jewish question in Germany and argued that especially the best among the younger Jewish generation were increasingly embracing Zionism, the national concept of Judaism. The wording "national minorities" instead of "sections of the population speaking a foreign language" would leave open the possibility, which might soon arise, of granting minority rights to the Jews. Cohn also invoked the work of the Peace Conference and nascent international law which would guarantee national-cultural rights to minorities, including the Jews, in the East of Central Europe. Since Germany strongly supported this tendency in the interest of the German minorities outside her frontiers and had extended the definition of a national minority far beyond the concept of language, she was duty-bound to protect her own minorities to the same extent.

Hugo Preuss, however, speaking for the government, and the spokesmen of the Social Democrats and the *Zentrum* found the draft satisfactory. The Constitution proceeded from the notion of the German citizen, not of a German in a *völkisch* sense, a fact deeply regretted by the DNVP-deputy and Professor of Constitutional Law Axel Freiherr von Freytagh-Loringhoven, later a follower of Hitler. The Jews, the spokesmen of the governmental parties held, did not need special protection in education, internal administration and courts of law, the fields specifically mentioned in Article 113. Their language was German, whether they were Zionists or not. The motion of the Independent Socialists was overwhelmingly defeated. Authoritative scholarly books on the Weimar Constitution followed the lines of thought of the majority, as far as the Jewish question was concerned, stating that most Jews were dedicated to assimilation, not to differentiation and that, as the Jews were divided among themselves about the meaning of the sociological structure of their community, there was no practical basis for the application of special legal principles.[35]

Cohn was the only Zionist among the Jewish members of the National Assembly. His group went along with its respected member, not because of his Zionist affiliation which meant nothing to his party or to the Marxist voters of Thuringia who had sent him to the Assembly. They were rather impressed with the suggestion of identifying their internationally-minded party with the new trends of international law. The German Jews themselves, however, did not share Cohn's opinion. The great majority of the Jews had voted for the German Democratic Party (DDP), a minority for the Social Democrats; the number of those who had cast their votes for the Independent Socialists was negligible. As matters stood in 1919, the Jews felt no need of supporting Cohn's demands. Those who were interested in Jewish matters could freely develop their religious, charitable and educational institutions, as well as scholarly Judaism, exercise the right of association and assembly and publish and read a Jewish press under the general laws of the country. Actually Cohn was the spokesman not of the official Zionist Organization which did not claim minority rights, but of a Zionist fraction, i.e. a small minority of the German Jews. He expected, however, that their number would increase, especially among the young Jews. Aware of the rising tide of antisemitism and of its impact on German public opinion, his idea was to open a new avenue in German constitutional law. If some day restrictive legislation followed the trend of public opinion, Jewish minority rights, he believed, might become meaningful and essential.

[35]National Assembly, February 28, 1919, p. 406; July 15, 1919, pp. 1571 f. - Axel Freiherr von Freytagh-Loringhoven, *Die Weimarer Verfassung in Lehre und Wirklichkeit*, Munich 1924, pp. 51-55; Hans Gerber, 'Minderheitenrecht', in Hans Carl Nipperdey, *Die Grundrechte und Grundpflichten der Reichsverfassung*, Berlin 1929, I, pp. 269-315; Gerhard Anschütz, *Die Verfassung des Deutschen Reiches*, Bad Homburg 1960, pp. 542 f.

It is important, therefore, to record Cohn's lone voice. In 1848, Gabriel Riesser had declined heatedly any separate status for the Jews, scornfully rejecting Moritz Mohl's motion for special laws for the "Jewish tribe". Full of optimism, Riesser envisioned a hopeful future. Seventy years later Oscar Cohn, viewing their future pessimistically, felt that a special status could provide a better protection. Whereas Riesser was overwhelmingly supported in Frankfurt, Cohn was overwhelmingly defeated in Weimar. The Jews were accorded equal rights in Frankfurt and the legal barriers separating them from their fellow citizens were broken down. In Weimar the law-makers rejected the possibility of a special status for the Jews, even when requested by a Jew to consider it. When the fight for the equality of rights appeared won and when the Jews seemed to have overcome all obstacles in law and fact and a point of culmination reached, Cohn remained unimpressed by these successes. His action in the National Assembly of Weimar implied a prophecy of doom for the Jews of Germany. The success of his motion would not have averted their fate. Its presentation, however, showed a remarkable insight into things that were to come in the not too distant future.

THE ANTISEMITIC MOVEMENT IN THE PARTIES OF THE RIGHT AND THE POLITICAL CLIMATE OF THE REPUBLIC

In 1869 and 1919, the right of the German Jews to equality was legalized within the framework of the law applicable to all. In 1869 hardly anyone, in 1919 no one opposed it. The parties which created the Weimar Constitution were resolved to uphold this right in political practice. Under the centre, left-centre and centre-right governments which ruled the *Reich* and most of its *Länder* until 1932, the provisions of the Constitution were, in general, observed; the practice which had evolved since the revolution continued. Jews were admitted to public office without any restrictions: to the Executive, all branches of the administration and the courts, a noteworthy accomplishment since the governments operated under unfavourable conditions and the majority enjoyed by the parties of the Weimar coalition in the National Assembly was not reaffirmed by the result of the first *Reichstag* election in 1920, and was never regained subsequently. The Jews also continued to take a prominent part in the cultural life of the nation. With their remarkable co-operation the constellation of a century earlier was revived. Germany prospered culturally while it lived in critical, sometimes ominous conditions politically, reactionary in the early nineteenth and troublesome in the early twentieth century. The Jews also enlarged their footholds in the professions. How their political, economic and social situation developed and how far the somewhat sweeping statement that they enjoyed full equality is to be qualified, will be discussed presently.

Not all segments of the German people were satisfied with the attitude of the governments toward the Jews. Six months only after the promulgation of the Constitution, on February 24, 1920, in Munich, the newly-founded National Socialist German Workers Party (NSDAP) issued a programme which challenged the entire development since the days of Moses Mendelssohn. Its paragraphs 4-6 were designed to throw back the Jews to their pre-emancipation status and read as follows:

> "4. Only fellow countrymen (*Volksgenossen*) can be citizens of the state. Only persons of German blood, regardless of their religious affiliation, can be fellow countrymen. No Jew can, therefore, be a fellow countryman.
>
> 5. Whoever is not a citizen of the state can be nothing but a guest in Germany and must live under the law applicable to aliens.
>
> 6. Only citizens of the state have the right to decide on the guidance and the laws of the state. We, therefore, demand that every public office of whatever nature, whether in the *Reich*, a *Land* or a municipality, be held by citizens only . . ."[36]

By its pre-war and immediate post-war history the Bavarian capital was pre-ordained for a proclamation in which anti-Jewish feelings played a preponderant part and were expressed in the most peremptory terms. The Conservatives were a Prussian party, led by the nobility with strong Protestant leanings, and had therefore always been unpopular in Bavaria. The DNVP, considered, at least in part rightly, as their successor, had no real foothold in the country and no chance of becoming a reservoir of the opposition from the right. Antisemitism was largely a middle-class movement in Bavaria; among the leadership it was less pronounced than in Prussia. A programme which appealed to the hopes, fears and prejudices of the middle class in general, and to its antisemitic emotions in particular, was likely to become popular. The establishment of the shortlived Bavarian "Soviet" Republic *(Räterepublik)* in April 1919 fanned the flames of antisemitism. The prominent appearance among its leaders of Jewish anarchists and Socialists had a considerable impact on the rural and urban population. Among them there were Eugen Leviné-Nissen, a Communist; high-minded literati, such as Gustav Landauer, a prophetic figure, violent in his language and moving in his sincerity; Ernst Toller, poet and playwright, who became military leader in the *Räterepublik* and on the occasion of his trial, drew praise from Thomas Mann and Carl Hauptmann, Boernstjerne Bjoernson and Romain Rolland for the lofty ideas and the high morality reflected in his writings; and Erich Mühsam, the Bohemian, a philosophical anarchist and dramatist; all politically completely inexperienced,

---

[36]Author's translation. There is no equivalent in English for the term *Volksgenosse*. It is linked with the emotive word *völkisch*. The German text reads:

4. Staatsbürger kann nur sein, wer Volksgenosse ist. Volksgenosse kann nur sein, wer deutschen Blutes ist, ohne Rücksichtnahme auf Konfession. Kein Jude kann daher Volksgenosse sein.

5. Wer nicht Staatsbürger ist, soll nur als Gast in Deutschland leben können und muss unter Fremden-Gesetzgebung stehen.

6. Das Recht über Führung und Gesetze des Staates zu bestimmen, darf nur dem Staatsbürger zustehen. Daher fordern wir, dass jedes öffentliche Amt, gleichgültig welcher Art, gleich ob in Reich, Land oder Gemeinde, nur durch Staatsbürger bekleidet werden darf . . .

unfit as political leaders and deeply disunited among themselves.[37] By the anti-semitic propagandists Jewish participation in such a revolutionary movement was stressed as typical and was exaggerated to such an extent that the *Räterepublik* was made to appear as a "Jewish" undertaking. This propaganda struck a note familiar to the Bavarian people for more than a century. The spirit of the National Socialist programme was not an isolated phenomenon. Antisemitism was equally rife in the numerous "patriotic associations", as well as among officers of the *Reichswehr* and among the armed right-wing volunteers who, less than a month after the publication of the Nazi programme, rose under the leadership of Wolf-gang Kapp and General Walter von Lüttwitz with the support of Ludendorff, against the government of the *Reich*. A failure in Berlin, the putsch became a success in Munich where the putschists installed a rightist government as an instrument of power "against the Jewish government of Berlin."

In Northern Germany the National Socialists were not favourably looked upon in the early years of the Republic. To the representatives of the reaction in Prussia they appeared as lacking in Prussian thoroughness and seriousness, as confused and romantic newcomers. The anti-Jewish emotions of a large section of the public were seized upon by the DNVP. They protected and co-operated with all the putschists and para-military associations, especially with the powerful *Stahl-helm,* and had radical racists in their midst. Part of these split away from them in 1922 and formed a *völkisch* group which subsequently merged with, and was eventually absorbed by the National Socialists. On the whole, however, the members of the DNVP were traditionalists, stalwarts of the monarchy, at least in their beginnings, and robust counter-revolutionaries. Former Conservatives were among their leaders. Biding their time in the first half of 1919, they soon sensed the ever-rising tide of opposition to the democratic regime burdened with, and unjustly made responsible for, the dire consequences of a war Germany had waged against the world. The Republic was shaken by Fascist and Bolshevist uprisings and seriously weakened by the fraternal rift between the two Socialist parties; the ranks of the Communists were swelled by left-wing deserters from the Socialist camp. The formation of new, embittered, well-organized and fanatical opposition from the left, supported by the Soviet Union, aggravated the problems of the Republic. The new leaders lacked governmental experience and were not ac-customed to the exercise of political power. They were, therefore, inclined some-times to overestimate the power of persuasion and sometimes to overreact to threatening popular moves. There was no trained democratic-minded personnel available to substitute for the cadres of administrators and judges inherited from the monarchy.

[37]Another Communist leader, Max Levien, has often erroneously been referred to as a Jew. He was the son of a German who had settled in Russia, and was naturalized in Bavaria. These and other facts have been reported by Immanuel Birnbaum, 'Der Spuk der Münche-ner Räterepublik', in *Süddeutsche Zeitung*, April 30th/May 1st. 1959, p. 4. About Lan-dauer see Paul Breines 'The Jew as Revolutionary. The Case of Gustav Landauer', in *LBI Year Book XII* (1967), pp. 75 ff.; about Toller, see the speech of Hugo Haase, his lawyer, at the trial of July 15, 1919, in *Hugo Haase. Sein Leben und Wirken*, ed. Ernst Haase Berlin 1929, pp. 249-254.

As early as in the summer of 1919 the DNVP considered the antisemitic potential as sufficiently strong to revive the antisemitic paragraph of the Conservative Party programme, adjusted to the new situation. After months of discussions which opposed the moderate wing and the radical faction the following text was agreed upon for the party programme and the proclamation to the *Reichstag* election of June 1920:

> "The Party combats every disintegrating, un-German spirit whether originating in Jewish or other circles. It takes a firm stand against the predominance of Jewry in government and public life which has been ever more fatefully present since the revolution. It urges that the influx of people of foreign origin across our frontiers be stopped."[38]

This statement, which was renewed on the occasion of all subsequent elections, has been described as a "compromise", because a proposal to exclude persons of Jewish ancestry from membership of the party was defeated by the followers of Westarp, the former Conservative floor leader of the *Reichstag;* they had a majority on the boards of the party and of its parliamentary groups. The text was nevertheless a victory for the radical wing. The moderates only reluctantly accepted the sentence in which the Jews were singled out for blame and their alleged predominance was castigated. They acquiesced because they felt that the radicals stood on firm ground among the rank and file of the party. This assumption proved correct and was especially confirmed when regionally leading party members put into practice the principle on which the radicals among the board members had been forced to retreat. In 1920, the well-known and nationally respected leader in the field of social work, Anna von Gierke, a DNVP-member of the National Assembly, the daughter of the famous jurist, Professor Otto von Gierke of Berlin University, was not renominated for the *Reichstag* because her mother had been of Jewish descent.[39]

Unlike the National Socialists, the DNVP was content to turn against the Jews in government and public life. The same point was expressly stressed in the Nazi programme. Since the Nazis demanded that the Jews be deprived of their rights as citizens and, therefore, were to be excluded *ipso facto* from access to public office, this paragraph was repetitious. Its incorporation discloses the propaganda value attributed to this specific demand.

Different as their origin and their objectives were, both parties operated and thrived in the same climate. The war had left a legacy of violence; human life was cheap, political murder an instrument of politics. Leading figures of the DNVP did not openly approve of murder, as did Hitler, but their increasingly passionate and immoderate propaganda against republican leaders, as well as their failure to take a strong stand against acts of violence, favoured and encouraged it. Murder was committed against Jews and non-Jews alike. Not only Rosa Luxemburg, Kurt Eisner, Gustav Landauer and Walther Rathenau, but also Karl Lieb-

---

[38]Author's translation.

[39]Liebe, *op. cit.*, pp. 24, 64 f., 107 ff., 115, 120. - In contrast to the case of Anna von Gierke, Reinhold Georg Quaatz, whose mother was also Jewish, won the nomination and election as a DNVP-deputy in Dresden-Bautzen; he was a high civil servant under the Empire and resigned in 1919.

knecht and the Catholic leader Matthias Erzberger were among the prominent victims. Hundreds of crimes were perpetrated against non-Jews by members of the Black *Reichswehr* and other secret or semi-secret para-military formations. The comments of part of the provincial press, mostly DNVP-orientated or so-called neutral newspapers with rightist affiliations, on the murders of Erzberger and Rathenau and on the premature death of *Reichspräsident* Ebert in 1925, reflecting the mood of the lower middle classes, especially in Eastern Germany, show an indescribably brutal cynicism and impassioned hatred against the Republic and its leaders.

The National Socialists did not create the climate of hatred. They found it among all the enemies of the Republic, monarchists as well as Communists, Fascist mercenaries as well as the Red Front Fighter Federation *(Roter Frontkämpferbund)*. But they were masters in whipping it up, they fed on it, expanded and exploited it.

THE DECLINE OF THE PAYS LÉGAL AND THE RISE OF THE PAYS RÉEL

The words of Louis Philippe pointing to the difference between the *pays légal* and the *pays réel,* used in quite a different context, are readily applicable to the Weimar Republic. While the functioning of its organs was legally determined by the Constitution, they often acted contrary to its text and spirit. The President of the *Reich* frequently recurred to Article 48 of the Constitution granting him extraordinary powers, even when the need for it was doubtful. The army arrogated to itself unconstitutional powers. Its illegal machinations included assistance and cover for the para-military rightist groups which without exception were antisemitic, and for secret rearmament in co-operation with the Soviet Union. These endeavours enjoyed the protection of governmental agencies and a majority of the parliament and, as far as the contacts with the Soviet Union were concerned, the benevolence and occasionally the help of the Communist Party. The courts applied the law unequally, favouring the law-breakers of the right and acting harshly against those of the left. They failed in their duty to protect the authority of the Republic. If the offenders were not simply acquitted, the judgments pronounced against those who grossly insulted leading figures were so shamefully lenient that even moderate *Reich* and state ministers gave up turning to the courts for the defence of their honour. The extremists of the right and the left and their armed formations fought, at times, each other and, at other times, joined hands to paralyse the institutions of the Republic by extra-parliamentary action.

For the gradual emancipation of the Jews which reached its peak under the Weimar system, the expansion of liberalism and the strengthening of the democratic forces had been a decisive factor. In the political parties to which they adhered, as well as in the organizations established for the defence of their interests, the Jews fought for the maintenance of democratic legality and tried to push back the anti-democratic forces.

The *pays légal* scored a triumph when, in 1920, the putsch of Kapp foundered on the general strike of the workers and the refusal of the civil servants to co-operate

The first Reich Conference of the Workers' and Soldiers' Councils in Berlin, December 1918

On the government rostrum seated, from left to right, Max Cohen-Reuss, Philipp Scheidemann, Otto Landsberg; seated, far right, Hugo Haase, Friedrich Ebert, Emil Barth

with the putschist government. It also developed greater strength in the five years of fallacious stability from 1924 onwards. This was reflected in the electoral results of those years. The Social Democrats registered impressive gains, the DNVP heavy losses and the National Socialists fell back from 32 seats in the spring of 1924 to 14 in December of the same year and twelve in the election of 1928. Before the economic crisis started, political radicalism was not solidly rooted in the mass of the citizens. Though they were far from feeling at home in the democratic Republic, they were ready to give it a chance whenever they felt that the situation improved. Ominously, however, the electoral victory of the left in 1928 drew the cadres of the *Zentrum* and of the DNVP to the right, thus foreshadowing disaster on the parliamentary scene. In the *Zentrum* the prelate Ludwig Kaas and Heinrich Brüning, both of the right wing, took the lead; in the DNVP Alfred Hugenberg, uncompromising and anxious to destroy the newly-constructed state, was elected floor leader instead of Count Westarp, under whose leadership the party had twice joined a governmental coalition. A year later, immediately after the death of Gustav Stresemann, the DVP, won over by him for constructive co-operation against the greatest odds, revived its previous oppositional tendencies. Thus the foundations for the building of new political fronts were being prepared.

Between 1919 and 1929 the situation of the Jews was little affected by the increase in strength of the DNVP. When, in 1928, the party declined from its peak of 111 in December 1924 to 78 in a *Reichstag* of 490, it was, together with the National Socialists, proportionately no stronger than the right had been in the pre-war *Reichstag*. Even in Bavaria the vehemence of antisemitism seemed to abate somewhat in the face of greater normalcy of public and private life.

The outbreak of the world economic crisis and its rapid expansion caused the abandonment of hope for the return of normal conditions and engendered fear and hatred. In municipal and state elections the ranks of the extremist parties, above all of the National Socialists, were swelled, mainly at the expense of the centre parties. The appointment, after the resignation of the government of the great coalition, of Heinrich Brüning as *Reich* Chancellor signalled the intention of the President of the *Reich* and his advisers to turn to the right in order to balance the growing strength of the National Socialists. Yet the dissolution of the *Reichstag* in the summer of 1930, without stringent necessity, resulted in their tremendous rise from 12 to 107 seats and a resounding defeat of the DNVP which was reduced from 78 to 41. A right-centre coalition without the National Socialists was made impossible, the *pays légal* defeated on the parliamentary level. In the light of all available evidence based on the results of the preceding local elections, Brüning's decision to wage a preventive electoral battle against the extremists was as hopeless an adventure as the waging of a preventive war against the major powers of Europe had been in 1914.

The results of the elections of 1930 narrowed the basis of action for the parties willing to uphold democratic principles. A semi-authoritarian regime ensued based on presidential decrees. A semi-legality was maintained by the approval of these decrees by *Reichstag* majorities. When Brüning was dismissed and a government of the right with no parliamentary basis was installed under Franz von Papen and new elections decreed, the National Socialists more than doubled their seats and the Communists who tried to outdo the rightists by nationalist slogans in their party platforms and proclamations increased their votes by 40 per cent. The two parties which, though irreconcilable, had the common objective of destroying the democratic Republic obtained a negatively effective majority. No government founded on, or tolerated by a majority could be established, parliamentary democracy was and remained dead throughout all stages of the further development which it is unnecessary to review here. The actions of the organs of the state still able to function were determined by the will of the aged President von Hindenburg, advised by changing cliques and camarillas.

During these years the situation of the Jews was influenced by various, often opposing factors: the reduction of parliamentary support for the constitutional rights which also protected the Jewish population, the governmental attitude, and the actions of the National Socialists and their armed bands.

The situation of the Jews was gravely undermined by the decrease in strength of the parties on which they could traditionally rely.[40] The Social Democrats receded gradually from their peak of 152 in 1928 to 120 in 1932, while the total membership of the *Reichstag* increased from 490 to 608. Among the parties of the centre, only the Catholic *Zentrum* was untouched by the dramatic changes. The Democratic Party in contrast, which had provided the main political home for the Jewish voters, and the DVP which, at least, was not openly antisemitic, were already seized with panic before the elections of 1930 and tried to save themselves by escaping from their past. The Democrats merged with Artur Mahraun's *Jungdeutscher Orden,* one of the anti-party, militarist and youth-glorifying leagues which did not accept Jews as members. The word "democratic" was dropped, the word "republican" avoided. Instead, the German State Party *(Deutsche Staatspartei)* formed; Mahraun qualified as the "Hitler of the centre", which sheds a significant light on the mood of the once democratic voters and their illusory hopes.[41] The DVP entered into a coalition with the National Socialists in Thuringia where they had trebled their votes to 11.3 per cent; with the help of the party of Stresemann, outraged more perhaps than any other statesman by

---

[40]On the democratic parties and the Jewish question see also *Entscheidungsjahr 1932. Zur Judenfrage in der Endphase der Weimarer Republik,* Ein Sammelband herausgegeben von Werner E. Mosse unter Mitwirkung von Arnold Paucker, Tübingen 1965, 1966 (Schriftenreihe wissenschaftlicher Abhandlungen des Leo Baeck Instituts 13), in particular the essays of P. B. Wiener, 'Die Parteien der Mitte [zur Judenfrage]' and Hans-Helmuth Knütter, 'Die Linksparteien [zur Judenfrage]'.

[41]Klaus Hornung, *Der Jungdeutsche Orden,* Düsseldorf 1958, pp. 97-107. Shortly after the election of September 1930, the members of the *Orden* left the *Staatspartei.* The expression "Hitler of the centre" was used by the Prussian Finance Minister Hermann Höpker-Aschoff. In a private talk with Otto Braun, Bernhard Falk, the Jewish floor leader of the *Staatspartei,* explained that the words "democratic" and "republican" had lost their appeal to the people at large and could not, therefore, appear in the name of the new party. On DDP and *Jungdo* see also P. B. Wiener in *Entscheidungsjahr 1932, loc. cit.,* pp. 292 ff. and Arnold Paucker in *LBI Year Book XIII* (1968), pp. 165-166.

the Nazis, a National Socialist became for the first time a minister in a German *Land*. The abandonment of their *raison d'être* by both parties was not rewarded by the voters. They lost heavily in the next elections and all but disappeared before the end of the Republic.

Inversely, the gains of the National Socialists had notable effects on neighbouring parties and on associations which had always leaned to the right. The DNVP, anxious to keep its followers, avoided polemics with the National Socialists and passed over in silence their frequent excesses. They were even swamped by their oratory. It was as depressing as it was revealing to see the followers of the von Winterfelds, von Kries, and other once respected Conservative leaders press around the speaker's rostrum in the Prussian Diet and shout their approval for the National Socialist floor leader Wilhelm Kube, one of the most disgusting Nazi leaders; not to speak of the younger members of the DNVP who had been reared in the atmosphere of demagogy. "How wonderfully he spoke", Baroness Helene von Watter, a physician, said ecstatically to her fellow-deputies of the DNVP.[42] They bowed to the plebeian and boisterous brand of nationalism and anti-semitism.[43]

The organs of government were wedded to the principle of the *Rechtsstaat* which had a longer tradition in Germany than democracy. In February 1932, *Reichs-minister* of the Interior Wilhelm Groener voiced strong disapproval of illegal anti-Jewish actions and declared that the constitutional rights of all citizens would be defended with the utmost firmness. When Brüning had to resign, the *Central-verein* acknowledged that he and his ministers had remained faithful to the constitution, maintained the law and safeguarded the constitutional equality of the rights of all Germans — a slightly exaggerated, but in the main true statement. In August 1932, shortly after the Nazis had won their crushing victory, the *Reichspräsident* let it be known that he disapproved of any attempt to restrict the constitutional, political and religious rights of the German citizens and of excesses against Jewish subjects of the *Reich*.[44]

[42]In his memoirs Willibalt Apelt, a great jurist and member of the Democratic Party reports the same experience: "All those tending politically to the right, which means the greater part of our relatives and acquaintances, were inebriated by nationalist phraseology and indulged in the idea of the so-called national rising. It was deeply distressing to see how many experienced and otherwise intelligent people were lacking in any sense of moral standards in relation to that movement and its people" (Willibalt Apelt, *Jurist im Wandel der Staatsformen. Lebenserinnerungen*, Tübingen 1965, pp. 224 f.).

[43]See also George L. Mosse, 'Die deutsche Rechte und die Juden', in *Entscheidungsjahr 1932*.

[44]*C.V.-Zeitung*, 1932, p. 53 (Groener), p. 233 (Brüning), p. 349 (Hindenburg). During his tenure as a member of Brüning's cabinet Groener was not influenced by antisemitic feelings such as he had expressed during the revolution (see above p. 31). He also found words of praise for Hilferding whom he called a decent man, a great financial scholar without much ambition, contrary to Schacht, his opponent, "a man of burning ambition and *Entgleisungs-manieren* who is already recommending himself as a candidate for the presidency, an excellent banker, but very controversial as a statesman" (Dorothea Groener-Geyer, *General Groener. Soldat und Staatsmann*, Frankfurt a. Main 1955, p. 262. In his will of April 1934 Groener wrote that he could not embrace National Socialism and warned the *Führer* to see to it in statesmanlike wisdom that the national will should never degenerate into national presumption, the biggest foe of the German people which had lost the war by indulgence in presumption (*ibid.*, p. 348).

In his thorough and enlightening analysis of the attitude of the central organs of government, Arnold Paucker dwells on Brüning's failure to include in one of his speeches a condemnation of the anti-Jewish excesses and a commitment to uphold the equality of rights of all citizens regardless of creed and origin, as suggested by Jewish organizations and pressed for in talks with governmental officials.[45] Doubtless this omission was intentional. Brüning thought of a coalition with the National Socialists and did not want to erect obstacles by committing himself to a cause which would have antagonized his prospective allies, a lugubrious advance-payment of a representative of the *Rechtsstaat* for a right-centre coalition, considered possible by him. But the immediate effect of this tacit concession of silence should not be overrated. It was known that Hindenburg rejected at that time the Nazi bid for power. Groener, the key figure in the second cabinet of Brüning as the head of the Ministries of Defence and of the Interior, was determined to maintain law and order and still enjoyed the confidence of the President. In Prussia the Socialist ministers of the Weimar coalition, Otto Braun as head of the government and Carl Severing as Minister of the Interior, spoke out and acted courageously against the National Socialists.

As long as these forces of the Executive co-operated, albeit with increasing friction — and this continued until the disastrous Prussian elections in April 1932 and the dismissal of Brüning shortly thereafter — the administration and the police were animated, in general, by the same spirit. In the face of mounting tensions they followed the regulations and orders of the central organs and tried to enforce the law. Even the courts which pronounced scandalous judgments in political cases and failed to protect Jews adequately against insults and defamation acted in accordance with the spirit of the law in civil cases. Basing themselves on the Civil Code and the law on fair competition they released judgments and issued interim orders, often accompanied by vigorous reasoning, against incitements to the boycott of Jewish firms and shops and untruthful allegations against individual Jews in newspapers, circulars and speeches.[46]

Nevertheless the task of the authorities became increasingly difficult and some of them wavered. The National Socialists were encouraged by their sweeping electoral victories to take their fights more and more to the streets. On October 13, 1930, parallelling the appearance of the 107 Nazis at the first meeting of the newly elected *Reichstag* in SA and SS uniforms as a show of defiance against the parliamentary system, Jews were beaten up and the windows of Jewish shops shattered in Berlin. New anti-Jewish riots broke out in the autumn of 1931. Desecrations of synagogues and Jewish cemeteries occurred, Jews were threatened, Jewish students were humiliated and excesses committed against them; incitements to boycott Jewish firms became more frequent. National Socialism also penetrated more deeply those strata of society which had always proved susceptible to it.

---

[45] Arnold Paucker, *Der jüdische Abwehrkampf gegen Antisemitismus und Nationalsozialismus in den letzten Jahren der Weimarer Republik*, Hamburg 1968, 1969, pp. 129-136; the documents pp. 217-235.
[46] *C.V.-Zeitung*, 1932, pp. 441, 516.

In 1931, the students, protagonists of racial antisemitism even before the time of William II, gave the National Socialist Students League a majority in the election to the boards of the General Students Committee in fifteen institutions of higher learning, including the University and Technical University of Berlin, and made it the biggest faction in thirteen others. The high school students were no less passionately attracted by the antisemitic movement. The attempt of the leadership of the German Association of Salaried Employees to bring its members into the camp of the moderate right failed; the 300,000 members mostly joined the National Socialists. Many public officials of the lower and middle ranks sensed the wind of change and turned to the Nazis.

In these conditions, after the coup of Papen against the Prussian Government and the *Reichstag* elections of July 1932, in the atmosphere of organized and whipped-up antisemitism, the number and scope of the incidents grew towards the end of the year. The terror increased mainly in East Prussia, Silesia and Schleswig-Holstein. There were Jews who left the small towns in which they felt endangered and took to the urban centres. But German-Jewish history of the year 1932 cannot be written exclusively on the basis of what concerned Jews alone. This was a year of a civil-war-like confrontation of uniformed Storm Troopers, Red Front Fighters and republican *Reichsbanner* men, of beer hall battles and political hysteria and of thousands of politically militant persons and attendants at meetings, trade union secretaries and newspapermen killed, wounded and assaulted. The Jewish situation had special features in so far as the Jews were unconditionally targets of the Nazi attacks without regard to their political activity, or non-activity. But numerous non-Jews also, whether active in public life or not, were exposed to violence. Moreover, the incidents of which the Jews were victims, often of a grave nature, did not become the norm. In 1932, the Jewish press continued to appear. Jewish associations operated freely, their members could meet and defend their rights in open and closed meetings and propagate and fight for their ideas and interests. Jewish firms were seriously threatened only in exceptional cases, Jewish physicians and lawyers were sought out and newspapers whose publishers or editors were well-known Jews had more readers and subscribers than the *Völkischer Beobachter* and its provincial derivatives. This writer, exposed as he was as a Jew and a Social Democratic member of Parliament, campaigned without major disturbances in five elections of the year 1932, outside and within the province of Silesia which had more than its fair share of leading Nazi Party members with criminal records. Other members of the *Reichstag* and the *Landtage* who were in the same position had a similar experience. But the fact that it was necessary for political activity to be carefully protected, that measures of protection had to be advertised, and women who wanted to attend were told they could rely on the precautions taken, and that nevertheless beer hall battles and bloody clashes occurred, denotes the direction in which the country was moving. This, however, is only by implication part of German-Jewish history. In fact it is the history of Germany in the year 1932.

To the Jews the *pays légal,* marked by the Weimar Constitution, tumultuously assailed, weakened and eroded by the forces of the *pays réel,* afforded a measure of safety and safeguard of their rights even in the twilight of the governments of von Papen and von Schleicher. This was ended only when Hitler was invested with the chancellorship and the *pays réel* substituted for the *pays légal* by a combination of governmental and monopoly party powers.

JEWS IN THE PARLIAMENTS OF THE WEIMAR REPUBLIC

Jews participated in the parliamentary life of the Weimar Republic, in the *Reichstag* as well as in the *Landtage,* exclusively as members of parties of the left.[47] Under the monarchy, some baptized Jews could be found in the Conservative and Free Conservative ranks. Since the time of William II, however, the racial aspects of antisemitism had gradually won prominence. No persons of Jewish descent were among the DNVP-deputies in the parliaments of the Republic. Nor were there Jews in the parliamentary ranks of the DVP, the party founded by Stresemann, who had started his career as a National Liberal, the party once denigrated as a "troop for the protection of the Jews" *(Judenschutztruppe).* Yet there was one notable exception. Jacob Riesser, baptized as a child, a nephew of Gabriel Riesser, a member of the board of directors of the *Darmstädter Bank* and Professor of Law in the University of Berlin, a man of unusual abilities and wide interests, was a member of the National Assembly and the successive *Reichstage* until, in 1928, he withdrew from parliamentary life because of his advanced age. He was held in high esteem by his party and, on its proposal, made a vice-president of the *Reichstag.*

Subject to this exception, the story of the Jews in parliamentary life of the Weimar Republic is, therefore, a story of their role in the parties of the left: the DDP, left of centre, the Social Democrats, the party of the moderate left, and the Communists, the party of the radical left. Moreover, at the beginning of the Weimar Republic, the Independent Social Democrats who, opposed to the approval of the war credits, had constituted themselves as a separate party in 1917, formed the opposition of the left at a time when the Communists were still insignificant. In 1920, they won an electoral victory, but disintegrated after the end of that same year and, faced with the demand for surrender to Soviet Communism on Soviet terms, split wide open at the Party Congress in Halle in 1922. While the majority of the rank and file joined the Communists, providing them with a mass basis, the remaining members and most of the leaders re-entered the unified Social Democratic Party. The history of the party is therefore brief but important for the purpose of this study inasmuch as Jews among the leading personnel of the Social Democrats had been attracted by the pacifist and internationalist views of the Independents during and after the war. Among the fifteen Jews in the *Reichstag* elected as Social Democrats in December 1924, ten were former Independents.

Contrary to the often wavering attitude of the former Progressive Party, the DDP accorded Jews their rightful place whenever it felt that a Jewish member was well fitted to fill a parliamentary position. In the National Assembly Ludwig Haas and Felix Waldstein, both members of the defunct *Reichstag,* and Bernhard Falk from Cologne were members of the DDP. Haas remained a representative of Baden until his death in 1930 and was the party's floor leader in the last years of his career. Falk was in the forefront of those who opposed the Rhenish separatists and federalists during the critical years from 1919 to 1923. He was later nominated for the Prussian Diet and was, from 1925, floor leader of his group.[48] Both discharged themselves effectively of the task of bringing the policy of their groups in line with that of the democratic ministers and vice-versa. In the later years of the Weimar Republic, too, the Democrats nominated Jews for the *Reichstag,* among them Georg Bernhard, the editor-in-chief of the *Vossische Zeitung* of Berlin, in 1928, and Gustav Stolper, the editor-in-chief of the famous economic weekly *Deutscher Volkswirt* in Hamburg, in 1930. Several other Jewish Democrats served in the Prussian Diet and the Diets of some smaller *Länder.* The DDP has often been blamed for its failure to nominate Hugo Preuss for membership of the National Assembly and the *Reichstag* and it may be that one of the reasons for this omission was the fear that the candidacy of the "Father of the Constitution" of the *"Judenrepublik"* could damage the chances of the party. Preuss was, however, nominated and elected to the Prussian Diet in which he served with distinction until his death.

Eugen Schiffer, a baptized Jew, was the most gifted member of the Democratic group. This versatile man exercized a real, although by no means felicitous influence on the events in the first crucial years of the Republic through a cautious but persistent resistance to a bold advancement of democratic institutions and to a democratic-minded appointments policy. He had risen to high parliamentary positions and, during the war, also to the highest rank in the civil service and was between 1919 and 1923 several times Minister of Finance and of Justice. He was a *Vernunftrepublikaner* who tended to the right and, after a futile attempt to merge the DDP and the DVP, abandoned politics. This extremely talented man, who after 1945, when almost ninety years of age, organized and headed the administration of Justice in the Soviet Zone of Occupation before he returned to the West to write his memoirs with many intentional lacunae, has not yet found a biographer.[49]

While Jews as voters opted mainly for the DDP, their proportion was almost as high among the Social Democratic leadership as it had been under the monarchy.

---

[47]Jewish members of the Provisional Reich Economic Council (*Vorläufiger Reichswirtschaftsrat*) are omitted. Most members of the Council were selected as representatives of the various branches of the national economy; ten were appointed by the government. There were several Jews among them.

[48]About Falk see Fritz Wahl, 'Bernhard Falk, ein rheinischer Patriot', in *Den Unvergessenen. Opfer des Wahns 1933-1945,* ed. Gustav Radbruch, Herman Maas, Lambert Schneider, Heidelberg 1952, pp. 105-122.

[49]Eugen Schiffer, *Ein Leben für den Liberalismus,* Berlin-Grunewald 1951; Fritz Hesse, *Von der Residenz zur Bauhausstadt,* Bad Pyrmont 1964, outlines Schiffer's extraordinary gifts (pp. 108 f., 114).

They accounted for an average of eight to ten per cent of the Social Democratic group of the *Reichstag* and for about seven per cent of the corresponding group of the Prussian Diet. The upswing of the Independent Social Democrats in the election to the first *Reichstag* brought to it a new group of leading Jewish parliamentary deputies. Rudolf Hilferding was outstanding among those who joined the reunified Social Democratic Party. He explored the application of the Marxist theory to the imperialist age and was the chief editor of the scholarly organ of the Party *Die Gesellschaft.* He skilfully adapted Marxist thought to the changing needs of the present and provided the altered practice of the party with a new version of the ideology for the benefit of the masses who were confused and bewildered in the years of transition. Paul Hertz became a hard-working, solid secretary of his *Reichstag* group and a down-to-earth financial expert. He was also instrumental in establishing an advisory body of young academically-trained party members to consolidate the parliamentary work in political, economic, financial and social matters and to supply material for new thought and direction. Siegfried Aufhäuser, a gifted organiser, succeeded in establishing a federation of white-collar worker associations as a counterweight to the antisemitic Association of Salaried Employees.

Of those who had remained in the Social Democratic ranks during the war, Hugo Heimann, clear-sighted and level-headed, courteous and conciliatory, was, from 1919 to 1932, chairman of the Main Committee of the *Reichstag.* He presided over more than a thousand meetings of the Committee which dealt with budgetary, financial and many constitutional matters. He also reformed the parliamentary control of the budget so thoroughly that the right of the *Reichstag* to consider and examine the appropriations was not only one on paper but became a reality to be faced by the Executive.[50] Ernst Heilmann, leader of the Social Democrats in the Prussian Diet and, after 1928, also a member of the *Reichstag,* deserves great credit for steadfastly impressing on the Socialist group the need for a consistent, subtle and open-minded policy in order to maintain the Weimar coalition. In co-operation with the Socialist ministers he thereby removed parliamentary obstacles to the continuation of the Socialist-led cabinet, contrary to the *Reichstag* group which often vacillated. Until 1932, the Prussian cabinet was thus enabled to pursue a progressive, substantial and enlightened appointment policy in the largest *Land* of the Republic.

During the years of the Weimar Republic some Jewish members of the Social Democratic Party died, among them the leader of the Independent Socialists Hugo Haase, and Emanuel Wurm. Others resigned because of their advanced age, such as Eduard Bernstein, Gustav Hoch, the industrious expert in social policy, and Hugo Heimann. Others again were not re-elected because of the dwindling strength of the party in the final years of the Republic. Among them were Julius Moses, a physician and an expert in all matters relating to health, and Adele Schreiber-

---

[50]Hugo Heimann, *Vom tätigen Leben,* published and introduced by Walther G. Oschilewski, Berlin-Grunewald 1949, pp. 34-38.

Krieger, a courageous and intelligent fighter for women's rights, elected in 1920 and again in 1928. Both failed to win re-election in 1932. There were fifteen Jews among a total of 131 in 1924 and among 152 in 1928; fourteen among 143 in 1930; twelve among 133 in July 1932 and ten among 121 in November of the same year. All ten, and likewise all Jews in the Social Democratic Party of the Prussian Diet, were re-nominated for the party-ticket of March 1933 in the election which took place under National Socialist terror in the countryside and threats, intimidation and interdiction of meetings of the Socialists and Communists everywhere in the country. Only in Wurttemberg, Berthold Heymann, a member of the Diet for more than twenty years, withdrew from the race after Wilhelm Keil, the regional Social Democratic Party leader, had been informed by the National Socialist president of the Diet that Heymann's presence would not be tolerated.

Taken all together, the Social Democrats pursued the same policy which they had practised under the monarchy in quite different conditions. Regardless of the violent and turbulent Nazi movement and in defiance of terrorist acts, Jews were presented as candidates as long as the Social Democratic Party existed. The Social Democrats were not shy even of making Jews leaders of the lists for some of the electoral districts. Hilferding led in Düsseldorf-East, Hertz in Merseburg in the province of Saxony, and Tony Sender, a high-spirited, attractive and intelligent woman, in Dresden-Bautzen.

As mentioned above, the Communists did not take part in the election to the National Assembly. In the first *Reichstag,* elected in June 1920, they occupied no more than two seats which went to Clara Zetkin and Paul Levi, disciple and friend of Rosa Luxemburg. At the time of the Revolution, most Jews among the political leadership of the radical left were attracted by the Independent Socialists rather than by the Communists. Later some of them were among the left-wingers of the Independents in the *Reichstag* and in the *Landtage* who joined the Communists. On the other hand, some of the Communists were horrified by the victimization of German workers in senseless putschist movements for Soviet Russian foreign policy interests; they split away and established a party of Communist heretics. Levi, expelled from the party, was among them. In the long run, however, the domination of the Third International by the Soviet Union foiled all attempts to set up viable autonomous Communist parties or to give the official Communist parties a direction not approved of by the Soviets. The period of the Weimar Republic is, therefore, filled with repeated changes of Communist leadership paralleling the political moves in the Soviet Union.

In the wake of the runaway inflation and the misery of the masses the Communists won their first electoral victory in May 1924, to be thrown back from 62 to 45 seats in December when the first beneficent effects of the policy of stabilization were felt. After this, the Communists increased their votes progressively and eventually occupied 100 seats in November 1932. In the same election the National Socialists won 196, the Social Democrats 121 seats. Many Jews and non-Jews lost leading positions in the Communist Party as a result of the frequently recurring party purges. A "rightist" ticket in the early twenties had to yield to a "leftist" ticket which, in turn, fought the "ultra-leftists" among whom two Jews, Iwan Katz and Werner Scholem, were prominent. Both were first members of the Prussian Diet, then also of the *Reichstag,* but neither was re-nominated in 1928. In 1925 Ernst Thälmann was built up as a *Führer* by the "leftists" among whom Ruth Fischer, daughter of a Jewish father and a non-Jewish mother, was a leading figure in 1924 and 1925; in 1927 she was expelled from the party. In 1928, a new triumvirate was formed, consisting of Thälmann, Hermann Remmele and Heinz Neumann, a Jew who made a lightning career in the party and was twenty-six years old at the time. He was a member of the *Reichstag* from 1930 to 1932. After 1931, however, he had many disagreements with Thälmann, who had the firm backing of Stalin, and was accused of activities prejudicial to the party and of grave political errors. Accordingly he was not re-nominated for the election of November 1932.

The Jews among the Communist members of Parliament had very different fates. Levi eventually joined the Social Democrats and became their most brilliant non-conformist; he died in 1930. He has been called the best forensic orator of the Weimar Republic.[51] He was admirable, indeed, in a *cause célèbre* in which he showed a public prosecutor to have favoured the murderers of Liebknecht and Luxemburg in flagrant violation of his duties. Arthur Rosenberg, a *Privatdozent* in the University of Berlin where he taught ancient history, a member of the Central Committee at the time of Ruth Fischer, left the party in 1927. He was the only Communist speaker after Levi's defection who was listened to attentively by the House. He wrote scholarly books about the origins and history of the Weimar Republic and about the history of Bolshevism and eventually emigrated to the United States. Katz and Scholem were seized in 1933 and sent to concentration camps. Scholem was murdered by the National Socialists, while Katz survived Auschwitz. Ruth Fischer became as violent in her opposition to Stalin and the Soviets as she had been in her espousal and reckless propagation of their cause before. Neumann was executed in the Soviet Union, a victim of the Stalinist purges.

Contrary to the upward trend of the Communist Party, the number of Communist Jewish deputies declined in the parliaments. Whereas six Jews were among the 62 Communists in the *Reichstag* of May 1924, from one to three served in the following periods of legislature and not a single Jew was among the 100 Communists in the last *Reichstag* of the decaying Republic. Whereas several Jews — Katz, Scholem, Rosi Wolfstein and Fritz Ausländer — were among the Communists in the Prussian Diet, no Jew was among the 57 of the last Diet of 1932. A perusal of the 565 names of the Communist lists for the electoral districts of

---

[51]Emil J. Gumbel, *Vom Fememord zur Reichskanzlei*, Heidelberg 1962, pp. 41 f. About Levi see Charlotte Beradt (ed.), *Zwischen Spartakus und Sozialdemokratie* (a selection from Levi's writings, speeches and letters), and Charlotte Beradt, *Paul Levi*, both Frankfurt a. M. 1969.

Prussia suggests that, with the possible exception of one or two, no Jews were nominated even for places on the lists in which there was no chance of being elected.

The question arises as to the motives for this omission. Jews are not easily inclined to accept unconditional obedience to a political master or rule. This may be one of the reasons why they disappeared from the Communist sectors of the German parliaments. Their complete omission from the lengthy electoral lists, however, also points to the deep distrust of Jewish intellectuals felt by the Communist bureaucrats who dominated the movement increasingly. Moreover the Communists tried repeatedly to establish contacts with rightists, including National Socialists, to lure them into the Communist camp; Jewish Communists even took a conspicuous part in these attempts: Karl Radek, in 1923, with his praise of the terrorist Albert Leo Schlageter; Ruth Fischer, in 1925, who called anyone attacking Jewish capitalism a working-class-fighter even though not yet aware of it, and exhorted her listeners to hang or trample down Jewish capitalists; and Heinz Neumann who formulated the nationalist Communist programme of national and social liberation of 1930, competing with the right in attacking the predatory Treaty of Versailles and the Young plan for enslaving the German people, and who tried to win over officers of the *Reichswehr* and National Socialists for the Communist cause.[52] In view of these efforts of leading Jewish party members it would be an irony of history if more research disclosed that the presentation of electoral lists free of Jews was also intended to disprove the suspicion fostered relentlessly by the National Socialists that Bolshevism was a Jewish conspiracy.

Summing up: Jews were nominated for election to parliamentary bodies of the Weimar Republic only by parties of the left. In the parliaments they were less numerous, in absolute figures and proportionately, than under the Empire, but there were several leading and influential figures among them. At the end of the Republic only the Social Democrats had Jews among their parliamentary representatives while the *Staatspartei* was virtually extinct and the Communists did not present Jews as candidates. In the *Reichstag* of November 1932, the last *Reichstag* elected under normal conditions, the Jewish members amounted to 1.7 per cent of the total, a percentage as low as it had been only twice since 1867, the year of the convening of the Constituent *Reichstag* of the North German Federation. The statement made above with reference to the period of the Empire, that "most of the people were averse to the exercise of public authority by Jews in legislative bodies" can be repeated with still greater validity with regard to the time of the Weimar Republic.

---

[52]Ossip K. Flechtheim, *Die Kommunistische Partei Deutschlands in der Weimarer Republik,* Offenbach/Main 1948, pp. 88 f. (Radek, Ruth Fischer); p. 173 (Heinz Neumann); p. 281 (text of the programme-declaration of August 24, 1930); Margarethe Buber-Neumann, *Von Potsdam nach Moskau,* Stuttgart 1957, pp. 162, 168-174, 278 ff.; Peter Lösche, *Der Bolschewismus im Urteil der deutschen Sozialdemokratie 1903-1920,* Berlin 1967, p. 275. - See also 'Dokumentation: Zu den Beziehungen zwischen der KPD und der kommunistischen Internationale', in *Vierteljahrshefte für Zeitgeschichte,* April 1968, pp. 177-208.

JEWS IN LEADING POSTS IN THE WEIMAR REPUBLIC

The governments of the Weimar Republic, observing the Constitution, continued the practice of granting Jews access to positions of the Executive which had started after the revolution. But while the authoritarian antisemitism of the Empire had disappeared with the *Obrigkeitsstaat*, popular antisemitism had immensely increased since 1916, as we have seen. In certain *Länder*, the composition of governments was determined by new constellations tending rather to the right after the shock of the revolution had been absorbed. Bavaria was a case in point, also Wurttemberg, where right-orientated governments were installed in 1920 and 1921 respectively. Even in Prussia, where after the election of 1921 the coalition including the Social Democrats was disrupted for a short while, a government of the centre, supported by the right, took disgraceful action against Eastern Jews residing in Germany. Their internment and the cruel treatment they received provoked widespread criticism by Jewish organizations and by the political left.[53]

Jews who had been appointed members of the Executive during the revolution continued in the same or other positions after democratic legality had been established. Preuss remained the spokesman of the government during the deliberations of the draft constitution prepared by him; Landsberg was the first Minister of Justice of the Republic. Both quit voluntarily because they disapproved of the adoption of the Treaty of Versailles. Schiffer served as Minister of Finance and, subsequently, twice as Minister of Justice, last in the cabinet of Joseph Wirth in which Georg Gradnauer of the right wing of the Social Democrats held the Ministry of the Interior while Walther Rathenau headed the Ministry of Reconstruction in 1921 and that of Foreign Affairs in 1922. His assassination by nationalist terrorists brought about a tremendous wave of mass demonstrations in all strata of the population such as the Weimar Republic was not to see again. But it also caused a shock which was never fully overcome. Thereafter, only two Jews were members of governments of the Republic. One was Hilferding, Minister of Finance in the governments of the great coalition, headed by Stresemann in 1923 and by the Social Democrat Hermann Müller from 1928 to 1930. The other was Curt Joel, a baptized Jew who had entered the *Reichsjustizamt* under the monarchy and risen to the highest post, that of *Staatssekretär* in the Republic. In this position he dominated the ministry from 1920 to 1931, through all the vicissitudes of politics during which the ministers, succeeding each other after short intervals, were not much more than titular heads. He was included by Brüning in his second cabinet, from October 1931 until his dismissal in May 1932. Regardless of his Jewish ancestry, although the Nazis had already become the largest party, Brüning picked the strongwilled man of the right, not affiliated to any party, who was endowed with extraordinary administrative abilities. His appointment pleased both the DNVP and the DVP. In his previous position Joel had sharply attacked his own minister Gustav Radbruch, a kindly, mild-mannered

---

[53]S. Adler-Rudel, *Ostjuden in Deutschland, 1880-1940,* Tübingen 1959 (Schriftenreihe wissenschaftlicher Abhandlungen des Leo Baeck Instituts 1), pp. 112-119.

scholar, in a cabinet meeting dealing with the planned ordinance for the protection of the Republic after the assassination of Rathenau, because Radbruch proposed to apply the ordinance against rightist radicals only.[54]

The appearance of Jews in the Executive was thus limited to seven or, disregarding the baptized Jews, to five persons. Baptized Jews had served as heads of ministries also under the Empire, Heinrich von Friedberg, for instance, as head of the department of Justice in the *Reich* and as Prussian Minister of Justice, and Rudolf Friedenthal, as Minister of Agriculture at the time of Bismarck. The ministries of all seven were furthermore of short duration. Landsberg, Preuss and Gradnauer served for less than six months, Rathenau and Joel for less than a year, Schiffer and Hilferding, all periods of service taken together, for less than two years.

The development in the *Länder* paralleled that of the *Reich*. Several members of the Executive who emerged in the period of the revolution continued in the first years of the Republic. Their ousting came about as part of the reorganization of governments, as a result of changes in party strength or of political events, such as the *Kapp-Putsch* of March 1920. In 1919, the Democrat Ludwig Haas resigned from the Ministry of the Interior in Baden, in March 1920 Paul Hirsch from his post as Prime Minister of Prussia. Berthold Heymann, Minister of Public Education, then of the Interior, in Wurttemberg and Heinrich Hugo Fulda, Minister of the Interior in Hesse, withdrew in 1921. No Jewish minister ever served in Bavaria after April 1919 or in any other German *Land* after 1921, except in Baden where Ludwig Marum remained, until 1929, as *Staatsrat,* an honorary post without responsibility for a special governmental department.

The mounting wave of antisemitism had an impact on the thinking of Jews and non-Jews alike when vacancies had to be filled. When the Prussian Minister of the Interior Albert Grzesinski resigned early in 1930, Ernst Heilmann, mentioned above as leader of the Socialist group of the Prussian Diet, would have normally been his successor. He made no effort, however, to attain this position. His private remarks leave no doubt that he was sadly and bitterly conscious of the fact that he could not be a candidate because of his Jewish origin. Any non-Jew holding the same position in the Diet and possessing similar qualifications would have been almost automatically appointed to the post. It was not, therefore, always a mere accident that, subject to the exceptions relating to Hilferding and Joel, Jews did not serve, after 1922, in positions of the Executive of the Weimar Republic.

Jews were granted access also to branches of the administration from which they had been excluded under the Empire. Previously, baptism had been an indispensable condition of admission to posts of authority. Paul Kayser rose to an influential position in the Foreign Office at the time of Bismarck, Curt Joel, already mentioned, in the *Reichsjustizamt* at the time of William II. In Prussia Friedrich Theodor Freund could look back on an impressive career when, shortly before the revolution, he became the highest civil servant in the Prussian Ministry

---

[54]Gustav Radbruch, *Der innere Weg. Aufriss meines Lebens*, Stuttgart 1951, p. 161.

of the Interior, a post in which he remained until his retirement upon reaching the age limit.[55] Robert Weismann, Otto Braun's *Staatssekretär*, too, started as a royal public prosecutor.

Careers, however, of unbaptized Jews such as Julius Hirsch as *Staatssekretär* in the *Reich* Ministry of Economics in the turbulent years from 1919 to 1932, and Hans Schäffer who entered the same ministry as a *Regierungsrat* and rose to the rank of *Ministerialdirektor* to become, from 1930 to 1932, *Staatssekretär* in the *Reich* Ministry of Finance would not have been possible. Nor would Hermann Badt, highly intelligent and agile, a man of indomitable activity, one of the representatives of Prussia in the *Reichsrat,* have been appointed *Ministerialdirektor* in the Prussian Ministry of the Interior and placed in charge of constitutional and other matters of prime importance. Even in outward-looking Hamburg Leo Lippmann was the first Jew to become *Staatssekretär (Staatsrat)* in 1920.[56]

It is not proposed to list here the names of all other Jewish high officials who served the Republic. This has been done by others. Suffice it to say that some Jews were included in the staff of almost all ministries of the *Reich* and Prussia and of many of the regional and smaller district agencies subordinated to them, political as well as technical.

The admission of Jews to posts of authority depended largely upon the degree to which governments were prepared to pursue a policy of reform of the administrative personnel inherited from the monarchy. This willingness was greatest in Prussia, ruled by the Weimar Coalition, and non-existent in Bavaria, governed by the right or by parties right of centre since 1920. In the two other largest *Länder,* Wurttemberg and Saxony, the number of Jews in administrative posts was insignificant. Yet so unforgettable a man, as Otto Hirsch, *Ministerialrat* in Stuttgart, later one of the two leading figures in the *Reichsvertretung der deutschen Juden* and murdered by the Nazis, was among them. Another was Hans Maier, *Ministerialrat* in Dresden, a specialist in questions of welfare, who committed suicide in the Nazi era.

Not only the political orientation of the governments, but also that of the individual ministers played a big role. In the *Reich,* the Ministries of Economics, Finance and Labour were more inclined to include Jews in their staffs than the *Reichswehr* which remained a state within the state; the grandfather of the present German Federal Minister of the Interior Ernst Benda was probably the only high official of Jewish origin in the *Reich* Ministry of Defence; and there were hardly any Jewish army officers. Jews were also infrequent in the diplomatic service of the Ministry of Foreign Affairs. Landsberg served as the first envoy to Belgium after the war, chosen probably because he had persistently opposed any open or hidden annexation of the country; Samuel Saenger, one of the editors of S.

---

[55]Kaznelson, *op. cit.,* p. 582 (Joel); p. 581 (Freund).
[56]About Badt see Otto Braun, *Von Weimar zu Hitler,* 2nd ed., New York 1940, p. 225.
  About Lippmann see Leo Lippmann, *Mein Leben und meine amtliche Tätigkeit,* ed. Werner Jochmann, Hamburg 1961.

Fischer's *Neue Rundschau,* steeped in German cultural life, represented Germany in Czechoslovakia; thereafter he was transferred to a high post in the Foreign Office. Later, however, Consul-General Moritz Schlesinger called himself rightly the only Jewish member of the diplomatic service.[57] Stresemann as well as his predecessors, including Walther Rathenau, were reluctant to touch the composition of the near-feudal staff of the ministry.

The same observations prove correct with regard to Prussia. Jews were more frequent in the Socialist-led than in the other ministries. Braun and the Ministers of the Interior Carl Severing and Albert Grzesinski wholly disregarded any anti-semitic attacks and chose their staff according to merit. Konrad Haenisch, Minister of Public Education in the first years of the Republic, assigned matters of the theatre to Ludwig Selig and of music to Leo Kestenberg. There were furious attacks on Badt and Hans Goslar, chief of the Press Office of the Prussian *Staats-ministerium* until Papen's coup of 1932, because of their Zionist affiliations and on Selig and Kestenberg because these two Jews were placed in charge of cultural affairs. All Socialist ministers but also Professor Carl Heinrich Becker who held the post of Minister of Public Education in 1921 and from 1925 to 1930, dis-regarded the anti-Jewish attacks. Under Severing and Grzesinski, too, Fritz Rathe-nau, tending politically to the moderate right rather than to the left, was in charge of aliens, minorities and border territories, a highly sensitive position in which he also dealt with Jewish questions with an irreproachable sense of justice. Otto Braun reports in his autobiography that his Minister of Finance, Hermann Höpker-Aschoff, who represented the right wing in the cabinet of the Weimar coalition, drew his attention to the fact that the four officials in the Press Office were Jews; he, Braun had not been aware of this fact since he did not pay atten-tion to matters like these, a statement which is absolutely true.[58].

Already under the monarchy, as mentioned above, Jews had an easier access to the administration of Justice than to posts in the multi-purpose administration reserved to the aristocracy and the upper class in general. Two Jews had served on the Supreme Court of the *Reich*; among the states Baden and Hamburg had been least restrictive. Under the Republic promotions became more frequent. The most significant feature, however, is revealed by a comparison of the development in Prussia and Bavaria.

Before 1914, in accordance with the authoritarian character of the Prussian government, Jews were not among the prosecutors who enjoyed a social standing superior to that of the judges and equal with that of the civil servants in the general state administration and no Jew was promoted to a post as director of a chamber of a district court or to that of president of a chamber (Senat) of a court of appeal. In Bavaria where the Executive was inspired by less hierarchical ideas

---

[57]Arnold Paucker, 'Searchlight on the Decline of the Weimar Republic. The Diaries of Ernst Feder', in *LBI Year Book XIII* (1968), p. 186 with footnote 120.
[58]Braun, *op. cit.,* p. 311. Braun wrote i.a.: "Their ability as press officers was decisive for me; the old Prussian administrators, grown up more or less under the autocratic regime, were often hardly capable of this type of work, as was revealed in practice."

Jews were not excluded from these posts. Contrary to this trend, the majority of the Bavarian Diet, dominated by the antisemitic leader of the Bavarian Catholic Centre Party, Georg Heim, adopted a resolution in 1902 urging as far as possible a numerus clausus for Jews in the Judiciary which should not exceed the proportional share of Jews in the population. The Ministers of Justice, however, paid hardly any attention to this illegal demand.

Under the Republic the situation was reversed. In Prussia, where the left-centre government lasted, Jews were appointed prosecutors and promoted to positions previously closed to them. An important assignment was given to Siegfried Rosenfeld as *Ministerialdirigent* in the Ministry of Justice. Young Jews trained in law were admitted to judgeships especially after Hermann Schmidt, a member of the *Zentrum*, was made Minister of Justice in 1925, a judge whose policy of appointments was inspired by great fairness and concern for the enlargement of the number of judges faithful to the democratic Republic. In Bavaria, however, where the forces of the right had taken the lead, the resolution of 1902, as illegal at the time of its adoption as it was under the Weimar Constitution, was made the basis of policy. Under various pretexts, but sometimes even with reference to the resolution, Jews were frequently refused admission to positions as judges under the Bavarian Minister of Justice Franz Gürtner.[59] He became *Reich* Minister of Justice in the Papen government and was confirmed in this position by Hitler, a well-deserved recognition of the services rendered by him to the National Socialist movement and to Hitler personally in the years of Weimar.

Jews were strongly attracted by new tasks and eager to explore unknown administrative territory while the officials who had become entrenched in tradition were to a large extent inclined to stick to routine. The interest of Jews in questions of labour and labour relations, a field in which the Weimar Republic has great accomplishments to its credit, was paramount. When the *Reich*-Law on the labour courts came into force in 1927, many Jews showed interest in appointments to these courts. Two scholars who have won national fame in their countries of adoption, Hans J. Morgenthau, Professor of Political Science and Modern History at the University of Chicago, and Otto Kahn-Freund, Professor of Law at the University of Oxford, began their careers as judges in German labour courts. Richard Joachim and Georg Flatow were assigned questions of labour law in the *Reich* Ministry of Labour and the Prussian Ministry of Commerce respectively;

[59]Sievert Lorenzen, *Die Juden in der Justiz*, 2nd ed., Berlin 1943, pp. 161-164 (Bavaria), pp. 165 f. (Prussia), pp. 166 f. (the other *Länder*). Lorenzen, a National Socialist judge, was given access to the records of the *Reich* Ministry of Justice to compile this antisemitic publication. It contains figures not otherwise available, but can be used only with great caution because of its definition of Jews according to Nazi principles. It results, however, from the statistics that Baden and Hamburg continued their liberal appointment policy and that Wurttemberg, Saxony and Hesse reversed the previously antisemitically inspired selection of judges. In Bavaria Mr. Jakob Kohnstamm, who applied for admission to the judiciary, general administration, post and railroad administration in 1928, was rejected everywhere under flimsy pretexts. The number of young Jewish judges in Bavaria was small compared with that of Jewish judges still appointed and promoted under the monarchy (Mr. Kohnstamm's letter of November 23, 1968, Beer Tuviah, Israel).

LUDWIG FRANK

HUGO HAASE

ROSA LUXEMBURG

KURT EISNER

PAUL LEVI

ERNST HEILMANN

PAUL HIRSCH

HANS SCHÄFFER

Flatow wrote the best-known commentary on the law dealing with the Works Councils, which had numerous editions. Two Jews were among the twelve "permanent arbitrators", provincial officials of the *Reich* Ministry of Labour who were in charge of the settlement of important labour disputes and related matters, namely Max Brahn for Upper Silesia, then for Rhineland-Westphalia, and Kurt Friedländer for Pomerania.[60]

In the institutions of higher learning to which Jewish scholars had won access under the monarchy but in which they were at a disadvantage, the number of Jewish full professors increased markedly. A thorough, though admittedly not fully exact scrutiny for the last years of the Republic discloses that approximately 120 Jews, including a considerable number of baptized Jews, were among a total of about 2,000 full professors in the last years of the Republic.[61] The situation in Bavaria differed again from that in the other *Länder,* especially in Prussia, Saxony, Baden and Hamburg. In 1931, only two Jewish full professors taught at Bavarian universities, Karl Neumeyer, whose university career started under the monarchy and who broke new ground in introducing the discipline of international administrative law, and Hans Nawiasky, a baptized Jew, who was mainly interested in federalism and published a treatise on the Bavarian Constitution. The Bavarian experience above all caused Richard Willstätter, Nobel Prize laureate in chemistry, to assert correctly that the appointment of Jewish scholars was often combated and prevented. In 1925 he resigned from his post at the University of Munich in protest, because the best-suited scholar for a chair of crystallography, highly recommended by the scholar who had vacated the chair because of his advanced age, was rejected by the Faculty for antisemitic reasons.[62] In Prussia, in contrast, the trend to propose and appoint university professors on the basis of merit alone became more pronounced when, early in 1930, Adolf Grimme, a Socialist with Protestant leanings assumed the post of Minister for Cultural Affairs.

Jews were occasionally appointed chiefs of regional administrative agencies and presidents of courts of law. A baptized Jew, Julius Lippmann, a member of the Prussian Diet before the revolution and of the National Assembly in 1919, was *Oberpräsident* of Pomerania between 1919 and 1930. When the *Oberpräsident* of Lower Silesia died, in 1929, Otto Landsberg, repeatedly mentioned, a Silesian who had great achievements to his credit in the fight against separatist movements

[60]Three of these four men, Brahn, Flatow and Joachim, outstanding among those instrumental for the development of the new labour laws and labour relations, perished in Auschwitz. As another field in which Jews displayed special talents that of press relations has already been mentioned (see above, p. 55). They were also frequently chosen as personal aides as, f.i., *Ministerialrat* Herbert Weichmann by Otto Braun (Braun, *op. cit.,* pp. 311 f.) who gives the reasons, confirmed by Weichmann's work, for his choice.

[61]E. G. Lowenthal, 'Die Juden im öffentlichen Leben', in *Entscheidungsjahr 1932,* pp. 76-79. - The percentage of full professors dismissed from the German universities between 1933 and 1936 was 10.9. Since this figure includes non-Jewish scholars and "half-Jews", it tends to confirm roughly Lowenthal's estimate; see Edward Yarnell Hartshorne jr., *The German Universities and National Socialism,* London 1937, pp. 93 ff.

[62]Willstätter in Kaznelson, *op. cit.,* p. VIII; Richard Willstätter, *Aus meinem Leben,* Weinheim, Bergstrasse 1949, pp. 341-351.

in Silesia during the revolution, was the first to be offered this position. Unwilling to abandon his prosperous law practice and his seat in the *Reichstag* where he continued to render great services to the Social Democratic Party, he declined. The president of the police in Cassel was a Jew. Still under the monarchy, Nathan Stein was appointed president of the district court of Mannheim, a post which he filled to the general satisfaction until his retirement in 1927. From 1924 to 1933 Ludwig Landmann was Mayor of Frankfurt. These appointments and offers respectively disprove any suspicion of discriminatory practices.

It is true, however, that no Jews were among the *Landräte,* the chiefs of the smaller administrative units of which more than 400 existed in Prussia and from 200 to 300 in the other *Länder* taken together. In the rural and small town districts the right-wing forces prevailed in the Protestant, those of the *Zentrum* Party in the Catholic parts of the country. In Prussia the appointment of a chief of any regional or smaller district agencies had to be approved by the respective representative bodies of the people, whose approval was not always easy to obtain. It was felt, therefore, that Jewish officials could make a better contribution from positions in the ministries or in the provincial or other larger-sized agencies. Moreover, the life of a Jewish official in a small or medium-sized town was anything but enjoyable. He was surrounded by oppressive hostility and had hardly any social contacts. Leading officials of the other agencies often shunned him. There were hardly common interests and no pleasant relations with the big landowners, the small farmers and the urban middle class. As to the administration of Justice, the present writer was repeatedly urged by the Prussian Minister of Justice to impress on the young Jewish judges the necessity of consenting to serve in a small or medium-sized town for several years at least; the crowding of Jewish judges in provincial capitals was unfavourably commented upon and should be avoided. It was possible to achieve this in several cases; only to be told some months later by the judges in question that life was made extremely difficult for them and for their families, and asked to plead with the minister on his behalf in order to obtain a transfer to a court in a city.

The perennial problems of the Republic, the *Reichswehr,* the Bavarian governments of the right and the political attitudes of the small town and rural population also interfered with the faithful and complete implementation of the Constitution which theoretically ensured equal access to public office to all citizens regardless of faith. These were, however, administratively or regionally limited impediments. On the whole, the governments of the *Reich* and the *Länder* did justice to the Jews in their efforts to gain access to and promotion in positions of authority and in the course of time to obtain recognition of their scholarly performance by attaining appointments to full professorships.

DETERIORATION IN ECONOMIC AND SOCIAL LIFE

While the endeavours of the Jews to gain entrance to all positions of the civil service reached their high mark in the Weimar Republic, their importance in the national economy declined. It was a reversal of the situation which had obtained a hundred years before. In the Weimar period they enhanced their social prestige by gaining admission to the *arcana dominationis ac imperii,* a rise indignantly registered by the majority of the population, while their situation in the national economy deteriorated, a process hardly noticed even by attentive observers. It presents a very different picture from the fiction of progressive control over the national economy, relentlessly put forward by the propaganda machine of the National Socialists.

This fiction was able to gain credence because of the persistence of the peculiarities of the occupational and social distribution of the Jewish population in the Weimar period. It is true that these peculiarities tended to decrease in certain branches of the economy in which they had been particularly evident. The share of Jews in commerce, banking and stock market activities declined from the high percentage reached in the second half of the nineteenth century. The gradual adaptation to the stratification of the total population can be proved statistically. However, it did not exend to all branches of economic, social and cultural pursuits and did not proceed at a pace so strikingly fast and visible as to act as a counterweight to Nazi propaganda. In 1925, almost half of the working Jewish population was still active in commerce and banking. Their share within the total had declined from 21 per cent in 1861 to 5 per cent in 1925. The number of Jewish private banks had decreased sharply.[63] But ordinary people do not read statistics and do not make comparisons with the past. Especially when constantly subjected to a ruthless, noisy and unrelenting propaganda, they interpret the indicated phenomena naively and in a simplified way.

These phenomena were the increasing urbanization of the Jewish population, the growth of their share in the professions, their control of the great department stores and a few big Jewish names in banking.[64]

Almost one third of the Jewish population of the *Reich* and one half of that of Prussia lived in Berlin. Their number also increased in provincial capitals of Prussia, such as Breslau and Cologne, as well as in Frankfurt. In cities of other German states where their number had been small, it grew rapidly. This trend, noticeable for a century, was accentuated by the effect of the territorial losses of Germany in the East and the West. Most of those Jews who had not taken part in the earlier exodus from the Polish parts of Prussia, now left the province of Posen and those parts of West Prussia and Upper Silesia which became part of newly restored Poland. They settled in the cities, preferably in Berlin where the opportunities of re-integration into economic life appeared favourable. The same holds true for the Jews of Alsace-Lorraine who opted for Germany. Many lawyers and physicians from these territories swelled the ranks of the corresponding

[63]H. Mommsen, 'Zur Frage des Einflusses deutscher Juden auf die deutsche Wirtschaft in der Weimarer Republik', in *Gutachten des Instituts für Zeitgeschichte II,* Stuttgart 1966, p. 361.
[64]A comprehensive survey of the participation of the Jews in economic life under the Weimar Republic may be found in Esra Bennathan, 'Die demographische und wirtschaftliche Struktur der Juden', in *Entscheidungsjahr 1932,* pp. 88-131.

professions in the big cities. Since most sons of well-to-do and middle-class Jews had attended universities in the last two decades of the Empire, the increase of the proportion of Jews in the professions continued rapidly. There were 16.3 per cent of Jews among the attorneys-at-law and, in addition, many lawyers employed as consultants in concerns, trusts and cartels or on the boards of joint-stock-companies, and more than 10.9 per cent among the physicians; one third of the physicians in Berlin were Jewish. The cultural elite formed by writers, artists, independent scholars and lawyers in the cities included a great many Jews. Though proportionately their share in the professions was, with 8.7 per cent, not excessive, compared with 6 per cent of the total population, its impact on the cultural life of the nation, especially in Berlin, was widely commented upon.[65] In addition, contrary to the trend in commerce and banking, their numbers in the professions had increased not only in absolute figures but also in proportion since 1907, the year of the last statistical survey of the Empire. The perennial complaints of the small shopkeepers and artisans about the crushing competition of the department stores, almost exclusively in Jewish hands, came into sharper focus in the times of a steep decline of production and trade and of social distress. Big Jewish names in banking, such as Carl Fürstenberg, Jakob Goldschmidt, Louis Hagen, M. M. Warburg, the Salomonsohns, Kurt Sobernheim, Oscar Wassermann were abundantly cited as indicators of an overwhelming Jewish participation in the devastating workings of predatory capital *(raffendes Kapital)*, contrasted by the Nazi propaganda with the producing capital *(schaffendes Kapital)*, represented by industrial pursuits.

The outward appearances, however, differed sharply from the actual decrease of the impact of the Jews on the German economy and from the deterioration of their social situation. Both were caused by several factors: the continuation of a trend which had prevailed since the Wilhelminian period; its accentuation and acceleration by the runaway inflation of the early twenties and by the economic crisis of the early thirties and its effect on the Jewish middle class; and the growth of antisemitism. These factors expressed partly structural changes in the participation of the Jews in German economic life and partly conditions by which the entire German post-war economy was affected between 1919 and 1933. They were closely interwoven, their interaction was obvious and the effect of each of them, considered separately, can therefore hardly be exactly determined.

As set forth previously, the free market economy in which the Jews had been pioneers and had prospered started yielding to new forms of economic life already in the last period of the Empire.[66] Cartels, concerns and trusts narrowed the role of the free entrepreneur and made the early capitalism look antiquated. The

---

[65]It should be noted that the figures include not only the professionals but also the white-collar and manual workers in the law and medical offices etc. It is not possible, therefore, to draw uncontestable conclusions from these figures, but it can be stated with certainty that the share of Jews among the professionals was higher than the figures suggest.
[66]See above pp. 22-3.

number of cartels increased from 300 in 1900 to 2,100 in 1930. In the same year 56,000 products were available at fixed market prices only. The German economy thus reached a new stage. It did not leave much room for the Jewish pioneering capacity from which Jews had benefited. The bureaucratic features of the depersonalized economy were not favourable to the integration of Jewish workers into the new forms of economic organization. The new huge economic bureaucracy was reluctant to hire Jews as professional and clerical workers. This trend coincided with the disappearance of many small businesses in commerce and banking in Jewish hands or with their absorption by big firms as a result of the inflation. Although the Jewish firms, taken together, employed more non-Jews than Jews, the majority of the Jewish white-collar workers obtained employment in Jewish-owned enterprises. They were, therefore, hard hit by the retrogression of the number of Jewish firms.

These developments were also reflected by the social statistics. Looking back over ten years of the Weimar Republic, in 1929, Leo Baeck observed in a sobering analysis that Jewish social assistance which, before 1914, had to take care exclusively of foreign Jews residing in Germany, was compelled to deal increasingly with cases of German Jews. They constituted one third of the total of Jewish cases at the time of the Republic.[67] In October 1932, 7,300 unemployed were registered in the Jewish Unemployment Office in Berlin, about 25 per cent of all employed Jews. It has been concluded that, assuming an analogous percentage for the entire *Reich,* about 30,000 out of 120,000 Jewish workers were idle.

Alfred Marcus and Jakob Lestschinsky, who have analyzed the economic plight of the German Jews thoroughly, wrote their studies in 1931 and 1932 respectively, at the height of the economic depression.[68] They, therefore, took an extremely pessimistic view of their economic future. Marcus felt that emigration and retraining of the young generation for skilled manual work was the solution. He asserted that many lawyers, physicians, tradesmen and commission-agents laboured under great difficulties and led a proletarian existence. He regretted that they nevertheless refused to consider careers as skilled workers for their sons. Lestschinsky spoke of the "collapse" of the Jewish middle and upper middle class and stressed the unemployment figures and the rapid increase of the number of wage earners in public enterprises with unfortunate consequences for the prospects of Jews of obtaining jobs. He also pointed to the bureaucratization of the professions. Lawyers were employed in increasing numbers by big corporations, physicians by state and city hospitals. Antisemitic appointment policy could, therefore, invade a domain on which it had previously had no impact because of the very nature of free professional work. Jewish actors and actresses could no

---

[67]Leo Baeck, 'Die jüdischen Gemeinden', in *Zehn Jahre deutsche Geschichte 1918-1928,* 2nd ed., Berlin 1928, p. 440.
[68]Alfred Marcus, *Die wirtschaftliche Krise der deutschen Juden,* Berlin 1931; Jakob Lestschinsky, *Das wirtschaftliche Schicksal des deutschen Judentums,* Schriften der Zentralwohlfahrtsstelle der deutschen Juden und der Hauptstelle für jüdische Wanderfürsorge, VII, Berlin 1933.

longer rely on being employed by provincial theatres.[69] Needless to say, Marcus and Lestschinsky wrote from purely economic points of view. They fully acknowledged the importance of antisemitism, but were far from taking into consideration the possibility of a takeover by a National Socialist government.

While many of their observations are irrefutable, the case has been overstated by these two writers and by those who have based their conclusion on their findings alone. Many of their statements are applicable to the entire German population. The figure of unemployed Jews in Berlin cannot be considered a criterion for that in other cities and towns without detailed research. Moreover it was one fourth of the whole smaller than that of the non-Jewish workers of whom about one third was idle. Jews had still good prospects in certain branches of the economy, e.g. in the textile and clothing trades. They also controlled most of the metal trade and were leading in certain branches of export trade. Most big department stores and many speciality shops remained in the hands of Jewish owners. The average income of the Jews, as stated by Marcus, had been five times as high as that of the total population before, and only 3.2 times as high after the First World War. But even so, though it reflects a deterioration of their social situation, it does not point to pauperization. Jews were on the boards of banks and firms of the manufacturing industry where they could exercise a certain influence in matters of staffing policy. The extension and intensification of social security legislation opened new areas of work also for Jewish physicians. The legal work connected with the concentration, transformation and intricate technicalities in the world of industry and trade provided opportunities for Jewish lawyers in a sector of business which was not unimportant. The cases of proletarization in these two professions increased, but remained marginal. The expectations of success could not be set as high as before, but were still justified to a certain degree. The Jews lost some positions in the national economy for good, but they could recover part of them by their flexibility, by their talents and industry. The last word appraising the economic and social situation of the Jews in the Weimar Republic cannot, therefore, be spoken without further and more thorough research.

IN RETROSPECT

"In the constitution of this country", observed Lord Wright in Liversidge v. Anderson in 1942, "there are no guaranteed or absolute rights; the safeguard of British liberty is in the good sense of the people and in the system of representative government which has been evolved". The participation of the Jews in the blessings of British liberty was founded on the admission of religious nonconformity; relief was given first to Protestant dissenters, then extended to Unitarians, in 1846 to Jews and, in a long process beginning at the end of the

---

[69]Lestschinsky, *op. cit.*, p. 168, quoting Leopold Jessner, Director of the Berlin State Theatre, from the *Berliner Jüdisches Gemeindeblatt*, September 1932.

eighteenth century and completed in 1926, also to Roman Catholics.[70] In France in contrast, freedom of opinion, including religious belief, was guaranteed by solemn documents. It was arrived at not as a result of a long evolution but by a revolutionary process. It was proclaimed by Article 10 of the Declaration of the Rights of Man and of the Citizen of 1789; Title I of the Constitution of 1791 guaranteed the practice of religion and the admissibility of all citizens to any employment and was followed, some weeks later, by a resolution which abolished all restrictions affecting members of the Jewish faith. All these texts emanated from the Constituant Assembly of France *"une et indivisible"*.

Unlike the emancipation of the Jews in the two great Western states, the emancipation of the German Jews originated not in a unified country but in the several states of Germany. Their constitutions, laws and political decisions were more essential for the fate of the Jews than Article 16 of the German Federal Act of 1815 and the articles on religious liberty in the abortive Constitution of 1849. Moreover, in almost every German state emancipation was reached in successive stages by various means, often after many setbacks.

The third common text, the Act of the North German *Reichstag* of 1869, did not innovate but, in the main, put the final stamp on the law as it had evolved and had been definitively shaped in the individual states during the liberal decade. Against the background of constitution-making of these years, restricted to purely organizational matters, the Act of 1869 is impressive as the only text in which one of the traditional human rights was enunciated. To use a term by which Hugo Preuss defined the purposes of the fundamental rights in the Weimar Constitution, it constituted a directive and a barrier *(Richtschnur und Schranke)*. It gave impetus to the elimination of the legal remnants of the pre-emancipation period and provided protection against possible future discriminatory legislation. During the monarchical period it was, therefore, more often quoted than any other legal instrument relating to Jewish emancipation. Although the Bismarckian *Reich* was not founded on the idea of representative government, the laws of the period of the foundation of the *Reich* were the work of an alliance between a semi-authoritarian government and the forces of the *grande bourgeoisie* which mainly controlled the German parliament during these years. They supplied "the good sense of the people" which seldom prevailed in German politics.

In fact, however, the Act of 1869, though reflecting the reality in private law and in economic and social activities and relations, was not applied in public life according to its letter and spirit. More particularly, most public services continued to be controlled by the several states of Germany. Decisions not infrequently arbitrary and contrary to the law of 1869 could not be appealed against. The law was not enforceable by the courts and by the Executive of the *Reich* against state governments unwilling to apply it and to abide by their own constitution and legislation consonant with it.

---

[70]Sir Cecil Carr, 'Human Rights and Fundamental Freedoms in the United Kingdom', *UN Yearbook on Human Rights for 1946*, p. 320.

The Constitution of 1919, on the other hand, included a re-affirmation of religious liberty in the framework of its part II on fundamental rights and duties of German citizens. By drafting and incorporating this part into the text of Weimar, the constituents joined their predecessors of Frankfurt and the French constituents of 1791. Apart from Soviet Russia — the Soviet Union did not yet exist at that time — they were the first to depict the dawn of a new era by a solemn enunciation of the fundamental rights and by their extension to economic and social activities and relations. But the Constitution had nothing to add to the guarantee of religious liberty as previously legalized; this guarantee had been complete in law before. The Constitution rather mirrored the transformation of the social forces, accomplished by the revolution, under which the actions of the Executive conformed more closely to the legal provisions. Since the federal structure of the *Reich* was weakened but not basically altered by the Weimar Constitution, anti-democratic forces in some *Länder* could make use of the possibility to act against its spirit. On the whole, however, the period of Weimar was the high mark of the application of the principles of equality and justice to the Jews. They were observed as long as representative government existed and the *Rechtsstaat* could be preserved, which means as long as "the good sense of the people" was not so fundamentally destroyed that the extremist parties of the right and the left, co-operating in the annihilation of the democratic Republic, could attain their common objective.

The period of emancipation coincided with the transition from the agrarian to the industrial economy, from early capitalism to the advanced phase of capitalism and with the formation of depersonalized and bureaucratized concerns and trusts. Large-scale migrations took place from the East to the West. The overwhelmingly rural and small-town society was dissolved, urban centres rapidly increased. Politically, the absolute monarchy yielded to a — largely fictitious — constitutional monarchy which collapsed in 1918 and to which, after the interlude of a short-lived parliamentary monarchy at the end of the war, and of the revolution, the Weimar constituents substituted a system of parliamentary democracy with some plebiscitarian features. The roots of conservative and authoritarian thought, however, were so strong and had so decisive an impact on the political preferences of the Germans that neither liberalism under the Empire nor democratic socialism under the Republic could conserve and consolidate the gains made during the short period of progress.

Structural, as well as political, changes in German social and political life were decisive for the status and the situation of the Jews during the entire period.

The transition from the agrarian to the industrial economy offered them unexpected opportunities. Not yet integrated into German economic and social life at the beginning of their emancipation, the Jews could successfully make use of the only traditional asset possessed by them: learning, training of the mind, interpreting, discussing. They were not, except in some localities of Southern Germany, part of the agrarian establishment out of which the urban proletariat arose, nor of the officialdom from which they were excluded. Handicraft, it is true, was a major field of occupation of the Jews in the Polish-inhabited parts of Prussia and efforts to increase the numbers engaged in crafts met with success in other parts of the country in spite of the resistance of the guilds and corporations. But when advancing capitalism affected these occupations unfavourably, they had few inhibitions to prevent them from turning to other pursuits. Thus, intellectual tradition, and lack of occupational roots as well as flexbility in worldly matters derived from centuries-old experience, helped the Jews to pioneer in the new openings offered by social change: private banking, commerce, import and export, certain branches of industry, and other industries neglected regionally. Moreover, they penetrated the professions in large measure, as they became accessible to them; lastly the legal profession within which, disregarding earlier individual cases, they had been able to establish lawyers' offices independently of official authorization since the sixties and the seventies. The Jewish population thus prospered mainly in the zones least controlled by the state, in the spheres of banking, commerce and the professions. When the turn of the tide came and the specific abilities of the Jews — individualism, a bold and enterprising spirit, anticipation of new opportunities — could no longer assert themselves in the capitalist era, as it had developed since the turn of the century, the prospects decreased and a serious strain and stress was felt in certain strata of the Jewish population. However, in the Republic of Weimar, too, they remained a middle-class and upper-middle-class group with a high percentage of graduates from institutions of higher learning. They suffered from the inflation and, subsequently, from the economic depression more severely than the agrarian population and the industrialists, but less than the other middle-class and working people.

Structurally, therefore, the regional, occupational and social evolution of the Jewish population was largely influenced by the long-range basic changes in German economic and social life during the 150 years of their participation in modern German developments. Politically, however, the reaction of the German people to this process underwent frequent modifications. The Jews were not seen by the Germans as the majority of Jews faithful to the philosophy of the *Centralverein* wished to be seen, namely, as a merely religious minority. Their sometimes differing intellectual approach as well as their occupational and professional distribution and peculiarities were generally noticed and increasingly interpreted as racial characteristics. They were not, however, rejected at all times and by all strata of German society. International developments, such as the great humanitarian movement of the second half of the eighteenth century and the wave of liberalism of the 1860s which led to world-wide changes, from the United States to Czarist Russia, were favourable to the beginning and the legal completion of the emancipation of the Jews. In times of national upswings — during the Revolution of 1848, in the decade of the foundation of the *Reich,* in the first months of the First World War — to a certain extent also in the years of prosperity starting before the turn of the century, a feeling of homogeneity which included the Jews, prevailed. In contrast, the reaction, following the abortive Revolution of 1848; the long-drawn economic depression after the mid-seventies, when Stoecker emerged as the sponsor and organiser of political antisemitism and Ahlwardt supplied its racial features; the forebodings of disaster in the last three years of the First World War, when Ludendorff at the General Headquarters and Colonel von Wrisberg in the War Ministry joined hands with the majority of the *Reichstag,* in a great diversionary manoeuvre, to whip up public opinion against the Jews; and imperial Germany's military defeat and collapse when, amidst a feeling of national humiliation and a wave of European anti-intellectualism, Hitler's and numerous other Fascist movements emerged, set the successive stages for focussing attention on the Jews as an alien, disruptive and sinister element, and blaming them, as profiteers in times of national catastrophe. At every stage, the popular ill-will toward the Jews became more impassioned.

To argue that the final extermination of the German Jews was an inevitable outcome of history would be extending determinist philosophy to its extreme. It is equally inadmissible to single out individual factors, such as the deep aversion of the Germans to Jews in posts of authority,[71] or real or alleged errors and weaknesses of leading statesmen, politicians and political parties of the Weimar Republic, as responsible for its downfall. The democratic Republic was born out of a transitory enraged rebellion of the people against the civil and military leaders who had misguided Wilhelminian Germany in peace and in war. Many of those, however, who felt outraged and betrayed by them, abandoned the Republic shortly after its birth and did not acknowledge the legitimacy of the norms which they had helped to establish; they did not rally to its defence when it was threatened; they did not contribute to the creation of a sufficiently extended and solid ground on which, regardless of party loyalty, a nation has to stand in order to survive difficult times and circumstances; they were not bound together by a recognition of certain common values. The traditional lack of the necessary measure of national unity led inevitably to the fall of the Weimar Republic. However, the victory of National Socialism was due to a combination of circumstances many of which were not of necessity bound to occur. Yet the statement of a German judge, made in 1966, to the effect that National Socialism had deep roots in the German people[72] does not hold true for the period from 1933 to 1945 alone. For it cannot be denied that a long historical process suggested the advent of a situation in which the possibility of the revocation of Jewish emancipation and the rule of violence loomed large.

---

[71]Thus Walter Gross, in *In Zwei Welten, loc. cit.,* p. 550: "As a result of a combination of historical circumstances the origins of which date back far into the nineteenth century, *the revolution and the Weimar Republic were born with the visible and important co-operation of Jewish politicians; the German Jews as well as the Republic paid for it with their lives"* (my italics).

[72]Hedwig Maier, 'Die SS und der 20. Juli 1944', in *Vierteljahrshefte für Zeitgeschichte,* Stuttgart 1966, p. 315.

Jewish Emancipation and Bourgeois Society

BY REINHARD RÜRUP

The nineteenth century is the century of the European bourgeois, of his technology and industry, his trade and economy, his art and science. The period between 1780 and 1870 spans that economic and political "dual revolution" which resulted in the political, social and cultural emancipation of the middle classes in Europe.[1] This fundamental transformation unfolds in England, France and Germany under different specific conditions, at different speeds, by different methods; nevertheless the process is the same in each case: the dissolution of the old European order with its corporate structure and mostly absolutist government and the emergence of a new bourgeois society dominated by the two watchwords of "Constitution" and "Machinery". The revolutionising force of thinking in terms of the Law of Reason found its expression in the Declaration of the Rights of Man, and of civil rights, in the demands for constitutions and political liberty. The economic and social development imparted to the bourgeois movement its élan as well as its optimistic view of progress, leaving no room for doubt that history had a sense and a purpose: the maturity and self-determination of the bourgeois.

In 1850 a highly reputed German encyclopedia told its readers that "properly considered, the whole history of mankind appears as one great process of emancipation, and all major social and political problems come under the general concept of 'emancipation issues' ".[2] All the "main purposes of life", another passage reads, could be reduced to a threefold emancipation — "economic-industrial, political and ethical-religious". Indeed, as contemporaries were more or less clearly aware, emancipation had become a constituent element of modern society, an essential principle of its structure: "The history of this society is the history of its emancipation".[3]

The emancipation of the Jews formed part of that general process of eman-

---

[1]Cf. in particular E. Hobsbawm, *Age of Revolution. Europe 1789-1848*, London 1962; Charles Morazé, *Das Gesicht des 19. Jahrhunderts*, 1959; F. Schnabel, *Deutsche Geschichte im 19. Jahrhundert*, 4 Bde., 1929-1937; Werner Conze (Ed.), *Staat und Gesellschaft im deutschen Vormärz*, 1962. The present paper represents preliminary reflections on a history of the problems of Jewish emancipation in Germany. They are based on a study of the Prussian, Bavarian, Wurttemberg, Baden and Hesse-Darmstadt official papers, of contemporary newspapers and journals, and above all of the proceedings of the State Diets. With a planned work of a more comprehensive nature in view I have refrained from discussing the opinions of other authors and giving further sources, but have confined myself to giving references to my quotations.

[2]K. H. Scheidler, 'Judenemancipation', in *Allgemeine Encyclopädie der Wissenschaften und Künste*, edited by Ersch and Gruber, Section 2, vol. 27, 1850, p. 254; cf. also K. H. Scheidler, 'Emancipation', *ibid.*, Section 1, vol. 34, 1840, pp. 2-12.

[3]F. Steinbach, 'Emanzipation', in *Religion in Geschichte und Gegenwart*, 3rd ed., vol. 2, 1958, p. 451.

cipation of bourgeois society; it was a chapter in the general story — certainly not the most important chapter but one of the most difficult and controversial. This, again, was a common European problem, although it presented itself differently and was tackled by different methods in each state. The course of this process of emancipation is closely linked with the general development of the modern bourgeois-industrial society: the fact that two main phases of Jewish emancipation — from 1780 to 1815 and from 1840 to 1870 respectively — can be observed in Central Europe, corresponds accurately to the changing dynamics of political and social development during that period. In more than one respect the history of Jewish emancipation mirrors the specific problems arising for each individual state through the genesis and growth of a modern society. The instance of Jewish emancipation sharply throws into relief the general range of problems of a process of emancipation based on the presumed identity of legal and real freedom. Since the old social order was constituted by law and the barriers blocking the new forces were legal in character, the task of the movement as a whole and the Jews in particular was first of all to shake off the legal fetters of a defunct world. But then it emerged, and especially in the case of the Jews, that legal equality was in itself no guarantee of social equality, and that the new society, too, was confronted with social problems which — so long as universal emancipation remained a utopia — required more for their solution than the mere break-up of outlived legal forms. When, following the severe economic crisis of the 1870s, not only the economic and political practice but the very norms of the liberal system came to be widely repudiated, Jewish emancipation, too, was once again open to question: the antisemitic movement took shape as the first counter-movement against industrial society and against the ideas of 1789.

Germany occupies a special place in a history of Jewish emancipation in Europe. Here for the first time the idea of emancipation was enunciated in programmatic form, and attempts were made at the same time to carry it into effect; here, again, the debate on emancipation was conducted for close on a century with an intensity not equalled in any other country in the world. There was hardly any other question that exercised both practical politics and public opinion to the same extent for scores of years, and none that was so controversial right across the board in all political camps. Here within a confined territory we find juxtaposed acutely contrasting attempts to solve the problem in the individual German states, ranging from full emancipation, later partly withdrawn, in the areas temporarily under French rule, to medieval legal conditions still surviving elsewhere in the middle of the nineteenth century. Some states had proportionately large Jewish populations, others harboured only very few Jews; some states were relatively advanced in their economic and political development, others preserved their traditional agricultural structure unchanged throughout the pre-revolutionary period up to 1848. Here, again, Germany occupied a special position: whereas the politically and economically most advanced states of Europe, such as England and France, had proportionately very small Jewish populations, the East European territories with their large Jewish populations exhibited political and social conditions in which the issue of emancipaton could scarcely arise. Germany was thus the country where the fate of European Jewry in general would largely be determined.

Jewish emancipation was not an offspring of pure theory, but a product of the social changes which, beginning in the latter years of the eighteenth century, marked the transition from the old society to the new. This does not mean, however, that the emancipation of the Jews took shape imperceptibly or spontaneously, for there was from the outset a clear awareness of the problem. Emancipation was conceived as a task, with specific goals in mind, in the light of a critical analysis of the contemporary situation. The debate opened in the decade preceding the French Revolution, but — a noteworthy omission — completely ignored the abolition of denominational barriers already introduced in North America. In 1781 Christian Wilhelm Dohm's epoch-making book *Über die bürgerliche Verbesserung der Juden* ("On the civil betterment of the Jews") was published in Berlin, and gave rise to an unusually wide-ranging and intense literary discussion. In 1787 the Academy in Metz chose as the topic for its essay competition the question "Are there means to make the Jews in France happier and more useful?", and in France, too, the question provoked a lively response for which the ground had been partly prepared by the German discussion. And it was not only the journalists and the scholars who debated such questions; governments also took them up: Joseph II led the way in Austria; and the Decrees of 2nd January 1782 remained for the time being the only practical steps. Other princes, stimulated by his example, soon followed suit, notably in Baden. In Prussia there was at first a period of waiting, as there was no hope of positive action in this matter on the part of Frederick the Great; but as early as 1787 a government commission started work on a draft bill concerning the future position of the Jews in Prussia. In France, finally, a similar commission under the chairmanship of Malesherbes had been appointed by the King, to discuss reform matters, even before the revolution. Thus the solution of the Jewish question was on the political agenda in all European states.

That a "Jewish question" existed at all was not self-evident. Indeed, whereas policy affecting the Jews — Jewry Statutes and taxes levied on Jews, as well as occasional persecutions and expulsions of Jews — had existed in Europe through the centuries, there had been no "Jewish question". The Jews had been looked upon as a "plague" by the Estates, or as a source of revenue by the princes, but they clearly did not present the world around them with a problem demanding a solution on principle. They lived outside the social order of the Estates, yet had a firm place in the mental picture of the world characteristic of those earlier times: they were seen as a social group with definite, seemingly immutable attributes, forming beyond doubt an integral part of the divine order of this world. Nor did this state of affairs undergo any significant change when, beginning in the seventeenth century, a few Jewish families acquired substantial wealth and entered into a new relationship with their Christian environment as financial partners of the princes and the nobility. It was only after the middle of the eighteenth century, when — especially in Berlin which, admittedly, occupied a unique position in this respect — a cultural Jewish upper stratum began to emerge together with the economic upper crust, that a more differentiated picture of Jewry gradually took shape. At the same time — and this turned out to be of decisive importance for the further development — the social world as a whole began to move, and the theories of the enlightenment gave rise to a new, secularised mode of thinking about the State which was no longer seen exclusively in terms of the Estates. In the light of that new thinking it became possible to see the Jewish question in a wider context. In Germany in particular, the long period of peace following the Seven Years' War and the rising agricultural boom from the 1770s onwards opened up opportunities for intensified activities devoted to domestic political reforms. Mercantilist and physiocratic theories aroused increasing interest on the part of princes and governments, manufactures were founded, agricultural techniques were improved, legal and administrative reforms paved the way for new developments, and a host of various educational projects served to train "useful" citizens, that is to say, citizens equipped with practical knowledge and skills. In not a few states government policy was dominated by the concepts of reform and experiment, supported and partly impelled by an enlightened public opinion which was manifested in a flood of journals serving the public weal and in patriotic pamphlets. And all these activities were inspired by a seemingly unbounded confidence in the capacities of the state as initiator and guide of all social change, as an instrument of reason in a world that appeared to be unreasonably designed.

It is under such conditions that the Jews, too, became a problem; the modern Jewish question arose as a question that was asked in order to determine the position of the Jews in modern society. The fundamental significance of the general tendencies of social development is reflected in the fact that Jewish emancipation was by no means an affair of philosemitism. Dohm always protested against the misunderstanding that credited him with having written an "apologia" for the Jews. In the nineteenth century, too, philosemitic tendencies played a very minor part among the champions of emancipation. The starting point for all endeavours towards emancipation was not so much any particular liking for the Jews but a critical view of the contemporary Jewish existence and the conviction that things simply could not stay as they were. The condition of the Jews and their position in the state were felt to be unbearable: unbearable not only, not even primarily, for the Jews, but for the state and the Christian population. The emancipationists shared the general opinion regarding the Jews — individual exceptions apart — as a "nuisance" and "a highly vexatious burden on our body politic" which ought to be shaken off. Not only were they distinct from the rest of the population through their religion, language, culture and descent, but they also constituted a largely uniform social group. For it was not the few rich Jews but the mass of the poor Jews who were the problem: the Jews who were debarred from the common trades and crafts, who lived predominantly by what had been called the "destitute trades" (peddling, pawnbroking and second-hand clothes trading), and whose poverty was often indescribable. They were "Protected Jews", but their Patents of Protection *(Schutzbriefe)* could be revoked at any time, and in many cases not even the eldest child could count with certainty on the right of marriage and settlement. All Jews, rich and poor alike, were combined in corporations within the political-religious framework of the regional Jewish body (*Landesjudenschaft*) in each state. They were subject to special regulations, were held collectively responsible for the payment of all the imposts levied on them — and in Prussia also in cases of theft and receiving — and had no share either in the rights or in the duties of the rest of the citizenry of a state. They were, in the words of a departmental expert opinion, "no more than subjects living on sufferance in the state and enjoying its protection without, however, being members of civic society".[4] In order to remedy this state of affairs it was necessary to think of new methods. The remedy of past centuries, the expulsion of the Jews across the state borders, was no longer acceptable in the age of enlightenment, nor did it promise a lasting solution. No better success was to be expected from the practice of restrictive decrees and threats of drastic penalties. The decisive part came to be played by a new interpretation of Jewish existence and its causes.

"The Jew is a human being even more than he is a Jew"[5] — this proposition became the foundation for all attempts at rethinking. A conviction took hold "that the Jews have been endowed by nature with the same capacity of becoming happier and better human beings, more useful members of society",[6] and there was also a ready explanation for the fact that that capacity had so far been very little in evidence. They were the product of past policies governing the treatment of the Jews. Their separation from the rest of the populace, their exclusive occupation with trade, their notorious propensity for haggling and usury were the outcome not of natural but of historical causes, and therefore amenable to change. "I may grant", Dohm wrote, "that the Jews may be morally more degraded than other nations; that they are guilty of a comparatively larger number of offences than the Christians; that their character on the whole is more inclined to usury and sharp trading practices, their religious prejudice more exclusive and unsociable; yet I must add that this admitted greater moral degradation of the Jews is a necessary and natural consequence of the oppressive conditions under which they have lived for so many centuries".[7] To change the Jews, then, it was necessary to change the conditions of their existence. They would have to be freed of the shackles of legal disabilities, they would have to be enabled to enter the civic society, and only after that could one expect their "civil betterment" and that "fusion" of Jews with Christians held to be the true aim of all endeavours.

The only way to solve the Jewish question — all progressive theoreticians and practitioners were agreed on this — was the way of emancipation, i.e. of liberation from the traditional legal disabilities. The manner of effecting that emancipation, however, remained undecided for the time being. Dohm pleaded on principle for

---

[4] Opinion by the Baden Counsellor Philipp Holzman, 1801, Karlsruhe State Archives 74/3691.
[5] Christian Wilhelm Dohm, *Über die bürgerliche Verbesserung der Juden*, 1781, p. 28.
[6] *Ibid.*, p. 130.
[7] *Ibid.*, p. 34.

"complete equality of rights with all other subjects",[8] but he believed at the same time that the "civil betterment" would inevitably require a prolonged process of education, to be supervised and guided by the state through the promulgation of educational legislation designed to overcome tendencies towards religious segregation and, above all, to induce a break-away from the exclusive occupation with trade. The "recasting of an entire people"[9] appeared as a task which the state, and the state alone, was capable of solving by reform measures that ought to blend resolution with discretion. Here again the Jewish question appeared to be embedded in the general tendencies of the age. "It is the great and noble business of government", said Dohm, "so to attenuate the exclusive principles of all those various societies that the common link that embraces all of them is not impaired; that each of these divisions shall stimulate only emulation and activity rather than dislike and distance; and that all of them are resolved in the great harmony of the state. Let the government allow each of those special groupings to indulge in its pride, even in innocuous prejudices; but let it also strive to instil yet more love in each of the members, and it will have achieved its great task when the nobleman, the peasant, the scholar, the artisan, the Christian and the Jew is, beyond and above all that, a *citizen*".[10] Here already we have the picture of a new society transcending the barriers of Estates, corporations and denominations, although under the state's leadership and authority. "The state as guardian and servant of civic society"[11] — this basic tenet of the authors of the Prussian General Code of State Law is time after time to the fore in the debate on Jewish emancipation.

There were other voices, however, which invoked the potent force of freedom also in the case of the Jews. Thus H. F. Diez wrote in 1783: "Whatever polish man ever acquired was the result of freedom. Give freedom to the Jews, and it will soon rejuvenate in them qualities wellnigh destroyed by the stifling pressure of centuries." [12] Conversely, there were other authors who emphasised the role of the state even more strongly than Dohm and held that the situation called for very prudent action — "for thus we shall follow nature in her measured progress and avoid a revolution with consequences that can never be predicted with absolute certainty".[13] F. v. Schuckmann therefore considered it necessary to gather some practical experience first of all, and he thought that the foundation of Jewish colonies — which Dohm had rejected — would be a particularly expedient way of attaining that end. He expressed doubts about the wisdom of granting complete equality of status suddenly and without preparation: "A sudden mixture of the Jews with the rest of the citizens would probably fail to relieve their

[8]*Ibid.*, p. 110.
[9]So passim in the Baden State papers, cf. R. Rürup, 'Die Judenemanzipation in Baden', in *Zeitschrift für die Geschichte des Oberrheins*, 114, 1966, p. 248.
[10]Dohm, *op. cit.*, p. 26.
[11]R. Koselleck, 'Staat und Gesellschaft in Preussen 1815-1848', in Conze, *loc. cit.*, p. 81.
[12]H. F. Diez, 'Über Juden. An Herrn Kriegsrath Dohm zu Berlin', in *Berichte der allgemeinen Buchhandlung der Gelehrten*, 1783, pp. 326f.
[13]F. v. Schuckmann, 'Über Judenkolonien. An Hrn. Geheimen-Rath Dohm', in *Berlinische Monatsschrift*, 1785, p. 54.

situation of its oppressiveness; driven by deep-rooted prejudice the citizens would still not accept them as brothers, a large part of the authorities would still not treat them on equal terms with the others, and no decree, however strict, however wise, could protect them against such conduct. What can decrees avail against prejudice, what can they achieve if the spirit of their execution has not yet ripened in the nation? ... So long, then, as the nation as a whole looks upon the Jews as an inferior kind of people and takes offence at being treated on a par with them; so long as prejudice against them rules the hearts of the greater part of the constituted Christian authorities and of the clergy who guide the people; for so long will it be impossible to protect them entirely from oppression by promulgating laws. For one thing, the inner content of human actions — tone and gesture — cannot be challenged before a court of law: for another, at the present stage the large majority of the newly accepted Jews would undeniably be lacking in the requisite civic capabilities, so that acts of oppression would rarely be without some semblance of justification, and in the end the Jewish cause would be set back further and brought lower than where it stands today".[14] These misgivings, as history was to show, were certainly not unjustified. The dismantling of existing prejudices was one of the central problems of any policy of emancipation. Even the advocates of the sudden introduction of equality, though optimistic, were not naive in this question. Dohm himself, who wanted to combine the granting of equality of status with educational measures involving fresh restrictions and special rights, reckoned that the process of social adjustment between Jews and Christians might take three to four generations.

In Germany the views represented by Dohm and partly by Schuckmann rather than those held by Diez prevailed. In the meantime, however, the Jewish question had been lifted practically as well as theoretically onto a new plane by the French Revolution. Although even the National Assembly had hesitated at first to grant full equality of rights to all French Jews, the case for Jewish emancipation, based as it was on the principles of the Revolution, was unanswerable. The Law of 13th November 1791 conferred immediate and unqualified equality on all French Jews. Henceforward there were two concepts of Jewish emancipation, sponsored respectively by Germany and France: one enlightened-etatist, the other liberal-revolutionary. Whereas in France action had been confined to one single act of emancipation leaving social integration to the unfettered interplay of social forces, opinion in Germany continued to look upon the state as an educational as well as legal institution, which accordingly was obligated to discharge its responsibility towards society also in respect of the Jews. Thus, in France reliance was placed on the integrating forces of society, in Germany on the state. Here emancipation was conceived not as a single act but as a prolonged process of social integration, and full equality was visualised only as the crowning achievement at the end of that road. Accordingly Jewish emancipation became in the German states largely the business of the bureaucracy, of that progressive civil service that was stamped

[14]*Ibid.*, pp. 55f.

with the die of the enlightenment, and often felt itself charged with the mission of educating the people for the tasks of the bourgeois-industrial society.

No further specific reforms were introduced in Germany before 1800. The statutes of Joseph II, although in substance continuing to stand until the Revolution of 1848, had little effect, and failed altogether to act as a model for imitation. The commissions appointed in a number of states worked only hesitantly and without marked success. In many cases they were important only inasmuch as they kept alive a general awareness of the existence of a "Jewish question", and as they gradually succeeded through the expert opinions and statistics which they produced on demand in convincing also the middle and lower ranks of administrative officials of the need for a solution. In Berlin alone a characteristic interim solution was introduced, a part payment, as it were, to the Jewish upper stratum, on account of the continually postponed general legislation. In 1791 the Berlin Banker Daniel Itzig received for himself and all his descendants — which meant, in fact, for the most influential Jewish families in Berlin — a patent of naturalization conferring on them the full rights of Prussian subjects. This underlined once more the exceptional position of the Berlin Jews: they exercised substantial economic influence; their ranks included a not inconsiderable number of scholars of repute; finally they even evolved a *salon* culture which had no parallel in the rest of Germany, with the possible exception of Vienna. Their social position permitted them to make their own emphatic claims for emancipation, instead of waiting for initiatives on the part of the government. Such a thing happened hardly anywhere else at that time, since the court agents in Southern Germany, though rich, were isolated individuals and did not form a special social group. Generally, then, emancipation was granted rather than fought for during the first phase of Jewish emancipation. For many years, continuing far into the period of the Holy Alliance, the driving force behind the development was the civil servants rather than the Jews.

Real progress was only set in motion in Germany under the influence of Napoleon, or rather as a result of the upheavals and changes of the Napoleonic era. Full emancipation was introduced in all the territories ruled directly or indirectly by France: first in the départements on the left bank of the Rhine, which had been incorporated within France, and later in the Grand Duchy of Berg and the Kingdom of Westphalia (Decree of 27. 1. 1808). At the same time, however, the territories on the left bank of the Rhine witnessed a setback which left its mark and permanently impaired the entire liberal concept of emancipation: on 17th March 1808 Napoleon issued a Decree which imposed on the Jews in the départements of Eastern France a number of humiliating trade restrictions based on a charge of usurous practice detrimental to the people *(le décret infâme)*. The Decree was introduced ostensibly as an educational measure and was limited at first to a period of ten years. The principle of equality was to remain intact. Yet the Decree marked an open breach with the revolutionary concept in France as well the state was now endeavouring to take corrective and educational action. The lifting of the disabilities was made conditional on the prior "improvement" of the Jews who were once more kept apart from the rest of society by being given a special status. In the subsequent German debates on emancipation, especially in the 1815-1848 period, Napoleon was invoked as the chief witness against abrupt emancipation: his measure of 1808 appeared as a factual refutation of the liberal concept of emancipation.

For the majority of the German states the need to legislate on the status of the Jews arose not from any definite theory but from practical exigencies as a result of the wide-spread changes in their state territory and their internal structure. The enlargement of the states had invariably entailed an increase in the Jewish population, all the more so as large numbers of Jews, in Southern Germany in particular, had settled precisely in the small and pocket-sized territories formerly under the immediate suzerainty of the Empire. Bavaria and Wurttemberg, for instance, had not allowed any Jews at all in their hereditary lands, whereas substantial numbers of Jews lived in the newly-acquired territories (not so much in Wurttemberg as in Bavaria which had about 50,000 Jewish subjects from 1815 onwards). Moreover, different Jewry Statutes were in force in each of the formerly independent territories, so that the governments of the new states were confronted with a welter of legal systems. In these circumstances the introduction of a comprehensive and unified code was essential in order to ensure efficient administration and promote the desirable integration of the various territories. Such uniform regulations were duly introduced in the various states within the framework of restructuring the system as a whole. The first instance is provided by the so-called Constitutional Edicts issued in Baden in 1807/8 and supplemented later by the specific Jewry Statute of 1809. Here the Jews were pronounced state citizens, and their legal position was substantially improved, although the improvement fell short of equality. Bavaria also introduced uniform regulations for the whole kingdom in 1813, which granted new rights to the Jews, yet largely denied the idea of emancipation. On the other hand, faced with the formidable difficulties of restructuring the whole system, not a few states refrained from attempting to legislate on the position of the Jews and confined themselves to administrative regulations on the basis of the existing laws. Emancipation virtually without qualifications was granted only in the Duchies of Anhalt-Bernburg and Anhalt-Köthen in 1810. These territories, however, had a distinctive and singular body of state law. In Austria nothing happened for scores of years; Wurttemberg, which had started with the preparations much earlier, did not enact a general Jewry Statute until 1828. Other states delayed legislation even longer, Saxony for instance, until 1838, Hanover until 1842.

The Prussian Law of 11th March 1812 represents a special case, as it was neither conceived under direct French influence nor prompted by the needs of territorial reorganization. It went back to the aspirations for emancipation at the close of the eighteenth century and belonged in the context of a comprehensive reform of the Prussian State. Among the German attempts at emancipation this Law represents the first summit of achievement. The drafts and various departmental opinions which preceded the enactment of the Edict — especially that of the Religious and Educational Affairs Section headed by Wilhelm von Humboldt — displayed a remarkable level of argument, and some of them went in their demands far beyond the terms eventually embodied in the Law. As a result of the Municipal Reform the Jews had already acquired civil rights in the Prussian towns. The next thing to do, therefore, was to establish a durable new system in tune with the aims of the comprehensive reform: "a society that is economically free, yet politically enveloped in the state".[15] Thus Jewish emancipation became an integral part of a vast reform project that was to remain unfinished, of that "revolution from above" intended to transform the social order resting on the Estates into the modern society under the guidance and supervision of the state. Yet, it was inherent in the underlying idea of that comprehensive reform that, despite many bold starts, the authorities did not see their way in the end to granting full equality of status to the Jews. Instead, once again, the Prussian Edict was given the character of an educational law. Nevertheless, the Jews received very far-reaching rights, and in respect of its material content that Edict did not appear to be too far removed from the French legislation. It was left to reactionary administrative practice after 1815 to make clear that, for all its advances this Law had not yet translated the fundamental ideas of the German emancipation debate into reality.

It seems surprising at a first glance that the question of Jewish emancipation in Germany should have been discussed at the Congress of Vienna, as the problem bears little relation to the other Congress topics. The specific point of departure was presented by the disputes of the cities of Frankfurt, Hamburg, Bremen and Lübeck with their Jews, who were to be stripped again of the rights granted during the French era. Metternich, Hardenberg and Humboldt, on the other hand, had reasons of their own for their vigorous efforts to bring about a comprehensive emancipatory solution at Confederate level: they were convinced that nothing short of uniform legislation in all states of the Confederation held out a promise of real success. Yet even the united efforts of Austria and Prussia were not sufficient to ensure a decision to that effect. Article 16 of the German Federal Act of June 8, 1815 merely contained a general assurance that the issue was to be discussed and settled by the Federal Assembly and a guarantee of the existing legal status of the Jews — which, however, was so worded as to apply to the rights granted "by" the states, not "in" the states, so that the preceding French legislation was practically excluded from the guarantee. The Federal Assembly actually made a few half-hearted beginnings in the following years, but never got beyond the stage of sittings of preparatory commissions. Article 16 was not implemented any more than the promise of a Constitution for the Confederate states in Article 13. Jewish emancipation thus continued to remain the concern of the individual states.

The first phase of Jewish emancipation was completed in 1815. Seen as a whole, it had increased rather than diminished the differences in the legal status of the Jews in Germany, new emancipatory legislation had been limited in scope

[15]Cf. Koselleck, in Conze, *loc. cit.*, p. 85.

in the few states which had attempted it at all. Yet, it had become clear in those years that even the states that had so far been hesitant would not be able to evade the problem in the long run.

At first, however, a period of reaction intervened in the sphere of Jewish emancipation as a result of the same causes that had ushered in the general reactionary movement. It was a reaction engendered in the first place by economic, above all agricultural crises, sharpened by the beginnings of social change, and motivated by the fear of liberal and democratic movements. The states started individually by way of administrative action to revoke or curtail rights previously granted, so that there could be no question for the time being of the foreshadowed extension of those rights. At the same time a fresh public discussion on the Jews was started with Article 16 of the German Federal Act as the point of departure, and in contrast to former occasions, the discussion was now dominated by voices hostile to emancipation. This marked the first break in the continuity of public opinion in the form in which it had been moulded by the principles of the age of enlightenment. A public critical of emancipation came into being in this way; it was to remain a potent negative factor impeding the social integration of the Jews. Traditional prejudices against the Jews were revived, new ones added. In the following decades it was generally accepted as an unchallengeable fact that the majority of the people, the rural population in particular, was not favourably inclined towards the Jews and rejected emancipation. "You may cut all roots of an old-established prejudice without altogether depriving it of all nutriments. It will suck them out of the air if need be", Moses Mendelssohn once said, and added: "In one word: reason and humanity raise their voices in vain; for grizzled prejudice is deaf".[16] True, there was no lack of opposing voices, yet the continuity of prejudice could no longer be overlooked. The most important result of this discussion was the fact that the Jewish question continued to arouse much public interest, and the very existence of that interest tended to make for isolation and thus militated against the gradual integration of the Jews.

In 1819 the discussion was overshadowed by the so-called "Hep! Hep!" movement, which started with a few incidents in Würzburg and swept in the late summer of that year through many German towns and regions. The movement led to persecutions of the Jews on a scale not witnessed for centuries. The material damage was in proportion not excessively large, but the general effect of that revolt of the old against the new age was staggering, for it brought the sudden revelation that even in the nineteenth century actions were possible that had been thought to belong to a remote past. These events opened frightening new vistas of things to come, disturbed the optimistic faith in progress of the educated middle class, and revealed an unsuspected seamy side of social change. The movement, indeed, was connected with the sense of crisis engendered by social change and accentuated by economic miseries; it was an answer not to the advances in the legal status of the Jews, but to the social tremors accompanying

---

[16]Moses Mendelssohn, *Vorrede zu Manasseh Ben Israel, Rettung der Juden*, 1782, pp. XIXf.

the transformation of society. The cause of Jewish emancipation, however, was severely affected, as the memory of that movement remained alive for decades, was more forcefully revived by the persecutions of spring 1848, and invariably loomed in the background behind the so-called "excesses" which, as a rule, were entirely insignificant incidents, but taken very seriously indeed by both the government and the Jews. Henceforward the sword of Damocles of the "people's wrath", frequently and by no means innocently invoked by some, was suspended over the issue of Jewish emancipation.

Between 1815 and 1848 the emancipation debate shifted largely to the constitutional states of South and South-West Germany, whereas Austria and Prussia refrained from fundamental changes up to the revolution, or at any rate till the eve of the revolution. In the years 1824-1828 all the Prussian Provincial Diets expressed negative views on the issue of emancipation, and the administration also set a reactionary course. Several rights previously granted — e.g. access to academic teaching posts — were revoked, and the interpretation of disputed provisions of the law went almost without exception against the Jews. The characteristic feature of Prussian policy on the Jewish question in those decades was the renewed uncertainty of law. Thus it was only a Royal Order of 30th August 1830 which finally decided that the Edict of 1812 was not valid in the territories newly acquired or regained by Prussia after 1812, that is to say in by far the greater part of the monarchy. This marked a retreat from the unity of law established in 1812 for the whole state territory. As a rule the authorities were satisfied to take over the legal provisions previously obtaining in the various territories. Only in the Province of Posen, where two-thirds of the Prussian Jews were living, was a new law introduced in 1833 which offered the Jews the opportunity of individual emancipation through the acquisition of a patent of naturalization. Uniform legislation settling the status of the Jews for the entire state had to wait until 1847, and even then special regulations were retained for Posen.

In the constitutional states of medium rank the practical measures adopted varied a great deal but the underlying principle was the same throughout. In all these states the authorities were holding on to the enlightened-etatist concept of gradual emancipation. This concept was most clearly expressed in the Württemberg Jewry Statute of 1828. The Stuttgart Government continued in the following years to declare over and over again that it was simply not true that "nothing more was needed than the lifting of the original oppression. Evils which arose in consequence of that oppression have become sufficiently important in themselves to be a subject of counter-measures, and those evils must be extirpated first of all".[17] This meant in practical terms: it was not enough to give the Jews free access to the common trades, but measures had to be taken simultaneously to combat peddling, second-hand clothes dealing and similar trades — in other words the only hope lay not in emancipatory but in educational legislation. Similarly it

[17]Minister of the Interior v. Schlayer, Second Chamber, 4.5.1836, p. 59.

was argued in Bavaria as late as 1846: "The mere granting of rights is of no help at all. The transformation of a people, of its national spirit and its modes of thought and action constitutes the most difficult task in politics — and we expect in supine inaction that it will be brought about simply by raising a few barriers and by uttering a few words".[18] An astounding confidence in the potentialities and abilities of the state was displayed time after time, even in the era of the bourgeois movement. In some states this attitude went so far as to give preference to administrative practice over legislative regulation. It was the intention of the government — so the First Chamber of Hesse-Darmstadt was told in 1823, to mention just one example — to "pursue meticulously that gradual course that must never be overlooked in the development of human capacities, and thus attain its goal by a longer, perhaps, but all the safer route. But its endeavours would end in failure if it attempted, without the gradual diffusion of improvement, to hasten towards the goal by means of legal measures". And it was added: "Let us, therefore, not disturb the State Government in its measured progress, let us not run ahead of time and experience".[19] As a result of such views — which were widely supported also in the Second Chamber — no attempt at comprehensive legislation was made in the Grand Duchy of Hesse-Darmstadt before the Revolution of 1848.

In the South German State Diets, questions of Jewish emancipation were subjects of debate through most of the 1815-1848 period, occasioned by Government Bills or by petitions. Here it became manifest that even the German Liberals were only reluctantly prepared to treat Jewish emancipation as a question of principle. In Baden, in the liberal Reform Diet of 1831, no more than two deputies voted for complete and immediate equality. The Liberals not only had misgivings about the popular mood, which was opposed to emancipation, but were in principle incapable of discarding the enlightened-etatist view which held that the Jews must first pass through a "preparatory school" on the way to freedom. In addition, a specific enlightened-liberal aversion to Judaism had taken shape. It was manifested, for instance, in the trend of liberal protestant theology, which formulated its critique of the ruling doctrine as a critique of Judaism in Christianity. The Talmud and rabbinical tradition were utterly repugnant to the rationalists and Liberals who found "ignorance, fanaticism and poor taste" peculiarly concentrated in Judaism. For centuries Jewry had not only stood outside the pale of society but kept aloof from history; the Jews — and this is where the Liberals took offence — had consistently closed their minds to progress; "Whereas everything is moved by time and subject to its development and transformation, the Jew alone offers defiance, standing immutable among us, a petrified living picture, as it were, of a bygone age, and his figure — like everything that runs counter to time — becomes loathsome".[20] Another influence pulling in the same direction was the anti-pluralistic doctrinaire attitude of some Liberals, which postulated a certain uni-

---

[18]Committee Report by Baron v. Gumppenberg, Second Chamber, 1846, 7th Suppl., p. 125.
[19]Committee Report v. Wreden, First Chamber, 18.11.1823, Suppl. LXIV, p. 9.
[20]Elucidations of the Wurttemberg draft bill "on the public conditions of the Israelites", Second Chamber, 1824, 4th Extraord. Suppl., p. 97.

formity of thought and action for the new society, as Rotteck especially repeatedly emphasised. No one, it is true, demanded that the Jews should become Christians, yet is was expected that they would cease to be Jews. The aim, clearly formulated in Wurttemberg in 1828 — though in a context referring to the Jewish attitude to trading — was "to let the Jew be dejudaised".[21] In general, no distinction was made between integration and assimilation of the Jews; in other words, integration could only be visualised in terms of assimilation. The hoped-for "fusion" of Jews with Christians, then, implied — although the Liberals had not consciously grasped this implication — that the Jewish question was to be solved by dissolving Judaism. Thus an element of intolerance was introduced into the liberal debates on emancipation. It made the further progress of emancipation considerably more difficult.

Controversies concerning a religious reform of Judaism — which had been advocated within Jewry since the days of David Friedländer by the Reform Movement — were at their height in the twenties. After 1830, the liberal demand for a reformation of Judaism receded into the background, nor was it taken up by the "Christian" policy of some states in the forties. The debate entered a new phase in which equality for the Jews was no longer demanded merely as an instrument of their "civil betterment" or of "civilization". From that time on Jewish emancipation was a question of principle — at any rate in its demands, if not in reality. Some, at least, of the spokesmen of liberalism rose in their arguments to the height of their principles. They declared that only freedom could educate for freedom, that nothing short of the abolition of all inequalities under the law could firmly implant the great ideal of the equality under the law among the people, that full equality alone was in harmony with the demands of the age and of justice. Statements pleading the need for education were met with the retort: "Civic virtue can spring only from civic freedom. Set the Jews free and they will soon acquire all the qualities that can only be gained in freedom and only be maintained in that same freedom".[22] The majority, however, was still unready to give up the statistical approach, that is to say the argument that further legislation ought to wait for proof of tangible progress, and that any abrupt changes must be avoided. Nevertheless, the conviction gained ground that full emancipation was ultimately inevitable: "The attempt to oppose it in a general way could at the most postpone that emancipation, but not suppress or frustrate it for ever".[23] In the Bavarian Second Chamber a deputy said in 1846: "I ask everyone whether he does not believe that emancipation will come one day, and the answer I get is: Indeed, that time is certain to come".[24] Jewish emancipation was not just a demand of the newspapers — as the Bavarian deputy Sepp put it — but of the age, that is to say, of bourgeois-liberal society. Even the statements hostile to emancipation were determined by the prevailing mood in those years;

[21]Commission Report v. Schlitz, Second Chamber, 1828, 2nd Extraord. Suppl., p. 12.
[22]Deputy Schott, Wurttemberg Second Chamber, 4.5.1836, p. 38.
[23]Deputy Lotheissen, Hesse-Darmstadt Second Chamber, 30.5.1836, p. 38.
[24]Deputy Sattler, Bavarian Second Chamber, 7.5.1846, p. 254.

they were protests, often formulated with a bad conscience and with many reservations. These were arguments which had no future in a society resolved to constitute itself on the foundations of the principles of freedom and justice, without tutelage by the state.

The common aim of all the efforts made towards emancipation, however varied in detail in their approach, was the social integration of the Jews who, after all, displayed not only religious and ethnic but also social group characteristics. The Jewish question appeared to be very largely a social question, since at the end of the eighteenth century the vast majority of Jews belonged to the rural and urban lower strata and lived precariously on meagre small-scale trading, peddling and second-hand clothes dealing. A fundamental change in their living conditions could only be expected to come from a change in their occupational pattern. This had been understood from the start of the emancipation debate, and all the governments made this problem their main concern. They had been supported since the twenties by Jewish associations for the promotion of crafts and agriculture among Jews. Everywhere the Jews were given access to the common trades, although rarely without exceptions, and frequently under conditions which subsequently impaired the practical value of those concessions (e.g. the absence of freedom of movement in the rural areas, which, especially in South Germany, often made it impossible for Jews to practise the trades they had learned). The progress made in the adoption of common trades was diligently watched by governments and regarded, as the case may be, either as a confirmation or as an occasion for a revision of their policies. The statistical data seemed to make that progress objectively measurable, and thereby provide a solid basis for policy. Governments and assemblies were only too ready to trust to figures as a substitute for argument. Actually the data on the occupations of Jews always required a particularly critical scrutiny, as the various administrations applied different standards of strictness, the Jews often declared several occupations, failed to practise trades they had learned or exercised them only as a sideline. Nevertheless, despite such reservations, the statistics presented a clear picture of the general trends of development.

For *Prussia* very detailed data are available, compiled on the basis of the 1843 census for the Unified State Diet of 1847.[25] Of the 206,050 Prussian Jews 127,414 lived in 1843 in regions with advanced laws on emancipation (including Posen Jews with patents of naturalization), while the civil rights of 78,636 were substantially curtailed. Of 62,185 gainfully occupied Jews 43.1% were active in trade, 19.3% in artisan trades, and 14.3% as labourers paid by the day and as servants. In addition there was a number of smaller groups: innkeepers and publicans (4.7%), scholars, artists and pedagogues (2.7%), rentiers and recipients of pensions (2.7%), farmers and fruit growers (1%), local government employees (1.3%), other independent trades (2.2%), finally recipients of alms (3.8%) and persons without definite source of income (4.9%). The large group of those engaged in commerce

---

[25]Supplements to the Memorandum on the Draft Decree concerning the Conditions of the Jews (1847), Part B: Deutsches Zentralarchiv Merseburg, Rep. 169 B 1a, B. 2.

can be further broken up into 1,140 wholesale merchants and bankers, 6,003 shopkeepers, 1,358 traders without shops and commission agents, and 13,238 small-scale traders, pedlars and second-hand clothes dealers (including 4,499 engaged exclusively in peddling and second-hand clothes dealing). Thus on the eve of the revolution Prussia still numbered 7.3% so-called needy traders among its Jewish population, to which presumably the great majority of the 4.9% without regular source of income should be added. To get a more accurate picture of the social structure of the Prussian Jews, however, it would be essential to make separate calculations for each province (the data for which are available). In *Bavaria* there were 57,498 Jews in 1848, and there are comparative figures for 1822 available.[26] In 1822 1.6% of the Bavarian Jews were engaged in artisan trades, 2.3% in agriculture and 95.1% in trade (including peddling); about 30% of the Jewish population was engaged in peddling. By 1848 conditions had substantially changed: agriculture 8.1%, artisans 24.2% trade 49.6%, other occupations 18.1%; but the pedlars still accounted for about 30% of the total Jewish population. For *Baden* occupational statistics are only available for 1833 and comparative figures for 1816.[27] Whereas in 1816 no less than 89% of the Jews in Baden lived by trade or by irregular trading, in 1833 32.5% of the 4,068 gainfully occupied Jews were engaged in artisan trades, agriculture, sciences and arts, 40.5% in regular trade, and only 27% in irregular trading. For *Wurttemberg,* finally, figures are available for various dates between 1812 and 1852.[28] Here the development seems to have shown the best results: whereas in 1812 85.5% of the Jews were described as hucksters, the proportion was only 38.9% in 1837 and 17.7% in 1852, while the numbers engaged in the professions and common trades had risen by 1852 to 5.4% in the sciences and arts, 10.3% in agriculture and 64.3% in the artisan trades and regular trade.

The statistics of the various states are not readily comparable, as the various occupations are grouped differently. Even so a general trend of social normalisation is clearly discernible. This trend was further reinforced by similar tendencies in the field of culture and education. Wurttemberg had the most striking successes to show; it had also pursued the most vigorous policy to bring about the desired change in the Jewish occupational pattern; on the other hand, it had the smallest Jewish population of all the states concerned. It should also be noted that in Northern Germany the Jews were not permitted to reside in the rural areas, whereas conversely the South German Jews belonged predominantly to the rural population and were not allowed into the towns. The influence of this fact on the occupational pattern is a subject deserving closer investigation.

Significant progress in legislation was only made in the aftermath of the Revolution of 1848. The first signs of a change came in the mid-forties with the

---

[26]Bavarian Second Chamber, 1850, 3rd Suppl., pp. 5-7 (the departmental files were destroyed in the Second World War).
[27]Baden Second Chamber, 27.9.1833, vol. 14, pp. 287ff., and General State Archives Karlsruhe 236/953.
[28]Main State Archives Stuttgart, Privy Council III, G 195.

start of a dynamic development of the economy and the transport system, which greatly accelerated the rate of social change in all spheres of society. Even before the revolution resolutions in favour of emancipation were adopted by several Estate Chambers; but the corresponding draft bills were not introduced in time; it was reserved for the revolution to enforce progress. Yet the beginning of the revolution witnessed not Laws on emancipation but persecutions of the Jews, which were far more violent even than had been the outrages of 1819. Disturbances occurred in Baden, Hesse, Silesia and a number of cities. The causes were economic and social, chiefly the results of crop failures and the weakening of the rural social structure induced by reform measures. Not only the Jews, but also rich priests and above all manorial castles and rent offices were the targets of revolt; everywhere "debtors sought out their creditors", as the report of a Baden investigation aptly put it.[29] But such excesses could not stop the revolutionary legislation for emancipation. In several states the revolution led to new initiatives in the field of legislation, but the decisive break-through was made in December 1848, when the Frankfurt National Assembly passed the "Fundamental Rights of the German People", which says in Article V inter alia: "The enjoyment of civil and political rights is neither dependent upon, nor restricted by religious creed." These provisions were either taken over by the individual states within the framework of the Fundamental Rights as a whole, or they were incorporated in the new Constitution, for instance in Austria in 1849, and even earlier in Prussia which as recently as 1847 had enacted a Jewry Statute of very different tendency.

Thus it seemed that after a struggle of more than two generations, the emancipation movement had at last reached its goal, and that equality of status had been achieved for the Jews. But that was a short-lived illusion. All too soon it became clear that after the failure of the 1848 Revolution, Jewish emancipation too, suffered new setbacks. In a not inconsiderable number of German states the rights granted to the Jews, together with the "Fundamental Rights of the German People", were declared null and void. Even in states where those rights were not explicitly revoked, there prevailed at best a renewed uncertainty of law. In Baden, equality of status had from the outset been confined to political rights, to the exclusion of the local civil rights which in practice were more important, as the prospects of a livelihood, residence and marriage depended on them. The difficulties that still had to be overcome were thrown into relief by the Bavarian debates of 1849/50 on a Government Bill providing for complete and immediate emancipation. Whereas the Second Chamber passed the Bill after prolonged discussions with several restrictions the Chamber of *Reich* Counsellors — having received petitions with 80,000 signatures pleading against Jewish equality — roundly rejected the Bill. In nearly all states the failure of the revolution was followed by restrictive administrative measures; in particular the rights of admission to state appointments in the judiciary, administration and the army for many years existed virtually only on paper. Prussia had again incorporated

[29]General State Archives Karlsruhe 318/2 (Zug. 1897 No. 10).

denominational equality in its revised Constitution of 1850, but during the subsequent period of reaction she developed restrictive administrative practices into a
fine art.

Even so, before long it became clear beyond doubt that in spite of all reactionary efforts the full consummation of emancipation was close at hand. The development could be slowed down but no longer arrested. The technical-industrial
advances, the prolonged economic boom, and the rise to ascendancy of liberal
ideas effected a fundamental transformation of the whole pattern of social
relations, which became manifest especially in South Germany which in this
respect had lagged far behind Prussia. Now Southern Germany introduced freedom of trade and occupation and freedom of movement, as well as new regulations
on the status of municipalities and parishes. While political reaction was still
dominant, the age of liberalism had begun. It was the age of economic and social
optimism and capitalist expansion. Jewish emancipation became an integral part
of the comprehensive new structure. Its completion, it appeared, must of necessity
follow the total legislative work of the period. It was no longer possible to challenge Jewish emancipation "in principle" without coming into conflict with the
norms and conventions of the new society. "In the last ten years the courage to
oppose Jewish emancipation in principle has drained away", the leader of the
Liberals in Baden said very aptly in 1860.[30] Indeed, as early as 1856 Hermann
Wagener, the publisher of the conservative *Kreuzzeitung* failed even to start
a debate in the Prussian House of Deputies on his motion to delete from the
Prussian Constitution the provisions on the equality of legal rights for all creeds
and denominations. Baden completed its emancipation legislation in 1862, Wurttemberg in 1861/64, and in 1861 Bavaria abolished at last the medieval restrictions on residence *(Matrikelzwang)*. In Northern Germany — where Prussia had
continued to maintain special provisions for Posen — a uniform settlement was
reached by the legislation of the North German Confederation of 3rd July 1869:
"All remaining restrictions of civil and political rights derived from the difference
in religious creed are hereby abolished. In particular, eligibility for participation
in municipal and state representation and for the holding of public office shall
be independent of religious creed." In Austria it was the liberal Constitution of
21st December 1867 which reaffirmed and consolidated the equal status of the
Jews, which, though not abolished in principle after the revolution, had in practice
been curtailed in many ways. With the extension of the Confederate Law of 1869
to the whole *Reich* territory on 16th April 1871 the emancipation legislation for
Germany had been finally completed.

Thus a development had been brought to its conclusion which had been
initiated nearly a century before. For three generations the "Jewish question" and
its solution had been contested, at times in bitter controversies: the demand for
emancipation had imprinted its stamp on that debate, but opposing voices had at

---

[30]Letter from A. Lamey to Grand Duke Frederick, 3.8.1862, General State Archives Karlsruhe, Grand-Ducal Family Archives 13, Correspondence with State Minister Lamey.

no time been absent. During the revolution and in the two following decades, as emancipation was actually translated into reality, people had at last discontinued the old debates. They saw Jewish emancipation as what it was: part of a wider development linked with the origin and rise of a bourgeois-liberal society. Liberalism, now in the ascendant, had brushed aside the statistics and resolved to apply a principle, leaving the establishment of social equilibrium — which in any case was well on its way — to the free interplay of social forces. It might have been presumed that within little more than another generation legal equality would be followed by the final disappearance of all remaining open or latent group tensions. In 1849 the Bavarian Minister von der Pfordten, when presenting the Emancipation Bill, said that: "...I believe that if we sanction this Bill in 1849, we shall earn gratitude for it, perhaps not by the year 1850 but by the year 1870 or 1880".[31] Such reasoning, however, presupposed that all would proceed smoothly and without disturbance, and that was precisely what Germany was not granted. Instead of a period of tranquil domestic development on the foundation of liberal principles, the country experienced three wars in succession. An extreme form of nationalism arose and made itself felt in the field of domestic politics as well, and finally a German Empire was established, which rested on foundations very different from those of the liberal society. Within a few years an economic crisis of unprecedented intensity shook the new Empire; as a result liberalism was plunged into a grave crisis which became the first fundamental crisis of bourgeois society itself. The sense of crisis found an outlet in an anti-liberal movement of a new type: antisemitism. The interval between emancipation and crisis was too short to allow the "Jewish question" and the continuing existence of "Jewry Statutes" right into the sixties to sink into oblivion. As early as 1861 the Bavarian *Reich* Counsellor v. Harless had given a warning — in a polemical manner, it is true, but not without factual justification: "It is an undeniable fact that the entire phraseology of the modern dictionaries of politics and various pamphlets is swept aside from time to time in a horrifying manner by the raucous uproar of savage persecutions of the Jews. And under the veneer of so-called civilization lies hidden a chasm of barbarity which, I fear, will erupt. Such eruptions may all too easily occur in our so-called cultured era."[32]

Now, it is certainly not permissible to imply a law of inevitability in historical development, for instance by assuming that the rise of antisemitism followed of necessity from the process of emancipation. Yet, a critical examination of the history of emancipation cannot overlook the fact that it was Germany where modern antisemitism had its origin and developed its characteristic features. That it should have been possible at all to pose the "Jewish question" anew and in an antisemitic sense within a few years of its supposed solution is a fact that needs explaining. In this connection it may be useful in conclusion to give a brief outline at least of some of the factors that prejudiced Jewish emancipation in

[31]Bavarian Second Chamber, 10.12.1849, p. 511.
[32]Bavarian First Chamber, 7.5.1861, vol. 1, p. 356.

Germany. Three groups of problems were to the fore:

1. the concept of gradual, phased emancipation,
2. the multiplicity of differing attempts at a solution in the various German states,
3. the attempt to emancipate the Jews in a society that was itself not, or only in part emancipated.

1. One of the very few champions of a resolutely liberal concept of emancipation — and in this respect unrepresentative of Germany — was Wilhelm von Humboldt. His departmental opinion on the draft of the Prussian Edict of Emancipation, written by him in 1809 when he was Head of the Religious Affairs Section in the Prussian Ministry of the Interior, may be considered one of the most important contributions ever made to the philosophy of emancipation.[33] Humboldt clearly distinguished "two systems" concerning the policy to be adopted: "one that wants to abolish segregation at one stroke, the other that wants to do it gradually". "Just, politic and consistent" in his view was immediate emancipation alone. Emancipation as an educational process he rejected in the first place on the grounds of principle, since "the State is an institution not of education but of law". At the same time he stated practical objections to a gradual establishment of equality: "for as a result of gradual abolition the very segregation that it sets out to liquidate is confirmed in all the spheres in which it has not yet been abolished and the new greater freedom redoubles the attention focused on the remaining restrictions, so that gradual abolition militates against itself". It was essential for the State to adopt a consistent attitude in order to ensure the permanent elimination of existing prejudices and to create the necessary psychological conditions for social integration. "Though they may admit that there are worthy Jews, no matter how many, the people will still not readily change their views about the Jews as such. They will always look upon the individuals as exceptions. It is not that the State ought to teach respect for the Jews. What it ought to do is to eradicate the inhumane and prejudiced mentality that judges a human being not by his specific qualities but by his descent and religion, and treats him not as an individual but as a member of a race with which he is considered to share certain characteristics of necessity. This the State can only do by saying loud and clear that it no longer recognises any difference between Jews and Christians."

That loud and clear pronouncement was not forthcoming from the German states for scores of years. They granted the Jews some rights, they also imposed duties on them, in some places they even treated them nearly as full citizens; yet in principle they continued throughout to make a distinction between Jews and Christians, however small that distinction may have been in the end. And every time a Law was promulgated that extended Jewish rights without making emancipation complete, it was inevitably pointed out that the Jews, as a matter of fact,

---

[33]Departmental opinion of 17.7.1809, for text see Ismar Freund, *Die Emanzipation der Juden in Preussen*, vol. 2, 1912, pp. 269-282; and Wilhelm v. Humboldt, *Gesammelte Schriften*, vol. 10, 1903, pp. 97-115.

were not yet "ripe" for the rights still withheld. Thus every advance brought a renewed reaffirmation of separateness. Other problems arose: the gradual advance towards equality allowed more or less marked discrepancies to appear between the legal and social status of the Jews. In this way the bad conscience of the Christian population lost its sting, and a mentality of raised expectations came into being which took for granted certain achievements from the Jews. "A people including in its ranks so many individuals who own factories, finance houses and even knightly estates", it was seriously argued in Bavaria by an opponent of emancipation, "a people where the rich are relatively so numerous cannot possibly have been so badly oppressed, or else they could not have acquired such wealth".[34] Along the path of a gradual advance towards equality even changes in the Jewish social structure which were in themselves desirable could thus become obstacles to further progress; indeed, in addition to Jewish poverty and lack of education of before, Jewish wealth and Jewish intelligence had suddenly become hindrances to the granting of further rights. The attempt to revise the effects of centuries of historical development, to remould an entire people and integrate it into a society of a different structure, needed patience. Individual assimilation, as the advocates of a liberal concept of emancipation were perfectly aware, would require several generations. Yet, the policy of emancipation by stages, advanced as one of circumspection and patience, was deficient in that very patience, since it insisted on seeing positive results before granting fresh rights. In theory the German governments, too, realised that the development set in motion would take time, yet over and over again they fell into the temptation of asking for results after too short a time. As early as fourteen years after the first emancipation Law it was asserted in Baden that "they had been offered all the opportunities of becoming like other people, and had been given the prize and reward in advance", so there was now "every reason" to "ask for the results".[35]

Gradually only it became apparent that one crucial problem of emancipation by stages lay in the difficulty of ever bringing the process to a conclusion: the hoped-for "opportune" moment never arrived. Instead the progressive shifts in the social structure and the growth in the economic importance of the Jews tended, if anything, to harden the resistance of broad sections of the people against the dismantling of the "last barriers". Accordingly a completion of the process was possible only within the framework of a comprehensive political concept of society which no longer laid stress on the "ripeness" of the Jews but on the "ripeness" of conditions. In effect in all German states the policy of emancipation eventually culminated with the very step with which it had started in France. However often governments and parliaments protested the continuity of their policy, the fact remained that it had not been possible to uphold the German concept of emancipation to the end. It was not the successes of a clearly defined policy concerning the status of the Jews, but the general social and political developments that had

---

[34]Bavarian Second Chamber, 7.5.1846, vol. 9, p. 150.
[35]Commission Report Dollmätsch, Baden Second Chamber 1823, vol. 11, p. X.

led to the completion of the legislation on emancipation. To the policy of a gradual advance to equality it was due, above all, that a "Jewish question" existed in Germany for close on a century, not only in the imagination of the enemies of the Jews but in the reality of the policy and legislation of the German states. Humboldt had been proved right with the statement which concluded the general section of his departmental paper: "Just as opinion is too timid towards the sudden granting of equality, so it seems to me that opinion is too bold in respect of the gradual process which fosters the two-fold dangers of both the old and the new state simultaneously while supposedly lessening both."[36]

2. The policy of a gradual or phased emancipation was further prejudiced by the absence of a uniform policy in the German states. This point also had already been grasped by Humboldt. In that question, where it was a matter of overcoming deeply rooted prejudices, he said, any one state would scarcely be able to make headway as long as prejudice was still tolerated and protected by law in the neighbouring state. At the Congress of Vienna, therefore, Austria and Prussia appropriately sought a comprehensive solution for the whole territory of the German Confederation, though without success. A memorandum on Article 16 of the German Federal Act put it very aptly: "If the greatest possible uniformity in Germany is desired on this point, there is a very weighty reason. For it is not possible to work with complete success for a betterment of the civic conditions of the Jews in one confederal state, unless the procedure in other states follows at least the same broad principles. Discrepancies in their situation in the various states would inevitably have an unsettling effect. The prejudices of the Jews and the prejudices against the Jews could never be overcome altogether while continuing to enjoy the protection of the law anywhere".[37] These points were fully borne out by the debates in the Chambers during the pre-revolutionary period as well as by the measures of the governments and administrative authorities; all too readily and all too often conditions in other states were invoked to justify particular state policies. In Baden the example of Alsace was adduced to demonstrate that complete emancipation did not succeed in improving the Jews, whereas in Wurttemberg the case of Baden was invoked to prove that the granting of any rights entailed only trouble and no progress. Not a few states pointed to Prussia with its relatively generous legislation of 1812 which, it was added, had not accomplished much either. The various factors which impaired the effectiveness of legislation in all those cases were ignored, such as the fact that the Edict of 1812 had only been introduced in a small part of the Prussian Monarchy and even there in a form riddled with reservations and inconsistencies. There was not the slightest readiness to admit that all legislation needs time to become effective. Before even beginning to gather experience on their home-ground politicians readily accepted that the experiment in their own state had been refuted in advance in some neighbouring state.

[36]Freund, *op. cit.*, vol. 2, p. 275.
[37]Memorandum (unsigned and undated) 'Über die bürgerliche Verbesserung der Juden'; Secret State Archives Munich, Kasten grün 90/96.

It is not easy to find satisfying answers to the question what were causes of the difficulties which beset the process of emancipation in the various states. Often one is tempted to attribute decisive importance to some specific legal provisions, only to find on closer inspection that their absence in the neighbouring territory did not lead to substantially different results. Conversely there are instances of textually identical laws producing vastly different effects in different states. Whereas in South Germany the Jewish question must be seen essentially in the context of agrarian development and the changes in village social structure, in Prussia it constitutes a predominantly urban problem. The crucial importance of local civil rights in South Germany has scarcely a parallel in Prussia. Again, the problem presents completely different aspects in states where at least some measure of freedom of occupation and of movement existed, as distinct from states with a guild constitution and severely restricted mobility. Thus each emancipation measure was built on specific preconditions, and each had its specific built-in faults. In spite of superficial similarities, then, one can hardly speak of uniformity; indeed it would be difficult to name two German states where the process of Jewish emancipation developed in identical ways. Here the absence of national unity became an obstacle to progress. The federalist structure of Germany generated tensions and friction which worked against emancipatory intentions. Thus the difficulties of Jewish emancipation mirror simultaneously the problematic aspects of the German Confederal Constitution in the bourgeois era.

3. When Marx in 1844 published his "Introduction" to the *Kritik der Hegelschen Rechtsphilosophie* he warned against the illusion that general, universal emancipation would result from the mere addition of partial emancipations. "In Germany", he said, "emancipation from the Middle Ages is possible only if it achieves at the same time emancipation from the only partial rectification of the Middle Ages. In Germany no kind of bondage can be broken without breaking every kind of bondage. In thorough-minded Germany there can be no revolution unless it be a thorough-going revolution".[38] Actually, the emancipation of bourgeois society in Germany took shape in a multitude of individual and uncoordinated episodes. The liberating overall revolution did not come any more than did wholesale comprehensive reform. Progress occurred sporadically in subdivisions of society, often unrelated to the political development or to other subdivisions. As the example of the South German States demonstrates, the existence of a Constitution was by no means a guarantee of a progressive economic and social structure. Modern municipal regulations and hoary guild statutes, civil rights and ancient imposts to manorial lords, monasteries and parsonages often existed incongruously side by side.

The legal status of the Jews was similarly at variance with other legal relations, some of them more advanced, others still more backward than theirs. And the discrepancies were invariably sources of tension. For the legal status of the Jews affected not only imagined but also at times very tangible interests of the Chris-

[38]Karl Marx, *Die Frühschriften*, edited by S. Landshut, 1953, pp. 223f.

tian citizens (share in accruing benefits, support in poverty, etc.). As long as no comprehensive reform, no new social order was brought into being, friction between variously developed sections of society was inescapable. When the progressive communes code was introduced in Baden in 1831, the legislators thought once again that emancipation in one sphere could be kept apart from that in another; so they declared that the status of the Jews should remain unchanged for the time being. Such reasoning, though formally correct, led in effect to a decisive worsening of the legal position of the Jews and a complete disruption of the policy of emancipation which had striven to bring Jews and Christians more closely together. What happened was that as a result of the communes code which abolished the old distinction between full citizens and protected subjects, 80,000 of the latter received full civil rights, and only the Jews — who had also counted as protected subjects — retained the old status. This meant that in the communes the distinction no longer lay between the full citizen and the protected subject, but between the Christian with full rights and the Jew with lesser rights. This is only one of many similar examples. The Prussian trades regulations of 1845 brought considerable improvements for many Prussian Jews; yet the communes codes issued at the same time in the various provinces contained new restrictions debarring Jews from holding office in local government. Contradictions both in legislation and in administrative practice were present everywhere. It was hardly possible under such conditions to achieve the desired educational effect.

Nor can it be overlooked that some of the opposition to Jewish emancipation was prompted by the conviction that other demands for emancipation were just as important or even more urgent. Rotteck, who objected to Jewish emancipation on many grounds, made the point that "the emancipation of the Christians and the emancipation of the Germans" ought to precede that of the Jews: "Let the latter take place when the former has been accomplished. If the former is not accomplished the latter will not be worth much either".[39] And Baron von Closen justified his criticism of the Bavarian Government's past policy on the status of the Jews by compiling an impressive catalogue of other "emancipations" that had not been tackled, ranging — in a rather wide interpretation of the term — from the "emancipation of children from ignorance and superstition by the better management of elementary schools" to the "emancipation of landowners from the 'tyranny of game' and from the 'absence of credits'" and the "emancipation of the Cabinet from external influences".[40] Such arguments again underlined the need to look upon Jewish emancipation not in isolation, but in the context of the political and social development as a whole.

The complications besetting Jewish emancipation in Germany flowed from the policy of the German states, which in its lurchings between progress and immobility failed to form, let alone to realize a coherent concept for the refashioning

---

[39] Baden Second Chamber, 27.9.1833, vol. 14, pp. 366f.
[40] Bavarian Second Chamber, 5.11.1831, vol. 22, pp. 98f.

of society. Where coordination between the regulations governing communes and trades, between the political and the economic constitution, between the development of industry and of trade policy was inadequate or non-existent, it could hardly be expected that Jewish emancipation alone should mesh smoothly with all other partial reform processes. It appeared, then, that the emancipation and integration of a minority with ethnic, religious and social characteristics within a society that is itself not or only partly emancipated presented a nearly insoluble problem. Thus the inquiry into the emancipation of the Jews in Germany leads of necessity to a wider inquiry into the whole problem of the "emancipation" of the Germans — an inquiry, that is, into German history in the age of the bourgeois revolution.

This English version of the preceding contribution is based on the author's essay originally written in German 'Judenemanzipation und bürgerliche Gesellschaft in Deutschland' which was published in *Gedenkschrift Martin Göhring. Studien zur Europäischen Geschichte*, edited by Ernst Schulin (Franz Steiner Verlag, Wiesbaden 1968).

Assimilation and Antisemitism in the German-French Orbit

in the Nineteenth and Early Twentieth Century

BY ROBERT A. KANN

I. SCOPE, METHOD AND CONCEPTS

This study* is concerned with the question of the relationship between anti-semitism and the progress of Jewish assimilation in core areas of Western and Central Europe. The setting in time refers to the period when Jewish eman-cipation, embodied in the formal equality of rights, remained technically fully intact. This means, broadly speaking, research in problems pertaining to the second half of the nineteenth century and the first quarter of the twentieth. It should be strongly emphasized that a mere pioneer inquiry of this kind can only sketch data and possible conclusions and must leave more comprehensive studies to future research. One essential premise for such a highly desirable undertaking in the future would be the intensification of socio-economic, particularly sta-tistical studies of Jewish-Gentile relations. The relative abundance of valuable material in the United States and pre-Hitler Germany in this respect is con-trasted by a woeful lack of data in many other countries, including France.

Before going into the problems of this study itself, it will be necessary to clarify a few terminological concepts. The term Jew as referred to here is bound to be largely determined by the statistical material used. In general available data have to be based on the association of the individual with a religious con-gregation irrespective of the significance of a lasting relationship. Problematical, however, is the question of the converted Jew and that of the Jew who has left the Jewish religious community but has not joined any other congregation.

As to the converted Jew, since he does not want to be identified with Jewry and is not identified with it by a sizeable part of the Gentile world, it is impossible to include him within the concept of Jewry as used in this study in even remotely precise terms. Quite different is the case of the individual who has left the Jewish religious community without joining any other. Here the former association with a major factor of ethnic affiliation, the religious-tra-ditional one, is not intentionally or unintentionally obscured by a new affiliation. For the sake of broader statistical representation this type of individual may well

*It is an abridged version of a study supported by the Institute of Human Relations of the American Jewish Committee, New York. This assistance is acknowledged with sincere thanks. - The longer version is deposited with the archives of the Leo Baeck Institute in New York and is available for use there.

be included in the statistical data which more comprehensive studies of this kind may require.[1]

A more difficult problem is the concept of antisemitism as used in this study. This does not concern the definition itself. The one given by Nathan W. Ackermann and Marie Jahoda, "antisemitism is any expression of hostility, verbal or behavioural, mild or violent, against the Jews as a group, or against an individual Jew because of his belonging to that group"[2] is certainly at least as good as any other and in fact probably better than most. The trouble is, however, that neither this nor any other definition can help us answer the cardinal question of how to gauge the intensity, the decline or rise of antisemitism in correlation with the development of emancipation and assimilation of Central and Western European Jewry. The authors of the above quoted study and one of them in conjunction with others[3] have indeed developed highly suggestive methods of measuring the degree of prejudice embodied in antisemitism. They are designed, however, for use in the present and future, not for the past that we are concerned with here.

The gauging of various trends of public opinion by approximation in the past may not actually present a completely insoluble problem of historical method,[4] but certainly one that cannot be handled within the modest frame of this paper. Consequently, like the overwhelming majority of students of history dealing in one way or another with the impact of drifts of public opinion, we are compelled to determine their intensity by the impact of external events. Obvious examples would be the double-edged influence of reaction and intense nationalism in Germany after the end of the Napoleonic wars, the social economic crisis of the 1870s and the formation of a clearly antisemitic, so-called Christian Social movement at about that time. As to France, the establishment and success of the strongly antisemitic League of Patriots and the *Action Française* in the 1880s and 1890s would seem to be of significance largely as a belated consequence of the lost war of 1870-71. However, the social conditions clearly indicating a change in public sentiments do not necessarily coincide with the external consequences of such a change. It might be suggestive to think here as an analogy of the notion of latency periods between the suffering of a traumatic experience and the emergence of its neurotic consequences, so well known to modern psychiatry. Anyway, the fact that public sentiments *qua* the past cannot be measured in a

---

[1]See at this point only two standard references of many: the classical work by Arthur Ruppin, *Soziologie der Juden*, Berlin 1930-31, 2 vols., cf. I, pp. 15-63 and Melville J. Herskovitz, 'Who are the Jews?', II, pp. 1151-1171, in Louis Finkelstein (ed.), *The Jews, their History, Culture and Religion*, New York, 2nd ed., 1955, 2 vols. For an evaluation of Jewish population statistics see Bruno Blau, 'Sociology and Statistics of the Jews', *Historia Judaica*, vol. XI/2, 1949, pp. 145-162; see *ibid.* in regard to Ruppin, in particular pp. 149-155, 160-162.
[2]Nathan W. Ackermann and Marie Jahoda, *Anti-Semitism and Emotional Disorder*, New York 1950, p. 19.
[3]Marie Jahoda, Morton Deutsch, S. W. Cook, *Research Methods in Social Relations with Special Reference to Prejudice*, New York 1951, 2 vols.
[4]Robert A. Kann, 'Public Opinon Research: a Contribution to Historical Method', *Political Science Quarterly*, vol. LXXIII, 1958, pp. 374-396, discusses this problem and lists some of the existing literature on the subject.

brief study but can only be deduced indirectly from the use of conventional data is a serious methodological weakness. Contrary to widespread practice it is recognized and frankly acknowledged here.

Finally, we have to take a close look at what is actually the central theme of this paper, the concept of equality. A democratic society hails the idea of equality of opportunity and equality of rights. There is no doubt that both are in a very real sense the premise and the tools of Jewish emancipation in the Western world. Yet there is a third category of equality, more difficult to define than the aforementioned, which plays a cardinal part in the analysis of our problem. We refer here to the notion of parity or at least similarity of social stratification between Jewry and the Gentile world. Can we speak of equality only if the members of the Jewish community fill the same types of occupational positions as the Gentiles according to approximately similar percentages?

The history of emancipation in the Western world has proved that this type of equality of occupation has existed and does exist at best by a limited degree of approximation. Long range observation in Western and Central Europe has shown on the other hand, that such kind of occupational assimilation had much less effect on Jewish-Gentile relations than frequently assumed by the liberal nineteenth-century Jewish and Gentile historiography. It very much seems as if two related but essentially different concepts had constantly been confounded: equality in regard to occupation and equality in regard to social status, either within or outside the same occupation. In the majority of industrial and commercial occupations, the free professions and public service, the primary factor determining social status is, quite obviously, the type of work within the occupation, which may range from huckster to wholesale dealer, from bank clerk to corporation president, from local reporter to editor-in-chief. Parity or similarity of social stratification should neither mean mere collective equality of opportunity nor of occupation, taken as a whole, but approximate equality within the ranks of occupations themselves, in other words, parity of status.

There is good reason to state so obvious a fact as the decisive importance of social status in evaluating Jewish-Gentile relations: namely, that nineteenth-century and even more recent Jewish historiography has so completely misread it. While the facts themselves have been recognized, though perhaps not sufficiently interpreted, by such eminent Jewish sociologists and statisticians as Arthur Ruppin, Jacob Lestschinsky and H. Silbergleit, historians following Heinrich Graetz's well-trodden trail have constantly adduced the success of individual Jews as Nobel Prize winners, bank presidents, ministers of state and outstanding figures in formative arts and literature as supreme evidence of the achievement of full equality of the Jews. No issue is taken here with the perhaps somewhat oversimplified view that the achievements and the success of individual Jews necessarily benefit the prestige of the Jewish community as a whole. The basic logical error should be exposed, however, which perceives outstanding and consequently atypical Jewish achievements as evidence of full Jewish equality, whereas in fact such achievements stand only for equality of opportunity. In every other respect their atypicality is the very essence of inequality, however desirable this may be in individual instances.

It is the thesis of this study that the problem of equality, similarity, or basic difference of social stratification is a key, if not *the* key issue of the whole success or failure of the course of Jewish assimilation. It is not claimed that the similarity or difference in social stratification is the only issue on which the success or failure of assimilation depends. In a sense other factors are equally or — according to some — perhaps even more important. Therefore we have to explain why just this one factor of social stratification and not any other has been singled out for closer scrutiny.

First it is held here that just this one factor, unlike many others, has been largely neglected in the previous literature on the subject.[5] We may, however, go farther than that. It is assumed here that the question of social stratification is indeed more basic than any other. Social disparity between the Jewish community and the Gentile environment is in itself neither good nor bad. Its wholesome or adverse effect must be judged according to specific conditions. Thus a favourable course of Jewish-Gentile relations is quite compatible with the existence of a moderate degree of disparity, as wide and lasting experience in several Western countries has amply shown. But wherever Jewish-Gentile friction does exist, disparity, difference in social stratification, always is the premise of Jewish identification on which all other issues are based. Without the experience of such disparity the Gentile world would not even become conscious of the existence of a problem of majority-minority relations. In an age where religious differences by themselves do not represent any longer the divisive force of three centuries ago, this factor of social inequality or disparity can be as little separated from our problem as the question of skin colour in a discussion of causes of prejudice against negroes. One may well raise the question whether, if this phenomenon of disparity should ever disappear completely, the identity of the Jewish people outside of a Jewish national state would or could be maintained. Hence, the importance of this problem for our discussion.

The general assumptions on which this study is based may be summarized as follows:

1. Jewish social equality — as differentiated from equality of rights — is to be measured not primarily in terms of individual opportunities and achievements. It should be gauged according to the degree of similarity of social stratification with the Gentile environment.

2. Within the whole range of social stratification the specific position within a social class is far more important for the determination of social status and

---

[5] A partial exception to this statement would be the work by A. Ruppin quoted above, also from a merely statistical viewpoint H. Silbergleit, *Die Bevölkerungs- und Berufsverhältnisse der Juden im deutschen Reich*, I, 1931, various studies by J. Lestschinsky, above all the statistical essay, 'Die Umsiedlung und Umschichtung des jüdischen Volkes im Laufe des letzten Jahrhunderts', *Weltwirtschaftliches Archiv*, vol. 32, 1930, and also Michel Roblin, *Les Juifs de Paris*, 1952.

consequently existence, degree or lack of discrimination than mere affiliation with the class itself.

3. The similarity of Jewish social stratification with the Gentile environment is a premise of the phenomenon of social antisemitism since the identification of the Jewish image and of the Jewish community depends primarily and increasingly on this factor.

II. SETTING AND CONDITIONS OF JEWISH EMANCIPATION IN GERMANY AND FRANCE

If one surveys the foundations of Jewish emancipation in Germany, one is struck by the fact that the noble social philosophy of a Moses Mendelssohn was so zealously concerned only with the issue of Jewish equality in its narrow sense, and so little with its actual operation on the social group level and the pragmatic possibilities of Jewish integration into the Gentile world. Indeed, the early theoretical contributions to the actual operation of the emancipatory programme had to come from the Gentile rather than from the Jewish community.[6]

This is actually much stranger than it seems at first glance. After all, the community organization of the ghetto — largely compulsory as it was — had only reached its peak as late as the sixteenth century, "the ghetto age."[7] Within such a ghetto the stratification of Jewish social life was on the whole far more restricted by extraneous forces than by the Jewish communal authorities. Mendelssohn himself was quite concerned with the problem that the tearing down of the ghetto walls should not mean the end of Jewish communal autonomy itself. Considering the wide and long experience in Jewish community life and administration, would it not have been strongly suggestive that the intellectual fathers of Jewish emancipation should have given thought and direction to the problem of the ways and means of actual integration of Jewry into the Gentile world?

The motivations of the advocates of enlightened reforms, Jews and Gentiles alike, may help to answer the question why this was not done. Marvin Löwenthal sees three main forces which prompted the beginnings of emancipation. First

---

[6]See particularly the treatise *Über die bürgerliche Verbesserung der Juden*, Berlin 1781, by the Prussian writer and archivist Christian Wilhelm von Dohm, discussed also in S. Dubnow, *Weltgeschichte des jüdischen Volkes*, vol. VII, Berlin 1930, pp. 376ff.; H. Graetz, *Volkstümliche Geschichte der Juden*, Vienna, n.d., vol. III, pp. 535ff.; see also Willy Cohn, 'Christian Wilhelm von Dohm', *Historia Judaica*, vol. XIII/2, pp. 101-108. References to the general history of French and German Jewry in this paper are, of course, to be found in the standard or popular histories of Jewry such as the above-noted by Dubnow and Graetz, H. M. Sachar, *The Course of Modern Jewish History*, Cleveland 1958 (notable for its up-to-date bibliography); A. L. Sachar, *A History of the Jews*, New York 1953; I. Elbogen, *A Century of Jewish Life*, Philadelphia 1946; J. Kastein, *History and Destiny of the Jews*, New York 1936, and quite a few others. Except in cases of direct quotation, no specific references will be made henceforward to these valuable general secondary sources and the use made of them in regard to established and widely known facts.

[7]A. L. Sachar, *op. cit.*, p. 252.

and subjectively the strongest, the appeal to reason, secondly sentiment and faith and finally — objectively the most powerful — the economic impact of the commercial and industrial revolution, the needs and mechanics of which inevitably made the ghetto walls burst.[8] No doubt, this last factor carried little positive weight with Mendelssohn and his intellectual friends and students but all the more the two others. Here one has to consider the fact that intellectual fathers of the emancipation like Holbach, Diderot or Voltaire personally were not any friendlier disposed toward the Jews than a practical reformer such as Joseph II in Austria. They all wanted primarily to reform an anachronistic social situation in principle rather than to undo a specific wrong. The German high-minded friends of Mendelssohn on the other hand were far more concerned with the rather sensational specimen of the noble Jew as an individual than with the social problems of a people. Small wonder then that a man of Mendelssohn's sensitive feelings (like Rousseau torn between the cold force of reason and the emotional sentiments of incipient Romanticism) did not want to burden the Jewish issue with any specific social demands which might smell even faintly of Jewish group interests. He preferred to stand exclusively on broad humanitarian principles. This hidden and only rarely formulated Jewish fear that social integration counselled or channelled by community leaders might be considered as selfish and materialistic, may well have been a weighty factor in preventing the orderly regulation of this integration by community counsel at the one and only time when this could have been possible without infringing on the rights of the individual.[9]

For different reasons we find this same lack of social counselling and channelling in the French emancipation as well. The German enlightened friends of Jewry, to mention only such noble names as Herder, Lessing or Kant, were primarily literary men and philosophers with scant interest in political reform. Only relatively lesser lights such as Dohm in Prussia or Sonnenfels in Austria (the latter a converted Jew himself) promoted actively the cause of Jewish emancipation. Primarily it depended on the princes. This meant an often hesitant and unwilling gradualism in reform with many ups and downs. All too active Jewish participation seemed to further the downs rather than the ups.

In France the success of Jewish emancipation prior to the French Revolution

[8]M. Löwenthal, *The Jews of Germany*, New York 1936, pp. 213ff. See also S. W. Baron, *The Jewish Community*, 1942, vol. 2, pp. 358ff.; Adolf Kober, 'Emancipation's Impact on the Education and Vocational Training of German Jewry', *Jewish Social Studies*, 1954, vol. XVI, pp. 3-32, 151-176. See further Charles L. Ozer, 'Jewish Education in the Transition from Ghetto to Emancipation', *Historia Judaica*, vol. IX, 1, 2, 1947, pp. 75-94, 137-158.
[9]The sermon of the enlightened reform preacher Mannheimer at the beginning of the Austrian March revolution of 1848 is illustrative in this respect. "What must now be done for us as Jews? For us, nothing! Everything for people and country . . . Now nothing for us! No petitions, no supplications, no prayers and laments for our rights! . . . First the right to live as a man - to breathe, to think, to speak, first the right of the citizen - the Jew comes afterwards! Let men not charge that always and everywhere we think first of ourselves! ..." Elbogen, *op. cit.*, p. 20.

was more modest than in the various German states. On the other hand all the great intellectual figures of the enlightenment from Voltaire to Rousseau are, as political philosophers, directly or indirectly involved in the demand for emancipation. This much broader intellectual foundation of the emancipation idea is reflected in the decisive victory of Jewish emancipation not — as in Germany — in terms of mere tolerance but of equality of rights achieved in the two stormy years in the Constitutional Assembly from August 1789 to September 1791. In spite of a certain amount of opposition, particularly from Alsatian deputies, there is no question about the decisiveness of emancipation, far beyond the specific Jewish issue, as one of the symbols of the creation of a united French nation under a constitution representing the common will of the people instead of the previous agglomeration of regional, occupational and denominational autonomous institutions, legally united by the mere common allegiance to the most Christian king. After all, this had represented the meagre substitute for the national state prior to 1789. There is no question that the immediate and demonstrable association between Jewish emancipation and French national rebirth — later minor restrictions notwithstanding — has given the Jewish achievement genuine depth in time.[10]

The reverse side of the picture is, of course, the fact that the Jewish community, even more so than in Germany, was the more passive beneficiary of a great ideological struggle. It was a victory of a sublime principle whose application included, among many others, the Jews. It was not the result of an active Jewish struggle. Indeed, so secondary did the specific issue appear to those who perceived history in terms of the "Declaration of the Rights of Man" that the citizenship oath to be taken by Jews provided for "the renunciation of all previous privileges and specific statutes valid in their favour."[11] Was it really conceivable to work openly and honestly for some kind of premeditated Jewish social integration at a time when under the spell of rising Jacobin egalitarianism any specific, often

---

[10]See L. Berman, *Histoire des Juifs de France,* Paris 1937, pp. 325-370; Anchel Robert, *Les Juifs de France,* Paris 1946, pp. 153-234, and on the proceedings in the Constitutional Assembly in particular Kurt Stillschweig, 'Die Judenemanzipation im Licht des französischen Nationsbegriffes', *Monatsschrift für Geschichte und Wissenschaft des Judentums,* 81, Berlin 1937, pp. 457-478. Of particular importance are, of course, the various articles by Zosa Szajkowski of which only the following can be mentioned here. As to pre-revolutionary history, 'The Jewish Status in Eighteenth Century France and the Droit D'Aubain . . .' (the right to confiscate the estate of a deceased citizen), *Historia Judaica,* vol. XIX/2, 1957, pp. 147-161. As to revolutionary history, see by the same author, *ibid.,* in particular, 'The Discussion and Struggle over Jewish Emancipation in Alsace and the Early Years of the French Revolution', vol. XVII/2, 1955, pp. 121-142; 'Jewish Autonomy debated and attacked during the French Revolution', vol. XX/1, 1958, pp. 31-46; 'The Demographic Aspects of Jewish Emancipation in France during the French Revolution', vol. XXI/1, 1959, pp. 7-36, 109-132, particularly pp. 129ff.

[11]Dubnow, *op. cit.,* VIII, p. 118; Stillschweig, *loc. cit.,* p. 474. See also Z. Szajkowski, 'The Attitude of French Jacobins toward Jewish Religion', *Historia Judaica,* vol. XVIII/2, 1956, pp. 107-120, and by the same author, 'Marriages, Mixed Marriages and Conversions among French Jews during the Revolution of 1789, *ibid.,* vol. XIX/1, pp. 35-54, and 'French Jewry during the Thermidorian Reaction', *ibid.,* vol. XX/2, pp. 97-108.

clearly discriminatory group regulations of yore were seen or construed as "privileges"? The Jewish community was bound to miss the opportunity of channelled assimilation under French Jacobinism no less than under German enlightened absolutism.

We may assume as follows:

1. Both German-Jewish and French-Jewish emancipation in the late eighteenth century failed conspicuously to channel the social transition from the ghetto to a free life in a Gentile world.

2. To German Jewry any planning in this respect would have appeared primarily as crass materialistic violation of the enlightened idea of individual human rights, to French Jewry as reactionary rearguard action on behalf of alleged ancient privileges versus liberty, equality and fraternity.

III. EMANCIPATION AND ECONOMIC DEVELOPMENT

Here the question arises whether social-economic conditions did not force Jewish assimilation in any case into a pattern of inevitable economic laws. There is a surprising degree of agreement on the part of adherents of a free as well as a planned economy, from Jewish Conservatives as well as Liberals, that the transition from a feudal economic political and economic social order to a regime of an economically and socially freer kind of capitalism was bound to lead to emancipation or assimilation anyway. There is, however, some disagreement as to whether this social process is just one major cause for emancipation and assimilation or *the* major cause. Such a controversy, however, is of far less importance than the positive or negative evaluation of the undisputed correlation between economic change and Jewish progress.

The process itself in its various stages is characterized by U. Z. Engelman quite aptly as follows:

a) The shifting of the centre of economic activity from the village to the town...

b) The increase in opportunities for engaging in gainful occupations... in particular commerce, industry and professions,

c) the abandonment of antisemitism as a state policy...

d) the abolition of the ghetto with its legal and physical demographic limitations, and finally,

e) the improvement in sanitary conditions which drastically reduced the Jewish death rate while the birth rate remained high.[12]

Some typical views may illustrate the problem. A. Ruppin, a first rank scholar of rather conservative leanings, hails the impact of the European economic transition on the fate of the Jews without reservation, as far as Jewish assimilation — but not Jewish ethnic consciousness and solidarity — is concerned.

[12]U. Z. Engelman, *The Rise of the Jews in the Western World*, New York 1944, pp. 87ff.

"The most important happening in the social life of the Jews since the eighteenth century . . . is the dissolution or the loosening of their ethnic homogeneity, of their feeling of belonging together, as well as their assimilation to the economic and cultural life of their Christian environment. Capitalism which in the eighteenth century replaced the system of guild organization by that of free competition and which opened to finance capital new opportunities for profit, had many features in common with Jewish occupational life. The Jew lost his character as alien body in economic life and began to integrate as organic part of the general economy. In connection with this, the legal separate status of the Jews yielded to the legally equal status with the Christians."[13]

This is also the view of J. Lestschinsky who as an outstanding demographer is fully aware of the social phenomena brought about by this process, though perhaps less so of its social consequences. He believes that prior to the development of a modern urban society, Jewry was so to speak merely injected or rather interpolated between the feudal rural and the peasant class, a social situation in which the Jews remained strangers to both these groups with an in-between social status. Thus socially, economically and culturally the Jew had to remain a *Klasseneinschiebsel.* The rapid and sweeping Jewish urbanization process in modern terms, welcomed unequivocally and somewhat uncritically by Lestschinsky, changed the situation radically and this by way of two processes:

"The environment during the last century became increasingly more 'Jewish', it branched off more and more urban classes, commercial elements, middle-men elements, dynamic in-between classes; the Jewish world, on the other hand, became more 'non-Jewish'. Increasingly working groups, producing groups developed, closer ties with the primary forms of economy, partly with agriculture and production were established."

In Germany in particular, the cultural emancipation and assimilation of the upper bourgeoisie preceded political emancipation while the reverse situation is true for the lower urban middle classes.

In general, the Jewish community:

". . . gradually loses its uncomplicated and undifferentiated structure [actually simple social stratification . . . R.A.K.] . . . thus this process of differentiation in the structure of Judaism and its assimilation . . . put an end to the exclusiveness of Jewry and the isolation from the interchange of economic forces and fights . . . [There] develops a socially and economically structured body, in many ways tied to and interwoven with all branches of economy and politics of the country. From a peculiar national class, a nation of diverse classes has emerged."[14]

Leaving the point entirely aside that here the issue is discussed as though it were the development of a "Jewish nation" similar to other nations, rather than the integration of the Jewish community into another nation, both Ruppin and Lestschinsky agree that this process of nation-like and nation-wide social stratification was fully successful. This view, though widely held, was opposed by many.

---

[13]Ruppin, *op. cit.*, II, pp. 103f., see also I, pp. 316f. on the specific consequences of technological advancement.

[14]Lestschinsky, *op. cit.*, pp. 124f., 599.

A basic study by the Austrian socialist Otto Bauer, directly concerned with the question of full assimilation of the Yiddish-speaking Polish workers, makes a point that may well be considered important beyond the Eastern European orbit, and this entirely apart from its socialist connotation. Like Lestschinsky, Bauer believes that emancipation after the seventeenth century proceeded in an order where the cultural assimilation of the top class, the upper bourgeoisie, was followed by that of the others; the intellectuals next, then the lower middle class and finally the workers. "These Jews adjust their culture to the culture of the European nations since the money economy, once represented only by the Jews, has become the economic organization of all European peoples..."[15]

This view, in several ways related to that of Lestschinsky, is certainly controversial in so far as it equates the ghetto economy with that of modern capitalism. But the following deduction is even more problematic. "This factual adjustment has finally led to the legal emancipation of the Jews, to the establishment of their legal equality with the Christians." According to Bauer this belief in the socio-economic lead and therefore natural course of assimilation inevitably encompasses the worker last and thus slows down and impedes the emancipatory process.[16]

The views presented thus far may differ as to the effect of assimilation on the Jews within a nation or on the Jews as a nation, they may disagree as to the status of the industrial or agricultural worker within the whole process, but the comprehensiveness of assimilation for Jews of all classes in modern times itself is not questioned. Bernard Weinryb, however, makes the point that the Jews during and after the enlightenment did not spread out into the occupational life of the society as a whole but merely filled the positions opened to them. This would mean — and here he points to the example of the seventeenth-century French Huguenot emigrants in Germany and the sixteenth-century Swiss Anabaptist settlers in Moravia — new business and previously unknown industries and trades.

Even these positions were held only as long as they appeared economically unattractive to the native population or as long as it had not acquired the necessary skill for competition in these new fields. As soon or as late as the host nation inevitably entered competition, social friction began. In the aforementioned cases such friction could, however, eventually be solved by the complete merger of the descendants of the immigrants with the native population.[17]

The analogy with the Jewish problem, though by no means complete, is obvious. The Jews did not actually move into stable positions opened to them but into new positions that required their special skill in certain fields, not yet commanded by the Gentiles. This in turn created or rather continued a lopsided

[15]Otto Bauer, *Die Nationalitätenfrage und die Sozialdemokratie*, 2nd ed., Vienna 1924, pp. 368f. - See also *LBI Year Book IV* (1959), pp. XVII-XX.
[16]Bauer, *op. cit.*, pp. 369, 371; see also the whole discourse pp. 366-381.
[17]Bernard D. Weinryb, 'The Economic and Social Background of Modern Anti-Semitism', in: K. S. Pinson (ed.), *Essays on Anti-Semitism*, New York 1946, pp. 17ff.

social stratification, right from the start of the emancipatory age. In addition, the new situation was aggravated by at least three factors. Some of the new positions to be filled outside the ghetto — by no means all, to be sure — were burdened in the eyes of the Gentile world with the memory of the odious and dubious financial privileges of the ghetto. The fact that the economic position into which the Jews were channelled, required permanent and even increased Jewish urbanization, aggravated rather than helped the course of further assimilation. Finally, the religious traditions and customs of long standing blocked complete integration.

Concerning the relationship between economic development and Jewish emancipation three main propositions, one generally accepted and two conflicting with each other, have to be investigated.

1. The direct connection between the Industrial Revolution, the gradual evolution of a modern capitalistic system and Jewish emancipation is generally affirmed.

2. It is widely held that the consequent vocational broadening of Jewish social stratification strongly furthered the process of Jewish assimilation.

3. In conflict with assumption 2) it may be argued that in the process of a fairly swift emancipation Jewry did not move into new positions opened to them without restrictions. Primarily they were forced into vocations for which Gentiles were insufficiently trained or which they abandoned or altogether rejected. This in turn complicated and to a point even invalidated the achievements of the emancipatory process.

IV. COURSE OF ASSIMILATORY PROCESS IN GERMANY AND FRANCE

Before attempting to support the above lines of reasoning with statistical evidence, the comprehensiveness of this sombre picture may be questioned. Obviously the Jews in commerce, finance and trade could be held to, kept in or crowded into a narrow strip of occupational life where such need or interest existed. This undoubtedly was the case in the still strongly feudal society of eighteenth-century Germany and largely true even in the era of continued German division from the end of the Napoleonic wars to the establishment of the German Empire in 1871. Considering the fact that progress of emancipation between 1792 and 1813 in Germany was far less an organic development than imposed by the foreign French administration, one may come to the conclusion that renewal of anti-Jewish feelings and partly renewed anti-Jewish legislation during the period of restoration and reaction from 1815 to 1848 and beyond, was not chiefly the consequence of a frustrated and backward looking Romantic nationalism and counter-revolutionary spirit; rather it was the continuation of a semi-feudal order, suspended but not destroyed by the Napoleonic wars.

The situation was somewhat different in France. True, the spirit of French government before 1789 was politically not any more progressive and in the later part of the pre-revolutionary eighteenth century far less efficient than the Austrian and Prussian administrations. Nevertheless the strong impact of government-controlled mercantilism in the late seventeenth century, the progress of industrialization and the financial operation of the Regency after the death of Louis XIV, had created an economic set-up far less dependent on the specific and generally frowned-upon massive Jewish participation than was the case in Germany. Although neither in finance, nor in trade or commerce did the pre-revolutionary French Jews hold a monopolistic position, as was exaggeratedly maintained, the consequences resulting from this social stigma were not entirely removed even by the radical egalitarian impact of the revolutionary experience.

Highly characteristic in this respect are again the actions of the two following regimes: that of Napoleon, who was the executor of the emancipatory inheritance of the revolution abroad, but only in a curiously twisted and questionable way its promoter at home as well. This refers of course to the unique, harsh and yet not ignoble experiment to force the Jews by temporary economic restrictive legislation into a social-economic merger with the Gentile world.[18] Not less significant is the policy of the ensuing Bourbon and Orleans regimes which, considering their general reactionary character, and the psychological impact of the lost wars notwithstanding, did not touch upon the emancipatory achievements, and even removed the relatively minor Napoleonic discriminatory decrees. The pre-revolutionary background of Jewish emancipation in France, the revolutionary experience, and the fact that the fallen Napoleonic regime appeared to be by no means favourable to the Jews on the domestic scene, exercised here a combined effect. Furthermore, the Industrial Revolution came earlier than in Germany, and in a setting of business of moderate size and free competition helpful to Jewish abilities. When German industrialization began to overtake the French rather rapidly in the 1870s, this came about in a semi-monopolistic frame of big banking and concentration of heavy industry quite out of line with previous Jewish experience and interests.

Whether one looks at German or French conditions, there can be no doubt, though, that neither country presented the Jewish future with conditions as favourable as those in the Anglo-Saxon world. In England the political and economic power of feudalism was seriously weakened, if not destroyed, as early as the seventeenth century. In the United States, it never existed, and neither did, by and large, the *privilegia odiosa* of the economic Jewish ghetto position.

At this point and before going into some of the statistical evidence pertaining to the course of assimilation, it might be convenient to compare very briefly and in barest outline the assimilatory pattern of French and German Jewry. While the profound intellectual influence of the French enlightenment, culminating in the great French Revolution of 1789, led to the sudden emancipation of the Jews, the German enlightenment, of more modest intellectual influence, brought about

---

[18]See Berman, *op. cit.*, pp. 371-394; A. Lemoine, *Napoleon I et les Juifs*, Paris 1900. The point could actually be made that Napoleon was primarily concerned not with Jewish assimilation but with the elimination of Jewish identity within the population of France. Discussion of this highly interesting problem would, however, transcend the limits of this paper.

relatively slow progress. On the other hand the Napoleonic period in France entailed limited retrogressive measures in regard to Jewry, whereas the conquests of the French armies on German soil led to a very limited victory of emancipation in Western Germany and, by indirect influence, by 1812 in Prussia as well. The reaction in France after a lost war, did not cause a set-back to Jewish assimilation. In several of the German states, above all in Prussia, however, administrative measures imposed new restrictions on the Jews after a victorious war.

Despite very little active Jewish participation, the French Revolution of 1789 had led to decisive improvement in the lot of the Jews; the German revolutions of 1848 — all too often minimized in their overall significance — show an active political and literary participation of the Jews with very little practical result as regards their civic position. The ensuing period of reaction, only gradually ebbing in the 1850s and 1860s ended with the complete legal — though by no means full social — emancipation in Germany. In France, a seemingly firm stabilization of emancipation, entailing full legal equality, was reached under the Bourbon and Orleans monarchy and continued under the second empire of Napoleon III.

Decisive changes in the climate of public opinion took place in both countries after the war of 1870/71 and, though won by the Germans and lost by the French, with very similar effect on the position of the Jews. In France the seemingly rather sudden rise of antisemitism illustrated by Paul Déroulède's League of Patriots, Drumont's publication of *La France Juive* and by the *Action Française,* culminated in the Panama scandal and above all in the Dreyfus affair. With the new century, the movement receded though not disappeared, to raise its head again in the 1930s and 1940s. As a significant French feature it might be noted that just as the emancipation of 1791 was initiated by a prelude of great intellectual brilliance, antisemitism of the era after 1870 was introduced by notable literary figures. They were not of comparable rank, but like Arthur de Gobineau, Hyppolite Taine, Maurice Barrès, Charles Maurras, of no mean intellectual status either.

In Germany such events as the switch from a moderate free trade policy to high protective tariffs at the end of the 1870s, and Bismarck's turning away from the Liberals and reconciliation with the Conservatives, are generally considered major causes for the rather sudden flare-up of antisemitic tendencies. The same holds true for the termination of the *Kulturkampf* and a new understanding with the Catholic Centre, paralleled to a point by the "realignment" between Vatican and Third Republic in France. This interpretation may be applied also to the anti-liberal aspects of Bismarck's fight to suppress the socialist workers' movement by way of the anti-socialist laws, the economic decline of the lower urban middle class left behind in the progress of rapid industrialization. Above all, as in 1814/15, there is the intolerance swelled by victorious nationalism, so remarkably absent in this particular field in France after World War I. As in France, the drive of the new antisemitism, spear-headed by the Christian Social petty bourgois party under the leadership of the Court Pastor Stoecker, reached its peak in the 1880s and early 1890s. Nationalist organizations like the pan-German League of 1891(94), though not primarily motivated by antisemitic considerations, nevertheless furthered antisemitic programmes. Intellectual sponsors of the antisemitic revival like Eugen Dühring, Paul de Lagarde, Julius Langbehn and Houston Stewart Chamberlain are lesser lights than their French counterparts. Yet antisemitism in Germany became more respectable due to the views of such men of brilliance, even genius, as the historian Heinrich von Treitschke and Richard Wagner. There never was and presumably never will be an antisemitic movement in history in which the mob does not play an important (though not necessarily the decisive) part. Unlike the situation in post-World War I Germany, neither in Germany nor in France, were the typical rabble rousers like Edouard Drumont or Hermann Ahlwardt either primary movers or primary leaders.[19] But Ahlwardt's electoral success induced the Conservatives to incorporate antisemitism in their programme.

Within the frame of this study it is, of course, impossible to analyze the political historical and psychological factors which have been advanced with good or less good reasons to explain the course of Jewish-Gentile relations, in the age of assimilation in Western and Central Europe. The interdependence of antisemitic movements in various countries, particularly in countries bordering on each other even to the extent of measures decreed from outside — vide Germany and her satellites under Hitler — may be considered as evident. But it would be highly controversial to assume that the same or very similar causes explain necessarily the same or similar antisemitic phenomena.

A few examples may illustrate the point. Antisemitism rose in Germany markedly after the lost First World War and in France after the war of 1870/71, but not after the Napoleonic wars. Rising nationalism furthered antisemitism in Germany after the victorious war of 1870/71 but not in France after 1918. Romanticism in Germany as well as in France may be considered in several ways as a conservative and backward-looking movement. Its influence on the revival of anti-Jewish feelings in Germany after the enlightenment is generally acknowledged; not so in France whose medieval tradition certainly was no less hostile to the Jews. While the argument of the alleged inordinate share of Jews in a Marxian labour movement played an important role in Germany, in France it was the charge of alleged Jewish subversive infiltration into the officers' corps of the army. The heavy and relatively rapid industrialization of the last third of the

---

[19]For literature on antisemitism in Germany and France in the nineteenth and early twentieth century see Paul W. Massing, *Rehearsal for Destruction. A Study of Political Anti-Semitism in Imperial Germany*, New York 1949; Waldemar Gurian, 'Antisemitism in Modern Germany', in Pinson, *loc. cit.*; B. Lazare, *Antisemitisme*, Paris 1903; R. F. Byrnes, *Antisemitism in Modern France*, New Brunswick 1950; Hannah Arendt, 'From the Dreyfus Affair to France Today', in Pinson, *loc. cit.*, See also the studies by Edmund Silberner pertaining to antisemitism among the leaders of the socialist labour movement in *Historia Judaica*, 'German Social Democracy and the Jewish Problem prior to World War I', vol. XV/1, 1953, pp. 3-48, and 'French Socialism and the Jewish Question, 1865-1914', *ibid.*, vol. XVI/1, pp. 3-38. Silberner perceives, after the Dreyfus affair, a decline of French antisemitism in the labour movement.

nineteenth century undoubtedly impaired the social and economic position of the lower middle class, those engaged in small retail business and crafts all over Western and Central Europe. Antisemitic reaction to such a development in Germany and Austria was much stronger than in France.[20] Differences of this kind could be elaborated almost *ad libitum*. All of them strengthen the belief that no single factor or combination of single factors, however valid in one country, can be applied to another country, even if adjacent to it and related to it by manifold historic and cultural ties.

To sum up:

1. The course of Gentile-Jewish relations from the end of the enlightenment to the post-World War I era is markedly different in Germany and France, not only in regard to the intensity of antisemitism but also due to fluctuations in time when antisemitic feelings and anti-emancipatory tendencies reached their peak.

2. While the interdependence of antisemitic movements in countries within the same cultural orbit is obvious, the tacit assumption that similar causes necessarily explain similar phenomena in different countries is not tenable.

3. A brief comparative survey of German and French conditions indicates that neither analogous political experiences nor similar intellectual trends produced comparable reactions in Germany and France. Rather limited similarities concerning reactions to the economic rise and crisis in both countries in the last quarter of the nineteenth century do not offer sufficient evidence to assume the existence of a genuine common denominator of Gentile-Jewish relations in France and Germany.

4. Since a survey of political, intellectual and economic conditions has failed to lead to general conclusions equally applicable to conditions in both countries, this analysis is bound to concentrate on the problem raised in Section I, the question of comparative social disparity per se.

V. STATISTICAL SURVEY

The original draft of this study included substantial statistical evidence to support the assumptions formulated and the questions raised and discussed in the four preceding sections as well as in the subsequent conclusions. Due to lack of space it has been decided to offer, in this revised version, a mere summary of statistical findings. The reader interested in more specific data is referred to the comprehensive report on file with the Institute of Human Relations.[21]

---

[20]See R. A. Kann, 'German-speaking Jewry during Austria-Hungary's Constitutional Period' and, by the same author, 'Hungarian Jewry during Austria-Hungary's Constitutional Period', *Jewish Social Studies*, vols. X, 1948, VII, 1945.

[21]This original report consists of 45 pages in typescript including 27 statistical main charts and their interpretations, as well as a number of observations based on additional statistical material. The original draft cites, of course, the specific references from which the data referred to in the revised version are taken.

As to the data selected and presented in the original report and abstracted here, the official

Some interpretative remarks on the statistical data are in order at this point. For once the German material is greatly superior to the French, in quantity as well as in quality, even though in many instances figures for Prussia, the most populous German state — comprising at the turn of the twentieth century more than three-fifths of the German population — have to be substituted for total German figures. It is suggestive to assume that greater interest for data on Jewish integration in Germany than in France offers circumstantial evidence that the assimilation process in Germany had to face greater impediments. In view of a number of striking parallels in German and French data such an interpretation should be accepted only with considerable reservations.

Secondly it should be emphasized that statistical data even in Germany, and particularly for the first half of the nineteenth century, are by no means standardized in the way of modern government statistics. Based on different sources and different methods these statistics are largely incongruous as to social groups, areas and periods covered. Data are frequently — and inevitably — based on mere estimates. In particular data concerned not merely with the general occupational set-up but with the specific status of individuals within an occupational group have largely to be derived by indirect methods.

Considering the limited means employed and the restricted data available, the achievements in the fields of Jewish community statistics should be considered outstanding.

French and German statistics offer only the scantiest material. The unchallenged standard work is the one by Arthur Ruppin noted before; A. Lestschinsky and particularly H. Silbergleit, *op. cit.*, proved likewise extremely useful. Valuable are also Jakob Segall, *Die beruflichen und sozialen Verhältnisse der Juden in Deutschland*, Berlin 1912, as well as U. Z. Engelman, 'Sources of Jewish Statistics', and N. Reich, 'Economic Structure of Modern Jewry', both in L. Finkelstein (ed.), *The Jews, their History, Culture and Religion*, 2nd edition, New York 1955, vol. II. See further in the third edition of this work published in 1960, the thoughtful essay by Simon Kuznet, 'Economic Structure and Life of the Jews', vol. II, 1596ff., with valuable statistics, bibliography, and very interesting conclusions. As to the latter, which are at variance with those presented in this paper, see below. See further B. Weinryb, 'The Economic and Social Background of Modern Anti-Semitism', in Pinson, *loc. cit.*, and U. Z. Engelman, *The Rise of the Jew in the Western World*, New York 1944, who summarize and interpret some of the existing material skillfully. W. Sombart, *Die Juden und das Wirtschaftsleben*, Leipzig 1911, contains important data though their interpretation has to be studied with caution. Of these contributions those by Ruppin, Lestschinsky, Sombart and Engelman are not confined to Germany but their emphasis is inevitably based on German data. As to French conditions, Michel Roblin, *Les Juifs de Paris*, Paris 1952, offers interesting data on a limited area. Zosa Szajkowski, 'The Growth of the Jewish Population of France; the Political Aspects of the Demographic Problem', *Jewish Social Studies*, 1946, vol. VIII, pp. 179-196 and 297-317 gives valuable background information but does not actually enter the field of occupational statistics. See also by the same author, *The Economic Status of the Jews in Alsace, Metz and Lorraine*, New York 1954. See further L. Berman, S. M. Dubnow, I. Elbogen, H. M. Sachar, *op. cit.* Since nearly all the material collected has to be based on various types of Jewish community census, two American studies which discuss techniques to be applied when faced with similar problems are of interest. H. S. Linfield, *The Communal Census of Jews; Methods used in Recent Years*, New York, Jewish Statistical Bureau, 1938 and by the same author, *Statistics of Jews and Jewish Organizations. Historical Review of the Ten Censuses, 1850-1937*, New York, American Jewish Committee, 1939, and Bruno Blau, 'Sociology and Statistics of the Jews', as quoted in note 1.

The statistical data submitted in the original report may be conveniently divided into three main groups. First there are a number of preliminary surveys which merely offer the background as to the percentages of German and French Jewry within the Jewish population of Europe altogether, the Jewish population of both countries in actual figures as well as percentages, external and internal immigration figures for both countries, and also figures on mixed marriages between Jews and Gentiles. It is noteworthy that the Jewish percentage of the population of Prussia between 1825 and 1880, was about static, that of Germany between 1880 and 1925 on the decline. In France the Jewish share in the population was on the rise until 1870, then, in spite of the loss of Alsace-Lorraine with a relatively strong Jewish population quota, there was little percentual change until the end of the First World War. In Prussia, Jewish population percentages fluctuated between 1.25 and 1.06 per cent in the century from 1825 to 1925, in Germany between 1.24 and 0.99 per cent from 1880 to 1921, in France between 0.38 and 0.4 per cent during that same period. While immigration figures from abroad were relatively minor in both countries prior to the First World War, Jewish internal migration was substantial. In Germany these moves were apparent in two directions, from the Prussian eastern provinces to Central and Western Germany and a substantial Jewish population increase in the capital of Berlin. A corresponding East-West movement is not demonstrable in France, but Jewish concentration in the German capital has its counterpart in the movement of French Jews to Paris. In either country there is a relatively strong Jewish agglomeration in big cities altogether, which in Germany exceeds in some instances the Jewish percentage in the total population by several hundred percent. According to Arthur Ruppin, agglomeration of Jews in great density in small areas slows down the assimilatory process, whereas mere urbanization, that is, the adjustment to city life in general, furthers it.[22] While the first assertion can easily be proved by experience from the times of the ghetto to the present, the second is accepted in this study only with reservations. As will be shown in the following, data of social disparity between Jews and Gentiles are connected not merely with agglomeration but with urbanization as well, even though the latter process has admittedly furthered Jewish adjustment in important aspects.

Concerning the related problem of mixed marriages, the objections raised against them on religious-traditional as well as sociological grounds are well known. On the other hand, these marriages tend to lessen the distinctions between Jewish and Gentile group images and in effect promote assimilation. German and German-Prussian figures within the half-century from the 1870s to the 1920s show a rise in mixed marriages of between 300 and 400 per cent.

The second group of statistical data presented in the original report is even more directly concerned with the specific topic of the study, namely the trend of Jewish occupational distribution in general as distinguished from the specific status of Jews within various occupational groups. Here statistical surveys under-

[22]Ruppin, *op. cit.*, I, p. 118.

taken in Prussia in 1816, 1834, 1843, and 1861 show a gradual but not spectacular spread from trade, commerce and crafts to industry, agriculture, free professions, and a limited share in civil service positions. Major divergences in the classification and summarization of jobs under various occupational groups demand, however, great caution in the interpretation of these figures.[23]

According to the first available occupational chart for the whole of Germany, in 1895, Jews in agriculture presented, in percentages of population figures, less than a tenth of their share in the population in industry, and in trade only slightly more than half. In commerce and finance on the other hand they exceed their population quota by some 700 per cent while they exceed their quota in free professions and civil service — both quite unjustifiably lumped together — by a mere 50 per cent.[24] Data for 1907 on Jewish representation in agriculture for Germany and Prussia comes closer to that of the total population, the percentual share in commerce and trade is somewhat in decline, civil service and free professions considerably on the rise; as to domestic service, Jewish representation is far below the overall German occupational picture. Finally, a comparative chart of Jewish and Gentile occupational distribution shortly before the National Socialist assumption of power in 1933 shows the Jewish occupational share in excess of that of Gentiles in commerce and credit (strongly), public service and free professions (slightly), Gentile occupational representation strongly in excess of Jewish in industry and handicraft, transport and communications and in domestic service.

As to France, figures for Paris[25] show — as in Germany — Jewish participation in trade and free professions considerably in excess of their share in population figures. On the other hand, the Jewish share in the manufacturing process — particularly in the textile industry — is well above the comparable figures in Germany, and in this respect much closer to the percentages of the total population.

Altogether figures quoted or referred to above, incongruous and incomplete as they are, show a fairly steady decline of the Jews in commerce, trade and crafts, a rather steady curve in regard to industry, and an increase in the percentual share in free professions and public service as well as (in a small way) in agriculture. Even though differences from the Gentile environment are still substantial — less marked in France — there is little doubt that the history of assimilation in both countries shows a continuous spread of Jewish occupations in the direction of closer approximation to the Gentile social stratification.

[23]In early statistics, trade, commerce, manufacturing, banking is summarized in one group. Others merge trade and innkeeping, a third survey lists innkeeping under communications. Examples of a similar kind could be offered ad libitum.
[24]As borne out by data assembled at different times and places, the number of Jews in the free professions was strongly on the rise whereas in civil service such an increase was kept down by only slightly camouflaged social restrictions. Hence this particular type of statistical classification gives a distorted picture of obvious facts.
[25]Paris represents a share of the Jewish population of France far in excess of the Jewish population quota of any large German city in relation to the Jewish population of Germany.

The question of social stratification leads to the third and more complex group of data, namely the determination of the evolution of the Jewish social status *within* each occupational group, compared to Gentiles. If we visualize that statistics comprise under industry labour as well as management, under finance, chairman of the board as well as bank clerk, under commerce in earlier statistics wholesale dealers as well as pedlars, it becomes clear that we face here the core of the problem.

If we take higher education in Western Europe as foremost premise of social status within any branch of occupation, it is suggestive to survey this topic first. According to statistics of general Prussian secondary schools at the beginning of the second and third decade of the twentieth century, Jewish students exceed their population quota by over 400 per cent in regard to preparatory schools, by over 700 per cent in regard to university education. We further find that within the educational institutions of university rank the quota of Jewish students of German citizenship tops their total population quota by about 400 per cent in universities, by more than 100 per cent in schools of commerce, by more than 50 per cent in technical colleges. In regard to specific fields of concentration, the percentage of Jewish students in law exceeds the population quota by nearly 600 per cent, in medicine by about 700 per cent, in the humanities roughly by 200 to 300 per cent, in the natural sciences by well above 300 per cent. At a time when Jews in France represented less than one half of 1 per cent of the population, they made up roughly between 10 and 15 per cent of the student body of the medical faculty of the University of Paris.

As to the ensuing problem of movement within specific occupational categories we have to proceed partly on the basis of mere estimates. According to H. M. Sachar and B. Weinryb some 20 per cent of the Prussian Jewish community were pedlars at the beginning of the nineteenth century, some 6 per cent only in 1852, just about 1 per cent in 1900. The number of regular Jewish retail and wholesale stores rose correspondingly. At the end of the nineteenth century when the Jewish share in banking exceeded the population quota by well above 300 per cent, Jews represented about 18 per cent of the owners or directors of banks in Germany as a whole, nearly 33 per cent in Berlin. This is a percentual increase above the population quota of 1800 per cent and 3300 per cent respectively. As to industry, Jews in 1910 filled about 13 per cent of the managerial positions in ten branches of production and about 24 per cent of the positions of board members of corporations, thereby exceeding their population quota by about 1300 and 2400 per cent respectively. On the other hand, Jews during the same period represented less than a third of their proportional share in the industrial labour group.

In the free professions, if properly separated from civil service, Jewish figures correspond roughly to those given in regard to graduate studies. Accordingly they exceed the Gentile quota by several hundred per cent. The Jewish share in civil service positions, on the other hand, is only slightly above their total population quota for the reasons referred to previously.

According to reliable sources, comparative figures for France as to Jewish doctors and lawyers in the period between the two World Wars are even farther in excess of the share in the total population. Representation in journalism, music and the theatre exceeds the Jewish population quota by as much as 1000 to 3000 per cent. On the other hand, the Jewish share in commerce in Paris is not considered excessive. As noted before, in at least one major industry requiring special skills — textiles — it comes much closer to the social stratification of the entire population than comparable German figures. Altogether it is fair to assume that the general trends of Jewish social stratification in various occupations are similar to those in Germany but, apart from the centres of concentration of Jewish population in Paris and the Alsace, by no means extreme.[26]

Summarization of the situation in Germany shows Jewish income tax returns in eight major German cities in 1905 in excess of the population quota by figures ranging from 200 to 700 per cent. For one other city of particularly strong Jewish concentration and also particularly strong Jewish wealth, Frankfurt am Main, the figures are even farther out of line. These findings regarding larger cities are fully confirmed by a pilot study which compares the income of Catholics, Jews, and Protestants in a larger, not predominantly metropolitan area, the Grand Duchy of Baden.

A final and particularly revealing issue is the question of percentage of independents and employees in each occupational group. A comparative survey of Jews and Gentiles for Prussia in 1907 shows these results: in commerce the proportional share of independent Jews exceeds that of independent Gentiles by nearly 100 per cent. Within the groups of employees, Jewish and Gentile white-collar workers are fairly evenly matched. On the other hand, in the labour group the proportional share of Gentiles in commerce exceeds that of the Jews by some 70 per cent. In industry and crafts the quota of Jewish independents is about 250 per cent above that of Gentile independents, in the group of white-collar workers it is over 350 per cent higher, in industrial labour it is less than 50 per cent of the Gentile quota. A far more complex chart for Germany as a whole in the post-World War I period confirms the above findings and reveals beyond this the existence of a continuous process of proportional increase of the occupational independence among Jews and a corresponding decline of Jewish manual labour, in excess of parallel movements among Gentiles.

Contrary to the opinion of an outstanding authority in the field[27] it is not held here that greater wealth or even higher social status are directly connected with the proportional number of independents in any occupation. In many instances the owners of the smallest shops in crafts and industry may be economically weaker than skilled industrial labour.

[26]In view of the fact that some of the figures pertaining to Jewish physicians were assembled by French authorities at the time of the German occupation in 1941, they have to be viewed with particular caution. These data, as interpreted by Roblin, *op. cit.*, pp. 104ff. are, however, in line with other French statistics in the field.
[27]See Ruppin, *op. cit.*, I, p. 378; see *ibid.*, also p. 365.

In Imperial Germany, where social prestige was foremost related to integration in the official hierarchy of civil service, independence offered at best a vicarious goal to the objective of status acquisition. Yet independence is of considerable significance for two other reasons. It offers great possibilities to make use of personal traits of flexibility, ingenuity and desire for change. Thus indirectly and in the long run such independence contributes to greater occupational and social disparity between Jews and Gentiles. This, however, is the foremost factor in this investigation.

VI. TENTATIVE CONCLUSIONS

We have attempted here to sketch the pattern of two social cycles which have constantly influenced the process of assimilation in exactly the opposite way. One is the horizontal advance of occupational spread within the Jewish community throughout the whole period. This course leads from the narrow confines of the vocational structure of the ghetto gradually to an occupational set-up more similar to — though not fully alike — that of the Gentile environment. This process clearly heads in the direction of lessening the social disparity between Jews and Gentiles. It works toward a corresponding decline in friction and toward a strengthening of the assimilatory process. The other process is vertical. Within each occupational branch, the traditional ones as well as the newly-gained ones, Jews advance to the top at varying but consistently greater speed than the Gentiles. The effect of this movement in the field of social relations is the exact opposite of the horizontal process. It increases and accentuates disparity, it adds to social friction. Even though it may give to individual Jews positions of highly meritorious and generally commended leadership, it works in balance against the success of assimilation.

Taking a long range view one may say that occupational spread was fairly successful in France as well as in Germany, though in France probably more so. There is no question that in either country, as shown in the statistical survey, the horizontal movement was still incomplete by the 1920s, particularly in industry and agriculture. The vertical process of rise in social status within each occupational group on the other hand[28] was generally, and increasingly, operative and clearly observable in any field where Jews believed they could make a gainful and distinguished career. This excluded by and large the potentialities of industrial labour or agricultural workers.

The resultant of both factors, one working in favour of, the other against the success of assimilation, determines the degree of social disparity between Jewish community and Gentile environment. The existence of this disparity to a greater or lesser degree is a cause — though clearly not the only one — of friction

[28]Barring those occupations from which Jews were still practically excluded such as officers in the armed forces (in peace time and with the exception of Bavaria) and many civil service positions in Imperial Germany.

between Jews and Gentiles. This disparity marks and illuminates the Jewish community as a target, if and when such conflict exists:

"In order that resentment and aggression released by economic hardship turn to a specific target, the target must be present in the minds of the embittered. Only because antisemitism already had a place in the political and cultural life of the nation, was it bound to be intensified with every intensification of socio-economic conflicts."[29]

This observation shows clearly why the first process of occupational spread was favourable to the course of assimilation and why the second was adverse, and this far beyond the economic sphere.

The vertical cycle moving toward increased disparity by way of disproportionate Jewish rise in social status is by no means to be equated with intentional selfish action, recklessly directed against the best interests of the Jewish community. It is on the contrary a perfectly typical manifestation of the driving forces of human nature, in operation wherever opportunity exists and where the individual has the necessary skill to make use of it. This moral and psychological explanation of a very human and inevitable process does not dispose of the fact, however, that it is one of the basic premises of social antisemitism. It stands to reason that Jewish improvements in social status, at the time when general economic conditions took an unfavourable turn, invited a harsher reaction than a movement which, in times of prosperity, worked merely at greater speed than that of the Gentile environment. Thus the rise of antisemitism in Germany in the 1870s may have been aggravated by the agricultural crisis and the steady deterioration of the status of the small artisan. In neither occupation were Jews strongly represented. Where the Jews were strong, in finance, banking and industrial management, the business outlook at that time was exceedingly bright. On the other hand, the relatively large quota of Jews among white-collar workers who were the chief victims of the German inflationary period in the 1920s, did not attenuate antisemitic feelings either. In public opinion this factor seemed to be more than balanced by greater potentialities for Jewish participation in public life after the Revolution of 1918, and thus only further illuminated their exposed position. In France similar social-economic cycles did occur, but there the powerful impact of the revolutionary tradition, unparalleled in Germany, radiated even into the darkness of the Boulanger, Dreyfus and Vichy crises.

There seems to be a counter argument against the detrimental influence of social disparity on the assimilatory process. It is the well-trodden way of identification of eminent individual achievement with success of the assimilatory process as a whole. This has already been referred to. Undoubtedly, outstanding services rendered by Jews in leading positions on behalf of the national and international community may have helped in a number of cases — by no means in all — to improve Jewish-Gentile relations. Yet, quite apart from the opposition and envy which many an outstanding achievement evokes, the relationship between outstanding services and high positions is frequently merely accidental.

[29]Massing, *op. cit.*, p. 249.

Besides and above all we are dealing here not with individual cases but with the impact of group movements.

All in all, relative paucity of the data presented here and the manifold variety of causes of antisemitic friction in general does not allow the interpretation of the course of Jewish assimilation in France and Germany by a strictly chronological comparison of social disparity and antisemitic friction. After all, highly important as the factors of occupational spread and social disparity are, Germany and France are not the only countries illustrative for a study of this kind. It might prove extremely interesting to compare conditions in non-feudal countries where social disparity has been reduced to a minimum, with countries of feudal tradition and an assimilation process impeded by excessive social disparity.

The interesting study by S. Kuznet, "Economic Structure and Life of the Jews",[30] arrives at the following conclusions, in some ways differing from mine, and which may be briefly summarized here.

The Jews outside Israel are perceived as permanent minority groups, characterized by and large by the two main factors of belonging to a group and distinctiveness from other groups. Such a static minority group has a deeply entrenched desire for cohesion and living in proximity. If it were otherwise, the group could not survive. But survival under such conditions exposes it to all kinds of restrictions and discriminations essentially dominated by non-economic motives on the Jewish as well as on the Gentile side. Furthermore Kuznet makes the point that the concept of "normal" Jewish social structure needs clarification.

Undoubtedly Kuznet's concept of the dominance of non-economic motives channelling the evolution of the Jewish social structure is correct. The question of the criteria of normalcy may be debatable, though it seems to me not entirely germane to our problem insofar as the question not of an abstract normalcy, but merely of deviation of the social structure of the Gentile world is the issue at stake.[31]

The main point of divergence on which Kuznet's and my own opinion hinges seems to me, however, the question of the static character of the minority which would lose its identity if it should overcome the needs for proximity and cohesion. Should this conclusion be proved as fully correct by pragmatic historical experience, then Kuznet's case would be strong indeed pertaining to the past, though, of course, it would still not decide the issue for the future.

I strongly believe, however, that this evidence does not at all point one way. As I see it, the history of the last three generations in Western Europe and America shows significant trends which reveal that the preservation of the identity of Jewry is neither exclusively nor necessarily determined by the factor of cohesion and proximity.

---

[30]In L. Finkelstein, *loc. cit.*
[31]*Ibid.*, see particularly pp. 1600ff. and 1658ff.

Additional studies in this field may well be based on testing of the following general propositions:

1. There is good reason to believe that horizontal occupational spread in the service of assimilation will continue.

2. There are equally sound reasons for the assumption that a vertical movement toward leading positions, by and large harmful to the process of assimilation, will likewise continue.

3. Either conclusion is backed by historical evidence throughout the assimilatory process of two foremost Western countries, France and Germany.

4. Germany, where social disparity became more conspicuous than in France, experienced the far more severe crisis in Jewish-Gentile relations.

5. This does not mean that social disparity is the unique or primary cause of friction between Jews and their Gentile environment. It does mean that disparity in the sense of exposure as a target is the premise of such friction.

6. The above assumption in no way implies a moral value judgment of the vertical cyclic process toward leading positions in various occupational groups. It is held here that this movement is a natural outcome of the free play of forces. It is intrinsically connected with the competitive aspects of human progress.

7. On the basis of the foregoing, two types of conflict must be faced. It is conceivable that the interest of the individual in personal progress may collide with that of the group. What is more important, the vertical cycle outlined above may be undesirable as impediment of the assimilatory process, but in a wider sense it may be constructive as incentive to human progress.

8. Such conflicts, seemingly inevitable in present-day society, may in the long run be remedied by progress in the direction of human reason rather than social affluence.

A Financial Tycoon

"Windsor-Cassel" - The Last Court Jew

Prolegomena to a Biography of Sir Ernest Cassel*

BY KURT GRUNWALD

FOREWORD

The story of Sir Ernest Cassel forms a fascinating chapter in the history of Jewish emancipation and assimilation, as well as in the record of that Jewish enterprise which had a significant share in the economic development of Europe and overseas. By the turn of the century this man of German-Jewish origin had become one of the most powerful figures in the very centre of money-power, the City of London, and influential at the Court of St. James.

If no full biography has been written hitherto, this seems to be due, primarily, to the absence of records. Cassel himself, in his talks with the Viennese journalist Sigmund Münz, in 1910, expressed his rather negative attitude towards historiography. He destroyed his correspondence with the late King Edward VII. In all the histories of Edward there is bound to be a gap that only Cassel could have filled, but he was no writer, nor did he consider it his duty to add to the historical knowledge of later generations.[1] Thus, he had probably also ordered that his own records should be destroyed. The present writer obtained confirmation that none were kept from Cassel's nephew, Sir Francis Cassel[2] and from the husband of his late grand-daughter, Viscount Mountbatten of Burma.[3]

Some of Cassel's letters, however, may still be found in the archives of his friends and associates. From the almost weekly exchange of letters over a period of forty years with Jacob H. Schiff, it is very likely that some are preserved in the American Jewish Historical Archives, Cincinnati, where part of the Schiff papers are deposited. As Professor Forest MacDonald is now writing a new biography of J. H. Schiff, our knowledge of his relations with Cassel too should soon be enriched. In Göteborg the archives of *Skandinaviska Banken A.B.* and of Cassel's company, the *Trafik A.B. Grängesberg-Oxelösund* probably contain much interesting material. In the course of sifting the archives of the *Deutsche Bank,* now apparently in progress, some other Cassel material may come to light; and in the Public Record Office in London some interesting "Casseliana" might be found. Cassel's correspondence with Max Warburg was destroyed in Hamburg during the war.

Of the notes published on Cassel — mentioned here in chronological order — the ones written on the basis of personal acquaintance are valuable, such as those

*This is a shortened version of a much longer manuscript which unavoidably had to be cut as lack of space prevented publication in full in this Year Book. - Ed.
[1] S. Münz, *Eduard VII in Marienbad*, Wien 1934, p. 217.
[2] Letter of 30.3.1967.
[3] Letter of 21.11.1966.

of Sir Sidney Lee (originally Levy) i.a. official biographer of Edward VII in 1925 and of the author of the article on Cassel in the *Dictionary of National Biography* (1927) who had been in Cassel's service for many years; as are those of the banker Saemy Japhet, the author of *Recollections of my Business Life* (London 1931) and of E. F. Benson, the noted author of *As We Were* (London 1932). P. H. Emden, if he did not know Cassel personally, certainly drew on the knowledge of people who did.

It is on some of these sources that Brian Connell, the biographer of the Mountbattens, leans. He also had the advantage of having at his disposal the unpublished notes of Miss Underhill, Cassel's secretary during the last eight years of his life. Thus his "portrait" of Cassel, apart from being an able appreciation of the man, can be considered an important primary source.

These "prolegomena" to a biography of Ernest Cassel are intended to shift the emphasis on Cassel as a Jew and as an entrepreneur and to probe deeper than was done before, as far as the sources permit. It is, admittedly, only a beginning, which, we hope, may encourage others to continue along the indicated lines.

I. THE LAST COURT JEW

When King Edward, after an enjoyable evening at the St. James's Theatre, asked the Marquis de Soveral whether he, too, had seen Oscar Wilde's new play *The Importance of being Earnest,* Lisbon's witty envoy answered, "No, Sire, but I have seen the importance of being Ernest Cassel."[4]

This often quoted witticism of the Portuguese diplomat, himself a favourite at Edward's court and in London Society, throws light on the extraordinary position held in those days by Sir Ernest Cassel, whose intimate relationship with the King had earned him the nickname "Windsor Cassel".

Cassel's position was, indeed, a unique one. He, as Emden put it

> ". . . fits into no category and cannot be classified under any heading; he was not a banker, nor the head of any great business house, he presided over no board and was not even a director in any of his companies. Yet, for many years, he was one of the most powerful, if not the most powerful financier who, in intimate friendship with most of the prominent people of two continents, acquired a unique personal position. He combined the art of a finished diplomatic negotiator with the gifts of a never-failing visionary, was perfectly straightforward in his methods, and reliability and discretion were the key-notes of his success."[5]

or as Sir Robert Vansittart said:

> "He exercised great influence in his time, not only in his own right as a magnate of money, but by acting as financial advisor to the King and all of the King's friends of both sexes. His shrewd judgment was of use to everybody, including himself and the nation."[6]

[4]See B. Connell, *Manifest Destiny*, London 1953, p. 66.
[5]P. H. Emden, *Jews of Britain*, London 1943, p. 334.
[6]Vansittart, *The Misty Procession*, London 1938, p. 61.

The period of Cassel's active business life, 1870-1910, was a time of rapid expansion of the world economy under the impact of a buoyant industrial capitalism, some aspects of which have led to its being stigmatized as the Age of Imperialism. In this period Cassel operated on a global scale, developing the Swedish iron and steel industry, railways in the U.S. and Mexico, building Nile dams in Egypt, forming central banks and agricultural banks in the Middle East.

It was, as Emden says,[7] his business to make money, and he made it in a relatively short time, not by extracting money from the countries where he operated but by enriching them. A "creative capitalism" distinguished his operations throughout.

They stand favourable comparison with many of the major, well-advertised projects in the developing countries of our own days. Some of these enterprises may have been inspired by his proximity to the throne. In this respect his position was unique indeed.

It was due to Cassel's sound financial advice that the Prince of Wales could indulge in the costly pastimes which he enjoyed so much and that his keeper of the Private Purse, Sir Dighton Probyn, could inform a surprised (parliamentary) commission set up to inquire into the financial position of the new sovereign, that Edward VII had ascended the throne "unencumbered by a single penny of debt".

Curiously enough, it was another Cassel, Joseph — in fact the first one of this name on record — who two centuries before had filled an almost identical position at the Court of the Wittelsbach Prince Elector at Cologne, the city in which Sir Ernest was born.

II. THE ANCESTORS

The art of finance seems to have been in the blood of the Cassels, ever since we find records of men of this name. The first, Joseph Cassel, was Court Jew to the Wittelsbach Prince Elector Joseph Clemens (1671-1723), Archbishop of Cologne from 1688.[8] Joseph Clemens introduced the system of the Court Jews to Cologne, as he found the subsidies of Louis XIV insufficient to satisfy his own expensive political ambitions and his lust for luxury.[9]

Joseph's son Hirtz Cassel (II) (ca. 1715) was Purveyor to the Court, and his grandson Meyer Cassel (III) held the lease on the elector's mint at Bonn during 1748-50, but moved later to Deutz. Of the latter's son, Joseph (IV) (1745-1781 or 1805?), the profession is unknown. He lived in Deutz, apparently in good circumstances, as he and his wife (née Hackenbroch) were able to present the synagogue there with a curtain for the *Tora* shrine. His son Moses, or Moises Joseph (V) (1771-1829; wife Gudula, née Wolff) had had a small bank — *Wechselstube* — in Cologne since 1822 which his son, Jacob (VI) (1802-1875)

[7]Emden, *Jews of Britain*, p. 334.
[8]F. L. Carsten, 'The Court Jews', *LBI Year Book III* (1958), p. 143.
[9]W. Treue, in *Monumenta Judaica*, Cologne 1963, p. 422.

inherited from him. Ernest Cassel (VII) was the youngest of Jacob's three children.[10]

The Cassels were a wide-spread family. Most of them, probably, were offspring of Joseph Cassel's sons.

Not long after Joseph Cassel (I) we come across another Court Jew, Loeb Benedict Cassel, who, coming from Offenbach, had settled in Friedberg (Hesse) in 1759 and had become the financial agent of the Count *(Burggraf)* of Friedberg. His son David Loeb Cassel (1766-1847), later known as Leopold Casseller, had become the founder of an important commercial enterprise in Frankfurt a.M.[11]

We do not know whether Loeb Benedict was among the ancestors or relatives of Ernest Cassel, nor one Wolf Cassel,[12] who obtained permission to settle in Cologne in 1798 (the same year, incidentally, as Salomon Oppenheim, who in 1801 transferred there the bank which he had established in Bonn in 1789 and which is still flourishing today). They were the first Jews to be allowed to settle in Cologne after three centuries, a right which not even the Archbishop could obtain for his Court Jews. Salomon Oppenheim became head of the young Jewish community, on whose council we find, from 1850, a Jacob Cassel, a cousin of Ernest's father, also named Jacob.[13]

In 1808, when on Napoleon's order the Jews had to adopt customary Christian names, we find in the *Register* of Names of the Jews of Cologne, as No. 18, Wolfgang, originally Wolf Cassel, still a bachelor at the age of thirty. In the same *Register* is listed as No. 9 Henri (Hayem) Cassel, a pawnbroker, aged thirty-four, with wife and four children (an older brother?), to whom the mayor of the city referred as a "solid citizen" *(guter Bürger)*.[14]

We have referred to Ernest's father's cousin Jacob Cassel, who in 1850 was one of the three elected as the leaders of the Jewish Community Council. In 1853 he was elected again, though as a deputy-councillor only.[15] But in 1864 he was among those who established the separatist, strictly traditional orthodox "Adass Yeshurun Synagogue" because they opposed the reform tendencies gaining strength in the community, which they feared would result in the alienation of youth from Judaism. In this synagogue Jacob Cassel, on the high holidays, took over part of the services in an honorary capacity, relieving the official cantor. And we are told that "the highly musical Cassel" instructed other members in the synagogal melodies.[16]

[10]Information received from Dr. Salomon Wolf, Jerusalem, historian of the Jews of Cologne.
[11]H. Gerlach, 'Ein grosser Frankfurter Handelsmann', *Frankfurter Allgemeine Zeitung*, 30.11.66.
[12]Z. Asaria, *Die Juden in Köln*, Cologne 1959, p. 65.
[13]Information from Dr. S. Wolf. See note 10.
[14]A. Kober, 'Das Namensregister der Kölner Juden von 1808', in *Mitteilungen des Gesamtarchivs der Deutschen Juden*, Berlin 1926, vol. 16.
[15]Carl Brisch, *Geschichte der Juden in Köln und Umgebung*, Mülheim a. R. [1879].
[16]Dr. S. Wolf, *Geschichte der Synagogen - Gemeinde Adass Jeschurun Köln*, 1957, p. 13 (Manuscript in the Jewish Historical Archives, Jerusalem; partly reproduced in Asaria, *op. cit.*, p. 246).

The other Jacob Cassel, Ernest's father, "had a small banking business in Cologne which yielded a moderate competence."[17] It had been established, as mentioned before, by his father. Ernest, born in Cologne on the third of March 1852, was the youngest of the three children of Jacob Cassel (died 1875) by his wife Amalia née Rosenheim (died 1874). His older brother Max (b. 1848) died in 1875; Ernest was to remain most devoted to his sister.

III. THE EARLY YEARS

"Cassel's early life", as his contemporary, Saemy Japhet,[18] was able to tell, "was happy. Home influence and his school education were in complete harmony, while the surroundings of his home were such as to exercise a wholesome and lasting influence on any intelligent youth." But Cassel's remark in his last year to Miss Underhill, his social secretary: "I think you must have had a very much happier home than I had when I was young," seems to contradict the impression which Japhet had received from Cassel's stories of his youth in Cologne.[19] He was an excellent pupil but left school at the age of fourteen. He entered, as an apprentice, the Bank of J. W. Eltzbacher & Co., whose owners, originally from Amsterdam, had opened in Cologne in 1858 and dealt mainly with financing larger industrial concerns and foreign business. The banks in Cologne became prime movers of the Rhenish industrial and railway development.[20] There is little doubt that the training received in this environment had a lasting effect on Cassel. Soon Cologne became too narrow in scope for his ambition, so in January 1869 he set out for England at the age of sixteen "... with a bag of clothes and his violin — the last occasion on which this musical instrument appears in his story ..."[21], and he arrived in Liverpool as an immigrant. He found a job as a clerk with a firm of grain merchants, Blessing, Braun & Co., who it seems also came from Germany. With them he stayed only a little over a year. In April 1870 he obtained a clerkship with the Anglo-Egyptian Bank in Paris. This, however, was of short duration, as, being a German subject, he had to leave Paris on the outbreak of the Franco-German War. He returned to England "with an introduction to the financial house of Bischoffsheim & Goldschmidt (in London) which was interested in the Franco-Egyptian Bank".[22]

There are several versions of how Cassel came to Bischoffsheim & Goldschmidt. According to the *Times* obituary,[23] it was Baron Hirsch who had introduced

[17]*Dictionary of National Biography (D.N.B.)*, vol. 1912-21, p. 97.
[18]S. Japhet, *op. cit.*, p. 125.
[19]B. Connell, *op. cit.*, p. 85.
[20]W. Treue, *Monumenta Judaica*, p. 445.
[21]Connel, *op. cit.*, p. 57. - It seems that Cassel was heir to his father's cousin's musical gifts. He is said to have been an able performer on the violin and, as he apparently told Benson, as a young boy he had dreamed of becoming a professional artist (Benson, *op. cit.*, p. 235). But "his father [had] offered him the choice of becoming a professional chess player as an alternative to a business career." (Connell, *op. cit.*, p. 56.)
[22]D.N.B., vol. 1912-1921, p. 97.
[23]*The Times*, London, 23.9.1921.

Cassel to them. More dramatic is the story that Cassel, on his return to London, chanced to hear that Louis Bischoffsheim, senior partner of Bischoffsheim & Goldschmidt, was looking for a confidential clerk, whereupon he sent in this application:

> "Dear Sirs,
>
> I apply for the position in your office and refer you to my former chiefs, Messrs. Eltzbacher, Cologne.
>
> Yours sincerely,
>
> Ernst Cassel"

Among the hundreds of applications, mostly in the verbose, flowery and self-praising style of those days, Cassel's straightforward and self-confident note made a deep impression upon Louis Bischoffsheim who said, "That's our man." This version was told by Sir Sidney Lee in 1925.[24] It was repeated by Saemy Japhet, a close business associate and compatriot in 1931, and afterwards by several authors of a later generation.

The account in the *D.N.B.* is reported to have been compiled by Mr. Geddes[25] who had started with Cassel as an office junior in 1893 and finished up as Managing Director of Sir Ernest's company (he died in 1955). It must, therefore, be considered authoritative as well. Münz's story that in 1870 Cassel had found a position with Bischoffsheim & Goldschmidt in Paris, but on the outbreak of the war was recommended by them to their London house, is probably based on hearsay.[26]

In the *Times* version, mentioned above, we are told that in the middle of the seventies Cassel was recommended by Baron Hirsch to Louis Bischoffsheim for some important and intricate job which he carried through with great success and thus became known to a few leading men in the City. According to the *Financial Times* obituary Cassel's rise was much less rapid than commonly supposed. His financial genius was recognised by his amalgamation of Vickers with Barrow Naval Construction (i.e. 1897). He subsequently became associated with Baron Hirsch.

Both these newspaper stories are quoted here, because they point at a special relationship between Cassel and Baron Hirsch, to which we shall revert in due course.

IV. PROVING HIS METTLE

Cassel was soon to show his unusual talents. Within a year his firm sent him to Constantinople, as Connel states, to look into the affairs of a Jewish firm there (in which Bischoffsheim had some interests), which had got into financial

---

[24]Sir Sidney Lee, *King Edward VII*, London 1925, pp. 60-62.
[25]Letter from Lord Mountbatten of Burma, 21.11.1966. - The actual article, however, is signed H. Ch. (Hugh Chisholm) who quotes as a source "Private Information". It would appear that Chrisholm edited a draft supplied by Geddes.
[26]Münz, *op. cit.*, p. 223.

difficulties.[27] It was expected that it would take at least a year to save something from the wreck, yet within three months Cassel was back at Bischoffsheims, investment intact, and with a substantial commission for himself.[28] In 1873, i.e. about the time of the above operation, the Bischoffsheims, jointly with the Ottoman Bank, formed the Bank of Constantinople. This, presumably, is the form which the rescue operation took.

Cassel had started work at an annual salary of £ 200, and then one day Henry Bischoffsheim offered him a rise to £ 500. "You mean £ 5,000, Mr. Bischoffsheim" was Cassel's reply. And Bischoffsheim quickly confirmed: "£ 5,000, of course."

Whether this story is true or not, the spectacular rise in Cassel's salary took place, according to Emden, after he had successfully settled a very complicated and unfortunate engagement "in connection with Nicaragua".[29] The firm had had considerable troubles with loans in many Latin-American countries whose default soon led to the appointment of a Parliamentary Committee in 1875. The enquiry produced criticism of the methods used by loan contractors such as Bischoffsheim & Goldschmidt.[30] The firm certainly offered ample scope to an ambitious and able troubleshooter. By 1878, the year he got married, Cassel had been able to put aside a capital of £ 150,000, largely made on commission earned by the liquidation of troublesome ventures, and probably also on some first investments of his own.

V. A LIFE-LONG FRIENDSHIP

JACOB HENRY SCHIFF (1847 - 1920)

It was Jacob H. Schiff, a native of Frankfurt a.M. who raised Kuhn, Loeb & Co. to a pre-eminence among American private banks, second only to J. P. Morgan & Co. He was a titan in the battles for control of American railroads, allying himself with Edward Harriman against James Hill and J. P. Morgan for control of the Northern Pacific.[31] He directed the firm from 1875 till his death in 1920, raising capital (much of it from Europe) to finance a rapidly industrializing United States.

Schiff's earliest personal relations with railway companies seem to have been i.a. with the Erie, and the Louisville & Nashville,[32] the two railroads in which Cassel was interested, the first on account of Bischoffsheim & Goldschmidt, the latter already on his own account. The reconstruction of the Erie, which, as Emden states, had failed in 1875, was another of Cassel's early successes for his

---

[27]Benson's version is that Cassel was lent by his employers for this task.
[28]Connell, *op. cit.*, p. 57.
[29]Emden, *Jews of Britain*, pp. 334-335.
[30]L. H. Jenks, *The Migration of British Capital to 1875,* New York & London 1927, pp. 269, 421-424; Emden, *Money Powers of Europe in the Nineteenth and Twentieth Centuries*, London 1937, pp. 330, 403; D. Joslin, *A Century of Banking in South America,* London 1963, pp. 9, 63.
[31]*New York Times*, 1.2.1967, on Kuhn, Loeb & Co. Centenary.
[32]C. Adler, *Jacob H. Schiff*, New York 1928, vol. I, p. 50.

firm.[33] And, according to Japhet, it was this business which brought him in contact with Schiff.[34] It was apparently in the spring of 1879 that Cassel, on one of his visits to New York, made Schiff's acquaintance through a mutual friend, Louis Marx. This acquaintance developed into "the closest friendship and the most intimate relationship which Schiff had with any man outside his own family..."[35] About fifteen hundred letters from Schiff to Cassel, dating from 1880, have been preserved,[36] and even the first of these gives some indication of the unique place which Cassel held in the circle of those with whom Schiff and his firm were doing business.[37]

Although Schiff was still a junior member of Kuhn, Loeb & Co., it was to him that Cassel looked for advice on the American market. And Schiff wrote to Cassel on 28.5.1883:

> "For many reasons we are seeking another brokerage connection in London, and while we are daily receiving many offers, our transactions require brokers specially qualified to form a desirable connection for us. It is after all no great feat to execute orders promptly on the Stock Exchange. What we have to stress especially is that our brokers shall always be on the alert, understand the American market well (which can easily be learned with a little practice), and call our attention to possible transactions in London. Their responsibility and credit must be beyond question, so that we can entrust them with large amounts of money; and they must be able to discount our remittances easily, and get renewals for us at the most favourable money rates."[38]

Cassel, at the time that letter was written, was still employed as manager of Bischoffsheim & Goldschmidt, a position from which he resigned a year later. Did that letter induce him to take that step, and was it meant to? After all, he never became a broker, and his relationship with Schiff or Kuhn, Loeb & Co., while it answered many of the requirements outlined in Schiff's letter, was one of principal to principal, and not of principal to agent. Thus Connell's conclusion that Cassel took that letter as a hint to resign from Bischoffsheim & Goldschmidt leaves some doubt in our mind.[39]

The two men had much in common. One of his successors described Schiff as "aggressively ambitious, adventurous, opinionated and strong-willed",[40] while Cassel was described by Margot Asquith as "a man of natural authority... dignified, autocratic and wise; with a power of loving those he cared for..."[41] It seems that these characterizations hold good for both men. They had both risen from a modest German-Jewish middle-class background to pre-eminence in the international financial world in relatively early stages of their careers. Adler calls Schiff "almost straitlaced".[42] Margot Asquith says of Cassel that "he had no small

---

[33]Emden, *Jews of Britain*, p. 335.
[34]Japhet, *op. cit.*, p. 127.
[35]Adler, *op. cit.*, vol. II, pp. 327, 329.
[36]The letters are kept in the American Jewish Historical Archives, Cincinnati.
[37]Adler, *op. cit.*, vol. I, p. 12.
[38]*Ibid.*, vol. I, p. 14.
[39]Connell, *op. cit.*, p. 63.
[40]Cf. note 31.
[41]See Adler, *op. cit.*, vol. II, p. 328.
[42]*Ibid.*

talk and disliked gossip". But in other ways they were as apart as the poles. Both were philanthropists on a large scale, but while Schiff took a deep personal interest in the progress of the many (largely educational) institutions he had generously endowed, this cannot be said of Cassel. He gave lavishly of his money, but not of himself. While Schiff was a deeply religious, observant and loyal Jew, Cassel did not hesitate, though out of loyalty to his dying wife's wishes, to change his religion. And different, too, were the pastimes they liked. Still, they enjoyed spending holidays together, particularly in the Swiss mountains which they both loved, or in Egypt. It was in 1890, in the autumn, when Schiff with his wife and their two children, and Cassel with his sister and her son, were exploring the lower ranges of Mont Blanc, that Frieda, Schiff's daughter (later to become Mrs. Felix Warburg), slipped and fell down a crevasse. Cassel without a moment's hesitation jumped after her and saved her from serious injury apart from a broken shoulder. Schiff, ready to jump after them, was kept back by Cassel's nephew (and later heir to the title) Felix. This incident deepened Schiff's friendship into a boundless devotion to Cassel.[43]

Schiff's almost weekly letters to Cassel over the four decades 1880-1920, which, though primarily devoted to business developments, usually contain family news, reflect an intimacy and warm personal note one rarely finds in a business correspondence. (Unfortunately those of Cassel's letters which may have been preserved in the Schiff archives have not yet been published.)

It had been the affairs of the Erie Railway which, in the late seventies, had brought Cassel to New York, and it had apparently been through him that Schiff had become involved in this business and had joined the board of the Erie company, from which he resigned in 1884.[44] The *D.N.B.*[45] does not mention the name of this company, but refers to Cassel's success, notably in the disentanglement of the affairs of the New York, Pennsylvania & Ohio Railway; British security holders, early in 1883, had arranged a lease to the Erie, a deal considered advantageous to both.[46] In 1893 both railroads were again in difficulties. Cassel and Schiff co-operated in negotiating an extension of maturing Prior Lien Bonds of the New York, Pennsylvania & Ohio. By the end of that year this operation had apparently been successfully concluded, and this seems to have terminated Schiff's and his firm's connection with Erie (and probably also Cassel's, by now on his own).

Schiff's resignation from the Erie board in 1884 may have been prompted by his preoccupation with a new railway business which in that year was suggested to his firm: the Louisville-Nashville Railway. After the financial crisis of 1884, the house of Wertheim & Gompertz, Amsterdam, had invited Kuhn, Loeb & Co. to join them in a syndicate for underwriting an issue of new Adjustment Bonds and Preferred Shares. While Kuhn, Loeb & Co. were unwilling to assume the

---

[43]Connell, *op. cit.*, pp. 63-64.
[44]Adler, *op. cit.*, vol. I, p. 51.
[45]*D.N.B.*, vol. 1912-21, p. 97.
[46]Adler, *op. cit.*, vol. I., p. 52.

moral responsibility for the bonds, they were willing to conduct negotiations for it in the U.S., provided Cassel would do the same in England. While this proposal was not accepted[47], it seems that the syndicate became financially interested in this railroad by the end of 1887. Between that time and the end of 1894 they were active in its development.

There were also other, possibly smaller, railway projects in which Schiff and Cassel were associated. They also co-operated in financing Mexican enterprises, particularly railways. In 1888, 1890 and 1893 Cassel negotiated loans for the Mexican government. When the latter, however, subsequently rejected his well thought out and carefully prepared plans (why, one wonders) he never again touched any business connected in any way with Mexico, a decision, as Emden comments[48], which worked to his advantage.

In 1899 Schiff asked Cassel whether he would be interested in American industrial securities, in which Kuhn, Loeb & Co. were investing, though in moderate amounts owing to the risk involved[49], and thus we see them, in that year, jointly interested in the American Beet Sugar Co.[50] A year later, in 1890, it is Cassel who interests Schiff in the shares of Anaconda, and from then onwards they collaborate with the Guggenheims in the development of their concern,[51] and its financing.

There was another field in which the two co-operated. In 1904, during the Japanese-Russian War, Japan tried to raise a £10 m. loan in London. The London bankers were willing to take up £5 m. at first, with a possible £5 m. to follow at a later date, but Japan needed the whole amount at once. Schiff was then on a visit in London. His sympathies were with Japan. He detested the Czarist regime because of its persecution of the Jews. So, after only short deliberation, apparently also after consultation with Cassel who was well-informed on international relations and economic conditions, he underwrote the other half of the Japanese loan. It was a pioneering enterprise, because the U.S. had not hitherto been a market for government loans. The British government was particularly pleased to be associated in this loan with U.S. interests. Edward VII gave a luncheon for Schiff and Cassel upon the conclusion of the loan negotiations.[52]

Schiff's house consistently refrained from negotiating any loan to Russia, and he disagreed with Cassel, who apparently thought that if the European (Jewish) bankers were to treat Russia, then under Stolypin, in a more conciliatory way, it would be to the advantage of the Russian Jews.[53] And indeed, "offers were made by agents of the Russian government", when Russia was pressed for funds, "to relax the restrictions upon the Jews in a particular province in exchange for a loan of fifty million dollars. Mr. Schiff invariably rejected such advances, declining

[47]*Ibid.*, p. 28.
[48]Emden, *Jews of Britain*, p. 336.
[49]Adler, *op. cit.*, vol. I, p. 27.
[50]*Ibid.*, p. 170.
[51]*Ibid.*, p. 255.
[52]*Ibid.*, p. 213.
[53]*Ibid.*, vol. II, pp. 140, 141.

to buy better treatment for a section of his correligionists which he held should be accorded them as a matter of right".[54] Kuhn, Loeb & Co. raised no loans for the Allies until the fall of the Czarist regime in 1917, when Schiff gave financial support to the Kerensky regime on which he had put high hopes for a betterment of the position of the Jews in Russia.[55] Lord Reading, who headed the British-French financial mission to the U.S. in 1915, appreciated Schiff's attitude.[56] (As Cassel was a member of that mission, it is surprising not to find his name in the Schiff story).

VI. GOLD FOR IRON

One of Cassel's earliest major operations, which took a quarter of a century to bring to its successful conclusion, took place in Sweden. Here he found "the first considerable scope for his abilities and his creative methods".[57]

The Railway Age came to Sweden rather late. Only in 1853/54 had the *Rijksdag* decided that the State was to build the main lines, with the aid of foreign loans, and to leave to private enterprise the construction of secondary lines. The first railway was opened in 1856; in 1862 the important Stockholm-Göteborg main line was completed.[58] The loans for the government-built lines were largely raised in London. And it was also predominantly British capital which had been invested in the construction of secondary lines. Thus the shares of the Royal Swedish Railway Co. Ltd. (incorporated in England in 1852 and opened in 1867), of the Swedish Central Railway Co. Ltd. (formed in 1869 and opened in 1873) and of the Oxelösund Railway were largely in the hands of British investors.[59] Among them were Bischoffsheim & Goldschmidt, who had locked up vast sums in the Swedish Central, which not only brought no return, but seemed to remain a losing venture. Cassel quickly realized not only that the three separate and rival lines which together connected the important iron deposits of Grängesberg with the Baltic port of Oxelösund should be combined in one concern, but also that the earnings and profitability of the railway depended on the quantity of ore carried. The working of the mines, however, proved un-remunerative: there was little demand for this phosphorus ore. But here Cassel was helped by a technological break-through: the invention in 1878/79 by two Englishmen, S. G. Thomas and S. Gilchrist, of the so-called Thomas-Process for the making of basic steel, even from phosphorus ore. It "was an event of world

---

[54]C. Adler, *Jacob H. Schiff. A Biographical Sketch*, New York 1921, pp. 16-17.
[55]*Ibid.*, p. 19.
[56]Adler, *Jacob H. Schiff*, New York 1928, p. 251.
[57]Emden, *Jews of Britain*, p. 335.
[58]I. Anderson, *Schwedische Geschichte*, Munich 1950, pp. 139-140; 404, see also Heckscher, *Economic History of Sweden*, London 1954, p. 219.
[59]Leading among these seems to have been the merchant banking house of Thomas, Bonat & Co., specialists in the Baltic trade, one of the Bank of England houses, which in 1859, jointly with Bischoffsheim & Goldschmidt, had formed a bank in Paris for industrial finance. They seem to have been the principal interested party in the English-Swedish Bank (1867-1870); Jenks, *op. cit.*, p. 176; also E. Soderlund, *Skandinaviska Banken, Dat Svenska Bank-väsendits historia, 1864-1914*, Stockholm 1964, p. 268.

import", as Landes states.[60] Cassel immediately took a deep interest in the new process and he apparently acquired the rights in it for Sweden. More important however: realizing the effect which the Thomas-Process (which had been introduced on the Continent at the same time) would have on the demand for Swedish ore, he bought a substantial interest in the struggling Grängesberg mines and possibly in steel mills and the railway company as well.

As far as the railway business is concerned, in 1883 talks took place on an equitable settlement between the Swedish banks and the English interests, united in the Swedish Association Ltd., a shareholders' pool. Cassel had joined the board of this Association in the summer of 1882 and visited Sweden for the first time in 1883, when an agreement was reached about debt conversion. From 1885 he served also on the board of the mining and railway companies, and became powerful in all the concerns in which the Association had an interest.

Meanwhile the effect of the Thomas-Process made itself felt. Exports rose from practically nil to 17,000 tons, then to 30,000. The railway's capacity was 20,000 and the traffic manager considered this an optimum. But by 1889 the exports to be carried exceeded 100,000 tons and by 1892 125,000 tons. Cassel had taken the sales in hand. So the board had not been wrong when, in spite of the traffic manager's pessimism, it had decided on investing heavily in expansion.

In 1894 Cassel had acquired a large interest in the above mentioned Swedish Association. His plan was to form a new company which would own the three hitherto separate railway concerns and harbour installations at Oxelösund, and have an option on the purchase of the mines. In June 1896 he came to Stockholm, together with his associate, Frederic Warburg, in order to carry out this scheme. Needing, as he did, local backing for this purpose, he discussed it first with his friends of the *Kreditbolaget*. Theodor Mannheimer, its Managing Director, while willing to join in the venture, objected to a number of details, such as Cassel's idea of selling the shares above par, which he found not suitable for Sweden. The talks with Cassel, according to the archives of the *Kreditbolaget*, were difficult and several times seemed to be on the verge of breaking up. But finally Cassel, who apparently could not find another partner of equal standing and reputation, gave in, also to the bank's insistence that Cassel should not be entitled to decide alone on the policies of the new concern. It was finally decided to incorporate the new concern as the Grängesberg Oxelösund Traffic Company, also owning the mines, with a capital of £995,000 or Kr. 19,050,000 (£785,000 for the railways and £210,000 for the mines). The allotment of *Kreditbolaget* was 2,826,000 Kr., held on its behalf by the Swedish Association. The subscribers were:

E. Cassel	Kr. 8,780,000
Swedish Association	8,564,000
F. E. Warburg	830,000
John Johnson	112,000
C. F. Liljevatch	674,000
Vollrath Tham	90,000
	Kr. 19,050,000

[60]D. S. Landes, 'Technological Change and Development in Western Europe, 1750-1914', in *Cambridge Economic History*, vol.VI/VII, Cambridge 1965, p. 486.

Cassel returned to Stockholm for the official formation of the company on 30th July 1896. It was not a very harmonious affair.

Mannheimer and Langenskiold disliked Cassel and did not care for his manner. The latter called him "The Great Mogul". Both were critical of his business methods. They were to have many dealings with him in the coming years. Both were on the board of the new company, which Cassel was not, and represented a more conservative element, opposing what they considered speculative expansion. They suspected Cassel of wanting to push up the price of the company's shares in order to sell them at a high price. In 1896 prices had reached 190. In 1897 Cassel, for his sales through a broker firm, realized 155/166, the Swedish Association 170, the *Kreditbolaget* 157/160.

Cassel did not sell below 140, but at this price he sold, even when the market was higher, to friends, bankers as well as to politically influential people and to journalists. Mannheimer called it "Cassel's greasing system". But the *Kreditbolaget* which, as Cassel's bankers, knew of these sales, could do nothing about it but transfer the yield to London. Eventually more than half of the shares were Swedish-held.

The *Kreditbolaget* had every reason to be satisfied with the deal. Not only was it the biggest and most profitable business they had ever had, but they had also gained as a client Sweden's biggest enterprise: the *Grängesberg Traffic Co.* The issue had helped to create a Swedish capital market. Cassel's enterprise had a "multiplier effect" on Sweden's economy which went beyond his own expectations.

The formation of the new concern came as a disappointment to the leaders of the Stockholm *Enskilde Bank*, the Wallenbergs, who had been protagonists of local investment in the mining industry and who had been interested in the Gällivare deposits. "The Englishman" Cassel, who held 95% of the shares of the new concern in his hands, was feared as a powerful opponent who had appeared on the scene and had consolidated his position, securing as an ally that very bank, *Skandinaviska Kredit A.B.*, with which K. A. Wallenberg[61] had been trying to co-operate and which was closely connected with *Skånes Enskilda Bank*[62] (i.e. the biggest Swedish Bank, *S. Kredit A.B.* being the second biggest).

The fear now persisted that Grängesberg would succeed in buying up Gällivare, and if so, it would be with Cassel's money, and ownership would virtually, if not technically — as Cassel was not on the board of directors — be in foreign hands.[63]

---

[61]The Wallenbergs' relations with Mannheimer were somewhat ambivalent. They, like many of the other private bankers, "resented the influence wielded by the cosmopolitans" in Swedish banking. This was true of the limited liability banks whose principal leaders were to a great extent Jews, with strong allegiances in foreign countries as well as in Sweden. This group included such men as Theodor Mannheimer and Henrik Davidson of the Skandinaviska Kredit A.B., Eduard Heckscher of Industrie Kredit A.B., and Louis Fraenckel of A.B. Stockholms Handelsbank. (Olle Gasslander, *History of Stockholm's Enskilde Bank till 1942*, Stockholm 1962, p. 277.)

[62]*Ibid.*, p. 234.

[63]*Ibid.*, p. 366.

Meanwhile Grängesberg was accused of doing its best to injure the reputation of its competitor.[64] And, after the attempt to make the government take over these mines had failed, Grängesberg in July 1903 succeeded in buying them. K. A. Wallenberg's letter to his brother at that time is an interesting postscript to that transaction:

> ". . . I am very glad to have finished with the mining business up there, and the right people have not got control, though the way it all happened has been nothing but scandalous. The very people who for years had been trying to undermine the whole thing by chatter and gossip and press intrigue have now rushed to buy, and paid far more than we thought reasonable. Last year Luorsavaara was supposed a rotten swindle, but now its 1,00 Kr. shares are worth 2,800 Kr. a piece. And the safety of our country has been preserved because Cassel, the London Jew, directs the companies!"[65]

VII. ARRIVÉ

Cassel, then, was already in flourishing circumstances when in 1878 he married Annette, daughter of Robert Thompson Maxwell of Croft House, Croft, Darlington. On the day of his marriage he became a British subject by legal naturalization. A happy married life was cut short by the early death of his wife in 1881, three years later. By her dying wish, not to be separated in the life hereafter, Cassel agreed to accept her creed, i.e. the Catholic faith, a fact which during his lifetime became known to few, and generally known only at his funeral.

"The interest in Sweden... laid the foundation of Cassel's fortune which in 1881, before he had reached the age of thirty, was already estimated to amount to £150.000."[66] And, adds the *D.N.B.*, "in the next fifteen years [i.e. by 1896] the increasing magnitude of his operations made him one of the wealthiest and most powerful financiers in the City of London.[67]

His association with the Bischoffsheims until 1884 was more on a profit-sharing than on a salaried basis. He never became a partner. And even when he severed his official connections with them and started out completely on his own, he continued to occupy part of their premises in Throgmorton Street. Only in 1898 did he take an office of his own in Old Bond Street which he occupied till he retired from active business in 1910.[68]

At first, in his independent business life, he had no success and we do not know precisely when Cassel's fortune changed, nor how, but it seems that the turning point must have been in about 1888/89. In 1899 Cassel tranferred his residence from 2 Orme Square, Bayswater, what would have been an "upper-middle class" address, to 48 Grosvenor Square, a distinctly "superior" address. Here he stayed until moving, in 1908, into his new and palatial "Brook House"

[64]*Ibid.*, p. 375.
[65]*Ibid.*, p. 378.
[66]Emden, *Jews of Britain*, p. 335.
[67]*D.N.B.*, vol. 1912-21, p. 97.
[68]*Ibid.*

on Park Lane.[69] This change of addresses can be taken as an expression of his rising fortunes.

We may guess that it was his meeting with Baron Maurice de Hirsch, Bischoffsheim's brother-in-law, which was of decisive importance for Cassel's career. Hirsch, as Saemy Japhet recalls:

> ". . . recognized genius wherever he found it. His admiration drew him to Cassel. He sponsored him in business as well as socially, and promised him that whenever he wanted to do some big thing on his own account he would support him to the fullest extent. From that moment Cassel became a power in the City. Even before that he had done business on his own account, under conditions that were sometimes difficult. Now, however, he was independent and on a level with the big City houses. And he made use of his opportunities."[70]

When Hirsch died in 1896, Cassel became one of the executors under his will. And more than that; Hirsch had been private banker and financial adviser to the Prince of Wales. Cassel, who had apparently been introduced to the Prince at a race-meeting about that time, "was to improve on these two functions. Where Hirsch had been an intimate, Cassel was to become Edward VII's closest personal friend".[71]

VIII. SOME IMPORTANT "MINOR" BUSINESSES

In 1897 Cassel was instrumental, so the *D.N.B.* records [72], in purchasing the Barrow Naval and Shipbuilding Construction Company for amalgamation with Vickers Sons & Co., and, after the merger of the Maxim Gun and Nordenfelt companies, in acquiring this combine also for Vickers. For some years thereafter he underwrote the chief financial issues for the Vickers company and its subsidiaries. Maxim Guns & Ammunition was bought for £1,353,334 and the whole sum was paid promptly, partly in cash, with Cassel's aid, and partly in Vickers shares.[73]

R. Neumann recalls that the *Economist* (1913/14) had to admit that the Foreign Office, in the course of its diplomatic labours, saw to it that Vickers and Armstrongs (then still competitors) got orders for munitions. The biggest English bankers (Rothschild, Cassel) made similar conditions when they were granting loans to foreign governments.[74]

As the *D.N.B.* tells us, Cassel took a leading part in the financing of the Electric Traction Co. Ltd. formed in 1894, which a year later underwrote the Central London Railways. It was opened in 1900, connecting the Bank with Shepherds Bush, and became popular as the Twopenny Tube.[75] As the

[69]*Ibid.*, p. 99.
[70]Japhet, *op. cit.*, p. 127.
[71]Connell, *op. cit.*, p. 65. On Hirsch and Edward VII see also S. Adler-Rudel, 'Moritz Baron Hirsch' in *LBI Year Book VIII* (1963), p. 38.
[72]*D.N.B.*, vol. 1912-21, p. 98.
[73]R. Lewinsohn, *The Man behind the Scenes -The Career of Sir Basil Zaharoff*, London 1929, p. 96.
[74]R. Neumann, *Zaharoff, the Armaments King*, London 1938, p. 157.
[75]*D.N.B.*, vol. 1912-21, p. 98; see also Emden, *Jews of Britain*, p. 337.

Times obituary comments,[76], the enterprise, though considered a great boon for London, was not a source of much profit to its promoters. Cassel himself remarked some time after the opening of the line, that the best way of making money would have been to let somebody else build it and to buy the land at its western terminal. There were discussions of other projects, such as a great shipping merger in 1902 or the establishment of huge steel works in India,[77] which, however, apparently came to naught.

IX. CASSEL IN EGYPT

In supplementing Lord Millner's classic *England in Egypt* (1889) by an appendix on the years 1892 to 1898, Sir Clinton Dawkins notes that... "The year *1898 will be a landmark* in the story of the British occupation".
In that year

> "the foundation stone was laid for the great Assuan dam, which will change the face of the country and constitute one of the noblest monuments to civil rule in the world. A first blow has been struck at the international top-hamper of modern Egypt by an arrangement for securing the extinction of the Daira Sanieh Debt in 1905. The increased facilities for credit afforded by the establishment of the National Bank with a right to issue notes will meet the need of commercial expansion and help to lower the rate of interest in the provinces."[78]

In February, 1898, the contract was signed for the construction of the Assuan dam and the Assiut Barrage, on June 21st the contract for the sale of the Daira Sanieh Estates was completed and on June 25th the Decree was promulgated for the creation of the National Bank of Egypt.[79] In his notes Sir Clinton omitted to mention, probably quite unintentionally, that it was one man, Ernest Cassel, who had made possible the realization of these three major and vitally important enterprises. Since law and order had been restored in Egypt, foreign capital had flowed into the country in a steady stream, but the importance of British investments had remained far below those of France, until Cassel's appearance on the banks of the Nile.

Cassel, as the *D.N.B.* states, had been interested in Egypt from early years.[80] As we have seen, he had been employed, though for a short while only in 1870, by the Anglo-Egyptian Bank in Paris, and during his years with the Bischoffsheims he had, no doubt, become well acquainted with the affairs of the Franco-Egyptian Bank, their affiliate since 1868.

The policy of increasing the water sources had started to occupy the authorities in the early nineties. By 1895 the technical questions seemed to have been solved. The cost of the whole scheme, prepared by Sir William Garston, providing for a dam at Assuan, a barrage at Assiut and accessory works,

[76]*The Times*, London, 23.9.1921.
[77]Reginald Viscount Esher, *Letters and Journals*, vol. I, pp. 332, 338-339.
[78]A. Milner, *England in Egypt*, 7th ed., London 1898, p. 380.
[79]*National Bank of Egypt, 1898-1948*, Cairo 1948, p. 15.
[80]*D.N.B.*, vol. 1912-21, p. 98.

was estimated at E£ 2,000,000. (It actually exceeded E£ 3,450,000 by its completion in 1902.)

Political difficulties prevented an early implementation of the project. The *Caisse de la Dette* (composed of representatives of France, England, Germany, Austria, Russia and Italy) which then controlled Egypt's finances, demanded that the contract be put up for tender. The government objected, claiming that the tendering firms would require at least two years to study the scheme and on receipt of their offers six months would be required to study the plans submitted, so that precious years would be lost; while a reputable firm of high standing, Messrs. Aird & Co., were willing to execute the Garston scheme straightaway. But time was lost, nevertheless, while an International Commission, as was usual in such disputes, sat on the scheme; eventually the contract was signed with Messrs. Aird. Of course the question arose of how to finance the scheme. Cassel was approached — by whom we do not know — and readily accepted the financial responsibility to the contractors. The Egyptian government undertook to repay him in a series of sixty half-yearly instalments of £78,613, from the date of the completion of the scheme. These payments corresponded to a thirty years' loan of £2 million at 6%. Thus Cassel earned the merit of bringing the scheme to accomplishment.

Cassel's second major transaction in that year, the *Daira Sanieh,* may have been an outcome of the first. It was evident that with the forthcoming availability of larger irrigation facilities, land prices were bound to rise sky-high. Thus investment in land was sound business. And an interesting proposition was soon made to Cassel by the Cairo banker Raphael Suares of Suares Bros., an old-established house of merchant-bankers. This firm had obtained the concession (or option thereof) for the purchase of the *Daira Sanieh* Estates for E£6 million, as well as for the establishment of the National Bank. Unwilling or unable to provide the entire capital necessary for the two ventures, Suares embarked for Europe and was advised to see Cassel. Offering a fifty percent share in the *Daira* scheme, Cassel said, "I know nothing of this class of business; what do you think it ought to yield?" When Suarez answered that he was looking for a profit of about E£ 1 million, the deal was concluded. Suarez's suggestion of Sir Eric Palmer, then Financial Adviser to the government at Cairo, as future head of the projected National Bank met with Cassel's approval.

The *Daira Sanieh* Estates (sugar plantations) had been pledged by the former *Khedive Ismail* as collateral for a loan in 1870 of £7,142,860 (of which he had actually received 75%, i.e. £5 million, from the Bischoffsheims) or over £9 million with accrued interest charges.[81] These estates were administered by a board of three, i.e. an Egyptian Director-General, one British and one French Controller, but showed a loss up to 1891 and unsatisfactory profits thereafter. Therefore, the option given to Suares for the purchase of the estates for £6,481,500, was to "free the administration of a millstone round its

[81]D. S. Landes, *Bankers and Pashas*, London 1963, pp. 339-340.

neck"; eventually the sales yielded over £13 million, which left a profit of over £6 million, of which the government got half, and one half went to the Suares-Cassel group. With them were associated a French group, headed by M. Cronier, which had just taken over the sugar works and refineries.[82]

The *Daira* transaction was apparently carried through by a limited company, the Deferred Shares of which were held by the concessionaires. They were quoted in 1905 at £108 (nominal value £1), ex £78 paid to the holders in the previous October. The manager of the *Daira Sanieh* Estates on behalf of Cassel was Victor Harari Pasha, who had resigned from the Ministry of Finance after years of distinguished service. But these substantial profits, so Guernville tells us, were nothing compared with those of the buyers of the land who had put up a down-payment with bills for the balance. Parcels were re-sold repeatedly before being eventually registered in the name of the final owner in 1905.[83]

Less fortunate was the French group, which had acquired the Sugar Works and Refineries of Egypt. Because of extreme mismanagement these were brought to the verge of bankruptcy. M. Cronier committed suicide (1904?) and another manager died suddenly. To save the basically sound enterprise from complete collapse, Cassel, Suares and other capitalists offered financial assistance on condition that the shareholders agreed to a standstill and did not force liquidation.[84]

The crowning event of that eventful year 1898 was the formation of the National Bank of Egypt Ltd. with an initial capital of £1,000,000. Of this Cassel subscribed 50,000 shares of £10 each, Messrs. C. M. Salvage, Alexandria, and Messrs. R. Suares Brothers & Co. 25,000 shares each. While the last two appear as corporate body, each subscribing for a quarter of the capital, Cassel appears in his own name only. But he, too, seems to have acted on behalf of a group. According to Crouchly, the Bank was formed "by a group of London financiers under Sir Ernest Cassel, in conjunction with some of the most important representatives of the local private banking houses".[85] The Bank, as Crouchly states, "was successful at once, as it had on the board the private bankers Cattaui, Rolo, Suares and Beyerli, who were closely connected with local trade and industry".[86]

In 1899 the Bank opened a Department for Agricultural Loans, lending to the peasants at 9%, a low rate compared to what the fellah usually had to pay to the money-lender. Loans were usually seasonal, secured by a lien on the crop. In 1902 it was set up separately (apparently at Lord Cromer's suggestion) as the Agricultural Bank of Egypt and financed (under Cassel's leadership) with £2,000,000. It was a pioneering venture in a country like Egypt, though its operations were handicapped in that it could not help the smaller cultivators

[82]A. B. Guernville, *New Egypt*, London 1905, pp. 52-53.
[83]*Ibid.*, p. 53.
[84]*Ibid.*, p. 69.
[85]A. E. Crouchly, *The Investment of Foreign Capital in Egyptian Companies and Public Debt*, Cairo 1936, p. 32.
[86]*Ibid.*, p. 32.

Sir Ernest Cassel

Cassel's daughter Maud

Cassel and grand-daughter Edwina

HENRY LOUIS BISCHOFFSHEIM
from a contemporary cartoon

JACOB HENRY SCHIFF
(1847 - 1920)

very much, owing to its inability to lend on the security of land inalienable under the Five Feddan Law. It was for this reason that in 1931 its place was taken by a kind of central bank for co-operative credit institutions.

The Bank, incidentally, must have benefited not only the cultivators, but its shareholders as well. The Founder Shares of a nominal value of £5 were worth £800 in 1905.[87]

From 1914 on Cassel was deeply involved in Egyptian affairs. He visited Egypt frequently, sometimes in the company of his friends, like the Schiffs, on holiday or on business. From the Diaries of Wilfred Scawen Blunt, the famous explorer and advocate of Egyptian nationalism in imperialist Britain, we know that some of these visits also had political purposes.

On June 25, 1903, he records in *My Diaries*: "The *Khedive* arrived in London yesterday, and is staying with the King's millionaire, Cassel, in Grosvenor Square."[88] And in the following pages we learn directly and from gossip (which is an important source for Blunt in general) that the *Khedive* had been prevented from visiting his friend (Blunt), as Cassel had advised him not to do so because it might offend the King (with whom Blunt apparently was persona non grata).[89]

In March, 1904 we learn from Blunt that Cromer was angry because "Cassel had lent His Highness half a million at 2½ percent to speculate with while Gorst as Financial Adviser granted Cassel concessions. The Khedive has been lectured and told to choose between being a Khedive or a tradesman. Gorst has had to leave Egypt..." (Cromer's regret in his annual report on Gorst's return to Britain was, for Blunt, just hypocrisy.) In the same entry we are told about various requests for concessions in Egypt . . . "Cassel, too, has been in treaty for a concession of all government land in Upper Egypt for some other prodigious sum . . ."[90] A month later, on April 5, 1904, Carton de Wiart said to Blunt that Cassel was a very bad influence on the *Khedive* in that he encouraged him in all his irregularities. Cromer disapproved of Gorst's intimacy with Cassel.[91]

Here our source of information on Cassel in Egypt peters out. Five years later, on August 8, 1909, the Diaries quote the gossipy doctor, Lyne Stevens, relating how the King received Cromer on his return from Egypt . . . to receive the Order of Merit. The King is reported to have said "I am happy to bestow this final honour on you, and all the more so because I hear so good an account of your work in Egypt from my friend Sir Ernest Cassel". This had incurred Cromer's venomous resentment.[92] Many entries in Blunt's Diaries are indicative of the misgivings which the "establishment", the landed aristocracy, had about the rising financial aristocracy, now favoured by the King.

[87]Guernville, *op. cit.*, p. 197.
[88]W. S. Blunt, *My Diaries*, London 1919, vol II, p. 63.
[89]*Ibid.*, p. 81.
[90]*Ibid.*, pp. 90, 91.
[91]*Ibid.*, pp. 97-98.
[92]*Ibid.*, p. 296.

On the philanthropic side of Cassel's activities the travelling eye clinics he endowed must be praised as a truly pioneering venture. Somewhere around 1902 he deposited with Lord Cromer £40,000, the interest on which fund was to be used for the equipping and operation of travelling eye-hospitals for the treatment of the prevalent eye-diseases, such as trachoma.[93]

X. TWO BANKS

A. *The Anglo-Austrian Bank*

A centenary article commemorating the formation of the Anglo-Austrian Bank in 1863 recalled that this Bank, in its varied history, had on occasion served as a field of operations for the two richest lone wolves in European banking, Baron Hirsch and Sir Ernest Cassel.[94]

We do not know what these operations were, nor when precisely Cassel had acquired an interest in this Bank. It had been established in 1863 by the London house of merchant bankers, Glyn, Mills & Co., which acted on Cassel's behalf in other transactions. The Anglo-Austrian had been active in the financing of Baron Hirsch's East Hungarian Railway and in the sale of his *Türkenlose* for the financing of his Oriental Railways. It had been active in the formation of banks in Central Europe and in the financing of industries. In the great crash of 1873 it was severely affected, but was one of the few survivors. Nevertheless, its operations during the next twenty years or so were limited to commercial banking. Only towards the end of the century had it again become a little more active. It seems that about that time Cassel and his friend, Karl Morawitz, one of Baron Hirsch's main assistants in the Oriental Railway venture, acquired larger parcels of shares. Morawitz's career in many respects resembled that of Cassel. He was born in Iglau (Bohemia) on 9th March 1846, and after finishing his education at a commercial high school, he entered the services of the banking firm Lippmann & Sons in Prague and of Philipp Elimeyer at Dresden. Having obtained an introduction to Henry Bamberger, head of the *Banque de Paris et des Pays Bas* he was engaged in 1868 as correspondent, though barely acquainted with French. In 1870, just twenty-four years old, he went to the Ottoman Bank as chief of control and right-hand man of the Bank's head, Charles Mallet. Compelled by the war of 1870 to leave Paris, he went to Vienna, where he had been in contact with Baron Gustav Springer and, introduced by Springer, he joined Baron Hirsch as financial manager of the Oriental Railways and later on as a member of their board. He maintained his residence at Brussels, though he spent more time in Paris and London. In 1885 he moved to Vienna and was in 1893 co-opted on to the board of the Anglo-Austrian Bank. In 1906 he was elected its president. The capital was increased from 48 to 60 million crowns, of which Cassel took one part and the Paris

---

[93]Guernville, *op. cit.*, p. 197.
[94]*Börsen-Zeitung*, 'Geschichte einer untergegangenen Bank', 5.9.1863.

Rothschilds another. Baron Gustav Springer, Alfred Rothschild's brother-in-law, became their representative on the board, which was joined also by the Bohemian coal magnate, Ignaz Petschek. In London an Advisory Council functioned, of which two partners of leading London merchant bankers were officials, and Cassel and some of his friends, like Joseph Chamberlain, were unofficial members.[95]

The secretary to the new president was the young Viennese economist, Felix Somary (orginally Smaragd) who was to become a well-known figure in international economic relations in due course. His memoirs, apart from some information on the Bank's history of expanding business, contain a few interesting episodes about meetings with Cassel in London and at his summer place at Riederfurka in the Swiss mountains. In the very early weeks of the new administration, the Bank, against its better judgment, yielded to the pressure of the Austrian government to participate in a loan to Russia, to be subscribed in Paris, Berlin and Vienna. The Viennese board had to agree without being able to consult with their London associates and Somary was sent to London to smooth their ruffled feelings.

Under Morawitz's direction, and with the backing of directors like Cassel, the Bank gained in profits and in standing. But the dissolution of the Habsburg empire in 1918 also sealed the Bank's fate. It eventually went into voluntary liquidation.

B. S. Japhet & Co.

In 1910 Cassel joined the private banking firm of S. Japhet & Co., London, as a sleeping partner with a capital of £200,000. Saemy Japhet, who came from Frankfurt, had originally opened his London bank as a branch. But in the course of time London had become the principal place of business. The continental branches were eventually sold. Japhet had the *Darmstädter Bank* as *commanditaire*, the agreement with which was due to expire at the end of 1909. Anxious to give his bank an English character, Japhet was looking for a replacement, and decided to approach Cassel directly. As he tells in his Recollections:

> "Cassel was the best listener I have ever met, but on the other hand I was more than careful not to say one word which was not absolutely necessary. So I remained silent after my first short statement, and he answered: 'I have always heard nothing but good about you and your firm and I am prepared to accept your offer . . .' "[96]

How accommodating Cassel could be in business dealings is shown in this case. He did not hesitate for one minute to annul a clause in the contract (which had remained from the old contract with the *Darmstädter Bank*) that displeased his partner-to-be. It was one forbidding Japhet & Co. permanent participation in any other firm.

[95] F. Somary, *Erinnerungen aus meinem Leben*, Zürich 1959, pp. 45, 47.
[96] S. Japhet, *op. cit.*, pp. 104-105.

When in 1921 S. Japhet & Co. became a limited company, Cassel took up a considerable parcel of shares and nominated (Sir) Sidney Peel[97] to the board, on which he served till his death in 1938. Thereafter Cassel's estate was represented on the board by his nephew, Sir Felix Cassel.[98]

XI. CASSEL AND "THE ESTABLISHMENT"

A. An Expensive G.C.B.

Cassel, as Lord Vansittart described him "... was a man of dour appearance, much generosity and considerable ambitions, which included power and a childish desire for the Grand Cross of the Bath..."[99] Indeed, as Magnus put it, Cassel's "austere personal habits... were not reflected in his attitude to decorations. He considered that he was entitled to purchase what he required."[100] These remarks refer to an incident which took place in 1908 when the Foreign Office was forced by the necessity of supporting British interests in Morocco to obtain a substantial sum for strengthening the Bank of Morocco (of which Cassel had been a co-founder in 1906). It was for this reason that Sir Edward Grey approached Cassel for a loan of £500,000 to that institution. Cassel agreed readily, but in return asked for the Grand Cross of the Order of the Bath. Grey was somewhat taken aback by this request, and stated that it was not in his power to grant it, but that he would report it to the Prime Minister.[101] And in 1909 Cassel finally achieved his ambition, and obtained the G.C.B. "Although displeased the King made no difficulty; and Grey", as Magnus says, "who cared personally as little for honours as he did for the great financier, was much amused."[102] But the incident was not forgotten by the "Establishment". As Lord Hardinge tells in his memoirs, he "got even with Cassel though he did not know it".[103] Hardinge refers here to the fact that he had advised Sir H. Babbington-Smith[104] to refuse the appointment as head of the National Bank of Turkey — in which Cassel had a share — at anything less than £10,000 a year, i.e. three times as much as Cassel had offered. Cassel finally gave in to this claim and Hardinge comments as follows: "This little transaction gave me great pleasure as a set-off to Cassel's G.C.B."[105]

Nor did Asquith and Grey seem to have forgotten the incident. In 1913 a list was prepared of about three hundred names of possible candidates for the peerage

[97]Lord Esher speaks of Sidney Peel, Cassel's right-hand man, as a man with an unusual flair for finance and especially for *haute finance*. It appears that Morley wanted to take Peel away from Cassel. Esher, *op. cit.*, vol. II, p. 175.
[98]Emden, *Jews of Britain*, pp. 337-338.
[99]Vansittart, *op. cit.*, London 1938, p. 61.
[100]Philip Magnus, *King Edward the Seventh*, London 1964, p. 259.
[101]Lord Hardinge of Penshurst, *Old Diplomacy*, London 1947, p. 164.
[102]Magnus, *op. cit.*, p. 259.
[103]Hardinge, *op. cit.*, p. 165.
[104]Sir Henry Babbington-Smith had been British representative at a series of congresses on financial matters, including the Ottoman Public Debt, and had also been Secretary to the Post Office, 1903-1909, when he became President of the National Bank of Turkey.
[105]Hardinge, *op. cit.*, p. 165.

to be submitted to the King in case the "packing" of the House of Lords should become necessary. We find among them names like those of Sir Edgar Speyer, the Rt. Hon. Arthur Cohen, Sir A. D. Kleinwort, Henry Oppenheim, R. C. Lehmann, N. Seligman, etc. as prospective peers, but Sir Ernest Cassel's name is strikingly absent.[106]

B. Frustrated in Egypt and Frustrated in Turkey

It was about the time of the affair of the Moroccan loan that Cassel happened to cause irritation to another section of the Establishment in an incident which Ronald Storrs recalls. Speaking of Sir Eldon Gorst, Cromer's successor as British Agent in Cairo (1907/08) he says "...By refusing an unneeded and unwanted loan of two million 'to steady the market' he incurred the resentment of high finance at home, thenceforth hostile in the local and the European Press..." And in a footnote he adds an (undated) extract from one of his letters home: "At the Gorst's on Tuesday I met Cassel and Murray Guthrie who are, I am informed, trying to force our government to borrow money from them. We don't want any — but they say we can have it so cheap..."[107]

Vansittart, referring to Storrs' memoirs, confirms the story. He describes Cassel at this occasion as follows:

> "He had grown sadder at the end of his heyday . . . time should never have been allowed to wear away from the memory of Cassel - a benefactor only sometimes self-interested - the noble fact that few men have done more for their fellows than he with his travelling eye-hospitals in a land where ophthalmic diseases claimed never less, and often more than fifty percent of the inhabitants. The fly-borne curse has been upon them since Exodus."[108]

And elsewhere in his book he recalls: "...we might have had the Baghdad Railway Concession, if we had listened to him."[109] Philip P. Graves who as a press-correspondent had shared a flat with Ronald Storrs in Cairo in those days, comments on a loan which Cassel was ready to grant in 1910 to the Young-Turkish government but which was prevented by the intervention of Downing Street, acting under French pressure. Graves says: "He [Cassel] retired angrily, but those who remembered the Press campaign, which he organized against Sir Eldon Gorst, because the British Agent in Egypt did not approve of an unnecessary loan, were not sympathetic."[110]

The comment is misleading. If Cassel "retired angrily", it happened most likely not because of a loss of profit, but because of the shortsightedness of British policy: the loan was granted by the Germans, who thereby re-established their strong position in Constantinople and their influence which four years later was to bring Turkey into the War on their side. It was the political rather than the financial implications of this and some other failures which made the far-sighted Cassel a disappointed man and "at heart the saddest of millionaires..."[111]

---

[106]Roy Jenkins, *Asquith*, London 1964, Appendix A, pp. 539-542.
[107]Ronald Storrs, *Orientations*, London 1939, p. 75.
[108]Vansittart, *op. cit.*, p. 90.
[109]*Ibid.*, p. 61.
[110]Philip Graves, *Briton and Turk*, London 1941, pp. 148-149.
[111]Vansittart, *op. cit.*, p. 61.

XII. . . . AND IN TURKEY

A. The Baghdad Railway

Cassel's preoccupation with schemes in Turkey seem to have anticipated those in Egypt by a decade, though it led to no results until much later. It had been here, actually, that in the early seventies he had had his first great success. He returned to the scene of his early triumph to suffer, as he saw it, his defeat almost four decades later.

On October 4th, 1888 Alfred Kaulla, Director of the *Württembergische Vereinsbank,* acting for the *Deutsche Bank* and the Anatolian Railway Company received a ninety-nine years concession for building a railway from Constantinople to Angora (Ankara). The members of the international *Dette Publique Ottomane* had favoured such a scheme. Its chairman, the British representative on this body, Sir Vincent Caillard, had tried in vain to form a British syndicate to sponsor the project. But the Germans (i.e. the *Deutsche Bank)* eventually made a start, and they had the political backing of Britain, Austria and Italy, all anxious to contain the ever-growing French influence and grip on Turkey.[112]

The line to Angora was completed in less than five years, i.e. by 1893, and at the Sultan's request it was, in spite of serious technical and financial difficulties, extended to Konia, which was reached in 1896.[113]

The Baghdad Railway project became one of the central issues of international politics for almost two decades. When the *Deutsche Bank* had entered the Turkish railway business, Bismarck had raised no objection, but had made it clear that the government accepted no responsibility for the protection of the company. He seems to have foreseen the struggle for influence which would arise over the Turkish railways.[114] But Bismarck had been dismissed and Wilhelm II voiced Germany's "Drang nach dem Osten". The situation is judged best by M. S. Anderson who says that: ". . . international competition for railway and other concessions for trade with the [Ottoman] empire and investment opportunities there, came to have an influence on the emotions of the nations involved, quite disproportionate to the real value of what was at stake."[115]

In 1899 the Anatolian Railway Co. had received a preliminary concession for the Konia-Baghdad line with an eventual extension to the Persian Gulf. This concession had first aroused little opposition, particularly as von Siemens, the Director of the *Deutsche Bank,* had come to terms with the French rivals, and he was now anxious for British participation. But in Britain public opinion had become increasingly sensitive to Germany's expansion in Turkey.[116]

Already in 1892 London's financial press had shown concern about Germany's ambitions in Asia Minor. Helfferich suspects that it was for this reason that Cassel

[112]H. Feis, *Europe, the World's Banker, 1870-1914*, vol. III, p. 341.
[113]*Ibid.*, pp. 343-344.
[114]*Ibid.*, p. 343.
[115]M. S. Anderson, *The Eastern Question*, London 1966, p. 264.
[116]*Ibid.*

carefully withdrew from the Anatolian railway business.[117] A new awareness arose of what was politically at stake: in 1899 Lord Curzon, Britain's viceroy in India, had concluded an agreement with the Sheik of Kuwait, putting that principality under British protection, and the idea of a German railway terminal next door to it outraged Britain's public opinion and made it imperative for her government to exclude all European rivals from the Persian Gulf.

Russia, too, had raised objections in 1899 to the German project, but a kind of settlement was reached by reserving northern Anatolia and Armenia for railways to be built by Russia.

In March, 1903 a definite concession was granted to the Baghdad Railway Co. (formed by the *Deutsche Bank* group and Ottoman Bank) for building the railway to Baghdad and Basra. The Bank's new head, Arthur v. Gwinner, had renewed his predecessor's attempts to find British partners, be it for political reasons or because German capitalists had shown doubts as to the profitability of the line. As the construction of the line was to be financed by the sale of Turkish government bonds, on the line of Baron Hirsch's *Türkenlose,* it was necessary to obtain the right for their official quotation in London and Paris. The British government had encouraged the London bankers to enter into negotiations with the Germans and promised its backing for the project, subject to the Germans agreeing to absolute equality for the British partners in the Baghdad Railway Co. It seems that these conditions had been accepted.[118] Thus Cassel again became active in the project. He and Sir Clinton Dawkins had already been approached in vain by v. Gwinner in London in 1901.[119] Lord Esher, according to his letter of 6th April, 1903, expected to accompany Cassel (whose aide he then was) and Lord Revelstoke (Baring Bros.)[120] to Berlin in connection with the Baghdad Railway. "Do you see" — he writes — "some of the newspapers have been attacking it because it is a German project and wish us to block it — or keep out of it — as we did when the Suez Canal was made."[121] And a day later he writes in his Notes:

> "It looks as if the Baghdad Railway scheme would fall through. Landsdowne sent for Cassel this evening, as there is a question in the House of Commons about it. My instinct tells me that the government will flinch. I don't care, although I think a lot of money will be made in it [a mistaken view]. The Germans will go on just the same and the railway will ultimately be made, only we shall be out of it. We never learn from experience."[122]

---

[117]Karl Helfferich, *Georg von Siemens,* Berlin 1923, p. 65.

[118]Feis, *op. cit.,* pp. 350 ff. See also A. v. Gwinner, 'The Baghdad Railway and the question of British Co-operation', *The Nineteenth Century and After,* June 1909, No. 388.

[119]Helfferich, *op. cit.,* p. 128.

[120]Baring Brothers were brought into these negotiations by Landsdowne himself to back the British group and to ensure their succes. Hitherto the negotiations had been carried on by Sir Clifton Dawkins of Morgan, Grenfell & Co., who was nervous that his firm was at the moment unpopular, having sponsored the transatlantic shipping combine, and by Cassel, who felt that as a naturalized citizen of German origin his position was delicate. (Cf. Feis, *op. cit.,* p. 350.)

[121]Esher, *op. cit.,* vol. I, p. 396.

[122]*Ibid.,* p. 397.

Though the government, particularly Balfour and Landsdowne, would have favoured a British participation which would have prevented the railway-project from becoming German-dominated and would have strengthened Turkey against Russia, it had to give in to the adverse pressure of press and Parliament. The German approach was turned down. The Foreign Secretary, in a later note, accused the bankers of yielding to public opinion. Had it not been for their scuttling, he would have been in favour of "sticking to our position".[123]

With the limited financial resources in hand the company built the first 200 kilometres from Konia to Bulgurli within nineteen months. Not till 1908 were the terms settled for the next two sections of 850 kilometres which was to bring the line to within 700 kilometres from the Gulf. But the Turkish revolution in 1908 and the reluctance of the Young-Turkish regime in granting financial privileges delayed progress. (Work on the tunnels through the Taurus mountains began only in 1913). The initially pro-Western government asked the *Deutsche Bank* again to seek British participation.[124] Von Gwinner visited Cassel in London in 1909 and consulted him, not only as a financier but also as a confidant of cabinet and King. Cassel suggested that the Baghdad-Basra line should be built by a company under British control. (When signing the final agreement with the Turkish government in March, 1911, the German group stated that for the Baghdad-Basra stretch a special arrangement would be made to satisfy British interests.)[125] This was the beginning of an all-round settlement, in which Turkey recognized Britain's special position on the Persian Gulf. In June 1914 a number of agreements were signed which seemed to promise collaboration without friction among the powers in the development of Turkey's resources. All this, however, was frustrated when, unexpectedly, at the end of July 1914 war broke out.[126]

B. The National Bank of Turkey

In 1909 the National Bank of Turkey was created[127] under Cassel's auspices, with the unofficial encouragement of the British Government.

The Young-Turkish government, which had come into power the year before, was looking for stronger economic ties with Britain. The British attitude is indicated by the following passage written by the Foreign Secretary Sir Edward Grey, in a memorandum:

> "I was distressed to find when I came into office [i.e. 1905], how completely we had been ousted from commercial enterprise in Turkey . . . [and] disappointed to find what a very poor set of financiers have got commercial enterprise in Turkey into their hands. It was, I suppose, inevitable under the old regime, for its methods were such that it did not attract the best class of financier. If Turkey puts its house in order, I hope that good financiers will come forward, and by degrees strengthen the British influence in such things as the Ottoman Bank, and to co-operate with the French at least on equal terms."[128]

---

[123]Feis, *op. cit.*, p. 351.

[124]The question of the Baghdad Railway was never off the agenda between the two governments during those years. On his visit to Windsor Castle in November, 1907, Wilhelm II told Sir Edward Grey (after an outburst against the Jews): "The concession is mine. You must come in on my terms or stay out. We have plenty of money." But in an audience

The new regime in Turkey desired to free itself from the yoke of the Ottoman Bank and the *Deutsche Bank;* therefore they aimed at the formation of a new group with which they could do business with regard both to concessions for enterprises and to loans for government and municipalities. They asked Nubar Pasha and Gulbenkian to align a group of bankers from England, Belgium, Holland and France; Germany and Austria were to be excluded.[129]

One of the principal participants, Calouste Gulbenkian, is quoted by his biographer, as follows:

"As far as Great Britain was concerned, the execution of this task depended on one man, Cassel, who at that time was indubitably the greatest expert on the finance and economic affairs of the Near East. It was natural that the guiding spirit of the ambitious transformation of the Nile Valley should also be entrusted with this financial and economic regeneration of the pitifully backward Ottoman Empire. With his plans centred around the bank which he was to establish, he immediately began to join finance groups which, in co-operation with the Young-Turkish government, would undertake the development of natural resources, particularly in Mesopotamia."[130]

According to Gulbenkian's record[131] the Young-Turks thought that there should be in Constantinople a centre of purely British financial influence.

After consultation of leading City figures, such as Lord Revelstoke (Baring Bros.), Lord Farringdon and Sir Ernest Cassel, it was decided that Cassel should proceed to Constantinople, on behalf of the "British Financial Consortium", to establish a bank on the pattern of the National Bank of Egypt. The British government seconded a distinguished civil servant, Sir Henry Babbington-Smith, to become chairman (governor) of the institution. Gulbenkian, who served as financial and economic adviser to the Turkish government in Paris and London, and who had been asked by Cassel to accompany him on his mission to Constantinople as a technical adviser, was nominated to the Executive Committee of the Bank as a director in London.

The National Bank was on the way to undermine the monopoly position which the Ottoman Bank had enjoyed under Abdul Hamid. It succeeded, according to the reports of the German ambassadors in Constantinople and Paris, owing to the collaboration of Sir Adam Block[132] in Constantinople and Cassel's representative in Paris (Gulbenkian).

---

given to Cassel, lasting three-quarters of an hour, he delivered practically a monologue on the need for a strong German navy, but said little on the Baghdad Railway. (Cf. Esher, *op. cit.*, vol. II, pp. 255, 266.)

[125]Helfferich, *op. cit.*, p. 144.
[126]For the full details of the history of the Baghdad Railway, see H. Feis *op. cit.*, pp. 342-360.
[127]D.N.B., vol. 1912-21, p. 95.
[128]Cf. A. S. I. Baster, *The International Banks*, London 1935, p. 107.
[129]F. C. Gerretson, *History of the Royal Dutch*, Leyden 1957, vol. III, p. 274.
[130]R. Hewins, *Mr. Five Percent, The Biography of Calouste Gulbenkian*, London 1957, pp. 72 ff.
[131]*Ibid.*, pp. 72 ff.
[132]Sir Adam Block, who, apart from his official position on the Debt Commission, also served as president of the British Chamber of Commerce in Constantinople, was called the unofficial ambassador of Britain's commercial interests in Turkey.

The French saw in Cassel "the scourge of the Entente".[133] His efforts to come to terms with the Germans on the Baghdad Railway question and Sir Adam Block's activities seemed to compete for France's established position. The opportunity for a French counter-attack came soon and was aided by British diplomats who disliked or distrusted Cassel.[134]

When Djavid Bey, Turkey's Foreign Minister, came to Paris to negotiate for an urgently needed loan, the Ottoman Bank, with the French government's concurrence, offered the loan under severe conditions. Turkey refused, also on the advice of Sir Adam Block.[135] Now Cassel promised Djavid Bey a loan of T£ six million, should his negotiations in Paris fail. The French ambassador, Jules Cambon, called on Sir Edward Grey and complained that Cassel's offer was in conflict with the spirit of the *Entente cordiale*. The Foreign Office through Sir Charles Hardinge (later Lord Hardinge of Penshurst) and Mr. (Sir) Louis Mallet made energetic representations to Cassel. He had to drop the project at the end of the year.[136] The Turks were told by Downing Street that this decision had been taken because the Baghdad Railway was considered "an enterprise which under the present conditions has not been conceived in the best interests of the Ottoman Empire, while it offers, as controlled at present, an undoubted menace to the legitimate position of British trade in Mesopotamia".[137] The Turks replied that it was a prerogative only of the Ottoman government to determine whether concessions were in Turkey's interest or not. And then, as the Russian ambassador to Turkey recalls, "the unexpected and unbelievable happened";[138] the resulting deadlock was skilfully used by the *Deutsche Bank* group. It issued the loan without strings attached and thereby regained at one stroke its predominant position held prior to the Young-Turkish revolution. Cassel's obvious chagrin gave some satisfaction to members of the British "Establishment". If he felt frustrated, it was not because of profits lost; it was rather because of the vaccillating policy of the Foreign Office which had prompted the formation of the National Bank as an instrument of competition with France, but later thwarted this policy. Moreover, while some people had thought the German initiative "unexpected and unbelievable", Cassel seems to have expected it. In order to prevent an independent German initiative in this field, Cassel, as the British ambassador to Berlin reported, had been in touch with German high finance and intended to issue the loan in co-operation with the *Deutsche Bank* (as junior partner). The failure of this loan, and in a wider sense of the Bank, and his policy, may have been one of the reasons why Cassel retired in 1910 from active business. After Cassel's death, the National Bank of Turkey was sold to the British Trade Corporation and was finally wound up in the late twenties.[139]

[133]Hallgarten, *Imperialismus vor 1914*, 2nd ed., vol. II, p. 423.
[134]*Ibid.*, vol. II, p. 172.
[135]Feis, *op. cit.*, p. 375.
[136]E. M. Earle, *Turkey, the Great Powers and the Baghdad Railway*, New York 1935, p. 225.
[137]Baster, *op. cit.*, p. 111.
[138]N. V. Tibaryskow, *Glimpses from High Politics*, New York 1931, p. 275.
[139]E. G. Mears, *Modern Turkey*, New York 1924, p. 375.

C. The Turkish Petroleum Company

The refusal of the loan to Turkey had certainly not strengthened the British claim for oil concessions, originally held by the Anatolian Railway Co. in 1901, but since lapsed or of doubtful validity. The Germans held a strong hand, claiming that the building of the railway was economically justified only by a concomitant exploration and exploitation of the natural resources which would supply the freight. The previous attempts of Gulbenkian and the Royal Dutch Shell group to obtain petroleum concessions in Mesopotamia had failed. Cassel "proffered that he was a great friend of the German Emperor and had great influence in German high finance",[140] and suggested an attempt at coming to terms with the Germans. Although he was reluctant that the National Bank should engage in oil speculation, he would, if Gulbenkian took an important share together with himself, arrange for contact to be established between Sir Henry Babbington-Smith with the head of the *Deutsche Bank*, v. Gwinner, and the German Chancellor.

The *Deutsche Bank*, anxious to get British financial backing, not only for petroleum exploitation but for its railway venture as well, eventually responded. In October, 1912 an agreement was reached for forming a British limited company, using the mantle of the African and Eastern concessions, a mining concern belonging to Cassel. Its name was later changed to the Turkish Petroleum Co.[141] For bringing in the mining rights of the Anatolian and Baghdad Railways (20 kilometres both sides of the track) and a *Lettre Viziriette* of 1883 promising German preferential mining rights, the *Deutsche Bank* received 20,000 out of the 80,000 shares free of charge. Of the remaining 60,000 shares Cassel and the National Bank held 28,000 and Gulbenkian 32,000, all paid in cash. Gulbenkian subsequently ceded 20,000 shares out of his holding to the Royal Dutch Shell group. These were vested in the Anglo-Saxon Petroleum Co., a British registered subsidiary for holding concessions in territories under the British crown.

The opportunity of reconciling British and German interests in the Turkish Petroleum Co. was not backed by the British government, which, "flushed with the sudden success of the all-British Anglo-Persian Oil Company, lost enthusiasm for the National Bank and its transformation into a rival oil company".[142] Sir Henry Babbington-Smith, as head of the National Bank, and Sir Ernest Cassel were told by the Foreign Office — about 1913 — that it was the desire of the British government that their interest should be transferred to the Anglo-Persian. Thereupon Cassel, together with his associates in the National Bank of Turkey, placed their holding of 28,000 shares at the disposal of the British government.

Cassel's efforts in Turkey, which he thought to be in the British economic and political interest, had been twice frustrated by the British authorities. Was this

---

[140]Hewins, *op. cit.*, p. 73.
[141]According to Seidenzahl the Turkish Petroleum Co. had been formed out of the Red Sea Oilfields Co. (F. Seidenzahl, *The Agreement concerning the Turkish Petroleum Co.*, Deutsche Bank, Studies No. 5, Autumn 1965, p. 15.)
[142]Hewins, *op. cit.*, pp. 76-77.

due only to objective economic and/or political considerations? Von Gwinner of the *Deutsche Bank* had written to the German Foreign Office in December, 1913:

> "Some trouble is . . . being caused not only by the Foreign Office's jealousy of Cassel, but also by their dislike of Sir Marcus Samuel, a former Lord Mayor of London, who is a conservative and belongs to the Deterding group. The Admiralty, for good reasons, abominates Sir Marcus."[143]

XIII. CASSEL AND THE CHURCHILLS

Winston Churchill referred to Cassel as "his father's old friend".[144] And in the recently published volume of *Letters of W. S. Churchill*, we find one by his father, Lord Randolph, to Frances, Duchess of Marlborough, of September, 1892, complaining about Winston's bad marks in the military examinations, saying "If he fails again, I shall think about putting him into business. I could get him something very good through Natty (Rothschild), or Horace (Farquharson) or Cassel . . ."[145]

It was Winston's brother Jack who was actually employed by Cassel. When in 1898 Jack was to accompany Cassel on a business trip to Egypt,[146] Winston wrote to his brother "Mind you try and make Cassel take you to Egypt. You can't push too much in all things".[147] And when Jack wanted to join up in the Boer War, 1899, Winston insisted that he should do so only with Cassel's approval.[148]

Winston Churchill himself said of Cassel: "He was a very great friend of mine." That was in the witness box in his law suit against Lord Alfred Douglas. Lord Douglas who, as Oscar Wilde's companion, had achieved some notoriety, had once been a promising young poet, but in the post-war years he had published an antisemitic yellow journal *Plain English*. In 1922 he had written a pamphlet *The Murder of Lord Kitchener and the Truth about the Battle of Jutland* in which he accused Churchill of having conspired with Cassel to publish a misleading *communiqué* about the Battle of Jutland in order to profit by the anticipated consequent fall in the value of British shares. Cassel allegedly had made £ 18,000,000 or even £ 48,000,000 on this deal, while Churchill got £40,000.

Churchill, suing Douglas for defamation (December 1923) proved that he did not write any such *communiqué* on that matter and the administrators of Cassel's estate gave evidence that Cassel did not buy or sell British stocks at that time. Lord Douglas was sentenced to six months' prison for slander.[149]

In the course of his evidence, Churchill stated that he had known Cassel since he was nineteen, and that "shortly after Lord Randolph's death in 1895 he got to know him very well". In 1905 when Churchill had taken a flat of his own,

---

[143]Seidenzahl, *The Agreement*, p. 22.
[144]W. S. Churchill, *My Early Life*, London 1937, p. 376.
[145]W. S. Churchill, *Letters*, ed. by Randolph Churchill, London 1966, vol. I, p. 181.
[146]*Ibid.*, p. 383.
[147]*Ibid.*, p. 436.
[148]*Ibid.*, p. 508.
[149]Cf. Oscar K. Rabinowicz, *Winston Churchill on Jewish Problems*, London 1956, pp. 33-34, 175-184.

Cassel, with Lady Randolph's permission, had furnished a library for him. In 1908, on his wedding day, he had received from Cassel a present of £500. And after Cassel's death he was given his watch and chain which, the family thought, was what the deceased would have wished. (On two occasions Churchill had asked Cassel to invest for him the royalties from his books and fees earned from his lectures.)

XIV. ANOTHER FAILURE: PEACE-MAKING[150]

Parallel with Cassel's endeavours, during the years 1908-1914, to come to an understanding with the Germans on the activities in Turkey were his efforts to bring about a relaxation in the tension growing between the two countries. In pursuing this end he kept in touch with Albert Ballin, the head of the HAPAG shipping company in Germany. Cassel's attempts to come to an understanding with the Germans in the economic as well as in the political sphere were not prompted, as many may have suspected, by any deep sympathies for his country of origin. Fearing that the growing economic power of Germany and her competition on the world markets could not be suppressed save by the force of arms, he wanted to find out whether a *modus vivendi* could be reached by which Britain's vital interests would be safeguarded.[151]

The deterioration in Anglo-German relations eventually caused concern also to some Germans who had originally favoured the German naval programme. Among them was Albert Ballin, whose remarkable achievements in the development of Germany's merchant navy had earned him the Emperor's respect and friendship.

Early in 1908, as Huldermann[152] and Rosenbaum[153] tell the story, Ballin was approached by British business friends, suggesting that it might be useful if he would discuss the problem of the Anglo-German tension with Cassel, who enjoyed the confidence of the British government and the King's friendship. Ballin was obviously chosen on account of his relationship with the Emperor. According to Stubmann[154] and Cecil[155] it was Max Warburg's introduction of Ballin to Cassel in the summer of 1908 which led to an exchange of views and an attempt to bring about talks to avoid competitive naval construction.

---

[150]This section is largely based, even when not specifically quoted, on the detailed and well-documented accounts given by Eduard Rosenbaum, 'Albert Ballin', *LBI Year Book III* (1958), pp. 257-299, and Lamar Cecil, *Albert Ballin, Business and Politics in Imperial Germany 1888-1918*, Princeton 1967.

[151]The Hamburg banker, Max M. Warburg, who remembers having been strongly influenced by Cassel during his apprentice years in London (1890-91), claims that Cassel, earlier than any other Britisher, foresaw that an Anglo-German armed conflict would mean the ruin of Europe. "Had his influence been stronger, with his entire striving for peace, for an honest understanding and sincere friendship, the tension in the Anglo-German relations would never have reached such a tragic magnitude." (M. M. Warburg, *Aus meinen Aufzeichnungen*, New York 1952, pp. 25-26.

[152]B. Huldermann, *Albert Ballin*, Berlin 1922, pp. 255 ff.

[153]Rosenbaum, *op. cit.*, p. 279.

[154]P. F. Stubmann, *Mein Feld ist die Welt - Albert Ballin*, Hamburg 1960, p. 200.

[155]Cecil, *op. cit.*, p. 161.

Ballin's campaign for Anglo-German naval talks got under way in the summer of 1908. In June, apparently at the behest and certainly with the knowledge of the *Kaiser*, Ballin met Cassel in London to discuss Anglo-German relations.[156] Cassel, stressing King Edward's concern over Germany's naval construction programme at this first meeting, thought that some day Britain, jointly with France and Russia, might ask Berlin at what point she intended to stop it. This, in Ballin's view, would be a *casus belli*. Other avenues would have to be found for relaxing the tension. An improvement in the difficult personal relations between Wilhelm II and his uncle Edward would be a first step.

In spring 1909 Cassel followed up Ballin's visit with warnings that German navalism was the very basis of Britain's mistrust of Germany. Ballin passed on these messages to the Imperial Chancellor von Bülow, and afterwards to the latter's successor Bethmann-Hollweg. And in June 1909, during the "Kiel Week", he suggested to the Emperor that he be authorized to initiate feelers with the British via Cassel, to bring about talks between Admiral Tirpitz, the instigator of Germany's navalism, and Sir John Fisher, the First Sea Lord. The *Kaiser* agreed, and Ballin discussed with Tirpitz the relevant questions of policy in a discreet approach. Then he wrote to Cassel that he would like to give him some "personal information" on the naval question. He was invited to London in June or July 1909. Here Cassel told him that Britain could no longer commit herself to a naval agreement with Germany, because of the recently announced naval programmes of France and the Habsburg monarchy, and that Britain would have to meet Germany's challenge by a naval construction programme sufficient for maintaining her naval superiority.

Ballin gave an account of these talks to the Emperor and Tirpitz, who were pleased, but the new Chancellor Bethmann-Hollweg and the German Foreign Office resented "the interference of an outsider" and insisted that any further negotiations be carried on through normal diplomatic channels. In August 1909 Ballin was told to stop his talks with Cassel. The Chancellor was backed by the British Ambassador to Berlin, Sir Edward Goshen and Count Wolff-Metternich, the German Ambassador in London, who did not like to be by-passed.

Cassel, however, used every opportunity to promote an understanding. There is evidence of a proposal he made to the German Colonial Secretary Dernburg for a ratio of 2 : 1 for the two fleets. But Count Metternich, as can be seen from his letter to the Chancellor, doubted very much whether Cassel had ever discussed the naval relations with Sir Edward Grey and decried the self-appointed negotiators.[157]

Nevertheless the Emperor, when attending the funeral of his uncle Edward in May 1910, had a long conversation with Cassel,[158] in which he ventured as his private opinion that Germany would approve of Britain's complete annexation

---

[156]*Ibid.*, p. 168.

[157]Rosenbaum, *op. cit.*, p. 283.

[158]As to Cassel's relations with the German Emperor, it is not quite clear when they had started and how. Bülow in his Memoirs, according to what he was told by von Marshall, the German diplomat, records that Wilhelm "was enthusiastically pro-Boer, because he ascribed the Jameson Raid (1895) to his uncle Edward, the Prince of Wales and the

of Egypt. But he asked this to be kept confidential, even from Sir Edward Grey, until he had talked to the Chancellor. The latter, obviously, did not agree.[159]

With Edward's death Cassel's position at court had changed and also at Downing Street his contacts seem to have become rather limited.

The failure of official diplomacy to make any progress on the way to an understanding made welcome a renewed initiative by Cassel and Berlin. It is difficult to judge today how it began.

According to Harold Nicolson's version (which Rosenbaum accepts) it was like this:

> "In the late winter of 1911 Sir Ernest Cassel . . . felt that the increasing rivalry between his homeland and his fatherland was leading both countries to the verge of disaster. He placed himself in communication with his friend, Albert Ballin of the Hamburg-America Line. Cassel was to tell the British government that the Emperor had expressed a wish to receive a Cabinet Minister in Berlin. Ballin was to tell the Emperor that the British government desired to send a special representative to Germany to discuss accommodation. The arrangement worked admirably. The Emperor signified his willingness to receive such an emissary; the British government was delighted to accept such an invitation. They selected Mr. Haldane as their representative. He arrived in Berlin on February 8, 1912."[160]

L. Cecil, however, considers that the first move in this second act of the drama came early in 1912, in a letter by Ballin in which he suggested to Cassel, who was due in Berlin in March for a meeting of the King Edward VII British-German Foundation,[161] to bring with him his friend Churchill, the new First Lord of the Admiralty. Cassel answered on January 9, 1912, that he had spoken to Churchill, who, according to him, felt that he — because of the peculiar limitations of his office — could not accept the invitation, unless he were to accompany the King on a State visit to Berlin. Cassel added that Britain was prepared to go very far in order to come to an understanding with Germany.[162] He passed on the correspondence with Ballin to the proper authorities.

What now followed, Churchill called the "Cassel Mission". According to his version, the initiative had come from the British cabinet and not from Ballin-

---

latter's two capitalist friends, Beit and *Cassel*, both, to mention incidentally, German Israelites." (Cf. Prince v. Bülow, *Memoirs 1897-1903*, New York 1931, p. 469.) In November 1907, on his ten-day visit to Windsor Castle, Wilhelm II, in a talk with Sir Edward Grey, spoke vehemently against the Jews. "There are too many of them in my country. They want stamping out. If I did not restrain my people, there would be Jew-baiting." (Cf. Esher, *op. cit.*, p. 255.) But it was on the occasion of this visit that Wilhelm II received Cassel in an audience lasting forty-five minutes, in which he spoke largely on Germany's need for a larger fleet, and little, apparently, on the Baghdad Railway which was probably the anticipated subject of the audience. (*Ibid.*, p. 266.)

[159]Rosenbaum, *op. cit.*, pp. 283-284.

[160]H. Nicolson, *Sir Arthur Nicolson, First Lord Carnock, A Study in the Old Diplomacy*, London 1930, p. 362. See also Rosenbaum, *op. cit.*, p. 284.

[161]It was to honour his friend's memory and to promote his aim of improving Anglo-German relations that Cassel in 1911 established the King Edward VII British-German Foundation with a capital of £210,000 (half for distressed Germans in England, and half for distressed Britons in Germany).

[162]Cecil, *op. cit.*, pp. 182-183.

Cassel.[163] Knowing of the formidable new Navy Law in preparation in Germany, the Chancellor of the Exchequer (Lloyd George) thought that a serious effort should be made to arrive at an understanding with Germany. So he and Churchill jointly consulted Sir Edward Grey, and then with the Prime Minister's concurrence invited Cassel to go to Berlin. "Sir Ernest was qualified for this task, as he knew the Emperor well and was at the same time devoted to British interests." Cassel returned on 30th January 1912, after a two days' stay in Berlin, with a cordial letter from the Emperor and a statement on the new Naval Law by the Chancellor. He had seen both accompanied by Ballin. The Cabinet thereupon decided to send Mr. Haldane, the Secretary of War, to Berlin for actual negotiations. A cable, drafted by Cassel, Churchill, Grey and Haldane, was despatched to Ballin, indicating the British government's willingness to discuss a naval understanding, on the basis of an alteration of the tempo of the new construction programme (i.e. spreading the six-year-programme over twelve years). On Berlin's acceptance, Haldane left for Berlin on February 6, accompanied by Cassel. There are considerable differences between Churchill's short account of the days between the Cassel Mission and Haldane's and the more detailed well-documented accounts by Rosenbaum and Cecil which, however, do not affect the earlier story.

On the very first day of the Haldane Mission's visit, Bethmann-Hollweg, who had never liked private diplomacy, suggested that Ballin and Cassel could now leave Berlin. Haldane forcefully objected and declared himself to be in need of Cassel's assistance. Ballin had to ask for the Emperor's intervention, who acquiesced in Haldane's request.

The Haldane Mission proved a failure, as Germany was not ready for real concessions in her naval programme and because of her insistence on a British declaration of neutrality. As a member of Wilhelm's entourage wrote to Ballin after Haldane's visit:

> "What I absorbed as an attentive listener for many hours is the impression that your great effort will be frustrated in the hands of the professionals, primarily because of inability, and partly due to bureaucratic superciliousness, we won't courageously grasp the chance . . ."[164]

---

[163]W. S. Churchill, *The World Crisis, 1911-1916*, London 1938, vol. I, pp. 71 ff. - Churchill's story, however, is supplemented by Sir Edward Grey's story, as told by G. M. Trevelyan, *Grey of Fallodon*, London 1937, (1945), p. 228: "Haldane's mission . . . originated from a suggestion conveyed through Sir Ernest Cassel and Herr Ballin that a British Mission should go over and pave the way for a *rapprochement*. Mr. Winston Churchill tells us that Lloyd George had helped to set the ball rolling; when it came back to Grey he understood that the invitation had the support of the Kaiser and he therefore considered that it ought to be accepted, though he had no great hopes of success." It would seem to this writer that Churchill, who recently (1911) had become First Lord of the Admiralty, when faced with the need of competing with the German construction programme, may, with the connivance of Lloyd George who as Chancellor of the Exchequer wanted to avoid if possible such a heavy expenditure, have suggested to his friend Cassel that he proceed privately in the way Harold Nicolson described.

[164]Huldermann, *op. cit.*, p. 270.

Sir Ernest Cassel, Albert Ballin, Felix Cassel and Max M. Warburg in 1913

Are we as welcome as ever?

Max Beerbohm's cartoon showing Ernest Cassel, Alfred Rothschild, Edward Lawson, Arthur Sassoon and Leopold Rothschild

But Bethmann-Hollweg asked Ballin to do what he could, through "private discreet support, to keep exchange of views going."[165]

Two years later, a last futile mediation attempt was made by the two friends. Early in 1914 Ballin wrote to Cassel that if Churchill and Tirpitz could be brought together, they might come to an understanding. Cassel reported that Churchill was eager for such an opportunity. Ballin suggested to the Emperor that Churchill be invited to the "Kiel Week" in June, but Wilhelm insisted that the British government, according to protocol, would first have to ask for his agreement, which then would be granted with pleasure. But, obviously, no such request had come forth. And a few weeks later the War started, a war which according to Ballin was "the most stupid of all wars, to prevent which no Bismarck was needed."[166]

XV. "ARE WE AS WELCOME AS EVER?"

It was under this caption that Max Beerbohm in a cartoon[167] shows Cassel, two Rothschilds, Lord Burnham and Arthur Sassoon before the door of Edward's successor. The underlying question was whether there would be a place in the new era for the great financiers of enterprise who, like Cassel, had done so much for Egypt's development, or his sponsor Hirsch, whose railway enterprise had opened up the Balkans? The question was justified: a curtain seemed to have fallen on an entire epoch.

In May, 1910, King Edward had died. His death was the end of Cassel's and some other financial knights' influential position at court. It was a moment to which some resentful members of High Society had been looking forward. As Lady C. had remarked to W. S. Blunt, "There will be a regular sweep of the people who used to be about the Court, the Jews and the second-rate women that the King preferred to his aristocracy because they amused him. The Prince of Wales [i.e. King George V.] hates all these and would have nothing to do with them."[168]

Many members of the Establishment and Society must have felt somewhat awkward when in the company of their late King whose "mind moved with a swiftness that could hardly fail to disconcert the slow-thinking among his advisors who would also be likely to find his frankness startling and his directness of

---

[165]Cecil, *op. cit.*, p. 192.

[166]C. P. Gooch, *Recent Revelations of European Diplomacy*, 4th ed., London 1940, p. 89.

[167]By chance we have two written accounts of the same afternoon in March, 1954, when Beerbohm referred to this cartoon. S. N. Behrman in his *Portrait of Max* (New York 1960, p. 220) recalls that Max said, "These five men, all of them Jewish financiers, are friends of Edward, coming for the first time to see the new King George the Fifth and being somewhat apprehensive, don't you know?" Edmund Wilson in an article in *Encounter* (No. 123, December 1963), on 'Meetings with Max Beerbohm', quotes the artist as saying, "Those . . . 'were the friends of Edward VII', and he went on to explain rather slyly that the occasion for this caricature had been the accession of George V . . . He added, after a second's pause, about the new king: 'Didn't need to borrow money so often, don't you know'. He said nothing about these friends being Jewish."

[168]Blunt, *op. cit.*, vol. II. p. 314.

purpose uncomfortable".[169] And it was because of that, probably, that "he felt himself most thoroughly at home with Jews and the French, of all the alien nationalities".[170]

Already when Prince of Wales his entourage had included "many Jews, a race for whose intelligence, cosmopolitan outlook and cynical wit [he] had developed a great predilection. It numbered actresses, society beauties, bankers and sportsmen, as well as ambassadors and the wittiest and most vivacious members of the old aristocracy".[171] In addition, ample resources were required to offer the Prince the lavish hospitality, the expensive entertainment and sports which he enjoyed so much.

It was probably on this basis that the unique relationship between Edward and Cassel had originated. They had first met some time in 1896 or 1897, apparently when Cassel was introduced to the Prince at a race-meeting as an executor of the late Baron Hirsch. It was the beginning of the happiest period in Cassel's life.

In his house at 48 Grosvenor Square Cassel entertained in grand style. In 1889 he started breeding race-horses, until 1894 in partnership with Lord Willoughby de Broke, and alone thereafter, and by 1896 he was racing his own horses, without, however, getting nearer to winning the Derby than second with "Hapsburg" in 1914. He also taught himself, with determination, to ride to hounds and to shoot, and became quite proficient in both sports. He could even aspire to being elected "Master of the Quorn", an affront to many of those "belonging" that was not forgotten even after his death.

> ". . . A full-blown German naturalized in England. Do you remember how he used to speak . . . how he looked when sitting on a horse? Do you think for a moment he could have been a Master of the Quorn? . . . I suggest his German accent . . . this suggestion is grotesque . . . It requires a man born and bred in the saddle for that position."

Thus the Attorney for the defence, Hayes, in the defamation law suit of Winston Churchill against Lord Douglas.[172]

Similar feelings, probably, prevented, in spite of the Prince's patronage, his election to the Jockey Club until 1908. Yet he never cared much for the society there or at the Marlborough Club, but preferred the brighter feminine company around Edward. He became a "feature of that smart and evanescent world which would have been incomplete without him and exercised much influence".[173]

To entertain his friends he bought in 1899 the estates of Moulton Paddocks, Newmarket. Here he had his stud-farm, here he organized his hunting parties, and here he frequently entertained the King, who invariably made Moulton Paddocks his home when staying at Newmarket.

---

[169]W. Steed, *Through Thirty Years*, New York 1922, vol. I, p. 237.
[170]Benson, *op. cit.*, p. 237.
[171]Connell, *op. cit.*, p. 242.
[172]Rabinowicz, *op. cit.*, p. 183.
[173]Vansittart, *op. cit.*, p. 61.

In 1912 he acquired Six Mile Bottom, Cambridge, and a year later Branksome Dene, Bournemouth; in 1917 Upper Hare Park, Cambridge. In Paris Cassel maintained a flat, always ready for him or for his friends. Just a month before his death he bought the *Villa des Lèdres* at Cap Ferrat, once the property of Leopold of Belgium, but he never set foot in it.

When he acquired Brook House, Park Lane, in 1905, it took three years, a pile of marble and a pile of money to rebuild it to Cassel's requirements. Six marble-lined kitchens catered for an oak-panelled dining-room designed to seat a hundred guests in comfort. The entrance hall was panelled in lapis lazuli alternating with green-veined cream-coloured marble. The library was furnished in cherrywood with black Wedgwood *cameos* inset under the bookshelves. A staff of thirty-one was required to run the household, among them, in the season, footmen in livery and with powdered hair.

Cassel had also become an art collector on a grand scale. He was one of Duveen's main customers. Valuable Renaissance bronzes, Dresden china, Chinese jades, old French and English furniture, and particularly a collection of English silver, including unique historical pieces, like the Wolsey beaker, the Bacon cup (1573) and the Blacksmith cup (1655) crammed the rooms and the basement strong-room. On the walls hung paintings by Botticelli, Van Dyck, Frans Hals, Murillo, Raeburn, Reynolds and Romney. And his library was full of rare volumes. As his friend Benson noted, he bought anything that was sufficiently expensive and of guaranteed quality, but all such were only the trappings suitable for a very wealthy man. He had no instinctive tastes for art or sport or literature.[174]

"There was about Cassel," says Benson, "something of that strange and barren inhumanity which is not rare among those whose abilities have long and exclusively been devoted to the acquisition of wealth. Often they lose all power of other enjoyments, and when the keenness for money begins to be blunted, there is no other savour for them in life, and this curious impotence to experience pleasure results."[175]

Endowed with "astonishing qualities of firm judgment, a strong will and an unerring will"[176], "a wonderful mathematical mind of unerring judgment"[177] Cassel showed a Midas touch in his "fanatical application to the acquisition of wealth."[178] "Hardened by a dozen years of fanatically hard work, in an age when there were no privileges without birth"[179] Cassel had accomplished within just over two decades what two or more generations of Rothschilds or Hirschs had achieved. And for that he had to pay a high price.

---

[174]Bearing in mind these statements by Benson (*op. cit.*, pp. 238-239) and Connell (*op. cit.*, p. 71) one is surprised and amused when reading in Birmingham's recent book *Our Crowd* that Cassel was Jacob H. Schiff's "guide" and mentor in art-collecting.
[175]Benson, *op. cit.*, p. 239.
[176]Connell, *op. cit.*, p. 54.
[177]*Ibid.*, p. 77.
[178]*Ibid.*, p. 55.
[179]*Ibid.*, p. 61.

Cassel has often been called a "Prince of Charity" — something of a misnomer. True, he had given away at least two million pounds sterling, a tremendous fortune in those days — three-quarters thereof during the last decade of his life. But these gifts were to him, like his race horses, his hunting parties and his collections, attributes of wealth, a status symbol. Some of the biggest contributions were gracious gifts to please his friends for purposes he had little interest in. The first big contribution, the biggest in fact, to be given to any charity up till then, was a gift of £200,000 to the King on his ascension to the throne, which was used for the erection of a tuberculosis hospital. And it was at the King's suggestion that he, in 1909, provided £46,000 as his half share for setting up (jointly with Lord Iveagh) the Radium Institute. Other gifts, such as the travelling eye clinics in Egypt, were connected with his wide field of activities. He also remembered the town of his birth, Cologne, which received a million marks for a women's sanatorium.

It was "not long before his death" (actually in 1919) that Richard Haldane visited his friend Cassel, a man "of great intelligence about the necessities of the British nation". Cassel who seemed to Haldane to be looking ill, surprised him by saying he would like to spend a million pounds on bettering the conditions of the poor. Haldane persuaded him to do something really constructive and Cassel agreed to a trust fund of £500,000, with Haldane, Balfour, Asquith and Sidney Webb as trustees, for the support of the Workers' Educational Association, the establishment of a faculty of Commerce in the London University (i.e. the London School of Economics) and sundry educational purposes; as well as £212,000 for founding a hospital for functional nervous diseases. Cassel was still able to participate actively in the early work of the trustees.[180]

An attempt by Israel Cohen to obtain a grant from this trust fund for the newly-established Hebrew University obviously did not find much support from the Webbs.[181] Nor do we find any other Jewish charitable institution among the recipients of Cassel's largesse. True, he had, as the *Jewish Chronicle* (23rd September 1921) noted in a short obituary, "for many years past dissociated himself from Judaism". He had indeed, in a rather dramatic way embraced Catholicism beside his wife's deathbed, but in spite of months of intensive study, had never been converted to the church's doctrine. As Connell says, "he remained a communicant without being able to accept the belief... the faith of his fathers was too strong".[182] One may question the correctness of those last words — Cassel was, as far as we know, rather an agnostic.

His early years were spent in a "Jewish environment"; — Bischoffsheim and Goldschmidt, Jacob H. Schiff of Kuhn, Loeb & Co., New York; Eduard Noetzlin of the *Banque de Paris et des Pays Bas,* Franz Philippson, Brussels; Wertheim & Gomperz, Amsterdam; Mannheimer in Goeteborg; Baron Hirsch; Albert Ballin and Max Warburg, Hamburg; Karl Morawitz, Vienna; Saemy Japhet, London;

---

[180]Haldane, *op. cit.*, pp. 317-318.
[181]J. Cohen, *A Jewish Pilgrimage,* London 1956, p. 171.
[182]Connell, *op. cit.*, p. 61.

Suares, Harari, Cattaui in Egypt; but the higher he climbed, the more alienated he was from Jewish elements.

His conversion had been kept a secret. Only on being sworn in as a Privy Councillor in 1902, on the Catholic Bible, did the fact become known to a few court functionaries. Again, when taking the oath in the Privy Council after King George V's ascent, Cassel's being sworn in together with the Catholic Councillors caused general surprise.[183] Would Baron Hirsch, one wonders, have made Cassel a shareholder and director in the Jewish Colonization Association, had he known this? And how is it to be explained that it did not affect Cassel's relationship with so loyal a Jew as Jacob Schiff?[184]

In the group surrounding King Edward there were also Louis Bischoffsheim, Cassel's former employer and Edward's intimate friends at the close of the century, the Rothschilds, the Sassoons, but it is not known what Cassel's relations were with them. There was one fundamental difference between the Rothschilds and Cassel: when King Edward in May 1907 was to meet the Russian Emperor at Reval, he received a letter from the Rothschilds requesting his intercession on behalf of the persecuted Russian Jews, and one from Cassel asking support concerning Russian loans. Cassel's "unashamedly self-interested, cold-blooded approach" gave rise to caustic commentaries in the King's entourage. As Hardinge wrote to Knollys on 4. 6. 1907: "It amuses me to see how the Jews, though hating the Russian government, are always ready to give them money, if they can 'make a bit' ".[185]

Was it really greed which drew Cassel to the Russian business, or did he sincerely believe, as he had written to Schiff, that by supporting the Stolypin regime, Jewish financiers abroad could achieve an amelioration in the situation of their Russian brethren?

The King knew more and understood better the implications for the British economy of Cassel's ideas, than the Establishment. After all, "the kinds of men to be found in the service of the State — and, more important, the kinds of incentives that impel them, are not necessarily those most conducive to innovation and economic growth".[186] And we can appreciate the uneasiness and antagonism which Cassel's close friendship with the King must have provoked. "Indeed, his position was to cause much active resentment in government circles and... he encountered much opposition."[187]

Theirs was a unique friendship. When they first met, in 1896, the relationship was one of mutual advantage. The Prince, addicted to extravagant expenditure, was glad to find a successor of proven judgment and integrity to the late Baron

---

[183]Blunt, *op. cit.*, vol. II, p. 314.
[184]It is significant that in 1903 Theodor Herzl and Lord Rothschild considered Cassel as a possible head for the organization to finance the Jewish Settlement of El-Arish (Th. Herzl, *Tagebücher*, vol. III, Berlin 1925, p. 326).
[185]Magnus, *op. cit.*, pp. 406-407.
[186]R. Cameron, *Banking in the Early Stages of Industrialization*, Oxford 1967, p. 320.
[187]Connel, *op. cit.*

Hirsch, who could advise him on profitable investment, and he enjoyed the entertainment which only people with resources like Cassel could offer. For Cassel a place in the Prince's company meant a short-cut into High Society in which a man's place and position was decided by family and not by fortune. The surprising fact that such a friendly relationship should have ripened into intimacy has caused some authors to look for the "psychological point of contact". Apart from a certain superficial resemblance, on which many authors commented, and a common Germanic guttural "r" in their accent they were as different as could be.

The Prince and later King, surrounded by courtiers and flatterers, learned that he could rely on the advice and opinion and the uncompromising honesty of Cassel, who, purged of most emotions by the pursuit of making money, had become an unbiased and objective observer of men and affairs in any other context.[188] And Cassel responded with a deep emotional loyalty to the friendship offered to him.

He was practically the last one to see the King, who had sent for him and insisted on sitting up, fully dressed, although breathless and speaking only with difficulty. Shortly afterwards he collapsed.

The day after his death the Privy Council was sworn in, and after the meeting, as Margot Asquith recorded, Cassel came over to see her and "we cried together on the sofa".[189]

As Margot Asquith said of Cassel, his was "a power of loving those he cared for which I find rare". Her view seems to contradict that of other sympathetic observers who considered him a kind man, but devoid of emotions. Still, his relation to the King seems to have been a deeply emotional one, as was his devotion to his daughter Maud, born in 1879. "Something in this fresh, young Englishwoman released in him all the pent-up emotions repressed under a forbidding exterior."[190]

A fortnight before his accession Edward had assisted at Maud's wedding to Wilfrid Ashley, the scion of a family which counted Lord Melbourne, Shaftesbury and Palmerston among its ancestors, and who was himself to become Lord Mount-Temple. The King was godfather to Edwina, their first-born daughter. Her sister Mary was born five years later. In 1911, a year after the death of Edward VII, Maud, too, died, from the same disease that had killed her mother. Cassel was desolate.

Soon after his wife's death Cassel brought his sister (Schoenbrunn), who had been divorced, and her children to live with him in London, and at his request they re-adopted her maiden name. Her son Felix Cassel, P.C., Q.C., who had been acting as Attorney-General, became, in a way, Sir Ernest's crown prince. He was married to Lady Grimstone, daughter of the Earl of Verulam. His sister, Anna Jenkins, mother of the Countess of Brecknock, now became Cassel's official

---

[188]*Ibid.*, p. 68.
[189]Margot Asquith, *Autobiography*, London 1936, p. 103.
[190]Connell, *op. cit.*, p. 61.

hostess, as her mother, who was ailing, lived at Bournemouth, in the place Cassel had bought for her.

In 1922 his grand-daughter Edwina was married to Lord Louis Mountbatten, a grand-nephew of Edward's. Cassel had not lived to see what would have been to him a fulfillment of all his dreams and ambitions: the ties of his friendship with Edward perpetuated in a family tie.

Cassel was a lonely man. Ever since Edward's death he had complained of his waning influence in high places though he was still used by the government for some special missions. And even after the war, a few months before his death, Ed. Arnhold, the German coal magnate who had been one of the trustees of Cassel's Anglo-German Foundation, wrote home from London on the 5th May 1921: "Cassel is not so completely without influence. Of his old friends Balfour and Churchill still are his pals. His son-in-law is an M.P., his nephew and crown prince is in a high position with the army and navy."[191] Nevertheless, Cassel had outlived himself. He was, as Vansittart said, "the saddest of millionaires".

It was towards the end of his days that Cassel once said to his secretary, Miss Underhill, "You know, money does not make for happiness."[192] Through his last decade, indeed, there runs a strong current of sadness.

The King, whose friendship had been the only real pleasure and happiness his material achievements had brought him, had died in 1910, and a year later he had lost his daughter. Furthermore, the operations and negotiations which he had started so auspiciously in Turkey, were suddenly disowned by the Foreign Office. Cassel was tired and disillusioned.

Then the war broke out which he had been so anxious to prevent. There was no doubt that he was loyal to his country of adoption. Still, there were tongues wagging... was it not strange that none of the heavy air-raids took place when Cassel stayed in London? Obviously, he had a specially designed wireless installed on the roof of Brook House by which he informed the German planes of his presence.[193]

Many of those who had enjoyed his hospitality, who had travelled and been treated at his expense, who had made big money on his advice, who had sat bright-eyed with expectation in the hope that he would ask them to be his guests when the King dined at Brook House, or to stay with him at the Paddocks when the King was there, now turned cold and elegant shoulders towards him. He was a "Hun", they said; but surely they had known that before? He was a Jew, they said; but that had not prevented those of Norman blood from refreshing themselves with his excellent champagne.[194]

There came to the surface now a resentment of the late King's friendship with a man who, without the privileges of lineage or birth, had penetrated into Society.

[191]E. Arnhold, *Ein Gedenkbuch*, Berlin 1928, p. 80.
[192]Connell, *op. cit.*, p. 56.
[193]Benson, *op. cit.*, p. 43.
[194]*Ibid.*, p. 245.

Quite characteristic is a remark of Lord Esher. Towards the end of 1907 Esher had written a letter, subsequently published, to the Navy League opposing the proposal of the House of Commons to reduce the Navy's budget. That the King was disturbed, seemed "very natural" to Esher; but that Cassel was critical was due to his "taking the German and Semitic point of view while the English will have to fight for their lives." The Cassels are "at home in all lands — equally rich, equally composed".[195]

Somewhere else we learn of a letter used by a certain peeress as an instrument to blackmail Cassel, which, when proved to be a forgery, was given up to him with humble apologies and the promise never to be naughty again.[196]. And we learn how Edward was once extremely displeased with the sister of a well-known peeress, who, after some fantastic dancing, playfully knelt before him whereupon he smilingly said "Thank you, Lady Salome, have you come to claim half my Kingdom?' "No King Herod" — she replied — "but do give me Sir Ernest Cassel's head on a charger."[197]

With such feelings prevalent in the more normal time of peace, it is not surprising that during the war Cassel's right to retain his membership in the Privy Council was challenged in court. At the end of 1915 Lord Reading presided over a Court of three judges before whom Sir George Makgill laid information against Cassel and Sir Edgar Speyer, calling upon them to show by what right they (as of German birth) claimed to retain their membership in the Privy Council, after the coming into force of the British Nationality and Status of Aliens Act of 1914. The verdict was in Cassel's and Speyer's favour.[198] Cassel had just returned from the U.S., where he had been a member of an Allied Mission to raise a war-loan of $500,000,000 and he himself had been a substantial subscriber. "The success of the law-suit in no way softened the hardness of the step taken against him. But he behaved with the utmost correctness."[199]

Cassel had been a financial genius, admired by many who did business with him. His quick decisions seem to indicate a reliance on instinct rather than on reasoning, but it may have been a mixture of both. The swiftness of his mind helped him to reach decisions while listening to a proposition. He was, as Japhet tells us, the best listener he ever met.[200] And Somary recalls "Once Cassel listened, he was possessed of a power I never saw a second time. He got out (from the speaker) everything, increasing his (the speaker's) self-assurance and helping him to clarify his mind."[201] As negotiator he was supreme. "My friend Cassel" — Ballin said — "no doubt, is an extraordinarily able negotiator. In my experience of many years in this field I hardly remember having met a man who through

---

[195]Esher, *op. cit.*, pp. 286-289, 295.
[196]Anonymous, *Uncensored Recollections*, London 1924, p. 219.
[197]*Ibid.*, p. 330.
[198]Lord Reading, *Rufus Isaacs, First Marquess of Reading*, II, London 1945, pp. 18-19.
[199]Emden, *Jews of Britain*, p. 346. - One will probably feel more sympathy with Sir Edgar Speyer, the patron of the arts in London, who resigned his membership in the Privy Council and left Britain for the U.S.
[200]Japhet, *op. cit.*, p. 104.

hours at a time could carry on a discussion with so much deliberation and such concentration on his purpose."[202]

If his method was not always admired, it may have been because Cassel, as Connell put it, "ploughed a lone, scrupulously honest and, let it be said, hard and ruthless furrow".[203]

His was a "flinty" personality; dark, stocky, with a slightly furtive air,[204] "a man of dour appearance, much generosity and considerable ambitions",[205] a "repressed nature, without charm and possibly hard and stubborn in his office in which he believed he could command".[206] His steely, cold glance[207] rarely brightened into a warm smile. His was not a personality easily inviting intimacy. Only a small number of those who established a social or business relationship with him on a basis of intellectual equality were able to bridge over his repressions towards his friendship and affection.

He had amassed a fortune. After having given away about two millions to charity, his estate, at depressed post-war prices, proved to be £7.5 million. And taking into account his lavish spending over the last twenty-five years, some observers calculate his total earnings over his life-time at approximately fifteen million pounds.

His fortune gave him power over men and institutions, but as Emden emphasizes, "to his credit it must be said that this power was not once misused by him and the genius of this financier was never directed to any other aim than the service of the Empire."[208] But empire building was a thing of the past, and a sharp eye could discern fine fissures in the Empire's structure.

Cassel died alone on the 21st September, 1921, sitting at his desk — "a pathetic figure, a sermon on the vanity of great wealth."[209]

Few of the Court Jews had a happy end. Some died on the gallows, like *Jud Süss,* or were disgraced and impoverished, like Samuel Oppenheimer, the most powerful among them. While they were loyally serving their masters, they earned the envy of the Establishment, the hatred of the masses. The death of the masters whose favours they enjoyed usually spelt the end of their positions at the seat of power.

Cassel's life was not threatened; nobody tried to deprive him of his fortune. But he was made to feel the loss of his position, to experience frustration and humiliation. He was suddenly made aware that he stood between two worlds, and belonged to neither; one he had rejected, the other had rejected him. He died in no-man's land.

[201]Somary, *op. cit.,* p. 95.
[202]Huldermann, *op. cit.*
[203]Connell, *op. cit.,* p. 50.
[204]*Ibid.,* pp. 60, 67.
[205]Vansittart, *op. cit.,* p. 61.
[206]Münz, *op. cit.,* p. 225.
[207]*Ibid.,* p. 216.
[208]Emden, *Jews of Britain,* p. 330.
[209]*Ibid.,* p. 343.

Vocational Training

The Ahlem Experiment

A Brief Survey of the "Jüdische Gartenbauschule"[1]

BY E. G. LOWENTHAL

Since the dawn of the Enlightenment, the unhealthy vocational and social structure of Jewish society, as inherited from the Middle Ages, and caused by restrictive legislation, has been recognized as one of the major obstacles to the integration of the Jews into society. But not much effective organized work was done in order to alter that situation. When the effects of emancipation began to make the anomaly of vocational distribution more perceptible, reasonable men of higher standing often raised their voice and made suggestions for remedy, but only rarely did this lead to practical results. One of the men who was not content to confine himself to admonitions but also took the initiative for practical steps was Moritz Simon (1837-1905). To him we owe one of the most salutary institutions, the horticultural school of Ahlem (near Hanover), which became a model for that type of training at the beginning of the twentieth century. It was established by the Simon Endowment, famous in Germany at that time. Its intentions and achievements deserve a historical appreciation, however cursory.

"Not by charity but by education for work alone can aid be brought to our destitute correligionists" (Nicht durch Almosen, sondern durch Erziehung zur Arbeit kann unseren armen Glaubensgenossen geholfen werden) — these words ascribed to Moritz Simon, are carved on the elaborate family-tomb in the Strangriede Jewish cemetery in Hanover where Moritz Simon is buried.[2] He was born in Hanover on November 27, 1837, and died in his native town on January 29, 1905. He never married. Moritz Alexander Simon, later known either as M. A. Simon or, sometimes, as A. M. Simon, was the son of Alexander Simon, an

---

[1] There has been no previous attempt to record the development of the school. As far as can be ascertained, even an incomplete set of source-material and relevant literature concerning either the school as such or the founding body is no longer available. Nevertheless, it was possible to gather substantial evidence and information from scattered sources, public German archives, the Wiener Library, London and private collections. Particular thanks are due to Mr. S. Adler-Rudel of the Leo Baeck Institute, Jerusalem, who put at my disposal his collection of Simon papers and Ahlem pamphlets. - The following brochures on Ahlem although not explicitly mentioned in the text or in the source references were likewise utilized for the survey: *Ahlem. Eine Kultur-Aufgabe der deutschen Judenheit* [1918]; *Die Israelitische Erziehungsanstalt zu Ahlem in Bild und Wort*; *Die Lehrer-Bildungsanstalt in Peine. Eine Neugründung der Simon'schen Stiftung zu Hannover*, Hanover 1911; *Plantage des Simon'schen Seminars für Gartenbau und Handfertigkeit in Peine (Einrichtung der Simon'schen Stiftung zu Hannover*); *Prospekt und Lehrplan der Israel. Gartenbauschule Ahlem bei Hannover*; *Satzung des Vereins "Hülfsfonds für ehemalige Lehrlinge der Israelitischen Erziehungsanstalt zu Ahlem"*; *Satzungen des "Vereins Ehemaliger Ahlemer"*; *Statut der Israelitischen Gartenbauschule Ahlem zu Ahlem bei Hannover*, Hanover 1919 (Neudruck 1934); *Die Ziele der Simon'schen Stiftung in Hannover* and annual reports and balance sheets of Ahlem for the years 1897, 1898, 1899, 1900, 1901, 1902, 1903 and 1905.

antique-dealer. After an apprenticeship with Ezechiel Simon, a banker, he went to the United States of America for some time.[3] In Hanover in 1852 he established, together with his father, the banking-firm of Alexander Simon. He was later appointed U.S. vice-consul there. At the time of his death the firm was in the process of liquidation.

HOW IT CAME ABOUT

In the eighties Simon had ample opportunity to study the deplorable economic situation and the shocking living conditions of many Jews who had then emigrated to the U.S.A. from East European countries. He thought of ways and means

> ". . . how to render assistance to our poor correligionists of Eastern Europe, how to remove the inevitably detrimental results of peddling and petty trading. In the instruction of youth in agriculture and in horticulture, in introducing them to the crafts, he saw a part of the solution of this significant social question. As soon as he perceived this he was moved by an indefatigable urge to transform his thoughts into practical realization."[4]

In the early stages of emancipation an awareness amongst the Jews in Germany as to the problem of their social adjustment became apparent and there was a growing resistance to the long-established prejudice that Jews allegedly were inclined exclusively towards certain lines of business, primarily commercial trades. Organizations came into being whose purpose it was to direct Jews towards agriculture and handicraft. Though this essay is devoted primarily to the period at the end of the nineteenth century and the first part of the twentieth, the fact that already in 1812 a *Gesellschaft zur Verbreitung der Handwerke und des Ackerbaus unter den Juden des Preussischen Staates* was formed must not be overlooked; this society continued all through the century and still existed, at least by name, in our time. In 1932, the chairman of this *Gesellschaft* was Georg Tietz in Berlin.[5] As from the end of the nineteenth century, the *Gesellschaft* had their own *Lehrlingsheim* in Berlin-Pankow, where twenty to twenty-five boys at a time were trained in various crafts.

Siegfried Klein (1888-1944), a Düsseldorf rabbi, in his book (quoted below)

---

[2]Cf. *Leben und Schicksal. Zur Einweihung der Synagoge in Hannover*, Hanover 1963, p.22. - Simon's death was caused by an accident in the bathroom of his Allee Strasse home; he died in hospital from severe burns. The local press of January 30, 1905, to February 2, 1905, reported on the tragic death of this well-known, noble Hanover citizen, particularly on the unselfish services rendered by him to his fellow-Jews and, above all, on the funeral on February 1, 1905, attended, amongst others, by some two-hundred Ahlem pupils; *Landrabbiner* Dr. Selig Gronemann (1843-1918) officiated.
[3]Cf. Bericht über die *Israelitische Erziehungsanstalt in Ahlem bei Hannover für das Jahr 1904*, Hanover 1905, p. 5.
[4]*Ibid.*, p. 5.
[5]Cf. *Führer durch die jüdische Gemeindeverwaltung und Wohlfahrtspflege in Deutschland 1932-33*, Berlin, n.d., p. 44. Some of Tietz's predecessors in this capacity were Lachmann-Mosse and Leopold Lesser (cf. *Handbuch der jüdischen Gemeindeverwaltung und Wohlfahrtspflege 1924-25*, Berlin, n.d., p. 216, and *Im deutschen Reich*, 1902, p. 240).

briefly mentions the founding of a more locally based organization at Münster/ Westphalia in 1825; this attempt, however, was a failure.

On April 18, 1880, following a suggestion circularised by the *Deutsch-Israelitischer Gemeindebund*, Leipzig, a *Verein zur Verbreitung der Handwerke unter den Juden* was founded in Düsseldorf.[6] On April 13, 1886, its name was changed to *Verein zur Verbreitung und Förderung der Handwerke unter den Juden*, and on October 28, 1900, it was given its final name. The intensive efforts of a few men actively engaged in Jewish communal work, primarily in the North of the Rhineland and in Westphalia, led to the creation of *Lehrlingsheime* in Düsseldorf (1887) and Cologne (1890).

In the course of time, a few more *Lehrlingsheime* opened, amongst them three in Berlin, that is to say besides the one mentioned above, one in 1882, connected with a Jewish orphanage, and another one in 1925.

Private and organizational efforts had thus succeeded in training young Jews in various crafts, though only in limited numbers.[7] On the other hand, nothing worth mentioning had been achieved in the field of agricultural training since the *Gesellschaft* had been founded in 1812 until in the last twenty years of the century Moritz Simon tried to carry this idea into effect. His ultimate aim was to direct young Jews at an early age to agriculture and manual skills. He rejected all suggestions of retraining adults. His strong outspoken views, time and again expressed like a *ceterum censo*, appeared to emanate from a mixture of political ideals, personal observations, and general consideration. In the first place, he set out to help the poor, above all Jewish children and adolescents; this was the humanitarian aspect. Secondly, he wanted to do something towards changing the detrimental social structure of the Jews in general by largely detaching them from the retail-trade, including peddling; this was the economic side of his scheme. And thirdly, he tried to counteract the anti-Jewish propaganda which also called for the boycott of Jewish business, this was his political point of view. In this connection, perhaps, another motive was taken into account (as far as German Jews were concerned): the trend towards social equalization.

A *Verein zur Förderung des Handfertigkeits- und Gartenbau-Unterrichts in den jüdischen Volksschulen* was founded in 1884 in Hanover by Moritz Simon "together with a number of intelligent people", as he himself put it.[8] It was realized that the success of his enterprise depended on the availability of a sufficient number of trained teachers for these subjects. With the consent and the co-operation of the *Bildungsanstalt für jüdische Lehrer* in Hanover,

---

[6]Siegfried Klein, *Festschrift zum 50jährigen Bestehen des Vereins zur Förderung der Handwerke und technischen Berufsarten unter den Juden*, Düsseldorf, April 14, 1930, priv. pr., p. 5.
[7]According to *Jüdisches Lexikon I* (1927), p. 926, up to 1898 in all 1,200 apprentices had been supported by the *Gesellschaft*. In April 1902, sixty-five apprentices were being trained under the supervision of six mechanics (*Im deutschen Reich*, 1902, p. 240). As regards agricultural training, the *Gesellschaft* had no significant success.
[8]Cf. A. M. Simon, *Soziales zur Judenfrage. Ein Beitrag zu ihrer Lösung*, published by I. Kauffmann, Frankfurt a. M., n.d., p. 5.

appropriate lessons were incorporated into the syllabus of the seminary. Similar efforts by other Jewish teachers' seminaries failed, as either the students were overburdened with other work or the number of teachers was too small.[8] At any rate, Simon's first efforts in this direction did not achieve their goal.

Yet, not easily discouraged, he made a further move.

In 1883, together with a few congenial men, he started the *Israelitische Erziehungsanstalt* at Ahlem near Hanover. (In 1919, it was renamed and henceforth known by the name *Israelitische Gartenbauschule Ahlem*). After this institution had been legalized in accordance with the Public Law (August/October, 1896), the first meeting of its Board *(Kuratorium)* took place in January 1897.[9] The members of this first Board were: Emil Berend, chairman, Semmy H. Oppenheimer and Eugen Rosenstiel, deputy chairmen, Leopold Fischer, secretary, Siegmund Federlein and Eduard Cohen, deputy secretaries. Soon after, at the request of the B'nai B'rith Lodge for Germany, Gustav Tuch, Hamburg, the deputy chairman of the *Verein zur Förderung der Bodenkultur unter den Juden Deutschlands,* briefly called *Bodenkulturverein,* was co-opted to the Ahlem Board.

The *Bodenkulturverein* had been founded in Berlin on October 24, 1897. The active participation of Gustav Tuch (1834-1909) was to be an important factor for the Ahlem movement. As a political economist, a writer on economics, a man well-versed in local government affairs, he had been quite a public figure in Hamburg. For a time, he was the president of the Henry Jones Lodge; he was also active in the Hamburg *Deutsch-Israelitische Gemeinde* and in the *Gesellschaft für jüdische Volkskunde* and helped many Jewish social welfare causes. A conference convened in Berlin on October 24, 1897, and attended by a large number of Jewish personalities from all parts of Germany, held the view "that the participation of German Jews in the agriculture of their homeland must be fostered by all the means at their disposal". To work for the support of the Ahlem school was regarded as one of the foremost tasks of this new organization. At its first general meeting (Berlin, January 16, 1898), *Oberamtmann* L. Cohn (Berlin) was elected chairman and *Privatier* Gustav Tuch deputy chairman. The first public appeal to join the *Bodenkulturverein* was signed by about one hundred well-known personalities, mostly living in Berlin, Hamburg and Poznan. In the early years, L. Cohn lectured in Berlin, Stettin, Poznan and Frankfurt/M. on the topic of the *Überführung der Juden zur Heimischen Bodenkultur,* whilst Tuch, as reported in the first Annual Report of the *Verein,* did much to bring about the success of the organization.[10]

---

[9]*Zweiter Bericht über die Israelitische Erziehungsanstalt zu Ahlem bei Hannover* (June 1, 1895, to September 15, 1897), Hanover 1897, p. 3.

[10]According to Felix A. Theilhaber (*Jüdisches Lexikon,* V (1930), p. 1174) the *Bodenkulturverein* at its height had a membership of some 2,000. It is supposed to have gone out of existence after World War I. Mention should be made also of Tuch's son Ernst, who helped in the building-up of the *Verein;* for a time, he acted as its Secretary General. Moritz Simon did not always share the views of Tuch jr. (cf. A. M. Simon, *Sollen sich Juden in Deutschland dem Handwerk, der Gärtnerei und der Landwirtschaft widmen?,* Berlin, n.d., p. 7).

Photo Hermann Friedrich, Hanover

MORITZ SIMON
(1837 - 1905)

Facsimile of the cover page of the first Ahlem report for the years 1893-1895

Fund-raising prospectus for Ahlem of the year 1902

Ahlem: In the school garden

Ahlem: Working in the orchard

The management of the Ahlem school was in the hands of the Executive Committee *(Vorstand)*. From the beginning, it consisted of: A. M. Simon, chairman, Georg Benfey, his deputy, Manfred Berliner,[11] secretary, Hermann Lichtenberg, his deputy, Gustav Cohen, Sartorius Rheinhold, S. Kayserling, L. Knoller, and Selly Meyerstein.

Ahlem pursued a twofold aim: it was to give a sound elementary school education to boys up to the age of fourteen, at the same time preparing them for, and acquainting them with, manual work, and to train boys over school-leaving age for agricultural and horticultural work.[12]

CAMPAIGNING FOR THE IDEA

It was probably around the turn of 1903 that A. M. Simon's little propaganda-leaflet *Soziales zur Judenfrage. Ein Beitrag zu ihrer Lösung* came out.[13] Judged by its emphatic style, it might just as well have been the printed version of the sort of lecture he delivered to Jewish audiences in an appeal for support. The impressions he gathered when he had toured the United States in the spring of that year and on an earlier visit to the Near East are described in some detail. The outline given is also an interim-statement of the conclusions drawn from the ten-year experiment of Ahlem. The leaflet is in a way the testament of this dynamic man whose life and thought was focussed on his one idea. Simon had been shocked by the working conditions of East European Jews who had arrived in the United States, in New York in particular, without sufficient experience of manual labour. Neither did he shut his eyes to the disadvantageous social structure of his fellow-Jews in Germany, a situation which he attempted to alleviate by prescribing his by then well-known formula. In his view, the training of young people in physical work meant, in the long run, less sacrifice than the numerous expensive efforts to settle unskilled adults in agricultural colonies abroad or commencing training at too late a stage. Simon was critical of the training-schools set up by the various Jewish colonization-organizations such as the ICA (Jewish Colonization Association), the Rothschild and Hirsch Funds, and by the Alliance Israélite Universelle. He also criticized the methods applied in Jewish orphanages in Germany and elsewhere. All the ideological and practical propaganda in favour of the Ahlem enterprise was based on Simon's ideas and aims. For example, Ludwig Klein,[14] a non-Jewish *Geheimer Regierungsrat*, when

---

[11]Hanover 1853-1931, headmaster of a private commercial school in Hanover, father of Cora Berliner (born in Hanover 1890, deported from Berlin 1942), one of the leading members of the *Reichsvertretung;* cf. *LBI Year Book II* (1957), pp. 309 ff., *Bewährung im Untergang*, ed. by E. G. Lowenthal, Stuttgart 1965, pp. 23 ff., and *Leben und Schicksal*, p. 88. The most famous of Manfred Berliner's brothers was Emil Berliner (Hanover 1851-Washington 1929), the inventor of the gramophone.

[12]*Erster Bericht über die Israelitische Erziehungsanstalt* . . . (1893-1895), Hanover 1896, p. 3.

[13]See note 8.

[14]*Rede des Herrn Geh. Regierungsrates Ludwig Klein zu Friedenau-Berlin, gehalten in einer vom Berliner Lokal-Komitee der Israelitischen Erziehungsanstalt Ahlem einberufenen Versammlung*, presumably 1902.

addressing a gathering in Berlin in 1902, expressed almost the same fundamental views as Simon himself. A lecture given by Simon at a Berlin meeting of the *Centralverein deutscher Staatsbürger jüdischen Glaubens* on February 22, 1904,[15] is sub-titled *Eine soziale Frage*; for in promoting his Ahlem idea, Simon always kept in mind the social welfare of children from needy Jewish families.

FINANCE

Ahlem was a private welfare institution, typical for the spirit of the age in which it was founded. The capital-stock donated by Moritz Simon in his lifetime (1892) amounted to 200,000 marks. It was chiefly used for the purchase of the estate, comprising sixty *Morgen*,[16] furthermore for the installation of the school, the living-quarters and the farm-buildings. By the end of 1905 another 15,000 marks and, by the terms of his will (see below), a further 100,000 marks was added.[17]

Besides the Simon Foundation and the assistance rendered by the *Boden-kulturverein*, there were several other Jewish Funds, all of them registered in Hanover, which made, though not all at regular intervals, more or less substantial contributions towards Ahlem's finances. Fairly large amounts originated from the Emma and Siegfried Brünn Foundation, the Minna and James Heinemann Foundation, the Joseph Berliner Foundation, the J. and M. Northmann Foundation, and the Sartorius Rheinhold Foundation. The latter (capital-stock: 30,000 marks), established on March 16, 1916, by Bertha Reinhold in memory of her late husband[18] made grants to a few indigent children enabling them to be admitted to Ahlem.

In addition, from the rather lengthy lists[19] incorporated into the Ahlem Annual Reports, it can be ascertained that there were at least another five different types of contributions and donations. Both annual and once-only payments ranged from 1 to 1,000 marks. The minimum of the so-called Benefactors' Payments was 300 marks; they sometimes went up to as high as five figure sums. Donations in kind were used for "extras". Children's collections, arranged mostly by Jewish teachers all over Germany at the High Festivals such as Rosh Hashanah and Chanukkah produced small amounts. At times individual pupils received financial support from various organizations such as the *Gesellschaft zur Verbreitung der Hand-werke und des Ackerbaus unter den Juden des Preussischen Staates.*[20]

---

[15]*Die Erziehung zur Bodenkultur und zum Handwerk, eine soziale Frage. Sonderdruck aus dem General-Anzeiger für die gesamten Interessen des Judentums*, Berlin C.2., n.d.
[16]One *Morgen* is roughly two-thirds of an acre.
[17]*Bericht* . . . 1904, p. 31.
[18]For many years Sartorius Rheinhold was a devoted Board member of the Simon Foundation. In February 1934, when the Rheinhold Foundation was dissolved, the capital was transferred to the Ahlem school.
[19]Quoting many names and places, thus giving some useful information also on certain aspects of German-Jewish communal history.
[20]See above p. 166 and *Im deutschen Reich*, 1902, p. 240.

When the school began functioning, the annual budget required was some 35,000 marks. By 1903, however, when the school had expanded both in scope and capacity, it was twice as big as in 1894. There was a steady increase from then on.

SIMON'S WILL AND THE SIMON FOUNDATION

On February 27, 1902, three years before his death, Moritz Simon made his will and had it registered with the *Königl. Amtsgericht 2 F* in Hanover on that day. In the first nine paragraphs he stipulated what he wanted to leave to his relatives. According to paragraph 10, the amount of 10,000 marks, called *Moritz Simonsches Legat,* was bequeathed to the "Emergency Fund for former Ahlem Pupils". In granting a further 100,000 marks to the *Israelitische Erziehungsanstalt* at Ahlem as such, Simon remarked:

> "On mature reflection I restrict my donation to this relatively insignificant amount, because I consider the permanent existence of the foundation only secured when it is regarded by all our correligionists as a common cause and supported by them accordingly."

A further 2,500 marks each were to go to four of Simon's close friends, "who had helped him in his endeavours to guide Jewish youth towards horticulture and manual skills". In his will, he asked each of the four potential recipients to accept the 2,500 marks in memory of him and to use them, at their convenience, for charitable purposes.

Seven of the thirty-three handwritten pages of Simon's testament constitute paragraph 11. It is there that the basis was laid for the *Alexander und Fanny Simon'sche Stiftung,* established by Moritz Simon in memory of his parents. The main provisions of the will as they affect the foundation are summarized below while the bulk of the relevant paragraph 11 is printed in the original German in an appendix to this essay.

Simon stipulates that the remainder of his property be earmarked for a foundation to be erected in the name of his parents, Alexander and Fanny Simon. The basic guide lines of the foundation were to be as follows: In recognition of the fact that the Jews had been forced by centuries of oppression and exclusion from industry, agriculture, the crafts, the civil service and the learned professions, to occupy themselves with commerce, and as it was in the interest of his correligionists and of the fatherland that they dedicate themselves to all lawful occupations, the aim of the foundation was to be to disseminate the profession of the crafts, agriculture and horticulture amongst the Jews. Jewish children, in particular younger pupils and orphans, were to be given instruction. Jewish teachers were to be aided to attend courses in agriculture and the crafts to enable them to prepare Jewish youth for vocational training. Special prizes were to be allocated to Jewish teachers who were particularly successful in this respect. Loans were to be made available to deserving and needy Jewish artisans and farmers. The foundation was to be empowered to receive additional donations.

The donors were to have the right to establish further subsidiary foundations in their own name under the administration of the main foundation provided that they conformed to its aims. Probity and economy were to be the rule. The founder hoped that his correligionists would follow his example by supporting similar enterprises.

The *Alexander und Fanny Simon'sche Stiftung* received the required Imperial approval on January 23, 1907, and commenced operating on August 15, 1907.

THE SCHOOL IN OPERATION

The school opened officially on June 2nd, 1893. At the very beginning, there were nine pupils in all, whilst the buildings had accommodation for a total of sixty pupils *(Zöglinge)* and two teachers. Boys up to the age of fourteen were called schoolboys, those older were regarded as apprentices; they had to sign on for three years. The schoolboys had the usual elementary lessons but were also given courses instructing them in light gardening and manual skills. The apprentices, on the other hand, worked primarily in the gardens and in the fields, supervised by a head-gardener and his assistants; in addition, they had to attend vocational training-courses in the various branches of horticulture and agriculture, and also their general knowledge of German, arithmetic, geography, etc., was not neglected.

The school observed strict neutrality from a Jewish political point of view. It was under the religious supervision of the Hanover *Landrabbiner*. Services were held daily.

During the first ten to twelve years of Ahlem's existence, up to the beginning of 1906, for which period the Annual School Reports are available, the total attendance rose from fifty-four pupils (in 1895) to ninety-four (in 1906), the average being in the neighbourhood of seventy-eight a year. Of these approximately seventy per cent were apprentices.

A special wing for young girls was added to the Ahlem campus at the end of 1902. In 1903, the attendance at the girls' school and domestic work training-centre was thirty-six; in 1905 it had risen to forty-six, of whom fifty per cent each were schoolgirls and trainees. The majority of either group was of German origin, fourteen came from smaller Jewish communities in Germany.

According to the second printed School Report (covering the two-year period June 1895 to September 1897), of the twenty-six pupils, eleven came from Saxony, five from the province of Hanover, four from Berlin, two from the Rhineland, and one each from Hesse-Nassau, West Prussia, Hamburg and Zürich. For the year 1900, the synopsis regarding the *Heimatsverhältnis der Zöglinge* (their geographical distribution) even distinguishes between schoolboys and apprentices. The former (thirty-nine) in their majority originated from Leipzig (seven), Berlin (five), the Rhine Province and the Province of Hanover (four each), from Hesse-Nassau (three), from Mainz, the provinces of Pomerania and

Poznan, from Bavaria and the Grand Duchy of Hesse (two each). The forty-six apprentices, on the other hand, included twenty-one foreigners; of these ten were from Austria, seven from Roumania, three from Russia, one from Switzerland; this breakdown indicates a comparatively strong East European element.

The first group of trained gardeners, twenty-nine in all, left school in 1898. Seventeen of them were able to find suitable employment in Germany. When the school began, fears had been expressed by some of the Jewish public that on completion of their training the boys would not find suitable jobs. Thereafter a breakdown of the geographical dispersion of the graduates *(Absolventen)* was included in the Annual Reports. As regards the first twenty-nine, of the remaining twelve five left for Austria, one went to St. Louis (Mo., U.S.A.) to take up work with the local Botanical Gardens. Two, for the purpose of continuing their training at higher horticultural or agricultural schools, proceeded to Jaffa/Palestine and Geisenheim/Rhine respectively. Two others stayed on until such time as suitable work in Germany was found for them. Only one trainee was reported as having left the calling altogether.

Looking at the figures of the Ahlem-trained assistants (as the *Absolventen* may be called), the statistical table below, based on the Annual Reports available, is made up only for a seven-year period, i.e. 1899 to 1905.

Year	Number of trainees leaving Ahlem
1899	12
1900	15
1901	16
1902	13
1903	12
1904	12
1905	8

Of the total 117 (as from 1898) fifty-four found employment in Germany. By the end of 1906, in all 134 gardeners had left Ahlem. During the period 1907 to 1913 their average yearly number was fifteen. For the middle of 1914 Katz[21] reported a total of 224. The average yearly "output" from 1915 to 1932 was at the rate of ten so that Weinryb's statement[22] made retrospectively to the effect that during the first thirty years of Ahlem the number of trained gardeners was 348 (or twelve per annum) is not far off; one third, according to Weinryb, was able to find work in Germany.

In World War I at least seventy-five former Ahlemer served in the German Armed Forces.[23] Up to the end of 1917, eighteen former pupils and two teachers had lost their lives in the war.[24] The girls' home at Ahlem was used as a military hospital.

[21]Cf. Eugen Katz, *Die Alexander und Fanny Simon'sche Stiftung zu Hannover, ihre Ziele und ihre Arbeiten von 1907-1914*, Hanover, June 1914, p. 33.

[22]Sucher B. Weinryb, *Der Kampf um die Berufsumschichtung. Ein Ausschnitt aus der Geschichte der Juden in Deutschland*, Jüdische Lesehefte, Nr. 13, herausgegeben von A. Leschnitzer im Auftrag der Reichsvertretung der Juden in Deutschland, Berlin 1936, p. 142.

[23]*Im deutschen Reich*, 1915, p. 126.

[24]*Ibid.*, 1917, p. 40.

Of the total 410 trainees who had left the school by 1932, 112 had found suitable employment in Germany.[25] 130 of the remaining 300 went abroad, i.e.

64 to America
36 to Palestine
9 to Poland
6 to the Argentine and Russia (3 each)
4 to Holland and Roumania (2 each)
11 to eleven different countries (1 each)

forty-five changed their trade, forty-eight died from natural causes or lost their lives in the war, and seventy-two were no longer traceable.

AFTER 1933

What happened at Ahlem in and after 1933? In introducing the Annual Report of the Simon Foundation for 1933, signed March, 10, 1934,[26] the Board issued the following statement:

> "With what clear perception and wise premonition our gracious founder, the Consul Simon, acted in propagating among German Jewry the necessity of vocational retraining and donating his entire property to the foundation in order to realize this good cause has been amply demonstrated by the events of the year 1933. The *Israelitische Gartenbauschule* Ahlem was the first German institution to adapt itself after the National Revolution to the new situation; it received a large number (about twenty-five) of young Jews aged twenty to thirty in order to effect their vocational retraining."

From the explanatory remarks accompanying a photo-reportage *Ein Tag in Ahlem bei Hannover,* published at about the same time in one of the major German-Jewish weeklies,[27] it transpired that on the then eighty *Morgen* Ahlem estate the following were in operation: a state-registered elementary school for boys aged six to fourteen; courses for apprentices, receiving either a three-year training as gardeners or a four-year training as tailors or cobblers, (commencing June 1933 under the heading *Berufsumschichtung)* a course for gardeners, aged fifteen to twenty-five, and a small department for the training of girls in domestic work.

The breakdown of the 104 persons living on the Ahlem estate shows that there were twenty-five pupils (schoolboys), thirty-five trainees (apprentices), thirty *Umschichtler,* five girls being trained in domestic work, and nine teachers.

Whilst for the first years of the Nazi era the usual Annual School Reports, whether in printed or in duplicated form, were not available, two comparatively short reports covering the periods May 1936 to May 1938 and May 1938 to June 1939 contain at least some statistical surveys giving information on the affairs

[25]Cf. the leaflet *Israelitische Gartenbauschule Ahlem 1893-1933*, p. 5.
[26]Hanover Municipal Archives.
[27]*C.V.-Zeitung*, 2. November 1933, No. 42.

of the school.[28] In either report the number of the pupils is given (1) according to categories and (2) for certain fixed dates; this is summarized as follows:

CATEGORY	Jan. 1, 1937	Jan. 1, 1938	Mar. 15, 1938	Dec. 15, 1938	June 15, 1939	
Gardeners' School	62	57	61	47	54	
Dept. for domestic work	9	8	9	7	13	
Cobblers' Training	1	2	2	1	2	
Tailors' Training	2	1	1	2	3	
Vocational pre-training *	—	7	16	14	22 }	**
Elementary school (6 forms; 8 teachers)	42	30	28	29	109 }	
Youth Aliyah (for boys and girls, aged 14-16)	—	—	—	—	39	
Total	116	105	117	100	242	

* i.e. *Berufsvorlehre*, its task being for a limited period to look after the general education and the physical skills of boys and girls of school-leaving age who were unable to find employment as apprentices.
**i.e. including non-residents.

Another statistical table illustrates the trend of emigration as follows:

DESTINATION	1933	1934	1935	1936	1937	1938	1939	Total
U.S.A.	9	—	—	2	2	12	1	26
Palestine	56	32	15	5	11	5	—	124
various countries (sixteen)								96
							Total	246

In the 1938/1939 Report, quoted above, it is pointed out that several attempts to have the school transferred abroad, either to Great Britain or Holland or to the U.S.A., failed.

In 1938 Ahlem was still the fifth largest Jewish agricultural training centre in Germany; it ranked next to Neuendorf (the former *Landwerk*[29], Winkel, Gross-Breesen[30] and Ellguth. These five between them, plus a further fifteen smaller centres, had a total capacity of 1,190. The percentage pertaining to Ahlem was close on 7.5.[31]

The minutes of the Simon Foundation Board Meeting, held in Hanover on June 25, 1939, a few weeks prior to the outbreak of World War II, throw some light on the financial position of the corporation; for it was reported that "quite recently representatives of the *Reichsvereinigung* had called in order to discuss current affairs, particularly in the light of the new course of events". As before, however, "Berlin" had held the view that as long as the institute's own funds

[28]Lower Saxony State Archives, Hanover.
[29]See p. 179.
[30]See Werner T. Angress 'Auswandererlehrgut Gross-Breesen', in *LBI Year Book X* (1965), pp. 168-187.
[31]*Arbeitsbericht der Reichsvertretung der Juden in Deutschland für das Jahr 1938*, p. 38.

were available and could be spent, financial support was not to be given. At that time, the Board members were: Paul Goldmann, Hanover, chairman; Alex Rehfeld, Hildesheim, deputy chairman; Fritz Gottschalk, Hanover, secretary; Max Schleissner, deputy secretary.

On October 19, 1939, six weeks after the outbreak of the war, the Education Department of the *Reichsvereinigung der Juden in Deutschland,* Berlin, over the signature of Paula Sara Fürst, reported to the *Regierungspräsident* of Hanover:

> "Auf Grund der 10. Verordnung zum Reichsbürgergesetz vom 4. Juli 1939 hat die Reichsvereinigung der Juden in Deutschland ab 1. Oktober 1939 die jüdischen Schulen in den nachstehenden Orten des Regierungsbezirks Hannover übernommen:
> Hannover,
> Ahlem."

On October 23, 1939, a letter addressed to the Simon Foundation in Hanover by the "Chef der Sicherheitspolizei und des SD" (signed Lischka), Berlin, ordered the ". . . incorporation of the *Alexander und Fanny Simon'sche Stiftung* into the *Reichsvereinigung der Juden in Deutschland.*"[32]

It may safely be assumed that during the first war years the Ahlem school continued functioning because only as late as July 23, 1942, did the *Regierungspräsident* of Hanover direct the Educational Officer of the Hanover-Land district to close the *Jüdische Gartenbauschule* and its elementary school immediately. On August 4th of that year it was confirmed that both schools had already been closed in June, 1942.[33]

THE TEACHING STAFF

It was not possible to obtain the necessary details in order to give a comprehensive picture of the teachers of Ahlem in chronological order. Instead, collecting from various and scattered sources as many names and relevant data as possible, only a somewhat abridged synopsis of the teaching staff employed can be given.

S. Bachrach, the first teacher to be engaged, stayed on until 1897. J. Hoexter already left in 1896. Bachrach's successor was Albert Silberberg. Born at Obersitzko (province of Poznan) in 1872, he served Ahlem from 1897 to 1929, when he retired to Hanover. He rose from teacher to *Erziehungsinspektor* and, subsequently, to Headmaster. When he died on April 30, 1934, in an obituary notice, signed by Hans Wolfes on behalf of the governing bodies of the school, Ahlem was described simply as "Silberberg's institution".[34] Kamm remained as teacher until 1899. Georg Feige was connected with Ahlem from 1899 to 1903, Blumen-

---

[32]Lower Saxony State Archives, Hanover.
[33]*Ibid.*
[34]*Erstrebtes und Erreichtes. Eine Jubiläumsschrift,* edited by the *Verein Ehemaliger Ahlemer* on the occasion of its 25th anniversary. Hanover-Linden 1929, p. 53. - Also *C.V.-Zeitung,* 10. Mai 1934, No. 19. - The idea of forming such an organization came first up in 1902. It was founded in 1903 as a *Verein ehemaliger Zöglinge* when its members numbered seventy-six. Later it also comprised former teachers.

feld until 1904. Lampel joined the teaching-staff in 1904, Meyerhof was a member from 1905 till 1906, Siegfried Jäckel in 1906. Ludwig Neumann lost his life in World War I. Levy Rosenblatt was Ahlem's second and last Headmaster. He was born at Beiseförth near Kassel in 1888 and appointed to the Ahlem post, as Silberberg's successor, on December 1, 1929. Previously he had held teaching positions with the Jewish orphanage at Paderborn (Westphalia) in 1920/1921 and with the Berlin municipality from 1921 to 1929. On July 1, 1939, he was also appointed chairman of the Simon Foundation.[35] Rosenblatt probably stayed on at Alhem until 1943, even after the school was closed. It is known that on March 15, 1943, he was taken to Terezin and nineteen months later deported to Auschwitz.[36] Prior to 1933 Alexander Moch,[37] for many years in Kenya, now in Israel, was in Ahlem; up to 1938 he was the administrator of *Landwerk* Neuendorf.[38] Martin Gerson (Czarnikau 1902—Auschwitz 1944) is likely to have been an Ahlem teacher in the years 1929/1930.[39] Moritz Rülf[40] taught at Ahlem from 1909 to 1914. Later he was, for many years, the minister of the Detmold Jewish community, passed the examinations as *Berufsschuloberlehrer* and *Diplomvolkswirt* and was called to Cologne to be in charge of the *Israelitische Kinderheim*. In 1942 he was a Board Member of the Cologne Jewish community.[41]

Other Ahlem teachers, as far as can be traced, were (in alphabetical order): Hermann Elter (1928/1929), Bruno Keith (1934), Ernst J. Mayford (1934-1939), Fred J. Perlstein (1925-1928), Siegfried Rothschild (1932), Julius Stein (1914-1923), Ruth Tennenhaus (1938/1939), José Tichauer (1930-1932), and Alfred Weiss (1932/1933).

SMALLER PROJECTS

The picture given of the Ahlem experiment and the Simon Foundation would be incomplete without at least mentioning three other, though on the whole short-lived, enterprises connected with it. Basically, they, too, conformed to what Moritz Simon had in mind.

In 1909, a farm at Steinhorst,[42] near Celle in Lower Saxony, was acquired by the Foundation jointly with the *Bodenkulturverein*,[43] the *Hilfsverein der deutschen Juden* and a few private individuals. Since this piece of property was in ruins, the purchase-price was very reasonable. Later, a Limited Company, called

---

[35]Letter addressed by the Simon Foundation to the Hanover Lord Mayor on July 1, 1939.
[36]*Bewährung im Untergang*, p. 141.
[37]*Erstrebtes und Erreichtes*, pp. 19 ff.
[38]See below p. 179.
[39]*Bewährung im Untergang*, pp. 58 ff.
[40]He contributed a short essay on the educational impact of Ahlem to *Erstrebtes und Erreichtes*.
[41]Cf. Zvi Asaria, *Die Juden in Köln von den ältesten Zeiten bis zur Gegenwart*, Cologne 1959, p. 384.
[42]Eugen Katz, *op. cit.*, and the propaganda leaflet *Das Lehrgut Steinhorst*, issued by the Simon Foundation, n.d., presumably in 1911, 4 pp., ill.
[43]See p. 168.

Land- und Lehrgutsgesellschaft, was set up to run the farm. Of the area of 900 *Morgen* two thirds consisted of moorland and heath. When acquiring the farm the idea was to have it under cultivation and make it pay within three years with the help of young Jewish agricultural trainees. They were to receive an all-round agricultural training including cattle- and horse-breeding. Up to 1914 two groups of trainees, in all twelve men, were ready to leave. According to the report for that year, they all found jobs, "without any difficulty", either as assistants or as administrators, with Jewish and non-Jewish landowners. During the war, Steinhorst was given up and sold.[44] In its stead the *Bodenkulturverein* took over some agricultural property at Buckow (Brandenburg), belonging to the Berlin Jewish community.[45]

In 1913, the *Simon'sche Seminar für Gartenbau und Handfertigkeit* opened at Peine (Lower Saxony). This institution, which incidentally was not restricted to Jews, was to train teachers in the subjects indicated. As compared with courses run by the State in Berlin and at Hagen and by the municipality of Munich, in the opinion of the Executive Committee (consisting of almost the same persons as the bodies governing Ahlem[46]) and its secretary, Eugen Katz, Peine was considered the only seminary of its kind in Germany, offering the most intensive training. That is why the syllabus,[47] forty-four hours per week, in summer and in winter, was filled to capacity. More than half the time was allotted to work in the gardens and to other manual work, whilst the rest of the time was used for lessons (in chemistry, physics, economics, methodology, etc.). However, because of the war, the seminary suffered considerably; a number of teachers lost their lives. Only in 1919 regular courses were resumed. But, during the ensuing years, the seminary experienced many vicissitudes with the result that in 1927, the whole undertaking having become a heavy burden to the Foundation, it had to be given up. The headmaster, Emil Alexander, was retired on a pension.[48]

As pointed out above,[49] Moritz Simon repeatedly stressed the view that his endeavours could only meet with success if young people were made to start manual work in their early years. With this in mind, school-gardens and training courses were installed and fostered by the Foundation. In the years 1918-1920 such installations, in most instances attached to Jewish elementary schools, were in operation, apart from Ahlem, in some forty German towns, both large and small. Amongst the cities were Berlin, Breslau, Hanover, Cologne, Königsberg, Leipzig and Mannheim; amongst the smaller places we find country-towns such as Bentheim (near the Dutch border), Binswangen (Bavaria), Rhina (Hesse), and Sohrau (Upper Silesia). The figure for 1913 was slightly higher.[50]

---

[44]Weinryb, *op. cit.,* p. 44.
[45]*Jüdisches Lexikon I* (1927), p. 927.
[46]Eugen Katz, *op. cit.,* p. 20.
[47]From the *Lehrplan mit Erläuterungen,* n.d. (Hanover Municipal Archives).
[48]From copies of typed minutes of either Foundation or Board Meetings 1918-1933 (Hanover Municipal Archives).
[49]See p. 169.
[50]Eugen Katz, *op. cit.,* p. 30.

AHLEM — A BYWORD

With all its shortcomings, Ahlem and all that belonged to the movement was a remarkable experiment. The idea conceived by Simon and his friends, springing from observation of things seen abroad and following certain political and humanitarian trends amongst Jews in Germany in the last two decades of the nineteenth century, made Ahlem a byword both as an institution and a name. Though remaining on a comparatively small scale, as far as the output went, the institution, after all, remained in existence for more than fifty years. This no doubt was an achievement considering that

(1) ORT commenced preparing its activities in Germany only in 1921,[51]

(2) the Hechaluz (*Deutscher Landesverband*, Berlin) for the Hachscharah training of future Palestine Chalutzim was founded only in 1922,[52]

(3) The *Reichsbund für jüdische Siedlung e.V.* and the *Jüdische Landarbeit G.m.b.H.* (Berlin) with their Gross-Gaglow (near Cottbus) agricultural settlement (and training facilities) began only in 1928,[53] and

(4) the labour service-style *Landwerk* Neuendorf (near Fürstenwalde/Brandenburg) for the training of unemployed Jews in agricultural and other manual work was set up only in the year preceeding the catastrophe.[54]

Berufsneuschichtung as contemplated and vigorously propagated by Moritz Simon and his circle in times of satisfactory economic conditions was indeed different from the *Berufsumschichtung* recognised as most desirable at the end of the twenties and considered inevitable after the events of the year 1933. The valuable experience gained over the many years of its existence meant that the Ahlem enterprise was able to give much help and guidance in the planning of the large-scale changeover process necessitated by the political and social upheaval and the rapid uprooting of Jewry as National Socialism consolidated its power in Germany.

[51]*Führer* . . ., p. 550. (ORT now stands for "Organization for Rehabilitation through Training).
[52]*Ibid.*
[53]*Ibid.*
[54]*Ibid.*, pp. 452-453.

APPENDIX

From the Will of Moritz Simon *

Meinen gesamten, nach Abzug der zur Ausführung der vorstehenden Verfügungen erforderlichen Mittel übrigbleibenden Nachlaß bestimme ich zu einer hiermit von mir errichteten Stiftung. Dieselbe soll zum Andenken an meine seligen Eltern den Namen

"ALEXANDER UND FANNY SIMON'SCHE STIFTUNG"

tragen.

Die Grundzüge der Verfassung der Stiftung bestimme ich wie folgt:

1. In der Erkenntnis, daß meine Glaubensgenossen infolge der Jahrhunderte währenden Unterdrückung und Ausschließung von Handwerk, Industrie und Landwirtschaft, vom Beamtenstand und den gelehrten Berufen sich notgedrungen dem Handel zuwenden mußten, daß es aber im Interesse meiner Glaubensgenossen und des Vaterlandes liegt, wenn sie sich allen rechtlichen Berufszweigen widmen, ordne ich als Zweck der Stiftung an: Hand- und Fabrikarbeit, Handwerk, Landwirtschaft, Garten- und Obstbau unter den Israeliten in größerem Umfange zu verbreiten.

2. Dieser Zweck soll vornehmlich durch folgende Mittel erreicht werden:

Aus den Einkünften der Stiftung sollen:

a) israelitische Kinder vom frühesten Alter an, namentlich in den Volksschulen, in jüdischen Waisen- und Erziehungsanstalten, auch insbesondere Handfertigkeitskursen oder in sonstiger Weise Handfertigkeitsunterricht erhalten sowie in den Handgriffen für Garten- und Obstbau und, wenn angängig, auch in Landwirtschaft unterwiesen werden.

Handfertigkeitsunterricht soll nur an solchen Anstalten unterstützt werden, in denen auch Hobelarbeit betrieben wird.

b) In Lehrerbildungsanstalten und Vorbereitungsanstalten oder in sonstiger Weise sollen angehende und tätige jüdische Lehrer praktische Kurse in Handfertigkeitslehre, in Garten- und Obstbau, Bienenzucht, und wenn angängig, auch in Landwirtschaft durchmachen; insbesondere sollen solche Anstalten, falls dieses zweckmäßig erscheint, Garten- und Ackerland zu Eigentum oder pachtweise erwerben, oder die sonst erforderlichen Veranstaltungen treffen, um die zukünftigen und auch bereits tätigen Lehrer für die Heranziehung der Jugend zum Landbau und zur Handfertigkeit zu befähigen.

Die aus dieser Stiftung geleisteten Zahlungen sollen nur zur Bestreitung der durch Handfertigkeit, Garten- und Landbau sowie Bienenkundeunterricht entstandenen Kosten verwandt werden dürfen, nicht etwa für die Bestreitung anderer, wenn auch an und für sich nützlicher Ausgaben.

Die Ziele der Simon'schen Stiftung, pp. 15-16.

Der Betrag von höchstens 1000 M. jährlich kann dazu verwandt werden, um an solche jüdische Lehrer Prämien zu verteilen, welche mit besonderem Eifer, Geschick und Erfolg Unterricht in Gartenbau und Handfertigkeit an jüdische Schüler erteilen. Es sollen jedoch nur solche Lehrer des Handfertigkeitsunterrichts berücksichtigt werden, die auch Hobelbankunterricht erteilen. Das Weitere hierüber zu bestimmen, überlasse ich dem Stiftungsvorstande.

c) Würdigen, fähigen, bedürftigen israelitischen Arbeitern, Handwerkern, Landwirten und Gärtnern sollen zur Ausübung ihres Berufes, namentlich bei Beginn ihrer Tätigkeit, wenn dieses dringend erforderlich, insbesondere in Form von Darlehen, Vorschüsse gewährt werden, welche je nach den Umständen zu niedrigem Zinsfuß verzinslich und nur ausnahmsweise unverzinslich sein sollen. Die zurückgezahlten Darlehen sollen dem Stiftungsgrundvermögen zugeschlagen werden. Trotz des Vereins „Hilfsfonds für ehemalige Lehrlinge der Israelitischen Erziehungsanstalt zu Ahlem" dürfen frühere Lehrlinge dieser Anstalt, wenn erforderlich, auch an den Wohltaten dieser Stiftung teilnehmen.

3. Ich bestimme ferner, daß ein Betrag von etwa 5% der Netto-Jahreseinkünfte der Stiftung nach bestem Ermessen des Stiftungsvorstandes für allgemeine Zwecke des Garten- und Obstbaues verwendet werden kann.

6. Das Vermögen der Stiftung besteht:

a) Aus meinem gesamten, nach Berichtigung der in meiner letztwilligen Verfügung angeordneten Erbteile, Vergabungen und Vermächtnisse übrig bleibenden Nachlaß, einschließlich der Ueberschüsse des Kosten- und Rentenfonds und der auflaufenden Einkünfte des Stiftungsfonds.

b) Aus dem etwa von dritter Seite der Stiftung zugewendeten Vermögen, zu dessen Annahme die Stiftung ermächtigt sein soll. Die Geber weiterer Beträge sollen auch berechtigt sein, unter ihrem Namen Nebenstiftungen zu errichten, welche unter Verwaltung der von mir gegründeten Stiftung gestellt werden können, sofern sie einen nach Ermessen des Stiftungsvorstandes den Zwecken der Hauptstiftung entsprechenden Zweck verfolgen.

8. Die Belegung des Vermögens der Stiftung soll stets in der solidesten Weise erfolgen. Es soll überall auf größte Sparsamkeit hingearbeitet werden, um auch anderen Anstalten hierin als gutes Vorbild zu dienen.

Ich hoffe, mit dieser Stiftung meinen Glaubensgenossen eine überaus nützliche Anregung gegeben zu haben, und erwarte, daß sie dieser Anregung durch Unterstützung gleicher Zwecke Folge geben werden.

Werkdorp Nieuwesluis

BY GERTRUDE VAN TIJN

When, following the Nazi seizure of power, German-Jewish refugees streamed into Holland, it had been realized that many would have to re-emigrate and were ill-equipped to do so. It was this consideration which led, in the beginning of 1934, to the foundation of the Jewish agricultural and manual training farm, the Werkdorp, to serve as an institution where young people could be trained in agriculture, horticulture, and various handicrafts.[1]

The foundation was officially registered at the end of February 1934 and on March 8th the first meeting of the committee took place. The foundation was named *Stichting Joodsche Arbeid* (Jewish Labour Foundation). Its task was to create and administer the Jewish training farm *Werkdorp Nieuwesluis*[2] in the Wieringer polder, thirty kilometres from the town of Alkmaar, on a newly-drained strip of land alongside the Zuijder Zee, placed for an indefinite period of time at the disposal of the Committee for Refugees from Germany.

The Council meeting of March 8th formally appointed the following members: Professor George van den Bergh[3], President; Mrs. Gertrude van Tijn, Secretary; Mr. Alfred Goudsmit, Treasurer; and as additional members: Professor David Cohen; Mr. Abraham Asscher; Mr. Sam van den Bergh (Member of the First Chamber); Mr. Isaac Hartogh; Mr. Siegfried Menko (Enschede) and Professor Engineer Dr. Dresden.

The additional (associate) members did not at any time take part in the decisions concerning the Werkdorp or its administration once it had been agreed in the first meeting to run the Werkdorp in accordance with the Jewish dietary laws. (This had been a very controversial issue.) However, the members of the committee, all leading personalities of Dutch Jewry, were ready to assist any time they were called upon for fund-raising or other activities. Thus Professor Dresden

[1] The writing of this brief survey of the history of the Jewish Werkdorp in the Wieringer polder almost thirty years after its liquidation would not have been possible without the co-operation of the following: American Jewish Joint Distribution Committee (JDC); The Central British Fund for Jewish Relief and Rehabilitation in London (Professor Norman Bentwich) and The Institute of Contemporary History and Wiener Library in London. The author would also like to mention the valuable help given by the former Werkdorp teacher, Fritz Hirsch, now in Australia (see note 4). Mr. Hirsch has kept in touch with many former pupils now scattered all over the world and the addresses he provided proved most useful. To all of these my sincere thanks.

[2] The original name had been "Werkdorp Wieringermeer" but had to be altered as this had caused confusion to the postal authorities.

[3] As Professor van den Bergh and Alfred Goudsmit have not been referred to often in this essay, it must be pointed out that from the start in 1934 until May 1940 they devoted considerable time to the Werkdorp and that all decisions were taken in regular board meetings and in close co-operation with the Director of the Werkdorp. Professor van den Bergh died some years ago. Alfred Goudsmit, now in his eighties, still takes an active part in Jewish social work in Holland.

came to the Werkdorp often and gave invaluable advice regarding the installations and the running of the various workshops.

From the very beginning the closest co-operation existed with the *Reichsvertretung der deutschen Juden;* the Joint Distribution Committee; the British Refugee Committee and, later (for emigration assistance) the HICEM in Paris.

In March 1934 the land, barracks etc. were formally handed over by the Dutch Government to the Foundation. The relationship with the government, the administration of the Wieringermeer polder as well as with all the other authorities, was excellent and it was to remain so during all the years of the Werkdorp's existence.

Originally the Werkdorp received 65 hectares, ground already prepared as part of the new polder, for agricultural and horticultural purposes. Eventually the Werkdorp was to extend to over 360 hectares. In addition the government provided barracks which had housed the polder workers, sufficient to accommodate 110 pupils; and we rented from the government one of the large, modern barns which in the beginning served partly for stabling and partly for the workshops. The Foundation also rented two large wooden houses; to dismantle these and erect them within the boundaries of the planned Werkdorp was one of the first tasks given to the pupils. These houses were used to house the manager, the staff and the girl pupils.

All new polders in Holland are subject to planning; farms as well as new towns are built and spaced in accordance with strict zoning and building laws. Permission from the government was needed and granted for the planned extension of the Werkdorp. The architect of the Wieringermeer polder drew up the plans for cheap and practical buildings to house the pupils as well as the plans for a large community building to contain dining-rooms and class-rooms as well as the synagogue. This building was planned in such a way that, hopefully, if one day no longer needed for refugees, it could be converted into a farmstead to fit in with the general polder plans.

We also had the help of the Wieringermeer administration when it came to the crucial task of engaging staff. Both the men who were to teach agriculture and horticulture were experts from the staff of the Wieringermeer polder, thoroughly acquainted with the quality of the virgin soil. Another Dutch expert taught husbandry and dairy-farming. Werkdorp pupils were to become later in Israel and elsewhere, firm advocates of Dutch agricultural methods and equipment. Dutch experts were also engaged to teach in the building and metalwork departments (plumbing, welding, training of blacksmiths, electrical installation etc.). A non-Jewish political refugee from Germany, *Meister* Hirsch, was in charge of the carpenter shop and also served as sports instructor. Eva Laufer, another refugee, the widow of a doctor, taught the girls; her three sons were admitted as pupils; Eva Laufer soon became the "mother" and confidante of the Werkdorp.

All these teachers were devoted to their pupils and full of understanding for the problems involved; all of them were experts in their fields, and all of them stayed until the bitter end or until, in the case of the building department, their task was finished. Yet if *Meister* Hirsch[4] and Eva Laufer deserve to be singled out here by name, it is because they were at the disposal of the pupils practically day and night, greatly assisting the manager in keeping things on an even keel. This was of importance because of the psychological difficulties of such a large and diverse group of men and women living so closely together — a subject to be discussed later.

The administrative staff and the assistants in the various departments were largely recruited from amongst the refugees. At the recommendation of the *Reichsvertretung* we engaged Dr. Hans Lubinski as Manager of the Werkdorp, a physician from Berlin and an educationalist who had already headed similar institutes in Lithuania and Germany. Dr. Lubinski brought his wife and three small children to Holland but was unable to live in the Werkdorp where in the beginning things were extremely primitive. Dr. Lubinski did a magnificent job during the initial difficult period but after a year and a half he decided to emigrate to Palestine. For some time he had been assisted by a young Palestinian and his wife, Moshe and Lea Katznelson, who had lived in the Werkdorp. After the departure of Dr. Lubinski they took over the management and to Moshe and Lea Katznelson must be given most of the credit for the success of the Werkdorp. If the manual training in the various departments, augmented by theoretical courses and classes in foreign languages (English, Hebrew and Spanish) was in excellent hands, the equally important aspect of the human factor was dealt with brilliantly by the young educator and his wife.

After the negotiations with the government had been completed and the staff had been engaged the board laid down the basic guidelines for admittance.

It may be mentioned here that throughout its existence the board worked together in absolute harmony. The avoidance of red tape and bureaucratic delays was remarkable and although the guidelines laid down age limits for admittance and although payment of fees had to be guaranteed by parents, the *Reichsvertretung,* or the Dutch Refugee Committee respectively, each case was examined on its merits and no suitable applicant was ever refused because too old, too young or because of lack of a sponsor.

The aim was to admit 150 pupils during the year to be extended — as facilities became available — to about 300. Two-thirds of the pupils were to be chosen by the *Reichsvertretung* from Jews still in Germany; about a third from refugees already in Holland; a few to be sponsored by the International Students Organization.

The age limits were 16 to 25 years; the charge for training and all living expenses was (Dutch guilders) fl 27.- per month in agriculture and horticulture and fl. 36.- per month in all manual training branches. The training period was to be roughly two years after which time the pupils were deemed ready to face life in a foreign country of their choice.

---

[4]Fritz Hirsch, a German anti-Fascist, later joined the Dutch resistance group Laren-Blaricum and was sentenced to death by a German tribunal in 1944. He managed to escape and lived in hiding until the liberation of Holland. After the war he emigrated to Australia.

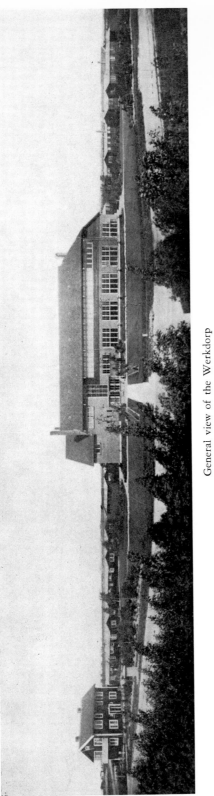

General view of the Werkdorp

Jewish youth at work in the Wieringermeer

Opening of the Werkdorp Community Centre on January 17th, 1937

Among those present: Dr. Arthur Hantke (extreme left); Dr. Bernhard Kahn (third from left);
James Macdonald, High Commissioner for Refugees (cont.)

The very large sums needed for building the Werkdorp were furnished by Dutch Jews and very generous contributions by the American Jewish Joint Distribution Committee (JDC) and the British Refugee Committee. Later the HICEM in Paris financed the costs of emigration. Dutch firms gave most of the modern, up-to-date equipment for the building, metal and carpenter shops as a gift.

Applicants for admission[5] had to submit a handwritten short biography, a photograph, a health certificate and had, after admittance, to sign a simple pledge to obey the rules laid down by the management for conduct in the camp.

These rules along with those concerning cleanliness, orderliness etc. stipulated significantly that the pupils were not allowed to take part in demonstrations and had to abstain from political activities of any kind. This may seem odd in retrospect but it must be remembered that the Jewish refugees were guests in a foreign country which became itself increasingly vulnerable to outside pressure. Also the pupils were told how and where they could lodge complaints and the management was given the right to expel pupils for valid reasons. Actually no pupil was ever expelled from the Werkdorp.

Thus all the preliminaries for beginning work and training in the Werkdorp had been completed and on March 13th, 1934 a small group of eleven boys and four girls clustered round two wooden barracks; dark specks on the vast, treeless, still only sparsely inhabited new polder. Two weeks later 48 pupils under the guidance of seven teachers started the task of building up the Werkdorp to a projected capacity of 300 pupils.

The first group was chosen exclusively from German-Jewish refugees already in Holland. They included a former lawyer; a chemical engineer; a physician; an actor; a music teacher; some students; sons of Jewish farmers; businessmen; boys from the lower middle class. In short, sociologically a group representative of the thousands who had fled Germany and were willing and ready to make the difficult transition to manual labour. They knew that only thus would they be able to have the chance to start a new life in a new country.

The following work schedule will demonstrate plans and priorities:[6]

Working scheme for the week of March 12th to March 19th, 1934

1. Building or Construction Group:
   1 foreman
   6 assistants
   Task: Erection of a canteen, re-building of a barrack as a bath-house.

2. Carpentry-Group:
   1 carpenter (cabinet-maker)

[5]The cover page of an application form and the top page of a prospectus are given in facsimile on the following page.
[6]The schedule is taken from a 'Memorandum on the agricultural and manual training farm "Werkdorp Nieuwesluis"' dated 16th March 1934, now in the possession of the Wiener Library, London.

WERKDORP
NIEUWESLUIS

ANMELDUNG
AUFNAHMEBEDINGUNG
KLEIDERVERZEICHNIS

STIFTUNG

JOODSCHEARBEID

Application form

BERUFS
UMSCHICHTUNG
HOLLAND

STIFTUNG

JOODSCHEARBEID

WERKDORP
NIEUWESLUIS

Prospectus

6 assistants
4-weeks' task:

Manufacture of 100 bed-frames for the assistants, manufacture of the necessary cupboards.

3. Locksmith-Group:
   1 locksmith
   6 assistants
   Task: Water Pipe-line and canalisation work, Installation of the bathroom, Installation of the canteen.

4. Painting-Group:
   1 painter
   6 assistants
   Task: Painting of the barracks.

5. Agricultural Group:
   1 teacher
   6 assistants
   Commencement of the work.

6. Gardening Group:
   1 teacher
   6 assistants
   Commencement of the work.

7. Household Group: (kitchen etc.)
   5 girls.

Thus in March 1934 the work was started. Six months later, on October 4th, 1934 the leading Dutch newspaper, the *Algemeen Handelsblad* started an article on a fund-raising drive for the Werkdorp with the following words:

> "The Werkdorp Nieuwesluis . . . only a small, almost invisible spot on the map of Europe - and yet a foundation of international importance whose name is known far beyond the polder and our country . . ."

This was true. From the very beginning the Werkdorp had the financial assistance of American and English Jewry. Many newspapers abroad gave publicity to the fact that the government of a small country giving asylum to thousands of refugees had had the foresight to grant land to enable a training farm to be founded. Professor Norman Bentwich, after a first visit to the Werkdorp, wrote an enthusiastic article about it in the *Manchester Guardian.* Throughout its existence a stream of prominent foreign visitors, both Jews and non-Jews, visited the Werkdorp. This included repeated visits by the then High Commissioner for Refugees at the League of Nations, later the first U.S. Ambassador to Israel, the late James G. Macdonald, who in October 1934 addressed a meeting on the Werkdorp in the Amsterdam Conservatory.[7]

---

[7] An invitation to this meeting is reproduced on the next page. It reads in translation: "The Council of the *Stichting Joodsche Arbeid* (Werkdorp Wieringermeer) and the *Comité voor Bijzondere Joodsche Belangen,* have the honour to invite you to join a meeting on

One year after the first shovel had turned the ground 130 young Jews were hard at work at their chosen occupations; learning while building the Werkdorp according to plan to become a beautiful, thriving, self-contained village.

They worked in the fields, the garden, and the newly-erected hot-houses; they raised poultry and took care of the growing herd of cattle; the twenty sheep and fourteen workhorses. They learned to handle tractors and other machinery. In the carpentry shop they made furniture and in the smithy shod horses, welded, made fixtures and repairs. They built wooden living quarters and laid bricks for the community building which was to form the centre of the village.

Amsterdam, 7 October 1934.
's-Gravenhekje 7

DE RAAD VAN BEHEER
VAN DE STICHTING JOODSE ARBEID (Werkdorp Wieringermeer)
EN
HET COMITÉ VOOR BIJZONDERE JOODSE BELANGEN

hebben de eer U uit te nodigen tot bijwoning van een bijeenkomst op Zaterdag 13 October a.s., des avonds te 20.30 ure in de Bachzaal van het Amsterdams Conservatorium, Bachstraat 7 te Amsterdam, waar gelegenheid zal bestaan met den Hogen Commissaris, den Heer James MacDonald, kennis te maken.

De Hoge Commissaris zal een toespraak houden en voorts zal de Heer Dr. Lubinski, directeur van het Werkdorp in de Wieringermeer, een lezing over het Werkdorp houden, waarbij een film van het Werkdorp zal worden vertoond.

De Raad van Beheer ziet Uw schriftelijk antwoord gaarne vóór 10 Oct. a.s. tegemoet.

One of the many voluntary helpers, the famous Dutch architect Paul Bromberg had drawn up the plans for this building. Architect Klein on behalf of the Wieringermeer administration saw to it that the building conformed in every detail to the strict building laws of the polder. This large building was an ideal training task for masons and carpenters; plasterers and painters; locksmiths and installers of lighting and heating, in short, everything connected with the building trade.

Saturday 13th October at 20.30 in the Bach Hall of the Amsterdam Conservatory, Bachstraat 7 in Amsterdam where you will have the opportunity to meet the High Commissioner, Mr. James Macdonald. The High Commissioner will address the meeting and Dr. Lubinski, the Director of the Werkdorp Wieringermeer will deliver a lecture and a film about the Werkdorp will also be shown. The Council requires a written answer before the 10th of October."

By March 1936, two years after the foundation of the Werkdorp, the plans were completed, except for the community centre, the ceremonial opening of which was planned for January 1937. The small wooden houses which served as living quarters were grouped in a wide circle around the community house. Each consisted of a dormitory for six and a common living-room.

Classes as well as the administration were still housed in the two wooden houses which the government had leased for a nominal fee. The large barn, also contributed by the government, was now used to capacity. It provided winter stabling for sixty cows, twenty sheep and fourteen workhorses. Wheat, oats, rye, winter barley, sugarbeet and other agricultural produce as well as cattlefeed were stored there.

The agricultural and horticultural branches were the only ones permitted by the government to sell surplus produce — that not used for the kitchen and the bakery of the Werkdorp — in the open market.

A budget drawn up by efficiency engineer J. van Tijn[8] (another of those who freely contributed of his time and knowledge) for the year 1935-1936 listed projected income from the farm as follows:

Income from crops fl. 10.992.— (a profit of fl. 1.725)

Income from horticulture dept. fl. 3.268,50 (a deficit of fl. 1,040,65)

Livestock: Income fl. 3.083,— (a deficit of fl. 2.460)

For poultry income and expenditure cancelled each other out (fl. 500)

Each year the acreage for the farm and the kitchen gardens was increased, showing growing profits. The Werkdorp never became self-supporting because of the high costs of maintenance; manual training and free scholarships. At the end of 1936 the Werkdorp covered 154 hectares. Of this about 90 hectares were under crops; 60 hectares grazing land and 3 hectares for the kitchen gardens.

The Wieringer polder administration used the Werkdorp as a testing station for shrubs and flowers etc. They thrived in the new soil and slowly the Werkdorp was transformed from a bleak collection of austere buildings, outlined against an immense horizon, into a miniature garden city surrounded by growing trees; each building the centre of multi-coloured flowerbeds and shrubs.

Up to October 1936, 317 pupils had been admitted of whom 162 had left, nearly all after having completed their training. They emigrated to:

Palestine	85
South America	15
South Africa	16
England	7
Italy	2
USA	1
other countries	7
	—
	133
For further education abroad	14
Left for reasons of health or unsuited	15
	—
	162

[8]Cf. 'Rapport von Ing. van Tijn für die *Stichting Joodsche Arbeid* über ihre finanzielle Lage in 1935' (33 pp.). On pp. 10 ff. 'Budget 1. Mai 1935 / 30. April 1936' (copies in the Wiener Library, London and the LBI, New York).

At that time another fifty pupils were ready and expecting early emigration.[9] Distribution over the various training branches was as follows:

    50 in agriculture and livestock
    30 garden, poultry and beekeeping
    15 carpentry
    30 building trades (including roadbuilding)
    30 girls in home economy[10]

The average age of the pupils was 24½ years. About 25% had originally been students or professionals; 40% had worked in some commercial capacity and 35% entered the Werkdorp directly after school. At that time there was also in the Werkdorp a group of twenty children aged 16 who were originally to have joined the children's Aliyah.

Up to October 1936 a total amount of fl. 280.000,-- had been spent in the Werkdorp. Of this amount:

raised in Holland	fl.	130.000,—
American Joint Distribution Committee	„	57.000,—
Central British Fund for German Jewry	„	26.000,—
Fees paid by parents; by the *Reichsvertretung* for pupils sent from Germany, as well as proceeds from harvest	„	67.000,—
	fl.	280.000,—[11]

Although new pupils were admitted as rapidly as possible, there was at that time a waiting list of 140.

There were some disappointments. After lengthy correspondence ICA had agreed to take five Werkdorp trainees for settlement in their farms in the Argentine. After arrival three of the group (two of whom had married girls not trained in the Werkdorp) decided to stay in Buenos Aires. Naturally, this did not improve the chances of future admittances from the Werkdorp.

On the other hand the leader of one of the new kibbutzim in Palestine which had admitted twenty-three of the Werkdorp pupils, wrote:

> ". . . the group had to live through an exceptionally hard winter in insufficient living quarters (tents) . . . and was asked to do heavy physical labour . . . We now know we can rely on them . . . It has also proved very helpful that the Werkdorp group was psychologically well prepared and were the only ones of the new arrivals who already spoke Hebrew."[12]

This was yet another tribute to the Werkdorp director, Moshe Katznelson, and one may well add here that today, more than three decades later, many former Werkdorp pupils hold responsible positions in the thriving agricultural settlements of Israel.

There was one rather serious incident during the year 1936; during a winter storm a chimney fire in one of the large wooden houses rented from the government spread and the whole house burned to the ground. The house had been

---

[9]LBI New York, 'Report regarding the *Stichting Joodsche Arbeid*, at the end of October 1936', 1.
[10]*Ibid.*, 2.
[11]*Ibid.*
[12]LBI New York, 'Bericht des Sekretariats der *Stichting Joodsche Arbeid* für das Jahr 1936' 5-6.

re-erected within the periphery of the Werkdorp — all but the community centre wooden structure — and the danger of the fire spreading was very great. Fortunately, the fire brigade, recruited some time before from among the pupils, managed to extinguish the flames before they spread further. However, insurance fully covered the loss. The house was not rebuilt because the community centre was planned to house the library (synagogue) and schoolrooms.

The year 1937 had started auspiciously. On January 17th the community centre was opened and visited by high Dutch government officials; representatives of the Wieringer polder administration; representatives from many foreign Jewish organizations; the High Commissioner James Macdonald; prominent Dutch Jews and many other invited guests. Bernhard Kahn who represented the American Joint Distribution Committee said on this occasion:

> "Our Dutch friends have recognized that the German Jews must go out to new countries not as refugees in distress and despair but as well-trained, hopeful pioneers. Therefore you have erected this institution here with your traditional ability and vision and with that Jewish heart that feels so strongly the needs and the tragedy of your brethren."

The next day the leading Dutch newspaper, the *Algemeen Handelsblad*, devoted a long article to the festivities in the Werkdorp. Reading it now, after more than thirty years, it is moving to find with what depth and sympathy and understanding this newspaper wrote of the Werkdorp and it inhabitants. In part the article read:

> "Two worlds in this new land. One large, one small . . . In the midst of the rapidly growing towns and farms on Holland's latest virgin soil . . . this brave small colony; people of a different race; different language; different customs . . . but with a tenacity bred out of pride . . . they do not succumb. Here, on a small piece of ground, generously given to them, they work together, helping each other to find a new life."

After the completion of the community centre the building trade department was liquidated. The few pupils not yet ready for emigration were absorbed by other training departments. After long discussions the board decided to follow the advice of Professor Dresden and continue training in the carpentry and locksmith shops, although these were largely responsible for the continued budget deficits.

For the first few years of the Werkdorp's existence we were able to base our survey on the annual reports which have survived in Jewish archives. Unfortunately it was impossible to trace copies of the annual reports for 1938 and 1939.[13] We are, therefore, unable to give exact figures for admittance, occupations and emigration.

Hitler's growing persecution of the Jews had involved the Werkdorp from its inception in March 1934. The invasion of Austria in March 1938, the occupation

[13]The only extant report from the year 1939 is a three-page memorandum 'The Jewish Werkdorp in Wieringermeer has existed for five years' dated 4th April 1939 (in the Wiener Library, London). Until the spring 1939 it gives the figure for emigration of Werkdorp pupils as 245; and in an incomplete breakdown lists 111 emigrants to Palestine, 20 to South Africa, 31 to the Argentine and 18 to North America.

of the Sudetenland later that year, all those events resulted in new waves of refugees coming to Holland; and always there was increased clamour for young people to be admitted to the Werkdorp. The farm itself had again been enlarged — a further 140 hectares were rented in 1939 — and now covered 360 hectares (at the beginning it had been only 40 hectares). Repairs and maintenance gave more than enough work to the carpentry shop and the smithy. The former also made some beautiful furniture which was auctioned off in a fund-raising drive for the Werkdorp.

In February 1938 the London Council for German Jewry made a £500 special grant to the Werkdorp to enable it to rebuild the lavatories and the showers and add a laundry. However, the Werkdorp never had enough girl students to tackle this extra job and the plans for a laundry were dropped. This reduced the building costs to £300.

In October 1938 we again were forced to make some changes in the plant as outlined in the following letter addressed to the Joint and the London Council dated October 6th, 1938.

STICHTING JOODSCHE ARBEID
Werkdorp Nieuwesluis

Secretariaat: Amsterdam, 's-Gravenhekje 7
October 6th, 1938

To the
American Joint Distribution Committee
Paris
Council for German Jewry
London

Dear Sirs,

A few weeks ago we received notice from the government that the smithy shop, consisting of an iron shed alongside the road and outside the farm property, would have to be removed immediately and would have to be rebuilt within the circuit of the Jewish village.

At the same time we had been considering the possibility of extending Wieringen. We received so many urgent demands to admit young people, either actually in concentration-camps or threatened with an expulsion-order that we felt we had to create a certain number of places, in order to be able to help in such emergencies. As we cannot rent more land and as the agricultural as well as the horticultural department cannot give work to more pupils than they have at present, we decided to not only rebuild the smithy shop, but to extend it at the same time. In this way it was possible to create 30 new places. These places will be reserved for urgent cases. How great is the need may be gathered from the fact that 23 of these places have already been promised.

The capital expenditure in connection with this extension is roughly a £1000,—. We are enclosing a detailed statement of the investment needed. Wieringen is constantly faced with the greatest financial worries; the extensive collection on behalf of the Refugee Committee, the Children's Alijah and the Zionistic drives make it difficult for us to raise money for Wieringen separately.

We realize that the exploitation costs will be increased through this new extension, but we feel that we should face these extra expenses. We hope, however, that your organisation will help us with the capital expenditure by increasing the subsidy for 1938.

Hoping to receive a favourable reply,   Yours sincerely,
Stichting Joodsche Arbeid
Gertrude van Tijn
Secretaresse

The council agreed to let us use the £200 left over from the shower-room complex and the JDC granted the rest. Thus again there was sufficient work for the carpenters and the smiths.

Very soon after, when the new places had barely been made available, a new disaster struck the German Jews. On November 10th a general pogrom, the *Kristallnacht,* swept through Germany following the assassination of the German Embassy official vom Rath in Paris.

Among the thousands of Jews thrown into concentration camps was a group of twenty pupils from a Jewish training farm Gross-Breesen who, with their director Professor Curt Bondy, had been interned in Buchenwald. After six weeks they were released on condition that they would leave Germany immediately. Many had emigration visas; also some countries, shocked by this new evidence of barbarism, did to some extent and for a short time relax immigration restrictions. All those who did not find another solution were admitted to the Werkdorp. Some leading Dutch professors obtained permission for Professor Bondy, an internationally known expert in social psychology and education, to come also to Holland.[14]

The Gross-Breeseners came to the Werkdorp a close-knit group — definitely non-Zionist — whose experience of communal living had been very different from life in the Werkdorp. They had been admitted to Gross-Breesen after Professor Bondy had personally interviewed each of them. The hundred or so who were admitted had practically all come from assimilated Jewish urban middle-class families.

Farming and some crafts were taught at Gross-Breesen and taught well. But a great deal of time and effort was devoted to education: "A systematic attempt to introduce to [the pupils] . . . a set of moral precepts by which [they were] . . . to be governed during their stay in Breesen and their future life overseas." Classical music, literature, current affairs were given equal time with theoretical and language courses. Attendance at religious (reform) ceremonies, cultural events and character-building *(Lebenskunde)* sessions was mandatory.

The Gross-Breeseners who came to the Werkdorp showed a high degree of maturity and impeccable manners in dress and at table. After their admittance Professor Bondy came frequently to the Werkdorp for lectures and counselling and a warm friendship developed between him and Moshe Katznelson.

Contrasting sharply with the Gross-Breesen policy the Werkdorp admitted applicants deemed suitable mostly on the basis of need. Not too much probing was done into their antecedents and none as to their ideological preferences. There were Zionists and non- or even anti-Zionists. Some were orthodox and quite a

[14]For the history of the training farm Gross-Breesen, established by the *Reichsvertretung der deutschen Juden* in February 1936 see Werner T. Angress, 'Auswandererlehrgut Gross-Breesen' in *LBI Year Book X* (1965), pp. 168-187. The information regarding Gross-Breesen given here is based on this essay.

few Reform Jews, others totally indifferent to the Jewish faith. The social background ranged from proletarian to middle or even upper middle class. Almost all professions were represented and even in age the pupils differed widely. Thus the Gross-Breeseners joined a far more diversified community, which ideologically at any rate never followed one distinct Jewish tendency.

Certain rules were enforced in the Werkdorp; but generally speaking the atmosphere was what would today be called "permissive". The Jewishness of the community was stressed; Jewish holidays were celebrated. There was special food on Friday nights; candles were lit and prayers said. Quite a few weddings were celebrated, also in accordance with Jewish law. Now and then a rabbi would visit us and, incidentally, make sure that the Jewish dietary laws were being obeyed. On Saturdays only the most necessary tasks were performed; the pupils were free to spend the day as they wished, even outside the village. There were organized cultural activities. Thus Dr. Erich Rosenberg (who headed the Welfare Department of the Jewish Refugee Committee in Amsterdam) gave a series of lectures on refugee problems as well as general socio-economic subjects. There were memorable musical events, such as a series of Mozart concerts given by Lili Krauss. The library was well stocked with books and records; magazines and newspapers were available. Never was attendance at any religious or cultural event mandatory.

Common interests, personal friendships, led to separate groupings; the Zionists were by far the largest and most cohesive group.

While the Gross-Breeseners were absorbed into the general life of the Werkdorp without any difficulties there had been a very different experience with another group. In the spring of 1936 some pupils were admitted who turned out to be confirmed Communists. Attempting to convert others to their beliefs, they caused a great deal of friction, particularly with the equally vocal and dedicated Zionists. (In those months a great deal of our time was consumed in deliberations how to overcome this serious problem). It was soon realized that tolerating the presence of an active Communist cell in the Werkdorp posed a real threat to its very existence in view of the stringent rules laid down by the host government and the official Dutch anti-Communist policies. Yet, expulsion of the group was, of course, inconceivable. It would have meant deportation to Germany and almost certain death.

The problem ultimately solved itself. The boys confided to Moshe Katznelson that they intended to leave the Werkdorp to make their way to Spain and fight in the Civil War for the Spanish Republic. One by one they left during the summer of 1936 and the tension within the community subsided.

It was estimated that after the November 1938 pogrom there were about 25,000 refugees in Holland. Even those who did not need financial assistance often came to the offices of the refugee committee for legal advice; assistance in emigration etc. The eighty or so employees (many of them volunteers) who worked in the welfare, housing, children, legal or emigration departments with their throngs of callers needed space. The refugee committee was offered for a nominal rental the use of an empty, modern, five-story diamond polishing factory.

The Amsterdam office of the *Stichting Joodsche Arbeid* (the Werkdorp) was also housed in this new building. The partitioning of the vast floor space, the painting and the making of furniture for the many offices gave meaningful employment to the pupils in the Werkdorp shops for a long time.

In the Werkdorp life went on, the cows were milked, the livestock was fed, sowing and reaping continued; it was hard work in the stables, the fields and the gardens.[15]

WOENSDAGAVOND

21 Juni 1939 te 8.30 ure

RADIOREPORTAGE

uit het Werkdorp in de Wieringermeer
door de V. A. R. A.

ter gelegenheid van het

Vijf-Jarig Bestaan

van het

WERKDORP

der Stichting „JOODSCHE ARBEID"

Vijf jaar Werkdorp Wieringermeer beteekent: honderden jonge Joodsche emigranten opgeleid voor een nieuw levensbestaan in andere landen.

Met Uw steun kunnen wij nog velen helpen.

Luistert . . . . . .

en doet wat gij kunt!

Het Bestuur:
Prof. Mr. Dr. G. VAN DEN BERGH, Voorz.
ALFR. GOUDSMIT, Penningm.
G. VAN TIJN-COHN, Secretaresse.

The once empty horizon was dotted with farms and barns, nestling in their groves of trees; here and there church spires pointed up towards the immense sky. It looked like a peaceful world; but in the Jewish village the pupils, most of whom still had families in Germany and who were constantly worried about their fate, knew better; not a single life had remained untouched by Nazi perse-

---

[15]Shortly before the outbreak of World War II the fifth anniversary of the Werkdorp was commemorated in a special broadcast. Part of a leaflet announcing this broadcast in a fund-raising campaign is reproduced here. "Wednesday Evening 21st of June 1939 at 8.30 p.m. Radio broadcast from the Werkdorp in the Wieringermeer through V.A.R.A. on the occasion of the Fifth Anniversary of the *Werkdorp* of the *Stichting Joodsche Arbeid.* Five years of the Werkdorp Wieringermeer means that hundreds of young Jewish emigrants have been trained for a new life in other countries. With your assistance we can still help many more. Listen and do what you can! The Board."

cution. And in September 1939 peace was to end for most of the rest of the
world for a long time. Though for many months the "phoney" war did not seem
to touch life in Holland most could read the writing on the wall.

Every effort was, therefore, made to speed up emigration. There had been one
lucky opportunity prior to the outbreak of the war. For some time two young
Palestinians had been in Holland trying to charter a boat to bring young Jews
from Holland to Palestine. It was a costly plan and the money would have to come
from an agency abroad. Fortunately through the good services of Sally Meyer in
Switzerland the money was made available and a boat, the SS "Dora" was
chartered.

In the summer of 1939 this project, so long in the planning, finally became a
reality. On July 15th, 1939 the SS "Dora" left Amsterdam for Palestine with
310 passengers on board, with few exceptions young people, among them about
fifty pupils from the Werkdorp.

In Antwerp the SS "Dora" took on another 157 passengers. Overloaded, ill
equipped, not very well provisioned, the SS "Dora" took six weeks — until
August 10th, to reach her destination. But luckily the British patrol boats did not
intercept her. Everything had been prepared for the reception of our pupils and
immediately after landing they were distributed among a number of kibbutzim —
indistinguishable from the old "legal" kibbutznicks. Most of them live in Israel
to this day.[16]

On May 10th, 1940 the Germans invaded Holland. The British Consulate
offered Moshe Katznelson and his family the chance to leave Holland together
with the other British subjects but he chose to stay with his charges. In July of
the same year he was interned in a Prisoner-of-War (not a concentration) camp
in Germany for the rest of the war's duration. His wife and son were after some
time repatriated to Palestine. A well-known Zionist, the lawyer Abel Herzberg,
took over the management of the Werkdorp on a temporary basis.

The Chairman of our Board, Professor George van den Bergh, was almost
immediately arrested and sent to Germany as a hostage. Our Treasurer, Alfred
Goudsmit, succeeded in leaving Holland with his family during the night of the
10th. His place was taken temporarily by an engineer Jules Cahen who, for a long
time, had taken a great interest in the Werkdorp.

I stayed at my post as head of the emigration department of the refugee
committee and secretary of the Werkdorp. However, because all private cars had
immediately been confiscated it was extremely difficult for me to reach the Werkdorp and most of the business was transacted by telephone.

On the whole life and work in the Jewish village went on — though with
mounting apprehension — outwardly undisturbed. The non-Jewish teachers and

---

[16]Many of them gathered together with Ambassador Gideon Raphael (who had chartered
the "Dora" in Holland) to celebrate the 25th anniversary of the landing.

foremen as well as the Jewish staff continued their work as before until the spring of 1941.

On March 20th, 1941 a telephone call from the German authorities informed me that all Werkdorp pupils would be brought to Amsterdam and we were ordered to find lodgings for them.[17] We arranged to have them brought to the diamond factory of Abraham Asscher to be distributed from there. When I tried to inform the Werkdorp of this it was already occupied by the Gestapo and I could not tell them what had been arranged.

Later I learned that seven buses had arrived; the boys were separated from the girls and all were given ten minutes to get ready to go to a destination unknown. The non-Jewish Dutch teachers of the agricultural and livestock departments were told to select the sixty best pupils so that the work on the farm could be carried on. The entire staff with the exception of Abel Herzberg was told to stay. The others were marched to the buses and driven away.

One can imagine only too well what it meant to these young people to be sent into the unknown at a time when the name of Mauthausen and other concentration camps were already more than just names to Jews in Holland. I shall never forget the expression of relief on the faces of those boys and girls when they realized they were in Amsterdam and saw me and others they knew ready to receive them.

A few days later we were told that the evacuation of the Werkdorp had been a mistake and that the pupils would be sent back. However, the negotiations dragged on and it was not until June when Professor Cohen, Jules Cahen and I were called to the Gestapo to discuss the arrangements for their return. Though the Germans had the names and addresses of the pupils they asked for a special list to facilitate collecting them and this list was given to them.[18]

During the same week, however, there had been a bomb outrage in the Schubertstraat in a house occupied by some German officers and situated in the fashionable South of Amsterdam where at that time many Jews were still living and where many of our Werkdorp pupils had been given hospitality. Thereupon the highest Gestapo official in Holland, *Generalkommissar* for Security Hanns Albin Rauter[19], ordered the arrest of 400 Jews, preferably refugees from Germany

---

[17]Apart from personal recollections the account of the liquidation of the Werkdorp and the deportation of its pupils is based on Gertrude van Tijn, *Contributions to the History of the Jews in the Netherlands from May 10, 1940 to June 1944*, a report written by the present writer after her release from Bergen-Belsen for the Joint Distribution Committee, and K. P. L. Berkley, *Overzicht van het ontstaan, de Werkzaamheden en het Streven van den Joodsche Raad voor Amsterdam*, Amsterdam 1945.

[18]On this see also J. Presser, *Ashes in the Wind. The Destruction of Dutch Jewry*, London 1968, p. 70. In the more comprehensive original Dutch edition, *Ondergang. De Vervolging en Verdelging van het Nederlandse Jodendom 1940-1945*, 's-Gravenhage 1965, 2 vols., the author gives further details of the subsequent fate of the Werkdorp and its pupils. Cf. vol. I, pp. 124, 420, 448-449 and vol. II, p. 15.

[19]On Rauter's activities and function in Holland see Presser, *op. cit.*, both versions, passim, and now also in particular Konrad Kwiet, *Reichskommissariat Niederlande. Versuch und Scheitern nationalsozialistischer Neuordnung*. Schriftenreihe der Vierteljahrshefte für Zeitgeschichte, Stuttgart 1968, passim. Rauter was executed as a war criminal by the Dutch in 1949.

who were to be sent to Mauthausen. This order was given on the very same day on which the pupils had been scheduled to return to the Werkdorp. I still believe that it had been the intention of the Amsterdam Gestapo to send the boys back but that this intention was foiled by the order for arrests given by higher officials in The Hague.

The Gestapo called on many houses listed as addresses for Werkdorp pupils but also on many others. Many Jews were arrested on the streets and in trams, all in the same district. The news spread like wildfire and many young Jews went into hiding. Among the 300 Jews who were finally detained and sent to Mauthausen were sixty Werkdorp pupils. Death notices for all of them began to arrive very shortly afterwards.[20]

Nobody was allowed to return to Wieringen and the Werkdorp was finally liquidated in August 1941. On the 1st of August 1941 the remaining pupils and the Jewish staff were brought to Amsterdam. The Dutch authorities were ordered to take over the Werkdorp and we were paid an indemnity for the community centre, livestock, equipment etc. the amount of which I cannot remember. The Germans tore down the wooden structures around the main building. The money was used to rent two houses; one, a home for younger pupils came under the management of Eva Laufer. The other house was used for a library and clubroom and housed older pupils. We were allowed to bring the equipment from the carpentry shop and the smithy to Amsterdam; there they were installed in one of the newly organized Jewish manual training schools.

In the early summer of 1941 Jules Gerzon had taken over as director of the Werkdorp and its pupils. He took a great interest in every single pupil and until after the houses had to be liquidated after the mass raids in 1942 he visited the homes every day. It was due to his great devotion and resourcefulness that many of the boys succeeded in going underground. Later he sent parcels to every one then in the Dutch camp in Westerbork until he himself was brought to Westerbork with his family in September 1943.

This was the last chapter in the history of the Werkdorp. In all about 300 people were in the Werkdorp when the Germans came to Holland.[21] 210 were taken to Amsterdam on March 20th, 1941; of those sixty died in Mauthausen. The remaining pupils were brought to Amsterdam on August 1st, 1941.

---

[20]According to K. P. L. Berkley, *op. cit.*, 31, the *Joodsche Raad* received the first death notices with regard to detainees of the June raid and the earlier one in February in June 1941. As the cause of death for such young and healthy men unlikely reasons - sunstroke, kidney infection and pneumonia - were given, and even the notorious "shot while trying to escape" was not lacking. In the course of the years 1941 and 1942 death notices were received for all those who had been detained in Mauthausen. See also Abel J. Herzberg, *Kroniek der Jodenvervolging*, n.p.n.d., pp. 96-98. - The terrible end of these young Jewish deportees to Mauthausen and the sixty Werkdorp pupils amongst them is described in Presser, *Ashes in the Wind*, pp. 53-54.

[21]Taking as a basis a two-year training, it is a conservative estimate that at least 1,000 pupils finished their training and that most of them managed to emigrate.

Some were still able to emigrate; many went underground; many were caught in later raids. How many of those in hiding and in camps survived is not precisely known.[22]

The tragic end of the Werkdorp is apt to make us forget that during the more than seven years of its existence much was achieved. Wieringen is now the old polder; the farmhouses already have the patina of weathered age but the community centre built by its pupils still stands and is used by the government as a manual training school. Thus, "the bricks we laid are alive to-day".

But a monument to the memory of the Werkdorp better than mere bricks is the many lives that were saved and the skills that were taught, enabling young German Jews in many countries, from Israel to Australia, from South America to Kenya to reconstruct their lives. Thus the Werkdorp certainly deserves to be recorded as a significant episode in the history of the organized emigration of German Jewry.[23]

In this bare outline of facts and figures we have attempted to show what it was that the *Stichting Joodsche Arbeid* endeavoured to achieve in its Werkdorp. Beyond the teaching of useful and needed skills "in the nightmare of the dark" the Werkdorp brought into the lives of many young Jews a ray of hope, a feeling of certainty that at some time in the future the light would shine again.

---

[22]Presser, *Ondergang*, vol. II, p. 15 gives, however, a table on the probable fate of those in training farms and *hachsharoth* in Holland after the Nazi invasion. He lists 299 Werkdorp pupils, 218 of whom were deported and 81 who went underground. There were 35 survivors amongst the deportees. All but ten of those who went into hiding survived the war (71); 21 of these reached Palestine illegally.

[23]The Werkdorp is mentioned briefly in the first volume to appear of the official Dutch history of the Second World War. See L. de Jong, *Het Koninkrijk der Nederlanden in de Tweede Wereldoorlog, 1 Voorspel,* Amsterdam 1969, p. 475.

Memoirs and Documents

Daniel Lessmann in Vienna and Verona

BY H. G. REISSNER

THE CORRESPONDENT

Daniel Lessmann (1794-1831) belonged to that first generation of German Jews after Moses Mendelssohn which had received a classical-humanist education. Born in Soldin, Neumark, the son of a petty merchant, Lewin Philipp (Gotthold Lessmann, after September 10, 1812), he attended the *Kgl. Joachimsthalsche Gymnasium*, Berlin from 1806 to 1812, and Berlin University in the years 1812 to 1817, with interruptions, however, as he had volunteered for the Prussian army in the wars against Napoleon of 1813 and 1815. Though he had studied and, during part of his military service, practised medicine, he decided not to follow it as a profession, but to devote his talents to literary pursuits. His travelogues, biographical sketches, translations, novels and poems appeared in journals and later on in books. In his day they were popular in Germany and Austria and received friendly comments from more formidable literary colleagues such as Heinrich Heine[1] and Heinrich Laube.[2] His publicistic and poetical endeavours were analysed in a German doctoral thesis almost a century after his death.[3]

Lessmann's active participation in the *Wissenschaftzirkel,* a Jewish group mainly of students of Berlin University, which existed from November 1816 to June 1817, and was first mentioned by S. Ucko.[4] It was described more fully in the present writer's biography of Eduard Gans.[5]

THE CORRESPONDENCE

When writing the Gans biography I had not been aware of a complete file of unpublished original letters written by Lessmann to various friends in Berlin during the years 1817 to 1825. They are now in the possession of YIVO Institute for Jewish Research in New York.[6] Chronologically linked to these letters is an unpublished Lessmann-manuscript of twenty pages *Knüttelversiges Disputatorium. Eine disharmonische Introduktions-Phantasie,* now in the Archives of the Leo

---

[1]*Reise von München nach Genua,* chap. XXVI, and various letters addressed to Moses Moser between January 9, 1824 and July 22, 1825, also to Joseph Lehmann on December 16, 1826, and 'Der Berliner Musenalmanach für 1830' in *Gesellschafter,* Berlin, December 28, 1829.
[2]*Moderne Charakteristiken,* vol. 2, No. 20, Mannheim 1835.
[3]Hertha Schumann, *David Lessmann,* typewritten, Leipzig 1920.
[4]'Geistesgeschichtliche Grundlagen der Wissenschaft des Judentums' in *Zeitschrift für die Geschichte der Juden in Deutschland,* 1934.
[5]*Eduard Gans. Ein Leben im Vormärz* (Schriftenreihe wissenschaftlicher Abhandlungen des Leo Baeck Instituts 14), Tübingen 1965, pp. 29ff.
[6]The archivist, Mr. Eliezer Lifschutz, had no idea by whom and when they were deposited.

Baeck Institute, New York.[7] It had previously changed hands amongst Austrian and German autograph dealers. Though not dated, the context makes it clear that it had been composed in Vienna some time between 1818 and 1820.

Lessmann's letters number fourteen. The first was written from his home town Soldin on October 12, 1817. Ten letters are dated from Vienna, between November, 17, 1817 and April 25, 1820. Two further letters were written from Verona, on April 14, 1821 and June 12/13, 1822 respectively. The last letter is dated from Doberan (a spa in Mecklenburg on the Baltic Sea), July 16, 1825.

Two of the letters were addressed to more than one party. Moses Moser appears as addressee altogether twelve times, and — each once — Joseph Hillmar; I. M. Jost; Eduard Normann; Adelheid Zunz; Leopold Zunz and Lessmann's own parents. The letters also contain repeated inquiries about, and messages to, other residents of Berlin, such as David Friedländer and his sons; members of the Lessmann and Normann families; Simon Veit etc. Some letters bear notations in Moser's and Normann's handwriting indicating the dates of their respective replies. Some Lessmann letters confirm receipt of replies from Berlin; but these counterparts are not included in the collection. Perusal of dates and contents, however, justifies the conclusion that the file is complete as far as Lessmann is concerned.

Added to the correspondence is one more letter, from the Viennese banking firm Arnstein & Eskeles to their Berlin business friends, M. Friedländer & Co., whose trusted employee Moses Moser was. It is undated, but requests information about the circumstances of Lessmann's death in 1831. It may, therefore, be assumed that the entire file had once formed part of Moser's estate.

THE CHRONOLOGY

The chronology indicated by Lessmann's letters is as follows: after the end of the summer-term 1817 he had left Berlin for his parental home in Soldin, apparently in the company of Moser who was visiting his own parents in neighbouring Lippehne. Lessmann spent the second half of October in Berlin in preparation for his trip South. He secured various letters of introduction to Viennese families. En route, he stopped at Dresden and Prague. He reached Vienna during the second week of November. An introduction from the Berlin banker Simon Veit to his Viennese business friend, Leopold Edler von Herz, yielded Lessmann an invitation to live in von Herz's house, as a tutor to the latter's son Adolph.[8] Early in 1820, Lessmann resigned this position and in April 1820, Count Moritz O'Donnell offered him the post of tutor to his seven-year-old son Maximilian in Verona. Lessmann accepted the offer readily as it seemed to fulfil his dream of an Italian trip. He returned to Germany late in 1823, possibly on account of his father's failing health (he died in November 1823). Lessmann's return to Berlin

---

[7]Presented by Dr. Fritz Bamberger, cf. *LBI News*, Spring 1968, p. 6.
[8]This particular detail escaped the attention of Hertha Schumann; she has him entering Count Moritz O'Donnell's service immediately.

ended the need for further written exchanges. There is only one later letter written while on summer vacation on July 16, 1825.

When Lessmann had begun his studies in 1812, the year of Prussia's emancipation edict, the admissibility, and actual admission, of Jewish university graduates to the exercise of professions other than medicine had yet to be tested. The final — negative — decision was to come only in 1822. So in 1817 hopes might still be harboured. Though he had chosen to give it up, his medical training and experience left lasting traces on Lessmann's mind. Medical terms repeatedly occur in his letters.

THE WISSENSCHAFTZIRKEL

As stated in the letter of December 20, 1817, Lessmann began having second thoughts in the course of 1816. In November 1816 he joined the *Wissenschaftzirkel*, a group of young men, all of approximately his own age and, like himself, steeped in secular, classical education, except for their senior, the self-taught Joseph Hillmar. Though all were of Jewish origin, the name of their circle was chosen to indicate that they were preoccupied with *Wissenschaft*. Enduring friendships, as well as acute antagonisms, crystallized instantaneously. All the letters Lessmann wrote home while away from Berlin, with the exception of the one to his parents, were addressed to members of this former "Circle", or to the wife of a member, Adelheid Zunz. They abound with assurances of deep personal devotion, particularly those meant for Moser (" . . . that I will always be yours with unshakeable brotherly fidelity", November 17, 1817; "your friend and brother who loves you infinitely", October 29, 1818). Conversely he refers to Eduard Gans in terms of a disappointment which is matched only by Heine's later outbursts of equally hurt friendship. "Woe unto us", Lessmann writes about Gans, while still in Soldin on October 12, 1817, "the days are past when we could count him as one of us. Entirely different spirits, entirely different regions have captivated this mosaic genius; how may we wretched caterpillars of the Helicon in any way at all reclaim this equerry of Pegasus". Moser apparently concurred in retrospect; for Lessmann's first letter from Vienna on November 17, 1817 continues with the "frank admission that I could never have tied myself to you closely so long as you fraternized with someone who recruits and dismisses his friends according to circumstances and pet ideas and who continuously and exclusively injects into this beautiful relationship of two souls the concept of a literary club". Moser may have pleaded mitigating circumstances on behalf of Gans in his answer, because on December 20, 1817 Lessmann takes issue once again: "You must excuse me, but relative to Gans I have spoken none too harshly . . . Gans, believe me, wishes each of his friends only to resound the echo of his own excellence, and the worst is that he now believes he can do without accepting advice." In another paragraph of the same letter a sarcastic message to Gans occurs: "I can assist the young *scribent* at Göttingen — if you have an opportunity to pass this on to him — with useful contributions, a.o., a "Love Story of the Colossus of Rhodes" which, beautified by elegant woodcuts, is peddled over here".[9] After repeated additional inquiries about Gans from Vienna (October 29, 1818 and January 26, 1819), however, Lessmann struck a more conciliatory note in his letter of April 14, 1821 from Verona: "Convey my handshake to excellent Gans who, as I have heard also from another source, has turned out quite an able human being; tell him I wish he would not let himself be deterred in his striving for what is true and noble, by paltry antipodes, and that he would finish with perseverance the course he forcefully began. 'Having willed what is good, with confidence and perseverance, leads to success'. But tell him also that I for one do not care to live in a country where it is possible to publicly defend a thesis denying a non-Christian's qualification for promotion to *Doctor utriusque juris.*"[10] The belated letter of July 16, 1825 contains two more, though good-humoured, gibes at Gans, author of the "Laws of Inheritance", and at his proverbial absent-mindedness.

In writing to and about the elder Hillmar, Lessmann was invariably polite and respectful. To Jost Lessmann was linked by plans for a joint literary venture, a continuation of lectures on Shakespeare they had severally given in the *Wissenschaftzirkel*; however, nothing came of it. A deep and lasting affection bound Lessmann to Leopold and Adelheid Zunz. Besides attending to various assignments on behalf of Zunz at the Hebrew manuscripts department of Vienna Imperial Library, Lessmann mused deeply on the psychological sources of Zunz's oft-professed cynicism. He referred to Zunz by his pet name *Löbel* (letter of July 16, 1825); in the same letter Lessmann stressed Adelheid Zunz's share in the attraction which the Saturday night reunions at the couple's Berlin home had for the "regulars".[11] Eduard Normann and his entire family also retained a special place in Lessmann's memories of earlier days. The Normanns came from Märkisch Friedland in the Neumark district of Brandenburg where Lessmann and Moser too had grown up. Normann's father — Jacob Moses *Nathan* until 1812[12] — had moved to Berlin after the turn of the century and was now living on income from investments in rural and urban property. His elder son Moritz Jacob administered a *Rittergut* (an East-Elbian manor, cultivated by hired farm hands). The younger son Eduard, born Märkisch Friedland 1794, — Lessmann's and Moser's friend — took over another *Rittergut*, Leppihn in Pomerania, late in 1818, much to Lessmann's consternation. He remembered Eduard Normann as possessed of "a character mature beyond his years and morally genuine" (letter of

---

[9]This refers to a prize essay 'The History and Constitution of the Island of Rhodes during the Macedonic Era', announced by the philosophical faculty of Göttingen University, which Gans was then undertaking.

[10]This has reference to one E. Th. Gaupp, a disciple of Savigny, whom Gans had just challenged on account of his antisemitic aggressiveness. Gans's rebuttal is included in the introduction of his legal treatise *Scholien zum Gajus*, Berlin 1821.

[11]Lessmann's regular attendance after his return to Berlin was also attested to in Zunz's letter to S. M. Ehrenberg of August 7, 1825, see Nahum N. Glatzer (ed.), *Leopold Zunz: Jude - Deutscher - Europäer* (Schriftenreihe wissenschaftlicher Abhandlungen des Leo Baeck Instituts 11), Tübingen 1964, p. 139.

[12]See Jacob Jacobson, *Die Judenbürgerbücher der Stadt Berlin 1809-1851*, Berlin 1962, p. 78, No. 172.

December 20, 1817). Twice thereafter he mused: "I cannot visualise him being joyful out there in his solitude" (January 26, 1819), and again: "His life in a village, mostly excluded from an exchange of ideas stimulating the spirit, displeases me; in view of his intellectual character I shall never be able to agree to this choice of a life on his part" (April 14, 1821). All the same, the memory of the hours once spent with Normann and the others "remains eternally as a precious legacy" (same letter). Mrs. Normann, the mother, provided Lessmann with an introduction to the Viennese family von Wertheimstein (letter of November 17, 1817); she also wrote to Lessmann personally (which he acknowledged on June 21, 1818).

Apart from these individual relationships, there was a lasting and formative impact of the now disbanded Berlin *Wissenschaftzirkel*. Lessmann's first letter from Vienna conveys greetings to Hillmar "and some other flotsam of the 'Circle' floating around in Berlin". On July 11, 1819 he adds once again "greetings to the fragments of the 'Circle' ". Talking of his own studies during the first winter in Vienna he laments: "What a pity that there is no more *Wissenschaftzirkel* where one may peddle one's wisdom and find tenfold reward for each drop of sweat in the speechless admiration of the audience." Lessmann even tried almost immediately to recreate something similar in Vienna. A prematurely optimistic report to Moser of December 20, 1817 says: "But read and be astonished: with the inception of the year 1818 there will rise a second *Wissenschaftzirkel*, like a phoenix, on the ruins of the dead one, on the banks of the Ister (i.e., the Danube), though, comprising twelve members, modelled approximately in accord with the same Constitution, omitting, of course, the fussy pedantry which seemed to denote the most interesting part of that former one." This, incidentally, was an oblique criticism aimed at Gans's management; the letter continued, indeed, with the harsh words on Gans quoted above. The undated letter of winter 1817/18 which followed repeated the announcement, but already with somewhat less exuberance, of "a *Deutero-wissenschaftzirkel*... which is in a certain month of its embryonic state and is to be promoted with all due seriousness.. Unfortunately, the project suffers a very bad initial deficiency: during the summer the majority lives dispersed in suburban homes, and I myself may perhaps prefer not to reside in Vienna after the beginning of June. The winter will, however, be gone within a few months, and it is, therefore, doubtful whether such a combination can still be formed this year".

LESSMANN'S STUDIES AND STYLE

Lessmann never reverted to this project in his letters, nor did he ever disclose the identity of the twelve prospective founder members. In all probability they belonged to the narrow general circle within which he moved, Jews of the new nobility who could afford suburban summer houses and who either had, or affected, certain intellectual leanings, and also their hangers-on, both Gentile and Jewish. In the event, the more superficial sociability of the *Ludlamshöhle* type (see below) proved more congenial and less spiritually taxing to them all. Neither in Vienna, nor later on in Verona does Lessmann appear to have formed any kind of intimate, personal intellectual attachment. The abundance of leisure in comfortable circumstances was detrimental to the formation of a mature literary style of his own. The first post-Mendelssohnian generation to which he belonged had imbibed a neo-humanist classical education; but he — and most of his like, possibly with the exception of Heinrich Heine — never managed to acquire true mastery over the substance of their formal learning. What E. M. Butler once described in general cultural terms as "The Tyranny of Greece over Germany" (the "danger of excess" as she aptly put it in the preface to the paperback edition of her study)[13] applied in an even more acute sense to the group to which Lessmann had belonged. His letters abound with references to, and quotations from, Greek and Roman poets and scholars, all quoted *in extenso* so as to lend more emphasis and authenticity to his personal feelings and thoughts. The reader must wind his way through a rank jungle of uncut growth.

Besides, the young generation of the 1810s and 1820s suffered from another handicap: the tyranny of Jean Paul's and De la Motte Fouqué's respective styles. This writer has previously drawn attention to the fatal dependence on Jean Paul under which members of the "Circle", particularly Zunz and Gans, laboured.[14] The undigested influence of Jean Paul is equally obvious with Lessmann. To this must be added in the latter's instance his fascination with De la Motte Fouqué's "sweet lyrical colibris" as Heine characterized that poet's verses in his *Romantische Schule.*

In the letter of April 14, 1821 Lessmann mentioned that he was rather busy for several journals in Austria and Italy, without identifying them.[15] Enclosed in Lessmann's letter to Moser of January 26, 1819, but detached from the file, had been his "first *specimen immortalitatis*" (perhaps a *Romanze* printed in *Wiener Zeitschrift?*). A self-mocking poem in Latin hexameters, 46 lines long, is incorporated in Lessmann's undated letter of winter 1817/18. Its first line reads:

> *Ille ego qui quondam Berolini lata vagatus*
> (I, the man who once tramped the broad streets of Berlin).

The afore-mentioned letter to Moser of April 14, 1821 had also originally had an enclosure, a poem, now detached, for publication in Berlin. The 1825 letter contained again some hexameters composed by Lessmann in German.

CONVERSION

Notions naively retained from early youth reflect the timeless, isolated nature of the spiritual ghetto into which Lessmann had been born and which he strove

---

[13]Beacon Press, Boston 1958.

[14]See 'Der Berliner "Wissenschaftzirkel" (1816/17) - Jean Pauls Einfluss auf den Stil von Leopold Zunz' in *Bulletin des Leo Baeck Instituts*, No. 22 (1963), pp. 101-112.

[15]Hertha Schumann furnishes the names of two, viz., *Wiener Zeitschrift* and *Wiener Conversationsblatt (Zeitschrift für wissenschaftliche Unterhaltung)* as well as titles of publications completed by Lessmann while away from Berlin.

DANIEL LESSMANN
(1794 - 1831)

Wien den 25 April 1820.

Dan Lessmann

Facsimile of a letter from Lessmann to his parents, dated Vienna, 25th April 1820

to discard. It is a strange psychological fact that such regressions occur all the more after formal separation. This reaction is germane to the entire group. Heine, for instance, continued to use, or perhaps he even emphasized, Jewish expressions and similes in his correspondence with Moser after he had converted to Christianity. It appears as though these men were anxious to demonstrate to their friends that they had remained the same as they had been before. Lessmann's last available letter from Doberan had been written about eleven months after his formal conversion which had taken place on August 19, 1824. At variance with all previous letters it carries a date according to the Jewish calendar, viz., "6785", although it is quite pathetic to observe that the figures in Lessmann's calculation were mixed up; 1825 C. E. would have corresponded to 5585. In the letter Lessmann describes to Moser how the Baltic Sea announces its proximity "murmuring as though it *davvens minche*" (i.e., recites the afternoon prayer in a subdued tone). Adding some lines for Adelheid Zunz he dubs a particularly tiny man whom he has encountered the "*gabbe* [i.e., secretary-spokesman] of the Pygmies".

For nearly a hundred years the fact of Lessmann's conversion had been known only through a remark in Moser's letter to Immanuel Wohlwill of September 11, 1824. In Albert Friedländer's translation it reads as follows:

> "Another friend did convert a short time ago, namely Daniel Lessmann. There was a time when I would have considered such a step reason to terminate a friendship. Now I find nothing spiritual within the Jewish community worthy of a noble battle. Amidst this universal dismemberment every individual has to see how he can come to terms with the particularities of *family ties* [my italics], etc. which may shackle him."[16]

Mention of "family ties" could be interpreted as a mere conjecture on the part of Moser in Lessmann's instance. But we know now from Hertha Schumann's perusal of the Berlin municipal police records that Lessmann had notified the authorities of his intention on May 3, 1824, stating precisely that "the death of his parents gave him freedom of action". The process of severance had, of course, been gradual, and had been completed years before. In his letter of July 11, 1818 Lessmann writes: "I swear by all by which free-thinkers like ourselves can swear . . ." And on January 29, 1819: "My entire religious activity at present consists in thinking" (*Mein ganzer jetziger Gottesdienst besteht im Denken*). This was not a stage through which Lessmann was going alone. Similarly Moser would write to his friend Wohlwill on September 18, 1825, the eve of the Jewish Day of Atonement: "If you can pray, do so on my behalf as well. However, I shall study philosophy for you."[17]

The cultural impact of Christianity on Western civilization began to fascinate Lessmann as the period of his residence in Catholic countries — Austria and particularly Italy — lengthened. Writing from Verona on April 14, 1821 he mentions that he is working on a three-volume opus "About the Influence of Christianity

---

[16]See Albert Friedländer, 'The Wohlwill-Moser Correspondence', in *LBI Year Book XI* (1966), p. 272.

[17]This is not quoted by Friedländer.

on Poetry, Painting and Sculpture"; he does not appear to have carried out this plan. His basic psychological ambivalence, however, crystallized with the passage of years. In the introduction — dated Berlin, June 12, 1830 — to one of his last publications, viz. *Das Wanderbuch eines Schwermüthigen* (The Travelogue of a Melancholic), p. 8, and writing in the first person singular, Lessmann stresses his "Christian consciousness". In a later episode, set at Bordeaux (p. 45), he refers to himself as a Protestant. Yet, while continuing his journey, the physiognomy of a fellow-traveller reminds him of a cantor in the Jewish temple: "With his features an entire past, *heder [Schulstube]* and cantor, juvenile delights and canings re-emerged before me in an achingly sweet sadness..." (p. 120).

Hertha Schumann presumes that the "true motive" for Lessmann's conversion was his wish to obtain a position at the Berlin Royal Library. She refers to a note by a Mrs. Wolff, published in the *Vossische Zeitung*.[18] This does not say precisely when he applied; it is, therefore, doubtful whether one fact had anything to do with the other. It is, however, safe to assume that so long as he resided in Vienna and, thereafter, in Verona, a formal break with Judaism was not mandatory.

JEWISH-CHRISTIAN CO-EXISTENCE

The attitude of the Viennese administration of that time was entirely pragmatic. Its main objective was to restrain infiltration of Jews from the provinces into the capital. In his first letter from Vienna of November 17, 1817 Lessmann wrote: "In regard to religion things over here are by no means as bad as I had been led to suspect beforehand." Seven months later, on June 21, 1818, he wrote to Eduard Normann: "I am no longer counted among a class of human beings which, being hated and despised, must keep aloof from all other branches of the state and go into hiding itself — a class whose members appear destined to arouse only animosity or envy, only contempt or regret. In one word, I am — baptised? God forbid, never shall I disown myself thus. But first of all, in Austria hatred between Jew and Christian is disappearing *(fällt fort);* one co-exists with one another on friendly, social terms, and rarely does anyone take note of the empty page between the Old and New Testaments. Over here the Jew has no rights, but he possesses the universal love of his fellow-citizens; without a permit he must not construct a house, but noble conduct *(edles Betragen)* gains him untarnished respect everywhere. I myself pass for a Protestant, although in this respect I am judged differently in society. Had I registered myself publicly as a Jew, I would have encountered many difficulties with the police."

VIENNESE JEWISH NOBILITY

When he emphasized *edles Betragen,* Lessmann probably had in mind the small group of Jewish families raised to the status of nobility, some explicitly with

---

[18]*Sonntagsbeilagen für das Jahr 1906,* pp. 287f.

the title *Edler von*. The Austrian government "tolerated", as the official formula went, 131 Jewish families in Vienna in 1802.[19] By 1820, this total had increased to only 135. The latter figure included nine families with various titles of nobility. The Rothschilds were in a special category because they were of German, not Austrian origin. Lessmann mentions five of the remaining eight as being known to him, viz., Arnstein; Eskeles; Herz; Neuwall; Wertheimstein. He may have met the other three — Hönigsberg; Lämel; Liebenberg — as well.

Lessmann had taken with him introductions to Barons Arnstein and Eskeles from Moser's principal Moses Friedländer, a nephew of the wives of the two Viennese bankers. Lessmann writes in his first letter from Vienna: "I have been received by Arnstein and Eskeles with his [sic] amiable hospitality; the two ladies display a particular kindness towards me. Mostly I meet company at their places, of which, so it appears, a great many are habitués at several houses. *Sometimes* [Lessmann's emphasis] the conversation turns on scholarly matters to which I may then contribute my mite, however *often* [again L's emphasis] also on visits and Brabant laces, to which I must learn to adjust myself gradually. The conversation is often in French. But one dines quite excellently and the pleasures of the table are enjoyed with all one's senses. I have also talked to the distinguished Madame Levy;[20] Dr. Hahn[21] who accompanies her has, hitherto, been nearly the only one of my generation with whom I cultivate a relationship. Through Madame Eskeles I am being introduced to *Hofrat* Hammer." The latter is the famous Orientalist in whom Zunz was interested: Joseph, later Freiherr von Hammer-Purgstall (1774-1856), was married to a Jewess, Karoline von Henikstein, the daughter of a banker, which may explain why Madame Eskeles had access to him. We learn from a remark in Lessmann's second letter that Madame Levy reported back to Berlin about her meeting with him.

As mentioned above, Lessmann had another written introduction from Normann's mother to Herr von Wertheimstein, presumably the family elder Hermann Samuel. Lessmann continues in the first letter: "Herr v. Wertheimstein and his family are rather amiable people."

The third introduction, which turned out to be the most relevant for Lessmann, was to Leopold Edler von Herz. It had been given by Simon Veit, one of the two then remaining partners of the Berlin banking firm Gebr. Veit. Von Herz was the son of Arnstein's late brother-in-law and business partner Salomon Edler von Herz. Leopold, sponsored by Friedrich von Gentz, had won Metternich's confidence in connection with financial transactions relative to the English subsidies to Austria; Gentz was — naturally, one may say — indebted to Herz[22], but Herz's influence was just at this time gradually being eclipsed by the emergence

[19]These and the following details are taken from Ludwig Bato, *Die Juden im alten Wien*, 1928 and Hans Tietze, *Die Juden Wiens*, 1933 respectively.

[20]The younger sister of the Baronesses Arnstein and Eskeles; about her see Eric Werner in *Hebrew Union College Annual*, XXVI, 1955, pp. 548f.

[21]Sigismund Samuel Hahn, M.D. (1791-1870), suggested as a candidate for membership in the *Culturverein*, 1821 - see Reissner, *Eduard Gans*, pp. 188f.

[22]See Jakob Baxa, *Friedrich von Gentz*, Wien 1965, pp. 168 and 271.

of Salomon von Rothschild on the Viennese scene. In his first letter, Lessmann describes Leopold von Herz as "a very upright *(bieder)* man who, in an outspoken oriental dialect, displays a sound understanding". Lessmann's second letter, written a month later on December 20, 1817, announces that Herz has offered him full board in his house and some pay in exchange for a few hours daily lessons which Lessmann is to give to Herz's son Adolph, and that Lessmann has already moved in. Lessmann continues that his own studies move in rather manifold directions. "Herr von Herz has a considerable library to which I carry the key in my pocket. I frequent the theatre without having to pay, my *hospes* owns a box." Five months later, on May 16, 1818, Lessmann notes that he has made the personal acquaintance of several musicians and composers. The next letter, dated July 11, 1818, adds: "As in our house the privileged modern languages are spoken with fluency — a fortunate fortuity true also of several other houses to which I have daily access — I am particularly happy in talking to foreigners, mostly knowledgeable men who travel for pleasure and to perfect their education. Generally, a host of travellers congregate here all the year round, in summer on account of the environs and amusements, in winter on account of the artistic treasures, as Vienna is, indeed, the antechamber to Italy."

The last two letters bear the date-line "Meidlingen", then a rural suburb of Vienna (nowadays Meidling, XII borough of the city of Vienna) where the Herz family spent the summer months. In other words, the annual exodus which Lessmann had anticipated as a drawback for the constitution of a *Wissenschaftzirkel* had materialised. Lessmann's *Knüttelversiges Disputatorium*, composed in 1818 or 1819 has as protagonists Herz's seven children, one Ignaz von Neuwall as a visitor and Lessmann as a recording secretary, together at work on a play in honour of the father's birthday.

Shortly after Lessmann's return from his trip to North Germany he left Herz's house, in January 1820, but continued to call on the family nearly every day.

LUDLAMSHÖHLE

It may be symptomatic that Lessmann failed to mention in his correspondence — and perhaps, even, to meet — two residents of Vienna publicly identified with Jewish affairs and personally known to his Berlin circle, i.e., Michael Lazar Biedermann (1769-1843) and his chief employee Löb Harzfeld (1756-1831). Both promoted the establishment of a branch of Jewish religious Reform in Vienna. Harzfeld also advised the Austrian authorities in reference to books published in the Hebrew language.[23] Lessmann seems to have preferred the company of people who dwelt in a kind of no-man's land, uninfluenced by religious tradition, Jewish or Catholic, of the kind described above. The neutral meeting ground of this group was a room called *Ludlamshöhle* in a Viennese restaurant, thus christened after A. G. Oehlenschlaeger's dramatic fairy tale which, on the 15th of December

---

[23]In the membership records of the Berlin *Culturverein* he is identified as "Herzfeldt, Wien, *K.u.K. Zensor*". See Reissner, *Eduard Gans*, pp. 184f.

1817, had just had its first performance.[24] They gave each other nicknames —
Daniel Lessmann went by the name Donel Lessly —, amused each other with
sometimes spontaneous, but often forced, humorous outpourings and observed a
droll ritual. This aroused the suspicion of the police and led eventually, in 1826,
to the disbandment of the association. The spirit of this light-minded group is
reflected in some passages of the Lessmann letters. On May 16, 1818, for instance,
he refers to the poet Grillparzer — whose tragedy *Sappho* he had seen and who
likewise frequented the *Ludlamshöhle* — as *Herr Grillenpatzer*. Lessmann preferred the Viennese theatre to that of Berlin. He liked "the gambolling *Kaschperl*
and the home-bred witticisms, dependent mainly on the Austrian dialect, for its
attraction". A little later, on July 11, 1818, he attempted a generalized comparison
between the typical "Berliner" and "Viennese". "The Berliner", he jotted down,
"thinks that he is educated, praises his own taste as the only beatification
(alleinseligmachenden), and rarely retracts his previous errors, either out of pride
or self-conceit; the Viennese is good-natured, acknowledges his absurdity, is willing
to take advice and turns inquisitively to the scholar after having seen through
the society-type to the very depths of his emptiness . . . . The Viennese is neither so
well nor so badly educated *(nicht so gebildet, aber auch nicht so verbildet)* as
the Berliner".

One ought not to take this comparison for more than what it reflects of Lessmann's own *éducation sentimentale*: eagerness to shed his own previous clumsiness
and willingness to assimilate the seductive atmosphere of his new surroundings.
His letter of June 21, 1818 is full of praise and admiration for the Austrian
scenery. Talking of Hungary, he points out that "this is, indeed, a remarkable
territory, blessed with all the products of the earth, a virile, cheerful tribe which is
lacking in nothing but culture. But the magnates will, advisedly, not permit this;
otherwise, they would cease to be magnates" (May 16, 1818).

VERONA

In the letter to his parents of April 25, 1820, Lessmann introduces the name of
Count Moritz O'Donnell whose acquaintance he says he had lately made at a
social gathering. Baron von Arnstein had been a protégé of the Count's father
Joseph, President of the *Hofkammer* until his death in 1810.[25] The family was of
Irish extraction. While in Venice in 1805, Count Moritz O'Donnell (1780-1843),
a professional military officer, had attracted the attention of Madame de Staël; in
1808, when she spent five months in Vienna, people considered him her
commissionaire.[26] The atmosphere of the house was cosmopolitan; conversation,
Lessmann stressed, was trilingual — German, French, "but mostly Italian". This

[24]See Ignaz Franz Castelli, *Memoiren meines Lebens*, München 1914, vol. 2, pp. 1-60.
[25]Hilde Spiel, *Fanny von Arnstein oder Die Emanzipation. Ein Frauenleben an der Zeiten-
wende. 1758-1818*, S. Fischer Verlag, 1962, pp. 355f.
[26]Jean Mistler, *Madame de Staël et Maurice O'Donnell*, Paris 1926, pp. 2 and 31.

was the man who entrusted to Lessmann the education of his elder son Maximilian while he, the father, was posted to Verona.

Lessmann's letters from Verona are not very rewarding as to content. However, the predominance of Italian themes in his later works indicates that Lessmann put his years in Verona to good, if not spectacular use.

NEW SLIPPERS

The Jewish flourishes with which the last Lessmann letter, written July 16, 1825, after his return from abroad and eleven months after his conversion, abounds, reflect his earlier sentiments and thoughts. Mentioning that a panorama of Berlin is due to open up at this Baltic spa next week, Lessmann ponders on how such a panorama would look to him. It is a day-dream, not dissimilar to the one Heinrich Heine had described, also in a letter to Moser, a year before, on July 20, 1824 [27]; Lessmann was probably not aware of its existence. In Heine's imagination the "host" of Israelites had been lined up for the exodus to Jerusalem with the members of the *Culturverein* busily occupied amongst them. Lessmann says: "Past and future will present themselves in the painting." He links the "old faithful" together, poking gentle fun at the little foibles of each: Gans's absent-mindedness; Moser's selfless absorption in the problems of others; Zunz's involvement with the date of birth of a rabbi who had lived during the Crusades. Finally Hillmar appears on the scene, entering a shop to buy a pair of new slippers. The merchant inquires how things are with the *Verein*. Hillmar answers:

> "It is just as with my old slippers whose incipient disintegration
> forces me to buy these new ones..."

[27]*Briefe von Heinrich Heine an seinen Freund Moses Moser*, Leipzig 1862, pp. 107-108.

Isaac Offenbach

BY A. W. BINDER *

HIS LIFE[1]

Isaac Judah Eberst was the father of Jacques Offenbach,[2] the famous composer, the 150th anniversary of whose birth was celebrated this year. Isaac was born on March 26th, 1779; he left his home town of Offenbach at the age of twenty, and went to seek his fortune in other towns along the Rhine. While learning bookbinding, he had a master who occasionally played the violin. One day, Eberst, driven by "musical instinct", plucked up enough courage to ask his employer whether he would allow him just to draw the bow over the strings. He succeeded to some extent and, from that day on, was allowed to use the violin during his spare time. He persisted and, self-taught, soon became proficient on the instrument. Later, in his own bookbinding shop, he engaged two men to do the work, while he devoted himself to teaching the violin, in addition to managing the business.

Isaac Eberst also possessed a beautiful tenor voice. This, together with a sound knowledge of Hebrew, qualified him later for the position of cantor in Deutz. where he married Marianne Rindskopf, daughter of one of the families residing there. In 1816 he became cantor of the community of Cologne, a position which he held with honour and dignity until his death in 1850. He later combined this position with that of acting rabbi in the same congregation. The charm of his personality, his wit and humour, made him many friends and earned for him an entrée into the select circles of society, where he soon became known as "the Offenbacher". This nickname became so well known that he finally discarded the name Eberst.

When Isaac Eberst — as he then was — arrived in Deutz in 1803 (he moved to Cologne in 1816), the political situation, as it affected the Jews, was in a state of flux. The era of enlightenment, which came to the Duchy of Cologne from France, manifested itself in the establishment of a new college in Bonn in 1777, where Jews were permitted to study but could not obtain a degree.

When the French occupied the left bank of the Rhine, which included Cologne

*We regret to announce that the author of this essay died shortly after his manuscript reached us and was being prepared for printing. - Ed.
[1]According to the manuscript biography written by Julie Offenbach-Grunwald, daughter of Isaac Offenbach.
[2]There is a great deal of confusion in available books of reference as to the real name of Jacques Offenbach's father. The Oxford Companion to Music, 8th ed., 1950, gives the name of Wiener, on the basis of information supplied by a grand-daughter of Offenbach's to the Radio Times (29th January 1932). Still more variants are to be found in other musical dictionaries. Most German or Jewish works of reference give Eberst or Eberscht; one anti-semitic publication has Ebersucht.

215

(they entered on October 6th, 1794), the Jews of the Rhenish Department became citizens of France.[3] This implied full equality before the law. In autumn 1797, the poll tax *(Körpersteuer)* for Jews on that bank of the Rhine was abolished.[4] Under the leadership of the Rabbi of Bonn seventeen families formed themselves into a Jewish community in Cologne on October 12th, 1801. When the consistorial system was decreed on March 17th, 1808, Cologne, where the Jews began to settle in 1798, was joined with Krefeld, with Leo Carlsberg as rabbi. On the same day, Napoleon's *décret infâme* was proclaimed in France, gravely affecting the position of the Jews.

After Napoleon's defeat the Prussians occupied the territory. Their Edict of March 11th, 1812, granted the Jews of Prussia almost complete equality, but the French Decree of 1808, which had discriminated against Jews in the conduct of trade, was not to expire until the end of 1818. This made it exceedingly difficult for Jews to engage in trade and commerce without special certificates which were not easily secured.

It was probably because the securing of a permit to conduct business had become too difficult that an educated man like Isaac Offenbach, with business experience and an engaging personality, chose the cantorate as a profession. Therefore he, like many another talented young man of that period with a good voice and Jewish knowledge, became a cantor in spite of the poor salary offered.

The Cologne community had been, since 1817, part of the Bonn Consistory; so the rabbi could only periodically preach in his various communities. The cantors of these communities were therefore often asked to preach and to perform certain rabbinical functions. Isaac Offenbach officiated in the capacity of both rabbi and cantor throughout his life.[5] His sermons showed depth and poetic feeling and a comprehensive command of biblical literature.

As mentioned before, Offenbach's salary was rather modest. In 1843, after about twenty years of service as cantor, he received only 43 *Thaler* for that year.[6] So he applied for an increase of a fixed salary of 80 *Thaler* and ten measures of cereal and Passover flour. From this income he had to support a family of a wife and ten children. True, the cantor also received some fees for serving at weddings and funerals and from the sale of synagogue seats, and special gifts from congregants on the High Holy-days.[7] Furthermore a cantor's wife supervised the ritual bath for women which yielded some additional income.[8]

Of the ten children of the Isaac Offenbach family, seven were daughters and three sons. Two of them, Jakob — later known as Jacques — and Julius — later Jules — were destined for fame in the world of music. To Jakob, his seventh child, the father presented a violin when he was six years old. The boy learned

[3] Adolph Kober, *History of the Jews in Cologne.* Jewish Publication Society of America, Philadelphia, p. 180.
[4] *Ibid.*, p. 181.
[5] See MSS biography of Julie Offenbach-Grunwald.
[6] Equivalent to $.
[7] Kober, *op. cit.*, p. 320.
[8] *Ibid.*, p. 236.

ISAAC JUDAH OFFENBACH
(1779 - 1850)

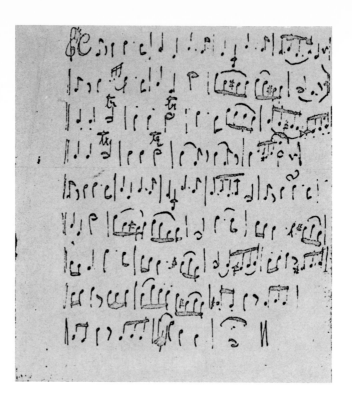

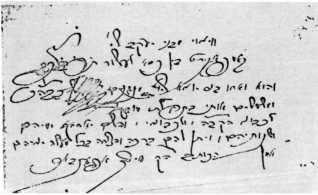

Facsimile of a composition for the Day of Atonement service
by Jacques Offenbach with an inscription by his father

quickly; at the age of eight he was already playing violin concertos and composing little songs. When Isaac Offenbach found out that his son showed extraordinary talent for the cello, which later he preferred to the violin, he was not content to leave him with his teachers in Cologne; he took him and his brother to the Paris *Conservatoire*, of which Luigi Cherubini was then the head. It was one of the chief musical centres in Europe.

Jacques and Jules returned each summer to Cologne for the vacation. Their home was a source of inspiration to them, as both father and mother were musical and in sympathy with their sons and what they were studying. Isaac Offenbach chose to send his sons to the Paris *Conservatoire* for their advanced musical studies rather than to Berlin because the political situation for Jews was easier in France than in Germany. In Germany it was very difficult for a Jew to rise to a high position in the world of music without embracing Christianity. This was not necessary in France; nevertheless, after Isaac Offenbach's death, his son Jacques did convert to Catholicism.

Isaac Offenbach's personal charm brought him many friends among the leading musical personalities in Cologne. His home was the meeting-place of artists, writers, lawyers and people of high standing in German society. He was organizer and member of the Cologne Musical Society which was established in 1812. It may be mentioned that in later decades many other Jews were active in this Society. In 1852, Wilhelm Hertz was its conductor, and in 1875 Anselm Cohen was among the leaders of the *Sing-Akademie* and also director of the Men's Chorus. Ferdinand Hiller (1811-1885) was in charge of the musical life of Cologne for three decades. Hard-working and self-sacrificing, he did much to raise the level of musical life there. Among his works are a musical setting of the 137th Psalm and an oratorio 'The Destruction of Jerusalem'. However, he too converted to Christianity.[9]

A noted contemporary of Isaac Offenbach was the artist David Levy Elkan, distinguished not only in his profession, but also by his enthusiastic interest in Jewish communal affairs. Among his works with a Jewish theme are a scroll of Esther and lithographic illustrations of the Hagaddah.

Thanks to the fame which the young Jacques Offenbach was gradually acquiring in Paris, Jacques Fromenthal Halévy, the French-Jewish composer, began a correspondence with Isaac with whom he had many things in common. For Halévy was very much interested in the music of the synagogue, having composed many settings for Hebrew liturgy, which may be found in the synagogue works of Solomon Naumbourg who, at that time, was chief cantor of Paris.

Between Isaac Offenbach and his son Jacques we find a strong resemblance in many respects. In some of the sprightly tunes to be found so abundantly in Jacques's work, we can see the father's influence. On the death of his wife in

[9]*Ibid.*, p. 311.

November 1840, Isaac Offenbach wrote to Jacques and Jules of their irreparable loss, expressing his feelings in a "poem" of rather rugged sentimental verses which is preserved in the manuscript biography written by his niece. Isaac was particularly attached to his son Jacques, as was this son to his father. Many times after his mother's death Jacques left his busy Parisian life and came with his wife and children to stay with his lonely father and comfort him. When, after a visit in 1848, Jacques returned to Paris, the family wrote that "the house became very quiet". Father and son never saw each other again. Isaac Judah Offenbach died on April 26th, 1850. He was considered one of the leading cantors of his day.[10]

THE MUSIC

The struggle over Reform which at the beginning of the nineteenth century shattered European Jewry had an impact also on synagogue music. In 1797 Israel Jacobson of Westphalia had organized a synagogue service without a cantor, introducing the organ and a mixed choir as well as the singing of Hebrew texts[11] to the tunes of German chorales and hymns. In their efforts to achieve emancipation many Jews sought to discard some of the traditional Jewish practices and the "oriental" character of their synagogue music. Getting away from the minor modes in the liturgy was considered an important element in early German Reform. The elimination of orientalisms had widespread effects, not only in the Western European countries, but also in the East. But the synagogue musicians of the latter part of the nineteenth century and of the twentieth century systematically brought back the original style, realising the danger of losing the musical tradition in which the synagogue service is embedded.[12]

During the first half of the nineteenth century the community of Cologne was orthodox, according to the Ashkenazi tradition, and had adopted the rite of the neighbouring city of Deutz.[13] There was no talk of reform,[14] until Rabbi Israel Schwarz became permanent rabbi in 1859. The music of Isaac Offenbach, therefore, mainly followed the orthodox tradition, though we find among his manuscripts some already scored for male chorus, dated Cologne, 1848,[15] as well as many prayers set to original tunes in waltz, minuet and polka rhythms.[16]

Synagogue music forms the bulk of the Isaac Offenbach Manuscript Collection. As a cantor, he was well versed in the style and traditional melodies of the

---

[10]His talents were many-sided. Besides his ability as cantor and rabbi he also wrote plays and poetry.
[11]A. Z. Idelsohn, *Jewish Music*, New York, p. 232.
[12]A. W. Binder, 'Cantorial Art in the Nineteenth Century', in *The Jewish People - Past and Present*, vol. III, p 336.
[13]Kober, *op. cit.*, p. 252.
[14]The elimination of the *piyutim*, for example, was not discussed until 1862.
[15]The manuscripts are to be found in the Library of the Hebrew Union College - Jewish Institute of Religion, New York City.
[16]See description of manuscripts in this article.

synagogue. He was, however, also a contemporary of the three great musical masters of that period, Mozart, Haydn and Beethoven, and there is evidence in Offenbach's music that the three composers were not without influence on him.

Offenbach's loyalty to the synagogue as well as his passion for general musical composition led him to divide his synagogual work (which, in his mature life, became his only means of musical expression) into two sections: a) compositions based on the traditional prayer motives and melodies; b) synagogue music in the style of the minuet, gavotte, polka, etc., bearing the stamp of the style of his contemporaries. Thus, while the major part of his works, like *Unessaneh tokef, Mechalkel Chaim, Kol Nidre, Kaddish lemussaf* are based upon the traditional modes and melodies known to Western Jews, many of his compositions are in the elegant style of Mozart and Haydn, customary at that time, when pianists during a public performance were in the habit of improvising on the popular tunes of the day. This was probably also done in the synagogue by improvising a minuet or a polka melody to some of the lighter portions of the liturgy, viz.: *Melech elion, Ki anu amcha, Lechoh Dodi.* We are made aware of the fact that Jews also came to the synagogue to be entertained by their cantors. For this was the only way most Jews could satisfy their hunger for music. This was also one of the reasons for the popularity of the *virtuoso* cantor who dominated the synagogue scene throughout the nineteenth and part of the twentieth centuries.[17]

Isaac Offenbach was constantly in the process of composition, as his works indicate. He could quite suddenly think of a new version to the *nussah* (text) of a certain prayer, or an entirely different tune, as late even as the day before Holy-day, jot it down, and probably sing it the next day at the service. In Offenbach's High Holy-day music we find the old style with which prayers, such as *Kaddish, Borchu, Kol Nidre* and others, were introduced on the High Holy-days. Usually, a long and florid wordless improvisation would be intoned by the cantor with the help of his musical assistants (most frequently a bass and a boy soprano) and this would finally culminate with the words of *Borchu, Yisgadal,* or *Kol Nidre.*

Most of the synagogue music of Offenbach is scored for the old combination prevalent in those days, namely cantor, discant and bass. But when choral music began to take root in the Austrian and German synagogues, Isaac Offenbach was not unmindful of it. It evidently took him a long time, probably fifteen or twenty years, to convince his congregation of the change; for his manuscripts do not show four-part writing until 1846. This we find in a complete Friday evening service, scored for male chorus and soprano.

When Solomon Sulzer introduced his music which simplified and often eliminated the florid portions of the *nussah hatefilah,* Isaac Offenbach followed suit with his own revised versions of this music.[18] Thus we find in his *Nigunim le-*

[17]Binder, *op. cit.*, p. 336.
[18]Idelsohn, *op. cit.*, p. 246.

yamim noraim,[19] an early version of the High Holy-day *Kaddish* before *Mussaf,* and later in the volume a simplified version showing the influence of the time. Offenbach did not go as far as Sulzer (who may have seemed too modern for his congregants).

Many of Offenbach's chants, for example *Unessaneh tokef* from the *Mussaf* High Holy-day liturgy[20] which ordinarily would be chanted in minor, are in a major key, again showing the influence of Solomon Sulzer and also of the ideas of Reform. Sulzer and the emerging fame of Lewandowski[21] had a tremendous impact on synagogue music in the East and West. In the place of improvised, unorganized singing, the ordered four-part boys' choir became more and more the norm as the century progressed.

In the large cities, large choirs were employed and choral singing was firmly entrenched by the mid-nineteenth century in Paris, Berlin, Vienna and other large European communities. The three great synagogue composers of the day were Sulzer in Vienna, Lewandowski in Berlin and Naumbourg in Paris. By the end of the century almost every city had a *Chor-Shul,* and the output of the composers of choral music increased by leaps and bounds, bringing forth a choral literature which stands as a monument to the preferences of European Jewry of the past.

Isaac Offenbach was a forerunner who, in his own way, succeeded in making his congregants aware of the new movement in synagogue music which began to stir when he arrived in Deutz in 1803 and which was in full bloom when he died in 1850.

[19]Cf. note 15.
[20]Cf. note 15.
[21]Idelsohn, *op. cit.,* p. 269.

THE ISAAC OFFENBACH MANUSCRIPT COLLECTION[22]

When one approaches the manuscript collection of Isaac Judah Offenbach, one becomes aware of his former vocation, namely bookbinding, which seems to manifest itself in later life as an avocation. Consequently, we find that most of his manuscripts are neatly bound and titled, always clearly and legibly written, *Nigunim le-yamim noraim,* sermons, addresses, poems and plays. This makes the study of them easy and pleasurable.

VIOLIN OBLIGATI TO SABBATH EVE SERVICE: Dated Cronberg, 1799-1800. Title pages show Isaac Judah Eberst, von Offenbach; containing violin obligati to several versions of *Lechoh Dodi* in the following forms alla polacco, minuet and siciliano. All spirited in style, rhythmic and joyous. The violin was one of the instruments used as accompaniment to the *Kabbalat Shabbat* service in those days. Isaac Judah Eberst held at this time the position of discant, as well as violinist.

FOR GUITAR(RE) (Published): Vols. II-III of a series entitled "Douze Sonatines Pour La Guitar(re)", containing practice pieces in the old dance forms, viz: march, rondo, polonaise and waltz.

Vol. XIII of a series entitled *Übungs-Stücke,* containing pieces for practice purposes, also in dance forms.

All the above show a gift of melody and rhythmic inventiveness but bear witness of the strong influence of Mozart and Haydn.

PURIM AND PASSOVER: Dated January 29, 1833, a pamphlet (MSS) containing humorous poems for Purim, written in Yiddish, some of them set to music. Music for the Passover Haggadah (published Cologne 1838), containing traditional melodies, such as *Echad mi yodea, Adir hu,* an original melody to *Chad Gadya* which has become quite well known; and melodies *Hodu, Chassel Siddur Pessach* and a German hymn for the Passover festival. A volume dated 1829, entitled *Nigunim le Pessach* containing Holy-day versions of the liturgy, including such compositions as *Tal, Hallel,* and various *Piyutim* etc.

HIGH-HOLY-DAY MUSIC: Two volumes entitled *Nigunim le-yamim noraim;* the first dated 1828-1829, contains almost all the liturgy to be sung by the cantor and his helpers. There are recitatives, chants and set-pieces. Another volume, entitled as above, but dated 1842, is a collection of many revised and completely

[22]This complete collection of manuscripts was presented to the Library of the Hebrew Union College - Jewish Institute of Religion in New York City in 1923 by two granddaughters of Isaac Judah Offenbach: Miss Isabella Grunwald and Mrs. S. Redlich, both residing in New York City. The gift was made through the late George Alexander Kohut. On the occasion of the 150th anniversary of the birth of Jacques Offenbach the Historical Archives of the city of Cologne arranged an exhibition which included amongst its exhibits a musical manuscript and a letter of Isaac Offenbach. Cf. Anna-Dorothee v. den Brincken, *Jacques Offenbach. Ausstellung des Historischen Archivs der Stadt Köln im Opernhaus aus Anlass der 150. Wiederkehr des Geburtstages des Komponisten am 20.6.1969,* pp. 6-9.

changed versions of the pieces found in the former volume. This, surely, was the personal copy which Isaac Offenbach used at the service. There are also helpers' parts.

PIECES COMPOSED BY SINGERS: It was the custom at that time for a singer or choir leader, when applying for a position, to bring an original composition to the cantor. This composition was intended to show the musical abilities of the applicant. In our collection, we find a piece by *Simcha hakaton* (Simchah, the little one), which contains nuances such as forte, crescendo, written in Hebrew characters. Another piece, by Abraham Alexander, shows style and imagination, and Haydnesque influence and a collection of High Holy-day chants for *Shemuel hakaton* (little Shmuel).

SABBATH MUSIC: A score very neatly bound, dated Cologne 1848, for male quartet, contains the entire *Kabbalat Shabbat*. It is the only volume which shows the use of the four-part choir. The arrangements prove a thorough knowledge and understanding of four-part writing.

MISCELLANEOUS: A volume containing various versions of the *Shabbat Mewarchim ha-chodesh* liturgy, according to the Holy-day or festival which it precedes. Soprano and discant parts of Sabbath and Holy-day services. Various chants for various parts of the year. *Semiroth* (home songs), pencil sketches and the musical notation of the chanting of *Akdemoth,* an Aramaic poem chanted on Shabuoth.

JACQUES' COMPOSITION: The collection contains a composition entitled Confession for the Day of Atonement service. It bears a felicitous inscription by his father which reads in translation as follows:

> "Confession" by my son, Jacques (may he live). Composed during the penitential days in the year 5602.

> He and his brother, my son Jules (may he live) sang in the synagogue, and assisted me in the mussaf service, for the honour of God, and my honour. May the Lord prolong their days and years, and give them blessing and success in all the works of their hands. Amen.

> signed - (Hakoton) Itzik Offenbach

The work is in F minor, scored for three parts, 3/4 time melodious and full of feeling. Isaac Offenbach evidently sang this work at the service during the rest of his career as cantor, for we find this version of *Ana tawo* repeated in his other volumes of High Holy-day compositions. This composition, dated 1842, at a time when Jacques was twenty-three years of age, reveals the fact that the boys came to assist their father as choristers even after they were already known as accomplished musicians. Jacques' biography tells us that in 1841 he gave a series of concerts of his own compositions in Paris.

JULES' COMPOSITION: A cradle song, setting of a German poem entitled *Wiegenlied* (lullaby) for medium voice, and piano accompaniment. The melody is in the German *lieder* style above a rocking accompaniment.

SERMONS, PRAYERS and other ADDRESSES: Neatly bound and titled as well as neatly and very patiently written is a sermon on a quotation from Psalm 34, delivered on November 2, 1836. In this group we also find Bar Mitzwah sermons, wedding addresses and prayers for various occasions.

CALENDAR AND MUSIC CHART: A very ingeniously thought-out calendar indicating holidays and seasons from 1860 to 2000.

A music chart indicating note values, rests, accidentals, evidently used in training choir boys in sight-singing.

PERSONAL: A biography of her family dated November 1902, by Julie Offenbach-Grunwald (his daughter) written while in the United States, in her own handwriting. She was eighty years old at that time. It is written in German with a great deal of feeling, sentiment and pride of family.

A PRAYER written by Isaac Offenbach for his deceased wife whom he loved so very dearly. In this prayer he speaks to his children of their great and irreplaceable loss. Attached is a list of dates from 1843 to 1862 indicating the anniversaries of her death.

August Belmont and the House of Rothschild

Four Letters from the Years 1848 and 1849

BY RAHEL LIEBESCHÜTZ

After the publication of a selection of letters from the Belmont family of Alzey in Year Book XII,[1] attention was drawn to the most prominent member, August Belmont (1813-90), by Professor Irving Katz's book,[2] a political biography giving full account of August Belmont's activities in the fields of politics and diplomacy. The four letters[3] we are presenting here shed some light on another sphere of his life. They deal with his relationship to the House of Rothschild, whose agent he was in New York, in the year preceding his engagement to Caroline, daughter of Commodore M. C. Perry.[4] We shall see that at this time his plans concerning his future life were by no means settled. He had not yet decided to make the United States his home, nor to continue as an agent of Rothschild, nor even to remain a banker. The letters are addressed to his brother-in-law and his sister, Stephan and Elisabetha Feist in Coblenz.

These were years when Europe was shaken by political unrest. In January 1848 the revolutionary movement started in Palermo and speedily spread to Paris, where it led to the resignation of King Louis Philippe and the establishment of a short-lived Republic. Risings in Vienna, Berlin and other parts of Germany followed. Alzey and Coblenz, where August's family lived, were quite near to the armed insurrection in the Palatinate in 1849.

Letter 1

From August Belmont in New York to Stephan Feist in Coblenz.   2nd May 1848.
August reassures the addressee on three points. First he talks of a business trans-action, which he has carried out on behalf of Rothschild and with which this House does not agree. Stephan has read about it in *The Times*. It is a loan of five million pesos granted to an unnamed *gouvernement* in America.[5] That the currency is given as pesos points to California as the debtor. Belmont maintained an office in this province, which had been recently acquired by the United States in the war with Mexico. During the transition period before California became a "state", the Spanish currency may still have been in use. Rothschilds are very vexed, but August is con-fident that they will not discredit his transaction in public, especially as the price of the loan is rising at the Stock Exchange. The second topic concerns the enormous losses which the houses of Rothschild in Paris and Vienna have suffered as a result of the revolutionary upheavals.[6] Will they remain solvent? August trusts that they will. But even in the unfortunate case of their not remaining so or of their having

---

[1]'The Wind of Change', *LBI Year Book XII* (1967), pp. 227-256.
[2]Irving Katz, *August Belmont. A political Biography*, New York & London 1968.
[3]The letters have come down to me as handwritten copies, carefully carried out by A.B.'s

to close down their business in America, Belmont - this is the third point - will not be affected by the disaster. He has earned money enough to be able to retire and to live comfortably in America or Europe.

...Für Ihre guten Nachrichten und das Interesse, das Sie meinethalben an den Tag legen, bin ich Ihnen äusserst verbunden. Sie haben jedoch dem Artikel in der Times eine falsche Auslegung gegeben und sich dadurch unnötige Sorgen gemacht. Rothschilds sind wegen der Ereignisse in Europa, der bedeutenden Verluste, die sie machen, sehr ärgerlich, und es ist schwer, es ihnen recht zu machen. Aber ich glaube nicht, dass sie daran denken, meine Transaktion öffentlich zu diskreditieren. Das Anlehen von 5 Millionen Ps steht übrigens heute 1½% höher als der Emissionspreiss, und es muss noch höher gehen, da viel europäisches Gold hierher kommen muss, *denn die Stocks dieses Gouvernements sind jetzt die sichersten in der Welt.* Die Capitalisten in Europa fangen an, leider zu spät für sie, daran zu glauben...

Was die Häuser Rothschild betrifft, so ist es gewiss, dass sie enorme Verluste erlitten haben, allein ich kann nicht glauben, dass es so schlimm mit ihnen aussieht; auch bin ich fest überzeugt, dass sie sich halten werden. Jedenfalls kann ich Ihnen im strengsten Vertrauen mitteilen, was Sie ausser Babette und meinem Vater niemand sagen wollen, dass selbst im schlimmsten Fall einer Suspension von R., was Gott verhüten möge, ich mich so situiert habe, dass ich weder dabei impliziert bin noch Geld verlieren kann. Freilich hört alsdann meine Agentur und deren Vorteil auf, und ich glaube selbst, dass Rothschild ihre Geschäfte in Amerika sehr einschränken, vielleicht ganz aufgeben, und ich bin ganz darauf gefasst. In diesem Fall gebe ich die Geschäfte ganz auf, da ich Gottlob genug habe, um überall, entweder hier oder in Europa, comfortable zu leben. Über alles dieses ist es jedoch zu früh zu sprechen, und ich empfehle Ihnen nochmals die strengste Verschwiegenheit. In ein oder zwei Monaten werden wir klar sehen. Ich werde Ihnen mehr sagen können...

---

father Simon. The spelling is Simon's. I have replaced it by modern spelling, as an attempt to imitate the correct spelling of the period, which August can be assumed to have used in the original, would have been rather arbitrary.

[4] Cf. a recent publication on Commodore Perry: S. E. Morison, *"Old Bruin", Commodore Matthew Calbraith Perry*, London 1968.

[5] A similar incident is mentioned without date in A. B.'s obituary, *New York Herald*, Nov. 25, 1890: "The Bank of Maryland had drawn bills on the Rothschilds on a credit opened by Belmont. The bills were sent to London and returned unaccepted. B's natural imperiousness had made him many enemies, and when it was known that B's name had not been honored by the Rothschilds the banking community was delighted. But B. refused to be frightened or dismayed. He declared that he was alright in this transaction, and he would not only compel the London House to honor the bills, but would make it pay damages to him for the trouble it had caused him . . . He kept his promise and so, far from ruining himself, he actually strengthened his position with the Rothschilds, who liked his pluck and sturdy courage."

[6] Cf. E. C. Conte Corti, *Das Haus Rothschild in der Zeit seiner Blüte*, Leipzig 1928, pp. 277-287.

Letter 2

August to his Sister Babett.   24th October 1848.
Belmont's future is unsettled. At the moment a journey to Europe, which he had
planned, must be shelved on account of the political unrest in France and Germany
as well as urgent business at home. As long as the present situation in Europe persists
he prefers to stay in U.S.A., where he enjoys political and personal freedom and is
able to carry on a profitable business, either as an agent or independently. If
conditions calm down, he will probably retire from business and settle in some place
near his family.[7] Regarding his agency, this will come to an end if his independence
should be threatened. James Rothschild in Paris intends to send his son Alphonso
(1827-1905) to New York. He hopes that Belmont will support him with his
experience. But August will not tolerate any infringement of his independence and
is determined to retire if his anticipations should turn out to be true. His appointment
as Consul General of Austria gives him a good social position in U.S.A. in any case.
For Germany he foresees no other future possibility but a return to an even more
oppressive despotism than that which obtained before the Revolution.

... Mein Plan, diesen Winter nach Europa zu reisen, hat sich wieder nicht
erfüllen lassen. Erstens hinderte mich daran der fortwährend gerüttelte Zustand
Frankreichs und Deutschlands, und anderenteils erlaubten es meine Geschäfte
nicht, obgleich die letzteren seit der französischen Revolution abgenommen haben.
Was ich in der Zukunft tun werde, kann ich leider bei dem besten Willen in
der Welt nicht sagen, denn vieles hängt von der Gestaltung der politischen Lage
Europas ab und vieles von den Absichten und Dispositionen Rothschilds in
betreff ihrer überseeischen Geschäfte. Im Augenblick sehe ich auf dem ganzen
Kontinent Europas mit Ausnahme von Spanien — und dieses Land bietet wenig
Anziehendes für einen permanenten Aufenthalt dar — nicht einen einzigen
Punkt, auf dem man sich mit Ruhe niederlassen könnte; und so lange dieser
Zustand fortdauert, ziehe ich es vor, in Amerika zu bleiben, wo ich zum wenigsten
im Genuss aller politischen und persönlichen Freiheit bin und entweder der
Agentur unserer Häuser oder für mich selbst profitable Geschäfte machen kann.
Wenn es, wie ich hoffe und wünsche, dorten[8] oder in Frankreich wieder ruhig
wird, so ziehe ich mich wahrscheinlich von den Geschäften zurück, und lebe,
wenn auch nicht ganz unter Euch, doch jedenfalls in Eurer Nähe.

Was die Fortsetzung meiner Agentur für Rothschilds betrifft, so liegt dieses
alles im Dunkeln, wird sich jedoch in der nächsten Zukunft entscheiden; und ich
habe mir vorgenommen, nichts zu poussieren, sondern dergleichen Dinge ruhig
kommen zu lassen.

---

[7]This plan for his future was not a passing fancy. On June 21, 1843 Babett in a letter to
Stephan quotes the following passage from a letter she has just received from August:
". . . Er [his father] hat mich in jüngsten Briefen sehr mit Heiratsprojekten heimgesucht,
allein ich habe und werde keine Lust zum Ehestande haben. Ich suche mir nach und nach
ein schönes Vermögen hier zu machen, und komme in späteren Jahren einmal mit G.H.
als reicher amerikanischer Onkel zu Dir zurück, um mich von Dir und Deinen lieben
Kleinen im Alter pflegen zu lassen, d.h. vorausgesetzt, dass Ihr dem lahmen Murrhaas ein
Erkerchen einräumen wollt."
[8]"dorten" in this correspondence always means the place to which the letter is directed; in
this case Germany.

Wie ich von James Rothschild höre, beabsichtigt er nächstens, seinen Sohn, einen jungen Mann von 21 Jahren, hierher zu senden, und ich glaube, dass diese Mission meine Trennung vom Hause zur Folge haben kann, obgleich ich *sicher* weiss, dass Rothschilds dies nicht wünschen und im Gegenteil vermutlich sehr gerne sehen, wenn ich dem jungen Mann zur Seite stehe und ihm mit meiner Erfahrung behülflich wäre. Ich bin jedoch zu lange in einer gänzlich unabhängigen Stellung gewesen, dass ich mich entschliessen könnte, irgend eine Position anzunehmen, die im geringsten unangenehm werden könnte; und, da ich Gottlob in pekuniärer Beziehung die [sic] Herren nicht bedarf, so werde ich, wenn es wirklich deren Absicht ist, mir Jemanden beizugeben, meine Demission einreichen.

Alle diese Befürchtungen und Prognostikationen sind jedoch nur Vermutungen, und es mag sich alles anders gestalten, als ich erwarte, und ich bitte daher, *unter keiner Bedingung irgend Jemanden* von dem Obigen zu sagen. Vorigen Monat habe ich von dem kaiserlichen neuen Ministerium[9] meine definitive Ernennung zum Österreichischen Generalkonsul empfangen, was mich[10] also, wenn ich mich auch vom Hause trennen sollte, immer eine sehr schöne Position in diesem Lande sichert; denn, obgleich die Amerikaner Republikaner sind, so geben sie auf dergleichen Dinge mehr, als man bei uns glauben sollte.

Ich folge mit vielem Bedauern und mit schwerem Herzen für die Zukunft dem Gange der Dinge, wo leider die Parteienwut und die Zügellosigkeit mit jedem Tag überhand nimmt. Wer weiss, wo dieses enden wird? Allein, ich sehe für Deutschland durchaus keine andere Rettung als eine neue *Reaktion,* welche die Gewalt wieder in die Hände der Gouvernements gibt; und in solchen Fällen hat uns die Erfahrung gelehrt, dass man von einem Extrem in das Andere fällt, so dass leider unser Vaterland nach meinen Befürchtungen unter einen drückenderen Despotismus fallen wird, als es vor den letzten Ereignissen hatte...

Letter 3

To his Sister.   5th March 1849.
Three months earlier, in a letter we do not possess, August has asked his sister's advice concerning his relationship to Rothschilds. He complains that he has not received an answer. He feels this to be the most difficult epoch of his life and this makes him conscious of his lack of friends and his isolation. He distrusts the Rothschilds. Although they write amiable letters, he believes that, being accustomed to flattery, they resent his independent style. But what annoys them even more is the fact that he has earned a fortune for himself and is carrying out business transactions on his own account. He thinks that they wish to keep him in a dependent position and to dismiss him, as soon as his services are no longer needed. James's son Alphonso has been in New York and is now staying at New Orleans. He behaves correctly, and yet August feels that he resents the reception given him by New York society.

[9]The successor of Prince Metternich, after the latter had lost his office in the Revolution. It was the confirmation of an appointment which Belmont held since 1844.

[10]Errors in the use of the pronouns "mir" and "mich" repeatedly occur in quotations from August's letters, although Simon Belmont, Babett and Stephan do not make such mistakes themselves. Two generations earlier even leading Hamburg merchants did not always differentiate correctly between Dative and Accusative. (P. E. Schramm, *Neun Generationen,* I, 177, Göttingen 1963.)

Although Belmont has done his best to have Alphonso treated with distinction, the scion of Rothschild was not shown more consideration by polite Society than his agent. This generation of men had been brought up on Schiller; Belmont describes the conflict between the strong and the weak in the language of Marquis Posa, Wallenstein, Tell.

Es sind nun über drei Monate, meine liebe, gute Schwester, dass ich Dir zuletzt schrieb, und doch habe ich bis zur Stunde auf zwei meiner Briefe noch keine Antworten von Dir. Dieses Schweigen deinerseits und von Seiten unseres guten Vaters befremdet mich umso mehr, da der Inhalt meiner letzten Briefe oder das, was ich Euch darin von der Mission des jungen Rothschild sagte, doch gewiss von Wichtigkeit (genug) für mich waren, um Euch zu interessieren, und ich vermisse mit wahrem Bedauern Eure Mitteilungen hierüber.

Entfernt von Freunden und Verwandten und in der schwierigsten Epoche meines Lebens ganz auf meine eigenen Resourcen verwiesen, wäre es ein süsser Trost für mich gewesen, den teilnehmenden und liebevollen Rat meiner geliebten Schwester zu empfangen, den ich nun schmerzlich vermisse. Seit ich Dir zum letzten Mal schrieb, hat sich wieder manches in meinen Ansichten und Beziehungen zu unserem Hause geändert, und obgleich dieselben mich [sic] fortwährend schreiben, mit vieler Freundschaft und Wohlwollen behandeln, und der junge Alphonso von New Orleans aus, wo er unsere Geschäfte besorgt, aufs freundschaftlichste schreibt, so habe ich doch die Überzeugung bekommen, dass weder er noch die Häuser es aufrichtig mit mir meinen.

Herren v. Rothschild, gewohnt dass man ihnen schmeichelt und auf jede Weise den Hof macht, können mir es nicht verzeihen, dass ich stets in allen meinen Beziehungen zu denselben eine unabhängige Stellung behauptet habe, von welcher ich entschlossen bin, nicht abzuweichen. Was sie jedoch noch mehr als dies erbittert, ist der Umstand, dass ich nicht allein in meinem Ton unabhängig bin, sondern auch, dass es mir gelungen ist, mich pekuniär so zu stellen, das heisst nur durch meinen Fleiss und günstige Operationen ein Vermögen zu erwerben, welches mir unter allen Verhältnissen genügend abwirft, um überall comfortable und vergnügt zu leben. Diese Herren wünschen, dass ich immer von ihnen abhängig geblieben sei, damit sie, solange es ihnen convenierte, von meinen Diensten und meinen Erfahrungen Nutzen ziehen könnten, und mich dann, wie Hanau,[11] vor die Tür setzen werden, wenn sie für ihre eigenen Söhne oder Neffen eine Position in diesem Lande hier schaffen wollen. Man sagt, ich sei zu grand Seigneur, hätte kein Recht, für meine Rechnung zu operieren, das heisst mit einem Wort: die Fabel von dem Wolf und dem Schaf ...

Du siehst daher, dass wenig Aussicht vorhanden ist, dass wir uns verständigen, besonders da Alphonso, trotz seiner ausserordentlichen Freundlichkeit und Intimität, wie ich es aus zuverlässiger Quelle weiss, falsch gegen mich ist und es mir nicht verzeihen kann, dass er während seines hiesigen Aufenthalts, trotz aller meiner Bemühungen zum Gegenteil und trotz seines Namens, nicht mit mehr

[11]This may refer to Ludwig Hanau, son of August's Uncle Isaac and employed in August's firm in New York.

Égard in der Gesellschaft behandelt wurde als ich, der ich sein Agent... Wenn ich meine Agentur aufgebe, so siehst Du mich jedenfalls noch vor künftigem Winter in Coblenz; dieses und das Glück, Dich nach so langer, langer Trennung wieder einmal zu umarmen, ist auch ein grosser Beweggrund für mich, die Geschäfte der Häuser aufzugeben. Denn so lange ich denselben vorzustehen habe, komme ich doch nie von New York weg.

Letter 4

To his Sister.   11th June 1849.

August has now received the advice from sister and father, which he had so urgently requested. He must have known his family well enough to anticipate what it would be. Both have entreated him to stay with Rothschilds; the words "vanity" and "susceptibility" were used. August insists that there is no vanity or susceptibility in his determination not to step down to the position of a clerk. It is hard to imagine that he would have let his decisions be influenced by family advice in any case. What he really wanted from them was interest in his doings and sympathy with his plight. However, meanwhile the tide has already turned in his favour. Alphonso is soon due to return to New York, but not for long. In the course of the following month he is going to sail for Europe. Although Belmont suspects that he may come back later, we know that he did not, and that Belmont's will had once more prevailed over that of the Rothschilds. This letter was written at the time of the armed rising in the Rhenish Palatinate. August is worried about his family and lack of correspondence adds to his anxiety. He hopes that Germany may not fall a victim to Socialists and Anarchists.

...Seit zwei Jahren empfangen wir in allen öffentlichen Blättern die schrecklichsten und beunruhigendsten Nachrichten von den Rheinprovinzen, wo sich die beiden Parteien gewaffnet gegenüberstehen,[12] und es an verschiedenen Plätzen bereits zu Blutvergiessen gekommen ist. Ich habe eine geliebte, einzige Schwester und einen lieben Vater in der Mitte dieser Unruhen, und keiner von beiden schreibt mir ein Sterbenswörtchen, so dass ich nun seit 14 Tagen in Unruhe bin und mit Zittern und Bangen der Ankunft des nächsten Steamers entgegensehe... Es sieht schlimm in dem guten Deutschland aus, allein ich hoffe, dass die gute Sache siegen wird, und dass unser schönes Vaterland nicht ein Opfer der Sozialisten und Anarchisten werden wird.

Ich bin Dir sehr verbunden für Deinen liebevollen und schwesterlichen Rat hinsichtlich meiner Stellung zu R. und habe denselben beherzigt, indem es mir zugleich viel Freude gemacht hat, bei dieser Gelegenheit zu sehen, wie sehr klar und richtig Du urteilst. Glaube mir, dass ich ebenso kalt und bedächtig die Sache beurteile wie Du, dass, wenn ich doch nach Allem zu dem Entschluss kommen sollte, meine Position aufzugeben, es aus wichtigeren und gründlicheren Motiven geschehen muss als einer lächerlichen Eitelkeit hinsichtlich einer mehr oder minder scheinbaren Unbehaglichkeit... Baron James in Paris, soviel höre ich indirekt, sucht seinen Sohn Alphonso hier zu etablieren, denn in Europa sind zu

---

[12]It was during this rising that Ludwig Bamberger, one of its leaders, used to ride to a mill near Alzey in the evenings after the fighting for rendezvous with Anna Belmont, his future wife and August's cousin. (L. Bamberger, *Erinnerungen*, Berlin 1899, pp. 176-196.)

viele von der Familie... und er möchte wahrscheinlich gar gerne meine Erfahrung dabei behalten. Ich bin hierzu ganz willig, wenn es in einer meiner Würde und der von mir bis jetzt gehabten Position angemessenen Stellung geschehen kann; allein, weder Du noch der Vater können es Eitelkeit oder Susceptibilität nennen, wenn ich nicht zur Rolle eines Commis heruntertreten will... Alphonso erwarte ich in 8 bis 10 Tagen von New Orleans. Er wird jedoch nicht lange hier bleiben, gedenkt schon im nächsten Monat nach Europa zu gehen, um alsdann vermutlich später hierher zurückzukommen. Ich verhalte mich natürlich fürs Erste ganz passiv und lasse die Sachen kommen...

Why, we may ask, was Belmont so ready to quit his exceptionally good position in the world of finance? I suggest that, as a man of boundless drive and enormous confidence in his ability for achievement, to be just a banker no longer satisfied him. Politics attracted him. A few months after he had written the last of this group of letters, all the problems concerning his profession and his definite residence with which they deal, were settled by his engagement to Caroline Perry. Now he would stay in America, would remain a banker, and through Caroline's uncle John Slidell would find his way into politics. Four years after his marriage, he resigned the agency for Rothschild while keeping up business connections with them, when he was appointed American Chargé d'Affaires at The Hague.

Rescue Efforts in the Iberian Peninsula

BY PEREZ LESHEM (FRITZ LICHTENSTEIN)

After reading 'A Chronicle of Rescue Efforts' by S. Adler-Rudel[1] I felt impelled to record the rescue efforts undertaken on behalf of the Jewish Agency for Palestine, with the participation of delegates of German Jewry, in Spain, Portugal, Tangier, Morocco and Algiers between 1943 and the end of World War II.

Adler-Rudel's chronicle summarizes the very beginning of those efforts in the Iberian Peninsula and mentions the tragic death of Wilfrid Israel[2], whose own report, in the form of his letter to the British Ambassador in Spain, cannot, for obvious reasons, do full justice to the strenuous efforts he made during his two months' stay in Portugal and Spain and to his own achievements. A moving tribute paid to him after his death by Heinz Wisla[3], a young refugee who emigrated to Palestine on SS "Nyassa" in January 1944, characterizes Wilfrid's approach to rescue work and his influence on the refugees. I have tried to piece together, as in a mosaic, a picture of the 2,500 Jews, refugees from Nazism, restored to a meaningful life in Palestine or elsewhere, and to illustrate the conditions — physical and psychological, social and material — in which these refugees found themselves. This may keep alive the memory of the days of suffering, hopelessness and despair which by organized action were turned into a new beginning.

During the winter months of 1942/43 alarming information reached the Jewish Agency in London and the Halutz movements in Britain — mainly composed of young people from "Greater Germany", who had been temporarily admitted into the United Kingdom for agricultural training before the outbreak of the war — that Jews were being deported from all parts of Nazi-occupied Europe to labour camps in the East and that, in fact, these were extermination camps.

At the time, this news sounded so utterly unbelievable and was so difficult to verify from where we were in the beleaguered island of Britain, that it became clear that emissaries would have to be despatched to neutral countries in order to establish contacts, to organize relief and attempt rescue in co-operation with whatever body, voluntary organization or government agency, offered itself.

Obviously, understanding and active co-operation on the part of the British Government were indispensable, and this made the choice of possible emissaries very restricted indeed. In spring, 1943, Wilfrid Israel and S. Adler-Rudel left the

---

[1]LBI Year Book XI (1966), pp. 213-241.
[2]Ibid., pp. 218-220.
[3]In Wilfrid Israel. July 11th 1899 - June 1st, 1943, Marsland Publications, London 1944, pp. 39-42. - Wisla later wrote a book on his experiences as a refugee and his emigration on the SS "Nyassa", Ben-Zwi Kalischer (Heinz Wisla), Vom Konzentrationslager nach Palästina. Flucht durch die halbe Welt, Edition Olympia-Martin Feuchtwanger, Tel-Aviv 1945 (Hebrew version, Ba Derech l'Eretz Israel, Am-oved 1945).

British Isles for the Iberian Peninsula and Sweden respectively, to gather reliable information and, if possible, to establish contacts with the Jewish underground leadership.

On 1st June, 1943, it was announced on the evening news in London that a British civil airliner on its way from Lisbon had been shot down by enemy fighters over the Bay of Biscay and was feared to be lost with its thirteen passengers and crew.[4] Knowing that Wilfrid Israel was scheduled to return from his mission about this date, I felt that a major disaster had struck our endeavours for relief and rescue. The work he had been doing for almost two months in Portugal and Spain would have to be carried on by somebody else.

The Jewish Agency in Jerusalem had hoped to send Walter Turnowsky to succeed Wilfrid Israel. He had been Director of "Peltours" for eighteen years and was greatly experienced in organizing transportation to Palestine. However, after many weeks, all efforts with the British military authorities in Cairo to secure visa and travel facilities failed.

Four Palestinian delegates of the General Federation of Jewish Labour in Eretz Israel (Histadrut) were then in London for Hehalutz work: A. Ben-Israel, Rafi Meisels, Otto Sinek and myself. By the nature of our work and by reason of the fact that we dealt primarily with Jewish youth from "Greater Germany", brought to the United Kingdom through the efforts of Anglo-Jewry and its institutions[5], we belonged to the group of people closely connected with the Jewish Agency (partially enumerated by Adler-Rudel)[6], who were anxiously watching the deterioration of the Jewish situation on the Continent.

It was against this background that, towards the end of August 1943, I was asked by the Jewish Agency in London to go to the Iberian Peninsula and to try to restore the links which Wilfrid Israel had forged in Spain and Portugal, and to carry on the efforts which he had begun by selecting refugees willing to go to Palestine. We would endeavour to ensure that as many Jews as possible, living in the Nazi-occupied Western countries, the Netherlands, Belgium, France and, possibly, Italy, could reach at least transient safety in the Peninsula.

The goal was clearly defined: relief and rescue through emigration to Palestine. At that time the Government of Palestine promised to add 150 immigration certificates for Jewish refugees in Portugal and Spain to the 400 granted in 1942, about a third of which had been distributed by Wilfrid Israel. These additional certificates were to be allotted by a representative of the Jewish Agency able to explain to potential immigrants the conditions of life in Palestine. Only some of them were Zionists, the rest were scantily acquainted with the way of life and the aspirations of the *Yishuv*.[7] Many just wanted to escape from the restricted and

---

[4]See Ian Colvin, *Flight 777*, Evans Brothers, London 1957, p. 200; on Wilfrid Israel see also *LBI Year Book III* (1958), H. G. Reissner, 'The Histories of "Kaufhaus N. Israel" and of Wilfrid Israel', pp. 239-256.
[5]E.g., the Agricultural Committee, Bloomsbury House, London W.C.1, under the energetic chairmanship of the late Rebecca Sieff.
[6]*Loc. cit.*, p. 214.
[7]Jewish inhabitants of Palestine.

ADMINISTRATION DES POSTES
Administração dos correios
du **PORTUGAL**
de
(À remplir par le bureau d'origine)
(A preencher pela estação de origem)

Envoi recommandé *encaixa*
Objecto registado

Lettre
Carta
Boîte   avec valeur déclarée de _____ 2)
Caixa   *com valor declarado*
Colis
Encomenda

Mandat de poste de _____ 2)
Vale do correio de

Déposé _____ au bureau de poste d _____ *Lisboa C*
Aceite na estação de

35604

le _____ 19 _____ sous le N.
em _____ *com o n.*

expédié _____ par M. _____
remetido _____ *por*

et adressé _____ à M. *Dr. Leo Baeck*
e endereçad _____ *a*

_____
(localidade) *Prot. Bocania*

1) Indiquer dans la parenthèse la nature de l'envoi
   (lettre, imprimé, etc.).
   Indicar no parêntese a classe do objecto
   (carta, impresso, etc.).
2) Biffer les indications inutiles.
   Riscar as indicações inúteis.

Timbre du bureau
renvoyant l'avis
*Marca de dia da
estação que devolve
o aviso*

AVIS DE **RÉCEPTION**
PAYEMENT
RECEPÇÃO
PAGAMENTO
AVISO DE

(À remplir par l'expéditeur qui mentionnera ci-dessous son
adresse complète)
*A preencher pelo remetente que indicará a seguir o seu
endereço completo*

(Lieu de destination, en gros caractères)
(Localidade de destino, em letras grandes)

Mr. Dr. Leo Baeck N.º L 156

(Rue et numéro)
(Rua e número)

(Pays de destination)
(País de destino)

Service des postes
Serviço postal

Le soussigné déclare que l'envoi
                          le mandat   mentionné d'autre part

O abaixo assinado declara que o objecto
                                   vale   *mencionado na frente desta fórmula*

A été dûment livré
              payé   le **30. VII. 1943** _____ 19 _____

foi devidamente entregue
                   pago   *em*

Timbre du bureau destinataire
Marca de dia da estação destinatária

Signature 1):
Assinatura:

du destinataire: de l'agent du bureau destinataire:
do destinatário: *do empregado da estação de destino:*

Dr. Leo Baeck

1) Cet avis doit être signé par le destinataire ou, si les règlements du pays de destination le comportent, par l'agent
du bureau destinataire et renvoyé par le premier courrier directement à l'expéditeur.

*Este aviso deve ser assinado pelo destinatário ou, quando os regulamentos internos o permitam, pelo empregado da
estação de destino e devolvido pelo primeiro correio, directamente, ao remetente.*

Card of acknowledgment, signed by Leo Baeck, for a food parcel sent by
Jewish aid organizations from Lisbon

The SS "NYASSA"

Embarkation for Palestine

Farewell celebration at Caldas da Reinha

Seated left: Joseph Schwartz, Director of European Joint;

DAVID BLICKENSTAFF

depressing circumstances of life in war-time Spain and Portugal and were eager to grasp any opportunity offered to them. As one of them, Heinz Wisla,[8] put it: ". . . most of us had not thought of going to Palestine until now, simply because there were no means of transport; we had finally reached the Atlantic Coast and were looking only for help from England or America."

The immigration certificates promised by the Mandatory Government to the Jewish Agency were limited both in time of validity and in kind. They were subdivided and sectionalized in four main categories: artisans, unskilled agricultural workers, orphans and capitalists. In addition, they were earmarked for certain age groups, for single people and for families.

My appointment and tasks were communicated by the Jewish Agency to Dr. Joseph Schwartz, the European Director of the American Joint Distribution Committee (JDC) and to Dr. James Bernstein, his opposite number in the HIAS-ICA Emigration Association (HICEM), who would extend their co-operation and that of their co-workers at their Lisbon European Head Offices. Mr. Isaac Weissmann, who acted on behalf of the World Jewish Congress (WJC), was likewise informed.

Meanwhile, the Political Secretary of the Jewish Agency in London, Mr. Joseph Linton (later to become Israeli Minister to Australia and New Zealand and Ambassador to Tokyo and Berne), prepared the ground with the British Foreign Office, which gave its blessing and accorded the necessary facilities. Mr. Linton introduced me to the Head of the Refugee Department, Mr. Osbert Peake. Mr. Peake advised me as to my contacts with H.M. Embassies which were informed by the Foreign Office of the nature of my mission and asked to assist me when necessary.

My departure was dependent on the transport to be allocated by the British Government. My Palestinian passport was endorsed with the exit permit, valid for departure before 14th December, 1943, for one journey only, to Portugal. At the beginning of October 1943 the Portuguese Embassy in London had received instructions to grant me an entry visa. My Palestinian passport, issued in Jerusalem on 7th March, 1939, for "all countries, except Spain" had been extended by the addition of Palestine passport No. 147724, dated London, 11th October, 1939, valid, after the outbreak of war, for "British Empire, Holland, Denmark, Sweden, France, Switzerland, Greece, Turkey, Egypt and Syria." This, again, was altered on 17th September, 1943. Whilst all these countries were cancelled, Portugal, Spain and Tangier were added. The passport was stamped "Not valid for any Military Zone Overseas", but on 19th April, 1944, endorsed in Lisbon "for travelling to French Possessions in North Africa."

Imperial Airways, as it then was, warned me to be ready for departure on "twelve hours' notice". A meeting point would be assigned the night before, and nobody was to accompany me beyond it. One evening about the middle of October, I was told over the phone to get ready for departure at Imperial Airways House

[8]In *Wilfrid Israel*, p. 40.

by 6 o'clock next morning, my luggage not to exceed 20 kg. I was not to leave the flat without further notice, but to stand by for a possible alteration of the schedule. This came promptly at 2 a.m., when I was informed that my departure had been postponed and that I might expect new orders after 6 p.m. next day. In the evening I was advised of my departure next morning, but in the small hours of the night the telephone rang again. This time we were told that I could not expect to leave before the beginning of the following week. Then the familiar game started again. Several marching orders were given and countermanded, so that we got used to interrupted nights and disbelieved an evening call, advising me to be at Airways House by 6 a.m.

There, next morning, a small group of people quickly disposed of their few suitcases and were led through a side exit onto a railway platform and into a dining car train which moved off while breakfast was served and daylight dawned. In war-time Britain, station names had been removed and replaced by very small nameplates, unreadable from a moving train. We stopped seemingly nowhere for about two hours, and the passengers hardly conversed even with their table partners.

When the two-carriage train came to a halt, we were told to alight and to hand over to the guard all letters written on the journey. They were subject to censorship, since we were considered already as being outside the United Kingdom. We were at Poole station. A waiting bus took us to customs control sheds within the harbour. Some seaplanes were rocking on the choppy water. Formalities over, our group split up. Taken to a launch, we soon reached one of the seaplanes. All windows were blacked out, with notices warning against interference and threatening arrest prominently displayed. The flight captain added a verbal warning and told us where to find blankets and lunch boxes. He apologized that the crew could give us only scant information before landing at our destination.

When finally the plane took off it was forenoon; we worked out that, all going well, we might land at Lisbon late in the evening. Little by little one began to converse with one's neighbours. We sat in fauteuils, two on opposite sides of a table. My neighbour turned out to be a French-born countess, married to a Spaniard. She was on her way to Algiers, General de Gaulle's headquarters, stopping over on a mission in the Peninsula. Opposite sat the Portuguese Naval Attaché at the London Embassy going home.

After a few hours in the air we touched water and a crew member came in to tell us that we would disembark and have a cup of tea — the best thing to have in any situation — before taking off for the onward flight. When we set foot on shore, unfamiliar lettering in a strange language made us wonder where we might be. People who had flown here previously, explained that we were in Eire, at Shannon Airport. An experienced war-time traveller gave us to understand that we would sweep out over the Atlantic by night to avoid detection from the near-by French coast with its German fighter and submarine bases. When dusk fell, the captain told us that in fifteen minutes a bus would take us to a country hotel, some twenty-five miles inland, where we would stay overnight, and the next day, at 4 p.m. it would bring us back for the take-off. The bus and we were all on time and after an hour's ride again we changed over to the launch and onto the plane, and shortly before 6 p.m. we were in the air again. To our surprise a crew member came from the cockpit informing us that the bus was standing by to take us back to the hotel because, owing to fuel leakage, we must turn back and previous arrangements held good for Thursday, our third day out of London.

Feeling by now quite at home, we spent the second spell of twenty hours. Embarkation and take-off had become routine and when we touched water on Friday, 29th October, at 2 o'clock in the morning, we knew it must be the Tajo and that we had arrived. Whereas transit passengers had hotel rooms reserved by the airline, we who were going neither to Gibraltar, Casablanca nor Algiers, had to make our own arrangements, which proved to be rather difficult. But with the help of the Air Terminal's office a double room was finally secured which I shared with the British Naval Attaché returning to his Madrid post. Later on, this companion for one night proved to be a valuable contact with the British Embassy in Madrid when I had to arrange transportation for emigrants from Spain and Tangier, with the help of the Ministry of War Transport in London.

From 1940 and until the end of the war, Lisbon was "the" door to Europe. It was a truly international city. Unlike Stockholm or Istanbul, which were also capitals of neutral countries, Lisbon offered easy lines of communication with the free Western world. Thus it had become a meeting-point of friends and foes alike. Here nationals of all the belligerent States tried to gather information, to establish contacts with Portuguese go-betweens, to keep their eyes open, their mouths shut and their ears pricked. Hotels were booked by long-term residents from all parts of the world. Relief and rescue organizations had made Lisbon their European headquarters. Consular representatives of "free" Governments, rivals of satellite Governments in occupied countries, worked, if not side by side, in proximity. To name only a few, there were de Gaulle's consular representative, M. Gorlier; the Dutch Legation with Dr. J. Luns (the present Dutch Minister of Foreign Affairs) on its staff, representing a country no longer master in its own house, was tolerated by the Portuguese Authorities; the Czech Government-in-exile in London was represented by Frantisek Cejka as consul.

While Europe sank deeper and deeper into ruin, Lisbon flourished, for neutrality paid handsome dividends. Some people grew rich overnight if they were clever or ruthless enough to seize the chance in dealings of all sorts.

A long-delayed cable to London, announcing my safe arrival, was dispatched in the early morning, but it was not before 9.30 a.m. that one could contact any office, including those of the Joint Distribution Committee (JDC) and HICEM. Eventually I met Dr. Joseph Schwartz, Director of the JDC European Office, in Rua Aurea, for an initial talk and survey of the relief work being done in the Peninsula. I was also introduced to his co-workers with whom I kept contact as they — though changing often in the course of the following two years — were more permanently available than Dr. Schwartz to whom Lisbon served merely as a foothold and stepping-stone for his own far-flung travels.

The same afternoon I had a useful meeting with the wife of Professor F. Wohlwill, originating from Hamburg, who had been very helpful to Wilfrid Israel.[9] She was familiar with the problem of the refugees as well as with local conditions in general, having lived in Portugal since Hitler's ascent to power. Her husband, who was Professor at Lisbon University and working as a neuropathologist, had wide connections and was greatly respected in the whole community. Through Mrs. Wohlwill's help the technical foundations of my work were quickly laid: two rooms with a Jewish family which provided me with an address, telephone and headquarters as the basis for organized work, and an excellent part-time secretary.

Next I met Dr. James Bernstein of HICEM and Professor Moise Amzalak, the head of the Jewish community, to whom I conveyed greetings from Dr. Weizmann. Professor Amzalak, a widely known economist, was Portugal's representative in his field at the League of Nations. He owned a large library comprising contemporary Hebrew books and old volumes of Judaica and religious dissertations. A friend of Salazar, he saw himself — as happens in such surroundings — above democratic community rules, a benevolent, but self-confident, and strong-willed *pater communitatis*.

I paid a visit to the Rabbi, Mendel Diesendruck, a learned man with a profound knowledge of Hebrew literature, a confirmed Zionist, with whom I soon established a lasting contact, and I also met the active members of the community. Gradually I learned about the division of the community into Portuguese and Ashkenazi groups, the former identical, on the whole, with the old resident families, the latter with the "immigrants" (who had settled in Portugal between the two World Wars). The majority of the Jews, in all about 1,600, lived in Lisbon. There was a small community in Oporto and a few families scattered in some small provincial places.

The war refugees were nearly all concentrated in two places of "assigned residence", about 350 at Caldas da Rainha, 140 km north of Lisbon, and 170 at Ericeira, 40 km from Lisbon on the Atlantic coast. Whilst the English expression "assigned residence" states a simple fact, the French term *"résidence forceé"* conveys the real significance of the position in which the refugees found themselves.

During my conversations I gained some insight into communal affairs and their bearing on relief and rescue work. Divisions within the community caused an unhealthy competition and arguments which occasionally degenerated into mutual recriminations. I always declined to be drawn into local strife. As a whole, Jewry in Portugal was in complete sympathy with the work which the Joint, HICEM, the WJC and the Jewish Agency were doing or trying to do. Understanding and moral support, however, varied according to each group's past experiences and

[9]On the Wohlwill family cf. *LBI Year Book XI* (1966), Albert Friedländer, 'The Wohlwill-Moser Correspondence', pp. 261-299 and subsequent correspondence.

immediate interests. Of the total Jewish population of 1,600, less than 400 were born in Portugal, while about 650 were Ashkenazi Jews, originating mainly from Poland and partly from Germany, while the remaining approximately 550 were war refugees who had reached Portugal after 1939, largely via Spain.

Portuguese Jews had returned to Portugal from Morocco, via Gibraltar and the Portuguese Isles (Cape Verde, Azores) only a few generations before. They were all well established in commerce, industry and the professions, while still owning considerable plantations in the islands. (This small community is assimilating rapidly and dwindling through mixed marriages and emigration to the U.S. and Brazil. Their social and cultural standards are high, but their wealth is gradually passing into Gentile hands — not only their landed property, but also valuable books and collections of specific Jewish interest).

The rediscovery of the Marranos and the study of their life during almost half a millennium, culminating in the establishment of a small museum in a disused, mediaeval synagogue at Tomar, about half-way to Coimbra, is due to the devoted research of Dr. Samuel Schwarz, a Russian-born Jewish mining engineer. When he died a few years after the war, all efforts to secure, for the Hebrew University or Israel Museum in Jerusalem his priceless library, with its many illustrated Jewish books and rare translations into Portuguese, proved in vain.

While the Portuguese Jews fully subscribed to the official approach to the new arrivals, but otherwise took no notice of the refugees, the Ashkenazi Jews maintained contact with those refugees who had permission to live in Lisbon or to visit the capital. They invited them to their homes, went to see them in their places of "assigned residence" and celebrated the Jewish holidays with them.

The representative of the World Jewish Congress in the Iberian Peninsula, Mr. Isaac Weissmann, was keenly interested in the rescue side of my work, as he thought that the approach of voluntary organizations was too legalistic and that they did not push rescue efforts hard enough. With his European-Jewish background, he found it difficult to understand the attitude of the American-educated leaders of the JDC or HICEM. The antagonism between the representatives of the three big Jewish organizations complicated relief and rescue work. Though I appreciated Mr. Weissmann's feelings, I also understood the hesitations and the more formal attitude of Dr. Schwartz's European Head Office of JDC. Although his co-workers in Lisbon changed repeatedly, all of them, as far as I could judge, gave remarkable service to relief work in the Peninsula and, later, in various countries of liberated Europe and North Africa where I met some of them again.

We were, after all, in foreign countries with whose laws we had to comply. The difference between the two approaches was, perhaps, as to whether or not one believed in the possibility of making the governments of these countries understand the peculiar position of Jewry in general and of Jewish refugees in particular. This could not be achieved in a short time or without endangering the immediate rescue work.

At the HICEM Office I learned of the practical aspects of Wilfrid Israel's work. There were lists of *Aliyah* candidates, which he had compiled in Spain and Portugal; people he had accepted, and others who were tentatively confirmed if and when more certificates became available. Then there were lists of applicants not yet interviewed and more who had come forward only after Wilfrid's departure. I was anxious to see them all, since by conversing with them I hoped to learn what standards had been applied.

The European Director of HICEM, Dr. James Bernstein, generously offered his office facilities. His second-in-command and the man actively concerned with matters of the Peninsula and Tangier, was M. Raphael Spanien, whom I had met in Paris some years before. He agreed that it would be most useful to go to Caldas da Rainha for a few days to meet the candidates who were eagerly looking forward to getting transport to Palestine. He offered to send with me his chief assistant who was familiar with the place and the local relief office, knew most of the active refugees and could organize my meetings and interviews, while also acting in a secretarial capacity. Whilst I preferred not to use any other organization's premises and working facilities, I accepted this offer gratefully, and we fixed the earliest convenient date for this first "field" visit.

Soon after my arrival at Lisbon I had presented myself at the British Embassy, where I was introduced to the First Secretary and to the Liaison Officer with the Portuguese Police, who dealt with visa appropriation, residence permits, extensions, etc. He was well acquainted with all branches of local government which even in matters exceeding their own competence, could get things done at central government level, if they were so inclined.

My contacts in the British Embassy, and those with representatives of Allied Powers and of Governments-in-exile were friendly throughout and in many respects of great help, whether in the case of my visa for Spain being applied for by the British Embassy, or whether enlisting their assistance in dealings with the Portuguese authorities; sometimes it was a matter of speeding up a telephone link or transmitting urgent reports to the Jewish Agency in London, or of forwarding books on Germany's warfare, such as *Blitzkrieg in Polen*, to the Wiener Library in London. I had permission from the British Authorities to purchase such books. Initially, my command of German was unsuspected in the German bookshop on Avenida de Liberdade, but later on I was apparently stamped as a British Intelligence Agent who disturbed the circles of the German Embassy in Lisbon and was to be "liquidated" by two Nazis. Their names and history and those of the German diplomat who suggested my liquidation became known to me by chance in 1966, when I served as Israel's first Consul-General in the Federal Republic of Germany.

Through contacts with the Netherlands Legation, I was able to receive first-hand reports on the situation of Jewry in Holland and on the three camps for detained Jews, Baarenfeld, Westerbork and Tyrs (which later was dissolved). I was also able to forward a report from a Jewish officer of the Foreign Service who returned from Greece and told me his observations regarding the attitude to, and the treatment of, Jews by the German Occupation Forces.

From Lisbon, food parcels could be dispatched to concentration camps in all parts of German-held Europe, and the signed or unsigned cards of acknowledgment permitted occasional conclusions as to the state of affairs there. The Joint and HICEM had long lists of German and French Jews to whom Lisbon firms were instructed to send regular food parcels. I added to these lists the names of several Palestinian civil internees at Ilag VIII Z *(Internierten-Lager VIII, Zivilisten)*. A card of acknowledgment signed Leo Baeck — astonishingly not Leo Israel Baeck, as he had to be called under Nazi law — from Theresienstadt is reproduced on another page.

I served in Lisbon also as a link between the Jewish Agency offices in Switzerland and those in Jerusalem and London. Even letters between Geneva and Lisbon, in two neutral countries, were censored by German interference. Information on atrocities in concentration camps inside Germany and German-occupied territories, which became known to the Red Cross and to Jewish organizations in Switzerland, often was transmitted through Lisbon to London, Jerusalem, New York and Istanbul where contacts with the underground in Eastern Europe had been established. Thus I kept in touch with Richard Lichtheim at Geneva, with the Palestine Office there, and with Adolf Silberschein who directed the placement of intellectual refugees and relief in Switzerland in close contact with the World Jewish Congress.

When meeting the refugees in Lisbon I listened to their wishes and answered their questions to the best of my ability. I tried to make them see the realities of the war-time situation. The difficulties which awaited them were in some respects even greater in Palestine where young and healthy people were needed, used to physical labour or adaptable and willing to start a new life different from that which they had led before. They had to be told that, although the Allies would finally defeat Hitler and liberate the conquered countries, pre-war conditions could nowhere be expected to return. Life would have to be rebuilt on new foundations, economically, socially and with a different spiritual outlook.

In these interviews I had to explain the nature of my mission and its limitations, imposed by the number of certificates granted by the Mandatory Government and by the measure of co-operation provided by the British authorities and the Jewish bodies, such as JDC, HICEM and WJC. All these were anxious to do their utmost to help those who wished to go to Palestine and to rescue any Jews who could be reached, especially those who came clandestinely over the border from occupied Europe into Spain.

These lectures not only acquainted the refugees with a new outlook, they raised their morale and strengthened their determination. For them it was, of course, difficult to form a picture of the situation on the distorted information provided by Portuguese news items in a language few of them knew, which was supplied from both belligerent sides.

Somewhat similar to the cultural activities arranged in the internment camps on the Isle of Man and elsewhere in Britain during the summer months of 1940, lectures, study circles, popular high school courses on many subjects and, particularly, Hebrew, Spanish and English classes, had been organized in the places of "assigned residence" in Portugal and Spain. The aim was twofold: therapeutical, to fight boredom, and practical, to gain or brush-up knowledge which might have a bearing on the hoped-for future. In Britain these activities were initiated and directed from within by utilizing the capabilities of the internees. They were less popular with the refugees in the Peninsula, scattered as they were over large areas and residing amongst people who led normal every-day lives. While in Britain the internees came from German-speaking countries and had a German cultural background, that of the refugees in Portugal and Spain was far more varied. Linguistic barriers and different educational standards fractionized the refugee communities. Moreover, their psychological outlook deteriorated as time dragged on with no solution in sight.

It may be understandable that in Portugal and Spain attempts to combat the lethargy of the refugees by cultural activities were short-lived despite an often enthusiastic initial beginning. The payments doled out by the organizations which supported and maintained the refugees, were strictly earmarked for given purposes and might not be spent at the recipient's will, except for a very small sum of pocket-money. Also mistakes were sometimes made by Jewish clerks and accountants which set off clashes and exacerbated frayed tempers.

Although the numerous refugees at Caldas da Reinha and the smaller group at Ericeira appreciated the material care which JDC extended to them, many were dissatisfied with the way in which this assistance was rendered. More independence, as to how the total amount at the disposal of the individual or the family could be spent, was clamoured for. It was understood that the Portuguese authorities set certain limits but many of the refugees wished to work. To be supported and guided like children caused discontent, indifference and despondency.

My appearance among the Jewish refugees revived their hopes for an early departure. They began to intensify their social and cultural activities, which now centred mainly on Palestine and Zionist topics. Hebrew courses for selected candidates were extended. There was a lack of text-books and teachers, but all available knowledge and material (prayer books, songs, etc.) was put to good use.

Most of these refugees expected an emissary of the Jewish Agency to solve all their problems; that the Jewish Homeland would restore to them the life they were used to; that everyone would get a certificate; that formalities could and would be dispensed with; that there need be no more filling in of forms, no fresh examinations; that a boat would bring them to Palestine speedily and safely. It was natural that the life that they had been forced to lead had given rise to illusions which were hard to destroy.

In autumn 1943, Canada offered to accept certain refugees, and immigration forms were distributed among married craftsmen with young children. It transpired that in interviews with immigration officers many a Jewish refugee, already listed for a Palestine certificate, changed his mind. Long discussions ensued in families, among friends, in groups emanating from the same township or country. The JDC and HICEM morally and technically supported the Canadian bid for skilled Jewish immigrants. Though both organizations were ideologically neutral, their representatives were then more knowledgeable as far as Canada or Latin America were concerned than in respect to Palestine.

Single people and young couples, especially those who belonged to Zionist youth movements knew their goal. It also became obvious that for the duration of the war emigration possibilities existed only for Palestine. Some people resolved to stay were they were and to go to Canada when the time came. Others took the advice of relatives and friends to accept jobs offered in South American countries as Allied victories in Southern Italy seemed to herald a successful conclusion of the war. The formation of the Jewish Brigade and the wish to fight Nazism, were decisive for those young refugees who could join the forces of their countries of origin in the United Kingdom and register with their consulates for trans-shipment, while former German and Austrian nationals saw a chance for enlisting in Palestine.

At the end of 1943 Palestine seemed safe enough. The war in the Mediterranean was practically over. But doubts began to appear as to whether Palestine would in fact provide the chances longed for. Most of the families hoped to resume their former life in new surroundings. Who could say what the Palestine of the White Paper with its restrictions on settlement might hold in store? An article in *The Times* by its Special Correspondent in Jerusalem on 2nd and 4th December 1943 under the heading "The Palestine Outlook", "Future of the White Paper Policy — Limits of Immigration" and "Dangers of Violence on both sides — Policies based on mutual Fears" was heatedly discussed.

Among the refugees, all age groups were represented; most trades and commercial skills could be found. Families with children, bachelors as well as spinsters pondered their chances in various countries which might eventually be open to them. And why not even wait and return to the place from which they came? Even if things had changed there drastically and destruction been wrought by the war, something worthwhile might still exist and compensation be claimed for losses sustained.

It seemed to me that everybody who was willing and appeared able to work in Palestine was acceptable. It was imperative that the largest possible number of persons which could be covered by each certificate should utilize these precious "passports to freedom". In other words: if a family certificate could be used by parents with more children — other qualifications being more or less equal — they should have preference over a smaller family. Younger people should rank before older candidates, as their contribution to Palestine's war effort would be greater and their integration easier and more successful than that of people less adaptable. Persons with close relatives in Palestine should enjoy preference over those with no family ties.

At first, in the late summer of 1943, it had seemed that at best a few hundred refugees in Spain and a few dozen in Portugal would utilize the certificates granted in winter 1942/43 by the Palestine Government to the Jewish Agency. But soon it became clear that, while certificates of some categories would not find applicants, of other categories there were too few. The immigration certificates authorized the British Passport Control Officers at the British Embassies in Madrid or Lisbon to issue entry visas for Palestine, but only part of these certificates were already at their disposal.

Meanwhile time passed and a vicious circle was created by the following dilemma:

a) Should we select and process candidates without waiting for all the necessary certificates to be deposited with the British Passport Control Officers?

b) Should we go on with the endeavours to charter a boat — anyway a well-nigh impossible undertaking — unless we could be sure of filling it with suitable immigrants duly provided with visas? How could we fix sailing dates from Lisbon and a Spanish port without being assured of the "Navy cert" or "Safe conduct" and *Freies Geleit* from the belligerents, a *conditio sine qua non* for the Government under whose flag the boat sailed as well as for any ship-owner whom we might approach? Who could — in time of war and scarcity of shipping space — tie down a neutral shipping company for an indefinite period without running up prohibitive costs?

c) Could we, on the other hand, afford to wait until the certificates, with their limited validity, arrived and only then start processing the candidates and hunt for a boat? Would time allow us to complete these drawn-out operations and coordinate them with all the authorities concerned?

As I learned from representatives of the JDC, the Junta for Shipping — a Government-controlled syndicate — was "in principle" prepared to let the SS "Nyassa" undertake the journey which the Joint was "in principle" ready to finance. "In principle" meant that a host of conditions had to be complied with and certain prerequisites fulfilled. These were dependent on different bodies outside Portugal with which the Portuguese authorities would have to deal.

Provided, then, that a) we could utilize in time all the certificates of which only an insufficient number was actually at my disposal, the remainder being merely promised by the Palestine Administration; b) we could complete the screening and medical examinations of the candidates; c) the British Passport Control Officers could issue the visas in time; d) overland transport from Northern Spain to a port in the South, probably Cadiz, could be secured and scheduled for embarkation on a given day; and e) the total number of immigrants would fill SS "Nyassa" to capacity — then the Joint was prepared to sign a contract for the boat.

Understandably enough, the Portuguese authorities would sanction the sailing through the Mediterranean only after obtaining formal assurances from the belligerents that the boat could proceed without hindrance and danger to its destination. The "Navy cert", the agreement allowing the boat's journey at a given time and along a prescribed route between agreed ports, had to be issued by the Allied Authorities, represented by the British Ministry of War Transport, and the *Freies Geleit* from the German High Command. Many conditions had to be complied with before these indispensable permits were finally granted.

Routes other than the direct sea voyage through the Mediterranean were also considered and explored by HICEM and the Joint. I was not in favour of North African overland transport in military vehicles. With elderly women and small children amongst them, I felt that the refugees were not physically able to cope with that. Furthermore, I doubted that the Allies would undertake civilian transport over vast distances of desert and among hostile populations and that they would provide food even if lorries and other facilities were put at their disposal.

Another "possibility" under consideration was the way around South Africa by a Portuguese boat to the Portuguese province of Mozambique, to Lourenço Marques and from there either by sea along the East coast of Africa via the Suez Canal to Haifa, or overland through the then British Colonies and Ethiopia.

As communications from Portugal and Spain with London or Jerusalem were hampered by scarcity of planes as well as by censorship, it was almost impossible for me to consult the Jewish Agency offices there and I had to make up my mind independently even in major matters. Though the British Foreign Office and Embassies allowed me an occasional urgent message sent by diplomatic pouch, I could not ask for such a favour too often. Besides, all communications forwarded officially through the Foreign Office, were, of course, subject to approval by the Embassy officers and to inevitable delay at the receiving end. Sometimes cables from London took up to five days, longer than those from Jerusalem, which usually reached us within 48 hours. The text of foreign language cables sent from Spain had to be given in Spanish as well and the correctness of the translation had to be certified. Even my letters from Lisbon to Madrid were often censored and delayed.

Because of all this we could not afford to adhere to ordinary business routine. The selection of candidates and their preparation for *Aliyah* could not be delayed until the certificates were safely deposited with the British Passport Control Officers nor could we wait for the agreement for the "Nyassa" to sail to be signed by JDC and the Portuguese shipping agency. We could not even wait for the conclusion of the negotiations between the Portuguese authorities and the belligerents. We just had to assume that everything would work out all right and on time and to act accordingly.

The nearer fulfilment came of the refugees' yearning to leave the "assigned residence" and to escape from what only yesterday had seemed to them an undignified life of tutelage, the more doubtful many became and the more reluctant to burn their bridges. There were enough candidates to fill the "Nyassa" to capacity with about 750 passengers, but the majority were in Spain and more scattered there than in Portugal. *Aliyah* from Spain would more deeply affect the Jews in German-occupied France, Belgium and Holland, and give a moral uplift to the Jewish factions in the underground movements, particularly in France. While there was no common frontier between Portugal and occupied Europe, the

Pyrenees did provide a slim chance of escape, in spite of the enormous physical difficulties involved. Thus the possibility of *Aliyah* from neutral Spain would encourage many Jews and particularly *halutzim* from Germany whom the war had overtaken in Holland, and who were supplied by the Dutch underground with false papers. Even so, some had been detected, arrested and never been heard of again, while to others this could happen at any moment. Yet news of a feasible *Aliyah* would set in motion a southward movement of endangered Jews. But before this final and decisive step was taken, they had to be sure that it was a practical proposition and not wishful thinking.

I decided to go to Spain before granting certificates in Caldas da Reinha and Ericeira to all applicants who came forward. I thought that about one fifth should be reserved for Portugal, where a few Jewish families, well established for many years, had also applied for *Aliyah*. Living in the smaller towns with adolescent daughters, they were apprehensive of approaching matrimonial problems in a Catholic country, and took advantage of their chance to go to Palestine on certificates of the "capitalist" category. When the British Embassy had obtained my Spanish visa and my coming had been announced to Mr. Blickenstaff by the Lisbon Joint, I took the plane to the Spanish capital on 15th December.

Madrid impressed me even more than Lisbon with its glittering lights and colourful illuminated advertisements — things one had forgotten during three-and-a-half years of black-out in London. Compared with Madrid, Lisbon seemed dull. Yet as a centre of world affairs during war-time Madrid was of lesser importance than Lisbon. Its importance for rescue work, on the other hand, outweighed that of Lisbon, because Spain had a common frontier with Nazi-occupied Europe. The country, and particularly Madrid, still showed the scars of the Civil War. The roads were in need of repair and the railways' rolling stock was depleted.

Spain was the goal of all refugees from Western Europe, French, Dutch or Belgian, as well as those numerous Germans and East-Europeans who had lived in France before 1939 or had sought safety there afterwards. The tortuous Pyrenean border not only divided two countries, but it created a kind of no-man's-land on the Continent, by isolating Nazi Europe from the Allied Countries.

In Madrid relief and rescue organizations had their offices. Quakers and Unitarians, whose mighty American parent bodies had brought relief to the victims of the Civil War, found in the refugees from Nazi persecution a new challenge. The Joint used their combined offices at Calle Eduardo Dato 20 under the direction of Mr. David Blickenstaff. The latter, a U.S. citizen, had headed the Quaker Relief group and had been *persona grata* both with the Republican Government and Franco's forces during the Civil War. He had been the only person allowed to cross the lines and had thus become thoroughly acquainted with conditions in Spain. In Madrid lived a privileged refugee group of all confessions and nationalities. They had partly financial means of their own to supplement the allocations received from the Joint. Some of these refugees had found employment in Mr. Blickenstaff's office.

Discussing the prospects for securing the SS "Nyassa", he told me what arrangements he and his office could make for the refugees to reach a suitable Spanish port of embarkation, and to care for their food and well-being whilst en route from Barcelona via Madrid to the south. He offered his office's and Dr. Block's assistance. Dr. Paul Block had been appointed by Wilfrid Israel to deal with the preparation of selected candidates and the registration and scrutinizing of new ones. He was well versed in the situation in the various places of "assigned residence" and at Miranda del Ebro camp. From time to time he was permitted to visit the places of "assigned residence" in the north. At that time, travelling in Spain was subject to special police permits for all residents. Police registration in the hotels often deprived one of one's passport for days.

Together with Dr. Block I discussed personal problems individually with about 150 people in Madrid. Compared with the mental and emotional strain of these interviews, the discussion of technical arrangements — with medical officers, the relief organizations or the Passport authorities — seemed a relaxation.

At the British Embassy I met the Naval Attaché with whom I had travelled on the plane from England, and the First Secretary, to whom I explained the subject of my mission. I informed him that additional certificates were to be communicated to the Embassy and that I would rely on the co-operation of the Passport Control Officer whom I would have to burden with a great deal of work over a comparatively brief period. He fulfilled my wish to meet the principal officers right away in order to coordinate the work which we expected. He also informed the Consul-General in Barcelona of my forthcoming visit and asked for his assistance.

The Passport Control Officer turned out to be a warm-hearted lady with deep understanding of the human aspect of the relief and rescue work. She outlined the details of the procedure as far as her office was concerned and the preparations which would facilitate and speed up her issue of the visas. Her office would do anything, she said, regardless of office hours or holidays, to get a transport ready in time, provided we submitted the travel documents and health forms as early as possible. We worked out that to utilize the full capacity of SS "Nyassa" at least one hundred more certificates would have to arrive at the Embassy three weeks prior to the sailing date at the latest.

Dr. Block shared my view that we should proceed as if all the certificates needed were actually in our hands. The candidates approved during my stay in Madrid would be processed under his supervision, additional applicants would be listed and could be selected on my return from Barcelona, where I was to go as soon as possible.

We urged the Jewish Agency in Jerusalem to ensure the speedy transmission by the Mandatory Government of the promised additional certificates to the British Embassy in Madrid which acted as distribution centre and had to pass on the certificate numbers to its counterpart in Lisbon.

Processing selected candidates in places of "assigned residence" in Spain meant lots of coordination work. They lived hundreds of miles apart, in small townships or camps and could not leave without police permits. For these they had to apply well ahead of intended journeys. Good, valid reasons for the application were required. Destination, date of departure and return were stated on these permits when granted. Police officers, local authorities and Government agents had to be convinced that the grant of such a permission was indeed warranted. The JDC office in Barcelona became in these matters a "trusted partner" of the local Spanish agencies.

Added to these cumbersome formalities was the ever-present transport problem. I realized this rather drastically when, soon after my arrival in Madrid, I had to enlist the help of the British Embassy to obtain a ticket for the night train to Barcelona. It appeared that a remunerative black market secured and disposed of all tickets for these trains which ran only every second day. It was a fourteen hours' journey.

Barcelona was the centre for rescue work and also the main base for relief in the northern provinces of Spain. The townships south of the French-Spanish border served as reception and absorption points for refugees entering Spain illegally for temporary residence. Lerida was the largest of such places of "assigned residence", which stretched from Figueras, the most easterly, via Pamplona to small villages in the neighbourhood of San Sebastian in the west. Refugees were scattered there in small numbers, often at first imprisoned, but generally soon freed and transferred to hotels and maintained by their respective consulates. For Jews deprived of their original German or Austrian citizenship and for other stateless persons the JDC shouldered financial responsibility and was accepted by the Spanish authorities in a quasi-consular capacity. By far the largest proportion of refugees who crossed the Pyrenees were Jews who fled from Southern France after it had been taken over by the German Forces in November 1942.

Whilst refugees under the protection of their consuls were also under their direction and, on the whole, left the Peninsula sooner or later to join the Allied Forces or to do work of national importance in Britain or overseas, stateless Jews were stranded, at least for the duration of the war, unless the Jewish Agency could procure certificates for their immigration into Palestine. By combining its public standing and special legal status with the material potentialities of the JDC, the Jewish Agency attained *de facto* a status similar to that of a consulate. Indeed, when I called on the British Consul-General in Lisbon, he told his senior staff jokingly that my rights and powers exceeded his own. If I accorded a certificate, and provided the security check revealed no objections, they would have to endorse a visa for Palestine without reference to London or Jerusalem, whereas he himself had to refer every visa application for Great Britain to his home authorities and to await their decision.

At Barcelona, the Joint occupied two floors of the Bristol Hotel, bustling with activity. Here new arrivals were registered; guides who had piloted a group of refugees across the border received their payment; bills were presented, refugees consoled, lectures given and all the needs, small and large, of the refugees dealt with. From here, groups in smaller provincial places, in Aragon and Navarre were administered, and permanent contact was maintained not only with Mr. Blicken-staff's office in Madrid, but also with the Spanish local and district authorities and the police. Dr. Samuel Sequerra from Lisbon was in charge. He received his instructions from the JDC's office in Lisbon. He facilitated my work and provided me with secretarial help.

Barcelona became the main single station of my work. Not only did the largest number of refugees reside in this town, with fairly large groups living in the towns and townlets of the northern frontier provinces, but here information could be obtained and contacts established with German-occupied France. The regular *Lufthansa* planes flying the Berlin-Lisbon route touched down first in Barcelona on neutral ground.

Besides being a busy harbour which has much in common with that of Mar-seilles, Barcelona is an important industrial centre, very different in character from Madrid. Dozens of Jewish non-refugee families lived here. Though not allowed to observe their holy days or to form Jewish associations, they were eager to meet an emissary from Palestine. To these Jews, Sephardim of Moroccan or Greek origin, it meant a chance of contact with Jewry and Palestine and they were determined not to let it slip. Quite a few families with numerous children were included in transports during the last eighteen months of World War II.

This was an aspect in our work of which we had been unaware in London. The several hundred Jews who lived in Spain, mainly at Barcelona, were small artisans, skilled in various crafts, in their forties and with many children. Though Spanish citizens, they were deprived of organized Jewish life. After the Civil War, synagogues could not re-open. The right of assembly at public places was severely restricted. To gather ten men at a private place for prayers would have constituted a grave risk. When these Sephardic families learned of a possible sailing to Pales-tine, they clamoured for admission and certificates. While physically safe as Spanish citizens, they felt their Jewishness was in danger.

The inclusion of Spanish citizens in our list meant additional complications and negotiations with the Spanish authorities. Anyone, citizen or refugee in "assigned residence" alike, needed an exit permit to leave the country. While it took some time for the Spanish authorities to grant it to refugees on the strength of their Palestine entry visas, for Spanish citizens it was still more difficult to obtain, since it involved a different Government department and the local authorities too. Yet, at long last, fifty such Spanish citizens were able to leave on SS "Nyassa" from Cadiz on 24th January 1944.

In Portugal, HICEM was charged with the technicalities pertaining to emigration matters. In Spain, the American relief organizations, the Society of Friends (Quakers), the Unitarians Service Committee and smaller organizations with which a close and smooth co-operation existed in all fields of relief work had an office in Madrid in which the JDC participated. Later on it became the repre-sentative and unified office of President Roosevelt's WRB (War Refugee Board) for the Peninsula, still under the direction of Mr. David Blickenstaff.

The overall picture and situation of refugees in Spain did not differ in any essential point from that in Portugal. They were mostly accommodated in small, poorly equipped hotels. Their numbers fluctuated. In little townships a few resided, in larger provincial centres, some dozens. Many had acquired some furniture, their own bedding and books. Some tried to learn and to keep abreast of developments in their professions, and all whiled away time by reading, studying languages, playing games. Old-timers who had been living in Spain for years and recent arrivals from France, young healthy men and women, old, sick, single and married people, with or without children of widely varying ages, were pressed by fate into unified communities. Many who had relatives in Canada, U.S.A., Australia or South America, hoped to proceed there but found that, at least as long as the war lasted, no such opportunities existed.

In autumn 1943, Allied victory seemed certain, but still far off and everybody realized that even after victory admission to overseas countries would be difficult to obtain and shortage of transportation would involve further delays. Everybody felt the prevailing situation humiliating and almost unbearable. Thus many begged to be considered as candidates for Palestine who might never have had it in mind to work on the land, to speak Hebrew, to regard themselves as observing or national Jews; but who could no longer bear an idle life as refugees. During preceding years of educational work for Hehalutz, I had had experience of the fact that many "good Zionists" were not able to master the difficulties and realities of life in Palestine, whilst many a Jew who was not an organized Zionist and knew little or nothing of Zionist ideology, integrated speedily and successfully.

On the already familiar pattern, my meetings and interviews took the best part of three weeks in Barcelona, at Lerida, capital of the province of that name and at the ill-famed Miranda del Ebro Camp, where political internees and refugees were held. Here were nearly thirty candidates whom Wilfrid Israel had accepted elsewhere. Rabbi Dr. Leo Ansbacher led the Jewish refugee group and acted on behalf of the Red Cross for all. I also visited a small number of *halutzim* from Germany who had crossed into Spain only a few days before, coming from Holland and awaiting their release from badly lit and primitive prison cells.

With Jews who were citizens of an Allied country and eager to join the war effort of its forces, we also kept contact. They were as much interested to hear about the situation in Palestine as we were to learn from them of their experiences concerning the situation of the Jews and the efforts being made for their survival in the regions from which they came. Though each of these Dutch, French or Belgian arrivals knew only a little of the whole picture, from combining their stories we learned a great deal about their contacts and the routes that they had covered. This proved most valuable for becoming acquainted with some aspects of underground work and the circles directing it.

It might be added that totalitarian Spain showed more active human understanding and generosity than a liberal, well-administered country in the heart of Europe. I do not know and did not hear of a single refugee who was refused

Deutsche Botschaft   Madrid, den 27.Januar 1944
in Spanien   ~~Geheim~~

Nr.353/44 g

| Auswärtiges Amt |
| In! II   2 4 3 g |
| 8 FEB 1944 |
| Anl. (/ ~~nach~~/ Dopp. d. Eing. |

Inhalt: Abtransport jüdischer Flüchtlinge aus Spanien
        und Portugal.

      1 Durchschlag

      Der portugiesische Dampfer "NYASSA" ist am 23.d.Mts.
aus Lissabon mit 245 jüdischen Flüchtlingen aus verschiedenen europäischen Ländern abgefahren. Am folgenden Tage lief er Cádiz an, wo
sich 573 jüdische Flüchtlinge aus Polen, Jugoslawien, Griechenland,
ehemaliger Tschechoslowakei, Belgien, Rumänien, Holland, Schweden
und Frankreich sowie Staatenlose eingeschifft haben. Der Dampfer
wird von Cádiz direkt nach Haifa laufen, wo die geflüchteten Juden
ausgeschifft werden, um sich in Palästina nieder zu lassen.

      Der Abtransport der geflüchteten Juden von der iberi-
schen Halbinsel geht auf amerikanische Initiative zurück. Mindestens
bei den Juden, die sich bisher in Spanien aufgehalten haben und in
Cádiz eingeschifft worden sind, handelt es sich um Personen, die bisher von der amerikanischen Botschaft bezw. der amerikanisch-jüdi-
schen Hilfsvereinigung J.O.I.N.T. unterstützt wurden und die Reise
nach Palästina auf Veranlassung der hiesigen amerikanischen Botschaft
angetreten haben. Zahlreiche dieser jüdischen Flüchtlinge sind nur
sehr widerwillig und offenbar nur unter Androhung der Einstellung
weiterer Unterstützung dazu bewogen worden, nach Palästina auszurei-
sen. Die Reise der Juden von Madrid, Barcelona und anderen grösseren
Städten Spanien's erfolgte in Sonderzügen, die auf die Initiative
der hiesigen amerikanischen Botschaft bereitgestellt wurden. Auf-
fällig war, dass z.B. der von Madrid ablaufende Sonderzug zum grösseren Teil aus Güterwagen bestand, in die die Juden zum Teil unter
erheblichen Protest verladen wurden. Jedem Juden war gestattet, einen
grossen Koffer mitzunehmen, ausserdem wurden ihm von der amerikanischen Botschaft bezw. der J.O.I.N.T. Ptas. 500.-- zur Bestreitung
der Reiseauslagen bis Haifa ausgezahlt. Zahlreiche der auswandernden
Juden, die gewisse Vermögenswerte nach Spanien gebracht bezw. hier er-
worben haben, haben diese zum Ankauf von Kaffee, Textilwaren und anderen Mangelwaren benutzt, die sie ohne Schwierigkeiten mitnehmen
konnten, da irgendeine Zollnachschau ihres Gepäckes nicht stattfand.

das
~~Auswärtige Amt,~~
~~Berlin.~~

            K213143   Die

                                478246

                                             C/0459

Dispatch of the German Embassy Madrid, dated 27th January, 1944
to the German Foreign Office

Die Passagekosten sind offenbar ebenfalls von amerikanischer
Seite bezahlt worden. Der Dampfer "NYASSA" fährt unter portugie-
sischer Flagge als Schiff einer in Lissabon ansässigen "Companhia
Nacional de Navegação". Nach den der Botschaft vorliegenden Nachrichten ist der Dampfer mit Hilfe eines portugiesischen Juden ge-
chartert, der hierfür Dollar 500.000.-- erhalten haben soll. Um den
Charakter des Schiffes als reinen Judentransporter zu tarnen und
die Reise bei einer Versicherungsgesellschaft decken zu können, hat
die Companhia Nacional de Navegação in portugiesischen Zeitungen,
u.a. im O Seculo vom 17.d.Mts., eine Anzeige aufgegeben, in der mit-
geteilt wird, dass der Dampfer am 23.Januar von Portugal nach Haifa, Alexandria, Port-Said, Lourenço Marques, Mormugao und Cochin
laufe und noch Passagiere 1. und 2.Klasse mitnehmen könne. Tat-
sächlich sind aber Passagen an dritte Personen so gut wie garnicht
verkauft worden, da beinahe alle verfügbaren Plätze durch jüdische
Passagiere in Anspruch genommen waren. Als Rückfracht wird der
Dampfer indische Baumwolle für Portugal laden.

Der Abtransport geht nach den der Botschaft vorliegenden
Nachrichten auf einen kürzlich auf der iberischen Halbinsel einge-
troffenen amerikanischen Juden B a k e r m a n zurück, der hier
als Beauftragter verschiedener amerikanischer Hilfsorganisationen
auftritt und ausserdem sich bemüht, unter den in Spanien befindli-
chen politischen Flüchtlingen, insbesondere den Franzosen, Spezia-
listen für die amerikanische Rüstungsindustrie anzuwerben. Die
Gründe, die die amerikanischen Stellen zum Abtransport der geflüchteten Juden veranlasst haben, sind nicht ganz klar. Da ein erheb-
licher Teil der Juden nur unter Anwendung wirtschaftlicher Druck-
mittel in die Ausreise eingewilligt hat, dürfte die Reise kaum
auf Initiative der Juden selbst zurückgehen. Da gleichzeitig hier
glaubwürdige Nachrichten vorliegen, dass nach Spanien geflüchtete
französische Juden, auch wenn sie in Marokko ihren Wohnsitz haben,
ein Einreisevisum nach Marokko verweigert und ihnen nur die Möglich-
keit der Ausreise nach Palästina gegeben wird, ferner offenbar geplant ist, alle nach Marokko geflüchteten Juden, die nicht vor 1939
in Marokko ansässig waren und ausserdem über wirtschaftliche Existenz

mittel

K 213143/

478247

Existenzmittel verfügen, ebenfalls nach Palästina abzutrans-
portieren, dürfte vielleicht die in hiesigen französischen
Kreisen geäusserte Ansicht zutreffen, dass die Amerikaner
durch den Abtransport der jüdischen Elemente verhindern wollen,
dass letztere nach der von ihnen als bevorstehend angesehenen
Besetzung Europa's an ihren früheren Wohnsitz zurückzuströmen
und dadurch antisemitische Reaktionen auszulösen, die den amerikanischen Besatzungstruppen nur Schwierigkeiten bereiten
würden.

    Es erscheint durchaus verständlich, dass die spani-
schen Behörden durch Bereitstellung von Sonderzügen und in
sonstiger Weise die Abreise der geflüchteten Juden erleich-
tert haben, da abgesehen von dem in Spanien nicht aus Gründen
der Rasse, aber aus Gründen des Glaubens vorhandenen Antisemitismus die hierher geflüchteten Juden sich durch zahlreiche
Betrügereien und sonstige strafbare Handlungen sehr unangenehm bemerkbar gemacht und den zuständigen Sicherheitsorga-
nen manche Sorgen bereitet haben.

                In Entwurf gezeichnet: Dieckhoff

           beglaubigt:

                                    Kanzler

K213144

478248

entry at the Spanish border or sent back into enemy territory. It would exceed the scope of this report to analyse the underlying reasons.

The very fact of my presence in Barcelona and the apparent progress in evacuating several hundreds of refugees to Palestine from the Iberian Peninsula encouraged the Jewish section of the Maquis (French resistance movement) to redouble its efforts to have people guided into Spain over the snow-clad mountains and to prepare young people and children for the spring months when the crossing would be less dangerous. The possibility of swelling this clandestine trickle from German-occupied Europe into Spain into a rivulet, employing Spanish guides and developing the random contact with the Maquis into a regular mutual information service was viewed by different people in different lights. The background of the persons in question, the tasks for which their organizations worked, their relationship to other agencies, to the financial sources — all these complex realities made long-term decisions impossible and led to divergent opinions and rivalries among the Jewish organizations which — quite rightly — regarded rescue and relief as their most pressing and noble task. Though the aims were identical, the daring was not.

I met some members of the Jewish section of the Maquis who had come to Spain to advise their organization on matters affecting the reception and prospects of those who were guided into Spain for transit to Palestine. They had contacted the Joint, HICEM and the World Jewish Congress and in due course forged an important link with their Toulouse Area Command for all of us. On the eve of the SS "Nyassa's" sailing, I received information that a delegate of the Jewish section of the Maquis would soon come to Spain to discuss these matters with me. However, it was only in May 1944, after my return to the Peninsula for a longer spell of work as delegate of the Jewish Agency for Palestine in the Iberian Peninsula and North Africa, that I met M. Croustillon for a lengthy exchange of information.

But prior to these developments, in December 1943 and well into January 1944, preparations for the first transport went on. Negotiations to enable the SS. "Nyassa" to sail were progressing. The missing certificates had not yet reached Madrid or Lisbon, and we were extremely anxious to secure these essentials in close co-operation with the JDC and HICEM.

Whilst the short December days went by rapidly in encouraging, selecting and processing refugees at Barcelona and Lerida, the authorities in Lisbon completed the legal formalities for the sailing of SS "Nyassa" and the Joint prepared to sign the contract with the ship's agent and the "Junta". During Christmas and New Year's day postal services as well as consular and Government offices came practically to a standstill, and health examinations could not take place. Travel permits for accepted candidates in the smaller places of "assigned residence" were delayed. The potential emmigrants were unable to sell their belongings or buy what they wished to take with them.

Finally, I arrived at the conclusion that a frank discussion of our problem with the British Ambassador in Spain, Sir Samuel Hoare (later Lord Templewood), might be useful and that his intervention with the Governments in London and Jerusalem might produce the long-awaited action by the Mandatory Government. I felt that Sir Samuel would be in a position to authorize the Passport Control Officer to issue the visas even without waiting for formal instructions and the knowledge of serial letters and numbers of the certificates. I felt all the more emboldened to approach the former British Foreign Secretary on humane grounds, since we knew that the Allies were anxious to relieve neutral countries of refugees and thereby encourage them to let others cross their borders. Therefore I asked the British Consul-General to request, through the Embassy, an appointment with Sir Samuel.

On 3rd January, 1944, I was informed at Barcelona of a telegram which JDC Lisbon had dispatched on 30th December to Mr. Blickenstaff, reading: "Nyassa sailing arranged for January 20th. Please make all arrangements. Advise us your progress". This was good news, but it made it even more imperative to have the certificates in hand without further delay. The news of the "Nyassa's" sailing in less than three weeks was received with great joy by all the candidates. It set others thinking whether they should not present themselves as candidates for joining the transport. The paper-work kept us working late into the nights. The British Passport Control Officers were swamped with application forms for travel papers and visas in preparation for the final granting of visas, once the certificates arrived.

The Consul-General at Barcelona depended upon his Madrid Embassy, where these matters were centralized for the whole of Spain. I decided to see the PCO in Madrid, who would have to carry an enormous burden in the very short time at our disposal. Also Dr. Block and Mr. Blickenstaff were eager to clarify the steps necessary to ensure the sailing of the boat with the greatest possible number of refugees. The Spanish authorities were required to co-operate in granting exit permits. Special trains had to be provided from Barcelona and Madrid to Cadiz, which was to be the Spanish port of embarkation. Provisions for about 570 people — amongst them children of all age groups and elderly, sick people — had to be prepared. Accommodation for such a large group at Cadiz was not only very expensive, but difficult to find. Departure from Barcelona of 420 people, who were to be joined in Madrid by the others, had to be timed for the arrival at Cadiz on 24th January, coinciding with the arrival of SS "Nyassa" from Lisbon. The agency in Spain of American Relief Organizations, with David Blickenstaff at its head, contacted the competent authorities in Madrid and, thanks to this, the overland transport went through without a hitch.

We were lucky to enlist the goodwill of Miss M. Gillot and her co-workers at the British Passport Control Office who subsequently worked throughout the night issuing the necessary papers. Some people received theirs whilst in transit in the special train in Madrid.

An additional reason for my short visit to Madrid between January 3rd and 6th, was to consult with Señor German Baraibar, the head of the European Department at the Spanish Foreign Office, regarding the admission of 73 Sephardic Jews, held by the Nazis at Athens and Perpignan. Several hundred Sephardic Jews, mostly from Salonika and detained in Bergen-Belsen, had been recognized by the Franco Government as Spanish citizens. On the strength of this they were to be released by the Germans and brought to Spain in the spring of 1944. The Spanish Government was helpful, knowing that the War Refugee Board could be trusted to see to it that these groups would not stay more than three months in Spain when they would be tranferred to the first UNWRA camp, then under construction near Fedhala, a village in Morocco between Casablanca and Rabat. During their stay in Spain, the Joint would maintain these Jews, thus even adding dollars to the Spanish Treasury. I based my request for the Athens and Perpignan groups on this precedent.

We raised the question whether Jews who would be allotted Palestine immigration certicates, but could not join the first transport on board SS "Nyassa", might be freed from "assigned residence" and await their departure in Spain. We discussed the question of release, in particular, from the Miranda del Ebro camp, where conditions were cramped and more difficult than elsewhere. No direct answers could be expected, but in the course of the following months some facilities were granted to Miranda camp inmates.

At the British Embassy, I learnt that the Ambassador was absent from Madrid, but my request for an urgent interview would be submitted to him on his return at the end of the week. I returned to Barcelona to help in the preparations of the candidates for the "Nyassa" sailing. Some anxiety was caused by the fact that nearly half of the Barcelona area candidates were not covered by the certificates actually at our disposal.

Saturday, 8th January, the British Consul-General informed me that the Ambassador would see me at his residence on Monday, the 10th, at 5 p.m. I tried immediately to book the first Iberia[10] flight to Madrid for that day, but was told, to my distress, that both planes scheduled to reach Madrid before 4 p.m. were fully booked. My explanations on the urgency of my trip produced the suggestion that I book one of the few remaining seats on the *Lufthansa* plane which, on its Berlin-Lisbon flight, lands at Barcelona and Madrid. Fully aware that with a Palestinian passport, I could not risk travelling on a German airliner, I booked a seat and immediately explained my predicament to the head of the Iberia's Barcelona office. Relying on the fact that I was a good customer, flying Iberia often on its Lisbon-Madrid-Barcelona route, I suggested that he go out with me on Monday morning to the airport and request one of his passengers to be good enough to swop tickets with me and travel half an hour later on the German plane. Finally he agreed and on Monday morning sent one of his officials with me to the airport. Luckily the plan worked: tickets were exchanged and names altered. I arrived in time at Madrid.

When I met Sir Samuel Hoare, we chatted about Palestine over a cup of tea.

[10]National Spanish Airline.

He had once visited the country and it so happened that he had seen the kibbutz of which I was a member. He questioned me on the collective way of life and showed his interest in a British-run country which to him seemed both romantic and strange. When I explained my plight to him, he listened attentively, made a few notes and said he would do what he could to help me. Hesitatingly I asked whether he would take it upon himself to authorize his Passport Control Officer to issue the visas in case the certificates from Jerusalem did not reach Madrid in time. His answer was that he trusted that they would arrive on time.

After more than half an hour, I left him with a feeling of relief. The preparations in Madrid for the transport were in full swing. I left next day for Lisbon and found the HICEM office there busy completing the formalities for 170 candidates from Portugal who would embark first. Early in January we cabled repeatedly to Jerusalem and London explaining time and again the difficulties arising out of the absence of certificates and our ignorance of categories and dispatch date. These cables were to convey the sense of urgency and desperation under which all of us laboured who were actively involved in this work. It was also suggested that we enlist the support of the High Commission for Refugees and of Miss Rathbone[11] in the negotiations with the Colonial Office. Finally a cable arrived on 12th January from the Jewish Agency Jerusalem saying that "Government cabled today Britconsul Lisbon 150 certificates without age or other restrictions also cabled Madrid ten youth certificates", and on 16th Jaunary a reassuring cable came also from the Jewish Agency London, dated 11th January. Now it was certain that on 23rd January SS "Nyassa" would sail filled to capacity. The Jewish community in Lisbon, its clubs and associations gave a farewell party for the refugees. Well-meaning speeches sped them on their way to Palestine. Lisbon's Jews never were as Zionist-inspired as in those days in January 1944. The Portuguese press announced the sailing date and hailed the coming event. Most local Jews and crowds of Gentiles gathered in the harbour to bid farewell and wish the refugees a safe landing in the Jewish Homeland. From Portugal 166 refugees sailed in SS "Nyassa". Four *halutzim* originating from Germany, who had trained in England, were given certificates in London to assist the refugees on the boat trip and, later, the Jewish Agency officials at Haifa on disembarkation.

Dr. David Schweitzer accompanied this first war-time transport on behalf of the Jewish relief organizations in U.S.A. when, on 23rd January, 1944, it sailed with 170 Jews and a hundred non-Jews, clergymen, Red Cross and relief workers for India on board. At Cadiz they were joined by six refugees from Tangier and 564 from Spain (138 from Madrid, 384 from Barcelona and 42 from Miranda camp, Uberagua, Nanclar de la Oca, Murguia and Lerida). About 40% of the passengers were Jews from "Greater Germany", many more had lived there till 1933 and had fled France and Belgium in 1940 before the invading German armies.

---

[11]Eleanor Rathbone, Independent Member of Parliament for the Combined English Universities, died in 1946, known and respected for her activities for refugees and underprivileged people.

A statistical break-down shows that of the total of the 170 passengers ex Lisbon
    68 were German Jews;
    74 Jews originating from Poland, but residing in Germany before 1933 or
        in Austria before 1938.
    The rest resided mostly in France till 1940.
Among the 564 passengers ex Cadiz were about
    50 residents of Spain, partly originating from Greece;
    151 Jews from Germany;
    260 residents of Germany before 1933 mostly of Polish origin;
    80 residents of France prior to 1940 but of Polish origin.

SS "Nyassa's" sailing in January 1944, almost five months before D-Day, was applauded in many quarters as a kind of break-through. The fact that refugees from Nazi oppression were evacuated from two European countries and from Tangier, where they were marooned, put heart into Jews still clandestinely living in Nazi-occupied Western Europe. All relief and rescue organizations, whose migration plans had not materialized so far, looked upon it with renewed hope. It showed the Governments of neutral countries that they need not indefinitely be saddled with the Jewish refugee problem, and this produced a more lenient attitude on the part of various district and local authorities. Officials in Government departments, Embassies and Consulates saw the human side of the event and attended to the formal work which they had to do with more than usual readiness, goodwill and understanding. A many-sided upsurge of sympathy allowed us to look forward to a continuation of this endeavour with good prospects.

My mission to the Iberian Peninsula was accomplished. While I began to prepare my report and the return journey to London I was urged by the Jewish Agency Jerusalem to continue the work in the Peninsula till the end of the war. I felt, however, that I should first report in person and in detail to the Agency and discuss the lines on which further work should proceed. Important technical matters, such as a new allocation of certificates and their categories, had to be settled. I indicated, therefore, that if desired I would return to Lisbon, but I wanted first to come to London to report and to prepare future activities.

After this had been agreed upon, it only remained for me to thank the heads of the Jewish community, the Joint, HICEM and War Refugee Board representatives, the Passport Control Officers and the diplomatic officers at the Embassies concerned for their unstinting and invaluable co-operation and having taken leave of them, I flew to the United Kingdom on 29th January, 1944. On the attitude of the various Governments I learned more during the continuation of my work between April 1944 and September 1945.

The Portuguese press reported extensively on the sailing of the boat in which the people took special pride as being of Portuguese registry, belonging to the Companhia Nacional de Navegacao with a Portuguese crew, and because it made history by crossing the Mediterranean in war-time. Other publications in Spain,

Palestine, U.S.A. and Great Britain as well as Jewish papers also carried the story. The *Manchester Guardian* on 25th January, 1944, published a short report, headlined "For Palestine at Last". The *Observer* wrote on Sunday, 23rd January, "750 Jews Sail for Palestine". Naturally, the *Zionist Review* (28th January) gave a more detailed account under the headings "The Way Home" and "God Speed the Ship". In its May 1944 issue, *Life in Palestine* devoted to the event an illustrated page entitled "On the Way to Eretz Israel — the Lesson of the 'Nyassa'". It concluded the report with the words: "Further 'Nyassas' must cross the waters now. Later it will be too late." In his report to the Annual Conference of the Zionist Federation on 31st January Dr. Weizmann singled out this action as being "on the credit side of the ledger".

After the arrival of SS "Nyassa" in Haifa port with 754 passengers, drawn from 21 nationalities and all walks of life, all the Hebrew papers reported at length and published interviews with Dr. Schweitzer and some of the newcomers. Among the British papers, the *Evening Standard* on 2nd February under the headline "Jewish Refugees reach Palestine", quoted the Master of the SS "Nyassa" as saying that the journey had been uneventful and the spirit of the passengers very high.

A German reaction is expressed in a dispatch of the German Embassy Madrid, dated 27th January, 1944, to the *Auswärtiges Amt*. It is inaccurate in almost every detail concerning persons and organizations although in Portugal and Spain these were common knowledge. The document reproduced in this essay speaks for itself.[12]

In the meantime, the Allied invasion of Hitler's "Fortress Europe" and the decisive blow in the West were expected to be imminent. In liberated France, Belgium, Holland and, eventually, occupied Germany, relief work and rescue activities needed strong and capable Jewish and Palestinian teams to attend to the pressing needs of starving, humiliated, sick and apathetic Jews of all age-groups who were known to be in concentration camps, in hiding, in monasteries or with friendly Gentile families. To add to relief and rescue, search and training centres, exchange of data, compilation of lists had to be organized and extended.

Lisbon soon became a transit station for Palestinian visitors who were either organizing these future activities or already awaiting their call to proceed in the wake of the Allied Armies to liberated areas. Meanwhile, being nearer their future assignments, they would try to gain first-hand knowledge in Lisbon of problems with which they would soon be confronted.

On Good Friday, 7th April, 1944, I returned to Lisbon to continue my work for the duration of the war. A small office of the Jewish Agency was established at Rua Castilho 30, Lisbon. Our rescue efforts were to include the — then still international — zone of Tangier as well as Morocco. At my disposal were still some immigration certificates in Madrid, unused by the "Nyassa" *Olim*, and the

[12]I obtained a photocopy of this report in September 1968 through the Embassy of the Federal German Republic in Israel. To the best of my belief it has not been published before. The document is reproduced in facsimile between pp. 248-9.

new schedule of 600 certificates granted by the Palestine Government as a result of the "Nyassa" sailing.

During my ten weeks' absence in London, some efforts undertaken in 1943 bore fruit. A few weeks before my return to the Peninsula, several hundred Sephardic Jews, mostly originating from Salonika and some from other small Greek towns, had been brought to Spain in a special train from Bergen-Belsen. As stated before, Franco's Government had been prevailed upon to recognise and claim them as Spanish citizens. They were evacuated to Fedhala in the summer, swelling the number of refugees already in Morocco. After due processing by us in September 1944, these Sephardic Jews were brought to Nuseirat in the south-west of Palestine, gradually released from the British detention camp there and largely integrated in the *Yishuv*.

Apart from this ethnically homogeneous group, there were hundreds of individual refugees from Germany, Austria, Hungary, Italy, France and Poland waiting anxiously at Tangier for their *Aliyah* or a definite absorption elsewhere. During the years 1944/45 a hundred or so refugees had been able to join the boats then sailing from Portugal and Spain to Palestine. Now a special boat, the Liberty ship "Asquanius", was put at our disposal for Tangier people by the British Shipping Office, following our negotiations in 1944 with it and with the Colonial Secretary at Gibraltar. She sailed from there on 27th April, 1945, with 248 refugees and some local Jewish families to Haifa where they landed on the last day of the war in Europe.

During the second period of my work in the Peninsula, I intensified my contacts with representatives of the Jewish Section of the Maquis. I met M. Joseph Croustillon in Spain and, later also M. Jules Yefroikin. We discussed and devised ways and means to help Jews in France in general, and young trained workers in particular, to escape to Spain. They were to serve the *Yishuv* in Palestine, or the Allied war effort. I knew already that, as an echo to the "Nyassa" sailing, many Jews, members of Hehalutz, helped by false papers issued by underground groups in Holland and France, had succeeded in crossing the Pyrenees. Some of them had worked their way south as workers for the German "Organisation Todt", building the Atlantic Wall near Bordeaux, in order to be nearer the Spanish border. They were a motley lot, stemming from Germany, which had deprived them of their citizenship by the Nuremberg Laws, from France, Holland or stateless, originating from East-European countries, though having lived and been educated in Germany since the early twenties. I visited the newcomers along the border from the Mediterranean to the Atlantic in the places of "assigned residence" and the children, who had been brought over from Youth-Aliyah-type homes in the south of France, by paid guides.

A first group of children had been brought to Portugal by the efforts of Mr. Isaac Weissmann who cared for them near Lisbon on behalf of the World Jewish Congress. The Joint set up a Children's Home at Barcelona under the direction of Laura Margolis, who later headed the Joint work in Sweden and in France, and, as Mrs. Jarblum, is now a devoted social worker in Israel.

The continuous arrival of children and young people soon necessitated another boat. The Portuguese liner "Guiné" sailed with refugees from Lisbon on 23rd October, 1944, to Tangier, where 88 additional refugees embarked and reached Haifa safely. Most of her passengers were young members of the German Hehalutz and Youth Movements who had gone underground in Holland and France during the war. After the Allied landings on the Riviera in August 1944 a landbridge between Switzerland and Spain was soon opened and permitted the departure of organized adult groups and of Youth Aliyah groups from Switzerland via Spain, on boats sailing from Barcelona under Charter to Haifa. These Youth Aliyah boys and girls originated from Germany and had been training in Holland and France when war broke out. They had been guided clandestinely into Switzerland for their safety and education. Their evacuation encouraged international bodies in Switzerland and the Swiss Government to admit survivors from death camps who had just been liberated in Germany, Czechoslovakia and Austria.

On 31st May, 1945, the Spanish liner "Plus Ultra" sailed with refugees from Lisbon, called at Barcelona for the embarkation of 155 children and 93 adults from Switzerland, was joined by more refugees in Spain, took 25 refugees at Algiers and some from Italy at Naples, and reached Haifa with almost 400 immigrants on 19th June.

When the war in Europe had ended, Relief Units and Allied help poured into the liberated areas. Concentration camps were dissolved. But repatriation or emigration were still far off. This situation imposed upon us additional tasks. We became a clearing house for lists of Jewish survivors in the camps of Germany, lists of Danish Jews and elderly German Jews deported to Theresienstadt, lists of Jewish intellectuals from Hungary in Mauthausen, lists of deportees in Vittel and other camps with thousands upon thousands of names. We were approached by Palestinian and U.S. Jews, by those in Spain and Portugal, Tangier and Morocco who sought information about their relatives and friends. We forwarded hundreds of lists to the Jewish Agency and to World Jewish Congress Offices in London and Jerusalem.

We were able to help 364 more displaced persons, as they now were, sending them on our fifth — and last — boat, the Portuguese steamer "Lima", on 27th August, 1945, from Lisbon to Haifa.

The eighteen months of intensified rescue efforts over a wider area, which followed the "Nyassa" sailing, were made possible by the success of the initial mission of October 1943 to January 1944. About two thousand people, refugees for years, displaced and homeless, could build their lives again in Palestine. Others went later from Spain and Portugal overseas, to Canada and the United States. The Jewish Agency's Immigration Department reported these activities to the 22nd Zionist Congress in Basle in December 1946 in sparse language, on less than two pages. This naturally could not encompass the human side, nor explain circumstances and background, or give an idea of the actual development of the story which I have tried to present.

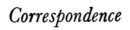

Correspondence

Notes on Organizational Problems of German Jewry

BY WALTER BRESLAUER

Jacob Toury's essay on the organizational problems of German Jewry in Year Book XIII[1] was bound to deal also with the *Verband der Deutschen Juden* (VDJ). I am very grateful to the Editor for referring readers, in a note on page 69, to my article on the VDJ in the Bulletin of the Leo Baeck Institute[2], though his remark that my point of view "is not always the same as that of Dr. Toury" is, I feel, rather an understatement.

Toury's survey of Jewish organizational activities at the turn of the century seems to me to be influenced — and its author not infrequently led astray — by a probably unconscious bias and this not only with regard to the VDJ. Such a bias may be easily induced in one of the younger generation by later events and by the author's present environment. This writer, twenty-five years older than Dr. Toury and active in Jewish public life in Germany from his early youth until 1936, would like to comment on some of Toury's statements.

I. Toury most assiduously uses all the Jewish periodicals, large and small. One is struck by the apparent completeness of the material available today in Israel; unfortunately this is not the case to the same extent in London.[3] However, other easily procurable sources, both relevant, and important, were apparently not consulted by the author.

They are:

a) The very informative articles in the *Jüdisches Lexikon,* for instance those on 'Gemeinden',[4] 'VDJ',[5] 'Frauenwahlrecht',[6] etc.

b) The annual *Handbuch der Jüdischen Gemeindeverwaltung und Wohlfahrtspflege.*[7]

c) All the publications of the VDJ.[8]

---

[1]'Organizational Problems of German Jewry. Steps towards the Establishment of a Central Organization (1893-1920)', *LBI Year Book XIII* (1968), pp. 57-90.

[2]'Der Verband der Deutschen Juden (1904-1922)' in *Bulletin des Leo Baeck Instituts,* No. 28 (1964), pp. 345-379.

[3]The following journals are, for instance, not available here in London: *Jüdische Rundschau,* 1907 and 1920, *Die Welt,* 1908, *Jüdische Rundschau, Breslau* and *Generalanzeiger.*

[4]Vol. II (1928), pp. 971 ff. (Authors: Ismar Freund, Josef Meisl and others).

[5]Vol. V (1930), p. 1166 (Author: R. Weiss).

[6]Vol. II (1928), pp. 780 ff. (Authors: Marcus Cohn, Siddy Wronsky).

[7]Edited by the *Deutsch-Israelitischer Gemeindebund* (DIGB) and in later years also by the *Zentralwohlfahrtsstelle der deutschen Juden.* The *Handbuch* is available in Londen for the years 1907, 1911, 1924/1925.

[8]They are quoted extensively in my article cited in note 2 above. (I received one of the *Korrespondenzblätter* of the VDJ from Jerusalem by courtesy of the Leo Baeck Institute. Perusal of them would have convinced Dr. Toury that the obscure pamphlet quoted by him (p. 72) which "soon" attacked the VDJ indulged in a baseless attack inasmuch as the VDJ

d) Ahron Sandler's article 'The Struggle for Unification'.[9]

e) The relevant Laws, most especially the *Preussische Judengesetz* of 1847 and Kollenscher's Commentary to it.[10]

II. Various remarks of Toury's culminate in his statement on "the long standing practice of managing Jewish communal affairs on an oligarchic basis. Even if Jews had wanted to hold democratic elections of their representatives", he says, "there existed no registers of voters and no other instruments for an orderly procedure."[11] This observation much astonished this writer who already in 1910 was active in the election campaign in the Berlin Jewish Community, conducted on the basis of a proper register of voters.[12]

A democratic electoral system exists if the right to vote is general, equal, secret and direct. Until 1918 votes for women and a proportional voting procedure were, however, nowhere considered essential.[13] Yet it is true that tendencies to establish proportional representation were not infrequent also before 1918. (Even now the system is not adopted in the UK and the USA, which are generally considered democratic countries.) Jewish communal affairs were regulated for more than half of German Jewry by the Prussian *Judengesetz* of 1847,[14] Section 41 of which reads:

> "All male members of the Synagogue Community who are of age, have an unblemished record, make an independent living and have not been in arrears with communal dues for the last three years, elect the representatives and these elect the Board for six years."[15]

Consequently the voting for the communal assembly *(Repräsentantenversammlung)* was equal and direct. In fact, nearly all the men were able to vote because the restrictions contained in the wording of section 41 as interpreted in Kollenscher's Commentary were of small importance.[16] The voting was in practice also

---

did in fact do extensive work and also that its public meetings, combined with its conventions, were attended by thousands.

[9]See *LBI Year Book II* (1957), pp. 76-84 which mentions the VDJ on p. 78; also *LBI Year Book VII* (1962), pp. 333 ff.

[10]*Die Rechtsverhältnisse der Juden in Preussen*, Berlin 1910.

[11]Toury, p. 72.

[12]Many others were conducted on such a basis both before and afterwards. For some election reports at random see *Allgemeine Zeitung des Judentums* (AZJ) 1910, pp. 85 ff. (Berlin), and 16.12.1910 (Munich), *Liberales Judentum*, vol. 1, p. 19 (Posen).

[13]Toury's stricture on p. 78 is therefore unjust as can easily be verified from Ismar Freund's article in *AZJ*, 1920, p. 218.

[14]It covered Prussia with the exception of the provinces conquered in 1866. The electoral laws for these areas and for the other German *Länder* were a mixed lot, some were democratic, others not. See *Jüdisches Lexikon*, II, pp. 971 ff.

[15]As to the composition of the Board see below.

[16]Kollenscher explained that everybody is of "unblemished record" except certain criminals (note 3 to section 41), that only lunatics, prisoners and bankrupts do not make an independent living, but that all members of a family such as children who are of age and domestic servants do so (note 4) and that whoever is not taxed at all is not in arrears (note 5). The provision concerning arrears was made innocuous after World War I by the granting of a respite for arrears in accordance with a regulation of the Prussian Ministry, dated 13.10.1919. See *Jüdisches Lexikon*, II, p. 975 and for Berlin AZJ, *Gemeindebote 43* of 1919.

secret.[17] After 1918 proportional representation was largely introduced and after a few years' struggle votes for women too.[18]

There were no difficulties with voting registers: the *Handbuch* gives the number of Jewish inhabitants and of those taxed for every Community. Taxes were generally based on a percentage of the State Income Tax;[19] the communities received the lists from the Inspector of Taxes and they could even have the taxes collected by the Inspectors.[20] The periodical State census giving religious affiliation was also at their disposal.

The *Handbuch* 1907[21] mentions that the census figures of 1905 had already become available. In 1911 the figures of 1910 had not yet come through. In 1924/25, several years had already elapsed since the last census, that of 1920, and several Communities, notably Berlin, made wildly inaccurate guesses as to the present number of Jewish inhabitants.

Although I could neither find any relevant discussions in the Jewish papers, nor remember such discussions myself, I have formed the opinion from my reading of the figures of the votes cast in communal elections that *before the war* Communities tended to make life easy for themselves by merely registering those members who had been taxed without making the corrections necessary according to Kollenscher's interpretation of the Act. On the other hand the figures of votes cast in *post-war elections* clearly show that a complete voting list of all adult Jewish inhabitants was prepared either with the help of the governmental census or otherwise. This is obvious, for instance, from the detailed figures of the voting for the *Landesverband* elections given in the *Jüdisch-Liberale Zeitung* of 26th February 1925 for the whole of Prussia and from the *Berliner Gemeindeblatt* of December 1930 for the last election to Community and *Landesverband,* when more than 77,000 Berlin Jews voted.

So much for communal elections. The VDJ was admittedly elected indirectly, namely, by the Boards of the Communities, and it also contained a minority of members of other groups, mainly in order to give representation to minorities, for example to the Zionists.[22]

---

[17]It was so to the best of my knowledge. See however below for some doubts in this respect.

[18]For elections under the proportional system in Breslau and Berlin see AZJ, 7.3.1920 and 20.6.1920. The introduction of the women's vote, contrary to the wording of the 1847 Act was justified by article 137(3) of the then new German Constitution and by a judgment of the German Supreme Court, dated 26.10.1921 (vol. 103, p. 91). Votes for women were demanded for example by the Berlin Liberals (*Jüdische Zeitung,* 25.9.1922) as well as by the Zionists. Only the orthodox party raised objections (see Sandler, *loc. cit.,* p. 79). Before February 1928 "votes for women" were accepted by most of the larger communities. Siddy Wronsky in *Jüdisches Lexikon,* II, pp. 780 ff. mentions fifteen communities but enumerates nineteen. Her list is probably incomplete. The Prussian Government agreed to the change (see *Jüdisches Lexikon,* II, p. 972).

[19]The percentage is given in the *Handbuch* 1911 for all Prussian and most other Communities and in the *Handbuch* 1924/25.

[20]See section 58 of the 1847 Statute. As regards the right of having Community taxes collected by the State this was made use of, to my knowledge, by the Breslau Community, but not by the Berlin Community.

[21]Cf. page III of the preface.

[22]See *Bulletin des Leo Baeck Instituts,* No. 28 (1964), p. 352.

Toury ends his survey unaccountably with the year 1920. The *Preussischer Landesverband Jüdischer Gemeinden* was elected in 1925 on a fully democratic basis.[23] It represented all of Prussia, that is to say two-thirds of German Jewry. Most of the *Länder* organizations had by then undergone a similar democratic reform.[24] The reasons why it proved impossible to form *one* organization representing all German Jews are lucidly set out by Sandler.[25] Toury states that the draft constitution for the whole of Germany which had unsuccessfully been presented by the DIGB in 1920 had been based "as of old upon action from the top downwards."[26] The meaning of this rather cryptic remark becomes clear from his quotation of Ismar Freund's leading article in the AZJ.[27] It appears that Toury's views were based on a counter-proposal then made by the Zionists to the effect that not only the Assembly but also the Council of the organization should be elected directly. This idea[28] was soon dropped by the Zionists. Sandler, himself one of the Zionist leaders, speaks of the DIGB democratic constitution.[29] The *Landesverband,* too, had a Council which was not based on direct elections.[30]

The *Reichsvertretung der deutschen Juden,* however, formed in 1933, was not democratically constituted.[31] Free elections under the Hitler regime were, of course, impossible.

III. Interwoven with Toury's survey of the attempts to establish a *Gesamtorganisation* are items of a wholly different character. This applies for instance to the "most desperate and most secret venture" reported under the slogan "Jewish Centre",[32] It concerns attempts to form a unified front of the two most important Jewish political organizations, the *Centralverein deutscher Staatsbürger jüdischen Glaubens* (C.V.) and the Zionists. In a democratic general election in Germany neither of them could — or would expect to — attract the votes of *all* Jews. This applies in effect also to the "Congress movement",[33] though at a time when for a few months *Volksbeauftragte* and *Arbeiter- und Soldatenräte* held sway in Germany the contours between representative bodies and political organizations may have become blurred in German Jewry too.

---

[23]See *Jüdische Rundschau,* 1924, p. 614; Sandler, *loc. cit.,* pp. 79-80; *Jüdisches Lexikon,* II (1925), p 1118 (Author: Dr. Kollenscher).

[24]See *Jüdisches Lexikon,* II, pp. 974 ff.

[25]The *Preussischer Landesverband,* but not its democratic constitution, is casually mentioned by Toury on pp. 79 and 89. A loose connection between the various *Landesverbände* in the form of an *Arbeitsgemeinschaft* was established on 4.3.1928 (see *Jüdisches Lexikon,* II, p. 1050).

[26]Toury, p. 89.

[27]AZJ 1920, pp. 218 ff. The relevant volume is not available in London.

[28]From Toury's point of view Israel, the United Kingdom and the Federal Republic of Germany, for instance, could not be considered democratically constituted.

[29]*Loc. cit.,* p. 78.

[30]The same applies to the draft statute adopted "almost unanimously" by the *Landesverband* in 1928 as stated by Sandler, *loc. cit.,* p. 83, as I for one, who was at that time the Vice-Chairman of the Liberal group in the *Landesverband* Assembly, can confirm.

[31]See also Toury, p. 90.

[32]*Ibid.,* pp. 72-76.

[33]*Ibid.,* pp. 84-88.

Representative Jewish bodies had no direct connections with political parties such as the *Freisinnige* in Wilhelminian Germany, though the C.V. may have had such relations.

It is not astonishing that Eugen Fuchs, who was a leader of the C.V., and Arthur Hantke and Alfred Klee, who were leaders of the Zionists, were involved in these political discussions although they were board members and Eugen Fuchs even a Vice-Chairman of VDJ. Their activities in different spheres of action were not contradictory.

The idea mentioned by Toury[34] of creating bodies similar to the national Jewish parties in Russia and Austria would have been completely unrealistic for Germany. I refuse to accept that Dr. Hantke, my father's and my law partner and cousin, propagated this, even if the idea had been put before him by some perhaps somewhat excitable people. He was a staunch Zionist all his life, but he was also a realist averse to wild-cat schemes. Dr. Kollenscher's action in Posen after the revolution which, according to Toury,[35] demonstrates the possibility of such plans, was possibly justified in the peculiar situation in this nationally mixed town.[36] It was also a very short-lived venture as very soon nearly all the Jews of Posen, Zionists as well as non-Zionists, left for Germany, amongst them the Zionist leaders Kareski and Kollenscher. They were, incidentally, the first Zionists to enter the Board of the Berlin Community in 1920, respectively in 1922.

IV. Toury complains[37] that the Jewish Communities and organizations were dominated by the so-called "notables", which refers to professional people or prosperous businessmen. The fact itself is undeniable. But there was really no social chasm dividing the Jews in community life. There was no class-conscious Jewish working class in Germany, nor was there, in general, any feeling amongst those of the middle classes whom Toury characterizes by the expression "small people", of being oppressed by these "notables".

The three parties which dominated Jewish communal life were the Liberals, the Zionists and the Orthodox. In the election to the *Preussische Landesverband* of February 1925 for instance 71 Liberals were elected, 31 Zionists and 14 Orthodox, apart from them five members of the Religious Centre Party and two from the *Poalei Zion*. There had been thirteen constituencies in ten of which there were contested elections, whereas in three of the smallest ones the parties divided the seats on a compromise basis. In the 1930 elections a compromise was achieved everywhere except in Berlin. The Berlin result was identical with those of the local elections of the same date. As a consequence the parties generally held their seats except that owing to the Berlin result the new offshoot of the Religious Centre Party, *Überparteiliche Vereinigung,* took a few seats from the Centre Party and probably one or two seats from the Orthodox. In the South

---

[34]*Ibid.*, p. 73.
[35]*Ibid.*, p. 77, note 89.
[36]See *LBI Year Book VIII* (1963), p. 230.
[37]Toury, pp. 73 and 75.

German States Bavaria, Wurttemberg, Baden and Hesse and in Hamburg the composition of the organizations were similar to those of Prussia except that in South Germany the Orthodox tended to be somewhat stronger in relation to the other two parties. In Saxony a Zionist majority would have been the consequence of democratic elections, but this could not come about on account of Saxony's particular electoral law.[38]

Now the three main parties were equally composed of "small people" and of others, and all three were inclined to elect "notables" to the leading positions. This is not to deny that there was a certain stratification amongst the Jews in Germany. I have explained elsewhere[39] that with the regrettable exception of Saxony and another small and irrelevant State there was, for instance, no legal discrimination against people without German nationality. There was, however, in this respect a distinct difference in the Jewish political allegiance. In Berlin, for example, the electoral districts near the centre of the town, inhabited mostly by poor Eastern Jews, had strong Zionist majorities. But it can be proved that this difference in allegiance was not decidedly influenced by *social* considerations. After the 1930 elections I noted that in my own electoral district in Berlin-Wilmersdorf there were five per cent more Zionist votes than in the other Wilmersdorf districts of a similar social character, the reason being that there lived in our district a comparatively greater number of Eastern Jews in comfortable circumstances. The same applied to a few other districts in the West of Berlin.[40]

When, for instance, in Berlin — which can be considered rather typical as one third of all German Jews resided there — the Zionists entered the Board of the Community as from 1920 their Board members were until 1936: three solicitors, one judge, one physician and one (very capitalistically minded) businessman;[41] after my emigration in 1936 there entered as replacements one more solicitor and a wealthy manufacturer.[42] The Religious Centre Party and its offshoot, the *Überparteiliche Vereinigung,* were, if possible, even more inclined to put "notables" in the front position than the other parties. The *Poalei Zion* may have had "small people" as adherents, but its leader and representative Dr. Oscar Cohn, a former Social Democratic deputy of the *Reichstag,* was also a solicitor and a generally respected figure. At that time a man of his stamp would certainly not have been considered by anyone as a "traitor to... the

---

[38]For details see *Jüdische Rundschau,* 1924, p. 211.

[39]Cf. *LBI Year Book VII* (1962), pp. 333-334.

[40]This development, which I have always very much regretted, does not seem so astonishing any longer after 1933. For instance, the German Jews who had immigrated to Palestine tended to swell there the ranks of Dr. Landauer's *Alijah Chadaschah* and later on in Israel Dr. Rosen's Progressive Party.

[41]Dr. Kollenscher, Dr. Klee, Dr. S. Hirsch - Tuchler - Dr. Sandler - Kareski. One should not be misled by the fact that the "notables" of the elder generation were called *Justizrat* or *Sanitätsrat.* These titles were conferred on all members of these professions after twenty years' practice and were, except in Bavaria, abolished in 1918. Otherwise the above-named professional men would have had these titles bestowed on them too.

[42]Dr. Sulzberger - Schmeidler.

Jewish cause". Such a view of Jewish Social Democrats as Toury avers existed in 1893,[43] I myself have never encountered in Jewish life — though it may still have been found at the beginning of the century.

Toury writes that "the Jewish craftsmen and other 'small people', who felt themselves neglected by the community-oligarchy tended to gather in special organizational frames such as artisans' clubs and *Volksvereine*".[44] I never encountered such a *Volksverein* in Berlin.[45] There existed, however, in Berlin (and as I believe also in one or two other places) a "Union of independent Jewish artisans" which, as regards communal policy, ended its rather chequered political career[46] by adhering to the Jewish majority party, the Liberals.[47]

[43]Toury, p. 53, note 3.

[44]*Ibid.*, p. 73.

[45]As Toury refers to the *Breslauer Jüdisches Volksblatt* and to the year 1903 there may well have existed a *Volksverein* in Breslau or other Silesian towns at such an early date. Later on the elections were fought also in Silesia between the three principal parties. To the *Preussischer Landesverband* six Liberals were elected from Breslau, two Zionists and two Orthodox, and from the rest of Silesia which formed one constituency two Liberals, one Conservative and one Zionist.

[46]At the 1910 election in Berlin the Liberals who won were opposed by a combined list which according to the *Welt* (1910, p. 1279) consisted of the Zionists and the Orthodox, but contained, if my memory does not fail me, three smaller organizations, amongst them the "Independent Artisans"; but in 1920 their President, Wolff (who was a master-upholsterer), was already a candidate of the Liberals and the Vice-President Wilhelm Marcus (a master glazier) who had opposed Wolff's candidature because he held that the artisans should remain independent (AZJ 1919; *Gemeindebote* No. 50, p. 1) himself entered the assembly of representatives as an Independent in 1922 as the result of a compromise. This compromise had been made palatable to the Liberals because Marcus was supposed to be a Liberal at heart. (*Jüdisch-Liberale Zeitung* 1922, No. 50.) Actually he soon joined the Liberals and was later the Vice-Chairman and one of the leading personalities of the Liberal group.

[47]Apart from Wilhelm Marcus the above-mentioned Wolff was likewise elected as a representative in 1930 and two more of the artisans as members of the *Landesverband* Assembly, all on the Liberal list. Artisans apart one or two more persons from each of the lists of the Liberals and Zionists were at that time elected who could be classified as "small people", e.g. employees and agents. Thus at the last democratic election before Hitler's seizure of power some break at least was made in the "notables" tradition.

Letters to the Editor

IMMANUEL WOLF-WOHLWILL

We print below excerpts from a letter in connection with the essay 'The Wohlwill-Moser Correspondence' in Year Book XI which reached us from a reader in Germany, giving some further details on the life of Immanuel Wohlwill, particularly in relation to the Jacobson school in Seesen. - Ed.

Bei Durchsicht der Akten der Jacobson-Schule in Seesen fand ich manche Einzelheiten über Immanuel Wohlwill, die im folgenden zusammengestellt sind.

Immanuel Wohlwill, bis 1822 Joel Wolf genannt, am 28.8.1798 als Sohn eines Lehrers in Harzgerode geboren, war vom 16. Juli 1811 an Freischüler in der Jacobson-Schule in Seesen und wurde am 28. Juni 1815 entlassen. In dem Notizenbuch der Schule heißt es "ein an Kopf und Herzen trefflicher junger Mann, der unserer Schule gewiss einst Ehre machen wird". Er wurde dann in die 3. Klasse des Grauen Klosters aufgenommen und studierte in Berlin seit 1819 Philosophie und Philologie und promovierte in Kiel zum Dr. phil. 1822 war er interimistischer Prediger am Neuen Israelitischen Tempel zu Leipzig, 1823 erster Lehrer der Israelitischen Freischule in Hamburg und in der Verwaltung des neuen Hamburger Tempels. In Hamburg heiratete er eine Tochter der Familie Warburg. Er und seine Nachkommen sind in den Stammtafeln der Familie Warburg zu finden. Am 8.7.1838 wurde er als Direktor in der Jacobson-Schule in einer Feierstunde eingeführt, bei der der Kurator der Schule (Meier?) Jacobson eine Rede hielt, die auch gedruckt wurde (Braunschweig 1838).

Die Kuratoren der Schule, Meier und Dr. Hermann Jacobson, schlossen am 4.7.1838 mit Wohlwill einen Anstellungsvertrag, in dem vereinbart wird, daß er einen Plan ausarbeiten solle, in dem seine Stellung aus Statuten geregelt werde. Ebenso solle er einen Erziehungs- und Unterrichtsplan für die Zöglinge aufstellen. In § 5 des Vertrages wird bestimmt, daß der Direktor den Gottesdienst im Tempel zu ordnen und zu leiten und bei religiösen Feiern angemessene religiöse Vorträge zu halten habe.

Dr. Wohlwill eröffnete am 10.4.1839 die Jacobson-Schule, die wegen Umbaus seit Mitte Juli 1838 geschlossen war, von neuem. Sie war nun als eine Höhere Bürgerschule und simultane Erziehungsanstalt eingerichtet worden mit 20 Freischülern und 19 Stadtschülern in zunächst zwei, dann drei Klassen. 1843 waren es bereits 122 Schüler, davon 68 Alumnen und 1844 wurde eine 4. Klasse eingerichtet. 1846 war die Zahl der Schüler auf 145 gestiegen, davon waren 25 Frei-, 61 Stadtschüler und 59 Pensionäre.

Immanuel Wohlwill starb am 2.3.1847 in Seesen. Sein Grabmal ist, wenn auch beschädigt, auf dem jüdischen Friedhof noch erhalten. Seine Witwe wird 1850 anlässlich des Verkaufes von Ländereien von ingesamt 6 Morgen, erwähnt, dann ist sie mit ihren Kindern nach Hamburg gezogen.

Auch eine Schwester Wohlwills, namens Dinah, lebte in Seesen und war mit dem Lehrer und späteren Hausvater Gerson Isaac Rosenstein verheiratet, der gleichfalls ein früherer Schüler der Jacobson-Schule war. Beider Grabmäler sind noch vorhanden. In einer Liste der Juden in Seesen vom 1.8.1851 wird Rosenstein mit seiner Familie aufgeführt. Seine Frau wird dort als eine "geborene Wolfsohn" bezeichnet, im Sterberegister aber als geborene Wohlwill geführt.

Seesen/Harz   GERHARD BALLIN

AUGUST BELMONT

In her letter to the editor (Year Book XI, 1966, p. 338), Dr. Rahel Liebeschütz takes issue with Dr. H. G. Reissner's statement (Year Book X, 1965, p. 78) that August Belmont (1813-1890) was originally named August "Schönberg" and that he had been baptized at an early age. As the biographer of Belmont (Columbia University Press, 1968), I fully support Dr. Liebeschütz's correction.

The false rumour started with Horace Greeley in the 1850s. Greeley, editor of the mass-circulation New York *Tribune*, was both an antisemite and an opponent of the Democratic Party. The economic, social and political successes of the German-born, Democratic-affiliated Belmont infuriated Greeley who, in 1853, outdid earlier attacks on Belmont's "Jew gold" by charging that the financier must have "Frenchified" an "original" name of "Schönberg". Belmont challenged Greeley to prove the contention, but Greeley ignored him. Still, the rumour took hold in many circles, and when Belmont died many obituaries recalled his "original" surname. The late financier's partner, Walter Luttgen, placed then a notice in New York newspapers stating that Belmont really had been born "Belmont".

Nevertheless, the recent best-seller *Our Crowd* (1967) contains a generally erroneous chapter on Belmont. There the "Schönberg" myth is revived, and the book's index contains some entries under "Schönberg, August".

The statement that Belmont was baptized or converted to Christianity is likewise erroneous. Belmont attended a Jewish school in Frankfurt during his early teens, but after coming to the United States in 1837 he ceased practising Judaism. In November, 1849, he married a devout Episcopalian, Caroline Slidell Perry, daughter of the famous Commodore, in the liberal Church of the Ascension. Belmont wrote the following to his sister Elisabetha (Dr. Liebeschütz's great-grandmother) a month before the wedding:

> "Caroline has put aside all prejudice in her esteem and love for me. And although she knows my origin and my religion, she has not requested any public or even secret apostasy or change of religion of any kind whatsoever.
> She knows my liberal views regarding religious beliefs. These views keep me at a distance from the old requirements of the Jewish Talmud and would prevent me from being led to baptism by her belief and she is completely content to let me keep my views and beliefs. Of course, this is extremely suitable to me. For although, as I told you, I have not had for years and years any connection with our correligionists in this country who are too disagreeable, I should not have liked to become a renegade, in consideration of the family."

For the rest of their lives Belmont and his wife lived near the New York church in which they had been married, and their six children were all baptized. Belmont's funeral service was held at this same church, but he was buried in a private cemetery. During his lifetime, he was never baptized nor confirmed in a Christian ceremony.

Indiana University   IRVING KATZ

Corrections

One of our readers in New York drew our attention to a mistake which occurred in the Introduction to Year Book XIII on page XXII. In the obituary devoted to the deceased Rabbi Hugo Hahn, former Rabbi of Essen, it was stated that the synagogue in that town was the work of the architect Erich Mendelssohn. We have now been informed that the building erected by Mendelssohn was not the synagogue but the *Jugendheim* where Hugo Hahn spent much of his time. The synagogue itself was the work of Edmund Körner.

We have been asked by Mrs. Carl Misch to correct the following error in the essay 'Search-light on the Decline of the Weimar Republic. The Diaries of Ernst Feder' in Year Book XIII (p. 183, note 102): Carl Misch was *not* editor of the *Pariser Tageblatt* but of the *Pariser Tageszeitung*.

Year Book XIII, p. 239, line 7 from below and index, p. 349 *for* Paul Epstein *read* Paul Eppstein (of the *Reichsvertretung*).

Abstracts of articles in this Year Book are included in *Historical Abstracts* and *America: History and Life.*

Post-War Publications on German Jewry

A Selected Bibliography of Books and Articles 1968

Compiled on behalf of

THE WIENER LIBRARY

by Bertha Cohn

The Wiener Library
4, Devonshire Street
London W. 1.

CONTENTS

I. HISTORY

    A. General   271
    B. Communal and Regional History
        1. Germany   271
        2. Austria   274
        3. Czechoslovakia   275
        4. Hungary   275
        5. Switzerland   276
    C. German Jews In Various Countries   276

II. RESEARCH AND BIBLIOGRAPHY

    A. Libraries and Institutes   276
    B. Bibliographies and Catalogues   277

III. THE NAZI PERIOD

    A. General   277
    B. Jewish Resistance   279

IV. POST WAR

    A. General   280
    B. Restitution   280

V. JUDAISM

    A. Jewish Learning and Scholars   280
    B. Jewish Life and Organisations   284
    C. Jewish Art and Music   284

VI. ZIONISM AND ISRAEL   284

VII. PARTICIPATION IN CULTURAL AND PUBLIC LIFE

    A. General   287
    B. Individual   289

VIII. AUTOBIOGRAPHY, MEMOIRS, LETTERS, GENEALOGY   306

IX. GERMAN-JEWISH RELATIONS

    A. General   308
    B. German-Israeli Relations   308
    C. Church and Synagogue   309
    D. Antisemitism   309
    E. Noted Germans and Jews   311

X. FICTION, POETRY AND HUMOUR   311

XI. Index   313

BIBLIOGRAPHY 1968

I. HISTORY

A. General

6892. *Die bürgerlichen Parteien in Deutschland.* Handbuch der Geschichte der bürgerlichen Parteien und anderer bürgerlicher Interessen Organisationen vom Vormärz bis zum Jahre 1945. In 2 Bänden. Band I: Alldeutscher Verband - Fortschrittliche Volkspartei. Hrsg. von einem Redaktionskollektiv unter der Leitung von Dieter Fricke. Berlin [East]: Das Europäische Buch, 1968. xv, 806 pp., tabs., bibls. after each chap. (Historisches Institut der Friedrich-Schiller-Universität Jena). [Incl. Antisemitische Parteien 1879-1894 (Dieter Fricke), pp. 36-40. Centralverein deutscher Staatsbürger jüdischen Glaubens (CV) 1893-1938 (Willy Menke), pp. 236-240.]

6893. *Germania Judaica.* Band II: Von 1238 bis zur Mitte des 14. Jahrhunderts. Hrsg. von Zvi Avneri. 1. Halbband: Aachen-Luzern. xxxix, 504 pp., front. illus., illus., maps, bibls. at ends of chaps. 2. Halbband: Maastricht-Zwolle. Pp. 505-1000, front. illus., illus., maps. bibls. at ends of chaps. Tübingen: J. C. B. Mohr (Paul Siebeck), 1968. (Veröffentlichung des Leo Baeck Instituts). [Vol. I: Von den ältesten Zeiten bis 1238. See No. 3676/YB. IX.]

6894. MIDAS, ERIC: *Eine Bittschrift christlicher Bürger zugunsten eines Juden an den Fürsten von Reuss aus dem Jahre 1846.* [In]: 'LBI Bulletin'. 11. Jg., Nr. 42. Tel Aviv, 1968. Pp. 116-124.

—— PAUCKER, ARNOLD: *Searchlight on the Decline of the Weimar Republic.* The Diaries of Ernst Feder. [See No. 7239.]

6895. RÜRUP, REINHARD: *Judenemanzipation und bürgerliche Gesellschaft in Deutschland.* [In]: Gedenkschrift Martin Göhring. Studien zur Europäischen Geschichte. Mit einem Geleitwort von Jacques Droz. Hrsg. von Ernst Schulin. Wiesbaden: Franz Steiner Verlag, 1968. Pp. 174-199.

6896. SCHRAMM, GOTTFRIED: *Die Ostjuden als soziales Problem des 19. Jahrhunderts.* [In]: Gesellschaft, Recht und Politik. Wolfgang Abendroth zum 60. Geburtstag. Neuwied: Luchterhand Verlag, 1967. 408 pp.

6897. STOBBE, OTTO: *Die Juden in Deutschland während des Mittelalters in politischer, sozialer und rechtlicher Beziehung.* Nachdruck der Ausgabe Braunschweig 1866. Amsterdam: Grüner, 1968. 312 pp., bibl. (pp. 308-310).

6898. *Zeitschrift für die Geschichte der Juden.* Hrsg. von Hugo Gold. Jg. V, Nr. 1, 2/3, 4. Tel Aviv: Olamenu, 1968, ports., illus., facsims. [Some selected contributions are listed according to subject.]

B. Communal and Regional History

1. Germany

6899. BADEN. HUNDSNURSCHER, FRANZ und GERHARD TADDEY: *Die jüdischen Gemeinden in Baden.* Denkmale, Geschichte, Schicksale. Hrsg. von der Archivdirektion Stuttgart. Stuttgart: W. Kohlhammer Verlag, 1968. xviii, 327 pp., cover facsim., front. illus., 225 illus., map. (Veröffentlichungen der Staatlichen Archivverwaltung Baden-Württemberg, Band 19).

6900. RÜRUP, REINHARD: *Die Judenemanzipation in Baden.* [In]: 'Zeitschrift für die Geschichte des Oberrheins'. Bd. 114. (Der neuen Folge 75. Bd.) Karlsruhe: G. Braun, 1966. Pp. 241-300.

6901. BERLIN. DÄHN, BRUNHILDE: *Berlin Hausvogteiplatz.* Über 100 Jahre am Laufsteg der Mode. Göttingen: Musterschmidt-Verlag, 1968, 249 pp., ports., illus., facsims., cover maps. [In the Berlin fashion or 'rag' trade Jews played a prominent part.

6902. HERZFELD, HANS unter Mitwirkung von GERD HEINRICH, eds.: *Berlin und die Provinz Brandenburg im 19. und 20. Jahrhundert.* Berlin: Walter de Gruyter, 1968. xii, 1034 pp., map.

6903. *Jüdische Trauungen in Berlin 1759-1813.* Mit Ergänzungen für die Jahre von 1723 bis 1759. Bearbeitet und herausgegeben von Jacob Jacobson. Mit einem Geleitwort von Hans Herzfeld. Berlin: Walter de Gruyter, 1968. xliii, 668 pp., ports., illus., bibl. (pp. 651-653). (Veröffentlichungen der Historischen Kommission zu Berlin. Bd. 28, Quellenwerke Bd. 4).

6904. KIENZL, FLORIAN: *Die Berliner und ihr Theater.* Berlinische Reminiszenzen. Berlin: Haude & Spenersche Verlagsbuchhandlung, 1968.

6905. MÜLLER, THORSTEN: *Berlins Ehrenbürger - Von Conrad Ribbeck bis Nelly Sachs.* Berlin: Haude & Spenersche Verlagsbuchhandlung, 1968. 156 pp., ports. [Incl. Otto Cassel, Hugo Heimann, Max Liebermann, Ferdinand Strassmann, Martin Kirchner, Otto Heinrich Warburg.]

6906. RACHEL, HUGO, JOHANNES PAPRITZ und PAUL WALLICH: *Berliner Grosskaufleute und Kapitalisten.* Neu hrsg., ergänzt und bibliographisch erw. von Johannes Schultze. Berlin: Walter de Gruyter, 1967. 3 vols. (Veröffentlichungen des Vereins für Geschichte der Mark Brandenburg. Bd. 32, 33, 34. Neudrucke Bd. 1, 2, 3). Bd. 1: Bis zum Ende des Dreissigjährigen Krieges. xli, 451 pp., 1 illus. Bd. 2: Die Zeit des Merkantilismus, 1648-1806. vii, 578 pp. [Incl.: Juden um 1700, pp. 26-66. Jüdische Handlungen unter Friedrich II. und seinen Nachfolgern, pp. 288-429.] Bd. 3: Übergangszeit zum Hochkapitalismus, 1806-1856. 336 pp., bibl. (pp. 315-336).

6907. SCHEFFLER, WOLFGANG: *Berliner Goldschmiede - Daten, Werke, Zeichen.* Mit 137 Abb. Berlin: Bruno Hessling, 1968. xxii, 647 pp. + 17 pp. illus.

6908. SIRAKOFF, MILTSCHO: *Berliner Läden und Geschäftshäuser von 1896 bis zur Gegenwart.* Berlin: Kiepert Verlag, 1967. 210 pp., illus. pp. 120-210.

6909. WALTHER, GERHARD: *Das Berliner Theater in der Berliner Tagespresse 1848-1874.* Berlin: Colloquium Verlag, 1968. 225 pp. (Theater und Drama. Bd. 32).

6910. BIELEFELD. MAASS, H. A.: *Zur Geschichte der jüdischen Gemeinde in Bielefeld in der brandenburgischen Zeit bis zur Emanzipation.* [In]: Historischer Verein für die Grafschaft Ravensburg. 65. Bericht. Bielefeld, 1966/67. Pp. 79-94.

6911. BONN. BRAUBACH, MAX: *Jüdischer Anteil an der Bonner Gelehrsamkeit.* [In]: 'Rheinische Vierteljahrs-Blätter'. Mitteilungen des Instituts für geschichtliche Landeskunde der Rheinlande an der Universität Bonn. Jg. 32, H. 1/4. Bonn: Ludwig Röhrscheid Verlag, 1968. Pp. 402-418. [Cf. No. 6226/YB. XIII.]

6912. BRAUBACH, MAX: *Kleine Geschichte der Universität Bonn, 1818-1968.* Bonn: Ludwig Röhrscheid Verlag, 1968. 70 pp., ports., illus.

6913. WENIG, OTTO, ed.: *Verzeichnis der Professoren und Dozenten der Rheinischen Friedrich-Wilhelms-Universität zu Bonn 1818-1968.* Bonn: Bouvier, Röhrscheid, 1968. xxv, 376 pp. (150 Jahre Rheinische Friedrich-Wilhelms-Universität zu Bonn, 1818-1968).

6914. BROMBERG. REHFELDT, KLAUS HELMUT: *Die preussische Verwaltung des Regierungsbezirks Bromberg 1848-1871.* Köln und Berlin: G. Grote'sche Verlagsbuchhandlung, 1968. 412 pp., illus., map, bibl. (Studien zur Geschichte Preussens. Bd. 11). Diss. Bonn. [Incl. references to Jews and to Jewish communities in the district.]

6915. ELBING. NEUFELD, S.: *Inneres Leben der Elbinger Gemeinde seit dem Bau der Synagoge.* (Fortsetzung von) *Geschichte der jüdischen Gemeinde Elbing.* [In]: 'Zeitschrift für die Geschichte der Juden'. Jg. 5, Nr. 2/3. Pp. 127-143. [See No. 6898, also No. 5030/YB. XI for Part I.]

6916. FRANCONIA. HOFMANN, HANNS HUBERT: *Ländliches Judentum in Franken.* [In]: 'Tribüne', Zeitschrift zum Verständnis des Judentums. Hrsg. Elisabeth Reisch. 7. Jg., H. 27. Frankfurt a. M.: Tribüneverlag, 1968. Pp. 2890-2904.

6917. FRIEDBERG. HERRMANN, FRITZ H.: *Aus der Geschichte der Friedberger Judengemeinde.* [In]: 'Wetterauer Geschichtsblätter'. Bd. 16. Friedberg/Hessen: Verlag Carl Bindernagel, 1967. Pp. 51-78.

6918. GODESBERG-MEHLEM. EILERS, ROLF: *Die Synagogengemeinde Godesberg-Mehlem.* Bad Godesberg: Verein für Heimatpflege und Heimatgeschichte, 1968. 21 pp.

6919. HAGUENAU (ALSACE). BLOCH, JOSEPH: *Histoire de la Communauté Juive de Haguenau des Origines à nos Jours.* Haguenau: Imprimerie du Bas-Rhin, 1968. 52 pp., illus., facsims. [One of the oldest Alsatian Jewish communities.]

6920. HAMBURG. ARON, WILLIAM: *Jews of Hamburg.* New York: American Jewish Committee of Hamburg Jews, 1967. 87, 105 pp., bibl. [Text in English and in Hebrew.]

6921. EPSTEIN, FELIX: *Gedanken und Erinnerungen anlässlich der Feier des 125-jährigen Bestehens des Israelitischen Krankenhauses in Hamburg am 6. September 1968.* Ein Ausschnitt aus der Geschichte des Hauses. No impr., 8 pp., front. port. [of Salomon Heine], illus., facsim.

6922. HESSE. HOLL, K.: *Antisemitismus, kleinbürgerliche Bewegung und demokratischer Liberalismus in Hessen.* Drei Briefe Philip Köhlers an Adolf Korell. [In]: 'Archiv für hessische Geschichte und Altertumskunde'. N.F. 30, 1.-2. Darmstadt, 1967/68. Pp. 150-159.

6923. MASCH, RÜDIGER: *Otto Böckel und die antisemitische Bauernbewegung in Hessen 1887-1894.* [In]: 'Wetterauer Geschichtsblätter'. Bd. 16. Friedberg: Verlag Carl Bindernagel, 1967. Pp. 113-147.

6924. HILDESHEIM. JAN, HELMUT VON: *Zur Geschichte der Hildesheimer Juden.* [In]: 'Hildesheimer Informationen', hrsg. vom Presseamt der Stadtverwaltung. H. 11, Nov. Hildesheim, 1968.

6925. HÜTTENBACH (FRANCONIA). BURKHARD, HUGO: *'Der Bimberle, Bamberle, Bomberle'.* Erinnerungen an eine Kehille. Mit einem Vor- und Nachwort von Jean Mandel und Arno S. Hamburger. Eine Dokumentarbetrachtung. Nürnberg: Verlag Richard Reichenbach, 1968. 44 pp., illus.

6926. KÖNIGSBERG i. PREUSSEN. GAUSE, FRITZ: *Geschichte der Stadt Königsberg in Preussen.* Bd. 1: Von der Gründung bis zum letzten Kurfürsten. Bd. 2: Von der Königskrönung bis zum Ausbruch des ersten Weltkrieges. Köln-Graz: Böhlau Verlag, 1968. 2 vols. (Reihe Ostmitteleuropa in Vergangenheit und Gegenwart. Hrsg. vom Johann-Gottfried-Herder-Forschungsrat, Bd. 10/1 und 10/2). [Many references to Jews in vol. 2.]

6927. KONSTANZ. LEIB, OTTO S.: *'Der Jude von Konstanz' - Woher und Wohin . . .* New Milford, Bergen County, N.J.: [Priv. pr.], 1968. 33 pp., tabs., facsim. [Mimeog.]

6928. LANDAU / PFALZ. HESS, H.: *Die Landauer Judengemeinde, ein Gang durch ihre Geschichte.* [In]: 'Landauer Monatshefte'. Jg. XVI, Nr. 8-11, Aug.-Nov., 1968. Pp. 14-22, 20-31, 2-15, 3-12.

6929. LÜBECK. WINTER, DAVID ALEXANDER: *Geschichte der Jüdischen Gemeinde in Moisling/Lübeck.* Mit einer Biographie des Verfassers von Hans Chanoch Meyer. Lübeck: Verlag Max Schmidt-Römhild, 1968. 224 pp., port., tabs. (Veröffentlichungen zur Geschichte der Hansestadt Lübeck. Hrsg. vom Archiv der Hansestadt. Bd. 20). [Dr. Winter was rabbi in Lübeck from 1921-1938].

6930. MARIENBURG. ZACHARIAS, RAINER, ed.: *Neues Marienburger Heimatbuch.* Geleitwort von Herbert Weichmann, Hamburg. Herford: Wendt Groll, 1967. 672 pp. [Incl.: Geschichte der Marienburger Synagoge.]

6931. MEMELLAND. KURSCHAT, HEINRICH A.: *Das Buch vom Memelland.* Oldenburg: F. W. Siebert, 1968. 644 pp., illus.

6932. NUREMBERG. MICHELFELDER, GOTTFRIED: *Die wirtschaftliche Tätigkeit der Juden Nürnbergs im Spätmittelalter.* [In]: Beiträge zur Wirtschaftsgeschichte Nürnbergs, hrsg. vom Stadtarchiv Nürnberg. Bd. 1. Nürnberg: Im Selbstverlag des Stadtarchivs, 1967. Pp. 236-260. (Beiträge zur Geschichte und Kultur der Stadt Nürnberg. Bd. 11/I).

6933. MÜLLER, ARND: *Geschichte der Juden in Nürnberg 1146-1945.* Nürnberg: Selbstverlag der Stadtbibliothek Nürnberg, 1968. 381 + xxiii pp., port. [of Heinrich Berolzheimer], illus., facsims., bibl. (pp. 348-356). (Beiträge zur Geschichte und Kultur der Stadt Nürnberg, Bd. 12).

6934. PALATINATE (ALSENZ). KOPP, AUGUST: *Die Dorfjuden in der Nordpfalz.* Dargestellt an der Geschichte der jüdischen Gemeinde Alsenz ab 1655. Meisenheim am Glan: Verlag Anton Hain, 1968. 458 pp., cover illus., illus., facsims., diagrs., tabs., maps, bibl. (pp. 436-438).

6935. POSEN. JACOBSON, JACOB: *Das Naturalisationsverzeichnis der jüdischen Gemeinde in Posen.* [In]: 'Zeitschrift für Ostforschung'. 17. Jg., H. 3. Marburg/Lahn: Elwert Verlag, 1968. Pp. 481-533. [A revised and enlarged report originally written by Georg Asch and Jacob Jacobson for the December 1938 issue of the 'Zeitschrift für die Geschichte der Juden in Deutschland', which could no longer be published. However, a photography of pageproofs of this report is in the Wiener Library, London. - Georg Asch perished in Poland. Jacob Jacobson, until his deportation to Theresienstadt director of the 'Gesamtarchiv der deutschen Juden' in Berlin, died in May 1968 during a visit to Germany. Ob. by Bernhard Brilling in 'Der Archivar', 22. Jg., H. 2, Mai. Siegburg (Rhld.), F. Schmitt, 1969. Pp. 234-236 [and by] Robert Weltsch in LBI YB. XIII, p. XXI, port.]

6936. PRUSSIA. FISCHER, HORST: *Judentum, Staat und Heer in Preussen im frühen 19. Jahrhundert.* Zur Geschichte der staatlichen Judenpolitik. Tübingen: J. C. B. Mohr (Paul Siebeck), 1968. viii, 232 pp., bibl. (pp. 220-228). (Schriftenreihe Wissenschaftlicher Abhandlungen des Leo Baeck Instituts. Nr. 20).

6937. RHINELAND. BÖCHER, OTTO: *Mittelalterliche Judenbäder.* Geschichte, Aufgaben, Bauweise der erhalten gebliebenen Mikvoth in Köln, Worms, Speyer, Friedberg/Hessen, Andernach, Offenburg. [In]: 'Ärzteblatt Rheinland-Pfalz'. Nr. 2. Mainz, 1968, illus.

6938. SIEGERLAND. BUSCH, HELMUT: *Die Stöckerbewegung im Siegerland.* Ein Beitrag zur Siegerländer Geschichte in der 2. Hälfte des 19. Jahrhunderts. Siegen: Stadtverwaltung, Forschungsstelle Siegerland, 1968. xvi, 256 pp., facsims. (Diss. Marburg 1964, Überarbeitung).

6939. THIEMANN, WALTER: *Von den Juden im Siegerland.* Siegen: Verlag der Gesellschaft für christlich-jüdische Zusammenarbeit, 1968. 57 pp.

6940. STRAUBING. SCHWARZ, STEFAN: *Aus der Geschichte der Juden in Straubing.* [In]: Festschrift zum 750-jährigen Bestehen der Stadt. Hrsg. von Karl Bosl im Auftrag der Stadtverwaltung Straubing, 1968. 10 pp., illus., facsims.

6941. SULZBURG. KAHN, LUDWIG: *Die Geschichte der Juden von Sulzburg.* [And]: *Chronologische Übersicht über die Geschichte der Juden in Sulzburg bis 1940.* [In]: 'Die Markgrafschaft', Beiträge aus Geschichte, Kultur und Wirtschaft des Markgräflerlandes. 19. Jg., H. 6-10, Juni-Okt., 1967, tabs.; H. 12, Dez., 1967 u. 20. Jg., H. 1-3, Jan.-März, 1968, tabs., bibl. Müllheim/Baden: Hebelbund, 1967/1968. [See also: Gustav Weil von Sulzburg. No. 7470.]

6942. WEST PRUSSIA. KORTHALS, OTTO: *Aus der Geschichte des Judentums in Westpreussen.* [In]: Westpreussen-Jahrbuch. Bd. 17. Hrsg. von der Landsmannschaft Westpreussen. Münster/W.: C. J. Fahle, 1967. Pp. 42-47. [And]: *Konfession und Muttersprache in den Volksschulen Westpreussens.* Auf Grund der Schulstatistik [comp. by] Willy Heidn. Bd. 18, 1968. Pp. 70-75. [References to Jews.]

6943. WOLFENBÜTTEL. SCHULZE, HANS: *Beiträge zur Geschichte der jüdischen Gemeinde in Wolfenbüttel.* Teil I: Die wirtschaftliche und bürgerliche Stellung der Schutzjuden. Teil II: Nachrichten über die Samsonschule, die Synagoge, den jüdischen Friedhof und den Samsonschen Legatenfonds. Herz Samson in Braunschweig (1783 bis 1794). [In]: Braunschweigisches Jahrbuch. Bd. 48-49. Braunschweig: Selbstverlag des Braunschweigischen Geschichtsvereins, 1967-1968. Pp. 23-61, 62-85, ports., illus., facsims.

6944. WÜRTTEMBERG. ISRAELITISCHE RELIGIONSGEMEINSCHAFT WÜRTTEMBERG, ed.: '5728 *Pessach-Festschrift*'. April. Stuttgart, 1968. 40 pp. [Incl.: Die Rolle der Juden im wirtschaftlichen und sozialen Leben der Stadt Schwäbisch Gmünd by Ernst Lämmle. Erinnerungen an meine Tätigkeit im Oberrat der Isr. Religionsgemeinschaft Württembergs by Julius Wissman. (He died August 1969).]

6945. ISRAELITISCHE RELIGIONSGEMEINSCHAFT WÜRTTEMBERG, ed.: *Rosch Haschana 5729/1968.* Stuttgart, 1968. 48 pp., ports., illus. [Incl. contributions on the history of the Jewish communities of Künzelsau, Kappel, Schwäbisch Gmünd.]

6946. STERN, BRUNO: *Meine Jugenderinnerungen an eine württembergische Kleinstadt und ihre jüdische Gemeinde.* Mit einer Chronik der Juden in Niederstetten und Hohenlohe vom Mittelalter bis zum Ende des Zweiten Weltkriegs. Stuttgart: W. Kohlhammer Verlag, 1968. xiv, 150 pp. + 49 ports., illus., facsims. (Lebendige Vergangenheit. Schriftenreihe. Bd. 4).

2. Austria

6947. BRILLING, BERNHARD: *Zur Geschichte der Juden in Österreichisch-Schlesien 1640-1737.* [In]: 'Judaica Bohemiae'. Jg. IV, Nr. 2. Praha: Státni Židovské Muzeum, 1968. Pp. 101-118.

6948. WEINZIERL, ERIKA: *Die Stellung der Juden in Österreich seit dem Staatsgrundgesetz von 1867.* [In]: 'Zeitschrift für die Geschichte der Juden'. Jg. V, Nr. 2-3. Pp. 89-96. [See No. 6898.]

6949. KLAGENFURT. SCHNEIDER, HERMANN TH.: *Ein Beitrag zur Geschichte der Juden in Klagenfurt.* [In]: 'Klagenfurt Stadtnachrichten und Amtsblatt'. Hrsg. Stadtmagistrat Klagenfurt. 18. Jg., Nr. 3 u. 5, März/Mai. Klagenfurt, 1968. Pp. 15-17, 21-24, illus., facsims., bibl.

6950. VIENNA. METZGER, H. M.: *Die Bibliothek der Wiener Kultusgemeinde, ihre Entstehung und Entwicklung bis zum Einmarsch der Deutschen in Österreich.* [In]: 'Die Gemeinde'. Nr. 121. 31. Jan. Wien, 1968. 25 pp.

6951. WECHSBERG, JOSEPH: *Sounds of Vienna.* Photographs by Werner Forman. Notes on the illustrations by Michael Raeburn. London: Weidenfeld and Nicolson, 1968. 298 pp., ports., illus.

3. **Czechoslovakia**

6952. DAN, ROBERT: *I. Jahrbuch der Gesellschaft für Geschichte der Juden in der Tschechoslowakischen Republik. II. Zeitschrift für die Geschichte der Juden in der Tschechoslowakei.* Zwei Inhaltsverzeichnisse. [In]: 'Zeitschrift für die Geschichte der Juden'. 5. Jg., Nr. 4. Pp. 177-201. [See No. 6898.]

6953. *(The) Jews of Czechoslovakia.* Historical Studies and Surveys. Vol. I. Publ. by The Society for the History of Czechoslovak Jews, New York. Philadelphia: The Jewish Publication Society of America, 1968. xxiii, 583 pp., cover maps, bibls. at end of chapters.

6954. 'Judaica Bohemiae'. Jg IV, Nr. 1-2. Praha, 1968. [No. 1 incl.: Les légendes juives pragoises (K. Krejči), pp. 3-19. Die wirtschaftliche Betätigung und die Berufe der Prager Juden vor ihrer Ausweisung im Jahre 1541 (J. Heřman), pp. 20-63. Čechen und Juden in altväterischer Zeit (R. Kestenberg-Gladstein), pp. 64-72. Nr. 2 incl.: Franz Janowitz (1892-1917) (Jiřina Hlavácová), pp. 119-137.]

6955. KWASNIK-RABINOWICZ, KURT (AHARON MOSHE): *Die jüdische Minderheit in der Tschechoslowakei.* Eine rechts-geschichtliche Analyse 1918-1939. Teil I-II. [No. impr., 196-?]. 360 pp., bibl. (pp. 342-356). [2 vols., mimeog., Diss. Amsterdam.]

6956. VYSKOČIL, JOSEF: *Českožidovské hnutí.* K. 90. Výročí Založení Spolku Českých Akademiků Zidů. (The Czech Jewish Assimilation Movement. On the 90th Anniversary of the Association of Czech Jewish University Students). [In]: 'Dějiny a Současnost'. Nos. 4-5, Prague, 1966. Pp. 18-21, 26-28, ports.

6957. BOHEMIA. SCHWARZENBERG, KARL FÜRST ZU: *Judengemeinden Schwarzenbergischer Herrschaften.* [In]: Schwarzenbergischer Almanach 1968. Hrsg. von den Schwarzenbergischen Archiven. Murau, Stmk., 1968. Pp. 284-298, bibl.

6958. MIKULASCH. BATO, YOMTOV LUDWIG: *Mikulasch, unser Städtchen.* [In]: 'Das Neue Israel'. H. 6, Dez. Zürich, 1968. Pp. 471-475. [Jecheskel Eduard Baneth, Samuel Fischer, Wilhelm Bacher were students of the Jewish school.]

6959. PRAGUE. BRILLING, BERNHARD: *Zur Geschichte des jüdischen Goldschmiedegewerbes in Prag: Die ersten Prager jüdischen Goldschmiede.* [In]: 'Zeitschrift für die Geschichte der Juden'. Jg. V, Nr. 1. Tel Aviv, 1968. Pp. 21-26, bibl. [See No. 6898.]

6960. URZIDIL, JOHANNES: *The Living Contribution of Jewish Prague to Modern German Literature.* Transl. from the German by Michael Lebeck. New York: Leo Baeck Institute, 1968. 26 pp. (The Leo Baeck Memorial Lecture, 11). [Also the original German text of the lecture]: *Der lebendige Anteil des jüdischen Prag an der neueren deutschen Literatur.* [In]: 'LBI Bulletin'. 10. Jg., Nr. 40. Tel Aviv: Bitaon, 1967. Pp. 276-297.

6961. TEPLITZ. BRILLING, BERNHARD: *Zur Geschichte der Juden von Teplitz im 18. Jahrhundert.* Rabbiner Nathan Utitz, 1678-1742. [In]: 'Zeitschrift für die Geschichte der Juden'. Jg. V, Nr. 4, Tel Aviv, 1968. Pp. 167-173. [See No. 6898.]

4. **Hungary**

6962. *The Synagogues of Hungary.* An Album by Imre Heller and Zsigmond Vajda. Ed. by Randolph L. Braham with the collaboration of Ervin Farkas. New York: Publ. for the World Federation of Hungarian Jews by the Diplomatic Press, 1968. xxxi, 197 pp., illus. [Introductory essay in Hebrew, English and Hungarian.]

5. Switzerland

6963. ISRAELITISCHE GEMEÌNDE BASEL, ed.: *Zum Zentenarium der Basler Synagoge, 1868-1968. Eine Festschrift.* [No impr.] Basel, 1968. 73 pp., port., illus., facsim., tabs.

6964. KAHN, LUDWIG: *Jüdische Bibliotheken. Vom Lesen.* Separatdruck aus dem Jüd. Taschenkalender der Israelitischen Fürsorge Basel, 1968/69. 12 pp. [With special reference to the 'Basler jüdische Gemeindebibliothek'.]

6965. KAHN, LUDWIG: *Zur Geschichte der jüdischen Gemeinden im Kanton Aargau und in der Regio Basiliensis.* Separatdruck aus dem Basler Volkskalender 1968. Basel: Verlag Cratander, 1968. Pp. 69-77, ports., illus., facsims., map.

C. German Jews In Various Countries

6966. BELMONT, AUGUST. KATZ, IRVING: *August Belmont. A Political Biography.* New York and London: Columbia University Press, 1968. xiv, 296 pp., front. port., ports., illus., facsim., bibl. (pp. 279-285). [Banker and diplomat, 1816-1890, saved the American Democratic Party from extinction. Cf. LBI YB. XII, p. XXV. Also Nos. 6286 and 6808/YB. XIII.]

6967. DEUTSCH, GOTTHARD. ROBERT, G. A.: *The Ordeal of Gotthard Deutsch.* [In]: 'American Jewish Archives'. Vol. XX, No. 2, Nov. Cincinnati: Hebrew Union College - Jewish Institute of Religion, 1968. Pp. 129-155, ports. [This distinguished scholar, (1859-1921), editor of the German-Jewish Weekly 'Deborah', was accused of pro-German sympathies during World War I.]

6968. FRANKFURTER, FELIX. *Roosevelt and Frankfurter: Their Correspondence, 1928-1945.* Annotated by Max Freedman. London: Bodley Head, 1968. 772 pp.

6969. (The) GUGGENHEIMS. HOYT, EDWIN P.: *The Guggenheims and the American Dream.* New York: Funk & Wagnalls, 1967. 382 pp.

6970. HIRST, HUGO. ARONSFELD, C. C.: *German Jew who backed Britain.* Lord Hirst and General Electric. [In]: 'Jewish Observer', Sept. 13, London, 1968. [Lord Hirst, born Hugo Hirsch in a Bavarian village, came to England in 1880.]

6971. O'CONNOR, RICHARD: *The German-Americans.* New York: Little, Brown, 1968.

6972. SCHIFF, JACOB H. ADLER, CYRUS H.: *Jacob H. Schiff: His Life and Letters.* Grosse Point, Mich.: Scholarly Press, 1968. 2 vols.

II. RESEARCH AND BIBLIOGRAPHY

A. Libraries and Institutes

6973. GERMANIA JUDAICA, ed.: *Arbeitsinformationen über Studienprojekte auf dem Gebiet der Geschichte des deutschen Judentums und des Antisemitismus.* Ausgabe 6. Köln: Kölner Bibliothek zur Geschichte des deutschen Judentums, 1968. 41 pp.

6974. LEO BAECK INSTITUTE. *Bulletin des Leo Baeck Instituts.* Hrsg. Hans Tramer. 11. Jg., Nr. 41-42. Tel Aviv: Verlag Bitaon, 1968. [A few contributions are listed according to subject.]

6975. *Year Book XIII.* Jews Amidst Political Turmoil. An annual Collection of Essays on the history and activity of Jews in Germany during the past century. Ed.: Robert Weltsch. London: East and West Library, 1968. xxiii, 358 pp., front. port. [of Hermann Cohen], ports., illus., facsims., bibl. [Individual contributions are listed according to subject.] [The editor's introduction incl. obituaries on Jacob Jacobson (1888-1968), Georg Herlitz (1885-1968), Hugo Hahn (1893-1967), Shaul Esh (1921-1968), Eugen Mayer (1882-1967).]

6976. LBI - NEW YORK. *LBI News.* Vol. IX, Nos. 1-2. Spring. Fall. New York: Leo Baeck Institute, 1968, ports., illus., facsims.

6977. REISSNER, HANNS G.: *Beiträge des Leo-Baeck-Instituts zu Firmengeschichte und Unternehmerbiographie.* [In]: 'Tradition', Zeitschrift für Firmengeschichte und Unternehmer-Biographie. Hrsg. Wilhelm Treue. 13. Jg., H. 2, Apr. München: Verlag F. Bruckmann, 1968. Pp. 90-104.

B. Bibliographies and Catalogues

6978. B'NAI B'RITH, WIEN, ed.: *Bücher von Autoren jüdischer Herkunft in deutscher Sprache.* Katalog zusammengestellt von Desider Stern. Zweite stark erweiterte Aufl. Wien, 1968. 407 pp. [With biogr. notes on the authors. 1st ed. see No. 6298/YB. XIII.]
6979. BROOKES, REUBEN S. and BROOKES, BLANCHE: *A Guide to Jewish Names.* Birmingham: Hebrew Congregation, Education Dept., 1967. 44 pp.
6980. *'C.V. Zeitung' 1922-1933.* Names and Subject Index. Comp. by Helen Kehr for the Wiener Library. London, [1968]. 148 pp. [Photocopy of typescript.]
6981. DAN, ROBERT: *Zeitschrift für die Geschichte der Juden in Deutschland.* Repertorium. [In]: 'Zeitschrift für die Geschichte der Juden'. V. Jg., Nr. 1. Pp. 27-49. [See No. 6898.]
6982. FREIMANN, ARON, ed.: *Katalog der Judaica und Hebraica.* Stadtbibliothek Frankfurt am Main. Band Judaica. Vorwort zur Neuauflage: Annie Fraenkel. Graz: Akademische Druck- und Verlagsanstalt, 1968. vi, xii, 646 pp. (Um ein Vorwort vermehrter Nachdruck der 1932 in Frankfurt am Main erschienenen Ausgabe).
6983. GERMANIA JUDAICA, ed.: *Geistes- und Kulturgeschichte.* Literaturbericht V. [In]: 'Germania Judaica', Mitteilungsblatt der Kölner Bibliothek zur Geschichte des deutschen Judentums. Neue Folge 26. VII. Jg., H. 4. Köln, 1968. 51 pp. [Literaturbericht I-IV see Nos. 4406/YB. X, 5061/YB. XI, 5682/YB. XII, 6302/YB. XIII.]
6984. *(The) Israel Honorarium.* New York: Educational Publishing Institute, 1968. 895 pp. [5 vols.] [A biographical dictionary of prominent Jews].
6985. ['Jewish Social Studies', New York] ROTHSCHILD, MAX M., comp.: *Jewish Social Studies.* Cumulative Index 1939-1964. Vols. I-XXV. New York: Conference on Jewish Social Studies, 1967. 148 pp.
6986. *Judaica Katalog.* Frankfurt am Main: Europäische Verlagsanstalt, 1968. [Catalogue of the publishing firm's 'Bibliotheca Judaica' series.]
6987. *Periodische Antinationalsozialistische Deutsche Exilpresse.* Auf Mikrofilm. Bonn: Mikropress, 1968. 11 pp. [Mimeog.] [A Catalogue.]
6988. *Post-War Publications on German Jewry.* A Selected Bibliography of Books and Articles 1967. Comp. on behalf of the Wiener Library by Bertha Cohn. [In]: LBI Year Book XIII. London, 1968. Pp. 289-341.
6989. SHAPIRO, LEON: *World Jewish Population.* A Statistical Report. [In]: American Jewish Year Book 1968. Vol. 69. Philadelphia: The Jewish Publication Society of America, 1969. Pp. 543-549.
6990. VERLAGSBUCHHANDLUNG GEORG OLMS, ed.: *Judaica und Hebraica.* Hildesheim, 1968. 24 pp. [A catalogue of 200 reprints of Judaica.]
6991. *Yad Vashem Studies* on the European Jewish Catastrophe and Resistance. Indexes to Vols. I-VI. Jerusalem: Yad Vashem, 1968. 111 pp.

III. THE NAZI PERIOD

A. General

6992. ADLER-RUDEL, S.: *The Evian Conference on the Refugee Question.* [In]: LBI Year Book XIII. London, 1968. Pp. 235-273, ports., illus., facsims.
6993. BADEN-WURTTEMBERG. SAUER, PAUL: *Die Schicksale der jüdischen Bürger Baden-Württembergs während der nationalsozialistischen Verfolgungszeit 1933-1945.* Statistische Ergebnisse der Erhebungen der Dokumentationsstelle bei der Archivdirektion Stuttgart und zusammenfassende Darstellung. Hrsg. von der Archivdirektion Stuttgart. Stuttgart: W. Kohlhammer Verlag, 1968. xvi, 468 pp., front. facsim., ports., illus., tabs., facsims. (Veröffentlichungen der Staatlichen Archivverwaltung Baden-Württemberg. Bd. 20).

6994. BALL-KADURI, K. J., comp.: *Testimonies and Recollections about Activities Organized by German Jewry during the Years 1933-1945.* Catalogue of Manuscripts in the Yad Vashem Archives. Supplements for the Years 1960-67. [In]: Yad Vashem Studies VII. Jerusalem: Yad Vashem, 1968. Pp. 205-219. [Part I in vol. IV, 1960, pp. 317-340. See No. 2024/YB. VI.]

6995. BERADT, CHARLOTTE: *The Third Reich of Dreams.* Transl. from the German by Adriana Gottwald, with an essay by Bruno Bettelheim. Chicago: Quadrangle, 1968. 170 pp. [In German: Das Dritte Reich des Traums. München:Nymphenburger Verlagsbuchhandlung, 1966. 151 pp.]

6996. BRESLAU. SCHAEFFER, RUDOLF F.: *Das religiös-liberale Schulwerk in Breslau 1933-1937.* [In]: '*LBI Bulletin*'. 10. Jg., Nr. 40. Tel Aviv, 1967. Pp. 298-308.

6997. BURKHARD, HUGO: *Tanz mal Jude!* Von Dachau bis Shanghai. Meine Erlebnisse in den Konzentrationslagern Dachau, Buchenwald, Getto Shanghai 1933-1948. Nürnberg: Verlag Richard Reichenbach, 1967. 207 pp., illus., facsims.

6998. FRIEDLANDER, ALBERT H[OSCHANDER]: '*Out of the Whirlwind*'. An Anthology and Reader of Holocaust Literature. New York: McGraw-Hill, 1968. 536 pp.

6999. GRÜBER, PROPST HEINRICH: *Erinnerungen aus sieben Jahrzehnten.* Köln: Kiepenheuer & Witsch, 1968. 429 pp., front port., ports., illus.

7000. KEMPNER, ROBERT M. W.: *Edith Stein und Anne Frank - Zwei von Hunderttausend.* Freiburg i. Br.: Herder Verlag, 1968. 190 pp. (Herder-Bücherei). [Cf. Albrecht Goes: Zwei von hunderttausend Opfern. [In]: 'Welt der Literatur', 27. Febr., Hamburg, 1969.]

7001. MAINZ. *Tagebuch einer jüdischen Gemeinde 1941-43.* Im Auftrag der Jüdischen Gemeinde Mainz hrsg. und kommentiert von Anton M. Keim. Mainz: v. Hase & Koehler Verlag, 1968. 112 pp., tabs., bibl. (pp. 109-112).

7002. MAINZ-KOBLENZ-TRIER. HEYEN, FRANZ JOSEF: *Nationalsozialismus im Alltag.* Quellen zur Geschichte des Nationalsozialismus vornehmlich im Raum Mainz-Koblenz-Trier. Boppard am Rh.: H. Boldt, 1967. xii, 372 pp. (Veröffentlichungen der Landesarchivverwaltung Rheinland-Pfalz, 9). [Pp. 125-163: Juden.]

7003. MEIER, KURT: *Kirche und Judentum.* Die Haltung der evangelischen Kirche zur Judenpolitik des Dritten Reiches. Göttingen: Vandenhoeck und Ruprecht, 1968. 153 pp.

7004. MEMMINGEN/BAVARIA. LINN, DOROTHEA: *Das Schicksal der jüdischen Bevölkerung in Memmingen 1933 bis 1945.* Stuttgart: Ernst Klett Verlag, 1968. 93 pp., tabs., map. (Aus den deutschen Landerziehungsheimen, H. 7). [See No. 3778/YB. IX.]

7005. MORSE, ARTHUR D.: *Die Wasser teilten sich nicht.* Aus dem Amerikanischen übertragen von Norbert Wölfl. Bern/München: Rütten & Loening, 1968. 365 pp., bibl. (pp. 357-359). [Engl. title: While Six Million Died. See No. 6334/YB. XIII.]

7006. MUNICH. HANKE, PETER: *Zur Geschichte der Juden in München zwischen 1933 und 1945.* München: Stadtarchiv, 1967. 353 pp., illus., tabs., facsims., bibl. (pp. 347-353). (Miscellanea Bavarica Monacensia, H. 3). (Neue Schriftenreihe des Stadtarchivs München).

7007. NIEMÖLLER, WILHELM: *Ist die Judenfrage 'bewältigt'?* [In]: 'Junge Kirche'. Eine Zeitschrift europäischer Christen. Beiheft 2. Mai. Dortmund, 1968. 20 pp.

7008. NOVEMBER POGROM. BALL-KADURI, K. J.: *30 Jahre nach dem Pogrom.* Die Kristallnacht war geplant. [In]: 'Aufbau', Nov. 8, New York, 1968, illus. [Articles of remembrance also in other Jewish periodicals.]

7009. *Reichskristallnacht. Pogrom. 9/10 November 1938.* Amsterdam: De Bezige Bij, 1968. 47 pp., front illus., illus., facsims.

7010. ROZENKRANZ, HERBERT: '*Reichskristallnacht*'. 9 November 1938 in Österreich. Wien: Europa Verlag, 1968. 72 pp. (Monographien zur Zeitgeschichte. Schriftenreihe des Dokumentationsarchivs des österreichischen Widerstandes).

7011. OBERHAUSEN. EMIG, ERIK: *Jahre des Terrors.* Der Nationalsozialismus in Oberhausen. Gedenkbuch für die Opfer des Faschismus. Hrsg. im Auftrage der Stadt Oberhausen, 1967. 259 pp. [Chaps. V-VI: Die Judenverfolgung. Die Opfer und ihre Schicksale, pp. 110-257.]

7012. PILCH, JUDAH, ed.: *The Jewish Catastrophe in Europe.* New York: American Association for Jewish Education, 1968. 230 pp.

7013. REITLINGER, GERALD: *The Final Solution.* The Attempt to Exterminate the Jews of Europe 1939-1945. 2nd Revised and Augmented Edition. London: Vallentine, Mitchell, 1968. xii, 668 pp., chronology, tabs., maps, bibl. (pp. 581-591). [First ed. 1953. See No. 128/YB. I.]

7014. ROBINSON, JACOB: *Cessation or Continuity of Community Councils during the Nazi Period.* Jerusalem: Institute for Contemporary Judaism of the Hebrew University, 1968.

7015. SENDER FREIES BERLIN, ed.: *Um uns die Fremde.* Die Vertreibung des Geistes 1933-1945. Berlin: Haude & Spener, 1968. 83 pp., illus. (Buchreihe des SFB, Nr. 9).

7016. SEYDEL, HEINZ, ed.: *Welch Wort in die Kälte gerufen.* Die Judenverfolgung des Dritten Reiches im deutschen Gedicht. Ausgewählt und hrsg. von Heinz Seydel. Berlin [East]: Verlag der Nation, 1968. 584 pp., biogr. notes on the authors, bibl. (pp. 568-575).

7017. SNOEK, JOHAN M.: *The Grey Book.* A Collection of Protests against Anti-Semitism and the Persecution of Jews Issued by Non-Roman Catholic Churches and Church Leaders during Hitler's Rule. Introduction by Uriel Tal. Assen (The Netherlands): Van Gorcum, 1968. xxvi, 315 pp., bibl. (pp.308-315).

7018. SPEAR, SHELDON: *The United States and the Persecution of the Jews in Germany, 1933-1939.* [In]: 'Jewish Social Studies', ed. by Conference on Jewish Social Studies. Vol. 30, No. 4, Oct. New York, 1968. Pp. 215-242.

7019. STETTIN. ROSENFELD, ELSE und LUCKNER, GERTRUD, eds.: *Lebenszeichen aus Piaski.* Briefe Deportierter aus dem Distrikt Lublin, 1940-1943. Nachwort von Albrecht Goes. München: Biederstein Verlag, 1968. 183 pp., tabs., map.

7020. STRÄTZ, HANS-WOLFGANG: *Die studentische 'Aktion wider den undeutschen Geist' im Frühjahr 1933.* [In]: 'Vierteljahrshefte für Zeitgeschichte'. 16. Jg., 4. H., Okt. Stuttgart: Deutsche Verlags-Anstalt, 1968. Pp. 347-372.

7021. THERESIENSTADT. EGEN, HORST: *Zeichnungen aus Theresienstadt.* [Chap. in]: Kinderzeichnungen und Umwelt. Bonn: H. Bouvier, 1967. 143 pp., illus. (pp. 50-59). (Abhandlungen zur Philosophie, Psychologie und Pädagogik. Bd. 38).

7022. ILTIS, RUDOLF and others, ed.: *Theresienstadt* (Terezin). Sammelband. Aus dem Englischen übertragen von Walter Hacker. Wien: Europa-Verlag, 1968, 343 pp., ports., illus. [For English ed. see No. 5092/YB. XI.]

7023. *Widerstand, Verfolgung und Emigration.* Studien und Berichte aus dem Forschungsinstitut der Friedrich-Ebert-Stiftung. Bad Godesberg: Friedrich-Ebert-Stiftung, 1967. [Papers read at a conference in Bergneustadt, Sept. 1966].

7024. YAHIL, LENI: *The Holocaust in Jewish Historiography.* [In]: Yad Vashem Studies VII. Jerusalem: Yad Vashem, 1968. Pp. 57-73.

B. Jewish Resistance

7025. HALPERIN, IRVING: *Spiritual Resistance in Holocaust Literature.* [In]: 'Yad Vashem Studies VII. Jerusalem, 1968. Pp. 75-82, bibl.

7026. MICHEL, HENRI: *Jewish Resistance and the European Resistance Movement.* [In]: Yad Vashem Studies VII. Jerusalem, 1968. Pp. 7-16. [Also a French ed.: La Résistance juive dans la Résistance Européenne. Jerusalem: Yad Vashem, 1968. 9 pp.]

7027. WULF, JOSEF: *'In Würde leben und sterben'.* Manuskript zu einer RIAS Berlin Sendung zum 25. Jahrestag des Warschauer Gettoaufstandes. Berlin, 1968.

IV. POST WAR

A. General

7028. CZECHOSLOVAKIA. ILTIS, RUDOLF, ed.: *Informationsbulletin*. Hrsg. vom Rate der jüdischen Gemeinden in der Tschechischen Sozialistischen Republik (früher Rat der jüdischen Gemeinden in Böhmen und Mähren) und vom Zentralverband der jüdischen Gemeinden in der Slowakei. Doppelnummer für die Berichtsperiode vom 17. April 1968 bis 6. Dez. 1968. Prag: Kirchenzentralverlag, 1968. 58 pp.

7029. THE WORLD JEWISH CONGRESS. THE INSTITUTE OF JEWISH AFFAIRS, ed.: *Jewish Aspects of the Changes in Czechoslovakia*. London, 1968. 26 pp. [Typescript.] (Background Paper No. 11).

7030. DAM, H. G. VAN: *Jüdische Gemeinschaft in Deutschland. Ergänzungsbericht bei der Ratsversammlung des Zentralrats der Juden in Deutschland am 23. Mai 1968*. Berlin: Zentralrat der Juden in Deutschland, 1968. 16 pp. [Supplementary to the 1967 report. Cf. No. 6360/YB. XIII.]

7031. FRANKFURT/M. JÜDISCHE GEMEINDE FRANKFURT, ed.: *Frankfurter Jüdisches Gemeindeblatt*. Amtl. Organ der Jüdischen Gemeinde. Jg. 1, 1968.

7032. GERMAN DEMOCRATIC REPUBLIC. BILGES, HANS-ERICH: *Wie leben heute die Juden in Mitteldeutschland?* Resignation kennzeichnet das Gemeindeleben. [In]: 'Welt', 22. Okt. Hamburg, 1968.

7033. KATCHER, LEO: *Post Mortem*. The Jews in Germany - Today. London: Hamish Hamilton, New York: Delacorte Press, 1968. 258 pp.

7034. LAMM, HANS: *Central Europe: West-Germany*. [Report in]: American Jewish Year Book 1968. Vol. 69. Prepared by The American Jewish Committee, New York. Philadelphia: The Jewish Publication Society of America, 1968. Pp. 477-490.

7035. LOWENTHAL, E. G.: *Jüdische Thematik an deutschen Universitäten*. [In]: 'Allgemeine'. Nr. XXII/42, 12. Jan. Düsseldorf, 1968.

B. Restitution

7036. BALABKINS, NICHOLAS: *West Germany and the Jews: Bonn's 'Moral Comeback'*. [In]: 'Orbis', A Quarterly Journal of World Affairs. Vol. XI. No. 3. Philadelphia: University of Pennsylvania, 1967. Pp. 897-902.

7037. BENTWICH, NORMAN: *The United Restitution Organisation (URO) 1948-1968*. The Work of Restitution and Compensation for Victims of Nazi Oppression. London: Vallentine, Mitchell, 1968. 47 pp. (Dedicated to the memory of Hans Reichmann and Frederick Goldschmidt who died 1964 and 1968 respectively.)

7038. KARLSBERG, B.: *German Federal Compensation- and Restitution-Laws and Jewish Victims in the Netherlands*. [In]: 'Studia Rosenthaliana'. Vol. II, No. 2. [Amsterdam], 1968. Pp. 194-244, bibl. (pp. 243-244).

7039. KÜSTER, OTTO: *Erfahrungen in der deutschen Wiedergutmachung*. Tübingen: J. C. B. Mohr (Paul Siebeck), 1967. 35 pp. (Recht und Staat in Geschichte und Gegenwart. H. 346/347).

7040. SCHÜRHOLZ, FRANZ: *Ergebnisse der deutschen Wiedergutmachungsleistungen in Israel*. Bonn: Bundeszentrale für Politische Bildung, 1968. 29 pp., bibl. (Schriften der Bundeszentrale für Politische Bildung).

V. JUDAISM

A. Jewish Learning and Scholars

7041. AGUS, JACOB B[ERNARD]: *The Vision and the Way*. An Interpretation of Jewish Ethics. New York: F. Ungar, 1966. ix, 365 pp.

7042. BAECK, LEO. BAECK, LEO: *Mahut ha-yahaduth. (Das Wesen des Judentums)*. Transl. into Hebrew with an introduction by Ernst Simon. Jerusalem: Leo Baeck Institute and Mossad Bialik, 1968.

7043. FRIEDLÄNDER, ALBERT H.: *Israel und die Diaspora bei Leo Baeck.* [In]: 'Freiburger Rundbrief', 1968. Pp. 38-41. [See No. 7535.]

7044. FRIEDLÄNDER, ALBERT H.: *Leo Baeck.* Teacher of Theresienstadt. New York: Holt, Rinehart and Winston, 1968. 294 pp., bibl. (pp. 277-288).

7045. BERNFELD, SIMON, ed.: *The Foundation of Jewish Ethics.* With a new Introduction by Samuel E. Karff. New York: Ktav, 1968. 265 pp. [The work was first publ. in Berlin, 1920: Die Grundlagen der jüdischen Ethik. First Engl. ed. 1929.]

7046. *Bibliotheca Rabbinica.* Eine Sammlung alter Midraschim. Zum 1. Male ins Deutsche übersetzt von August Wünsche. Reprograf. Nachdruck der Ausgabe Leipzig 1880/81. Hildesheim: G. Olms, 1967. Vols. 1-5.

7047. BILLIGHEIMER, S.: *On Jewish Translations of the Bible in Germany.* [In]: Abr-Nahrain. An Annual. Publ. by the Department of Middle Eastern Studies, University of Melbourne. Vol. VII, 1967/68. Leiden: E. J. Brill, 1968. 34 pp.

7048. BIRD, THOMAS E., ed.: *Modern Theologians, Christians and Jews.* Introduction to the works of M. Buber [and others]. Notre Dame, Ind.: University of Notre Dame Press, 1967. xii, 224 pp., bibl. (pp. 201-202, 221-222). [Incl. Martin Buber (L.D. Streiker, pp. 1-17). Abraham Yoshua Heschel (F. A. Rothschild, pp. 169-182).]

7049. BOROWITZ, EUGENE B.: *A New Jewish Theology in the Making.* Philadelphia: Westminster, 1968. 230 pp. [An examination and evaluation of the teachings of Leo Baeck, Mordecai M. Kaplan, Martin Buber, Abraham Joshua Heschel and Joseph Baer Soloveitchik.]

7050. BOROWITZ, EUGENE B.: *How Can a Jew Speak of Faith Today?* Philadelphia: Westminster, 1968. 221 pp. [A companion vol. to above.]

7051. BUBER, MARTIN. BEEK, M. A. and J. SPERNA WEILAND: *Martin Buber.* Personalist and Prophet. Glen Rock, New Jersey: Newman Press, 1968.

7052. BERGMAN, HUGO: *Briefe Martin Bubers.* (Zum 90. Geburtstag). [In]: 'Isr. Wochenblatt', 68. Jg., 9. Febr., Zürich [and] 'MB', 9. Febr., Tel Aviv, 1968. [Cf. also No. 6383/YB. XIII. The letters are addressed to Gusta Strumpf-Rechaw and to Hugo Bergman.]

7053. CENTRE NATIONAL DES HAUTES ETUDES JUIVES, ed.: *Martin Buber. L'homme et le philosophe.* Introduction par Robert Weltsch. Symposium. Bruxelles: Editions de l'Institut de Sociologie, Université Libre de Bruxelles, 1968. 76 pp., bibl. [Papers delivered by Gabriel Marcel: L'anthropologie philosophique de Martin Buber. Emmanuel Levinas: La Pensée de Martin Buber et le judaïsme contemporain. André Lacoque: Martin Buber: de l'individu à la personne.]

7054. GERSON, MENACHEM (HERMANN): *Chinuch Umischpacha Bamiziuth Hakibbuz.* Seminar Hakibbuzim Oranim Al Jedei Sefarit Poalim, Merchaviah, 1968. [Incl. an essay: Martin Buber und das deutsche Judentum.]

7055. GOES, ALBRECHT: *Erinnerungen an Martin Buber.* [In]: 'Neue Rundschau'. 79. Jg., 3. H. Frankfurt a. M.: S. Fischer, 1968. Pp. 448-458.

7056. HILBURG, ERWIN K. J.: *Der Chassidismus.* Martin Buber und der Neo-Chassidismus. [In]: 'Germania Judaica', Mitteilungsblatt der Kölner Bibliothek zur Geschichte des deutschen Judentums. Neue Folge 24/25. VII. Jg., H. 2/3. Köln, 1968. 32 pp., bibl. (pp. 30-32).

7057. JACOB, E.: *Martin Buber, traducteur et exégète de la Bible.* [In]: 'Revue d'Histoire et de Philosophie Religieuses'. 48, 4. Strasbourg, 1968. Pp. 321-328.

7058. KURZWEIL, Z. E.: *Martin Bubers Erziehungslehre und die Moderne.* [In]: 'Zeitschrift für Pädagogik'. Jg. 14, Nr. 2. Apr. 1968. Pp. 129-143.

7059. MISRAHI, ROBERT: *Martin Buber, philosophie de la relation.* Présentation, choix de textes, bibliography. Paris: Editions Seghers, 1968. 192 pp., ports., illus., bibl. M.B. pp. 113-184, bibl. (pp. 187-189).

7060. MURTI, V. V. RAMANA: *Buber's Dialogue and Gandhi's Satyagraha.* [In]: 'Journal of the History of Ideas'. Vol. 29, No. 4, Oct.-Dec. Philadelphia, 1968. Pp. 605-613. [On the exchange of letters between Buber and Gandhi at the beginning of 1939 concerning the position of Jews in Germany.]

7061. OLIVER, ROY: *Martin Buber. Der Wanderer und der Weg.* Aus dem Englischen von Dorothea Fischer-Barnicol. Mit einem Vorwort von Hans Fischer-Barnicol. Heidelberg: Lambert Schneider Verlag, 1968. 168 pp. [For English ed. see No. 6390/YB. XIII.]

7062. ROLLINS, E. WILLIAM: *Albrecht Goes, Man of Dialogue.* The personal and literary relationship of Goes to Martin Buber. Nashville, Tenn.: Vanderbilt University, 1968.

7063. ROSENBLÜTH, PINCHAS ERICH: *Martin Buber.* Sein Denken und Wirken. Hannover: Niedersächsische Landeszentrale für Politische Bildung, 1968. 88 pp. (Schriftenreihe der Niders. Landeszentrale — Deutsch-jüdisches Gespräch).

7064. WEHR, GERHARD: *Martin Buber in Selbstzeugnissen und Bild-Dokumenten.* Reinbek bei Hamburg: Rowohlt, 1968. 153 pp., front. port., ports., illus., facsims., bibl. (pp. 145-150). [Cf. Ernst Simon: Ein bedenkliches Buber-Buch. [In]: 'NZZ', 11. Mai, Zürich, 1969 [and] Gerhard Wehr: Entgegnung auf eine Kritik, 'NZZ', 11. Juli 1969.]

7065. COHEN, HERMANN. COHEN, HERMANN: *Das Prinzip der Infinitesimal-Methode und seine Geschichte.* Ein Kapitel zur Grundlegung der Erkenntniskritik. Einleitung von Werner Flach. Frankfurt a. M.: Suhrkamp, 1968 229 pp. (Theorie (Reihe) 1).

7066. GRÜNEWALD, PINCHAS PAUL: *Hermann Cohen.* Hannover: Niedersächsische Landeszentrale für politische Bildung, 1968. 81 pp. (Schriftenreihe der Niders. Landeszentrale — Deutsch-Jüdisches Gespräch).

7067. LIEBESCHÜTZ, HANS: *Hermann Cohen and his Historical Background.* [In]: LBI Year Book XIII. London, 1968. Pp. 3-33, front. port., port., facsim.

7068. LÖWITH, KARL: *Philosophie der Vernunft und Religion der Offenbarung in H. Cohens Religionsphilosophie.* Heidelberg: Carl Winter Universitätsverlag, 1968. 34 pp. (Sitzungsberichte der Heidelberger Akademie der Wissenschaften. Philosophisch-historische Klasse, Jg. 1968. 7. Abhandlung). [A much shorter version of this text appears in 'Neue Rundschau', 79. Jg., H. 4. Frankfurt a. M.: S. Fischer Verlag, 1968. Pp. 644-660.]

7069. MELBER, JEHUDA: *Hermann Cohen's Philosophy of Judaism.* New York: Jonathan David, 1968. 503 pp.

7070. RIEGNER, HEINRICH: *Hermann Cohen.* Buenos Aires: Ejecutivo Sudamericano del Congreso Judio Mundial, 1968. 32 pp. (Grandes Figuras del Judaismo, XXVII). [Germ. original see No. 1673/YB. V.]

7071. WEISS-ROSMARIN, TRUDE: *Hermann Cohen.* On the 50th Anniversary of his Death. [In]: Jewish Book Annual. Vol. 26. Publ. by Jewish Book Council of America. New York, 5729/1968-1969. Pp. 88-93, bibl.

7072. EBAN, ABBA: *My People.* The History of the Jews. New York: Behrman House/Random House, 1968. 534 pp., illus.

7073. FRIEDMANN, GEORGES: *Das Ende des jüdischen Volkes?* Deutsch von Gilbert Strasmann. Reinbek bei Hamburg: Rowohlt Verlag, 1968. 274 pp., front. illus. (Rowohlt Paperback. 67). [For French ed. see No. 5188/YB. XI, for English transl. No. 6400/YB. XIII.]

7074. GRAETZ, HEINRICH. MICHAEL, REUVEN: *The unknown Heinrich Graetz.* From his diaries and letters. [In]: LBI Year Book XIII. London, 1968. Pp. 34-56.

7075. MAHLER, EDUARD: *Handbuch der jüdischen Chronologie.* Hildesheim: G. Olms, 1967. xiv, 635 pp. (Grundriss der Gesamtwissenschaft des Judentums). [Photogr. reprint of the ed. Frankfurt a. M. 1916. - E. Mahler, 1857-1945, orientalist and astronomer.]

7076. MELCHIOR, MARCUS. MELCHIOR, MARCUS: *Gelebt und Erlebt.* Berlin: Verlag Annedore Leber, 1968. 180 pp. [Autobiography, transl. from the Danish. Transl. into English by Werner Melchior: A Rabbi Remembers, New York: Lyle Stuart, 1968.]

7077. MENDELSSOHN, MOSES. MENDELSSOHN, MOSES: *Schriften zur Philosophie, Aesthetik und Apologetik.* Mit Einl., Anm. und einer biogr.-histor. Charakteristik Mendelssohns hrsg. von Moritz Brasch. (Reprogr. Nachdruck der Ausgabe Leipzig, 1880). Hildesheim: G. Olms, 1968. Bd. 1: Schriften zur Metaphysik, Ethik sowie zur Religionsphilosophie. lxxxx, 537 pp., front. port. Bd. 2: Schriften zur Psychologie, Aesthetik sowie zur Apologetik des Judentums. vi, 602 pp.

7078. ALTMANN, ALEXANDER: *Eine neuentdeckte Moses Mendelssohn-Korrespondenz zur Frage des Selbstmords.* [In]: 'Zeitschrift für Religions und Geistesgeschichte'. Bd. XX, H. 3. Köln: E. J. Brill Verlag, 1968. Pp. 240-258.

7079. ALTMANN, ALEXANDER: *Moses Mendelssohn's Gesammelte Schriften.* Neuerschlossene Briefe. Zur Geschichte ihrer Herausgabe. [In]: 'LBI Bulletin'. 11. Jg., Nr. 42. Tel Aviv, 1968. Pp. 73-115.

7080. ALTMANN, ALEXANDER: *Moses Mendelssohns Kindheit in Dessau.* [In]: 'LBI Bulletin'. 10. Jg., Nr. 40. Tel Aviv, 1967. Pp. 237-275, facsim.

7081. MEYER, HERRMANN M. Z. /TOURY, JACOB: *Koheleth Mussar.* Berichtigungen, Ergänzungen, Meinungen. [In]: 'LBI Bulletin'. 11. Jg., Nr. 41. Tel Aviv, 1968. Pp. 48-65. [With ref. to: Die Anfänge des jüdischen Zeitungswesens in Deutschland. See No. 6440/YB. XIII.]

7082. TOURY, JACOB: *On the Authorship of 'Koheleth Mussar'.* [In]: Kirjath Sepher. Bibliographical Quarterly of the Jewish National and University Library. Vol. XLIII, No. 2. March. Jerusalem, 1968. Pp. 279-284. [In Hebrew. An extract in German is cont. in: Die Anfänge des jüdischen Zeitungswesens in Deutschland'. See No. 7081.] ['Kohelet Mussar' (Sittenprediger), the first Hebrew periodical in Germany, was founded by Moses Mendelssohn in 1750.]

7083. (The) MENDELSSOHN FAMILY. HENSEL, SEBASTIAN: *The Mendelssohn Family, 1729-1847.* New York: Greenwood Press, 1968. 2 vols., ports., illus. [A reprint from letters and journals. First German ed.: Berlin: Behr, 1879. 3 vols.]

7084. ROTENSTREICH, NATHAN: *Jewish Philosophy in Modern Times.* New York: Holt, Rinehart & Winston, 1968. 282 pp., bibl. [Incl. Moses Mendelssohn, Samson Raphael Hirsch.]

7085. ROTHMAN, JACK: *Minority Group Identification and Intergroup Relations: An Examination of Kurt Lewin's Theory of Jewish Group Identity.* New York: Research Institute for Group Work in Jewish Agencies, 1967. 263 pp. [Kurt Lewin (1890-1947), psychologist. Cf. Nos. 4124, 4125/YB. IX; 5984/YB. XII.]

7086. SCHOLEM, GERSHOM. SCHOLEM, GERSHOM: *Dankwort an der Stiftungsfeier der Universität Zürich.* [In]: 'Neue Zürcher Zeitung'. 5. Mai. Zürich, 1968. [Speech on receiving the hon. doctorate, on April 29th, of Zurich University.]

7087. *Studies in Mysticism and Religion.* Presented to Gershom G. Scholem on his Seventieth Birthday. Ed. by E. E. Urbach, R. J. Zwi Werblowsky and Ch. Wirszubski. Jerusalem: The Magnes Press. The Hebrew University, 1967. 387 pp. + 235 pp. in Hebrew, bibl. G.S. [Essays in English, German, French, incl.: Das Religiöse bei Kafka (Werner Kraft). Geistiger Kontakt der Juden mit ihrer Umgebung im Mittelalter in Deutschland (J. F. Baer). Produktivität der mystischen Lehren in Deutschland (J. Dan). Hugo v. Hofmannsthals jüdische Legenden (Ernst Simon).]

7088. URBACH, E. E.: *On Gershom Scholem.* [And]: *The Kabbalah and its Downfall.* On the Theories of Gershom Scholem by Yisrael Rosenzweig. [In]: 'Molad'. New Series. Vol. 1, No. 4, Febr./March. Jerusalem, 1968. Pp. 437-441, 442-451. [In Hebrew.]

7089. SPANIER, MEIER. LOEWENBERG, ERNST L.: *Meier Spanier.* Leben und Wirken eines deutschen Juden. [In]: 'LBI Bulletin'. 11. Jg., Nr. 41. Tel Aviv, 1968. Pp. 1-31. [Cf. also No. 6427/YB. XIII.]

7090. STEIN, LEOPOLD. ARNSBERG, PAUL: *Der Frankfurter Rabbiner Dr. Leopold Stein.* Würde eines Rabbiners oder Autorität des Gemeindevorstandes. [And]: *Entgegnung* von Rudolf M. Heilbrunn. [In]: 'LBI Bulletin'. 10. Jg., Nr. 40. Tel Aviv, 1967. Pp. 336-339. [Leopold Stein, 1810-1882.]

7091. STEIN, SIGMUND. DICKINSON, JOHN K.: *German and Jew.* The life and death of Sigmund Stein. Chicago: Quadrangle Books, 1967. xii, 339 pp. [S. Stein, 1896 Hesse-1944 Auschwitz. Cf. Kurt R. Grossmann: Die deutsch-jüdische Symbiose. Symbol ihrer Entstehung und ihres Untergangs - das Schicksal Sigmund Steins. [In]: 'Rheinischer Merkur'. 13. Sept., Köln, 1968, ports.]

7092. STEINHEIM, SALOMON LUDWIG. HABERMAN, JOSHUA O.: *Salomon Ludwig Steinheim's Doctrine of Revelation.* [In]: 'Judaism'. Ed.: Steven S. Schwarzschild. Vol. 17, No. 1, Winter. New York: The American Jewish Congress, 1968. Pp. 22-41. [1789-1866, physician and philosopher].

B. Jewish Life and Organisations

7093. BRILLING, BERNHARD: *Das erste Gedicht auf einen deutschen Rabbiner aus dem Jahre 1752*. Ein Beitrag zum Emden-Eibenschütz-Streit. [In]: 'LBI Bulletin'. 11. Jg., Nr. 41. Tel Aviv, 1968. Pp. 38-47, facsim. [The Jacob Emden-Jonathan Eibenschütz conflict of 1750 in Altona.]

7094. 'C.V.'. LOWENTHAL, E. G.: *Schutzjude oder Staatsbürger?* Vor 75 Jahren wurde der Central-Verein deutscher Staatsbürger jüdischen Glaubens gegründet. [In]: 'Allgemeine'. Nr. XXII/52. 22. März. Düsseldorf. [Also in]: 'AJR Information'. Vol. XXIII, No. 5, May. London, 1968.

—— *C.V. Zeitung 1922-1933*. Names and Subject Index comp. by Helen Kehr for the Wiener Library. London [1968.] 148 pp. [Photocopy of typescript.]

7095. FRANK, JULIUS I. *In memoriam Julius Frank I.* 'Unser Dackele', geb. 10. April 1886 - Gest. 27. Februar 1968. Unser Vorsitzender 1930-1968. Hrsg.: Salia. März/Sept. New York, 1968. [x], 18, 32 pp., front. port., ports.

7096. *'Mitteilungen der Gesellschaft für Jüdische Volkskunde'*. Unter Mitwirkung hervorragender Gelehrter hrsg. von Max Grunwald. Reprogr. Nachdruck, H. 1-10, Hamburg 1898-1902. New York/London: Johnson, 1968, illus. (Gesellschaft für Jüdische Volkskunde).

7097. REICHSVEREINIGUNG DER JUDEN IN DEUTSCHLAND. ESH, SHAUL: *The Establishment of the 'Reichsvereinigung der Juden in Deutschland' and its Main Activities*. [In]: 'Yad Vashem Studies'. Vol. VII. Jerusalem: Yad Vashem, 1968. Pp. 19-38, facsim.

7098. SCHWARZBAUM, HAIM: *Studies in Jewish and World Folklore*. Berlin: Walter de Gruyter, 1968. viii, 603 pp., bibl. (pp. 369-373). (Fabula. Reihe B: Untersuchungen. Bd. 3).

7099. TOURY, JACOB: *Organizational Problems of German Jewry*. Steps Towards the Establishment of a Central Organisation (1893-1920). [In]: LBI Year Book XIII. London, 1968. Pp. 57-90, ports.

7100. WOYDA, BRUNO. BRESLAUER, WALTER: *In Memory of Bruno Woyda*: [In]: 'AJR Information'. Vol. XXIV/2, Febr. London, 1969. [Further obituaries in: 'MB', 3. Jan., 1969; 'Allgemeine', 10. Jan.; Aufbau, 17. Jan. 1969.] [A member of the Council of Jews from Germany. He died 23 Dec. 1968 in London.]

C. Jewish Art and Music

7101. GUTFELD, LUDWIG: *Jewish Art from the Bible to Chagall*. Transl. by William Wolf. New York: Yoseloff (London distribs.: W. H. Allen), 1968. 128 pp., illus.

7102. IDELSOHN, A[BRAHAM] Z[WI]: *Jewish Music in its Historical Development*. New York: Schocken Books, 1967. xi, 535 pp., facsims., music. scores. [First publ. 1929.]

7103. TAMMUZ, BENJAMIN and MAX WYKES-JOYCE: *Art in Israel*. Philadelphia: Lippincott, 1967. 338 pp., 288 illus.

7104. WERNER, ERIC: *From Generation to Generation: Studies in Jewish Musical Tradition*. New York: American Conference of Cantors, 1967. 168 pp.

7105. ZUNZ, LEOPOLD: *Die synagogale Poesie des Mittelalters*. Bd. 1: Im Auftrag der Zunzstiftung hrsg. von Aron Freimann. 2., nach dem Handexemplar des Verfassers berichtigte und durch Quellennachweise und Register verm. Aufl. Reprograf. Nachdruck der Ausgabe Frankfurt a. M., 1920. vi, 584 pp. Bd. 2: Die Riten des synagogalen Gottesdienstes. Reprograf. Nachdr. der Ausgabe Berlin, 1859. 249 pp. Hildesheim: G. Olms, 1967. 2 vols.

VI. ZIONISM AND ISRAEL

7106. BENTWICH, NORMAN: *The Hebrew University of Jerusalem: A Historical Survey*. Neuchatel: Editions de la Baconniere, 1968. [An account of the development and expansion of the university from its opening in 1925 to the end of 1967. Cf. also No. 7112.]

7107. BERGMAN, SHMUEL HUGO. SHOCHETMAN, BARUCH and SHLOMO SHUNAMI, comps.: *The Writings of Shmuel Hugo Bergman.* A Bibliography 1903-1967. Jerusalem: The Magnes Press - The Hebrew University - The Jerusalem Philosophical Society, 1968. 1786 entries.

7108. WELTSCH, ROBERT: *Hugo Bergman zum 85. Geburtstag.* [In]: 'AJR Information'. No. XXIII/12, Dec., London 1968 [and in]: 'MB', Nr. 51. 20. Dez., Tel Aviv, 1968, port. [Another tribute by Viktor Kellner.]

7109. BIRNBAUM, ERNST: *Roter Davidstern über Israel.* Die erste Geschichte des Magen David Adom. Mit einem Geleitwort des Präsidenten des MDA in Israel, Eliahu Elath, und einem Vorwort des Vorsitzenden des MDA, Joseph Kott. Velbert: Blick und Bild Verlag S. Kappe, 1968. 136 pp., 28 illus.

7110. BÖHM, ADOLF. PREUSS, WALTER: *Adolf Böhm und die Zeitschrift 'Palästina'/ Dreissig Jahre nach ihrem Ende.* [In]: 'MB', 14. Juni. Tel Aviv, 1968.

7111. BUBER, MARTIN: *Israel und Palästina.* Zur Geschichte einer Idee. (Ungekürzte Ausgabe). München: Deutscher Taschenbuch Verlag, 1968. 167 pp. (dtv-Taschenbücher, 494). [The Hebrew original was publ. by Schocken, Jerusalem, 1945. First German ed. Zurich: Artemis-Verlag, 1950. Engl. transl. New York: Farrer Strauss & Young, London: East and West Library, 1952.]

7112. BUBER, MARTIN, BERTHOLD FEIWEL, CHAIM WEIZMANN: *Eine jüdische Hochschule.* Jerusalem: The Hebrew University, The Magnes Press, 1968. 36, 36 pp. [German and Hebrew on opposite pages. First publ. in 1902, republ. with a Hebrew translation on the occasion of the 50th anniversary of the laying of the foundation stone of the Hebrew University on Mount Scopus. Cf. also No. 7106.]

7113. *'Deutscher Palästina-Verein'.* Zeitschrift. (Bis 1945: Deutscher Verein zur Erforschung Palästinas). [Reprints of]: Jg. 1-25, Leipzig, 1878-1902; Jg. 26-35, Leipzig, 1903-1912. Nendeln, Liechtenstein: Kraus Reprint, 1968. 2 vols.

7114. ESH, SHAUL (1921-1968). BAUER, Y.: *Shaul Esh, in memoriam.* [In]: 'The Jewish Journal of Sociology'. Vol. 10, No. 2, Dec. London, 1968. Pp. 287-288. [Further tributes by Jacob Robinson in 'Yad Vashem Studies'. Vol. VII. Jerusalem: Yad Vashem, 1968. Pp. 17-18, port.; Ernst Simon in 'MB', 12. Apr., Tel Aviv; 'Aufbau', 19 Apr., New York; 'AJR Information', No. XXIII/6, June, London, 1968. Robert Weltsch in LBI Year Book XIII, London, 1968, port.]

7115. *Frieden im Nahen Osten.* Zum arabischen-israelischen Konflikt: Ernst Bloch, Iring Fetscher, Rolf Rendtorff, Heinz Joachim Heydorn. Frankfurt a. M.: Europäische Verlagsanstalt, 1967. 43 pp.

7116. HERLITZ, GEORG. BEIN, ALEX: *Dr. Georg Herlitz.* (1885-1968). Versuch einer Würdigung zu den Schloschim. [In]: 'MB', 9. Febr. Tel Aviv, 1968. [Tributes also in: 'Der Archivar', Mitteilungsblatt für deutsches Archivwesen. 22. Jg., H. 2, Siegburg (Rhld.), 1969. (Alexander Bein); 'MB', Nr. 3, 19. Jan., Tel Aviv, 1968 (by Siegfried Moses); 'Das Neue Israel', Febr. Zürich (by S. Neufeld); LBI Year Book XIII, London, 1968, port. (by Robert Weltsch).]

7117. HERZL, THEODOR. HERZL, THEODOR: *Der Judenstaat.* Neudruck der Ausgabe Leipzig und Wien, Breitenstein, 1896. Osnabrück: Verlag Zeller, 1968. 86 pp., bibl. (Milliaria, 12).

7118. *Israel.* [Issue of]: 'Merian', Das Monatsheft der Städte und Landschaften. 21. Jg., H. 6, Hamburg: Hoffmann und Campe, 1968. 109 pp., ports., illus., map.

7119. *Jerusalem.* Text: Willy Guggenheim. Aufnahmen: Annemarie Meier. Zürich/Freiburg i. Br.: Atlantis Verlag, 1968. 186 pp. with 118 illus.

7120. *Jerusalem.* Text von Gabriella Rosenthal. Farbaufnahmen von Werner Braun. München: Andermann Verlag, 1968. 104 pp., 40 colour plates, maps. [Available in German, English and French.]

7121. *Jerusalem. Sacred City of Mankind.* A History of Forty Centuries. Ed. by Teddy Kollek and Moshe Pearlman. London: Weidenfeld and Nicolson, 1968. 288 pp., 214 illus., maps.

7122. KATZ, KARL, P. P. KAHANE, MAGEN BROSHI: *Von Anbeginn. Vier Jahrtausende Heiliges Land im modernsten Museum der Welt.* Photos von David Harris. Einführung von Philip Hendy. Deutsch von Ulla Leippe. Hamburg: Hoffman und Campe, 1968. 288 pp., illus., facsims. [Engl. ed.: From the Beginning. London: Weidenfeld and Nicolson, 1968.]

7123. KENYON, KATHLEEN M[ARY]: *Jerusalem - die heilige Stadt von David bis zu den Kreuzzügen.* Ausgrabungen 1961-1967. Bergisch Gladbach: Gustav Lübbe Verlag, 1968. 235 pp., illus., drawings, maps. (Aus dem Englischen von Joachim Rehork: 3000 Years of History).

7124. KIMCHE, JON: *The Unromantics.* The Great Powers and the Balfour Declaration. With a Preface by Lord Sieff. Publ. under the auspices of the Anglo-Israel Association. London: Weidenfeld and Nicolson, 1968. xiii, 87 pp. [Chap. I: Britain faces defeat and the German challenge in the East. Chap. II: Germans plan 'to liberate Russian Jewry'.]

7125. LEHMANN, SIEGFRIED. SIMON, ARYEH: *Erziehung zum Wesenhaften.* Zur Erziehungslehre Siegfried Lehmanns. [In]: 'MB'. Nr. 44, 1. Nov. Tel Aviv, 1968. [1892-1958. Founder of Ben Shemen.]

7126. LEVIN, SHMARYA. *Forward from Exile.* The Autobiography of Shmarya Levin. Transl. and edited by Maurice Samuel. Philadelphia: The Jewish Publication Society of America, 5728/1967. xxiii, 419 pp. [The first German ed. of the autobiography appeared in 1932/33.]

7127. LOEWY, WILHELM: *Zwanzig Jahre Israel - in Wort und Bild.* Tel Aviv: Bronfman Books Publishing Co., 1968. 152 pp. with 260 illus. (Ein Bildbericht).

7128. MEIER-CRONEMEYER, HERMANN: *Kibbuzim - Geschichte, Geist und Gestalt.* Hannover: Verlag für Literatur und Zeitgeschehen, 1968. 250 pp.

7129. RÖHRING, HANS-HELMUT: *Die Entstehungsgeschichte des Staates Israel.* [In]: 'Aus Politik und Zeitgeschichte', Beilage zur Wochenzeitung 'Das Parlament'. Hrsg. Bundeszentrale für politische Bildung. Nr. B 2/68, 10. Jan. Bonn, 1968, 38 pp.

7130. RUPPIN, ARTHUR. RUPPIN, ARTHUR: *My Life and Work. The Autobiography and Diaries.* Ed. by Alex Bein. Transl. from the German by D. Saphir. Tel Aviv: Am Oved, 1968. 3 vols., ports., facsims. [In Hebrew.]

7131. PINNER, LUDWIG: *Das Siedlungswerk Arthur Ruppins im Lichte unserer Zeit.* Zum 25. Todestag. [In]: 'MB', Nr. 1, 5. Jan. Tel Aviv, 1968. [Articles also appeared in 'Isr. Wochenzeitung', 2. Febr., Zürich, 1968, port [and] 'Münchner Jüdische Nachrichten', 2. Febr., München, 1968.]

7132. SCHOCKEN, SALMAN. SCHOCKEN, GERSHOM: *Ich werde seinesgleichen nicht mehr sehen.* Erinnerungen an Salman Schocken. [In]: 'Der Monat'. 20. Jg., H. 242, Nov. Berlin, 1968. Pp. 13-30. [Salman Schocken, 1877-1959.]

7133. SONTHEIMER, KURT, ed.: *Israel - Politik, Gesellschaft, Wirtschaft.* Ein Sammelband. München: R. Piper Verlag, 1968. 364 pp., bibl. (pp. 311-356). [Cf. No. 6456/YB. XIII.]

7134. *Textbuch zur Geschichte Israels.* In Verbindung mit Elmar Edel und Riekele Borger hrsg. von Kurt Galling. Tübingen: J. C. B. Mohr (Paul Siebeck) Verlag, 1968. xi, 109 pp., maps.

7135. ULBRICHT, WALTER: *Antwort auf aktuelle Fragen.* Anhang: *Dokumente zur israelischen Aggression und zu ihren Hintergründen.* Berlin [East]: Dietz Verlag, 1967. 79 pp., front. illus., map.

7136. WARBURG, OTTO. WILK, CURT: *Der dritte Präsident im Weltzionismus.* Zum 30. Todestag Prof. Otto Warburgs am 10. Januar. [In]: 'Das Neue Israel', Febr., Zürich, 1968 [and in]: 'Boletin Informativo', Febr., Buenos Aires, 1968.

7137. WEIZMANN, CHAIM. *The Letters and Papers of Chaim Weizmann.* English Edition. Series A: Letters. Vol. I: Summer 1885 - 29 October 1902. Ed. by Leonard Stein in collaboration with Gedalia Yogev. London: Oxford University Press, 1968. xlii, 447 pp., front. port., ports., illus., facsims., biogr. index (pp. 408-428).

VII. PARTICIPATION IN CULTURAL AND PUBLIC LIFE

A. General

7138. ARENDT, HANNAH: *Men in the Dark Times.* New York: Harcourt, Brace & World, 1968. 272 pp. [Incl. Rosa Luxemburg, Hermann Broch, Walter Benjamin.]

7139. BERTHOLD, MARGOT: *Weltgeschichte des Theaters.* Stuttgart: Kröner Verlag, 1968. xii, 522 pp., 454 ports. and illus., bibl. (pp. 495-500).

7140. *Biographien bedeutender Chemiker.* Eine Sammlung von Biographien. Hrsg. von Karl Heinig. Red. Bearbeitung: Wolfgang Eisenhuth [and others]. Stark bearb. und ergänzte Aufl. Berlin [East]: Verlag Volk und Wissen, 1968. 311 pp.

— BRAUBACH, MAX: *Jüdischer Anteil an der Bonner Gelehrsamkeit.* [See No. 6911.]

7141. CARTER, JOHN / PERCY H. MUIR: *Bücher, die die Welt verändern.* Hrsg. von Kurt Busse, München: Prestel Verlag, 1968. 800 pp., illus., biogr. notes, bibl. [Incl. Einstein, Freud, Marx.]

7142. *Deutsche Literatur im 20. Jahrhundert.* Strukturen und Gestalten. Begründet von Hermann Friedmann und Otto Mann. 5., veränderte und erweiterte Aufl., hrsg. von Otto Mann und Wolfgang Rothe. München: Francke Verlag, 1968. 390, 456 pp. biogrs., bibls. [2 vols.] [Vol. 1 incl.: Ferdinand Bruckner, Karl Kraus, Else Lasker-Schüler. Vol. 2 incl.: Hugo von Hofmannsthal, Alfred Döblin, Franz Kafka, Hermann Broch, Franz Werfel, Elisabeth Langgässer, Ernst Toller, Carl Zuckmayer.]

7143. *Deutsche Nobelpreisträger.* Deutsche Beiträge zur Natur- und Geisteswissenschaft, dargestellt am Beispiel der Nobelpreisverleihungen für Frieden, Literatur, Medizin, Physik und Chemie. Verfasst von Armin Hermann [and others] unter Gesamtredaktion von Armin Hermann. München: Heinz Moos Verlag, 1968. 172 pp., front. illus., ports., illus., diagrs., facsims., bibl. (pp. 161-167).

7144. DIWALD, HELLMUT: *Der jüdische Beitrag zur gegenwärtigen Internationalität der deutschen Kultur.* [In]: Auswärtige Kulturbeziehungen. Hrsg. von Berthold Martin. Bd. 3. Neuwied: Hermann Luchterhand Verlag, 1966. Pp. 51-68.

7145. ETTINGHAUSEN, MAURICE L[EON]: *Rare Books and Royal Collectors.* Memoirs of an Antiquarian Bookseller. New York: Simon and Schuster, 1966. 220 pp.

7146. EXILE LITERATURE. *Exil-Literatur 1933-1945.* Bad Godesberg: Inter Nationes, 1968. 72 pp., facsims., bibl.: Werke deutschsprachiger Autoren im Exil [and] Deutschsprachige Exil-Zeitschriften 1933-1945, pp. 63-74. [Papers read at a conference in Luxemburg, January 1968, by: Willy Brandt, Pierre Grégoire, Carl H. Lueders, Kurt Köster, Golo Mann, Hans Mayer. The speeches made by Willy Brandt and Pierre Grégoire also in 'Tribüne', 7. Jg., H. 25, 1968, pp. 2710-2714. Golo Mann's speech in: 'Neue Rundschau', 79. Jg., H. 1, Frankfurt a. M.: S. Fischer, 1968. Pp. 38-49.]

7147. RÖDER, WERNER: *Die deutschen sozialistischen Exilgruppen in Grossbritannien, 1940-1945.* Hannover: Verlag für Literatur und Zeitgeschehen, 1968. 322 pp., tabs., bibl. (pp. 299-312). (Schriftenreihe des Forschungsinstituts der Friedrich-Ebert-Stiftung).

7148. SCHEU, FRIEDRICH: *Die Emigrationspresse der Sozialisten 1938-1945.* Wien-Frankfurt: Europa Verlag, 1968. 44 pp.

7149. SCHLÖSSER, M[ANFRED]: *Deutsch-Jüdische Dichtung des Exils.* [In]: 'Emuna', Blätter für Christlich-Jüdische Zusammenarbeit. 3. Jg., Nr. 4. Frankfurt a. M., 1968. Pp. 250-265.

7150. SENDER FREIES BERLIN, ed.: *Um uns die Fremde.* Die Vertreibung des Geistes 1933-1945. Berlin: Haude & Spenersche Verlagsbuchhandlung, 1968. 83 pp., ports., illus. (Buchreihe des SFB, Bd. 9).

7151. WEGNER, MATTHIAS: *Exil und Literatur.* Deutsche Schriftsteller im Ausland 1933-1945. 2. durchgesehene und ergänzte Aufl. Frankfurt a. M.: Athenäum Verlag, 1968. 247 pp., bibl. (pp. 226-241). (Athenäumbücher zur Dichtkunst).

7152. GAY, PETER: *Weimar Culture - The Outsider as Insider.* New York: Harper & Row, London: Secker & Warburg, 1968. 197 pp., ports., illus. [Incl. Alfred Adler, Albert Einstein, Hannah Arendt, Kurt Weill.]

288 *Bibliography*

7153. HAMBURGER, ERNEST: *Juden im öffentlichen Leben Deutschlands.* Regierungsmitglieder, Beamte und Parlamentarier in der monarchischen Zeit 1848-1918. Tübingen: J. C. B. Mohr (Paul Siebeck), 1968. xxii, 595 pp., bibl. (pp. 563-584). (Schriftenreihe Wissenschaftlicher Abhandlungen des Leo Baeck Instituts. 19). [Cf. Review by Egmont Zechlin in 'Zeit', Okt. 4, Hamburg, 1968, illus.]

7154. HEIMPEL, HERMANN, THEODOR HEUSS, BENNO REIFENBERG, eds.: *Die grossen Forscher, Erfinder, Ärzte.* [And]: *Die grossen Dichter, Philosophen, Historiker.* Auswahl aus: Die grossen Deutschen. Berlin: Propyläen-Verlag, 1966/1968. 502 pp., ports., 453 pp., ports. [2 vols.] (Genius der Deutschen). [Selection from: Die grossen Deutschen. Deutsche Biographie. Berlin: Propyläen-Verlag bei Ullstein, 1956-1957. 5 vols. See No. 1125/YB. III.]

7155. IHERING, HERBERT: *Von Reinhardt bis Brecht.* Mit einem Vorwort von Rolf Badenhausen. Reinbek b. Hamburg: Rowohlt Verlag, 1968.

7156. INSTITUT FÜR MARXISMUS-LENINISMUS BEIM ZK DER SED, ed: *Illustrierte Geschichte der Novemberrevolution in Deutschland.* Berlin [East]: Dietz Verlag, 1968. 390 pp., ports., illus., facsims., maps, tabs., diagrs.

7157. *Jüdischer Geist in Geschichte und Gegenwart.* 6 Vorträge. Hrsg. von Peter Schneider und Hermann J. Meyer. Mainz: Johannes-Gutenberg-Universität, 1968. 71 pp. (Studium generale der Johannes-Gutenberg-Universität).

7158. KRAFT, WERNER: *Rebellen des Geistes.* Stuttgart: W. Kohlhammer, 1968. 162 pp.

7159. LANE, BARBARA MILLER: *Architecture and Politics in Germany, 1918-1945.* Cambridge, Mass.: Harvard University Press, 1968. 278 pp., illus., plans, bibl. (pp. 217-229). [References to Erich Mendelsohn and other German Jews, also to antisemitism.]

7160. LANGE, FRIEDRICH ALBERT: *Über Politik und Philosophie. Briefe und Leitartikel 1862 bis 1875.* Hrsg. und bearb. von Georg Eckert. Duisburg: Walter Braun Verlag, 1968. 707 pp., ports., facsims. (Duisburger Forschungen. Schriftenreihe für Geschichte und Heimatkunde Duisburgs). [Incl. Karl Marx, Leopold Sonnemann, Max Hirsch, Adolph Samter, Hermann Cohen.]

7161. LIPTZIN, SOL: *Germany's Stepchildren: The Jews in Germany from Varnhagen to Zweig.* London: Harper & Row, 1967. 298 pp., illus. [First publ. 1944. Cf. also No. 2693/YB. VII.]

7162. *Maler des Impressionismus.* (Ausstellungskatalog). Bearb.: Peter Krieger. Hrsg. durch Aussenamt der Staatl. Museen. Fotos: Walter Steinkopf. Berlin: Staatl. Museen, Nationalgalerie, 1967. 34 pp. text und illus. + 32 pp. illus. (Bilderhefte der Staatlichen Museen Berlin, Stiftung Preussischer Kulturbesitz, H. 3).

7163. MANN, GOLO: *The History of Germany since 1789.* Transl. from the German by Marian Jackson. London: Chatto & Windus, 1968. xii, 547 pp., bibl. (pp. 537-540). [Incl. chaps. on Heinrich Heine, Karl Marx, Ferdinand Lassalle, Walther Rathenau. - First publ. in German under the title 'Deutsche Geschichte des 19. und 20. Jahrhunderts', Frankfurt a. M.: S. Fischer Verlag, 1958.]

7164. MANN, GOLO: *Prinz Max von Baden und das Ende der Monarchie in Deutschland.* [In]: 'Merkur', 22. Jg., H. 8 (244), Aug. Stuttgart: Ernst Klett Verlag, 1968. Pp. 727-750. [Incl. Kurt Hahn's decisive rôle, as a close adviser of the prince, in the last episode of Imperial Germany's history. Incl. also Max Warburg.]

7165. MAYER, PAUL: *Ernst Rowohlt in Selbstzeugnissen und Bilddokumenten.* Hamburg: Rowohlt Verlag, 1968. 229 pp., front. port., ports., illus., facsims., chronology, bibl. (pp. 226-229). (rowohlts monographien, 139). [Many of the publisher's authors and friends were German Jews.]

7166. *Menschheitsdämmerung.* Ein Dokument des Expressionismus. Mit Biographien und Bibliographien neu hrsg. von Kurt Pinthus. Rev. Ausg. mit wesentl. erw. bio-bibliographischem Anhang. 8. Aufl. Reinbek b. Hamburg: Rowohlt Verlag, 1968. 384 pp., illus. (Rowohlts Klassiker der Literatur und der Wissenschaft, 55/56/56a: Deutsche Literatur. Bd. 4). [First publ. 1920. See No. 1912/YB. V.]

7167. PIATIGORSKIJ, GREGOR: *Mein Cello und ich.* Aus dem Amerikanischen von Else Winter. Tübingen: Rainer Wunderlich Verlag Hermann Leins, 1968. 280 pp., ports. [Refs. to Albert Einstein, Carl Flesch, Jascha Heifetz, Otto Klemperer, Fritz Kreisler, Yehudi Menuhin, Nathan Milstein, Artur Rubinstein, Artur Schnabel, Arnold Schönberg, Rudolf Serkin, Bruno Walter, Stefan Zweig.]

7168. POLITZER, HEINZ: *Das Schweigen der Sirenen.* Studien zur deutschen und österreichischen Literatur. Stuttgart: Metzlersche Verlagsbuchhandlung, 1968. 436 pp.

7169. 'QUERSCHNITT'. *Faksimile-Querschnitt durch den Querschnitt.* Hrsg. von Wilmont Haacke und Alexander Baeyer. München: Scherz Verlag, 1968. 208 pp., ports., illus., facsims., bibl. (Facsimile Querschnitte durch Zeitungen und Zeitschriften. 11. Bd.) [The literary magazine was founded by the art-dealer and publisher Alfred Flechtheim in 1921. Many Jews were contributors to it. In 1936 it was prohibited by the Nazis on account of 'zersetzendem Intellektualismus'.]

7170. RITTER, GERHARD A. und SUSANNE MILLER, eds.: *Die deutsche Revolution 1918-1919.* Berlin: Fischer-Bücherei, 1968. 381 pp.

7171. SCHONBERG, HAROLD C.: *The Great Conductors.* London: Victor Gollancz, 1968. 384 pp., ports., illus. [Part 3 of a trilogy. Part 1: The Great Pianists. 1965. 448 pp., ports., illus. Part. 2: The Great Singers (by Henry Pleasants), 1967. 382 pp., ports., illus.]

7172. STEINMANN, ULRICH: *Gründer und Förderer des Berliner Volkskunde-Museums.* Rudolf Virchow, Ulrich Jahn, Alexander Meyer Cohn, Hermann Sökeland, James Simon. Sonderdruck aus: Staatliche Museen zu Berlin. Forschungen und Berichte. Berlin [East]: Akademie-Verlag, 1967. Pp. 71-112, ports., facsims., bibls. (Kunsthistorische Beiträge, Bd. 9). [Alexander Meyer Cohn (1853-1904), banker, art collector, pp. 82-86, port., facsim., bibl. James Simon (1851-1932), pp. 93-112, port., facsim., bibl.]

7173. STUTSCHEWSKY, JOACHIM: *Jüdische Musikverlage.* Historische Bilanz. [In]: 'Das Neue Israel'. 21. Jg., H. 2, Aug. Zürich, 1968. Pp. 109-115, facsims.

7174. SWIRIDOFF, PAUL: *Portraits from German Economic Life.* Text by Günther Neske. Portraits, vol. 2. Pfullingen: Günther Neske Verlag, 1967. 218 pp., ports. (Swiridoff Picture Books. Vol. 15). [Vol. 14: Portraits from German Intellectual Life. See No. 5852/YB. XII.]

7175. WALLMANN, JÜRGEN P.: *Argumente.* Informationen und Meinungen zur deutschen Literatur der Gegenwart. Aufsätze und Kritiken. Mühlacker: Stieglitz Verlag, 1968.

7176. WALLWITZ, ALICE GRÄFIN, ed.: *Panorama 1918.* Ein Jahr im Spiegel der Presse. Eingeleitet von Dietrich Bracher. München und Bern: Scherz Verlag, 1968. 159 pp., ports., illus., facsims., chron. (Panoramen der Geschichte. 7. Bd.).

7177. WEGNER, KONSTANZE: *Theodor Barth und die Freisinnige Vereinigung.* Studien zur Geschichte des Linksliberalismus im wilhelminischen Deutschland (1893-1910). Tübingen: J. C. B. Mohr (Paul Siebeck), 1968. xii, 159 pp. (Tübinger Studien zur Geschichte und Politik, 24).

7178. 'WELTBÜHNE'. DEAK, ISTVAN: *Weimar Germany's Left-Wing Intellectuals.* A Political History of the 'Weltbühne' and its Circle. Berkeley and Los Angeles: University of California Press, 1968. xii, 346 pp., ports., illus., facsims., bibl. (pp. 321-334). [Chap. II: Die Weltbühne and its editors: Siegfried Jacobsohn, Kurt Tucholsky, Carl von Ossietzky. Appendixes: Biographies of members of the Weltbühne circle.]

7179. *(Der) Zentralrat der deutschen sozialistischen Republik 19.12.1918—8.4.1919 - Vom Ersten zum Zweiten Rätekongress.* Bearb. von Eberhard Kolb unter Mitwirkung von Reinhard Rürup. Leiden: E. J. Brill, 1968. lxxvii, 830 pp. (Quellen zur Geschichte der Rätebewegung in Deutschland 1918/19).

B. Individual

7180. ADLER, MAX. HEINTEL, PETER: *System und Ideologie.* Der Austromarxismus im Spiegel der Philosophie Max Adlers. München: R. Oldenbourg Verlag, 1967. 412 pp. [Cf. No. 6501/YB. XIII.]

7181. ADLER, VICTOR. LANZER, WANDA und ERNST KARL HERLITZKA, eds.: *Victor Adler im Spiegel seiner Zeitgenossen.* Wien: Verlag der Wiener Volksbuchhandlung, 1968. 237 pp.

7182. ADORNO, THEODOR W. ADORNO, THEODOR W.: *Eingriffe.* Neun kritische Modelle. 5. Aufl. Frankfurt a. M.: Suhrkamp Verlag, 1968. 173 pp. (edition suhrkamp. 10).

7183. ADORNO, THEODOR W.: *Impromptus.* 2. Folge neu gedr. musikalischer Aufsätze. Frankfurt a. M.: Suhrkamp Verlag, 1968. 184 pp., bibl. T. W. A. (edition suhrkamp. 267). [Cf. Norbert Linke: Die Schwierigkeit über Musik zu schreiben. [In]: 'Welt der Literatur'. Nr. 1, 2. Jan. Hamburg, 1969.]

7184. *Über Theodor W. Adorno.* Mit Beiträgen von Kurt Oppens, Jürgen Habermas u.a. Frankfurt a. M.: Suhrkamp Verlag, 1968. 150 pp., bibl. (pp. 143-149). (edition suhrkamp. 249).

7185. ALTENBERG, PETER [i.e. Richard Engländer]. HATVANI, PAUL: *Chronist der Nebenwelt.* Peter Altenberg zum 50. Todestag. [In]: 'Frankfurter Allgemeine Zeitung', Nr. 9, 11. Jan. Frankfurt a. M., 1969, illus. [1859-1919].

7186. TRAMER, HANS: *Arthur Schnitzlers Altenberg-Stück.* [In]: 'LBI Bulletin'. 11. Jg., Nr. 42. Tel Aviv, 1968. Pp. 125-152.

7187. ANDRIAN, LEOPOLD. SCHUMACHER, HORST: *Leopold Andrian.* Werk und Weltbild eines österreichischen Dichters. Wien: Bergland Verlag, 1967. 140 pp., ports., illus. (Österreich-Reihe. Bd. 340/342). [Leopold Andrian, 1875-1951, a grandson of Giacomo Meyerbeer. Cf. No. 2196/YB. VI, No. 3339/YB. VIII, also No. 7509.]

7188. ARENDT, ERICH. ARENDT, E[RICH]: *Gedichte.* Rostock: Hinstorff Verlag,, 1968. 608 pp. [Publ. on the occasion of the 65th birthday of the author who lives in East Berlin.]

7189. BAB, JULIUS. *Julius Bab (1880-1955) und das Theater der Republik 1918-1933.* Ausstellungskatalog der Akademie der Künste, hrsg. von Walther Huder, Bua Knoll und Ilse Bauer. Berlin, 1967.

7190. BALLIN, ALBERT. CECIL, LAMAR: *Albert Ballin.* Wirtschaft und Politik im Deutschen Kaiserreich. Hamburg: Hoffmann und Campe, 1968. 338 pp., ports., illus.

7191. BENJAMIN, WALTER. BENJAMIN, WALTER: *Illuminations.* Edited, with an Introduction, by Hannah Arendt. Transl. by Harry Zohn. New York: Harcourt, Brace & World, 1968. 280 pp. [For German ed. see No. 2714/YB. VII.]

7192. ARENDT, HANNAH: *Walter Benjamin.* I. Der Bucklige. II. Die finsteren Zeiten. III. Der Perlentaucher. [In]: 'Merkur', Deutsche Zeitschrift für europäisches Denken. 22. Jg., H. 1/2 (238), Jan.-Febr., H. 3 (239), März, H. 4 (240), Apr. Stuttgart: Ernst Klett Verlag, 1968. Pp. 50-65, 209-223, 305-315. [Also]: *Walter Benjamin und das Institut für Sozialforschung - Noch Einmal.* H. 10 (246), Okt. 1968.

7193. BELMORE, H. W.: *A New Study of Walter Benjamin.* (Rolf Tiedemanns Studien zur Philosophie Walter Benjamins). [In]: 'German Life and Letters'. N.S., Vol. XXI, No. 4, July. Oxford: Basil Blackwell, 1968. Pp. 345-350.

7194. HAAS, WILLY: *Zwiegespräche, die zu visionären Wortgebilden führen.* Mystiker und Marxist - Walter Benjamin in seinen Briefen. [In]: 'Die Welt der Literatur'. 18. Jan. Hamburg, 1968, port. [Cf. Nos. 6785-6787/YB. XIII.]

7195. HEISSENBÜTTEL, HELMUT: *Zu Walter Benjamins Spätwerk.* [In]: 'Merkur'. 22. Jg., H. 1/2 (238), Jan.-Febr. Stuttgart: Ernst Klett Verlag, 1968. Pp. 179-185.

7196. REICH, WILLI: *Kontroverse um Walter Benjamin.* Eine Dokumentation. [In]: 'Neue Zürcher Zeitung'. 1. Sept. Zürich, 1968.

7197. *Über Walter Benjamin.* Mit Beiträgen von Theodor W. Adorno, Ernst Bloch, Max Rychner, Gershom Scholem, Jean Selz, Hans Heinz Holz und Ernst Fischer. Frankfurt a. M.: Suhrkamp Verlag, 1968. 173 pp., bibl. (pp. 165-173). (edition suhrkamp Bd. 250).

7198. *Walter Benjamin - Towards a Philosophy of Language.* [In]: 'The Times Literary Supplement'. Vol. 67, Aug. 22. London, 1968. Pp. 885-887.

7199. *Walter Benjamin (I).* Der Benjamin-Nachlass im Deutschen Zentralarchiv Potsdam. Text-Rekonstruktionen. Beaudelaire-Fassungen u.a. [In]: 'Alternative', Zeitschrift für Literatur und Diskussion. Nr. 56/57, Okt.-Dez. Berlin: Alternative Verlag, 1967.

7200. *Walter Benjamin (II).* Die Lesbarkeit der Bilder (Hildegard Brenner). Brief an Asja Lazis (Walter Benjamin). Nachbemerkungen zu einer Polemik oder Widerlegbare Behauptungen der Frankfurter Benjamin-Herausgeber (Rosemarie Heise). Wie es zu den Eingriffen in Benjamins Texte kam oder Über die Herstellbarkeit von Einverständnis (Helga Gallas). Die Diskussion in der 'Frankfurter Rundschau'. Kleine Bibliografie zur Diskussion über Interpretation und Edition der Werke Benjamins. [In]: 'Alternative'. Nr. 59/60, Apr.-Juni. Berlin: Alternative Verlag, 1968. Pp. 45-93, port.

7201. BEREND-CORINTH, CHARLOTTE. *Charlotte Berend-Corinth (1880-1967).* Gemälde, Graphik. Ausstellungskatalog, zusammengestellt von Charlotte Berend-Corinth und Thomas Corinth. Berlin: Staatl. Museen, National-Galerie, 1967. 16 pp + 16 pp. illus.

7202. SCHULTZMAN, MONTY: *Die Malerin Charlotte Berend-Corinth.* Eine Künstlerin unserer Zeit. München: Bruckmann, 1967. 63 pp., front. port., illus. (pp. 21-60).

7203. BERNSTEIN, EDUARD. RADEZUN, GÜNTER: *Zum Kampf Eduard Bernsteins gegen die marxistische Lehre vom Staat und von der proletarischen Revolution.* [In]: Beiträge zur Geschichte der deutschen Arbeiterbewegung. Hrsg. vom Institut für Marxismus-Leninismus beim ZK der SED. 8. Jg. Berlin [East], 1966. Pp. 446-460.

7204. BILBO, JACK. BILBO, JACK [i.e. Hugo Baruch (1907-1967)]: *'Pfui Teufel!.* Aphorismen. Hamburg: Matari Verlag, 1968. 64 pp. [Cf. his autobiography 'Rebell aus Leidenschaft', No. 4003/YB. IX.]

7205. BLOCH, ERNST. BLOCH, ERNST: *Atheismus im Christentum.* Zur Religion des Exodus und des Reichs. Frankfurt a. M.: Suhrkamp Verlag, 1968. 364 pp. (Gesamtausgabe Werke, Bd. 14).

7206. BLOCH, ERNST: *Widerstand und Friede.* Aufsätze zur Politik. Frankfurt a. M.: Suhrkamp Verlag, 1968. 112 pp. (edition suhrkamp. 257).

7207. MAIHOFER, WERNER: *Ernst Blochs Evolution des Marxismus.* [In]: Die Neue Gesellschaft. Nr. 15. Bielefeld, 1968. Pp. 259-266.

7208. *Über Ernst Bloch.* Mit Beiträgen von Martin Walser, Jürgen Habermas, Ivo Frenzel [and others]. Frankfurt a. M.: Suhrkamp Verlag, 1968. 150 pp., bibl. (pp. 133-149).

7209. WERCKMEISTER, O. K.: *Ernst Blochs Theorie der Kunst.* [In]: 'Neue Rundschau'. 79. Jg., H. 2. Frankfurt a. M.: S. Fischer, 1968. Pp. 233-250, bibl. (pp. 249-250).

7210. BLUM, JULIUS. RONALL, JOACHIM O.: *Julius Blum Pasha.* An Austro-Hungarian Banker in Egypt (1843-1919). [In]: 'Tradition', Zeitschrift für Firmengeschichte und Unternehmer-Biographie. Hrsg. Wilhelm Treue. 13. Jg., 2. H., April. München: F. Bruckmann Verlag, 1968. Pp. 57-80, cover port., ports., bibl. [Egyptian finance minister 1879-1890, later director of the 'Österreichische Kreditanstalt'.]

7211. BOAS, FRANZ. KORN, B.: *Franz Boas, ein jüdischer Anthropologe und Rassenforscher.* [In]: 'Emuna', Blätter für Christlich-Jüdische Zusammenarbeit. 3. Jg., Nr. 4. Frankfurt a. M., 1968. Pp. 243-249. [The anthropologist (1858-1942), born in Minden, worked from 1886 in the USA.]

7212. BORCHARDT, RUDOLF. BORCHARDT, RUDOLF: *Gedichte.* Auswahl und Einleitung von Theodor W. Adorno. Frankfurt a. M.: Suhrkamp Verlag, 1968. 114 pp. (Bibliothek Suhrkamp. Bd. 213).

7213. BORCHARDT, RUDOLF: *Der leidenschaftliche Gärtner.* Hrsg. von Marie Luise Borchardt unter Mitarbeit von Ernst Zinn und Ulrich Ott. Stuttgart: Ernst Klett Verlag, 1968. 433 pp. (Gesammelte Werke in Einzelbänden, Bd. 8).

7214. *Rudolf Borchard: Auswahl aus dem Werk.* Zusammengestellt und mit einem Nachwort versehen von Helmut Heissenbüttel. Stuttgart: Ernst Klett Verlag, 1968. 232 pp.

7215. BORN, MAX. VOGEL, HEINRICH: *Physik und Philosophie bei Max Born.* Berlin [East]: Deutscher Verlag der Wissenschaften, 1968. 180 pp., ports.

7216. BROCH, HERMANN. BROCH, HERMANN: *Zur Universitätsreform.* Aus dem Nachlass hrsg. und mit einem Nachwort von Götz Wienold. Frankfurt a. M.: Suhrkamp Verlag, 1968 (edition suhrkamp. Bd. 301).

7217. BAUMANN, WALTER: *Hermann Broch und die Lyrik.* [In]: 'Colloquia Germanica'. Nr. 2. Bern, 1967. Pp. 174-205.

7218. DURZAK, MANFRED: *Hermann Broch.* Der Dichter in seiner Zeit. Stuttgart: W. Kohlhammer Verlag, 1968. 234 pp., bibl. (pp. 222-229). (Reihe 'Sprache und Literatur'. Bd. 43).

7219. DURZAK, MANFRED: *Hermann Brochs Anfänge.* Zum Einfluss Weiningers und Schopenhauers. [In]: 'Germanisch-Romanische Monatsschrift'. N.F., Bd. XVII/3. Heidelberg, 1967. Pp. 293-306.

7220. KANTZENBACH, FRIEDRICH WILHELM: *Broch und Jahnn als religiöse Denker.* [In]: 'Hochland'. H. 3. München: Kösel Verlag, 1968.

7221. STEINECKE, HARTMUT: *Hermann Broch und der polyhistorische Roman.* Studien zu Theorie und Technik eines Romantyps der Moderne. Bonn: H. Bouvier Verlag, 1968. 221 pp. (Bonner Arbeiten zur deutschen Literatur. Bd. 17). (Diss. Bonn).

7222. SUCHY, VIKTOR: *Hermann Broch und der Roman.* [In]: 'Literatur und Kritik'. Österr. Monatsschrift. H. 26/27. Juli/Aug. Wien, 1968. Pp. 391-403.

7223. BROD, MAX. BROD, MAX: *Das Unzerstörbare.* Stuttgart: Verlag W. Kohlhammer, 1968. 240 pp.

7224. *Max Brod,* born 27 May, 1884 in Prague - died 20 Dec. 1968 in Tel Aviv. Obituaries in almost all Jewish newspapers and periodicals and in some leading German and Swiss papers, also in 'The Times', London, and 'New York Times '(both on Dec. 21, 1968).

7225. BRUNNER, CONSTANTIN [i.e. Leo Wertheimer, 1862-1937]. BRUNNER, CONSTAN-TIN: *Science, Spirit, Superstition.* A Selection from his work by Abraham Suhl, revised and edited by Walter Bernard. London: Allen & Unwin, 1968. 648 pp.

7226. BUKOFZER, WERNER. BUKOFZER, WERNER: *Splitter.* Prosa der Begegnungen. Neuwied: Hermann Luchterhand Verlag, 1968. 104 pp. (Mainzer Reihe, Bd. 22). [Born 1903 in Berlin, the actor has lived in Israel since 1939.]

7227. CASSIRER, ERNST. CASSIRER, ERNST: *Philosophie und exakte Wissenschaft.* Einleitung und Kommentar von H. G. Gadamer. Frankfurt a.M.: Vittorio Klostermann Verlag, 1968. (Quellen der Philosophie. Bd. 7).

7228. CELAN, PAUL. CELAN, PAUL: *Ausgewählte Gedichte. Zwei Reden.* Nachwort von Beda Allemann. Frankfurt a. M.: Suhrkamp Verlag, 1968. 170 pp., bibl. P. C. pp. 167-170 (edition suhrkamp).

7229. NEUMANN, PETER HORST: *Wortnacht und Augennacht.* Zu einem Gedicht Paul Celans. [In]: 'Neue Rundschau'. 79. Jg., H. 1. Frankfurt a. M.: S. Fischer, 1968. Pp. 88-99.

7230. CHAGALL, MARC. *The Jerusalem Windows of Marc Chagall.* Text and Notes by Jean Leymarie. Transl. from the French by Elaine Desautels. New York: George Braziller, London: Michael Joseph, 1968. 111 pp. + 84 illus.

7231. DÖBLIN, ALFRED. DÖBLIN, ALFRED: *Reise in Polen.* In Verbindung mit den Söhnen des Dichters hrsg. von Walter Muschg. Weitergeführt und mit einem Nachwort versehen von Heinz Graber. Olten und Freiburg i. Br.: Walter Verlag, 1968. 376 pp. (12. Bd. der 'Ausgewählten Werke'). [Döblin visited Poland in 1924. This work was first publ. by S. Fischer, Berlin, 1925.]

7232. DÖBLIN, ALFRED: *Die Vertreibung der Gespenster.* Autobiographische Schriften, Betrachtungen zur Zeit, Aufsätze zu Kunst und Literatur. Hrsg. und mit einem Nachwort versehen von Manfred Beyer. Mit Fotos, Zeichnungen, Dokumenten. Berlin [East]: Rütten & Loening, 1968. 450 pp., ports., illus., facsim.

7233. GRASS, GÜNTER: *Über meinen Lehrer Döblin und andere Vorträge.* Olten-Freiburg i. Br.: Walter Verlag, 1968. 77 pp.

7234. PEITZ, WOLFGANG, comp.: *Alfred-Döblin-Bibliographie 1905-1966.* Freiburg i. Br.: Eckhard Becksmann Verlag, 1968. 99 pp. (Materialien zur deutschen Literatur. Bd. 1).

7235. EHRENSTEIN, ALBERT. EHRENSTEIN, ALBERT: *Gedichte und Prosa.* Hrsg. und eingeleitet von Karl Otten. Neuwied: Luchterhand Verlag, 1968. 512 pp., bibl. A. E. pp. 502-506. [The literary estate of this writer and poet (1886-1950) is in the Hebrew University Jerusalem.]

7236. EINSTEIN, ALBERT. MICHELMORE, PETER: *Albert Einstein - Genie des Jahrhunderts.* Hannover: Fackelträger Verlag, 1968. 220 pp.

7237. *Relativitätstheorie und Weltanschauung.* Zur philosophischen und wissenschaftlichen Wirkung Albert Einsteins. Berlin [East]: Deutscher Verlag der Wissenschaft, 1967. 291 pp.

7238. EISLER, HANNS. NOTOWICZ, NATHAN und JÜRGEN ELSNER: *Hanns Eisler.* Quellennachweise. Hrsg. im Auftrag des Hanns-Eisler-Archivs bei der Deutschen Akademie der Künste zu Berlin [East]. Leipzig: Deutscher Verlag für Musik, 1966. 174 pp. [Cf. No. 4650/YB.X.]

7239. FEDER, ERNST, PAUCKER, ARNOLD: *Searchlight on the Decline of the Weimar Republic. The Diaries of Ernst Feder.* [In]: LBI Year Book XIII. London, 1968. Pp. 161-234, ports. [Ernst Feder (1881-1964), political journalist and editor.]

7240. FEUCHTWANGER, LION. LEUPOLD, HANS: *Lion Feuchtwanger.* Leipzig: Bibliographisches Institut, 1967. 88 pp.

7241. FREUD, SIGMUND. ANDREAS-SALOME, LOU: *Lebensrückblick.* Grundriss einiger Lebenserinnerungen. Aus dem Nachlass hrsg., mit Erläuterungen und einem Nachwort versehen von Ernst Pfeiffer. Frankfurt a. M.: Insel Verlag, 1968. 334 pp., ports., illus. [A friend and follower of Freud. Cf. also No. 6088/YB. XII.]

7242. *Freud and Anthropology.* [In]: 'The Times Literary Supplement'. March 21. London, 1968.

7243. GOMBRICH, E. H.: *Freuds Ästhetik.* [In]: 'Literatur und Kritik'. Österr. Monatsschrift. H. 19, Nov. Wien, 1967. Pp. 511-528. [French version in]: 'Preuves'. No. 217. Paris, 1968. Pp. 24-35. [For English version see No. 5901/YB. XII.]

7244. GRINSTEIN, ALEXANDER: *On Sigmund Freud's Dreams.* Detroit, Mich.: Wayne State University Press, 1968. 484 pp.

7245. MACINTYRE, ALASDAIR C[HALMERS]: *Das Unbewusste.* Eine Begriffsanalyse. Mit einem Abriss 'Freuds Theorie' von Richard Stanley Peters als Einleitung. Aus dem Engl. übersetzt von Gudrun Sauter. Frankfurt a. M.: Suhrkamp Verlag, 1968. 139 pp. (Theorie. Reihe 2). [Engl. title: The Unconscious.]

7246. MURARKA, DEV: *Freud makes a comeback in Russia.* [In]: 'The Observer'. 23 June, London, 1968.

7247. PLÉ, ALBERT: *Freud et la Religion.* Paris: Editions du Cerf, 1968. 144 pp.

7248. ROBERT, MARTHE: *Die Revolution der Psychoanalyse.* Leben und Werk von Sigmund Freud. Frankfurt a. M.: Fischer Bücherei, 1967. 364 pp. [For Engl. ed. see No. 5905/YB. XII.]

7249. SAJNER, J.: *Sigmund Freuds Beziehungen zu seinem Geburtsort Freiberg (Příbor) und zu Mähren.* [In]: 'Clio Medica'. 3, 2 May. Oxford, 1968.

7250. SCHARFENBERG, JOACHIM: *Sigmund Freud und seine Religionskritik als Herausforderung für den christlichen Glauben.* Göttingen: Vandenhoeck und Ruprecht, 1968. 221 pp. (Habil.-Schrift Tübingen).

7251. SCHÖNAU, WALTER: *Sigmund Freuds Prosa. Literarische Elemente seines Stils.* Stuttgart: Metzlersche Verlagsbuchhandlung, 1968. vii, 296 pp., bibl. (pp. 276-290). (Germanistische Abhandlungen. 25).

7252. VESZY-WAGNER, LILLA, comp.: *Gesamtregister der Bände I-XVII* (der Gesammelten Werke in Einzelbänden, chronologisch geordnet). Band XVIII. Frankfurt a. M.: S. Fischer Verlag, 1968. xxxv, 1098 pp.

7253. WOLMAN, BENJAMIN B.: *The Unconscious Mind: The Meaning of Freudian Psychology.* Englewood Cliffs, N.J.: Prentice-Hall, 1968 (Spectrum Books).

7254. FREUND, LEOPOLD. FREUND-EIBUSCHÜTZ, HEDY: *Erinnerung an den Begründer der Röntgentherapie.* Prof. Dr. Leopold Freund zum 100. Geburtstag. [In]: 'Aufbau'. 5. Apr. New York, 1968. [1868-1943].

7255. FREUNDLICH, OTTO. SPIES, WERNER: *Otto Freundlich in Paris.* Eine vielbeachtete Ausstellung des Malers und Bildhauers. [In]: 'Frankfurter Allgemeine Zeitung'. 20. Febr. 1968, illus. [1878-1943 Maidanek].

7256. FRIEDLAENDER, MAX J. LUZZATO, G. L.: *La Personalità di Max Friedlaender e il suo Ebraismo.* [In]: 'La Rassegna Mensile Di Israel'. Gia diretta da Dante Lattes. Vol. XXXIV, N. 2 (Terza Serie), Febr. Milano, 1968. Pp. 111-114, ports. [Art historian (1867-1958)].

7257. FROMM, ERICH. FROMM, ERICH: *Das Menschliche in uns.* Konstanz: Diana Verlag, 1968. 199 pp.

7258. GOLL, YVAN. GOLL, YVAN: *Gedichte. Eine Auswahl.* Mit 14 Gedichten von Claire Goll. Hrsg. und mit einem Kommentar versehen von René A. Strasser. Meilen: Magica Verlag, 1968. 438 pp. [Yvan Goll, orig. Lang, 1891-1950.]

7259. GRABOWSKY, ADOLF. THIERBACH, HANS, ed.: *Adolf Grabowsky. Leben und Werk.* Festschrift zum 80. Geburtstag dem Altmeister der politischen Wissenschaften gewidmet. Köln, Berlin: Carl Heymanns Verlag, 1968. [1880-1969. Founder and co-editor of 'Zeitschrift für Politik'.]

7260. HAASE, HUGO. CALKINS, KENNETH R.: *The Election of Hugo Haase to the Co-Chairmanship of the SPD and the Crisis of the pre-war German Social Democracy.* [In]: 'International Review of Social History'. No. XIII/2. Assen/Amsterdam: Internationaal Instituut voor Sociale Geschiedenis, 1968. [1863-1919].

7261. HAHN, KURT. SCHWARZ, KARL: *Die Kurzschulen Kurt Hahns.* Ihre pädagogische Theorie und Praxis. Ratingen bei Düsseldorf: Henn Verlag, 1968. 287 pp., illus., bibl. (pp. 234-280). [Kurt Hahn with the Prince of Baden founded the 'Landerziehungsheim Salem' after the First World War.]

7262. HARDEN, MAXIMILIAN. WELLER, B. UWE: *Karl Kraus und Maximilian Harden.* [In]: 'Publizistik'. Bd. XIII, H. 1, Jan.-März. Konstanz/Bremen: B. C. Heye, 1968. Pp. 44-53.

7263. HASENCLEVER, WALTER. RAGGAM-LINDQVIST, HELGA MIRIAM: *Das Leid als menschliche Grunderfahrung im Leben und Werk Walter Hasenclevers.* Wien: Phil. Diss., 1968. vii, 264 pp., pp. 265-434 + vl pp. bibl. [2 vols., typescript].

7264. HEIMANN, MORITZ. ROHNER, LUDWIG: *Moritz Heimann.* Essay. [In]: 'Neue Zürcher Zeitung'. Nr. 43, 21. Jan., Zürich, 1968 [Also]: *Moritz Heimann. Centenary of his Birth* (Fritz Friedlaender). [In]: 'AJR Information'. No. XXIII/7, July, London, 1968.

7265. HEINE, HEINRICH. *Heinrich Heine: Sämtliche Schriften.* Dünndruckausgabe in 6 Bänden. Hrsg. Klaus Briegleb. Bd. 1: Buch der Lieder und andere frühe Schriften. München: Karl Hanser Verlag, 1968. 884 pp. (Hanser Klassiker).

7266. *Heinrich Heines Werke.* Hrsg. und eingeleitet von Hermann Rudolf Leber. Bearbeitet und für die Gegenwart gedeutet. Klagenfurt: Kaiser Verlag, 1968. 1184 pp.

7267. *Heinrich Heine in 4 Bänden.* Hrsg.: Christoph Siegrist, Wolfgang Preisendanz, Eberhard Galley, Helmut Schanze. Essays der Herausgeber, Einleitung von Hans Mayer. Frankfurt a. M.: Insel Verlag, 1968. 2850 pp. (Insel-Bibliothek Deutscher Klassiker). (Bd. I: Gedichte. Bd. II: Reisebilder. Bd III: Schriften über Frankreich. Bd. IV: Schriften über Deutschland.)

7268. BRANSCOMBE, PETER: *Heine: Selected Poems.* Transl. and ed. by Peter Branscombe. London: Penguin Books, 1968. 263 pp. [In German with English translation.]

7269. *Heine-Jahrbuch 1969.* Hrsg. vom Heine-Archiv. Schriftleitung: Eberhard Galley. 8. Jg. Hamburg: Hoffmann und Campe, 1968. 132 pp., port., illus.

7270. KURZ, PAUL KONRAD: *Künstler, Tribun, Apostel - Heinrich Heines Auffassung vom Beruf des Dichters.* München: Wilhelm Fink, 1967. 249 pp. [Author is a Jesuit and teaches at the University of Munich.] (Diss. München, 1964).

7271. OWEN, CLAUDE R.: *Heine im spanischen Sprachgebiet.* Eine kritische Bibliographie. Münster/Westf.: Aschendorff, 1968. L, 336 pp. (Spanische Forschungen der Görres-Gesellschaft. Reihe 2. Bd. 12).

7272. SANDOR, A. I.: *The Exile of Gods.* Interpretation of a theme, a theory and a technique in the work of Heinrich Heine. The Hague: Mouton, 1967. 192 pp. (Anglica Germanica. British Studies in Germanic Languages and Literature, 9).

7273. SEIFERT, SIEGFRIED, comp.: *Heine-Bibliographie 1954-1964.* [And]: *Ergänzungen oder Berichtigungen der Heinrich-Heine-Bibliographie von 1817-1953.* Berlin [East] und Weimar: Aufbau Verlag, 1968. xiii, 395 pp. [2640 entries. For Heine-Bibliographie von 1817-1953, comp. by Gottfried Wilhelm and Eberhard Galley see No. 4687/YB. X.]

7274. WINDFUHR, MANFRED: *Heinrich Heine - Revolution und Reflexion.* Stuttgart: J. B. Metzler, 1968. x, 300 pp.

7275. HEINE, SALOMON. KRAMER, GERHARD FRIEDRICH and ERICH LÜTH: *Salomon Heine in seiner Zeit.* Gedenkreden zu seinem 200. Geburtstag. Hamburg: Hans Christian Verlag, 1968. 22 pp., front. port. (Vorträge und Aufsätze. Hrsg. vom Verein für Hamburgische Geschichte H. 16). [Banker, philanthropist, 1767-1844.]

7276. HEINE, THOMAS THEODOR. LANG, LOTHAR, ed.: *Thomas Theodor Heine.* Berlin [East]: Eulenspiegel-Verlag, 1968. 156 pp., illus. pp. 1-100. (Klassiker der Karikatur. Bd.1).

7277. HERSCHEL, SIR JOHN. LOCKE, RICHARD ADAMS: *Sir John Herschel's merkwürdige astronomische Entdeckungen am Kap der Guten Hoffnung, den Mond und seine Bewohner betreffend.* Aus dem Englischen nach der deutschen Ausgabe von 1836. Fürth/Saarland: Bleymehl, 1965. 173 pp. (Sammlung Antares. Bd. 12). [An account of the great astronomical discoveries made by Sir John Herschel (1792-1871), at the Cape.]

7278. (CARL) HEYMANNS VERLAG. *Zur Geschichte von Carl Heymanns Verlag.* [In]: Von Manuskripten und Büchern. Ein kleines Brevier für Autoren, Buchhändler und verständige Leser. Köln: Carl Heymanns Verlag, 1967. 128 pp. (18 pp.).

7279. HILDESHEIMER, WOLFGANG. HILDESHEIMER, WOLFGANG: *Begegnung im Balkanexpress. An den Ufern der Plotinitza.* Zwei Hörspiele. Mit einem autobiographischen Nachwort. Stuttgart: Reclam, 1968. 71 pp. (Reclams Universalbibliothek Nr. 8529).

7280. HILFERDING, RUDOLF. HILFERDING, RUDOLF: *Das Finanzkapital.* Eingeleitet von Eduard März. Frankfurt a. M.: Europäische Verlagsanstalt, 1968. 480 pp. [Member of the Reichstag, Minister of Finance. 1877-1941, died in a Nazi prison.]

7281. HIRSCH, AUGUST. HIRSCH, AUGUST: *Über die historische Entwicklung der öffentlichen Gesundheitspflege.* Rede, gehalten zur Feier des Stiftungstages der militärärztlichen Bildungsanstalten am 2. August 1889. (Unveränderter Nachdruck). Bad Reichenhall: Kleinert, 1967. 46 pp. [Medical historian (1817-1894), founder of the 'Deutsche Gesellschaft für öffentliche Gesundheitspflege, 1872.]

7282. HIRSCH, ERNST E. *Berliner Festschrift für Ernst E. Hirsch.* Dargebracht von Mitgliedern der Juristischen Fakultät zum 65. Geburtstag. Berlin: Duncker und Humblot, 1968. viii, 265 pp., front. port. [During his exile advisor to the Turkish Government on legal questions. Now professor at the FU Berlin.]

7283. HIRSCH, SIEGMUND. OTTO JUNKER GMBH, ed.: *Siegmund Hirsch: Revolution im Messing, 1908-1928.* Lammersdorf, 1967. 194 pp. [Aron Hirsch of Halberstadt and his descendants were the founders of the 'Hirsch-Kupfer-Messingwerke' which played an important rôle in the German metal trade.]

7284. HODDIS, JAKOB VAN (i.e. Hans Davidsohn). RICHTER, FRITZ: *Jakob van Hoddis und sein 'Weltende'.* [In]: Jahrbuch der Schlesischen Friedrich-Wilhelms-Universität zu Breslau. Bd. XIII. Würzburg: Holzner Verlag, 1968. Pp. 313-321. [1887-1942, expressionist].

7285. HÖNIGSWALD, RICHARD. HÖNIGSWALD, RICHARD: *Philosophie und Kultur.* Schriften aus dem Nachlass, Bd. 6. Hrsg. von Günter Schaper und Gerd Wolandt. Bonn: H. Bouvier, 1967. 317 pp. [Philosopher, 1875-1947.]

7286. ORTH, ERNST WOLFGANG: *Bedeutung, Sinn, Gegenstand.* Studien zur Sprachphilosophie Edmund Husserls und Richard Hönigswalds. Bonn: H. Bouvier, 1967. 215 pp.

7287. HOFMANNSTHAL, HUGO VON. BAUER, SYBILLE, ed.: *Hugo v. Hofmannsthal.* Darmstadt: Wissenschaftliche Buchgesellschaft, 1968. x, 464 pp. (Wege der Forschung. Bd. 183).

7288. GOLDSCHMIT, RUDOLF: *Hugo von Hofmannsthal.* Velber b. Hannover: Friedrich Verlag, 1968. 100 pp., ports., illus. (Friedrichs Dramatiker des Welttheaters. Bd. 43).

7289. HOPPE, MANFRED: *Literatentum, Magie und Mystik im Frühwerk Hugo von Hofmannsthals.* Berlin: De Gruyter, 1968. 140 pp., bibl. (pp. 130-135). (Quellen und Forschungen zur Sprach- und Kulturgeschichte der germanischen Völker, N.F. 28 (152).

7290. NÜCHTERN, EVA-MARIA: *Hofmannsthals Alkestis.* Bad Homburg v. d. Höhe: Gehlen Verlag, 1968. 60 pp. (Frankfurter Beiträge zur Germanistik. Bd. 6).

7291. PICKERODT, GERHART: *Hofmannsthals Dramen.* Kritik ihres historischen Gehalts. Stuttgart: Metzler Verlag, 1968. 283 pp., bibl. (pp. 269-271). (Studien zur allgemeinen und vergleichenden Literaturwissenschaft. Bd. 3).

7292. RÖSCH, EWALD: *Komödien Hofmannsthals.* Die Entfaltung ihrer Sinnstruktur aus dem Thema der Daseinsstufen. 2. erw. Aufl. Marburg: Elwert Verlag, 1968. 269 pp., bibl. (pp. 261-269). (Marburger Beiträge zur Germanistik. Bd. I).

7293. SCHMID, MARTIN ERICH: *Symbol und Funktion der Musik im Werk Hugo von Hofmannsthals.* Heidelberg: Universitätsverlag Carl Winter, 1968. 179 pp.

7294. WITTMANN, LOTHAR: *Sprachthematik und dramatische Form im Werke Hofmannsthals.* Stuttgart: W. Kohlhammer Verlag, 1968. (Studien zur Poetik und Geschichte der Literatur. Bd. 2).

7295. HORKHEIMER, MAX. HORKHEIMER, MAX: *Kritische Theorie.* Gesammelte Schriften und Aufsätze. Eine Dokumentation. Hrsg. von Alfred Schmidt. Frankfurt a. M.: S. Fischer Verlag, 1968. xiv, 376 pp., xi, 358 pp. [2 vols.]

7296. GOLDSCHMIDT, HERMANN LEVIN: *Zur Kritik der instrumentellen Vernunft.* Zu einer Sammlung von Aufsätzen und Vorträgen Max Horkheimers. [In]: 'Neue Zürcher Zeitung'. 26. Mai, Zürich, 1968. [Cf. also No. 6600/YB. XIII.]

7297. JACOB, BERTHOLD. ARNAU, FRANK: *Menschenraub.* Alexander P. Kutjepow, Berthold Jacob, Jésus de Galindez, Ben Bella, Adolf Eichmann, Antoine Argoud, Ben Barka, Moise Tschombé, Isang Yun. München: Kurt Desch Verlag, 1968. 232 pp. [The journalist Berthold Jacob (1898-1944), was abducted from Switzerland to Germany in 1935, and from Portugal in 1941. He died in a Gestapo prison.]

7298. JACOBOWSKI, LUDWIG. JEZIORKOWSKI, KLAUS: *Jacobowskis Nachlass.* Eine Ausstellung in Wiesbaden. [In]: 'Frankfurter Allgemeine Zeitung'. 24. Apr., Frankfurt a. M., 1968. [The literary estate of the poet and writer (1868-1900) was found by Mr. Fred Benno Stern and was transferred to the Hessische Landesbibliothek in Wiesbaden. Cf. No. 5933/YB. XII. See also 'MB', 5. Juli, Tel Aviv, 1968.]

7299. *Gedenken an Ludwig Jacobowski.* [In]: 'Inter Nationes', Deutsche Kulturnachrichten. 11. Jg., H. 4, Apr. Bad Godesberg, 1968.

7300. KAFKA, FRANZ. ALBÉRÈS, R. M. and PIERRE DE BOISDEFFRE: *Kafka: The Torment of Man.* Transl. by Wade Baskin. London: Vision Press, 1968. 103 pp.

7301. BINDER, HARTMUT: *Kafka und seine Schwester Ottla.* Zur Biographie der Familiensituation des Dichters unter besonderer Berücksichtigung der Erzählungen 'Die Verwandlung' und 'Der Bau'. [In]: Jahrbuch der Deutschen Schillergesellschaft. Bd. XII. Stuttgart: Alfred Kröner Verlag, 1968. Pp. 403-456.

7302. CANETTI, ELIAS: *Der andere Prozess*. Kafkas Briefe an Felice. Teil 1 und 2. [In]: 'Neue Rundschau'. 79. Jg., H. 2 und 4. Frankfurt a. M.: S. Fischer Verlag, 1968. Pp. 185-220, 586-623.

7303. CARROUGES, MICHAEL: *Kafka versus Kafka*. Tuscaloosa: University of Alabama, 1968. 144 pp. [A graphological analysis of Kafka's handwriting and his relationship to Judaism and Zionism.]

7304. EMRICH, WILHELM: *Franz Kafka*. Transl. from the German by S. Z. Buehne. New York: Ungar, 1968. 561 pp., bibl. [Publ. in German in 1958. See No. 1496/YB. IV.]

7305. GREENBERG, MARTIN: *The Terror of Art: Kafka and Modern Literature*. New York: Basic Books, 1968. 241 pp. [Kafka's influence on modern European and American writing.]

7306. HODIN, JOSEF PAUL: *Kafka und Goethe*. Zur Problematik unseres Zeitalters. Hamburg: Odysseus Verlag, 1968. 99 pp., illus.

7307. HÖCK, WILHELM: *Franz Kafka*. [In]: *'Der junge Buchhandel'*, Beilage zum Börsenblatt für den Deutschen Buchhandel. Nr. 1. 2. Jan. Frankfurt a. M., 1968. Pp. 1-7. (Tagebücher der Literaturgeschichte. Eine Aufsatzreihe).

7308. *Infelice - Franz Kafka's Courtship*. [In]: 'The Times Literary Supplement'. July 4. London, 1968. Pp. 1-2, port.

7309. JANOUCH, GUSTAV: *Gespräche mit Kafka*. Aufzeichnungen und Erinnerungen. Erweiterte Ausgabe. Frankfurt a. M.: S. Fischer Verlag, 1968. 268 pp. [First publ. 1951. See No. 608/YB. I.]

7310. JONAS, KLAUS W.: *Die Hochschulschriften über Franz Kafka und sein Werk*. [In]: 'Philobiblon'. Eine Vierteljahrsschrift für Buch- und Graphiksammler. Jg. XII, H. 3. Hamburg: Ernst Hauswedell Verlag, 1968. Pp. 194-203.

7311. KRAFT, WERNER: *Franz Kafka*. Durchdringung und Geheimnis. Frankfurt a. M.: Suhrkamp Verlag, 1968. 215 pp. (Bibliothek Suhrkamp Bd. 211).

7312. LOOSE, GERHARD: *Kafka und Amerika*. Frankfurt a. M.: Vittorio Klostermann Verlag, 1968. 92 pp., bibl. [On Kafka's novel 'Der Verschollene'.]

7313. MISSAC, P.: *Walter Benjamin et Franz Kafka*. [And]: W. Benjamin: *Lettre à Gershom Scholem*. ('... ce que je pense du 'Kafka' de Brod'). [In]: 'Les Nouveaux Cahiers'. No. 15. Autumn. Paris, 1968. Pp. 47-56.

7314. OSBORNE, CHARLES: *Kafka*. Edinburgh: Oliver and Boyd, 1967. iv, 120 pp., bibl. (pp. 119-120). (Writers and Critics).

7315. PASLEY, MALCOLM: *Rilke und Kafka*. *Zur Frage ihrer Beziehungen*. [In]: 'Literatur und Kritik'. Österr. Monatsschrift. H. 24. Mai. Wien, 1968. Pp. 218-225.

7316. POLITZER, HEINZ: *Franz Kafka, der Künstler*. Frankfurt a. M.: S. Fischer, 1968. 536 pp., bibl. (pp. 512-525). (Broschierte Studienausgabe). [First German ed. 1965. See No. 5348/YB. XI.] [Cf. Johannes Urzidil: Sisyphos war ein Junggeselle. Zu Heinz Politzers Kafka-Buch. [In]: 'Merkur'. 22. Jg., H. 5 (241), Mai. Stuttgart: Ernst Klett Verlag, 1968. Pp. 461-465.]

7317. ROBERT, MARTHE: *Das Alte im Neuen. Von Don Quichotte zu Franz Kafka*. Aus dem Franz. übersetzt von Karl August Horst. München: Carl Hanser Verlag, 1968. 320 pp. (Reihe: Literatur als Kunst). [For French ed. see No. 4101/YB. IX.]

7318. TORBERG, FRIEDRICH: *Der Mann, der nie über Kafka schrieb*. Eine Erzählung. [In]: 'Der Monat'. 20. Jg., H. 237, Juni. Berlin, 1968. Pp. 33-44.

7319. URZIDIL, JOHANNES: *There Goes Kafka*. Transl. into English from the expanded edition of 'Da geht Kafka'. Detroit, Mich.: Wayne State University Press, 1968. 232 pp. [German ed. see No. 5959/YB. XII.]

7320. WEBER, ALBRECHT, CARSTEN SCHLINGMANN u. GERT KLEINSCHMIDT: *Interpretationen zu Franz Kafka*. Das Urteil, Die Verwandlung, Ein Landarzt, Kleine Prosastücke. München: Oldenbourg Verlag, 1968. 140 pp., bibl. (Interpretationen zum Deutschunterricht).

7321. WELTSCH, FELIX: *Franz Kafka: Datiut v'Humour b'Hayav*. Jerusalem: The Bialik Institute, The National Publishing House, 1968. 128 pp. [German ed.: Religion und Humor im Werk Franz Kafkas. Berlin: Herbig, 1957. See No. 1216/YB. III.]

7322. KARMÁN, THEODORE VON. KARMÁN, THEODORE VON: *Die Wirbelstrasse*. Mein Leben für die Luftfahrt. Hamburg: Hoffmann und Campe Verlag, 1968. 434 pp., ports., illus. [Theodore von Karmán (1881-1963), physicist and mathematician, was the son of the philosopher Moritz Kleinmann (1843-1915), professor at Budapest University.]

7323. KAUFMANN, FRITZ. KAUFMANN, FRITZ: *Das Reich des Schönen*. Bausteine zu einer Philosophie der Kunst. Nachwort von Hans-Georg Gadamer. Stuttgart: W. Kohlhammer Verlag, 1960. 405 pp., front. port., bibl. F.K. pp. 394-396. [Art philosopher, 1891-1958.]

7324. KELSEN, HANS. METALL, RUDOLF ALADÁR: *Hans Kelsen*. Leben und Werk. Autorisierte Biographie Wien: Verlag Franz Deuticke, 1968. viii, 220 pp., front. port., bibl. (pp. 163-216). [Prof. Kelsen is the author of the Austrian Republican Constitution.]

7325. KISCH, EGON ERWIN. EINSTEIN, SIEGFRIED: *Ein Magier mit melancholischen Augen*. Zur Erinnerung an Egon Erwin Kisch (1885-1948). [In]: 'Israelitisches Wochenblatt'. 68. Jg., Nr. 13, 29. März. Zürich, 1968. [And]: *Der rasende Reporter aus Prag*. [In]: 'Aufbau'. 5. Apr. New York, 1968.

7326. POLACEK, JOSEF: *Egon Erwin Kisch 1914-1930*. Bausteine einer Biographie. [In]: 'Philologica Pragensia'. Nr. X/3. Praha, 1967. Pp. 129-146.

7327. KOESTLER, ARTHUR. KOESTLER, ARTHUR: *Analyse d'un Miracle*. Naissance d'Israel. Traduit par Dominique Aury. Paris: Calmann-Lévy, 1967. 326 pp., map. [Orig. title: Promise and Fulfilment. Publ. 1949. Autobiographical.]

7328. KOESTLER, ARTHUR: *Drinkers of Infinity*. Essays 1955-1967. London: Hutchinson, 1968. 291 pp.

7329. KOESTLER, ARTHUR: *Das Gespenst in der Maschine*. Aus dem Englischen übertragen von Wolfram Wagmuth. Wien: Fritz Molden Verlag, 1968. 399 pp., bibl. (pp. 384-391). [Engl. title: The Ghost in the Machine.]

7330. KOESTLER, ARTHUR: *Der göttliche Funke*. Der schöpferische Akt in Kunst und Wissenschaft. Übertragung aus dem Englischen von Agnes von Cranach und Willy Thaler. Bern: Scherz Verlag, 1968. 532 pp., bibl. (pp. 521-525). (Das moderne Sachbuch). [Engl. original: The Act of Creation.]

7331. KOESTLER, ARTHUR: *What's Wrong With Us?* [The article is based on the speech he made in Copenhagen when accepting the Sonning Prize, awarded for contributions to European culture.] [In]: 'The Observer Review'. 28 April. London, 1968, port.

7332. CALDER, JENNI: *Chronicle and Conscience: A Study of George Orwell and Arthur Koestler*. London: Secker & Warburg, 1968. 303 pp.

7333. KOLMAR, GERTRUD. [Gertrud Chodziesner]. KOLMAR, GERTRUD: *Die Kerze von Arras*. Ausgewählte Gedichte. Auswahl und Nachwort: Uwe Berger. Berlin [East]: Aufbau Verlag, 1968. 130 pp. [1894-1943].

7334. KRAFT, WERNER: *Zeit aus den Fugen*. Aufzeichnungen. Frankfurt a. M.: S. Fischer Verlag, 1968. 244 pp.

7335. KRAUS KARL. KRAUS, KARL, ed.: *Die Fackel*. Neuausgabe von Heinrich Fischer. 922 Nummern in 37 Jahrgängen. Bd. 1-4, Jg. I und II, Nr. 1-72; Bd. 5-8, Jg. III und IV, Nr. 73-134. München: Kösel Verlag, 1968. (Literarische Zeitschriften in Neudrucken).

7336. KRAUS, KARL: *Nachts*. Aphorismen. München: Dtsch. Taschenbuch-Verlag, 1968. 120 pp. (dtv. Nr. 493).

7337. KRAUS, KARL: *Weltgericht*. Hrsg. von Heinrich Fischer. Frankfurt a. M. und Hamburg: Fischer-Bücherei, 1968. 236 pp. (Fischer-Bücherei, Nr. 895).

7338. HAAGE, PETER: *Streber unterm Vorwand es zu sein*. Die Kontroverse zwischen Karl Kraus und Egon Friedell. [In]: 'Stuttgarter Zeitung'. Nr. 201, 31. Aug. Stuttgart, 1968, illus.

7339. HARTL, EDWIN: *Karl Kraus im Spiegel der Literaturgeschichte oder Literaturgeschichte im Spiegel von Karl Kraus?* [In]: Österreich in Geschichte und Literatur. H. 4. Wien, 1968.

7340. KOHN, CAROLINE: *Karl Kraus als Lyriker*. Paris: Verlag Marcel Didier, 1968. vi, 183 pp., facsims. (Germanica. Collection publ. sous la dir. de Maurice Coleville. No. 11).

7341. KRAFT, WERNER: *Es war einmal ein Mann* ... Über die 'Dritte Walpurgisnacht von Karl Kraus'. [In]: 'Merkur'. H. 10 (246), Okt. Stuttgart: Ernst Klett Verlag, 1968. Pp. 926-935. [Also]: Hilde Spiel/Fritz J. Raddatz: *Wer verteidigt nun Karl Kraus?* Ein Offener Brief und eine Antwort. Pp. 965-967.

7342. RADDATZ, FRITZ J.: *Der blinde Seher*. Überlegungen zu Karl Kraus. [In]: 'Merkur', Deutsche Zeitschrift für europäisches Denken. XXII. Jg., H. 6 (242), Juni. Stuttgart: Ernst Klett Verlag, 1968. Pp. 517-532. [Cf. *Der blinde Leser*. Überlegungen zum Karl Kraus-Unverständnis des Fritz J. Raddatz und Genossen (Josef Konrads). [In]:

'Werkhefte'. Zeitschrift für Probleme der Gesellschaft und des Katholizismus. 22. Jg. Nr. 12, Dez. München, 1968.]

7343. WEIGEL, HANS: *Karl Kraus oder Die Macht der Ohnmacht*. Versuch eines Motivenberichts zur Erhellung eines vielfachen Lebenswerks. Wien: Fritz Molden Verlag, 1968. 342 pp., ports., illus., facsims. (Glanz und Elend der Meister). [Cf. Curt Hohoff: 'Glanz und Elend des Karl Kraus'. [In]: 'Merkur'. 22. Jg., H. 6 (242). Juni. Stuttgart: Ernst Klett Verlag, 1968. Pp. 563-566. [And]: Manfred Müller: Stichwörter aus der Kulisse. [In]: 'Frankfurter Rundschau', 7. Sept. 1968.]

—— WELLER, B. UWE: *Karl Kraus und Maximilian Harden*. [See No. 7262.]

7344. KRONSTEIN, HEINRICH. BIEDENKOPF, KURT HANS [and others], ed.: *Das Unternehmen in der Rechtsordnung*. Festgabe für Heinrich Kronstein aus Anlass seines 70. Geburtstages am 12. September 1967. Karlsruhe: C. F. Müller, 1967. 392 pp., front. port., bibl. H.K. pp. 387-392.

7345. LANDAU, EDMUND. TURAN. P., ed.: *Abhandlungen aus Zahlentheorie und Analysis*. Zur Erinnerung an Edmund Landau (1877-1938). Berlin [East]: Deutscher Verlag der Wissenschaften, 1968. 350 pp., port. [Mathematician, co-founder of the Hebrew University Jerusalem.]

7346. LANDAUER, GUSTAV. LANDAUER, GUSTAV: *Zwang und Befreiung*. Eine Auswahl aus seinem Werk. Eingeleitet und hrsg. von Heinz-Joachim Heydorn. Köln: Jakob Hegner Verlag, 1968. 274 pp., bibl. (pp. 272-274). (Hegner-Bücherei). [Incl. essays on Martin Buber (written 1913) and Walter Calé (1881-1904), written 1907.]

7347. KALZ, WOLF: *Gustav Landauer*. Kultursozialist und Anarchist. Meisenheim am Glan: Verlag Anton Hain, 1967. 161 pp., bibl. G.L. pp. 146-152, bibl. (pp. 152-161). (Schriften zur politischen Wissenschaft. Bd. 6). [Correction to No. 6645/YB. XIII.]

7348. LANDSTEINER, KARL. BATO, YOMTOV LUDWIG: *Die Tragik der Assimilation*. [In]: 'Das Neue Israel'. 21. Jg., H. 4, Okt. Zürich, 1968. Pp. 275-276, illus. [Karl Landsteiner (1868-1943), bacteriologist, emigrated to the USA during the First World War. He lost a claim for damages against the editors of the Encyclopaedia 'Who's Who in American Jewry', publ. 1937, because he had always tried to hide the fact that he was a Jew.]

7349. LASKER-SCHÜLER, ELSE. LASKER-SCHÜLER, ELSE: *Hebräische Balladen*. Mit 4 in Farben gedruckten Kupferstichen von Otto Rohse. Hamburg: Otto Rohse Presse, 1968. 28 pp. [This edition has won a prize as one of the most beautiful German books in 1968.]

7350. LASKER-SCHÜLER, ELSE: *Leise sagen*. Ausgewählt und mit einem biographischen Nachwort versehen von Karl-Heinz Sühnhold. Berlin [East]: Aufbau Verlag, 1968. 140 pp.

7351. HERZFELDE, WIELAND: *Else Lasker-Schüler - Dichtung und Wirklichkeit*. [Report on a lecture delivered by a board member of the East German PEN to the German PEN Centre at the 'studio dumont' in Cologne, Oct. [In]: "Frankfurter Allgemeine Zeitung'. 16. Okt. 1968.]

7352. KUPPER, MARGARETE: *Der Nachlass Else Lasker-Schülers in Jerusalem*. Ein Bericht. [In]: Literaturwissenschaftliches Jahrbuch. N.F. Nr. 9. München, 1968. Pp. 243-283.

7353. LASSALLE, FERDINAND. GROTE, HEINER: *Sozialdemokratie und Religion*. Eine Dokumentation für die Jahre 1863 bis 1875. Tübingen: J. C. B. Mohr (Paul Siebeck), 1968. xi, 253 pp., bibl. [Chap. II: Der Lassallekult.]

7354. HIRSCH, HELMUT: *Ferdinand Lassalle*. Eine Auswahl für unsere Zeit. Frankfurt a. M.: Büchergilde Gutenberg, 1968.

7355. NA'AMAN, SHLOMO: *Ferdinand Lassalle*. Deutscher und Jude. Eine sozialgeschichtliche Studie. Hrsg. von der Niedersächsischen Landeszentrale für Politische Bildung, Hannover, 1968. 151 pp., bibl. (pp. 106-107). (Schriftenreihe der Niedersächsischen Landeszentrale für Politische Bildung. Deutsch-jüdisches Gespräch).

7356. LAUTERPACHT, HERSCH. FEINBERG, N.: *Hersch Lauterpacht, Jurist and Thinker*. [In]: 'Israel Law Review'. 3, 3. July. Jerusalem, 1968. Pp. 333-344. [Sir Hersch Lauterpacht (1897-1938), Prof. of International Law at Cambridge University and judge at the International Court at The Hague.]

7357. LESSER, ERNST JOSEF. AMMON, ROBERT: *Ernst Josef Lesser und sein Beitrag zur Entdeckung des Insulins*. [In]: 'Mannheimer Hefte'. In Verbindung mit der Gesellschaft der Freunde Mannheims und der ehemaligen Kurpfalz hrsg. von H. R. Fuchs u.a. H. 1. Mannheim, 1968. Pp. 29-37, ports., facsim. [of a letter from Theodor

Heuss to his brother-in-law E. J. Lesser]. [1879-1928, biochemist and Zionist.]
7358. LESSER, JONAS. LESSER, SERAFINE, ed.: *Jonas Lesser (1895-1968) zum Gedächtnis.* London: Priv. pr. [1968]. 62 pp., front. port. [Author.]
7359. LEVISON, WILHELM. HÜBINGER, PAUL EGON: *Wilhelm Levison (1876-1947).* [In]: Bonner Gelehrte. Beiträge zur Geschichte der Wissenschaften in Bonn. Bonn: H. Bouvier, Ludwig Röhrscheid Verlag, 1968. Pp. 311-331, bibl. (Festschrift: '150 Jahre Rheinische Friedrich-Wilhelms-Universität zu Bonn, 1818-1968'). [Medievalist.]
7360. LIDZBARSKI, MARK. BAUMGARTNER, WALTER: *Mark Lidzbarski (1868-1928).* [In]:'Neue Zürcher Zeitung', 14. Juli. Zürich, 1968. [Noted Semitist, Prof. at Göttingen University. Converted Jew.]
7361. LOEWI, OTTO. LEMBECK, FRED und WOLFGANG GIERE: *Otto Loewi.* Ein Lebensbild in Dokumenten. Biographische Dokumentation und Bibliographie. Berlin/ Heidelberg: Springer Verlag, 1968. xiii, 241 pp., front. port., ports., illus., facsims., bibl. O.L. [Incl. an autobiographical sketch, written in English, in 1960.] [1873-1961, pharmacologist, Nobel prize for medicine 1936.]
7362. LUBITSCH, ERNST. WEINBERG, HERMAN G.: *The Lubitsch Touch.* A critical study of the great film director. New York: E. P. Dutton, 1968. 300 pp., ports, illus. [1892-1947.]
7363. LUXEMBURG, ROSA. LUXEMBURG, ROSA: *Politische Schriften III.* Hrsg. und eingel. von Ossip Kurt Flechtheim. Frankfurt am Main: Europäische Verlagsanstalt, 1968. 156 pp., bibl. (pp. 150-151). (Politische Texte). [For vols I-II see No. 5987/ YB. XII.]
7364. ARENDT, HANNAH: *Rosa Luxemburg.* [In]: 'Der Monat'. 20. Jg., Nr. 243, Dez. Berlin, 1968. Pp. 28-40.
7365. FETSCHER, IRING: *Rosa Luxemburg oder Die betrogene Revolution.* [In]: 'Merkur'. 22. Jg., H. 1/2 (238). Jan.-Feb. Stuttgart: Ernst Klett Verlag, 1968. Pp. 156-161. [With ref. to the two biographies by Paul Frölich and Peter Nettl, see Nos. 6657 and 6659/YB. XIII.]
7366. RÜHLE, JÜRGEN: *Rosa Luxemburg oder die Freiheit des anderen.* Analysen, Darstellungen und Selbstzeugnisse einer menschlichen Revolutionärin. [In]: 'Die Welt der Literatur'. 1. Febr. Hamburg, 1968, facsim.
7367. MAHLER, GUSTAV. MAHLER, GUSTAV: *X. Symphonie.* Faksimile nach der Handschrift. Hrsg. von Erwin Ratz. Nachwort von Arnold Schönberg. Meran: Laurin Verlag; München: Verlag Walter Ricke, 1968.
7368. KRALIK, HEINRICH: *Gustav Mahler.* Eine Studie. Hrsg. und eingel. von Friedrich Heller. Wien: Österr. Bundesverlag Lafite, 1968. 70 pp., ports., facsims., music score.
7369. MAHLER, ALMA: *Gustav Mahler.* Memories and Letters. Transl. by Basil Creighton. Revised and edited by Donald Mitchell. London: John Murray, 1968. 369 pp., ports., illus. [Incl. letters omitted from the 1947 edition.]
7370. MAIMON, SALOMON. BERGMAN, S. HUGO: *Salomon Maimon et les débuts de la parapsychologie scientifique.* [In]: 'Revue Métapsychique'. N.S. 9. Mars. Paris, 1968. Pp. 9-21. [For German version see No. 5788/YB. XII.]
7371. KLAPP, ECKHARD: *Die Kausalität bei Salomon Maimon.* Meisenheim am Glan: Hain Verlag, 1968. 106 pp. (Monographien zur philosophischen Forschung. Bd. 52). (Diss. München).
7372. MARCUSE, HERBERT. MARCUSE, HERBERT: *Der eindimensionale Mensch.* Neuwied: Luchterhand Verlag, 1968. 282 pp.
7373. MARCUSE, HERBERT: *Ideen zu einer kritischen Theorie der Gesellschaft.* Frankfurt a. M.: Suhrkamp Verlag, 1968. (edition suhrkamp. Bd. 300).
7374. MARCUSE, HERBERT: *Kultur und Gesellschaft.* Frankfurt a. M.: Suhrkamp Verlag, 1967. 183 pp. (edition suhrkamp. Bd. 101, 135).
7375. MARCUSE, HERBERT: *Negations.* A Collection of Essays. London: Allen Lane The Penguin Press, 1968. 289 pp.
7376. MARCUSE, HERBERT: *Psychoanalyse und Politik.* Frankfurt a. M.: Europäische Verlagsanstalt, 1968. 78 pp. (Kritische Studien zur Philosophie).
7377. HABERMAS, JÜRGEN, ed.: *Antworten auf Herbert Marcuse.* Mit Beiträgen von Alfred Schmidt, Fritz Haug, Claus Offe, Joachim Bergmann, Heide Berndt, Reimut Reiche. Frankfurt a. M.: Suhrkamp Verlag, 1968. 161 pp., port. (edition suhrkamp. Bd. 263).
7378. HOLZ, HANS HEINZ: *Utopie und Anarchismus.* Zur Kritik der kritischen Theorie Herbert Marcuses. Köln: Pahl-Rugenstein, 1968. 134 pp. (Politik, Wissenschaft, Zukunft. Bd. 1).

7379. MARX, HEINRICH. MONZ, HEINZ: *Die rechtsethischen und rechtspolitischen Anschauungen des Heinrich Marx.* [In]: *Archiv für Sozialgeschichte.* Hrsg. von der Friedrich-Ebert-Stiftung. Band VIII. Hannover: Verlag für Literatur und Zeitgeschehen, 1968. Pp. 261-283. [The father of Karl Marx presented a petition concerning Napoleon's decree against the Jews of 1808.]

7380. MARX, KARL. MARX, KARL und FRIEDRICH ENGELS: *Über Kunst und Literatur.* Werke Bd. 1-2. Auswahl und Red.: Manfred Kliem. Frankfurt a. M.: Europäische Verlagsanstalt, 1968. 671, 795 pp.

7381. ALTHUSSER, LOUIS: *Für Marx.* Aus dem Französischen von Karin Brachmann und Gabriele Sprigath. Frankfurt a. M.: Suhrkamp Verlag, 1968. 216 pp. (Theorie. Reihe 2). [French title: Pour Marx.]

7382. ANDREW, EDWARD: *Marx and the Jews.* [In]: 'European Jewry'. Vol. 3, No. 1. Summer. Amsterdam/London, 1968. Pp. 9-14, bibl. [The same issue cont.]: *Judaism and Marxism.* First European Dialogue. Pp. 30-40. [A short report on a preliminary meeting.]

7383. AVINERI, SHLOMO: *The Social and Political Thought of Karl Marx.* New York/ Cambridge University Press, 1968. viii, 268 pp., bibl. (pp. 259-264). (Cambridge Studies in the History and Theory of Politics).

7384. BERLIN, ISAIAH: *Karl Marx. Sein Leben und sein Werk.* Aus dem Englischen übersetzt von Curt Meyer-Clason. Nach der 3. engl. Auflage rev. und erw. Ausgabe. Frankfurt a. M./Berlin: Ullstein Verlag, 1968. 208 pp. (Ullstein-Bücher Nr. 4003). [First Engl. ed. 1939.]

7385. BLOCH, ERNST: *Über Karl Marx.* Frankfurt a. M.: Suhrkamp Verlag, 1968. 178 pp., bibl. (edition suhrkamp. Bd. 291). [Bloch's speech 'Marx, aufrechter Gang, konkrete Utopie' was delivered at the Symposium at Trier, organised by the German UNESCO-Commission, on the occasion of the 150th anniversary of the birth of Karl Marx.]

7386. BÖLL, HEINRICH: *Karl Marx.* [Chap. in]: Aufsätze, Kritiken, Reden. Köln: Kiepenheuer & Witsch, 1967. 510 pp. (pp. 84-102).

7387. CARMICHAEL, JOEL: *Karl Marx.* London: Rapp and Whiting, 1968. 262 pp., bibl. [Incl. an examination of his article on the Jewish question.]

7388. CORNU, AUGUSTE: *Karl Marx und Friedrich Engels.* Leben und Werk. Bd. 1: 1818-1844. Bd. 2: 1844-1845. Bd. 3: 1845-1846. Berlin [East] und Weimar: Aufbau Verlag, 1962/1968. Vol. 2, 410 pp., bibl. (pp. 379-396); Vol. 3, 492 pp., bibl. [Vol. 1 is out of print, a new ed. is in preparation.]

7389. DORNEMANN, LUISE: *Jenny Marx.* Der Lebensweg einer Sozialistin. Berlin [East]: Dietz Verlag, 1968. 330 pp., ports., illus., bibl. (pp. 327-330). [Karl Marx married Jenny von Westphalen in 1843.]

7390. FEUER, LEWIS S.: *Karl Marx and the Promethean Complex.* [In]: 'Encounter'. Dec. London, 1968. Pp. 15-32, facsim. [An extract in German transl. under the title]: *Karl Marx' jüdischer Selbsthass'* [In]: 'MB', 17. Jan. Tel Aviv, 1969.

7391. FISCHER, ERNST: *Was Marx wirklich sagte.* Biographische Daten, Anmerkungen, Register. Unter Mitarbeit von Franz Marek. Wien: Fritz Molden Verlag, 1968. 188 pp.

7392. GEMKOW, HEINRICH: *Karl Marx.* Eine Biographie. In Zusammenarbeit mit O. Hoffmann u.a. hrsg. vom Institut für Marxismus-Leninismus beim ZK d. SED. Berlin [East]: Dietz Verlag, 1968. 445 pp., ports., illus., maps.

7393. HIRSCH, HELMUT: *Karl Marx und die Bittschriften für die Gleichberechtigung der Juden.* [In]: Archiv für Sozialgeschichte. Hrsg. von der Friedrich-Ebert-Stiftung. Bd. VIII. Hannover: Verlag für Literatur und Zeitgeschehen, 1968. Pp. 229-245.

7394. *Karl Marx 1818-1968.* Neue Studien zu Person und Lehre. Mainz: v. Hase & Koehler Verlag, 1968. 239 pp., cover port., illus. [Cont.: Karl Marx und das Judentum (Hans Lamm), pp. 11-66. Die soziale Lage der elterlichen Familie von Karl Marx (Heinz Monz), pp. 67-129. Katholische Kirche und Marxsche Kapitalismuskritik (Oswald v. Nell-Breuning), pp. 131-143. Marginalien zum christlich-marxistischen Dialog heute (Martin Stöhr), pp. 145-163. Recht und Staat im Denken des jungen Marx (Werner Maihofer), pp. 165-239. [Cf. No. 7403.]

7395. *Karl Marx, 1818-1968.* Mensch, Werk, Wirkung. Auswahl der neueren Literatur. Hrsg.: Volksbüchereien der Freien Hansestadt Bremen. Bibliographischer Bearbeiter: Rudolf Ernemann. Dortmund: Stadtbücherei, Stadt- und Landesbibliothek, Institut für Zeitungsforschung, 1968. 63 pp.

7396. *Karl Marx' Dokumente seines Lebens.* Hrsg. M. Kliem. Mit 70 Bilddokumenten. Leipzig: Reclam Verlag, 1968.

7397. MASSICZEK, ALBERT: *Der menschliche Mensch - Karl Marx' jüdischer Humanismus.* Wien: Europa Verlag, 1968, 654 pp., gen. table, bibl. (pp. 629-640). [Cf. Eine neue Karl-Marx-Deutung (Fritz Lothar). [In]: 'Isr. Wochenblatt', 17. Jan. 1969. See also No. 7403].

7398. MAYER, HANS: *Karl Marx und die Literatur.* [In]: 'Merkur'. 22. Jg., H. 9 (245), Sept. Stuttgart: Ernst Klett Verlag, 1968. Pp. 813-827.

7399. MONZ, HEINZ: *Das Karl-Marx-Geburtshaus in Trier.* Grundrisszeichnung: Johann Monz. Trier: Karl-Marx-Haus-Verwaltung, 1967. 44 pp., illus.

7400. PAYNE, ROBERT: *Marx.* London: W. H. Allen, 1968. 582 pp., ports., illus.

7401. ROSDOLSKY, ROMAN: *Zur Entstehungsgeschichte des Marxschen 'Kapitals'.* Frankfurt a. M.: Europäische Verlagsanstalt, 1968. 288, 304 pp. [2 vols. in one.]

7402. RUBEL, MAXIMILIAN, comp.: *Marx-Chronik.* Daten zu Leben und Werk. Aus dem Franz. von Anjuta Dünnwald. München: Carl Hanser Verlag, 1968. 162 pp. (Reihe Hanser. 3).

7403. RUHLE, JÜRGEN: *Die Mode, Marx als Juden zu interpretieren.* Zwei neue Untersuchungen zur Person und Sache. [In]: 'Welt der Literatur', Nr. 10, 8. Mai. Hamburg, 1969, illus. [With ref. to: Albert Massieczek: Der menschliche Mensch. See No. 7397. [And]: Karl Marx 1818-1968. Neue Studien zu Person und Lehre. See No. 7394.]

7404. MENDELS[S]OHN, ERIC[H]. *Erich Mendelssohn.* Ausstellung der Akademie der Künste und des Vereins Dt. Bauzentrum in der Akademie der Künste vom 14. Jan. bis zum 4. Febr. 1968. Ausstellungskatalog: Julius Posener und Peter Pfankuch. Berlin: Akademie der Künste. Essen: Verein Dt. Bauzentrum, 1968. 119 pp., front. port., illus.

7405. MENDELSSOHN-BARTHOLDY, FELIX. MENDELSSOHN-BARTHOLDY, FELIX: *Aquarellenalbum.* 13 Schweizer Ansichten aus dem Jahre 1847 aus dem Besitz des Mendelssohn-Archivs der Staatsbibliothek, Preussischer Kulturbesitz. Hrsg. von Max F. Schneider und Cécile Hensel. Berlin: Staatsbibliothek, Preuss. Kulturbesitz, Mendelssohn-Archiv. Tutzing: Kommissionsverlag Hans Schneider, 1968. 2 pp. + 13 pp. illus.

7406. MEYER, GEORG HEINRICH. HACK, BERTHOLD, comp.: *Auf den Spuren von Georg Heinrich Meyer.* Problem eines Porträts nebst Quellentexten und einem unveröffentlichten Brief von Hermann Broch. [In]: 'Börsenblatt für den Deutschen Buchhandel'. 24. Jg., Nr. 52, 28. Juni. Frankfurt a. M., 1968. Pp. 1558-1567. [Publisher (1858-1931)].

7407. MISCH, GEORG. KÖNIG, JOSEF: *Georg Misch als Philosoph.* Nachrichten der Akademie der Wissenschaften in Göttingen. I. Philologisch-Historische Klasse. Jg. 1967, Nr. 7. Göttingen: Vandenhoeck & Ruprecht, 1967. 243 pp., front. port., bibl. G. M. pp. 239-242. [Incl. short biography of the philosopher (1878-1965).]

7408. MISCH, LUDWIG. MISCH, LUDWIG: *Neue Beethoven-Studien und andere Themen.* Mit einem [biographical] Vorwort von Paul Mies. Hrsg.: Beethoven-Haus, Bonn. München-Duisburg: G. Henle Verlag, 1968. 222 pp. [The posthumously publ. book of the music-critic and scholar (1887-1967), cont. an essay on Adolf Bernhard Marx (1795-1866), the first prof. of music at Berlin University and co-founder of 'Sternsches Konservatorium'.]

7409. MORUS (i.e. LEWINSOHN, RICHARD). MORUS: *Eine Weltgeschichte der Sexualität.* Ungekürzte Ausg., 5. Aufl. Reinbek b. Hamburg: Rowohlt Verlag, 1967. 377 pp. (rororo Taschenbuch Ausgabe Nr. 6617/6619). [Physician and writer on economic affairs (1894-1968).]

7410. MÜHSAM, ERICH. MÜHSAM, ERICH: *War einmal ein Revoluzzer.* Bänkellieder und Gedichte. Berlin[East]: Henschel Verlag, 1968. 111 pp., illus. (Klassische kleine Bühne.)

7411. MÜNZENBERG. WILLI. SPERBER, MANES: *Willi Münzenberg.* [In]: 'Merkur', 22. Jg., H. 10 (246), Okt. Stuttgart: Ernst Klett Verlag, 1968. Pp. 948-955. [A review essay on: Willi Münzenberg. Eine politische Biographie (Babette Gross). See No. 6688/YB. XIII.]

7412. NOETHER, MAX. DICK, AUGUSTE: *Mathematiker aus Mannheim.* [In]: 'Mannheimer Hefte', H. 1. Mannheim, 1968. Pp. 26-28, ports. [Max N. (1844-1921). Incl. also his daughter Emmy (1882-1935) and his son Fritz (1884-?).]

7413. NORDAU, MAX [orig. Südfeld]. NORDAU, MAX: *Degeneration.* Transl. from the second edition of the German work. With an introduction by George L. Mosse. New York: Howard Fertig, 1968. xxxiv, 566 pp. [The work was written in 1892 and first publ. in English in 1895.]

7414. OPPENHEIMER, JOSEPH SÜSS. EIDELBERG, S.: *A Note on Joseph Süss Oppenheimer's Death Sentence.* [In]: 'Jewish Social Studies'. Vol. 30, No. 4, Oct. New York, 1968. Pp. 272-274. ['Jud Süss', Court Jew (1692-1738).]

7415. OPPENHEIMER, ROBERT J. KIPPHARDT, HEINAR: *In the Matter of Robert J. Oppenheimer.* Transl. from the German by Ruth Spiers. New York: Hill & Wang, 1968. 128 pp. [For German original see No. 4775/YB. X.]

7416. PANOFSKY, ERWIN. PANOFSKY, ERWIN: *Idea.* A Concept in Art Theory. Transl. by Joseph J. S. Peake. Columbia, South Carolina: University of South Carolina Press, 1968. [Art historian (1892-1968). Obituary by Eduard Hüttinger in 'Neue Zürcher Zeitung', 31. März and an appreciation by Bruno Snell in 'NZZ', 29. Dez. 1968.]

7417. RATHENAU, WALTHER. BRANDT, WILLY: *Deutsche Aussenpolitik nach zwei Weltkriegen.* [And]: *Rathenau als Wirtschaftler* (Hans Constantin Boden). Zwei Reden zum 100. Geburtstag Walther Rathenaus (auf der Veranstaltung der Ernst-Reuter-Gesellschaft der Förderer und Freunde der Freien Universität Berlin am 6. Okt. 1967). Berlin: Berlin-Verlag, 1967. 25 pp., port. [The speech by Willy Brandt also in]: 'Der Monat', 19. Jg., H.230, Nov. Berlin, 1967. Pp. 7-17.

7418. HELLIGE, HANS DIETER: *Wilhelm II. und Walther Rathenau.* Ein Gespräch aus dem Jahre 1900. [In]: 'Geschichte in Wissenschaft und Unterricht'. Zeitschrift des Verbandes der Geschichtslehrer Deutschlands. Jg. 19, H. 9, Sept. Stuttgart: Ernst Klett Verlag, 1968. Pp. 538-544.

7419. LAMM, HANS: *Walther Rathenau.* Denker und Staatsmann. Hrsg. von der Niedersächsischen Landeszentrale für Politische Bildung. Hannover, 1968. 111 pp. (Schriftenreihe der Niedersächsischen Landeszentrale für Politische Bildung. Deutschjüdisches Gespräch).

7420. POIS, ROBERT A.: *Walther Rathenau's Jewish Quandary.* [In]: LBI Year Book XIII. London, 1968. Pp. 120-131, ports.

7421. ROSENBAUM, EDUARD: *Rathenau - A Supplementary Note.* [In]: LBI Year Book XIII. London,1968. Pp. 132-134.

7422. SCHULIN, ERNST: *Walther Rathenau.* [In]: 'Der Monat'. 20. Jg., H. 237, Juni. Berlin, 1968. Pp. 45-56.

7423. REINHARDT, MAX. CLAUSS, VOLKMAR: *Max Reinhardt im Spiegel der Wiener Theaterkritik.* Von den schauspielerischen Anfängen bis zum Beginn der Josefstädter Direktionszeit. Phil. Diss. Wien, 1968. vii, 426 pp. [Typescript].

7424. KNÖLKE, BÄRBEL DOROTHEE: *Hugo von Hofmannsthals Bühnenschaffen - geprägt und beeinflusst durch Max Reinhardt und sein Theater.* Phil. Diss. Wien, 1967. 207 pp. [Typescript].

7425. *Max Reinhardt Ausstellung 1968.* 17. Mai bis 15. Juni, Akademie der Bildenden Künste Wien. Veranstalter: Gesellschaft für Wiener Theaterforschung, Theatersammlung d. Österr. Nationalbibliothek, Max Reinhardt-Forschungs- und Gedenkstätte Salzburg. Katalog: Hans Hüttner, Edda Leisler, Gisela Prossnitz. Linz: Draschny, 1968. 24 pp. + 4 pp. ports., illus.

7426. *Max Reinhardt - Sein Theater in Bildern.* Einleitung: Siegfried Melchinger. Hrsg. von der Max-Reinhardt-Forschungsstätte Salzburg von Edda Leisler, Gisela Prossnitz und Otto Schindler. Velber b. Hannover: Friedrich Verlag, 1968. 162 pp., front. port., facsim., illus. (pp. 21-140), Inszenierungsverzeichnis (pp. 145-157).

7427. RÖSSLER, KARL. FIGHTER, REMUS: *Karl Rösslers Geheimnis.* Zur 20. Wiederkehr seines Todestags am 13. Februar. [In]: 'Frankfurter Rundschau'. 14. Febr. Frankfurt a. M., 1968. [1864-1948. The best known of his many comedies: 'Die Fünf Frankfurter'.]

7428. ROTH, JOSEPH. BÖNING, HANSJÜRGEN: *Joseph Roths Radetzkymarsch.* Thematik, Struktur, Sprache. München: W. Fink, 1968. 220 pp. [See No. 5580/YB. XI.]

7429. BRONSEN, DAVID: *Phantasie und Wirklichkeit.* Geburtsort und Vaterschaft im Leben Joseph Roths. [In]: 'Neue Rundschau'. 79. Jg., H. 3. Frankfurt a. M.: S. Fischer, 1968. Pp. 494-505.

7430. HACKERT, FRITZ: *Joseph Roth.* [In]: 'Deutsche Vierteljahrsschrift für Literaturwissenschaft und Geistesgeschichte'. 43. Jg., H. 1. Stuttgart: J. B .Metzler, 1968. Pp. 161-186.

7431. (The) ROTHSCHILDS. DRUON, MAURICE: *Ces Messieurs de Rothschild (1817-1967)*. Paris: P. Tisné, 1967. 59 pp., front. port., ports., illus., facsims., gen. table.

7432. VERITY, W.: *The Rise of the Rothschilds*. [In]: 'History Today'. Vol. 18, No. 4, Apr. London, 1968. Pp. 225-233.

7433. SACHS, HANS JOSEF. SACHS, HANS J.: *Der Zahnstocher und seine Geschichte*. Eine kulturgeschichtlich-kunstgewerbliche Studie. Nachdruck der Ausgabe Berlin 1913. Hildesheim: Georg Olms Verlag, 1967. viii, 52 pp., illus. (Kulturgeschichte der Zahnheilkunde in Einzeldarstellungen I). [The author has added a new introduction describing the fate of his unique collection of toothpicks during the Nazi period.]

7434. SACHS, NELLY. *Almanach für Literatur und Theologie*. Hrsg. von Dorothea Sölle. Wolfgang Fietkau, Arnim Juhre, Kurt Marti. Wuppertal: P. Hammer Verlag, 1967. 192 pp. [Incl.: Das Werk der Nelly Sachs (I. Drewitz). The vol. incl. also: S. J. Agnons episches Werk (M. Gertner). Die Dichtung der Psalmen (D. Michel).]

7435. BERENDSOHN, W. A.: *Nobel Prize Winner Nelly Sachs*. [In]: 'Universitas'. Jg. 10, Nr. 3. Stuttgart, 1968. Pp. 215-227.

7436. HOLMQVIST, BENGT, ed.: *Das Buch der Nelly Sachs*. Frankfurt a. M.: Suhrkamp Verlag, 1968. 439 pp., bibl. N.S. pp. 419-432. [Part I cont. poetry by Nelly Sachs from the last 20 years. Part II contributions on Nelly Sachs by Beda Alleman, Hans Magnus Enzensberger, Walter Jens, Siegfried Melchinger and others. The introduction by the ed.: 'Die Sprache der Sehnsucht' concerns life and work of Nelly Sachs.]

7437. SCARPI, N. O. [i.e. FRITZ BONDY]. *Geburtstagspost für N. O. Scarpi*. Von Freunden und seinem Verleger Werner Classen mit herzlichen Glückwünschen überreicht. [Zürich], 18. April 1968. [69 pp.], drawings, facsims., bibl. N.O.S.

7438. SCHELER, MAX. HARTMANN, WILFRIED, comp.: *Max Scheler Bibliographie*. Stuttgart: Friedrich Frommann Verlag, 1968.

7438a. MADER, WILLI: *Max Scheler*. Die Geisteshaltung einer Philosophie und eines Philosophen. Innsbruck, 1968. 180 pp., port., illus., bibl. (pp. 174-180). (Diss. Phil. Innsbruck).

7439. SCHIFFER, EUGEN. WEBERSINN, GERHARD: *Eugen Schiffer*. [In]: Schlesische Lebensbilder. Hrsg. von der Hist. Kommission für Schlesien. 5. Bd. Würzburg: Holzner Verlag, 1968. Pp. 148-157. [1860-1954. Minister of Justice and Finance Minister. Converted Jew.]

7440. SCHLOSSMANN, ARTHUR. WUNDERLICH, PETER: *Arthur Schlossmann (1867-1932) und die Kinderheilkunde in Dresden*. [And]: *Arthur Schlossmann und die Düsseldorfer Kinderklinik*. Festschrift zur Feier des 100. Geburtstages am 16. Dezember 1967. Düsseldorf: Triltsch Verlag, 1967. xxiv, 123 pp.,ports., illus., facsim. (Düsseldorfer Arbeiten zur Geschichte der Medizin. H. 27).

7441. SCHNITZLER, ARTHUR. SCHNITZLER, ARTHUR: *Aphorismen und Betrachtungen*. Hrsg. von Robert O. Weiss. Frankfurt a. M.: S. Fischer, 1967. 528 pp.

7442. SCHNITZLER, ARTHUR: *Dramen*. Mit einem Nachwort von Manfred Diersch. Berlin [East]: Aufbau Verlag, 1968. 530 pp.

7443. HORWATH, PETER: *Arthur Schnitzlers 'Professor Bernhardi'*. Eine Studie über Person und Tendenz. [In]: 'Literatur und Kritik'. Österreichische Monatsschrift. H. 12-13, März-Apr. Salzburg: Otto Müller Verlag, 1967. [Both issues of the periodical cont. various contributions on Schnitzler. - Correction to No. 6714/YB. XIII.]

7444. JUST, GOTTFRIED: *Ironie und Sentimentalität in den erzählenden Dichtungen Arthur Schnitzlers*. Berlin. E. Schmidt Verlag, 1968. 149 pp. (Philologische Studien und Quellen. H. 42).

7445. MELCHINGER, CHRISTA: *Illusion und Wirklichkeit im dramatischen Werk Arthur Schnitzlers*. Heidelberg: Carl Winter Verlag, 1968. 138 pp. (Beiträge zur neueren Literaturgeschichte. Folge 3, Bd. 7). (Diss. Hamburg).

7446. REY, WILLIAM HENRY: *Arthur Schnitzler*. Die späte Prosa als Gipfel seines Schaffens. Berlin: E. Schmidt Verlag, 1968. 198 pp.

7447. URBACH, REINHARD: *Arthur Schnitzler*. Velber bei Hannover: Friedrich Verlag, 1968. 134 pp., ports., illus. (pp. 97-112), bibl. A. Sch. pp. 128-134. (Friedrichs Dramatiker des Welttheaters. Bd. 56).

7448. URBACH, REINHARD: *Schwätzer sind Verbrecher*. Bemerkungen zu Schnitzlers Dramenfragment 'Das Wort'. [In]: 'Literatur und Kritik'. Österreichische Monatsschrift. H. 25, Juni. Wien, 1968. Pp. 292-304.

7449. VACHA, BRIGITTE: *Arthur Schnitzler und das Wiener Burgtheater, 1895-1965*. In 2

Teilen: 1. Chronik. 2. Rekonstruktion und Vergleich. Wien: Phil. Diss., 1968. xxxxi, 252 pp., 175, 89 pp. [2 vols. Typed.]

7450. SCHÖNBERG, ARNOLD. NEWLIN, DIKA: *Self Revelation and the Law - Arnold Schönberg in his Religious Works*. [In]' 'Yuval', Studies of the Jewish Music Research Centre. Ed. by Israel Adler, Hanoch Avenary and Bathja Bayer. Jerusalem: The Magnes Press, The Hebrew University, 1968. (Die Jacobsleiter, Moses und Aaron, Kol-Nidré).

7451. PAYNE, ANTHONY: *Schönberg*. London: Oxford University Press, 1968. 61 pp., port., illus., music scores. (Oxford Studies of Composers, No. 5).

7452. REICH, WILLI: *Arnold Schönberg oder Der konservative Revolutionär*. Wien: Verlag Fritz Molden, 1968. 328 pp., ports., illus., music score, bibl. (pp. 321-323). (Glanz und Elend der Meister).

7453. SIMMEL, GEORG. SIMMEL, GEORG: *Das individuelle Gesetz*. Philosophische Exkurse. Hrsg. und eingeleitet von Michael Landmann. Frankfurt a. M.: Suhrkamp Verlag, 1968. 261 pp., bibl. G.S. pp. 256-260. (Theorie, Reihe 1).

7454. BROCK, ERICH: *Georg Simmel*. Zum 50. Todestag (28. Sept.) [In]: 'Neue Zürcher Zeitung', 29. Sept. Zürich, 1968, port.

7455. SIMON, JAMES. STEINMANN, ULRICH: *Some Notes on James Simon*. [In]: LBI Year Book XIII. London, 1968. Pp. 277-282. [Cf. also No. 7172.]

7456. STAMPFER, FRIEDRICH. MATTHIAS, ERICH, ed.: *Mit dem Gesicht nach Deutschland*. Eine Dokumentation über die sozialdemokratische Emigration. Aus dem Nachlass von Friedrich Stampfer, ergänzt durch andere Überlieferungen. Bearbeitet von Werner Link. Düsseldorf: Droste Verlag, 1968. 700 pp. (Veröffentlichungen der Kommission für Geschichte des Parlamentarismus und der politischen Parteien). [1874-1957. Political journalist, member of the 'Reichstag'.]

7457. STERNHEIM, CARL. STERNHEIM, CARL: *Gedichte, Frühe Dramen*. Hrsg. und eingeleitet von Fritz Hofmann. Berlin [East]: Aufbau Verlag, 1968. 620 pp., front. port. (Gesammelte Werke in sechs Bänden. Bd. 1).

7458. SUSMAN, MARGARETE. SUSMAN, MARGARETE: *Das Buch Hiob und das Schicksal des jüdischen Volkes*. Mit einem Vorwort von Heinrich Schlier und einer Einführung von Hermann Levin Goldschmidt. Freiburg i. Br.: Herder Verlag, 1968. 238 pp. (Herder-Bücherei Nr. 318). [First publ. Zürich, 1948.]

7459. TOLLER, ERNST. SPALEK, JOHN M.: *Ernst Toller and his Critics*. A Bibliography. Publ. by the Bibliographical Society of the University of Virginia. Charlottesville, Va.: The University Press of Virginia, 1968. xxii, 919 pp., port.

7460. TORBERG, FRIEDRICH. TORBERG, FRIEDRICH: *Golems Wiederkehr und andere Erzählungen*. Frankfurt a. M.: S. Fischer Verlag, 1968. 184 pp. (Gesammelte Werke. Bd. 6).

7461. TUCHOLSKY, KURT. TUCHOLSKY, KURT: *Warum lacht die Mona Lisa?* Gedichte, Lieder und Chansons. Berlin [East]: Henschel Verlag, 1968. 214 pp., illus. (Lizenz des Rowohlt Verlags).

7462. TUCHOLSKY, KURT: *'What If - ?' - 'Was Wäre, Wenn'*. Satirical Writings of Kurt Tucholsky, transl. by Harry Zohn and Karl F. Ross. New York: Funk and Wagnalls, 1968. 238 pp. [Tucholsky's satirical prose and verse from 1916 to 1932. The 26 poems in the vol. are printed in the German original and Ross' translation.]

7463. POOR, HAROLD L.: *Kurt Tucholsky and the Ordeal of Germany, 1914-1935*. New York: Charles Scribner's Sons, 1968. 297 pp.

7464. WALBERER, ULRICH: *Kurt Tucholsky als Theaterkritiker*. Von der aesthetischen zur ethischen Theaterkritik. Wien: Phil. Diss., 1968. 170 pp., bibl. (pp. 162-170). [Typescript.]

7465. URZIDIL, JOHANNES. URZIDIL, JOHANNES: *Der Autor als Selbstkritiker*. [In]: 'Schweizer Monatshefte'. 47. Jg., März. Zürich, 1968.

7466. TRAPP, GERHARD: *Die Prosa Johannes Urzidils*. Zum Verständnis eines literarischen Werdegangs vom Expressionismus zur Gegenwart. Bern: Verlag Herbert Lang, 1967. 235 pp.

7467. VARNHAGEN VON ENSE, RAHEL. VARNHAGEN, RAHEL: *Lichtstreifen und Glutwege*. Aufzeichnungen. Hrsg. von Rahel E. Steiner. Frankfurt am Main: Insel Verlag, 1968. 109 pp., front. port. (Inselbücherei Nr. 882).

7468. HOHOFF, CURT: *Wo die Seele spazieren geht*. Aus Anlass der Briefe Rahel Varnhagens in vier Bänden. [In]: 'Merkur'. 22. Jg., H. 11 (247), Nov. Stuttgart: Ernst Klett Verlag, 1968. Pp. 1052-1055. [See No. 6822/YB. XIII.]

7469. VEIT, DAVID. ZONDEK, THEODOR: *Dr. med. David Veit (1771-1814)*. [In]: 'Hamburgische Geschichts- und Heimatblätter'. Bd. 8, H. 5, Okt. Hamburg: Verein für Hamburgische Geschichte, 1968. Pp. 120-128, facsim., bibl. (pp. 127-128).

7470. WEIL, GUSTAV. KAHN, LUDWIG: *Gustav Weil von Sulzburg*. Orientalist und Geschichtsschreiber. [In]: 'Die Markgrafschaft'. 19. Jg., H. 11, Nov. Müllheim (Baden): Hebelbund, 1967. Pp. 13-14, bibl. [1808-1889. The translator of 'The Thousand and One Nights'. See also No. 6941.]

7471. WELTSCH, FELIX. WELTSCH, FELIX: *Hessed v'Heruth. (Gnade und Freiheit)*. Untersuchungen zum Problem des schöpferischen Willens in Religion und Ethik. Transl. into Hebrew by Shmuel Shihor. Jerusalem: Leo Baeck Institute in co-operation with Mossad Bialik, 1968. 139 pp. [Biographical-philosophical introduction by Max Brod. Appendix by S. Hugo Bergman. The work was first publ. in 1920.]

7472. WELTSCH, FELIX: *Das Wagnis der Mitte*. Mit einer Einleitung von Max Brod: *Felix Weltsch, der Philosoph des Werdens und der Mitte*. Stuttgart: Kohlhammer Verlag, 1968. [Orig. publ. 1936.]

7473. WERNER, ERIC. COHEN, JUDITH, comp.: *Bibliography of the Publications of Eric Werner*. Tel Aviv: University, 1968. 12 pp., front. port. [Musicologist.]

7474. WITTGENSTEIN, LUDWIG. WITTGENSTEIN, LUDWIG: *Vorlesungen und Gespräche über Ästhetik, Psychologie und Religion*. Übers. und eingeleitet von Eberhard Bubser. Hrsg. von Cyrill Barrett. Göttingen: Vandenhoeck und Ruprecht, 1968. 111 pp. (Kleine Vandenhoeck-Reihe, Nr. 267-269).

7475. BORGIS, ILONA: *Index zu Ludwig Wittgensteins 'Tractatus logico-philosophicus' und Wittgenstein-Bibliographie*. Freiburg/München: Alber Verlag, 1968. 113 pp. [Cf. No. 2887/YB. VII.]

7476. PITCHER, GEORGE: *Die Philosophie Wittgensteins*. Eine kritische Einführung in den Tractatus und die Spätschriften. Übertragen von Eike von Savigny. Freiburg und München: Karl Alber Verlag, 1968. 396 pp.

7477. *Über Ludwig Wittgenstein*. Mit Beiträgen von Norman Malcolm u.a. Zusammengestellt unter Mitarbeit von Ulrich Steinvorth. Frankfurt a. M.: Suhrkamp Verlag, 1968. 172 pp., bibl. (pp. 157-171). (edition suhrkamp. 252).

7478. WOLFENSTEIN, ALFRED. FISCHER, PETER: *Alfred Wolfenstein, der Expressionismus und die verendende Kunst*. München: W. Fink, 1968. 251 pp., bibl. A.W. und bibl. (pp. 236-251). [1888-1945 (suicide). Poet, translator, dramatist.]

7479. WOLFF, THEODOR. SCHWARZ, GOTTHART: *Theodor Wolff und das 'Berliner Tageblatt'*. Eine liberale Stimme in der deutschen Politik 1906-1933. Tübingen: J. C. B. Mohr (Paul Siebeck), 1968. ix, 311 pp., bibl. (pp. 288-303). (Tübinger Studien zur Geschichte und Politik. Nr. 25).

7480. WOLFSKEHL, KARL. NYLAND-VERWEY, MEA, ed.: *Wolfskehl und Verwey*. Die Dokumente ihrer Freundschaft 1897-1946. Heidelberg: Verlag Lambert Schneider, 1968. 377 pp., ports., facsims., bibl. (pp. 357-358). (Veröffentlichungen der Deutschen Akademie für Sprache und Dichtung Darmstadt, 40).

7481. RUBEN, MARGOT, comp.: *Karl Wolfskehl und die Rupprecht-Presse*. Eine Auswahl in Briefen und Aufsätzen. [In]: 'Imprimatur'. Ein Jahrbuch für Bücherfreunde. Neue Folge. Bd. V. Wiesbaden: Otto Harrassowitz Verlag, 1967. Pp. 20-37, facsim.

7482. ZUCKMAYER, CARL. ZUCKMAYER, CARL: *Scholar zwischen gestern und morgen*. [In]: 'Neue Rundschau'. 79. Jg., H. 1. Frankfurt a. M.: S. Fischer Verlag, 1968. Pp. 1-15. [His 'Festrede' on the occasion of his becoming an hon. citizen of the Ruperto-Carola University Heidelberg (Nov. 1967).]

7483. HERDAN-ZUCKMAYER, ALICE: *Die Farm in den Grünen Bergen*. Illustrierte, überarbeitete Neuausgabe. Frankfurt a. M.: S. Fischer Verlag, 1968. 240 pp., ports., illus.

7484. MERTZ, WOLFGANG, ed.: *Carl Zuckmayer*. Eine Auslese. Wien: Ueberreuter Verlag, 1968. 317 pp., ports., illus.

7485. ZWEIG, ARNOLD. ZWEIG, ARNOLD: *Baruch Spinoza*. Porträt eines freien Geistes 1632-1677. Darmstadt: Joseph Melzer Verlag, 1968. 61 pp. [Written 1960.]

7486. BAUM, HANS-WERNER: *Arnold Zweig: Leben und Werk*. Berlin: Zentralinstitut für Bibliothekswesen, 1967. 24 pp., front. port., bibl. A.Z. pp. 17-22.

7487. HILSCHER, E[BERHARD]: *Arnold Zweig*. Leben und Werk. Berlin [East]: Verlag Volk und Wissen, 1968. 182 pp. (Schriftsteller der Gegenwart. 22).

7488. *Zum Tode von Arnold Zweig (1887-1968)*. [Obituaries in most Jewish newspapers and periodicals and in many German as well as in several English papers, during November and December 1968.]

7489. ZWEIG, STEFAN. ARENS, HANNS, ed.: *Stefan Zweig im Zeugnis seiner Freunde.* Hrsg. und eingeleitet von Hanns Arens. München: Langen-Müller Verlag, 1968. 292 pp., front. port., ports., illus., facsims., bibl. St. Z. [Rev. and enlarged ed. of 'Stefan Zweig - Der grosse Europäer', publ. 1956.]

7490. FREUND, JOACHIM HELLMUT, ed.: *Stefan Zweig - Eine Auslese.* Ausgewählt und hrsg. von Joachim Hellmut Freund. Einführung von Richard Friedenthal. Wien/Heidelberg: Carl Ueberreuter Verlag, 1968. 317 pp., ports., illus.

7491. HEILBUT, I. G.: *Stefan Zweig, Motive für einen Freitod.* [In] 'Areopag'. 3. Jg., Nr. 2. Mainz, 1968. Pp. 139-150.

7492. MAITLIS, J.: *Stefan Zweigs Stellung zum Jiddischen.* [In]: 'Isr. Wochenblatt'. 68. Jg., Nr. 48. 29. Nov. Zürich, 1968. Pp. 5-7, facsims.

VIII. AUTOBIOGRAPHY, MEMOIRS, LETTERS, GENEALOGY

7493. ANDERS, GÜNTHER [i.e. Günther Stern]: *Zähle.* Aus den philosophischen Tagebüchern 1944 bis 1948. [In]: 'Merkur'. 22. Jg., H. 9, Sept. Stuttgart: Ernst Klett Verlag, 1968. Pp. 828-836. [Cf. No. 6783/YB. XIII.]

7494. (The) BENEDICT FAMILY. RAPHAEL, JACOB: *Die Stuttgarter Familie Benedict im 19. Jahrhundert.* [In]: 'LBI Bulletin'. 11. Jg., Nr. 41. Tel Aviv, 1968. Pp. 32-37.

7495. BÖRNE, LUDWIG: *Briefe.* Neu bearbeitet und hrsg. von Inge und Peter Rippmann. (Sämtliche Schriften in 5 Bänden). Bd. 4: Briefe 1, cxx, 1366 pp., illus.; Bd. 5: Briefe 2. Nachtrag, xxviii, 1164 pp., illus. Darmstadt: Verlag Joseph Melzer, 1968. [2 vols., cont. correspondence with Henriette Herz. Letters to Friedrich von Cotta, Julius Campe and the correspondence with Jeanette Wohl. For vols. 1-3 see No. 4623/YB. X.]

7496. CRONER, FRITZ: *Ein Leben in unserer Zeit.* (Deutsch-Schwedische Emigranten Symbiose). Autobiographie. Frankfurt a. M.: Büchergilde Gutenberg, 1968. 398 pp., front. port. [The autobiography was publ. 1966 in Swedish.]

7497. EHRENBERG, EVA. RIAS BERLIN, ed.: *Kleine Welt - grosse Welt.* Sendung von Karla Höcker zum Buch von Eva Ehrenberg: 'Sehnsucht, mein geliebtes Kind'. Bekenntnisse und Erinnerungen. Berlin, 1968. 17 pp. [Typescript.] [The autobiographical book was publ. 1963. See No. 4199/YB. IX.]

7498. EINSTEIN, ALBERT. *Albert Einstein - Arnold Sommerfeld: Briefwechsel.* Hrsg. und kommentiert von A. Heimann. Geleitwort von Max Born. Basel: Verlag Benno Schwabe, 1968. 126 pp., illus., facsims. [60 letters written between 1912 and 1949. Arnold Sommerfeld (1868-1951), physicist. Cf. review by Alfred Brunner in 'NZZ', 24. Mai, Zürich 1969.]

7499. LARSEN, EGON: *Albert Einstein - Poet, Helper and Inventor.* [In]: 'AJR Information'. Vol. XXIII, No. 1, Jan. London, 1968. [Author has looked through appr. 60 unknown and unpubl. letters which Einstein wrote to Dr. Gustav Bucky and which have since been auctioned by Christie's, London for £15,000.]

7500. (The) FEUCHTWANGER FAMILY. GRUNWALD, KURT: *The Feuchtwangers.* A Family of Bankers. [In]: 'AJR Information'. Vol. XXIII/6, June. London, 1968.

7501. FREUD, SIGMUND. FREUD, SIGMUND: *Brautbriefe.* Briefe an Martha Bernays aus den Jahren 1882-1886. Ausgewählt, hrsg. und mit einem Vorwort von Ernst L. Freud. Frankfurt a. M.: Fischer-Bücherei, 1968. 143 pp., ports., illus. (Fischer-Bücherei, 899).

7502. FREUD, SIGMUND: *Briefe 1873-1939.* Ausgewählt und hrsg. von Ernst L. und Lucie Freud. 2. erw. Aufl. Frankfurt a. M.: S. Fischer Verlag, 1968. 538 pp., ports., facsims.

7503. FREUD, ERNST L., ed.: *Sigmund Freud/Arnold Zweig: Briefwechsel.* Frankfurt a. M.: S. Fischer Verlag, 1968. 202 pp., cover ports., facsims.

7504. GODAL, ERIC. GODAL, ERIC: *'Kein Talent zum Tellerwäscher'.* Hamburg: Verlag Hoffmann und Campe, 1968. 314 pp., illus. by the author. [The autobiography of the artist (1898-1969).]

7505. HAMELN, JENTE. ROSENSTOCK, WERNER. *The Descendants of Jente Hameln.* An Interesting Genealogy. [In]: 'AJR Information'. Vol. XXII/11, Nov. London, 1968. [Based on a work by Ludwig Lazarus not yet published.]

7506. HILLER, FERDINAND. HILLER, FERDINAND: *Briefwechsel mit B. Auerbach, H. Levi, E. Pasqué, J. Stockhausen und N. W. Gade.* Aus Ferdinand Hillers Briefwechsel. Beiträge zu einer Biographie Ferdinand Hillers von Reinhold Sietz. Bd. 6. Köln: Volk Verlag, 1968. 185 pp. (Beiträge zur rheinischen Musikgeschichte. H. 70). [Conductor, Composer, Pianist, (1811-1885).]

7507. HOFMANNSTHAL, HUGO VON. *Hugo v. Hofmannsthal/Harry Graf Kessler: Briefwechsel 1898-1929.* Hrsg. und Anm. von Hilde Burger. Frankfurt a. M.: Insel Verlag, 1968. 608 pp., bibl. (pp. 597-604)

7508. ITALIAANDER, ROLF, ed.: *Hofmannsthal/Willy Haas: Ein Briefwechsel.* Mit einer Einführung von Rudolf Hirsch. Berlin: Propyläen Verlag, 1969. 116 pp., facsims. (Sonderdruck für die Freunde der Verlage Propyläen-Ullstein).

7509. PERL, WALTER H., ed.: *Hugo v. Hofmannsthal/Leopold von Andrian: 'Briefwechsel'.* Frankfurt a. M.: S. Fischer Verlag, 1968. 582 pp. [Cf. No. 7187.]

7510. MARX, KARL. GUNNEMANN, HEDWIG, ed.: *Karl Marx: Briefe an Ferdinand Freiligrath.* Autographenausstellung zum 150. Geburtstag. Dortmund: Stadt- und Landesbibliothek, 1968. vi, 32 pp. (Ausstellungskatalog).

7511. MARX, KARL [and] FRIEDRICH ENGELS: *Briefe.* Hrsg. vom Institut f. Marxismus-Leninismus beim Z.K. d. SED. Werke. Bd. 36: April 1883-Dez. 1887. xxvii, 939 pp., illus., facsims., bibl. (pp. 854-885). Bd. 39: Jan. 1893-Juli 1895. xxvii, 785 pp., ports., illus., facsims., bibl. (pp. 616-646). Berlin [East]: Dietz Verlag, 1968.

7512. MENDELSSOHN-BARTHOLDY, FELIX. MENDELSSOHN-BARTHOLDY, FELIX: *Briefe.* Bd. I: Briefe an deutsche Verleger. Gesammelt und hrsg. von Rudolf Elvers. Mit einer Einführung von Hans Herzfeld. Berlin: Walter de Gruyter, 1968. xxx, 399 pp., port., bibl. (pp. 383-387). (Veröffentlichungen der Historischen Kommission zu Berlin).

7513. NEUMANN, ROBERT. NEUMANN, ROBERT: *Vielleicht das Heitere.* Tagebuch aus einem anderen Jahr. München: Kurt Desch, 1968. 608 pp.

7514. SACHS, MAURICE. SACHS, MAURICE: *Der Sabbath.* Eine Chronique Scandaleuse. Deutsch von Herbert Schlüter. Nachwort von François Bondy. München: Verlag R. Piper, 1967. [Autobiography. Author was born 1906 as Maurice Ettinghausen, adopted his mother's maiden name Sachs, turned first a Catholic, later a Protestant, to become, during the Nazi period, a Jew again. He was arrested and shot by the Gestapo in Hamburg, April 1945.]

7515. SCHNITZLER ARTHUR. SCHNITZLER, ARTHUR: *Jugend in Wien.* Eine Autobiographie. Hrsg. von Therese Nickl und Heinrich Schnitzler. Mit einem Nachwort von Friedrich Torberg. Wien: Fritz Molden Verlag, 1968. 384 pp., ports., illus., chronology.

7516. SPIEL, HILDE. SPIEL, HILDE: *Rückkehr nach Wien.* Tagebuch 1946. München: Nymphenburger Verlag, 1968. 155 pp.

7517. STERN, ARTHUR. STERN, ARTHUR: *In bewegter Zeit.* Erinnerungen und Gedanken eines jüdischen Nervenarztes. Jerusalem: Rubin Mass, 1968. Cover drawing by R. Dayan, bibl. A.St. [The neurologist and author, born in Sohrau (Upper Silesia), celebrated his 90th birthday, in June 1969, in Jerusalem.]

7518. STERNBERG, JOSEF VON. STERNBERG, JOSEF VON: *Ich - Josef von Sternberg.* Erinnerungen. Aus dem Englischen von Walther Schmiedling. Velber bei Hannover: Friedrich Verlag, 1967. 374 pp., front. port., ports., illus. [English title: Fun in a Chinese Laundry, publ. 1965.]

7519. SZIGETI, JOSEPH. SZIGETI, JOSEPH: *With Strings Attached.* Reminiscences and Reflections. New York: Knopf, 1967. 376 pp. [The autobiography of the violinist was first publ. 1947. For German ed. see No. 3520/YB. VIII.]

7520. TAU, MAX. TAU, MAX: *Auf dem Weg zur Versöhnung.* Hamburg: Hoffmann und Campe, 1968. 251 pp. [Part 3 of his memoirs. For parts 1-2 see Nos. 4879/80/YB. X.]

7521. TERGIT, GABRIELE. TERGIT, GABRIELE, comp.: *Autobiographien.* Eine Sammlung des PEN-Zentrums deutschsprachiger Autoren im Ausland. 2. Aufl. London, 1968. 108 pp. [A revised and enlarged version of the 1959 ed. See No. 1831/YB. V.]

7522. WALTER, BRUNO. *Der Briefwechsel mit Bruno Walter.* [In]: Emil Bock: Briefe. Hrsg. von Gundhild Kacer-Bock. Stuttgart: Verlag Urachhaus, 1968. 436 pp., ports., facsim. [Mainly correspondence between 1941 and 1959.]

7523. WELTLINGER, SIEGMUND. WELTLINGER, SIEGMUND: *Jugenderinnerungen und Alterserkenntnisse eines deutschen Juden.* Berlin: Gesellschaft für Christlich-Jüdische Zusammenarbeit, 1968. 19 pp. (Vortrag gehalten am 10. Jan. 1968).
7524. WESTMAN, STEPHAN K. WESTMAN, STEPHAN K.: *Surgeon with the Kaiser's Army.* London: William Kimber, 1968.185 pp. [Obstetrician, Gynaecologist (1894-1968). See No. 2380/YB. VI.]
7525. ZOFF, OTTO. ZOFF, OTTO: *Tagebücher aus der Emigration (1939-1944)* Mit einem Nachwort von Hermann Kesten. Heidelberg: Verlag Lambert Schneider, 1968. 293 pp. (Veröffentlichungen der Deutschen Akademie für Sprache und Dichtung, Darmstadt. Aus dem Nachlass hrsg. von Liselotte Zoff und Hans-Joachim Pavel). [Author, 1890-1963.]
—— ZWEIG, ARNOLD. FREUD, ERNST L., ed.: *Sigmund Freud/Arnold Zweig: Briefwechsel.* Frankfurt a. M.: S. Fischer Verlag, 1968. 202 pp., cover ports., facsims. [Cf. No. 7503.]

IX. GERMAN-JEWISH RELATIONS

A. General

7526. GROSSMANN, KURT R.: *The Problem of Forgetting.* Thoughts on the Nazi Crimes Trials. [In]: 'Patterns of Prejudice'. Ed.: C. C. Aronsfeld. Publ. by the Institute of Jewish Affairs, in association with the World Jewish Congress. Vol. 2, No. 6, Nov.-Dec. London, 1968. Pp. 10-16.
7527. MANN, GOLO: *Germany - Today and Tomorrow.* [In]: 'The Wiener Library Bulletin', publ. in conjunction with the Anti-Defamation League of B'nai B'rith, New York. Ed. Ernest Hearst. Vol. XXII, No. 2. New Series No. 11, Spring. London: Weidenfeld & Nicolson, 1968. Pp. 2-4. [This analysis of the new Germany concluded his address delivered at the opening of the Luxemburg exhibition of 'German Literature in Exile 1933-1945'.]

B. German-Israeli Relations

7528. *Deutschland zeigt seine Bücher.* [Report on an exhibition in Israel.] [In]: 'MB', 18. Oktober. Tel Aviv, 1968. [The exhibition catalogue conts. a preface by the German Ambassador Knoke, and an Introduction by Max Brod. [Also]: *Culture without 'Kultur-Propaganda'* (Erich Gottgetreu). [In]: "AJR Information'. Vol. XXIII/No. 12, Dec. London, 1968. [And]: *Deutsche Bücher in Israel.* (Moshe Tavor). [In]: 'FAZ', 10. Okt., Frankfurt a. M., 1968.
7529. KIESINGER, GEORG: *Frieden für das tapfere und kluge israelische Volk.* Bericht eines Interviews mit dem Bundeskanzler von Rolf Vogel. [In]: 'Deutschland-Berichte'. 4. Jg., Nr. 5. Bonn, 1968. Pp. 2-8.
7530. SCHLEE, EMIL: *Begegnung mit Israel.* Eindrücke und Erlebnisse einer Offenbacher Jugendgruppe. Illustrationen von Dina Kraus. 2. Aufl. Offenbach a. M.: Stadtverwaltung, Schuldezernat, 1968. 63 pp., illus.
7531. *Studieren in Jerusalem.* 'Woche der Hebräischen Universität' in Frankfurt. [In]: 'FAZ', 5. und 17. Jan., Frankfurt a. M. 1968. [Also]: Das Fazit der 'Woche der Hebräischen Universität'. [In]: 'MJN', 2. Febr. München, 1968. [And]: Ein jüdisches Selbstporträt. (Referat von Ernst Simon). [Report in]: 'FAZ', 22. Jan. [and in]: 'MB', 9. Febr. 1968.
7532. WALICHNOWSKI, TADEUSZ: *Israel and the German Federal Republic.* Transl. from the Polish. Warsaw:Interpress Publishers, 1968. xvi, 199 pp., bibl. (pp. 196-199). [Also in German]: Israel und die Bundesrepublik. [Antisemic, anti-Zionist book.]
7533. WEISSBERG, JOSEF [and others]: *Dikduk ha-laschon hagermanit.* (Grammatik der deutschen Sprache). Jerusalem: Magnes Press, The Hebrew University, 1968. 268 pp. Förderer: Fritz Thyssen Stiftung, Deutscher Akademischer Austauschdienst, Alexander von Humboldt-Stiftung, Goethe Institut).

7534. BORCHSENIUS, POUL: *Two Ways to God.* Foreword by the Rev. The Lord Soper. Transl. from the Danish. London: Vallentine, Mitchell, 1968. 218 pp.

7535. *'Freiburger Rundbrief'.* Beiträge zur Förderung der Freundschaft zwischen dem Alten und dem Neuen Gottesvolk im Geiste beider Testamente. Hrsg. von Willehad P. Eckert, Rupert Giessler, Georg Hüssler, Ludwig Kaufmann, Gertrud Luckner u.a. XX. Folge. Nr. 73/76. Dez. Freiburg i. Br.: Deutscher Caritasverband, 1968. 155 + xxv pp. [Incl.: 30 Jahre danach. ... Zum 9. Nov. 1968. Busstagspredigt geh. am 16. Nov. 1938 von Helmut Gollwitzer. Der Segensspruch (Hugo Bergman). Begegnung zwischen christlicher Scholastik und jüdischer Philosophie an der Hebräischen Universität Jerusalem (P. Marcel/Jacques Dubois). Entwicklungen im Nahen Osten. See also No. 7043.]

7536. ISAAC, JULES: *Jesus und Israel.* Wien: Hans Deutsch Verlag, 1968. [The work was written whilst in hiding from the Nazis and first publ. in French in 1946.]

7537. LAUER, S.: *Das Verhältnis zwischen Christen und Juden in heutiger jüdischer Sicht.* [In]: 'Christlich-Jüdisches Forum'. Mitteilungsblatt der Christlich-Jüdischen Arbeitsgemeinschaft in der Schweiz. Nr. 40. Juni. Zürich, 1968.

7538. LICHTENBERG, JEAN-PAUL: *Stärke und Schwäche der Erklärung über die Juden.* [In]: 'Concilium', Nr. 5. Internationale Zeitschrift für Theologie. Einsiedeln: Benziger Verlag, Mainz:Matthias-Grünewald Verlag, 1968.

7539. LOUIS GABRIEL, SISTER: *Christian-Jewish Relations and the Ecumenical Movement.* Bulletin 15, Winter. London: Centre for Biblical and Jewish Studies, 1968/69. 15 pp.

7540. MAYER, EUGEN: *An Ecumenical Experiment.* [In]: LBI Year Book XIII. London, 1968. Pp. 135-141, facsim. [Concerning the journal (of 1837) 'Unparteiische Universal-Kirchenzeitung für die Geistlichkeit und die gebildete Weltklasse des protestantischen, katholischen und israelitischen Deutschlands']. [Eugen Mayer died Dec. 1967 aged 85. [See]: 'MB', Nr. 2, 12. Jan. Tel Aviv, 1968. LBI Year Book XIII, London, 1968.]

—— MEIER, KURT: *Kirche und Judentum.* Die Haltung der evangelischen Kirche zur Judenpolitik des Dritten Reiches. [See No. 7003.]

7541. PFISTERER, RUDOLF: *Juden, Christen, getrennt, versöhnt.* 2. erw. Aufl. Gladbeck: Schriftenmissions-Verlag, 1968. 72 pp. (Wahrheit und Wagnis).

—— SNOEK, JOHAN M.: *The Grey Book.* A Collection of Protests against Anti-Semitism and the Persecution of Jews Issued by non-Roman Catholic Churches and Church Leaders during Hitler's Rule. Introduction by Uriel Tal. [See No. 7017.]

D. Antisemitism

7542. BIEBERSTEIN, JOHANNES ROGALLA VON: *Die These von der Verschwörung der Philosophen, Freimaurer, Illuminaten und 'geheimen Gesellschaften', 1789-1825.* Ein Beitrag zur Geschichte von Konterrevolution und gesellschaftlicher Emanzipation. Hausarbeit für die akademische Abschlussprüfung. Ruhr-Universität Bochum, 1968. 131 pp., bibl. (pp. 113-131). [Mimeog.] [Pp. 93-111: Exkurs: Die These von der Verschwörung und 'die Juden'.]

7543. BUNDESZENTRALE FÜR POLITISCHE BILDUNG, ed.: *Rechtsradikalismus in der Bundesrepublik im Jahre 1967.* Beilage zur Wochenzeitung 'Das Parlament'. B. 15/68, 10. April. Bonn, 1968. 40 pp., illus., facsims., diagrs., maps, tabs.

7544. CARSTEN, FRANCIS L.: *Der Aufstieg des Faschismus in Europa.* Frankfurt a. M.: Europäische Verlagsanstalt, 1968. 307 pp. ('res novae' - Veröffentlichungen zu Politik, Wirtschaft, Soziologie und Geschichte. Bd. 65). [Introd. chap.: Nationalismus und Antisemitismus vor 1914.]

7545. CERNY, BOHUMIL: *Der Mord in Polna.* Prag: Armee-Verlag, 1968. [In Czech]: *Vražda v Polné.* Praha: Vyd. časopisu MNO, 1968. 215 pp., ports., illus., facsims., bibl. (Magnet 9/68). [A critical analysis of the ritual murder trial of Leopold Hilsner, in 1899, whose death sentence was subsequently changed to life imprisonment. He was reprieved in 1916 after Thomas G. Masaryk and others had pleaded for a retrial.] [See also No. 7546.]

7546. CERVINKA, FRANTIŠEK: *The Hilsner Affair.* [In]: LBI Year Book XIII. London, 1968. Pp. 142-157, ports. [See also No. 7545.]

7547. CUTLER, A.: *The Origins of Modern Anti-Semitism, a new Hypothesis*. [In]: 'Judaism'. Vol. 17. No. 4, Fall. New York, 1968. Pp. 469-474.

7548. FLANNERY, E.: *The Anguish of the Jews: 2000 Years of anti-Semitism*. London: Collier-Macmillan, 1967. 328 pp. (Quest Books).

7549. GIVET, JACQUES: *La Gauche contre Israel?* Essai sur la néo-antisémitisme. Paris: Jean-Jacques Pauvert, 1968.

7550. *(Das) Judentum am Scheideweg*. [Special no. of]: 'Nation Europa'. XVIII. Jg., H. 7, Juli. Coburg: Nation Europa Verlag, 1968. 64 pp., illus.

7551. KIRSCHNER, BRUNO: *Deutsche Spottmedaillen auf Juden*. Bearbeitet und hrsg. von Arie Kindler. Mit einem Vorwort von Siegfried Moses. München: Ernst Battenberg Verlag, 1968. 92 pp., 76 illus. (Veröffentlichung des Leo Baeck Instituts).

7552. LOEWENSTEIN, RUDOLPH M[AURICE]: *Psychoanalyse des Antisemitismus*. Aus dem Französischen übersetzt von Lothar Baier. Frankfurt am Main: Suhrkamp Verlag, 1968. 174 pp., bibl. (pp. 167-174). (edition suhrkamp 241). [French title: Psychoanalyse de l'Antisémitisme. Publ. 1952.]

7553. MASSICZEK, ALBERT, ed.: *Antisemitismus*. Die permanente Herausforderung. Beiträge von Otto Breuer, René Marcic, Albert Massiczek, Erica Wantoch. Wien: Europa Verlag, 1968. 116 pp.

7554. *(Das) Oberammergauer Passionsspiel in seiner ältesten Gestalt*. Zum ersten Male hrsg. von August Hartmann. (Neudruck der Ausgabe Leipzig: Breitkopf und Härtel, 1880). Wiesbaden: M. Sändig, 1968. vi, 269 pp.

7555. PAUCKER, ARNOLD: *Der jüdische Abwehrkampf gegen Antisemitismus und Nationalsozialismus in den letzten Jahren der Weimarer Republik*. Hamburg: Leibniz-Verlag, 1968. 311 pp., cover facsim., facsims., bibl. (pp. 291-302). (Hamburger Beiträge zur Zeitgeschichte. Band IV). [Concerns primarily the defence work of the Centralverein deutscher Staatsbürger jüdischen Glaubens.]

7556. PERLS, HUGO: *Die Komödie der Wahrheit*. Essays. Bern-München: Francke Verlag, 1967. [Incl. Die Wurzeln des Antisemitismus.]

7557. PHELPS, REGINALD H.: *Hitlers 'grundlegende' Rede über den Antisemitismus*. [In]: 'Vierteljahrshefte für Zeitgeschichte'. Hrsg. von Hans Rothfels und Theodor Eschenburg. 16. Jg., 4. H., Okt. Stuttgart: Deutsche Verlags-Anstalt, 1968. Pp. 390-420. [Speech delivered at a public meeting in Munich on 13 August, 1920, on the subject: 'Warum sind wir Antisemiten?'. The text of the speech, a 30 page typescript, is in the Bundesarchiv at Koblenz.]

7558. PHILIPPSON, JOHANNA: *Constantin Frantz*. [In]: LBI Year Book XIII. London, 1968. Pp. 102-119, facsims. [Constantin Frantz (1817-1891) was the author of two antisemitic pamphlets: 'Ahasverus oder die Judenfrage' (1844) [and] 'Der Nationalliberalismus und die Judenherrschaft' (1874).]

7559. POLIAKOV, LÉON: *Histoire de L'Antisémitisme*. Vol. III: *De Voltaire à Wagner*. Paris: Calmann-Lévy, 1968. 506 pp., bibl. (pp. 483-489). (Collection 'Liberté de l'Esprit'). [Vol. I incl.: L'Antisémitisme activé: Allemagne. Luther - L'Allemagne après Luther. Et passim. See No. 830/YB. I. For English transl. of vol. I see No. 5539/YB. XI.]

7560. REICHMANN, EVA G.: *Flucht in den Hass*. Die Ursachen der deutschen Judenkatastrophe. 5. Aufl. Frankfurt am Main: Europäische Verlagsanstalt, 1968. 324 pp., bibl. (pp. 308-319)). (res. novae. Veröffentlichungen zu Politik, Wirtschaft, Soziologie und Geschichte. [Paperback] Bd. 68). [First publ. in English under the title: Hostages of Civilisation. London: Gollancz, 1950. See No. 832/YB. I. First German ed. 1956. See No. 1023/YB.II.]

7561. SAMUEL, MAURICE: *Blood Accusation: The Strange History of the Beiliss Case*. London: Weidenfeld & Nicolson, 1967. 320 pp.

7562. SCHEIDL, FRANZ J.: *Deutschland und die Juden in Vergangenheit und Gegenwart*. Wien: Scheidl-Verlag, 1968. 321 pp.

7563. SCHEIDL, FRANZ J.: *Was der Nationalismus aus Juden machte*. Wien: Scheidl-Verlag, 1968. 95 pp., tabs. (Israel, Bd. 3). [Anti-Zionist].

7564. SCHEIDL, FRANZ J.: *Weltprotest der Christenheit: Jerusalem der ganzen Menschheit*. Wien: Scheidl-Verlag, 1968. 52 pp. (Israel, Bd. 4).

7565. *Verachtet, Gehetzt, Verstossen*. Die Verfolgung des Menschen aus rassischen, politischen und religiösen Gründen. Baden-Baden: Signal-Verlag Hans Frevert, 1968. 224 pp., illus., bibl.

7566. WEINZIERL, E.: *Antisemitismus in der österreichischen Literatur 1900-1938*. [In]: 'Mitteilungen des Österreichischen Staatsarchivs'. Nr. 20. Wien, 1967. Pp. 356-371.

E. Noted Germans and Jews

7567. ADENAUER, KONRAD: *Fragmente, 1959-1963.* Erinnerungen, Bd. 4. Stuttgart: Deutsche Verlagsanstalt, 1968. 375 pp., ports., illus., facsims. [Incl. Begegnung zwischen De Gaulle und Ben Gurion in New York, März 1960. Cf. Kurt Loewenstein in 'MB', 7. Febr. Tel Aviv, 1969.]
7568. BUCER, MARTIN. COHEN, CARL: *Martin Bucer and his Influence on the Jewish Situation.* [In]: LBI Year Book XIII. London, 1968. Pp. 93-101. [Martin Bucer, also Butzer or Bucerus, 1491-1551. Christian Reformer.]
7569. GEORGE, STEFAN. MAYDELL, BODO FREIHERR VON: *Stefan George und das Judentum.* Zur 100. Wiederkehr des Geburtstages des Dichters am 12. Juli. [In]: 'Aufbau'. No. XXXIV/27. July 5. New York, 1968.
7570. *Stefan George 1868, 1968.* Der Dichter und sein Kreis. Eine Ausstellung des Deutschen Literaturarchivs im Schiller-Nationalmuseum Marbach a. N. vom 25. Mai - 31. Okt. 1968. Ausstellungskatalog hrsg. von Bernhard Zeller, Werner Volke, Gerhard Hay u.a. München: Kösel Verlag, 1968. 422 pp., ports., illus., facsims. (Sonderausstellungen des Schiller-Nationalmuseums, Katalog Nr. 19).
7571. HEGEL, GEORG WILH. FRIEDRICH. AVINERI, SHLOMO: *Hegel revisited.* [In]: 'Journal of Contemporary History'. Eds. Walter Laqueur, George L. Mosse. Vol. 3, No. 2, April. London: Weidenfeld and Nicolson, 1968. Pp. 133-147.
7572. KANT, IMMANUEL. AXINN, S.: *Kant on Judaism.* [In]: 'The Jewish Quarterly Review'. Vol. 16, No. 1 (59), July. Philadelphia, 1968. Pp. 9-23.
7573. LESSING, GOTTHOLD EPHRAIM. *Gotthold Ephraim Lessing.* Hrsg. von Gerhard und Sibylle Bauer. Darmstadt: Wissenschaftl. Buchges., 1968. vi, 447 pp. (Wege der Forschung. Bd. 211). [Incl.: Die Weisheit in Lessings Nathan (F. Brüggemann, (1925). Humanität bei Lessing (B. von Wiese (1932). Lessing, Mitwelt und Nachwelt (H. Mayer (1953). Lessings Parabel von den drei Ringen (H. Politzer (1958).]
7574. MANN, HEINRICH. MANN, HEINRICH: *Politische Essays.* Die Auswahl besorgte H. M. Enzensberger. Der Text folgt Heinrich Mann, Essays 1-3. Berlin [East]: Aufbau-Verlag, 1954-1962). Frankfurt a. M.: Suhrkamp Verlag, 1968. 202 pp. (Bibliothek Suhrkamp. Bd. 209). [Incl.: Die Deutschen und ihre Juden (1936), pp. 146-152.]
7575. MANN, THOMAS [and] HEINRICH. WYSLING, HANS, ed.: *Thomas Mann/Heinrich Mann: Briefwechsel 1900-1949.* Frankfurt a. M.: S. Fischer Verlag, 1968. lxi, 371 pp., cover facsims. (Auf Grund der 1965 von der Deutschen Akademie der Künste zu Berlin [East] im Aufbau-Verlag veröffentlichten, von Ulrich Dietzel redigierten Ausgabe, in erweiterter Form hrsg. von Hans Wysling). [Conts. references to German Jews. Cf. Brüderlichkeit als Schicksal (Kurt Loewenstein) [In]: 'MB', 12. Sept. Tel Aviv, 1969.]
7576. VIRCHOW, RUDOLF. KÜMMEL, W.: *Rudolf Virchow und der Antisemitismus.* [In]: 'Medizinhistorisches Journal'. Jg. 3, Nr. 3. Hildesheim, 1968. Pp. 165-179.
7577. WAGNER, RICHARD. GUTMAN, ROBERT W.: *Richard Wagner, the Man, his Mind and his Music.* London: Secker & Warburg, 1968. 544 pp. + 32 pp. ports. and illus. [Cf. H. W. Freyhan: Wagner's Racialist Virus. A new Appraisal of the Composer. [In]: 'AJR Information'. No. XXIV/9, Sept. London, 1969.]
7578. TAPPERT, WILHELM: *Wörterbuch der Unhöflichkeit.* Richard Wagner im Spiegel der Kritik. München: Deutscher Taschenbuch-Verlag, 1967. 134 pp. [First publ. 1876, 2nd ed. 1903.]

X. FICTION, POETRY AND HUMOUR

7579. ADLER, HANS G.: *Panorama.* Roman in zehn Bildern. Olten: Walter Verlag, 1968. 580 pp., front port.
7580. AGNON, S. Y.: *A Guest for the Night.* Transl. by Misha Louvish. London: Gollancz, 1968. 485 pp. [For German version see No. 4950/YB.X.]
7581. ALONI, JENNY: *Die silbernen Vögel.* Erzählungen. München: Starczewski-Verlag, 1968, 68 pp., illus.
7582. AUSLÄNDER, ROSE: *36 Gerechte.* Gedichte. Hamburg: Hoffmann und Campe Verlag, 1968. 64 pp.

312 *Bibliography*

7583. CELAN, PAUL: *Fadensonnen.* Gedichte. Frankfurt a. M.: Suhrkamp, 1968. 128 pp.
7584. DAVID, ERWIN J.: *'Wege'.* Wege eines deutschen Juden und seiner Zeitgenossen. Die Lebensgeschichte des Julius Oppenberg. Roman. Frankfurt a. M.: Europäische Verlagsanstalt, 1968. 288 pp. [Autobiographical novel.]
7585. DOMIN, HILDE: *Das zweite Paradies.* Roman in Segmenten. München: Verlag R. Piper, 1968. 200 pp. [The experience of exile, and of the return to Germany.]
7586. ERMANN, LEO: *Schlussakkord und kämpferischer Neubeginn.* Jerusalem: Priv. printed, 1968. 181 pp. [In German and Hebrew.]
7587. FRIED, ERICH: *Befreiung von der Flucht.* Gedichte und Gegengedichte. Hamburg und Düsseldorf: Claassen Verlag, 1968. 138 pp.
7588. FRIED, ERICH: *Zeitfragen.* Gedichte. München: Carl Hanser Verlag, 1968. 93 pp. (Reihe Hanser. Bd. 5).
7589. GOURI, HAIM: *The Chocolate Deal.* New York: Holt, Rinehart & Winston, 1968. 142 pp. (Transl. from the Hebrew by Seymour Simckes). [A symbolic novel about Jewish survivors of Nazi concentration camps in a German city.]
7590. GRIMMELSHAUSEN, HANS JAKOB CHRISTOFFEL VON: *Des vortrefflich keuschen Josephs in Egypten Lebensbeschreibung samt des Musai Lebens-Lauff.* Hrsg. von Wolfgang Bender. Tübingen: N. Niemeyer, 1968. xxiv, 174 pp., illus., facsims.
7591. HABE, HANS: *Christopher and his Father.* Transl. from the German by Michael Bullock. New York: Coward-McCann, 1968. 320 pp. [A young German, whose father served the Nazis, tries to expiate his father's sins by working on a kibbutz and taking a Hebrew name.]
7592. KALÉKO, MASCHA: *Das himmelblaue Poesie-Album der Mascha Kaléko.* Mit 25 Illustrationen von Bele Bachem. Berlin: Blanvalet Verlag, 1968. 96 pp.
7593. KISHON, EPHRAIM: *Arche Noah, Touristenklasse.* Neue Satiren aus Israel. Aus dem Amerikanischen übertragen von Friedrich Torberg. Reinbek b. Hamburg: Rowohlt Verlag, 1967. 170 pp. (rororo Taschenbuch. Ausg. 756). [Engl. title: Noah's Ark, Tourist Class.]
7594. KISHON, EPHRAIM: *Kishons beste Geschichten.* Die ausgewählten satirischen Geschichten wurden von Friedrich Torberg übersetzt. Berlin: Herbig Verlag, 1968. 328 pp. (Die Bücher der Neunzehn).
7595. KISHON, EPHRAIM: *Pardon wir haben gewonnen.* Satiren mit Cartoons von Dosh. Ins Deutsche übertragen von Friedrich Torberg. München: Langen-Müller, 1968. 185 pp.
7596. *'Meine jüdischen Augen'.* Jiddische Lyrik aus Polen. Aus dem Jiddischen von Hubert Witt. Einmalige bibliophile Ausgabe mit 14 ganzseitigen Original-Punzenstichen von Hermann Naumann. Leipzig: Reclam Verlag, 1968. 160 pp.
7597. PEREZ, JIZCHAK LEJB: *Der Golem.* Aus dem Jiddischen übersetzt und mit 7 Original-Holzschnitten von Peter Richter. Freiburg i. Br.: Syrinx-Presse, 1967. 17 Bl. (Quadrate, Bd. 1).
7598. *(Des) Rebben Pfeiffenrohr.* Eine Sammlung jiddischer Erzählungen in der Übersetzung von Alexander Eliasberg. Mit einem 'Vorwort' von Rudolf J. Neumann. München: Deutscher Taschenbuch Verlag, 1968.
7599. ROKEAH, DAVID: *Ijara.* Hebräisch-Deutsch. Übersetzung von Benigna Chilla und Ruth Geyer. Frankfurt a. M.: Heiderhoff Verlag, 1968. 36 pp. (Reihe ars poetica, Bd. 5).
7600. SCHOLEM ALEJCHEM: *Der behexte Schneider.* Erzählung. Aus dem Jiddischen von Max Reich. Mit Illustrationen von Anatoli Kaplan. Berlin [East]: Verlag Volk und Welt, 1968. 128 pp., illus.
7601. SINGER, ISAAC BASHEVIS: *Gimpel der Narr.* Ausgewählte Erzählungen. Hamburg: Rowohlt Verlag, 1968. 367 pp. [Written in Yiddish, transl. into English. Transl. into German from the English version.]
7602. STRAUSS, GEORG: *'Vita nuova in Kanaan'.* Roman einer Liebe. Genf und Hamburg: Verlag Kossodo, 1968. 260 pp.
7603. WERFEL, FRANZ: *Das Lied von Bernadette.* Roman. München/Zürich: Droemer/Knaur, 1968. 426 pp. (Knaur Taschenbücher, Nr. 170). [Lizenz des Fischer Verl., Frankfurt a. M. First publ. 1941.]

Index to Bibliography

Abendroth, Wolfgang, 6896
Adenauer, Konrad, 7567
Adler, Alfred, 7152
Adler, Cyrus H., 6972
Adler, H. G., 7579
Adler, Israël, 7450
Adler, Max, 7180
Adler, Victor, 7181
Adler-Rudel, S., 6992
Adorno, Theodor W., 7182-7184, 7197, 7212
Agnon, S[amuel] J[osef], 7434, 7580
Agus, Jacob B[ernard], 7041
Albérès, R. M., 7300
Alexander von Humboldt Stiftung, 7533
Allemann, Beda, 7228, 7436
Aloni, Jenny, 7581
Alsace, 6919
Alsenz (Palatinate), 6934
Altenberg, Peter [Richard Engländer], 7185-7186
Althusser, Louis, 7381
Altmann, Alexander, 7078, 7079, 7080
Altona, 7093
Amercian Jewish Congress, 7092
American Jewish Year Book, 6989, 7034
Ammon, Robert, 7357
Andernach, 6937
Anders, Günther [Günther Stern], 7493
Andreas-Salomé, Lou, 7241
Andrew, Edward, 7382
Andrian, Leopold von, 7187, 7509
Anglo-Israel Association, 7124
Anti-Defamation League of B'nai B'rith, 7527
Antisemitism, 6922, 6923, 6973, 7017, 7159, 7533, 7542-7566, 7576
Antisemitism, Austrian, 7566
— Antisemitic Parties, 6892, 6938
Archiv für Sozialgeschichte, Hannover, 7379, 7393
Arendt, Erich, 7188
Arendt, Hannah, 7138, 7152, 7191, 7192, 7364
Arens, Hanns, 7489
Argoud, Antoine, 7297
Arnau, Frank, 7297
Arnsberg, Paul, 7090
Aron, William, 6920
Aronsfeld, C. C., 6970, 7526
Arts and Crafts, Jews in, 6907, 6959
Asch, Georg, 6935
Assimilation, 7348
Auerbach, B., 7506

Aury, Dominique, 7327
Ausländer, Rose [Scherzer-Ausländer], 7582
Austria, 6947-6951, 7010, 7566
Austromarxismus, 7180
Avenary, Hanoch, 7450
Avineri, Shlomo, 7383, 7571
Avneri, Zwi, 6893
Axinn, S., 7572

Bab, Julius, 7189
Bachem, Bele, 7592
Bacher, Wilhelm, 6958
Baden, 6899-6900
Baden-Wurttemberg, 6993
Baden-Württemberg, Veröffentlichungen der Staatl. Archivverwltg., 6899, 6993
Badenhausen, Rolf, 7155
Baeck, Leo, 7042-7044, 7049
Baer, J. F., 7087
Baeyer, Alexander, 7169
Baier, Lothar, 7552
Balabkins, Nicholas, 7036
Balfour Declaration, 7124
Ball-Kaduri, K. J., 6994, 7008
Ballin, Albert, 7190
Baneth, Jecheskel Eduard, 6958
Bankers, Jewish, 7172, 7210, 7500
Barrett, Cyril, 7474
Baruch, Hugo see Bilbo, Jack
Baskin, Wade, 7300
Basle, 6963, 6964
— Isr. Fürsorge, 6964
Bato, Yomtov Ludwig, 6958, 7348
Bauer, Felice, 7302, 7308
Bauer, Gerhard, 7573
Bauer, Ilse, 7189
Bauer, Sybille, 7287, 7573
Bauer, Y., 7114
Baum, Hans-Werner, 7486
Baumann, Walter, 7217
Bavaria, 7004
Bayer, Bathja, 7450
Bayern see Bavaria
Beek, M. A., 7051
Beethoven-Haus, Bonn, 7408
(The) Beiliss Case, 7561
Bein, Alex, 7116, 7130
Belmont, August, 6966
Belmore, H. W., 7193
Ben Barka, 7297
Ben Bella, 7297
Ben Gurion, David, 7567
Ben Shemen, 7125
Bender, Wolfgang, 7590

Benedict Family, 7494
Benjamin, Walter, 7138, 7191-7200, 7313
Bentwich, Norman, 7037, 7106
Beradt, Charlotte, 6995
Berend-Corinth, Charlotte 7201-7202
Berendsohn, Walter A., 7435
Berger, Uwe, 7333
Bergman, S. H., 7052, 7107-7108, 7370, 7471, 7535
Bergmann, Joachim, 7377
Berlin, 6901-6909
— Hausvogteiplatz, 6901
— Historische Kommission, Veröffentlichungen der, 6903, 7512
— Mendelssohn-Archiv der Staatsbibliothek, 7405
Berlin, Isaiah, 7384
'Berliner Tageblatt', 7479
Bernard, Walter, 7225
Bernays, Martha, 7501
Berndt, Heide, 7377
Bernfeld, Simon, 7045
Bernstein, Eduard, 7203
Berolzheimer, Heinrich, 6933
Berthold, Margot, 7139
Bettelheim, Bruno, 6995
Beyer, Manfred, 7232
Bibliotheca Rabbinica, 7046
Bieberstein, Johannes Rogalla von, 7542
Biedenkopf, Kurt Hans, 7344
Bielefeld, 6910
Bilbo, Jack [Baruch, Hugo], 7204
Bilges, Hans-Erich, 7032
Billigheimer, S., 7047
Binder, Hartmut, 7301
Bird, Thomas E., 7048
Birnbaum, Ernst, 7109
Bloch, Ernst, 7115, 7197, 7205-7209, 7385
Bloch, Joseph, 6919
Blum, Julius, Pasha, 7210
B'nai B'rith Vienna, 6978
Boas, Franz, 7211
Bock, Emil, 7522
Boden, Hans Constantin, 7417
Böcher, Otto, 6937
Böckel, Otto, 6923
Böhm, Adolf, 7110
Böhmen see Bohemia
Böll, Heinrich, 7386
Böning, Hansjürgen, 7428
Börne, Ludwig, 7495
Bohemia, 6954, 6957
Boisdeffre, Pierre de, 7300
Bondi, Fritz see Scarpi, N. O.
Bondy, François, 7514
Bonn, 6911-6913
Borchardt, Marie Luise, 7213
Borchardt, Rudolf, 7212-7214
Borchsenius, Poul, 7534
Borger, Riekele, 7134
Borgis, Ilona, 7475

Born, Max, 7215, 7498
Borowitz, Eugene B., 7049, 7050
Bosl, Karl, 6940
Bracher, Dietrich, 7176
Brachmann, Karin, 7381
Braham, Randolph L., 6962
Brandt, Willy, 7146, 7417
Branscombe, Peter, 7268
Brasch, Moritz, 7077
Braubach, Max, 6911, 6912
Braun, Werner, 7120
Brecht, Bertolt, 7155
Brenner Hildegard, 7200
Breslau, 6996
— Jahrbuch der Schlesischen Friedrich-Wilhelms Universität, 7284
Breslauer, Walter, 7100
Breuer, Otto, 7553
Briegleb, Klaus, 7265
Brilling, Bernhard, 6935, 6947, 6959, 6961, 7093
Broch, Hermann, 7138, 7142, 7216-7222, 7406
Brock, Erich, 7454
Brod, Max, 7223-7224, 7313, 7471, 7472, 7528
Bromberg, 6914
Bronsen, David, 7429
Brookes, Blanche, 6979
Brookes, Reuben S., 6979
Broshi, Magen, 7122
Bruckner, Ferdinand (Theodor Tagger), 7142
Brüggemann, F., 7573
Brunner, Alfred, 7498
Brunner, Constantin, 7225
Buber, Martin, 7048, 7049, 7051-7064, 7111-7112, 7346
Bubser, Eberhard, 7474
Bucer, Martin [also Butzer or Bucerus], 7568
Bucky, Gustav, 7499
Buehne, S. Z., 7304
(Die) bürgerlichen Parteien in Deutschland, 6892
Bukofzer, Werner, 7226
Bullock, Michael, 7591
Bundesarchiv Koblenz, 7557
Bundesrepublik, 7543
Bundeszentrale für politische Bildung, Bonn, 7040, 7129, 7543
Burger, Hilde, 7507
Burkhard, Hugo, 6925, 6997
Busch, Helmut, 6938
Busse, Kurt, 7141

Calder, Jenny, 7332
Calé, Walter, 7346
Calkins, Kenneth R., 7260
Campe, Julius, 7495
Canetti, Elias, 7302
Carl Heymann Verlag, 7278

Carmichael, Joel, 7387
Carrouges, Michel, 7303
Carsten, Francis L., 7544
Carter, John, 7141
Cassel, Otto, 6905
Cassirer, Ernst, 7227
Catholic Church, 7017
Cecil, Lamar, 7190
Celan, Paul, 7228-7229, 7583
Cemeteries (Jewish), Wolfenbüttel, 6943
Central-Verein deutscher Staatsbürger
    jüdischen Glaubens (C.V.), 6892, 7094,
    7555
'C.V. Zeitung', 6980
Centre National Des Hautes Etudes Juives,
    Bruxelles, 7053
Černy, Bohumil, 7545
Červinka, František, 7546
Chagall, Marc, 7101, 7230
Chassidismus see Hasidism
Chilla, Benigna, 7599
Chodziesner, Gertrud see Kolmar, Gertrud
Christian-Jewish Cooperation, Society for,
    6939
'Christlich-Jüdisches Forum', 7537
Classen, Werner, 7437
Clauss, Volkmar, 7423
Cohen, Carl, 7568
Cohen, Hermann, 6975, 7065-7071, 7160
Cohen, Judith, 7473
Cohn, Alexander Meyer, 7172
Cohn, Bertha, 6988
Coleville, Maurice, 7340
Cologne, 6937
Conference on Jewish Social Studies, 6985,
    7018
Corinth, Thomas, 7201
Cornu, Auguste, 7388
Cotta, Friedrich von, 7495
Council of Jews from Germany, 7100
Court Jew, 7414
Cranach, Agnes von, 7330
Creighton, Basil, 7369
Croner, Fritz, 7496
Cutler, A., 7547
Czech Jewish University Students,
    Association of, 6956
Czechoslovakia, 6952-6961, 7028-7029

Dähn, Brunhilde, 6901
Dam, Hendrik George van, 7030
Dan, J., 7087
Dan, Robert, 6952, 6981
David, Erwin J., 7584
Davidsohn, Hans see Hoddis, Jakob van
Dayan, Ruth, 7517
De Gaulle, 7567
Deak, Istvan, 7178
Desautels, Elaine, 7230
Dessau (Anhalt), 7080
Deutsch, Gotthard, 6967

Deutsche Akademie der Künste, Berlin-East,
    7238, 7575
Deutsche Akademie für Sprache und
    Dichtung, Darmstadt, 7480, 7525
Deutsche Demokratische Republik (D.D.R.)
    see German Democratic Republic
Deutscher Akademischer Austauschdienst,
    7533
'Deutscher Palästina-Verein', Zeitschrift,
    7113
Deutsches Literaturarchiv im Schiller-Natio-
    nalmuseum Marbach a. N., 7570
Dick, Auguste, 7412
Dickinson, John K., 7091
Diersch, Manfred, 7442
Dietzel, Ulrich, 7575
Diwald, Hellmut, 7144
Döblin, Alfred, 7142, 7231-7234
Domin, Hilde, 7585
Dornemann, Luise, 7389
Dortmund, Institut für Zeitungsforschung,
    7395
Dosh, —, 7595
Dresden, 7440
Drewitz, Ingeborg, 7434
Droz, Jacques, 6895
Druon, Maurice, 7431
Dubois, Jacques, 7535
Dünnwald, Anjuta, 7402
Düsseldorf, 7440
Duisburg, Schriftenreihe für Geschichte und
    Heimatkunde Duisburgs, 7160
Durzak, Manfred, 7218-7219

Eban, Abba, 7072
Eckert, Georg, 7160
Eckert, Willehad, 7535
Economics, Industry, Trade, Jews in, 6901,
    6977, 7174, 7190
Edel, Elmar, 7134
Egen, Horst, 7021
Ehrenberg, Eva, 7497
Ehrenstein, Albert, 7235
Eibenschütz, R. Jonathan, 7093
Eichmann, Adolf, 7297
Eidelberg, Shlomo, 7414
Eilers, Rolf, 6918
Einstein, Albert, 7141, 7152, 7167, 7236-
    7237, 7498-7499
Einstein, Siegfried, 7325
Eisenhuth, Wolfgang, 7140
Eisler, Hanns, 7238
— Hanns-Eisler-Archiv, 7238
Elath, Eliahu, 7109
Elbing (Town), 6915
Eliasberg, Alexander, 7598
Elsass see Alsace
Elsner, Jürgen, 7238
Elvers, R[udolf], 7512
Emancipation (Jewish), 6895, 6900
Emig, Erik, 7011

Emigrants, 7456, 7496
Emrich, Wilhelm, 7304
'Emuna', Blätter für Christlich-Jüdische Zusammenarbeit, 7149, 7211
Engels, Friedrich, 7380, 7388, 7511
Engländer, Richard see Altenberg, Peter
Enzensberger, Hans Magnus, 7436, 7574
Epstein, Felix, 6921
Er[d]mann, Leo, 7586
Ernemann, Rudolf, 7395
Erringhausen, Maurice L[eon], 7145
Eschenburg, Theodor, 7557
Esh, Shaul, 6975, 7097, 7114
Ettinghausen, Maurice see Sachs, Maurice
'European Jewry', 7382
Evian Conference, 6992
Exil-Literatur, 6987, 7146-7151, 7527
Expressionism, 7166, 7478

Farkas, Erwin, 6962
Fashion Trade, Jews in, 6901
Feder, Ernst, 7239
Federal German Republic, 7543
Feinberg, Nathan, 7356
Feiwel, Berthold, 7112
'Felice' see Bauer, Felice
Fetscher, Iring, 7115, 7365
(The) Feuchtwanger-Family, 7500
Feuchtwanger, Lion, 7240
Feuer, Lewis S., 7390
Fietkau, Wolfgang, 7434
Fighter, Remus, 7427
Fischer, Ernst, 7197, 7391
Fischer, Heinrich, 7335, 7337
Fischer, Horst, 6936
Fischer, Peter, 7478
Fischer, Samuel, 6958
Fischer-Barnicol, Dorothea, 7061
Fischer-Barnicol, Hans, 7061
Flach, Werner, 7065
Flannery, Edward H., 7548
Flechtheim, Alfred, 7169
Flechtheim, Ossip K[urt], 7363
Flesch, Carl, 7167
Forman, Werner, 6951
Fraenkel, Annie, 6982
Franconia, 6916, 6925
Frank, Anne, 7000
Frank I. Julius, 7095
Franken see Franconia
Frankfurt/Main, 7031, 7531
— Jewish Community of (new), 7031
Frankfurter, Felix, 6968
Frantz, Constantin, 7558
Freedman, Max, 6968
Freiburg (Přibor), 7249
'Freiburger Rundbrief', 7043, 7535
Freie Universität Berlin, 7417
Freiligrath, Ferdinand, 7510
Freimann, Aron, 6982, 7105
Frenzel, Ivo, 7208

Freud, Ernst L., 7501, 7502, 7503
Freud, Lucie, 7502
Freud, Sigmund, 7141, 7241-7253, 7501-7503
Freund, Joachim Hellmut, 7490
Freund, Leopold, 7254
Freund-Eibuschütz, Hedy, 7254
Freundlich, Otto, 7255
Freyhan, Wilhelm, 7577
Fricke, Dieter, 6892
Fried, Erich, 7587, 7588
Friedberg (Hesse), 6917, 6937
Friedell, Egon, 7338
Friedenthal, Richard, 7490
Friedländer, Max J., 7256
Friedlander, Albert H[oschander], 6998, 7043, 7044
Friedla[e]nder, **Fritz, 7264**
Friedmann, Georges, 7073
Friedmann, Hermann, 7142
Friedrich II., 6906
Friedrich-Ebert-Stiftung, 7023, 7147, 7379, 7393
Fritz Thyssen Stiftung, 7533
Frölich, Paul, 7365
Fromm, Erich, 7257
Fuchs, H. R., 7357

Gabriel, Sister Louis of Sion, 7539
Gadamer, Hans Georg, 7227, 7323
Gade, N. W., 7506
Galindez, Jésus de, 7297
Gallas, Helga, 7200
Galley, Eberhard, 7267, 7269, 7273
Galling, Kurt, 7134
Gandhi, Mahatma, 7060
Gause, Fritz, 6926
Gay, Peter, 7152
Gemkow, Heinrich, 7392
George, Stefan, 7569-7570
— Stefan George Kreis, 7570
German Democratic Republic, 7032
German-Israeli Relations, 7528-7533
German-Jewish Relationship, 7526-7527
Germania Judaica, 6893
Germania Judaica, Kölner Bibliothek zur Geschichte des deutschen Judentums, 6973, 6983
— Mitteilungsblatt der, 6983
Gerson, Menachem (Hermann), 7054
Gertner, Meir, 7434
Gesellschaft für Christlich-Jüdische Zusammenarbeit see Christian-Jewish Co-operation Society
Gesellschaft für Jüdiche Volkskunde, Mitteilungen der, 7096
Geyer, Ruth, 7599
Giere, Wolfgang, 7361
Giessler, Rupert, 7535
Givet, Jacques, 7549
Godal, Eric, 7504

Godesberg-Mehlem, 6918
Göhring, Martin, 6895
Görres-Gesellschaft, 7271
Goes, Albrecht, 7000, 7019, 7055, 7062
Goethe Institut, 7533
Goethe, Johann Wolfgang von, 7306
Gold, Hugo, 6898
Goldschmidt, F[rederick], 7037
Goldschmidt, Hermann Levin, 7296, 7458
Goldschmit, Rudolf, 7288
Goll, Claire, 7258
Goll, Ivan, 7258
Gollwitzer, Helmut, 7535
Gombrich, E. H., 7243
Gottgetreu, Erich, 7528
Gottwald, Adriana, 6995
Gouri, Haim, 7589
Graber, Heinz, 7231
Grabowsky, Adolf, 7259
Graetz, Heinrich, 7074
Grass, Günter, 7233
Greenberg, Martin, 7305
Grégoire, Pierre, 7146
Grimmelshausen, Hans Jakob Christoffel von, 7590
Grinstein, Alexander, 7244
Gross, Babette, 7411
Grossmann, Kurt R., 7091, 7526
Grote, Heiner, 7353
Grüber, Propst Heinrich, 6999
Grünewald, Pinchas Paul, 7066
Grunwald, Kurt, 7500
Grunwald, Max, 7096
Guggenheim Family, 6969
Guggenheim, Willy, 7119
Gunneman, Hedwig, 7510
Gutfeld, Ludwig, 7101
Gutman, Robert W., 7577

Haacke, Wilmont, 7169
Haage, Peter, 7338
Haas, Willy, 7194, 7508
Haase, Hugo, 7260
Habe, Hans, 7591
Haberman, Joshua, 7092
Habermas, Jürgen, 7184, 7208, 7377
Hack, Berthold, 7406
Hacker, Walter, 7022
Hackert, Fritz, 7430
Haguenau (Alsace), 6919
Hahn, Hugo, 6975
Hahn, Kurt, 7164, 7261
Halperin, Irving, 7025
Hamburg, 6920-6921
— Isr. Krankenhaus, 6921
— Verein für Hamburgische Geschichte, 7275, 7469
Hamburger, Arno S., 6925
Hamburger, Ernest, 7153
Hameln, Jente, 7505
Hanke, Peter, 7006

Harden, Maximilian, 7262
Harris, David, 7122
Hartl, Edwin, 7339
Hartmann, August, 7554
Hartmann, Wilfried, 7438
Hasenclever, Walter, 7263
Hasidism, 7056
Hatvani, Paul (Hirsch, Paul), 7185
Haug, Fritz, 7377
Hay, Gerhard, 7570
Hearst, Ernest, 7527
(The) Hebrew University of Jerusalem, 7106, 7112, 7235, 7345, 7531
Hegel, Georg Wilh. Friedrich, 7571
Heidn, Willy, 6942
Heifetz, Jascha, 7167
Heilbrunn, Rudolf M., 7090
Heilbut, Iven George, 7491
Heimann, A., 7498
Heimann, Hugo, 6905
Heimann, Moritz, 7264
Heimpel, Hermann, 7154
Heine, Heinrich, 7163, 7265-7274
— Heine Archiv, 7268
— 'Heine-Jahrbuch 1969', 7269
Heine, Salomon, 6921, 7275
Heine, Thomas Theodor, 7276
Heinig, Karl, 7140
Heinrich, Gerd, 6902
Heintel, Peter, 7180
Heise, Rosemarie, 7200
Heissenbüttel, Helmut, 7195, 7214
Heller, Friedrich, 7368
Heller, Imre, 7275
Hellige, Hans Dieter, 7418
Hendy, Philip, 7122
Hensel, Cecile, 7405
Hensel, Sebastian, 7083
Herdan-Zuckmayer, Alice, 7483
Herlitz, Georg, 6975, 7116
Herlitzka, Ernst Karl, 7181
Herman, Jan, 6954
Hermann, Armin, 7143
Herrmann, Fritz H., 6917
Herschel, Sir John, 7277
Herz, Henriette, 7495
Herzfeld, Hans, 6902, 7512
Herzfelde, Wieland, 7351
Herzl, Theodor, 7117
Heschel, Abraham J[oshua], 7048, 7049
Hess, H., 6928
Hesse, 6917, 6922-6923, 6937
— Archiv für Hessische Geschichte und Altertumskunde, 6922
Heuss, Theodor, 7154, 7357
Heydorn, Heinz-Joachim, 7114, 7346
Heyen, Franz Josef, 7002
Heymann, Carl, 7278
Hilburg, Erwin K. J., 7056
Hildesheim, 6924
— Presseamt der Stadtverwaltung, 6924

Hildesheimer, Wolfgang, 7279
Hilferding, Rudolf, 7280
Hiller, Ferdinand, 7506
Hilscher, Eberhard, 7487
Hilsner, Leopold, 7545, 7546
— (The) Hilsner Case, 7545, 7546
Hirsch, August, 7281
Hirsch, Ernst E., 7282
Hirsch, Helmut, 7354, 7393
Hirsch, Max, 7160
Hirsch, Paul see Hatvani, Paul
Hirsch, Rudolf, 7508
Hirsch, Samson Raphael, 7084
Hirsch, Siegmund, 7283
— Hirsch-Kupfer-Messingwerke, 7283
Hirst, Hugo (Hirsch, Hugo), 6970
Historische Kommission für Schlesien, 7439
Hitler, Adolf, 7557
Hlavácová, Jirina, 6954
Hoddis, Jakob van (Hans Davidsohn), 7284
Hodin, Josef Paul, 7306
Höck, Wilhelm, 7307
Höcker, Karla, 7497
Hönigswald, Richard, 7285-7286
Hoffmann, O., 7392
Hofmann, Fritz, 7457
Hofmann, Hanns Hubert, 6916
Hofmannsthal, Hugo von, 7087, 7142, 7287-7294, 7424, 7507-7509
Hohenlose (Wurttemberg), 6946
Hohoff, Curt, 7343, 7468
Holl, K., 6922
Holmqvist, Bengt, 7436
Holz, Hans Heinz, 7197, 7378
Hoppe, Manfred, 7289
Horckheimer, Max, 7295-7296
Horst, Karl August, 7317
Horwath, Peter, 7443
Hospitals (Jewish): Hamburg, 6921
Hoyt, Edwin P., 6969
Huder, Walther, 7189
Hübinger, Paul Egon, 7359
Hüssler, Georg, 7535
Hüttenbach (Franconia), 6925
Hüttinger, Eduard, 7416
Hüttner, Hans, 7425
Hundsnurscher, Franz, 6899
Hungary, 6962
Husserl, Edmund, 7286

Idelsohn, A[braham] Z[wi], 7102
Iltis, Rudolf, 7022, 7028
Institut für Marxismus-Leninismus, 7156, 7203, 7392, 7511
Institute of Jewish Affairs, London, 7029, 7526
Isaac, Jules, 7536
Israel, 7040, 7109, 7118, 7127, 7129, 7133, 7327
(The) Israel Honorarium, 6984
Italiaander, Rolf, 7508

Jackson, Marian, 7163
Jacob, Berthold, 7297
Jacob, E., 7057
Jacobowski, Ludwig, 7298-7299
Jacobsohn, Siegfried, 7178
Jacobson, Jacob, 6903, 6935, 6975
Jahn, Ulrich, 7172
Jahnn, Hans Henny, 7220
Jan, Helmut von, 6924
Janouch, Gustav, 7309
Janowitz, Franz, 6954
Jens, Walter, 7436
Jerusalem, 7119-7123, 7230, 7352, 7531, 7564
Jewish Art, 7101, 7103
Jewish Art and Music, 7101-7105
Jewish Book Council of America, 7071
Jewish Journal of Sociology, 7114
Jewish Music, 7102, 7104, 7105
(The) Jewish Publication Society of America, Philadelphia, 6989, 7034, 7126
Jewish Quarterly Review, 7572
Jewish Social Studies, New York, 6985, 7018, 7414
Jeziorkowski, Klaus, 7298
Johann-Gottfried-Herder-Forschungsrat, 6926
Jonas, Klaus W., 7310
Journal of Contemporary History, 7571
'Judaica Bohemiae', 6954
Judaica Katalog, 6986
'Judaism', New York, 7547
(Das) Judentum am Scheideweg, 7550
Juhre, Arnim, 7434
(Otto) Junker GmbH, 7283
Just, Gottfried, 7444

Kabbala, 7088
Kacer-Bock, Gundhild, 7522
Kafka, Franz, 7087, 7142, 7300-7321
Kahane, P. P., 7122
Kahn, Ludwig, 6941, 6964-6965, 7470
Kaleko, Mascha, 7592
Kalz, Wolf, 7347
Kant, Immanuel, 7572
Kantzenbach, Friedrich Wilhelm, 7220
Kaplan, Anatoli Lwowitsch, 7600
Kaplan, Mordecai Menahem, 7049
Kappel (Wurttemberg), 6945
Karff, Samuel E., 7045
Karl Marx 1818-1968, 7394, 7403
Karlsberg, B., 7038
Karmán, Theodore von, 7322
Katcher, Leo, 7033
Katz, Irving, 6966
Katz, Karl, 7122
Kaufmann, Fritz, 7323
Kaufmann, Ludwig, 7535
Kehr, Helen, 6980
Keim, Anton M., 7001
Kellner, Viktor, 7108
Kelsen, Hans, 7324

Kempner, Robert M. W., 7000
Kenyon, Kathleen M[ary], 7123
Kessler, Harry Graf, 7507
Kesten, Hermann 7527
Kestenberg-Gladstein, Ruth, 6954
Kibbuz, 7128
Kienzl, Florian, 6904
Kiesinger, Georg, 7529
Kimche, Jon, 7124
Kindler, Arie, 7551
Kipphardt, Heinar, 7415
Kirchner, Martin, 6905
Kirschner, Bruno, 7551
Kisch, Egon Erwin, 7325-7326
Kishon, Ephraim, 7593-7595
Klagenfurth, 6949
Klapp, Eckhard, 7371
Kleinmann, Moritz, 7322
Kleinschmidt, Gert, 7320
Klemperer, Otto, 7167
Kliem, Manfred, 7380, 7396
Knölke, Bärbel Dorothee, 7424
Knoke, Karl Hermann, Deutscher Bot-
    schafter, 7528
Knoll, Bua, 7189
Koblenz (Coblence), 7002
Köhler, Philip, 6922
Köln see Cologne
König, Josef, 7407
Königsberg i. Pr., 6926
Köster, Kurt, 7146
Köstler, Arthur, 7327-7332
Kohn, Caroline, 7340
Kolb, Eberhard, 7179
Kollek, Teddy, 7121
Kolmar, Gertrud (Chodziesner Gertrud),
    7333-7334
Kommission für Geschichte d. Parlamenta-
    rismus und der politischen Parteien,
    Veröffentlichungen der, 7456
Konrads, Josef, 7342
Konstanz am Bodensee, 6927
Kopp, August, 6934
Korell, Adolf, 6922
Korn, B., 7211
Korthals, Otto, 6942
Kott, Joseph, 7109
Kraft, Werner, 7087, 7158, 7311, 7334,
    7341
Kralik, Heinrich, 7368
Kramer, Gerhard Friedrich, 7275
Kraus, Dina, 7530
Kraus, Karl, 7142, 7262, 7335-7343
Krauss, Samuel, 6990
Kreisler, Fritz, 7167
Krejci, Karel, 6954
Krieger, Peter, 7162
Kronstein, Heinrich, 7344
Kümmel, W., 7576
Künzelsau, 6945
Küster, Otto, 7039

Kupper, Margarete, 7352
Kurschat, Heinrich A., 6931
Kurz, Paul Konrad, 7270
Kurzweil, Zvi E., 7058
Kutjepow, Alexander P., 7297
Kwasnik-Rabinowicz, Kurt (Aharon Moshe),
    6955

Lacoque, André, 7053
Laemmle, Ernst, 6944
Lamm, Hans, 7034, 7394, 7419
Landau (Pfalz), 6928
Landau, Edmund, 7345
Landauer, Gustav, 7346-7347
Landmann, Michael, 7453
Landsteiner, Karl, 7348
Lane, Barbara Miller, 7159
Lang, Lothar, 7276
Lange, Friedrich Albert, 7160
Langgässer, Elisabeth, 7142
Lanzer, Wanda, 7181
Laqueur, Walter Ze'ev, 7571
Larsen, Egon, 7499
Lasker-Schüler, Else, 7142, 7349-7352
Lassalle, Ferdinand, 7163, 7353-7355
Lattes, Dante, 7256
Lauer, S., 7537
Lauterpacht, Sir Hersch, 7356
Law, Jews in, 7282, 7324, 7344, 7356
Lazarus, Ludwig, 7505
Lazis, Asja, 7200
Lebeck, Michael, 6960
Leber, Hermann Rudolf, 7266
Lehmann, Siegfried, 7125
Leib, Otto S., 6927
Leippe, Ulla, 7122
Leisler, Edda, 7425, 7426
Lembeck, Fred, 7361
Leo Baeck Institute, 6977, 7042, 7471
— Bulletin, 6894, 6960, 6974, 6996, 7079,
    7080, 7081, 7089, 7090, 7093, 7186,
    7494
— Schriftenreihe Wissenschaftlicher Ab-
    handlungen des, 6936, 7153
— Veröffentlichung des, 6893, 7551
— Year Book XIII, 6935, 6975, 6992,
    7067, 7074, 7099, 7114, 7116, 7239,
    7420, 7421, 7455, 7540, 7546, 7558, 7568
— New York, 6960, 6976
— Leo Baeck Memorial Lecture 11, 6960
— News, 6976
Lesser, Ernst Josef, 7357
Lesser, Jonas, 7358
Lesser, Serafine, 7358
Lessing, Theodor, 7573
Leupold, Hans, 7240
Levi, Hermann, 7506
Levin, Rahel see Varnhagen von Ense, Rahel
Levin, Shmarya, 7126
Levinas, Emmanuel, 7053
Levison, Wilhelm, 7359

Lewin, Kurt, 7085
Lewinsohn, Richard see Morus
Leymarie, Jean, 7230
Lichtenberg, Jean-Paul, 7538
Lidzbarski, Mark, 7360
Liebermann, Max, 6905
Liebeschütz, Hans, 7067
Link, Werner, 7456
Linke, Norbert, 7183
Linn, Dorothea, 7004
Liptzin, Solomon, 7161
Locke, Richard Adams, 7277
Loewenberg, Ernst L., 7089
Loewenstein, Kurt, 7567, 7575
Loewenstein, Rudolf M., 7552
Loewi, Otto, 7361
Löwith, Karl, 7068
Loewy, Wilhelm, 7127
Loose, Gerhard, 7312
Lothar, Fritz, 7397
Louis Gabriel, Sister, 7539
Louvish, Misha, 7580
Lowenthal, Ernst G., 7035
Lubitsch, Ernst, 7362
Luckner, Gertrud, 7019, 7535
Lübeck, 6929
— Archiv der Hansestadt, 6929
Lueders, Carl H., 7146
Lüth, Erich, 7275
Luther, Martin, 7559
Luxemburg, Rosa, 7138, 7363-7366
Luzzatto, Guido L., 7256

Maass, H. A., 6910
Macintyre, Alasdair Chalmers, 7245
Mader, Willi, 7438a
Mähren see Moravia
März, Eduard, 7280
Magen David Adom, 7109
Mahler, Eduard, 7075
Mahler, Gustav, 7367-7369
Mahler-(Werfel), Alma, 7369
Maihofer, Werner, 7207, 7394
Maimon, Salomon, 7370-7371
Mainz, 7001, 7002
Maitlis, Jaacob J., 7492
Malcolm, Norman, 7477
Mandel, Jean, 6925
Mann, Golo, 7146, 7163, 7164, 7527
Mann, Heinrich, 7574, 7575
Mann, Otto, 7142
Mann, Thomas, 7575
Mannheim, 7357, 7412
Marcel, Gabriel, 7053
Marcel, P., 7535
Marcic, René, 7553
Marcuse, Herbert, 7372-7378
Marek, Franz, 7391
Marienburg, 6930
Marti, Kurt, 7434
Martin, Berthold, 7144

Marx, Adolf Bernhard, 7408
Marx, Heinrich, 7379
Marx, Jenny, 7389
Marx, Karl, 7141, 7160, 7163, 7379-7403,
    7510-7511
Marxism, 7207
Masaryk, Thomas G., 7545, 7546
Masch, Rüdiger, 6923
Massiczek, Albert, 7397, 7403, 7553
Matthias, Erich, 7456
Max von Baden, Prinz, 7164, 7260
Maydell, Bodo, Freiherr von, 7569
Mayer, Eugen, 6975, 7540
Mayer, Hans, 7146, 7267, 7398, 7573
Mayer, Paul, 7165
Medicine, Jews in, 7154, 7281, 7357, 7361,
    7409, 7440, 7469, 7517, 7524
Meier, Annemarie, 7119
Meier, Kurt, 7003
Meier-Cronemeyer, Hermann, 7128
'Meine jüdischen Augen', 7596
Melber, Jehuda, 7069
Melchinger, Christa, 7445
Melchinger, Siegfried, 7426, 7436
Melchior, Marcus, 7076
Melchior, Werner, 7076
Memelland, 6931
Memmingen (Bavaria), 7004
Mendels(s)ohn, Eric(h), 7159, 7404
(The) Mendelssohn Family, 7083
Mendelssohn, Moses, 6990, 7077-7083, 7084
Mendelssohn-Bartholdy, Felix, 7405, 7512
Mendelssohn-Archiv der Staatsbibliothek in
    Berlin, 7405
Menke, Willy, 6892
Menuhin, Yehudi, 7167
Mertz, Wolfgang, 7484
Metal Trade, Jews in, 6969, 7283
Metall, Rudolf Aladár, 7324
Metzger, H. M., 6950
Meyer, Georg Heinrich, 7406
Meyer, Hans Chanoch, 6929
Meyer, Hermann J., 7157
Meyer, Herrmann M. Z., 7081
Meyer-Clason, Curt, 7384
Meyer-Cohn Alexander, 7172
Meyerbeer, Giacomo, 7187
Michael, Reuwen, 7074
Michel, D., 7434
Michel, Henri, 7026
Michelfelder, Gottfried, 6932
Michelmore, Peter, 7236
Midas, Eric, 6894
Mies, Paul, 7408
Mikulasch, 6958
Miller, Susanne, 7170
Milstein, Nathan, 7167
Misch, Georg, 7407
Misch, Ludwig, 7408
Misrahi, Robert, 7059
Missac, P., 7313

Mitchell, Donath, 7369
Monz, Heinz, 7379, 7394, 7399
Moravia, 7249
Morse, Arthur D., 7005
Morus (Lewinsohn, Richard), 7409
Moses, Siegfried, 7116, 7551
Mosse, George L., 7413, 7571
Mühsam, Erich, 7410
Müller, Arnd, 6933
Müller, Manfred, 7343
Müller, Thorsten, 6905
München see Munich
Münzenberg, Willi, 7411
Muir, Percy H., 7141
Munich, 7006
Murarka, Dev, 7246
Murti, V. V. Ramana, 7060
Muschg, Walter, 7231
Music, Jews in, 7167, 7171, 7173, 7367,
    7408, 7450, 7473, 7506, 7512, 7519,
    7522

Na'aman, Shlomo, 7355
Napoleon I, 7379
Naumann, Hermann, 7596
Nell-Breuning, Oswald v., 7394
Neske, Günther, 7174
Netherlands, 7038
Nettl, John Peter, 7365
Neufeld, S., 6915, 7116
Neumann, Peter Horst, 7229
Neumann, Robert, 7513
Neumann, Rudolf J., 7598
Newlin, Dika, 7450
Nickl, Therese, 7515
Niedersächsische Landeszentrale für Poli-
    tische Bildung, Hannover, Schriftenreihe
    der, 7063, 7066, 7355, 7419
Niederstetten (Wurttemberg), 6946
Niemöller, Wilhelm, 7007
Nobel Prize, 7143, 7361, 7435
Noether, Emmy, 7412
Noether, Fritz, 7412
Noether, Max, 7412
Nordau, Max, 7413
Notowicz, Nathan, 7238
November Pogrom 1938, 7008-7010, 7535
Nüchtern, Eva-Maria, 7290
Nürnberg, Stadtarchiv und Volksbücherei,
    6932
Nuremberg, 6932-6933
Nyland-Verwey, Mea, 7480

Oberammergauer Passionsspiel, 7554
Oberhausen (Ruhr), 7011
O'Connor, Richard, 6971
Österreich see Austria
Österr. Staatsarchiv, Mitteilungen des, 7566
Offe, Claus, 7377
Offenbach a. M., 7530
Offenburg, 6937

Oliver, Roy, 7061
Oppenheimer, Joseph Süss, 7414
Oppenheimer, Julius Robert, 7415
Oppens, Kurt, 7184
Orth, Ernst Wolfgang, 7286
Orwell, George, 7332
Osborne, Charles, 7314
Ossietzky, Karl von, 7178
'Ostjuden', 6896
Ott, Ulrich, 7213
Otten, Karl, 7235
Ottla, 7301
Otto Junker GmbH, 7283
Owen, Claude R., 7271

Palatinate, 6928, 6934
Panofsky, Erwin, 7416
Papritz, Johannes, 6906
Pasley, Malcolm, 7315
Pasqué, E., 7506
'Patterns of Prejudice', 7526
Paucker, Arnold, 7239, 7555
Pavel, Hans-Joachim, 7525
Payne, Anthony, 7451
Payne, Robert, 7400
Peake, Joseph J. S., 7416
Pearlman, Moshe, 7122
Peitz, Fritz, 7234
PEN Centre, German, 7351
PEN Zentrum deutschsprachiger Autoren im
    Ausland, London, 7521
Perez, Jizchak Lejb, 7597
Perl, Walter H., 7509
Perls, Hugo, 7556
Peters, Richard Stanley, 7245
Pfalz see Palatinate
Pfankuch, Peter, 7404
Pfeiffer, Ernst, 7241
Pfisterer, Rudolf, 7541
Phelps, Reginald H., 7557
Philippson, Johanna, 7558
Philosophy and Learning, Jews in, 7154
    7157, 7359, 7360, 7370, 7407, 7413,
    7438, 7453, 7470, 7474
Piatigorskij, Gregor, 7167
Pickerodt, Gerhart, 7291
Pilch, Judah, 7012
Pinner, Ludwig, 7131
Pinthus, Kurt, 7166
Pitcher, George, 7476
Plé, Albert, 7247
Pleasants, Henry, 7171
Pois, Robert A., 7420
Polacek, Josef, 7326
Poliakov, Léon, 7559
Politics, Jews in, 7153, 7177, 7179, 7203,
    7239, 7260, 7346-7347, 7353, 7363,
    7380, 7411, 7417, 7456, 7479
Politzer, Heinz, 7168, 7316, 7573
Polna, 7545, 7546
Poor, Harold L., 7463

Posen, 6935
Posener, Julius, 7404
Prague, 6959-6960
Preisendanz, Wolfgang, 7267
Preuss, Walter, 7110
Preussen see Prussia
Prinz Max von Baden see Max von Baden
Prossnitz, Gisela, 7425, 7426
Prussia, 6914, 6936
Publishing, Jews in, 7278, 7406

'*Querschnitt*', 7169

Rabbis, 6929, 6961, 7093
Rabinovic, Salom see Scholem Alejchem
Rachel, Hugo, 6906
Raddatz, Fritz Joachim, 7341, 7342
Radezun, Günter, 7203
Raeburn, Michael, 6951
Raggam-Lindqvist, Helga Miriam, 7263
Raphael, J., 7494
Rathenau, Walther, 7163, 7417-7422
Ratz, Erwin, 7367
'*(Des) Rebben Pfeiffenrohr*', 7598
Rehfeldt, Klaus Helmut, 6914
Rehork, Joachim, 7123
Reich, Max, 7600
Reich, Willi, 7196, 7452
Reiche, Reimut, 7377
Reichmann, Eva G., 7560
Reichmann, Hans, 7037
Reichsvereinigung der Juden in Deutschland, 7097
Reifenberg, Benno, 7154
Reifenberg, Elise see Tergit, Gabriele
Reinhardt, Max, 7155, 7423-7426
— Forschungs- und Gedenkstätte Salzburg, 7425, 7426
Reisch, Elisabeth, 6916
Reissner, H. G., 6977
Reitlinger, Gerald Roberts, 7013
Rendtorff, Rolf, 7114
'Res Novae', Veröffentlichungen zu Politik, Wirtschaft, Soziologie und Geschichte, 7544, 7560
Resistance, Jewish, 7025-7027
Restitution, 7036-7040
Rey, William Henry, 7446
Rhineland, 6937
RIAS Berlin, 7027, 7497
Richter, Fritz, 7284
Richter, Peter, 7597
Riegner, Heinrich, 7070
Rilke, Rainer Maria, 7315
Rippmann, Inge, 7495
Rippmann, Peter, 7495
Ritter, Gerhart A., 7170
Ritual Murder, 7545, 7546, 7561
Robert, G. A., 6967
Robert, Marthe, 7248, 7317
Robinson, Jacob, 7014, 7114

Röder, Werner, 7147
Röhring, Hans-Helmut, 7129
Rösch, Ewald, 7292
Rössler, Carl, 7427
Rohner, Ludwig, 7264
Rohse, Otto, 7349
Rokeah, David, 7599
Rollins, E. William, 7062
Ronall, Joachim O., 7210
Rosdolsky, Roman, 7401
Rosenbaum, Eduard, 7421
Rosenblüth, Pinchas, 7063
Rosenfeld, Else, 7019
Rosenkranz, Herbert, 7010
Rosenstock, Werner, 7505
Rosenthal, Gabriella, 7120
Rosenzweig, Yisrael, 7088
Ross, Karl F., 7462
Rotenstreich, Nathan, 7084
Roth, Joseph, 7428-7430
Rothe, Wolfgang, 7142
Rothfels, Hans, 7557
Rothman, Jack, 7085
Rothschild, Max M., 6985
Rothschilds, 7431, 7432
Rowohlt, Ernst, 7165
Rubel, Maximilian, 7402
Ruben, Margot, 7481
Rubinstein, Arthur, 7167
Rühle, Jürgen, 7366, 7403
Rürup, Reinhard, 6895, 6900, 7179
Ruppin, Arthur, 7130-7131
Rychner, Max, 7197

Sachs, Hans Josef, 7433
Sachs, Maurice (Ettinghausen, M.), 7514
Sachs, Nelly, 6905, 7434-7436
Sajner, J., 7249
Salem (School), 7261
Salia, 7095
Samson, Herz, 6943
— Samsonschule Wolfenbüttel, 6943
Samter, Adolph, 7160
Samuel, Maurice, 7126, 7561
Sandor, A. I., 7272
Saphir, D., 7130
Sauer, Paul, 6993
Sauter, Gudrun, 7245
Savigny, Eike von, 7476
Scarpi, N. O. (Fritz Bondi), 7437
Schaeffer, Rudolf F., 6996
Schanze, Helmut, 7267
Schaper, Günter, 7285
Scharfenberg, Joachim, 7250
Scheffler, Wolfgang, 6907
Scheidl, Franz Josef, 7562-7564
Scheler, Max, 7438, 7438a
Scheu, Friedrich, 7148
Schiff, Jacob Henry, 6972
Schiffer, Eugen, 7439
Schillergesellschaft Deutsche, 7301

Schindler, Otto G., 7426
Schlee, Emil, 7530
Schlier, Heinrich, 7458
Schlingmann, Carsten, 7320
Schlösser, Manfred, 7149
Schlossmann, Arthur, 7440
Schlüter, Herbert, 7514
Schmid, Martin Erich, 7293
Schmidt, Alfred, 7295, 7377
Schmiedling, Walther, 7518
Schnabel, Artur, 7167
Schneider, Hermann Th., 6949
Schneider, Max Friedrich, 7405
Schneider, Peter, 7157
Schnitzler, Arthur, 7186, 7441-7449, 7515
Schnitzler, Heinrich, 7515
Schocken, Gershom, 7132
Schocken, Salman, 7132
Schönau, Walter, 7251
Schönberg, Arnold, 7167, 7367, 7450-7452
Scholem, Alejchem, 7600
Scholem, Gershom, 7086-7088, 7197, 7313
Schonberg, Harold C., 7171
Schopenhauer, Artur, 7219
Schramm, Gottfried, 6896
Schürholz, Franz, 7040
Schulin, Ernst, 6895, 7422
Schultze, Johannes, 6906
Schultzmann, Monty, 7202
Schulze, Hans, 6943
Schumacher, Horst, 7187
Schwäbisch Gmünd, 6944, 6945
Schwarz, Gotthart, 7479
Schwarz, Stefan, 6940
Schwarzbaum, Haim, 7098
Schwarzenberg, Karl Fürst zu, 6957
Schwarzschild, Steven S., 7092
Science, Jews in, 7140, 7154, 7211, 7277
    7322, 7345, 7348, 7357, 7412, 7498
Seifert, Siegfried, 7273
Selz, Jean, 7197
Sender Freies Berlin (SFB), 7015, 7150
Serkin, Rudolf, 7167
Seydel, Heinz, 7016
Shapiro, Leon, 6989
Shihor, Shmuel, 7471
Shochetman, Baruch, 7107
Shunami, Shlomo, 7107
Sieff, Lord, 7124
Siegerland, 6938-6939
Siegrist, Christoph, 7267
Sietz, Reinhold, 7506
Simckes, Seymour, 7589
Simmel, Georg, 7453, 7454
Simon, Aryeh, 7125
Simon, Ernst, 7042, 7064, 7087, 7114, 7531
Simon, James, 7172, 7455
Singer, Isaac Bashevis, 7601
Sirakoff, Miltscho, 6908
Snell, Bruno, 7416
Snoek, Johan M., 7017

Sökeland, Hermann, 7172
Sölle, Dorothee, 7434
Soloveitchik, Joseph Baer, 7049
Sommerfeld, Arnold, 7498
Sonnemann, Leopold, 7160
Sonning Prize, 7331
Sontheimer, Kurt, 7133
Soper, Lord, 7534
Spalek, John M., 7459
Spanier, Meier, 7089
Spear, Sheldon, 7018
Sperber, Manes, 7411
Speyer, 6937
Spiel, Hilde, 7341, 7516
Spiers, Ruth, 7415
Spies, Werner, 7255
Spinoza, Baruch, 7485
Sprigath, Gabriele, 7381
Stampfer, Friedrich, 7456
Stein, Edith, 7000
Stein, Leonard, 7137
Stein, Leopold, 7090
Stein, Sigmund, 7091
Steinecke, Hartmut, 7221
Steiner, Rahel E., 7467
Steinheim, Salomon Ludwig, 7092
Steinkopf, Walter, 7162
Steinmann, Ulrich, 7172, 7455
Steinschneider, Moritz, 6990
Steinvorth, Ulrich, 7477
Stern, Arthur, 7517
Stern, Bruno, 6946
Stern, Desider, 6978
Stern, Fred Benno, 7298
Stern, Günther see Anders, Günther
Sternberg, Josef von, 7518
Sternheim, Carl, 7457
Sternsches Konservatorium, Berlin, 7408
Stettin, 7019
Stiftung Preussischer Kulturbesitz, Berlin,
    7162
Stobbe, Otto, 6897
Stockhausen, J., 7506
Stöcker, Adolf, Stöckerbewegung, 6938
Stöhr, Martin, 7394
Straetz, Hans-Wolfgang, 7020
Strasmann, Gilbert, 7073
Strasser, René A., 7258
Strassmann, Ferdinand, 6905
Straubing, 6940
Strauss, Georg, 7602
Strumpf-Rechaw, Gusta, 7052
Stutschewsky, Joachim, 7173
Stuttgart, 6899, 7494
Suchy, Viktor, 7222
Südfeld, Max see Nordau, Max
Sühnhold, Karl-Heinz, 7350
Süss-Oppenheimer, Joseph, 7414
Suhl, Abraham, 7225
Sulzburg, 6941
Susman, Margarete, 7458

Sweden, 7496
Swiridoff, Paul, 7174
Switzerland, 6963-6965
Symbiose (German-Swedish Emigrants' Symbiosis), 7496
Synagogues:
— Basle, 6963
— Elbing, 6915
— Hungarian, 6962
— Marienburg, 6930
— Wolfenbüttel, 6943
Szigeti, Joseph, 7519

Taddey, Gerhard, 6899
Tagger, Theodor see Bruckner, Ferdinand
Tal, Uriel, 7017
Tammuz, Benjamin, 7103
Tappert, Wilhelm, 7578
Tau, Max, 7520
Tavor, Moshe, 7528
Teplitz, 6961
Tergit, Gabriele (Reifenberg, Elise), 7521
Thaler, Willy, 7330
Theatre, Jews in the, 7139
Theresienstadt, 7021-7022, 7044
Thiemann, Walter, 6939
Thierbach, Hans, 7259
Tiedemann, Rolf, 7193
Toller, Ernst, 7142, 7459
Torberg, Friedrich, 7318, 7460, 7515, 7593, 7594, 7595
Toury, Jacob, 7081, 7082, 7099
'Tradition', Zeitschrift für Firmengeschichte und Unternehmerbiographie, 6977, 7210
Tramer, Hans, 6974, 7186
Trapp, Gerhard, 7466
Treue, Wilhelm, 6977, 7210
'Tribüne', Zeitschrift zum Verständnis des Judentums, 6916
Trier, 7002, 7385, 7399
Tschombé, Moise, 7297
Tucholsky, Kurt, 7178, 7461-7464

Ulbricht, Walter, 7135
UNESCO, 7385
Ungarn see Hungary
United States of America (U.S.A.), 7018
Universities: — 7035
— Berlin, Freie Universität, 7417
— Bochum, Ruhr Universität, 7542
— Bonn, Rhein. Friedrich-Wilhelms-Universität, 6911-6913, 7359
— Breslau, Schles. Friedrich-Wilhelms-Universität, 7284
— Heidelberg, Ruperto-Carola-Universität, 7482
— Jerusalem, Hebrew University, 7531
— Mainz, Johannes-Gutenberg-Universität, 7157
— Zurich, 7086
Urbach, E. E., 7087, 7088

Urbach, Reinhard, 7447, 7448
Urzidil, Johannes, 6960, 7316, 7319, 7465-7466
Utitz, Nathan, 6961

Vacha, Brigitte, 7449
Vajda, Zsigmond, 6962
Varnhagen von Ense, Rahel [also Levin-Varnhagen], 7161, 7467-7468
Veit, David, 7469
Verachtet, Gehetzt, Verstossen, 7565
Verband d. Geschichtslehrer Deutschlands, Zeitschrift des, 7418
Verein f. Geschichte der Mark Brandenburg, Veröffentlichungen des, 6906
Verity, W., 7432
Verlagsbuchhandlung Georg Olms, 6990
Verwey, Albert, 7480
Veszy-Wagner, Lilla, 7252
Vienna, 6950-6951, 6978, 7515, 7516
— Akademie der Bildenden Künste, 7425
Virchow, Rudolf, 7172, 7576
Vogel, Heinrich, 7215
Vogel, Rolf, 7529
Volke, Werner, 7570
Voltaire, François-Marie, 7559
Vyskocil, Josef, 6956

Wagmuth, Wolfram, 7329
Wagner, Richard, 7559, 7577-7578
Walberer, Ulrich, 7464
Walichnowski, Tadeusz, 7532
Wallich, Paul, 6906
Wallman, Jürgen P., 7175
Wallwitz, Alice Gräfin, 7176
Walser, Martin, 7208
Walter, Bruno, 7167, 7522
Walther, Gerhard, 6909
Wantoch, Erica, 7553
Warburg, Max M., 7164
Warburg, Otto, 7136
Warburg, Otto Heinrich, 6905
Weber, Albrecht, 7320
Webersinn, Gerhard, 7439
Wechsberg, Joseph, 6951
Wegner, Konstanze, 7177
Wegner, Matthias, 7151
Wehr, Gerhard, 7064
Weichmann, Herbert, 6930
Weigel, Hans, 7343
Weil, Gustav, 6941, 7470
Weiland, Sperna, 7051
Weill, Kurt, 7152
Weimar Republic, 7239, 7555
Weinberg, Herman G., 7362
Weininger, Otto, 7219
Weinzierl, Erika, 6948, 7566
Weiss, Robert O., 7441
Weiss-Rosmarin, Trude, 7071
Weissberg, Josef, 7533
Weizmann, Chaim, 7112, 7137

Weller, B. Uwe, 7262
'(Die) Weltbühne', 7178
Weltlinger, Siegmund, 7523
Weltsch, Felix, 7321, 7471-7472
Weltsch, Robert, 6935, 6975, 7053, 7108, 7114, 7116
Wenig, Otto, 6913
Werblowsky, Zwi, 7087
Werckmeister, O. K., 7209
Werfel, Franz, 7142, 7603
'Werkhefte', Zeitschrift f. Probleme der Gesellschaft und des Katholizismus, 7342
Werner, Eric, 7104, 7473
Wertheimer, Leo see Brunner, Constantin
Westman, Stephan K., 7524
West Prussia, 6942
Widerstand, Verfolgung und Emigration, 7023
Wien see Vienna
(The) Wiener Library, London, 6980, 6988
(The) Wiener Library Bulletin, 7527
Wienold, Götz, 7216
Wiesbaden, Hessische Landesbibliothek, 7298
Wiese, Benno von, 7573
Wilhelm II, German Emperor, 7418
Wilhelm, Gottfried, 7273
Wilk, Curt, 7136
Windfuhr, Manfred, 7274
Winter, David Alexander, 6929
Winter, Else, 7167
Wirszubski, Ch., 7087
Wissmann, Julius, 6944
Witt, Hubert, 7596
Wittgenstein, Ludwig, 7474-7477
Wittmann, Lothar, 7294
Wölfl, Norbert, 7005
Wohl, Jeanette, 7495
Wolandt, Gerd, 7285
Wolf, William, 7101
Wolfenbüttel, 6943
Wolfenstein, Alfred, 7478
Wolff, Theodor, 7479
Wolfskehl, Karl, 7480-7481

Wolman, Benjamin B., 7253
World Jewish Congress, 7029, 7526
Worms, 6937
Woyda, Bruno 7100
Wünsche, August, 7046
Wulf, Josef, 7027
Wunderlich, Peter, 7440
Wurttemberg, 6944-6946
— Israelitische Religionsgemeinschaft, 6944, 6945
— Oberrat d. Israel. Religionsgemeinschaft, 6944
Wykes-Joyce, Max, 7103
Wysling, Hans, 7575

Yad Vashem Archives, 6994
Yad Vashem Studies, 6991, 6994, 7024, 7025, 7026, 7097, 7114
Yahil, Leni, 7024
Yiddish, 7492
Yogev, Gedalia, 7137
Yun, Isang, 7297

Zacharias, Rainer, 6930
Zechlin, Egmont, 7153
'Zeitschrift für die Geschichte der Juden', 6898, 6915, 6948, 6952, 6959, 6961, 6981
'Zeitschrift für die Geschichte der Juden in Deutschland', 6935, 6981
'Zeitschrift für die Geschichte des Oberrheins', 6900
'Zeitschrift für Ostforschung', 6935
Zeller, Bernhard, 7570
Zentralrat der Juden in Deutschland, 7030
Zinn, Ernst, 7213
Zoff, Liselotte, 7525
Zoff, Otto, 7525
Zohn, Harry, 7191, 7462
Zondek, Theodor, 7469
Zuckmayer, Carl, 7142, 7482-7484
Zunz, Leopold, 7105
Zweig, Arnold, 7485-7488, 7503
Zweig, Stefan, 7489-7492

List of Contributors

BINDER, Abraham W., Mus. B., Dr. Hon., b. 1895 in New York, d. 1966. Composer, conductor, musicologist, Professor of Liturgical Music at Hebrew Union College-Jewish Institute of Religion, Director of Music at 92nd Street Young Men's and Young Women's Hebrew Association, New York. Published works include a.o. sacred music, songs, arrangements of Jewish folk music, chamber and orchestral pieces.

BRESLAUER, Walter, Dr. jur., b. 1890 in Berlin. From 1931-1936 *Verwaltungsdirektor* of the Jewish Community, Berlin. Now an International Laywer living in London. Author of *The Private International Law of Succession in England, America and Germany* (1937); and of articles in legal journals in England and Germany, contributor to Jewish periodicals and newspapers. Vice-President of the Council of Jews from Germany. (Contributor to Year Book VIII).

GRUNWALD, Kurt, Dr. rer.pol., b. 1901 in Hamburg. Studied in Vienna. Now lives in Jerusalem. Formerly Manager of Union Bank of Israel Ltd. Author of a.o. *Türkenhirsch. A. Study of Baron Maurice de Hirsch* (1966); *Industrialization in the Middle East* (with Dr. J. O. Ronall, 1961); and of numerous articles in political and economic periodicals. (Contributor to Year Book XII).

HAMBURGER, Ernest, Ph. D., b. 1890 in Berlin. Lives now in New York. Formerly held office in the Prussian Ministry of the Interior and was a member of the Prussian Diet. In Paris, Lecturer at the Institute of Comparative Law and Editor, *Cahier de la Presse*. In New York, Professor, École Libre des Hautes Études. From 1946 to 1958, Consultant and First Officer, United Nations Secretariat; Editor, *UN Yearbook on Human Rights*. Author of *Juden im öffentlichen Leben Deutschlands. Regierungsmitglieder, Beamte und Parlamentarier in der monarchischen Zeit 1848-1918* (1968); and of many essays and articles on international relations, constitutional law, human rights, etc. Member of the Executive Committee of the LBI New York. (Contributor to Year Book IX).

KANN, Robert A., Dr. jur., Ph.D., b. 1906 in Vienna. Professor of History at Rutgers University, New Jersey. Author of *The Multinational Empire* (1950, revised edition 1964); *The Habsburg Empire* (1957); *A Study in Austrian Intellectual History* (1960); *The Problem of Restoration* (1968) etc.; and of many essays in scholarly journals. (Contributor to Year Book XII).

LESHEM, Perez (formerly Fritz Lichtenstein), b. 1903 in Chemnitz. Lives now in Jerusalem. Between 1932 and 1950 European delegate of the Central Federation of Jewish Labour in Palestine (Histadruth) and of the Jewish Agency. From 1950 in the Israeli Foreign Service. Until retirement Israeli Consul-General in the Federal Republic of Germany. Author of articles on education and vocational training in Hebrew periodicals.

LIEBESCHÜTZ, Rahel née Plaut, M.D., b. 1894 in Leipzig. Lives in Liverpool. Formerly Lecturer in Physiology at Hamburg University. Now voluntary social worker. Author of papers on Metabolism and Comparative Physiology. (Contributor to Year Book XII).

LOWENTHAL, Ernst Gottfried, Dr. rer.pol., b. 1904 in Cologne. Lives now in London and Berlin. Journalist. Formerly Assistant Editor of the *C.V.-Zeitung*; Editor of the *Zeitschrift für die Geschichte der Juden in Deutschland* (1930-1938); *Philo-Atlas* (1938); *Bewährung im Untergang* (1965); Co-editor of *Lexikon des Judentums* (1967), etc. Member of the London Board of the LBI, and LBI representative in Germany. (Contributor to Year Book XI).

REISSNER, Hanns G., Ph.D., b. 1902 in Berlin. Lives now in New York. Professor of History, New York Institute of Technology, Old Westbury, N.Y., and Lecturer in History, Queens College of the City University of New York. Author of *Eduard Gans — Ein Leben im Vormärz* (1965); and of many books and papers on modern general and Jewish history and sociology. Co-editor of *Lexikon des Judentums* (1967). Fellow of the Leo Baeck Institute, New York. (Contributor to Year Books II, III, IV and X).

RÜRUP, Reinhard, Dr. phil., b. 1934 in Rehme/Westf. *Oberassistent* at the Friedrich-Meinecke-Institut der Freien Universität Berlin. Publications on eighteenth-century and contemporary history, Jewish emancipation, and antisemitism. Co-editor of *Quellen zur Geschichte der Rätebewegung in Deutschland, 1918/19*, vol. 1.

van TIJN-COHN, Gertrude F., b. 1891 in Braunschweig. Lives now in Portland (Oregon) USA. Journalist and social worker, formerly representative of the Joint Distribution Committee in Holland. Writer of weekly news columns and book reviews.

Index

General Index to Year Book XIV
of the Leo Baeck Institute

Ackermann, Nathan W., 93
Action Française, 93, 104
Adass Yeshurun Synagogue, Cologne, 122
Adler-Rudel, S., XXII, 165n, 231-2
Agricultural training see Jewry, German,
    vocational training
Ahlem Israelitische Gartenbauschule (horti-
    cultural school), XXI-XXII, 165-181;
    governing bodies, 168, 169, 176; Peine,
    178; teaching staff, 176-7; Verein ehe-
    maliger Zöglinge, 176n
Ahlwardt, Hermann (antisemitic agitator),
    20, 26, 66, 105
Akademie für die Wissenschaft des Juden-
    tums, X
Alexander, Abraham, 222
Alexander, Emil (headmaster of Peine), 178
Alliance Israélite Universelle, 169
Altmann, Alexander, Xn, XI
American Federation of Jews from Germany,
    VII
American Jewish Historical Archives, Cin-
    cinnati, 119
American Joint Distribution Committee
    (JDC), 182n, 183, 185, 190, 192, 193,
    197n, 233-55 passim
Amzalak, Moise (economist), 236
Anderson, M. S., 142
Ansbacher, Leo (rabbi), 248
Antisemitism, IX, XVII, XVIII, XX, XXI,
    17, 19, 20, 21, 22, 23, 24, 25, 26, 27, 28,
    31, 32, 33, 35, 37, 38, 40, 43, 45, 46, 52,
    53, 55, 57, 60, 61, 62, 68, 85, 92, 93, 96,
    99, 104, 105, 106, 113, 114, 148, 167,
    267; Ahlwardt, 20, 26, 66, 105; Bismarck
    and, 17; Chamberlain, 105; Class, 20;
    Deutschnationaler Handlungsgehilfen-
    verband, 23, 45, 48; Deutschnationale
    Volkspartei, 38, 39; Dühring, 105; in
    France, 93, 104-6; German Conservatives,
    20; in German Students' movement, 22,
    23-4, 25, 45; Lagarde, 24, 105; Langbehn,
    24, 105; Stoecker, 20, 24, 28, 66, 104;
    Treitschke, 24, 105; Voltaire, XVII;
    Wagner, 105; in youth movement, 24, 25.
    See also Pogroms, Racialism, Ritual
    Murder
Apelt, Willibalt (jurist), 43n
Arendt, Hannah, XIV
Arnheim, Fischel (liberal politician), 19
Arnhold, Eduard (industrialist), 159
Arnstein & Eskeles (banking house), 204,
    211
Arnstein family, 211, 213
Ashley, Maud née Cassel, 158, 159
Ashley, Wilfrid (Lord Mount-Temple), 158
Asquith, Herbert Henry (British Prime
    Minister), 140, 152, 156
Asquith, Margot, 126, 158
Asscher, Abraham, 182, 197
Assimilation, XIV, XV, 80, 92-115
Aufhäuser, Siegfried (Socialist politician), 48
Auschwitz, 177
Ausländer, Fritz (Communist politician), 50
Avineri, Shlomo, XVII, XVIII, XIX

Babbington-Smith, Sir Henry (British civil
    servant), 140, 145, 147
Badt, Hermann (Prussian civil servant), 54
    55
Baeck, Leo, 61, 239
Balfour, Arthur James, later Earl of, 144,
    156, 159
Ballin, Albert, 149-53, 156, 160
Bamberger, Anna née Belmont, 229
Bamberger, Fritz, XVIn, 204n
Bamberger, Henry (banker), 138
Bamberger, Ludwig (politician and econo-
    mist), 16, 19, 24, 229
Bankers, Jewish, 10, 13, 17, 22, 23, 59, 60,
    61, 62, 82, 119-61 passim, 203-14 passim,
    224-30 passim
Baptism see Conversion
Barbasch, Ludwig (jurist), 30
Bar-Dayan, Chaim, XIn
Barrès, Maurice (French novelist and poli-
    tician), 104
Bauer, Bruno (Protestant theologian and
    historian), XVIII
Bauer, Otto (Austrian Socialist politician),
    101
Bavarian Räterepublik, 37, 38
Bebel, August (Socialist leader), 21
Becker, Carl Heinrich (Prussian Minister for
    Cultural Affairs), 55
Beerbohm, Max, 153
Behrman, S. N., 153n
Beilis, Mendel (accused of ritual murder), 24
Beit, Alfred (financier), 151n
Belmont family, 267; August, 224-30, 266-7;
    Caroline née Perry, 224, 230, 267; Simon,
    224-30
Benda, Ernst (German Federal Minister of
    the Interior), 54

Benfey, Georg, 169
Ben-Israel, A., 232
Benson, E. F., 120, 123n, 125n, 155
Bentwich, Norman, 182n, 187
Berend, Emil, 168
Bergen-Belsen, 251, 255
Bergh, George van den, 182, 195, 196
Bergh, Sam van den, 182
Berlin Jewish Community, 74, 178, 260-5;
 communal elections, 260-5
Berlin, Sir Isaiah, XVI
Berliner, Cora (of the Reichsvertretung),
 196n
Berliner, Emil (inventor and philanthropist),
 169n
Berliner Foundation, 170
Berliner, Manfred (headmaster), 169
Bernhard, Georg (editor of 'Vossische
 Zeitung'), 47
Bernstein, Eduard (Socialist politician), 21,
 30, 48
Bernstein, James (European Director of
 HICEM), 233, 236, 238
Berr, Cerf (French Jewish leader), XV
Berufsumschichtung see Jewry, German,
 vocational training
Bethmann-Hollweg, Theobald von (German
 Imperial Chancellor), 26, 33, 150, 151,
 152, 153
Beyerli (banker), 136
Biedermann, Michael Lazar, 212
Bischoffsheim & Goldschmidt (banking
 house), 123-5, 126, 129, 132, 134, 135,
 156
Bischoffsheim, Henry Louis, 124, 125, 133,
 157
Bismarck, Otto von, IX, 10, 15-20, 28, 33,
 53, 63, 104, 142
Bjoernson, Boernstjerne, 37
Blickenstaff, David, 244, 245, 247, 250
Block, Sir Adam, 145, 146
Block, Paul, 245, 249
Blunt, Wilfred Scawen (explorer), 137, 153
B'nai B'rith, 168
Börne, Ludwig, XIV
Bondy, Curt (educationalist), 193
Boycott, 44, 167
Brahn, Max (jurist), 57
Braun, Otto (Prime Minister of Prussia),
 42n, 44, 53, 55, 57n
Breitscheid, Rudolf (Socialist politician), 31
Breslau Jewish Community, 261
Breslau Rabbinical Seminary, VII
Breslauer, Bernhard (Jewish liberal leader),
 263
British Refugee Committee, 183, 185
Bromberg, Paul (Dutch architect), 188
Bruck, Moeller van den (nationalist writer),
 24n
Brüning, Heinrich (German Chancellor), 41,
 42, 43, 44, 52

Brünn Foundation, 170
Buchenwald, 193
Bülow, Prinz Bernhard von (German
 Imperial Chancellor), 150
Burnham, Lord, 153
Butler, E. M., 208

Cahen, Jules, 196, 197
Caillard, Sir Vincent, 142
Cambon, Jules (French ambassador), 146
Carlsberg, Leo (rabbi), 216,
Carové, F. M., XIX
Cassel family, 121-3, 158-9
Cassel, Annette née Maxwell, 132, 156, 158
Cassel, David Loeb (Leopold Casseller),
 merchant, 122
Cassel, Sir Ernest, 119-61; and Ballin, 149-
 53; and Churchill, 148-9, 151-2; conver-
 sion, 127, 132, 156, 157; and Edward VII,
 119, 120, 121, 128, 133, 144, 153, 154,
 157-8, 159-60; and Baron Hirsch, 124,
 133, 154; and Schiff, 125-9, 157
Cassel, Sir Felix, 127, 140, 158, 159
Cassel, Sir Francis, 119
Cassel, Jacob (father of Ernest Cassel), 122,
 123
Cassel, Joseph (Court Jew), 12, 122
Cassel, Loeb Benedict (Court Jew), 122
Cattaui (banker), 136, 157
Cecil, Lamar, 149, 151, 152
Central British Fund for Jewish Relief and
 Rehabilitation, London, 182n, 190
Centralverein deutscher Staatsbürger jüdi-
 schen Glaubens (C.V.), 28, 43, 65, 170,
 262, 263
Chamberlain, Houston Stewart (writer), 105
Chamberlain, Joseph (British statesman), 139
Cherubini, Luigi (composer), 217
Christian Social Movement (Germany), 24,
 93, 104-5
Churchill family, 148, 149
Churchill, Winston, 148-9, 151, 152, 153,
 154, 159
Class, Heinrich (nationalist politician), 20
Clemens, Joseph (Archbishop of Cologne),
 121
Closen, Baron von, 90
Cohen, Anselm (musician), 217
Cohen, Arthur, 141
Cohen, David, 182, 197
Cohen, Eduard, 168
Cohen, Gustav, 169
Cohen, Hermann, Xn
Cohen, Israel, 156
Cohen-Reuss, Max (Socialist politician), 30
Cohn, Hermann (politician), 31
Cohn, L., 168
Cohn, Marcus, 259n
Cohn, Oscar (Socialist politician), 34-6, 264
Cologne Jewish Community, 177, 215-6, 218
Conversion, XI, XIII-XIV, 16, 19, 20, 21,

46, 53, 92, 217, 267; August Belmont, 267; Börne, XIV; Cassel, 127, 132, 156, 157; Court Jews, XI; Heine, XIV; Lessmann, 208-10; of Mendelssohn's descendants, XIn, XIII; Offenbach, 217; Rahel Varnhagen, XIII
Connell, Brian, 120, 124, 156, 161
Council for German Jewry, London, 192-3
Council of Jews from Germany, VII
Court Jews, Court bankers, XI, 10, 121-2, 161
Cromer, Lord (British statesman), 136, 137, 138, 141
Cronier, M., 136
Crouchly, A. E., 136
Croustillon, Joseph, 249, 255
Curzon, Lord (British statesman), 143

Davidson, Henrik (banker), 131n
Dawkins, Sir Clinton, 134, 143
Declaration of the Rights of Man, 4, 63, 67, 98
Delbrück, Klemens von (nationalist politician), 32
Department stores, 14, 59, 60, 62
Dernburg, Bernhard (German Colonial Secretary), 150
Déroulède, Paul (French poet and politician), 104
Deutsche Demokratische Partei (DDP), Staatspartei, 30, 32, 33, 35, 42, 43n, 46, 47, 51; Jews in, 46-7
Deutsche Volkspartei (DVP), 32, 41, 42, 46, 47, 52
Deutsch-Israelitischer Gemeindebund (DIGB), 167, 259n, 262
Deutschnationaler Handlungsgehilfenverband, 23, 45, 48
Deutschnationale Volkspartei (DNVP), 32, 35, 37, 38, 39, 40, 41, 43, 46, 52
Diderot, Dénis, XVII, 97
Diesendruck, Mendel (rabbi), 236
Diez, Heinrich Friedrich von (orientalist and diplomat), 72, 73
Dohm, Christian Wilhelm von (writer and archivist), XV, XVI, XVIII, 4, 69, 70, 71, 72, 73, 96n, 97
Douglas, Lord Alfred, 148, 154
Dresden, Professor, 182, 183, 191
Dreyfus Affair, 104, 105n, 113
Drumont, Edouard Adolphe (French writer), 104, 105
Dühring, Eugen (philosopher), 105
Düringer, Adelbert (nationalist politician), 33
Ebert, Friedrich (First President of German Republic), 30, 40
Edward VII (of England), 119, 120, 121, 128, 133, 137, 140, 141, 144, 149, 150, 151, 153, 154, 157-8, 159, 160
Ehrenberg, Samuel Meyer, 206n

Eisner, Kurt (Socialist politician), 30, 32, 39
Elbogen, Ismar, XXIII
Elimeyer, Philipp (banker), 138
Elkan, David Levy (artist), 217
Ellstätter, Moritz (Minister of Finance in Baden), 15
Eltzbacher, J. W. & Co. (banking house), 123, 124
Emancipation, IX-XXI, 3-115, 165, 166; in Austria, 6-8; Edict of Toleration of 1782, 7, 69; of British Jewry, 62-3; of Eastern Jewry, 101; of French Jewry, XIV-XVII, 4, 63, 73, 74-5, 97-9, 102-6; Prussian Edict of 1812, IX, 5, 6, 10, 18, 75-6, 78, 86, 88, 104, 205, 216; Prussian Law of 1869, IX, XIX, 3, 4, 15-7, 63, 84
Emden, Paul H., 120, 121, 125, 127, 161
Emigration of German Jews, XXII, 61, 174, 175, 185, 189-90; to Holland, XXIII, 182-99; from the Iberian Peninsula, XXIII, 231-56; to Palestine, XXII, 174, 175, 189, 190, 231-56, illegal to P., 196, 199n; to South America, 174, 189, 190; to Spain, 244, 246, 248-9; to the USA, 174, 175, 189
Engelman, U. Z., 99, 107n
Enlightenment, X, XV, XVII, 70, 71, 74, 77, 98, 101, 103, 105, 106, 165, 215
Eppstein, Paul (of the Reichsvertretung), 267
Erzberger, Matthias (Zentrum politician), 40
Esher, Lord, 140n, 143, 160
Eskeles family, 211

Falk, Bernhard (politician), 42n, 47
Falkenhayn, Erich von (Prussian Minister of War), 26
Farringdon, Lord, 145
Federlein, Siegmund, 168
Feist family, Stephan (Salomon), 224-7; Elisabetha née Belmont, 224-30, 267
Finkelstein, Karl von, XIIn
Fischer, Leopold, 168
Fischer, Ruth (Communist politician), 50, 51
Fischer, Samuel (publisher), 54-5
Fisher, Sir John (British First Sea Lord), 150
Flatow, Georg (jurist), 56, 57
Flottenverein, 20
Foissac, Jean Baptiste Annibal Aubert Dubayet (French antisemite), XVII
Fortschrittliche Volkspartei (Progressive Party), 19, 20-1, 25, 26, 28, 30, 46
Fouqué, Friedrich Heinrich Karl, Freiherr de la Motte- (poet), 208
Fraenkel, Louis (banker), 131n
Frank, Ludwig (Socialist politician), 21
Frankfurt a. Main Jewish Community, 5, 8-9, 76, 111
'Frankfurter Zeitung', 19
Frankfurt National Assembly of 1848, 3, 4, 34; Jewish question at, 11-3, 16, 34, 36, 83

Fraternities, German, 22, 23-4, 25, 45
Fraternities, Jewish, 24
Frederick the Great (King of Prussia), 69
Freisinnige Volkspartei, 263
French Revolution, XVI, XVII, 4, 8, 69, 73, 97, 103, 104
Freud family, XIV
Freud, Ernst, XIV
Freud, Jacob (father of Sigmund Freud), XIV
Freud, Sigmund, XIV
Freund, Friedrich Theodor (German civil servant), 53-4
Freund, Ismar, 259n, 260n, 262
Freytagh-Loringhoven, Axel Freiherr von (nationalist politician), 35
Friedberg, Heinrich von (Prussian Minister of Justice), 53
Friedberg, Robert (liberal politician), 21
Friedenthal, Rudolf (Prussian Minister of Agriculture), 16, 53
Friedländer & Co. (banking house), 204
Friedländer, Albert H., 209
Friedländer, David (Reformer of Judaism), 80, 204
Friedländer, Kurt (jurist), 57
Friedländer, Moses (banker), 211
Fuchs, Eugen (Chairman of the C.V.), 263
Fürst, Paula Sara (headmistress of Jewish school), 176
Fürstenberg, Carl (banker), 60
Fulda, Heinrich Hugo (politician), 53

Gans, Eduard (jurist and philosopher), 203, 205, 206, 207, 208, 214
Garston, Sir William, 134, 135
Gaupp, E. Th., 206n
Gauss, Karl Friedrich (mathematician), 15n
General Federation of Jewish Labour (Histadrut), 232
Gentz, Friedrich von (Austrian statesman), 211
George V (of England), 153, 157
Gerzon, Jules, 198
Gesellschaft zur Verbreitung der Handwerke und des Ackerbaus unter den Juden des Preussischen Staates, 166, 167, 170
Gestapo, 197, 198
Gierke, Anna von (German politician), 39
Gierke, Otto von (jurist), 39
Gobineau, Joseph Arthur de (French orientalist and poet), 104
Goethe, Johann Wolfgang von, XII
Goldmann, Paul, 176
Goldschmidt, Jakob (banker and philanthropist), 60
Goldschmidt, Levin (jurist), 15, 16, 17
Gorst, Sir John Eldon (British statesman), 137, 141
Goshen, Sir Edward (British ambassador), 150

Goslar, Hans (Prussian civil servant), 55
Gottschalk, Fritz, 176
Goudsmit, Alfred, 182, 195, 196
Gradnauer, Georg (German Minister of the Interior), 30, 52, 53
Gräfe-Goldebee, Albrecht von (German politician), 33
Graetz, Heinrich (historian), 94
Graves, Philip P., 141
Greeley, Horace (American editor), 267
Grey, Sir Edward (British Foreign Secretary), 140, 144, 146, 150, 152
Grillparzer, Franz (Austrian poet), 213
Grimme, Adolf (Prussian Minister for Cultural Affairs), 57
Groener, General Wilhelm (Reichswehrminister), 31, 43, 44
Gronemann, Selig (rabbi), 166n
Gross-Breesen, 175, 193-4
Gruenewald, Max, VII-VIII
Grunwald, Isabella, 221n
Grzesinski, Albert (Prussian Minister of the Interior and President of the Berlin Police), 53, 55
Guernville, A. B., 136
Gürtner, Franz (German Minister of Justice), 56
Gulbenkian, Calouste, 145, 147
Guthrie, Murray, 141
Gwinner, Arthur von (banker), 142, 144, 147, 148

Haas, Ludwig (politician), 30, 47, 53
Haase, Hugo (Socialist politician), 21, 30, 31, 38n, 48
Haenisch, Konrad (Prussian Minister for Cultural Affairs), 55
Häusser, Ludwig (historian and liberal politician), XXI
Hagen, Louis (banker), 60
Hahn, Hugo (rabbi), VII, 267
Hahn, Sigismund Samuel (physician), 211
Haldane, Richard Burdon (British Secretary of War), 151, 152, 156
Halévy, Jacques Fromenthal (composer), 217
Hamburg, Deutsch-Israelitische Gemeinde, 168; Gesellschaft für jüdische Volkskunde, 168
Hamburger, Ernest, XVI, XIX, XXI
Hammer-Purgstall, Joseph Freiherr von (orientalist), 211
Hanau family, Isaac H., 228; Ludwig, 228
Hanover, Bildungsanstalt für jüdische Lehrer, 167; Verein zur Förderung des Handfertigungs- und Gartenbau-Unterrichts in den jüdischen Volksschulen, 167
Hantke, Arthur (Zionist leader), 263
Harari (banker), 157
Hardenberg, Karl August von (Prussian statesman), IX, 5, 7, 9, 10, 18, 76
Hardinge of Penshurst, Lord (British states-

man), 140, 146, 157
Harless, Adolf von (theologian), 85
Hartogh, Isaac, 182
Harzfeld, Löb, 212
Hauptmann, Carl (writer), 37
Hebrew, XIn, XIV, XXI, XXIIIn, 184, 190, 212, 215, 218, 221-3, 236, 240, 248
Hebrew Union College - Jewish Institute of Religion, New York, 221n
Hebrew University Jerusalem, 156, 237
Hechaluz, XXII, 179, 231, 232, 248, 255
Heckscher, Eduard (banker), 131n
Hegel, Georg Wilhelm Friedrich, and Judaism, XVII-XVIII
Heilmann, Ernst (Socialist politician), 48, 53
Heim, Georg (Zentrum politician), 31, 56
Heimann, Hugo (Socialist politician), 48
Heine, Heinrich, XIV, 203, 205, 208, 209, 214
Heinemann Foundation, 170
Helfferich, Karl (German politician), 142, 143n
Hell, François J. A. (French antisemite), XVII
Henikstein, Karoline von, 211
Herder, Johann Gottfried, 97
Hertz, Paul (Socialist politician), 48, 49
Hertz, Wilhelm (conductor), 217
Herz, Adolph von, 204
Herz, Leopold Edler von, 204, 211, 212
Herz, Salomon Edler von, 211
Herzberg, Abel J., 196, 197
Hertzberg, Arthur, XV, XVII
Heuss, Theodor (First President of the German Federal Republic), 31
Heymann, Berthold (Socialist politician), 30, 49, 53
HICEM (HIAS-ICA Emigration Association), 183, 185, 233-53 passim
Hilferding, Rudolf (Socialist politician), 43n, 48, 49, 52, 53
Hilfsverein der deutschen Juden, 177
Hiller, Ferdinand (composer), 217
Hillmar, Joseph, 204, 205, 206, 207, 214
Hindenburg, Paul von, 26, 27, 41, 42, 43, 44
Hirsch, Fritz, 182n, 183, 184
Hirsch, Julius (Staatssekretär), 54
Hirsch, Baron Maurice de, XXII, 123, 124, 133, 138, 143, 153, 154, 155, 156, 157-8, 169
Hirsch, Paul (Socialist politician), 30, 53
Hirsch, Otto (Director of Reichsvertretung), 54
Hirsch, Sally (German Zionist), 264n
Hitachduth Olej Germania, VIII
Hitler, Adolf, VIII, 24, 27, 28, 31n, 35, 39, 42, 43, 46, 56, 66, 92, 105, 191, 236, 239, 254, 262, 265n
Hoare, Sir Samuel (Lord Templewood), British ambassador to Spain, 250, 251-2

Hoch, Gustav (Socialist politician), 48
Höpker-Aschoff, Hermann (Prussian Minister of Finance), 42n, 55
Hohenborn, Adolf Wild von (Prussian Minister of War), 26
Holbach, P. H. Dietrich, Baron von (philosopher), XVII, 97
Homberg, Herz (educationalist), XIn
Hugenberg, Alfred (nationalist politician and publisher), 41
Huldermann, Bernhard, 149
Humboldt, Wilhelm, Freiherr von (Prussian statesman), 76, 86, 88

ICA (Jewish Colonization Association), 157, 169, 190
Israel, Wilfrid, 231-2, 236, 237, 238, 245, 248
Itzig, Daniel (banker), 74
Iveagh, Lord, 156

Jacobson family, 266
Jacobson, Israel, 218
Jacobson school, Seesen, 266
Jacoby, Johann (liberal politician), 19
Jahoda, Marie, 93
Japhet, Saemy (banker), 120, 123, 124, 126, 133, 139, 156, 160
Japhet & Co., S. (banking house), 139, 140
Jarblum, Laura née Margolis, 255
Jewish Agency (for Palestine), VIII, 231-56 passim
Jewry, British, 62-3
Jewry, Dutch, 182-99
Jewry, Eastern, XV, 263; emancipation of, 101; in Germany, 52, 264; as immigrants in the USA, 166, 169; Czarist persecution of, 128-9, 157
Jewry, French, XIV-XVIII, 4, 63, 73, 74-5, 97-9, 102-6
Jewry, German, attempts at unification, 259-65; demographic distribution, 59, 81, 108; emigration from Nazi Germany, XXIII, 61, 175, 182-99; in German parliamentary life, 19, 21, 46-51; during November Revolution, 28-31; occupational structure, XXI, 9-10, 22-3, 59-62, 64-5, 81-2, 108-13, 165, 166, 167, 169; process of emancipation, IX-XXI, 3-115; in public service 17-9, 29-31, 52-8; vocational training, XXI-XXIII, 61, 81, 165-99, 231
Jewry, Portuguese, 237, 244
Jewry, Spanish, 247
Joachim, Richard (jurist), 56, 57n
Joel, Curt Walter (German Minister of Justice), 52-3
Joseph II (Emperor of Austria), 7, 69, 74, 97
Jost, Isaak Markus (historian), 204, 206
Jüdische Landarbeit GmbH, Berlin, 179

Jüdischer Volksverein, Berlin, 265
Jüdisch-Liberale Partei, 261, 263, 265
Jungdeutscher Orden (Jungdo), 42
Jurists, Jewish, 17, 18-9, 22, 25, 30, 55-8, 60, 62

Kaas, Ludwig (Zentrum politician), 41
Kafka, Franz, XXII-XXIII
Kafka, Ottla, XXIII
Kahl, Wilhelm (politician), 34
Kahn, Bernhard (General-Secretary of the Hilfsverein), 191
Kahn-Freund, Otto (jurist), 56
Kann, Robert A., XV, XVI
Kant, Immanuel, 97
Kapp-Putsch, 38, 40-1, 53
Kapp, Wolfgang (nationalist politician), 38, 40
Kareski, Georg (German Zionist), 263, 264n
Kartell-Convent der Verbindungen deutscher Studenten jüdischen Glaubens (K.C.), 24
Katz, Eugen, 173, 178
Katz, Irving, 224
Katz, Iwan (Communist politician), 50
Katznelson, Lea, 184
Katznelson, Moshe, 184, 190, 193, 194, 196
Kaulla, Alfred (banker), 142
Kayser, Paul (German civil servant), 53
Kayserling, S., 169
Keil, Wilhelm (Socialist politician), 49
Kerensky, Alexander (Russian statesman), 129
Kestenberg, Leo (musician and Prussian civil servant), 55
Klee, Alfred (German Zionist), 263, 264n
Klein (Dutch architect), 188
Klein, Ludwig, 169
Klein, Siegfried (rabbi), 166
Kleinwort, Sir A. D., 141
Knoller, L., 169
Körner, Edmund (architect), 267
Kohnstamm, Jakob (jurist), 56n
Kohut, George Alexander, 221n
Kollenscher, Max (German Zionist), 260, 261, 262n, 263, 264n
Kommunistische Partei Deutschlands (KPD), Communists, Spartacists, 29, 32, 38, 40, 42, 46, 49-51, 194; Jews in, 49-51
Kosch, Raphael Jakob (liberal politician), 19
Krauss, Lili (pianist), 194
Kreutzberger, Max, VII-VIII
Kristallnacht *see* Pogroms, Germany, November 1938
Kube, Wilhelm (Nazi leader), 43
Kuhn, Loeb & Co. (banking house), 125, 126, 127, 128, 129, 156
Kulturkampf, 27, 104
Kuznet, S., 114

Lachmann-Mosse, Hans (publisher), 166n
Lagarde, Paul Anton de (orientalist and philosopher), 24, 105

Landauer, Georg (German Zionist), 264n
Landauer, Gustav (Antimarxist Socialist), 37, 38n, 39
Landes, David S., 130
Landmann, Ludwig (Mayor of Frankfurt), 58
Landsberg, Otto (Socialist politician), 30, 31, 52, 53, 54, 57
Landsdowne, Marquis of (British statesman), 143, 144
Langbehn, Julius (writer), 24, 105
Lasker, Eduard (politician), 16, 19, 27
Laube, Heinrich (writer and theatre director), 203
Laufer, Eva, 183, 184, 198
Lavater, Johann Kaspar (theologian), X
Lee, Sir Sidney (Levy), 120, 124
Lehmann, R. C., 141
Leo Baeck Institute, VII-VIII, 165n, 189n, 259n; New York Archives, VII-VIII, XIV, 92n, 189n;, 203-4
Leshem, Perez (Fritz Lichtenstein), XXIII, 231-56
Lesser, Leopold, 166n
Lessing, Gotthold Ephraim, 4, 97
Lessmann, Daniel, XIV, 203-14; Conversion, 208-10
Lessmann, Gotthold (Lewin Philipp), 203
Lestschinsky, Jakob (economist), 61, 62, 94, 100, 101, 107n
Levi, Paul (Socialist politician), 49, 50
Levien, Max (Communist politician), 38n
Leviné-Nissen, Eugen (Communist politician), 37
Lewandowski, Louis (composer), 220
Lichtenberg, Hermann, 169
Lichtheim, Richard, 239
Liebeschütz, Hans, XVII
Liebeschütz, Rahel, 266, 267
Liebknecht, Karl (Leftist Socialist politician), 29, 39-40, 50
Linton, Joseph (Israeli ambassador), 233
Lippman, Leo (Staatssekretär), 54
Lippman, Julius (politician), 57
Lippmann & Sons (banking house), 138
Lloyd George, David (British statesman), 152
Löwenthal, Marvin, 96
Louis XIV (of France), 103, 121
Louis Philippe (of France), 40, 224
Lubinski, Hans, 184, 188
Ludendorff, General Erich, 26, 27, 28, 29, 31, 66
Lüttwitz, Walter von (general), 38
Luttgen, Walter (American financier), 267
Luxemburg, Rosa (Leftist Socialist politician), 29, 39, 49, 50

MacDonald, Forest, 119
Macdonald, James G. (High Commissioner for Refugees), 187, 188, 191
Magnus, Philip 140

Mahraun, Artur (leader of Jungdeutscher Orden), 42
Maier, Hans (German civil servant), 54
Makgill, Sir George, 160
Malesherbes, Chrétien Guillaume de Lamoignende (French statesman), 69
Mallet, Sir Louis, 146
Mann, Thomas, 37
Mannheimer, Isaak Noah (preacher), 97n
Mannheimer, Theodor (banker), 130, 131, 156
Marcus, Alfred (economist), 61, 62
Marcus, Levin, XIII
Marcus, Wilhelm (Jewish liberal representative), 265n
Marlborough, Frances, Duchess of, 148
Marranos, 237
Marum, Ludwig (politician), 53
Marwitz, Alexander von der, XII
Marx, Karl, XVIII, 89
Marx, Louis, 126
Maurras, Charles (French writer), 104
Mauthausen, 107, 198, 256
Maxwell, Robert Thompson, 132
Meinecke, Friedrich (historian), 28
Meisele, Rafi, 232
Meisl, Josef, 259n
Mendelssohn, Erich (architect), 267
Mendelssohn, Joseph, XIn
Mendelssohn, Moses, X, XI, XIII, XV, 4, 37, 77, 96, 97, 203
Menko, Siegfried, 182
Metternich, Klemens von, Fürst, 76, 211, 227
Meyer, Sally (Swiss), 196
Meyerstein, Selly, 169
Middle Ages, XI-XII, XX, XXI, 89, 165
Millner, Lord Alfred (British statesman and writer), 134
Mirabeau, Honoré Gabriel, XVII
Misch, Carl (journalist and historian), 267
Mixed marriages, 108
Mohl, Moritz (politician), 12, 36
Montesquieu, XVII
Morawitz, Karl (banker), 138-9, 156
Morgenstern, David (liberal politician), 19
Morgenthau, Hans J. (political scientist), 56
Moser, Moses, 204, 205, 206, 207, 208, 209, 211, 214
Moses, Julius, 48
Mountbatten, Lady Edwina, 158, 159
Mountbatten of Burma, Viscount Louis, 119, 120, 124n, 159
Mühsam, Erich (anarchist dramatist), 37
Müller, Hermann (Socialist German Chancellor), 52
Münz, Sigmund (journalist), 119, 124

Napoleon I, 4, 18, 74, 75, 103, 122, 203, 216
Napoleon III, 104

National Liberal Party (Germany), 15, 19, 20, 21, 27, 46
Nationalism, German, XVI, 85, 93, 104, 105
National Socialism, Nazi era, VII, VIII, X, XVI, XX, XXII, XXIII, 4, 24, 36, 38, 39, 40, 41, 42, 43, 44, 45, 49, 51, 52, 54, 56, 59, 60, 62, 66, 109, 179, 195, 231, 238, 241, 244, 253
Naumbourg, Samuel (cantor and composer), 220
Nawiasky, Hans (jurist), 57
Neuendorf, 175, 177, 179
Neumann, Heinz (Communist politician), 50, 51
Neumann, R., 133
Neumeyer, Karl (jurist), 57
Nicolson, Harold, 151, 152n
Noetzlin, Eduard (banker), 156
Normann, Eduard, 204, 206, 207, 210
Normann family, 204, 206, 207, 211
Northmann Foundation, 170
November Revolution, 28-31
numerus clausus, 56

O'Donnell, Count Moritz, 204, 213
Oehlenschlaeger, Adam Gottlob (Danish poet), 212
Offenbach-Grunwald, Julie, 215, 223
Offenbach, Isaac Judah (Eberst), father of Jacques Offenbach, 215-23; compositions, 218-23; manuscript collection, 218, 221-3
Offenbach, Jacques, 215, 216-8, 222
Offenbach, Jules, 216-7, 223
Offenbach, Marianne née Rindskopf, 215-8, 223
Oppenheim, Henry, 141
Oppenheim, Salomon (banker), 122
Oppenheimer, Joseph Süss (Jud Süss), 161
Oppenheimer, Samuel (Court Jew), 161
Oppenheimer, Semmy H., 168
ORT (Organisation for Rehabilitation through Training), 179
Orthodoxy, Jewish, XIII, XV, 122, 261, 263, 264, 265n
Ostmarkenverein, 20

Palmer, Sir Eric, 135
Pan-Germanism, 20, 105
Papen, Franz von (German Chancellor), 42, 45, 46, 56
Paucker, Arnold, 44
Paulskirche see Frankfurt National Assembly
Paulus, Heinrich Eberhard Gottlob (Protestant theologian), XX
Peake, Osbert (British civil servant), 233
Peel, Sir Sidney, 140
Perry, Commodore Matthew Calbraith, 224, 267
Petscheck, Ignaz (industrialist), 139
Pfordten, Ludwig Karl Heinrich, Freiherr von der (Bavarian statesman), 85

Philippson, Franz (banker), 156
Poalei Zion, 263, 264
Pogroms, 28, 31; autumn 1930 and 1931,
   44; Germany, November 1938, 193, 194;
   during 1848 Revolution, XVIIIn, 13, 77,
   83; in Southern Germany, 9, 77-8, 83; in
   the Ukraine, 1918, 29n
Posen Jewry, 263
Probyn, Sir Dighton, 121
Preuss, Hugo (political scientist), 27-8, 30,
   31, 33, 35, 47, 52, 53, 63
Preussischer Landesverband jüdischer Gemeinden, 261, 262, 263, 265n

Radbruch, Gustav (German Minister of
   Justice), 52-3
Racialism, Racism, XVII, XXI
Radek, Karl (Communist politician), 51
Railway building, Jews and, 10, 125, 127-9,
   130-2, 133-4, 138, 142-4, 153
Raphael, Gideon (Israeli ambassador), 196n
Rath, Ernst vom (German diplomat), 193
Rathbone, Eleanor (British M.P.), 252
Rathenau, Fritz (Prussian civil cervant), 55
Rathenau, Walter, 26, 39, 40, 52, 53, 55
Rauter, Hanns Albin (Nazi Generalkom-
   missar for Security in Holland), 197
Reading, Lord (Rufus Daniel Isaacs),
   Viceroy of India, 129, 160
Redlich, Mrs. S., 221n
Reform Judaism, Reform Movement, 80,
   122, 212, 218
Rehfeld, Alex, 176
Reichsbanner Schwarz-Rot-Gold, 45
Reichsbund für jüdische Siedlung e.V., 179
Reichsvereinigung der Juden in Deutschland,
   175, 176
Reichsvertretung der deutschen Juden, VII,
   VIII, 54, 169n, 183, 184, 190, 193n, 262,
   267
Reichswehr, 38, 51, 54, 58
Reinhold family and Reinhold Foundation,
   169, 170
Remmele, Hermann (Communist politician),
   50
Revelstoke, Lord, 143, 145
Revolution of 1848, XVIIIn, 9, 10, 11-3,
   65, 74, 79, 82, 83, 85, 97n, 224, 226-7
Richter, Jean Paul Friedrich (writer), 208
Riesser, Gabriel (politician), 12, 15, 19, 36,
   46,
Riesser, Jacob (politician), 46
Ritual murder, 24, 25
Rolland, Romain, 37
Rolo (banker), 136
Romanticism, XVI, 97, 102, 105
Rosen, Pinchas (Felix Rosenblüth), German
   Zionist, later Israeli Minister of Justice,
   264n
Rosenbaum, Eduard, 149, 151, 152
Rosenberg, Arthur (historian), 50

Rosenberg, Erich, 194
Rosenblatt, Levy (headmaster of Ahlem),
   177
Rosenfeld, Siegfried (Prussian civil servant),
   56
Rosenstein, Dinah née Wohlwill 266
Rosenstein, Gerson Isaac, 266
Rosenstiel, Eugen, 168
Rosenzweig, Franz, Xn
Roter Frontkämpferbund, 40, 45
Rothschild, Alfred, 139
Rothschild, Alphonso, 226-30 passim
Rothschild, James, 226-29 passim
Rothschild, Salomon von, 212
Rothschilds, 9, 133, 139, 153, 155, 157,
   169, 211, 224-30
Rotteck, Karl von (historian), 9, 80, 90
Rousseau, Jean-Jacques, 97, 98
Rürup, Reinhard, XIV, XV, XVI, XX, XXI
Ruppin, Arthur (sociologist), 94, 99, 100,
   107n, 108

SA, 44, 45
Sachar, H. M., 110
Saenger, Samuel (editor), 54
Salomonsohn, Adolph (banker), 60
Salomonsohn, Arthur (banker), 60
Salons, Jewish, 4, 74
Samuel, Sir Marcus (Lord Mayor of London),
   148
Sandler, Ahron (German Zionist), 260, 262,
   264n
Sassoon, Arthur, 153, 157
Savigny, Friedrich Karl von (jurist), 206n
Schacht, Horace Greely Hjalmar (President
   of the Reichsbank), 43n
Schäffer, Hans (Staatssekretär), 54
Schiff, Jacob Henry (banker), 119, 125-9,
   137, 155n, 156, 157
Schiffer, Eugen (politician), 21, 30, 47, 52,
   53
Schiller, Friedrich von, 228
Schlageter, Albert Leo (nationalist), 51
Schleicher, General Kurt von (German
   Chancellor), 46
Schleissner, Max, 176
Schlesinger, Moritz (Generalkonsul), 55
Schmidt, Hermann (Prussian Minister of
   Justice), 56
Scholem, Werner (Communist politician),
   50
Schreiber-Krieger, Adele (Socialist politi-
   cian), 48-9
Schuckmann, Friedrich von (Prussian states-
   man), 72, 73
Schumann, Hertha, 204n, 208n, 209, 210
Schwartz, Joseph (European Director of
   Joint), 233, 235, 236, 237
Schwarz, Israel (rabbi), 218
Schwarz, Samuel, 237
Schweitzer, David (of Joint), 252, 254

Selig, Ludwig (Prussian civil servant), 55
Seligman, N., 141
Sender, Tony (Socialist politician), 49
Sepp (Bavarian deputy), 80
Sequerra, Samuel, 247
Severing, Carl (Prussian Minister of the Interior), 44, 55
Sieff, Rebecca (Woman Zionist), 232n
Siemens, Johann Georg von (banker), 142, 143n
Silberberg, Albert (headmaster of Ahlem), 176, 177
Silbergleit, Heinrich (economic historian), 94
Silberschein, Adolf, 239
Simon, Alexander, 165, 171
Simon, Ezechiel (banker), 166
Simon, Fanny, 171
Simon, Moritz Alexander (banker and philanthropist), XXII, 165-181; Simon Foundation, 165-181 passim; will, 171-2, 180-1
Simson, Eduard von (politician), 16, 19
Sinek, Otto, 232
Singer, Paul (Socialist politician), 21
Slidell, John, 230
Sobernheim, Kurt (banker), 60
Somary, Felix (Smaragd), 139, 160
Sombart, Werner (economist), 107n
Sonnemann, Leopold (editor of 'Frankfurter Zeitung'), 19
Sonnenfels, Joseph, Freiherr von (Austrian writer), 97
Sozialdemokratische Partei Deutschlands (SPD), Social Democrats, XIX, 21, 22, 25, 28, 29, 30, 32, 33, 34, 35, 38, 41, 42, 45, 46, 47, 48, 49, 50, 52, 58, 104, 264, 265; Jews in, 21, 48-9, 51
Soveral, Marquis de (diplomat), 120
Spanien, Raphael, 238
Spanish Civil War, 194, 244, 247
Speyer, Sir Edgar (banker), 141, 160
Springer, Baron Gustav, 138, 139
SS, 44
'Staatsbürger-Zeitung', 25
Staël-Holstein, Germaine, 213
Stahlhelm, 38
Stalin, Joseph, 50
Stein, Baron Karl vom (Prussian statesman), 5
Stein, Nathan (jurist), 58
Sterling, Eleonore, XXIII
Stern, Moritz Abraham (mathematician), 15n
Stern-Täubler, Selma, IX
Stichting Joodsche Arbeid (Jewish Labour Foundation), Holland, 182-99
Stoecker, Adolf (antisemitic leader), 20, 24, 28, 66, 104
Stolper, Gustav (economist), 47
Stolypin, Peter A. (Russian statesman), 157

Storrs, Sir Ronald (British Colonial Secretary), 141
Strauss, Leo (philosopher), XIn
Stresemann, Gustav (German statesman), 27, 32, 41, 42, 46, 52, 55
Stubmann, P. F., 149
Suares, Raphael (banker), 135, 136, 157
Sulzer, Solomon (cantor and composer), 219, 220
Synagogue music, 218-23

Talmud, XXI, 79, 267
Täubler, Eugen, IX, Xn, XVI
Taine, Hyppolite (historian), 104
Terezin (Theresienstadt), 177, 239, 256
Thälmann, Ernst (leader of German Communist party), 50
Thalheimer, August (Socialist politician), 30
Tietz, Georg, 166
Tijn, Gertrude van, 182, 192, 195
Tijn, Jacques van, 189
Tirpitz, Alfred von (Admiral), 150, 153
Toller, Ernst (dramatist), 37, 38n
Tramer, Hans, XIn
Treitschke, Heinrich von (historian), 24, 105
Toury, Jacob, XVIIIn, 259-65 passim
Tuch, Ernst, XXII, 168
Tuch, Gustav, 168
Tuchler, Kurt (German Zionist), 264n
Turnowsky, Walter, 232

Überparteiliche Vereinigung, 263, 264
Ucko, Siegfried (educationalist), 203
Unabhängige Socialdemokratische Partei Deutschlands (USPD), Independent Social Democrats, 29, 30, 31, 32, 34, 35, 38, 46, 49; Jews in, 46, 49
Underhill, Miss (Ernest Cassel's secretary), 120, 123, 159
Universities, Jews at, 10-1, 14, 15, 18, 57, 110, 205
UNWRA, 251
d'Urquijo, Raphael, XIIn

Vansittart, Sir Robert (diplomat), 120, 140, 141, 159
Varnhagen von Ense, Karl August (writer), XIIn
Varnhagen von Ense, Rahel (Rahel Levin), XII-XIII, XIV
Vaterlandspartei, 28, 29n
Veit, Gebr. (banking house), 211
Veit, Moritz (publisher and politician), 19
Veit, Simon (banker), 204, 211
Verband der Deutschen Juden (VDJ), 259, 261, 263
Verein deutscher Studenten, 24
Verein für Cultur und Wissenschaft der Juden (Culturverein), XIV, 214
Verein zur Förderung der Bodenkultur unter den Juden Deutschlands (Bodenkultur-

verein), XXII, 168, 170, 177, 178
Verein zur Verbreitung und Förderung der Handwerke unter den Juden, 167
Vienna Congress, Jewish Question at, 3, 4, 6-8, 11, 16, 76, 88
'Völkischer Beobachter', 45
Voltaire, XVII, 97, 98
'Vossische Zeitung', 47

Wagener, Hermann (editor of 'Kreuzzeitung'), 84
Wagner, Richard, 105
Waldstein, Felix (politician), 26, 47
Wallenberg, K. A. (banker), 131, 132
Wandervogel, 24
Warburg family, 266
Warburg, Felix, 127
Warburg, Frederic, 130
Warburg, Frieda née Schiff, 127
Warburg, Max M. (banker), 60, 119, 149, 156
Wassermann, Oscar (banker), 60
Watter, Helene von (nationalist politician), 43
Webb, Beatrice, 156
Webb, Sidney, 156
Weichmann, Herbert (Ministerialrat, later Lord Mayor of Hamburg), 57n
Weimar Constitution, XIX, 3, 4, 32-6, 45, 56, 63, 64
Weimar Republic, XIX, 3, 24, 27, 32-62, 65-6
Weinryb, Bernard, 101, 110, 173
Weismann Robert (Staatssekretär), 54
Weiss, R., 259n
Weismann, Isaac, 233, 237, 255
Weizmann, Chaim, 236, 254
Werkdorp Nieuwesluis, XXIII, 182-99
Wertheim & Gompertz (banking house), 127, 156
Wertheimstein family, 207, 211
Westarp, Kuno, Graf von (nationalist politician), 39, 41
Westerbork, 198, 238

Wiener Library, XXII, 165n, 182n, 185n, 189n, 238
Wilde, Oscar, 120, 148
William I (of Germany), 15, 16, 17
William II (of Germany), 20, 25, 29, 45, 46, 53, 142, 144n, 147, 150, 151, 152, 153
Willoughby de Broke, Lord, 154
Willstätter, Richard (chemist), 57
Wirth, Joseph (German Chancellor and Minister of the Interior), 52
Wilson, Edmund, 153n
Wisla, Heinz, 231, 233
Wissenschaftszirkel, Berlin, 203, 205, 206, 207
Wohlwill family, 236, 266
Wohlwill, Immanuel, 209, 266
Wolff (Jewish liberal representative), 265n
Wolff-Metternich, Graf Paul (German ambassador), 150
Wolfstein, Rosi (Communist politician), 50
World Jewish Congress (WJC), 233-56 passim
Wrisberg, Ernst von, 27, 66
Wronsky, Siddy, 259n, 261n
Wurm, Emanuel (Socialist politician), 30, 48

Yiddish, 101, 221
YIVO Institute for Jewish Research, New York, 203
Youth movement, German, 24, 25
Youth movement, Jewish, 31, 241, 256

Zentralwohlfahrtsstelle der deutschen Juden, VIII, 259n
Zentrumspartei (German), 27, 31, 32, 35, 41, 42, 56, 58, 104
Zetkin, Clara (Communist politician), 49
Zionist movement, Zionism, 34, 35, 55, 193, 194, 232, 240, 241, 248, 252, 254, 256, 261, 262, 263, 264, 265n
Zunz, Adelheid, 204, 205, 206, 209
Zunz, Leopold, 204, 206, 208, 211, 214
Zweig, Ferdynand, XV

RECENT PUBLICATIONS OF THE
LEO BAECK INSTITUTE

Schriftenreihe wissenschaftlicher Abhandlungen des Leo Baeck Instituts

17

Hans Liebeschütz

Das Judentum im deutschen Geschichtsbild von Hegel bis Max Weber

1967. XII, 360 Seiten

*

18/1

Ruth Kestenberg-Gladstein

Neuere Geschichte der Juden in den böhmischen Ländern

Erster Teil

Das Zeitalter der Aufklärung

1780 - 1830

1969. XVI, 418 Seiten

*

19

Ernest Hamburger

Juden im öffentlichen Leben Deutschlands

Regierungsmitglieder, Beamte und Parlamentarier
in der monarchischen Zeit 1848 — 1918

1968. XXIV, 595 Seiten

*

20

Horst Fischer

Judentum, Staat und Heer in Preussen im frühen 19. Jahrhundert

1968. VIII, 232 Seiten

J. C. B. Mohr (Paul Siebeck), Tübingen

RECENT PUBLICATIONS OF THE LEO BAECK INSTITUTE

Germania Judaica

Band II: Von 1238 bis zur Mitte des 14. Jahrhunderts

Herausgegeben von Zvi Avneri

1968. 1. Halbband: XXXIX, 504 Seiten. 2. Halbband: IX, Seiten 505 — 1000

J. C. B. Mohr (Paul Siebeck), Tübingen

Bruno Kirschner

Deutsche Spottmedaillen auf Juden

Herausgegeben von Arie Kindler

1968. 92 Seiten, 76 Abbildungen, 1 Farbtafel

Ernst Battenberg Verlag, München

*

Elias Auerbach

Pionier der Verwirklichung

1969. 414 Seiten

Deutsche Verlags-Anstalt, Stuttgart

PUBLICATIONS OF THE LEO BAECK INSTITUTE

The Leo Baeck Memorial Lectures

No. 12 Emil L. Fackenheim: Hermann Cohen — After Fifty Years

No. 13 Robert Weltsch: Max Brod and his Age (In preparation)

FORTHCOMING

Hans Liebeschütz

Von Georg Simmel zu Franz Rosenzweig
Studien zum Jüdischen Denken
im deutschen Kulturbereich

*

*A Second Symposium on the Jewish Question
in Twentieth-Century Germany*

Deutsches Judentum
in Krieg und Revolution 1916-1923

Ein Sammelband herausgegeben von
WERNER E. MOSSE
unter Mitwirkung von Arnold Paucker

J. C. B. Mohr (Paul Siebeck), Tübingen